**Accounting for
Managerial Analysis**

**The Willard J. Graham Series in Accounting**

Consulting Editor
ROBERT N. ANTHONY  *Harvard University*

# Accounting for Managerial Analysis

**JAMES M. FREMGEN,** D.B.A., C.P.A.

Professor of Accounting
Naval Postgraduate School

 Third Edition • 1976

RICHARD D. IRWIN, INC.  Homewood, Illinois  60430
Irwin-Dorsey International  Arundel, Sussex  BN18 9AB
Irwin-Dorsey Limited  Georgetown, Ontario  L7G 4B3

Third Edition

*First Printing, February 1976*

ISBN 0-256-01777-8
Library of Congress Catalog Card No. 75-28947
*Printed in the United States of America*

LEARNING SYSTEMS COMPANY—
a division of Richard D. Irwin, Inc.—has developed a
PROGRAMMED LEARNING AID
to accompany texts in this subject area.
Copies can be purchased through your bookstore
or by writing PLAIDS,
1818 Ridge Road, Homewood, Illinois  60430.

*For Eleanor, James, and Steve*

# Preface

Tʜɪs third edition continues the basic theme of the first two—the uses of accounting information by management for planning, control, and decision making. The text also includes three chapters on cost accounting. This material, of course, is important and useful in itself. Moreover, it is a very helpful background for studying certain managerial uses of cost data. The book is intended primarily for a one-semester or one-quarter course in management accounting following a course in financial accounting. It could also be used in a cost accounting course with a heavy emphasis on managerial considerations.

## Major Changes

This revision entails more substantial structural changes in the text than was found in the previous edition. There are now 17 chapters instead of 19. The former three chapters on budgeting have been reduced to two. Similarly, the three chapters on standards and standard costs have been condensed into two; and the introduction to standards is no longer separated from the discussion of variances from standard costs. The concluding chapter dealing with reporting practices has been eliminated, although the material on reporting exceptions is included in Chapter 10. The chapter on divisional performance measurement has been moved up to the section dealing with analysis for planning and control. The chapter on the role of costs in pricing decisions now follows immediately after the one on incremental profit analysis. These changes of sequence should improve the logical flow and the continuity of subject matter.

Chapter 1 is completely new. It introduces the student to the nature and objectives of management accounting rather than simply describing the functions of the industrial accountant. A comparison and contrast with financial accounting is presented to set the subject of management accounting in its proper perspective.

Chapter 4 has been substantially revised. The material on inventory methods and cost-flow assumptions has been omitted, as the student will have studied these topics in financial accounting. The section on process costing has been expanded to include both the average cost and the Fifo methods.

Chapter 5, dealing with the allocation of indirect costs, is new in this edition. It presents both the management accounting and the financial accounting implications of indirect cost allocations, and it introduces the student to cost accounting standards.

The two chapters on budgeting represent substantial revisions of the earlier materials. Chapter 6 not only presents the general framework for periodic budgeting but also links budgeting to the logically antecedent subjects of planning and programming. Chapter 7 consolidates material previously covered in two chapters and is completely rewritten. The material dealing with the cost of capital has been moved back to the first chapter on capital budgeting, where it is most pertinent.

Chapter 10 has been revised to emphasize the control implications of variances from standard costs from the outset rather than to defer those implications to a subsequent chapter. In Chapter 13, a section dealing with the analysis of the causes of a variation in profit has been added.

Chapter 17 has been expanded to include a section on the management of capital investment projects. The tables of present values in the appendix are now the conventional tables based upon discrete annual discounting rather than continuous discounting. This change was the one suggested most often by users of the previous editions.

As in the second edition, every effort has been made to provide an adequate variety of problems. Many of the problems are very short and are designed simply to test the student's understanding of specific points in the chapters. There are also longer problems, many of which require the student to integrate two or more subjects in the analysis of a single situation.

## Acknowledgments

I am deeply indebted to the many users of the previous edition who have taken the time to write to me with suggestions for improving the book. My own students were most responsive to my request for criticisms and suggestions prior to the preparation of this revision. I owe an enormous debt of gratitude to Robert N. Anthony of the Graduate School of Business Administration, Harvard University. He reviewed both the previous edition and the manuscript for this revision very carefully and made numerous suggestions that have improved the text. In addition, his work on management control systems has been invaluable to me in developing my own thoughts on the subjects of planning and control.

C. W. Elliott of Louisiana State University and William J. Grasty of Murray State University have thoroughly reviewed and criticized the previous edition and made many helpful recommendations. My colleague, David C. Burns, reviewed much of the manuscript for this revision and offered many constructive suggestions. Commander James F. Schumann provided valuable assistance with the section on program planning in the Department of Defense. The flaws that remain in the book are my responsibility alone. I sincerely hope that future users will call them to my attention.

Monterey, California
*January 1976*

JAMES M. FREMGEN

# Contents

**part three**
ANALYSIS FOR DECISION MAKING

# INTRODUCTION

# chapter 1

# The Nature
# and Objectives of
# Management Accounting

IN ADDITION to his many sins against Christmas, Ebenezer Scrooge may be held accountable for a notable disservice to the profession of accountancy. By placing Bob Cratchit on a high stool, bent over a dusty ledger, with a long quill pen in his hand and a green eyeshade over his brow, Scrooge perpetuated a caricature of the accountant which persisted long after that miser's reconciliation with his fellow men. Happily, this image has been dispelled. Accountants have guided the fortunes of some of the largest business corporations in America and have filled creditably some of the most responsible positions in government. A principal reason for this advancement of the accounting profession is the fact that managers have come to appreciate the importance of accounting data and analyses in the effective administration of an enterprise. Thus, the accountant has become a member in good standing of the management team. The central theme of this book is the usefulness of accounting information in the management of an organization. Most of the discussions and illustrations in the text are presented in the context of a business enterprise. However, much the same type of information and analysis is equally useful in the management of a governmental or a nonprofit organization.

Managerial applications of accounting data are not the only important aspect of modern accounting development, of course. The public reporting responsibilities of the accountant, and particularly the independent certified public accountant, are essential to the smooth functioning of our vast capital markets. These responsibilities extend far beyond the limits of a single firm. However, the uses of accounting information within a firm by management are sufficiently important and distinct to warrant separate study. Thus, the subject of this text is management accounting, that particular set of accounting information that is useful in the various functions of enterprise management.

## MANAGEMENT ACCOUNTING AND FINANCIAL ACCOUNTING COMPARED

The reader of this book is presumed to be familiar with the basic principles of financial accounting that underlie the financial statements published by an enterprise for the use of outside parties. Hence, it may be helpful to begin the study of management accounting by comparing and contrasting it with financial accounting. All accounting, of course, has certain common characteristics. First, accounting is concerned primarily with financial information. Nonfinancial information is also of importance, but much of it lies outside the scope of accounting. The essential function of accounting is to provide financial information that will be useful to someone for purposes of decision making. There are many different users of accounting information, and the natures of the decisions that confront them vary widely. Thus, different information may be needed for different users and for different decisions. The task of the accountant is to provide relevant and reliable financial information to meet these varied needs. The major differences between financial accounting and management accounting relate to the nature of the users of the information and their objectives, the scope and focus of the information, and the criteria for evaluating the quality of that information.

### Users and Their Objectives

Financial accounting is concerned chiefly with users outside the enterprise for which the financial statements are presented. For a large business corporation, these outside users will include present and prospective stockholders, creditors, customers, financial analysts, employees and their bargaining agents, and a variety of government agencies. Their purposes are to make decisions regarding their relationships with the corporation. For example, a stockholder may wish to decide whether to purchase stock in the corporation, hold stock purchased earlier, or sell his or her holdings. A creditor may wish to decide whether to extend credit to the firm, the term for which credit should be allowed, and the specific provisions of the loan agreement. Employees may wish to determine the amount of increased wages that the firm could reasonably afford to pay them. A government agency might want to know whether the firm has earned excessive profits, whether it wields monopoly power in its industry, or simply whether its financial statements conform to prescribed standards of full and fair disclosure. In each case, the financial information about the firm is taken as an indication of the appropriate course of action for the outside party to take with regard to the firm. That party does not contemplate making a decision *for* the firm but, rather, a decision *about* the firm.

Management accounting, as the term implies, is concerned with financial information for the use of management. Thus, it deals with data about the firm for the benefit of those inside the firm. The objective of the inside user is to make decisions for the firm itself. Accounting information is an important input to the manager in managing the affairs of the enterprise. The manager is interested in setting or in evaluating a course of action for the enterprise.

## Scope and Focus of Information

Financial accounting generally presents information about an entire entity. Thus, the annual income statement summarizes the results of operations for an entire firm or, perhaps, for a consolidated unit of two or more related corporations. Similarly, the balance sheet presents all of the assets, liabilities, and owners' equity of the firm. This broad scope is consistent with the objectives of outside users. They can make decisions regarding their relationships to the entity as a whole. A stockholder can buy stock in the corporation only; he or she cannot purchase a share in a single division or some other segment of the company. A potential creditor must assess the risk of lending money to the corporation; he or she cannot lend money only to a successful product line and thus protect that investment from the perils implicit in an unprofitable product line. This is not to say that information about segments, such as product lines, is not useful to outside parties. It is useful to them, however, only as a detailed expansion of information about the entire entity.

The management of an organization can and does make decisions respecting only one particular segment of the total entity. For example, management may decide to discontinue operations in one division, to raise the price of a single product, or to replace a particular asset. Thus, management accounting must be capable of providing relevant financial information about such segments of the firm. Of course, management accounting may also provide information about the entity as a whole; but the focus of management accounting is more often on some segment of the enterprise. This focus is consistent with the observed fact that management decisions typically are limited to only one part of the firm at a time. Decisions regarding the entire entity are rare (e.g., the decision to start a firm or to liquidate it).

### Criteria for Accounting Information

The dominant criteria for evaluating financial accounting information are generally accepted accounting principles. These principles are established by authoritative bodies, such as the Financial Accounting Standards Board and the Securities and Exchange Commission, or by long usage in practice. Thus, their essential characteristic is that they are generally accepted throughout the business and financial community. The managers of a particular company may not like a particular accounting principle, but they are constrained to use it because of its general acceptability. Inasmuch as financial accounting reports will be used by a large number of diverse parties, it is reasonable that they be governed by general principles. The credibility of financial statements would be seriously impaired if every firm were free to establish and use its own accounting principles. The users must recognize and accept the basis on which published statements are prepared, or those statements will effectively communicate no useful information.

Management accounting information is for the use and benefit of the management of a single enterprise. Thus, it need not be constrained by generally accepted principles. The primary criterion for management accounting information is usefulness. If a particular bit of information or a particular measurement principle is found to be useful for management's purposes, then it is good management accounting. Thus, the development of management accounting practices is based more on logic and experience than on general acceptability. Of course, we would certainly expect that generally accepted principles of financial accounting should be logical and proven by experience also. Further, there is every reason to expect that management accounting practices that are proven to be successful in one firm will spread and become widely accepted. Nevertheless, the essential criterion is that they are effective for the management of the individual firm. The management accounting concepts and techniques presented in this book are ones that have been found to be useful in a large number of enterprises. However, no authoritative body has sanctioned their use or denied the use of alternative practices.

## COST ACCOUNTING

Cost accounting is the process of recording, classifying, allocating, and reporting the various costs incurred in the operations of an enterprise. It is an important part of the total accounting activity of a business firm, and particularly of a manufacturing company. It is not a third basic type of accounting, however. Rather, it is an integral part of both financial and management accounting.

## Financial Accounting Applications

As regards financial accounting, cost accounting activities are directed primarily toward the correct classification and measurement of the cost data that are reported on the income statement and in the balance sheet. These activities relate to the determination of periodic net income and to the valuation of inventories. They are, appropriately, guided by the dictates of generally accepted accounting principles. Although financial accounting is not the central theme of this book, it is essential that the student have a basic knowledge of cost accounting as it relates to financial reporting. Many of the managerial applications of cost data are based upon financial accounting records and classifications. Thus, it is important to understand how these records are developed and what adjustments to the data they contain may be necessary for managerial purposes. Chapters 3, 4, and 5 present the fundamental concepts and procedures of cost accounting as it relates to the financial accounting function.

## Management Accounting Applications

The management accounting applications of cost accounting derive from and are determined by the needs of management in particular situations. Cost data are very useful to managers in planning, controlling, and evaluating business operations and in making specific decisions among alternative courses of action. In this context, costs should be classified, measured, and reported in whatever manner best satisfies the requirements of management, regardless of conformity to generally accepted accounting principles. Hence, cost records prepared for financial accounting purposes may require modification before they are suited to management's purposes. Part Two (Chapters 6 through 12) and Part Three (Chapters 13 through 17) are concerned chiefly with the management accounting aspects of cost accounting—as well as with other financial data and techniques useful to management. In some cases, however, the managerial and financial accounting applications are so interwoven that separate discussion can be based upon different points of view only, not upon wholly different concepts. The use of standard costs (Chapters 9 and 10) is an example of such a case.

## ECONOMIC MOTIVATION

Every organization is created and operated with the intention of achieving some specific goal or, more often, a set of goals. A business firm, for example, has a primary objective of producing and selling a product or service that is in demand. A government agency's principal objective is to provide a particular service to the public. A nonprofit institution may also offer its services to the public, or it may provide them only to some limited group. All of these organizations probably also recognize such other explicit goals as survival, growth, stability of employment for their workers, and reputations as "good corporate citizens" of the communities in which they operate. In addition, every organization must recognize certain explicit economic objectives, even if its primary purpose is not economic in nature. Any organization must use economic resources in the conduct of its operations. It must incur costs to obtain these resources, and it must have some source of revenue to provide the capital necessary to operate. Thus, regardless of its primary purpose for existence, every enterprise has very direct economic motivations.

In a business enterprise, the economic motivation is likely to be one of the most important factors in the minds of its owners. They must obtain a satisfactory profit on their investment if they are to continue to commit their capital to that business. If the profit objective is not met, the business firm will be unable to remain in operation for very long. Thus, economic considerations tend to be paramount in the minds of management also. Economic aims are very important in governmental and nonprofit activities, too. Even though such organizations do not seek a profit, they must seek sufficient revenues to sustain their intended operations. Further, they must manage their resources carefully so that they can perform their services without incurring excessive costs. A nonbusiness entity may strive either to maximize the amount of services it performs within the constraint of a fixed amount of cost to be incurred or to minimize the costs incurred in performing a fixed level of service. In either case, the goal is to attain an optimal relationship between benefits (the services rendered) and costs. This goal is not basically different from that of a business enterprise, in which the relationship between benefits (revenues from sales of goods and services) and costs is referred to as profit.

A basic premise of most management accounting practices is that any organization is motivated, at least partially, by economic considerations. Given a choice, any enterprise would prefer to produce a given volume of output at the lowest possible cost. Management would prefer to control the flow of resources into and out of the entity rather than to be surprised by the results of totally unforeseen events. A business firm would prefer an alternative that would increase its profit by a larger amount than any other feasible alternative. Of course, these economic motivations do not operate in a vacuum. Noneconomic objectives also exist and may sometimes conflict with economic goals. For example, the least costly method of disposing of industrial waste may cause pollution of public water resources. Thus, a firm's management may elect to incur a higher cost in order to avoid antisocial behavior, even though no direct, measurable benefits accrue to the firm as a consequence. Economic motivation is implicit in the nature and the structure of management accounting information. This information, of course, is only part of the total inputs to the management decision-making process. Other, noneconomic information may be considered more important and more persuasive in certain instances. Nevertheless, economic or financial information is always relevant to management. This book is concerned only with relevant financial information for management use. It does not purport to deal with the total process of management or to present all of the pertinent considerations for decision making.

## PROFESSIONAL ACTIVITY IN MANAGEMENT ACCOUNTING

Whether one regards management as a profession or simply as an occupation, he can hardly question its importance in any economically developed or developing society. Management offers a challenging and rewarding career. As accounting information is essential to effective management, accountants have become important members of the management hierarchy. Not surprisingly, then, organizations of accountants particularly interested in management applications have arisen and flourished. Their common purposes are to enhance the capabilities and the stature of their members and to advance the notion of professionalism in management accounting. The three principal American organizations in this area are the Financial Executives Institute, the Institute of Internal Auditors, and the National Association of Accountants. Each of these associations has a widespread membership that participates in the activities of local chapters as well as in the national organization. Each publishes a periodic journal containing articles and news items of particular interest to management accountants. Each includes members who are not actually accountants but who share an interest in the development of financial information for management. Such other organizations as the American Accounting Association, the American Institute of Certified Public Accountants, and the American Management Association have also turned their attentions to matters specifically related to management accounting.

In 1972, the National Association of Accountants announced a new program designed to recognize and enhance the professional status of management accounting. It created an Institute of Management Accounting whose function is to administer and issue a Certificate in Management Accounting (CMA). The CMA is awarded to candidates who successfully complete a five-part examination and have had at least two years of related professional experience. This certificate may be viewed as a managerial parallel to the CPA certificate granted to accountants in public practice. The CPA certificate, of course, is a license to practice, issued by a state or territory. The CMA, on the other hand, is issued by a private organization and conveys no legal status or privilege that the holder did not previously enjoy.

In light of recent and prospective developments in American and international business, it is difficult to imagine that the role of accountants and of management accounting will do anything but increase in importance. These developments do not mean that all managers will one day be accountants or that the roles of other specialists will decline. The need for specialized knowledge and skill in such areas as production, marketing, engineering, research, and personnel administration will continue to grow also. Further, the role of the accountant as a technical specialist will not disappear; but his or her special functions will pervade more and more of the general management and decision making in all types of organizations. Thus, while the manager need not be an accountant, he or she must be able to understand and interpret accounting information with considerable facility. Similarly, the accountant must understand the requirements of management in all of the phases and functions of the entity. If these twin requirements are not met, the accountant will be unable to provide the information needed by management and/or the manager will be unable to use the information that is received. Accountants and managers must be able to communicate freely and effectively. The manager must be familiar with accounting concepts and techniques, and the accountant must be aware of all of the operations and the problems of the firm. The purpose of this book is to contribute to the manager's understanding of how accounting information can be helpful in the informed pursuit of the basic goals of the organization, to increase the accountant's appreciation of the needs of management, and to enhance the abilities of both to adapt accounting practices to the ever changing needs of business and nonbusiness enterprises.

## QUESTIONS FOR DISCUSSION

1. What is management accounting? How does it differ from financial accounting?

2. "Management accounting is nothing but cost accounting with a fancy new name." Discuss this allegation.

3. What are the criteria for good corporate financial reports to the public? What are the criteria for good financial reports to management? Are they the same in both cases? If not, why not?

4. "Management accounting information is important to business firms, of course, but it is not relevant to governmental agencies. Since a government does not have to make a profit, it need not be concerned with such matters as control of revenues and costs or making the most economical decisions." Do you agree with this assertion? Explain your position.

5. Is accounting a profession? Is management a profession? What is the essential nature of professionalism? Can there be such a thing as a professional management accountant?

6. "If management accounting is performed properly, it will provide all of the information management needs for the successful conduct of business operations." Discuss the validity of this claim.

7. "This can't be an accounting text. There wasn't a single number in that whole first chapter." Discuss this comment.

part one

COSTS AND
COST ACCOUNTING

chapter **2**

# Cost Concepts
# and Classifications

**B**ROADLY, a cost is a sacrifice of economic resources. While this simple definition is perfectly true, it is not sufficient to make the concept operationally meaningful. There are various ways of defining and measuring the economic resources sacrificed in a variety of circumstances. Thus, there are various different concepts and classifications of cost. In financial accounting, the term "cost," used without modifiers, has a fairly generally accepted meaning. In management accounting, however, there are a great many different concepts of cost, each intended to convey a very specific and distinct meaning. Unfortunately, cost terminology in this latter area has not been established with complete uniformity. Different accountants use different terms to describe the same concept of cost, and a single term may be used to denote different concepts. The terminology employed in this volume follows that which appears to have attained a substantial degree of acceptance and which seems to be most useful.

## HISTORICAL AND FUTURE COSTS

### Historical Costs

In financial accounting, the term "cost" almost invariably means *historical cost* or *actual cost*. This is defined by the Committee on Terminology of the American Institute of Certified Public Accountants as follows:

15

*Cost* is the amount, measured in money, of cash expended or other property transferred, capital stock issued, services performed, or a liability incurred, in consideration of goods or services received or to be received.[1]

In other words, historical cost is the measurable monetary value of goods or services sacrificed in exchange for other goods or services. The measurability of the cost in monetary terms is essential to the concept. One of the traditional requisites of the recording function in accounting has been the existence of objective, verifiable evidence in support of each transaction to be recorded. As accounting deals with business information in terms of money, this objective evidence must not only demonstrate the reality of the transaction but also provide for its accurate measurement in monetary terms. The cost data reported in conventional financial statements are almost exclusively historical costs. The accurate measurement of the costs incurred is not the only problem concerning them, however. There is also the very important question of in which financial statement, the balance sheet or the income statement, they are to be reported.

**Expired and Unexpired Costs.**    All historical costs may be classified as either unexpired or expired. An *unexpired cost* is one which has the capacity of contributing to the production of revenue in the future. It is the measured monetary value of the expenditure for goods or services which can be of use in the future revenue-producing activities of the firm. Thus, an unexpired cost is an asset and is reported on the balance sheet as of the end of an accounting period. The cost of salable merchandise on hand affords a good example of an unexpired cost. Such a cost can contribute to the production of revenue in the future because the merchandise acquired at that cost can subsequently be sold. An *expired cost* is one which cannot contribute to the production of future revenues. Such revenue-producing capacity as this cost had has either already been consumed in the production of revenue or has been lost without benefit to the firm. The first type of expired cost, that which has been consumed in the production of revenue, is called an *expense.* An example is the cost of merchandise which has been sold. The second type, which has expired with no benefit to the enterprise, is generally described as a *loss.* An illustration of a loss is the cost of uninsured merchandise destroyed by fire. Both expenses and losses are reported in the income statement.

Many of the most complex and controversial accounting problems relate to the separation of expired and unexpired costs in preparing financial reports. Alternative accounting principles may resolve these problems differently. The measurement of cost expiration depends not only upon

---

[1] Committee on Terminology, American Institute of Certified Public Accountants, *Accounting Terminology Bulletin No. 4: Cost, Expense, and Loss* (New York, 1957), p. 1.

the occurrence of transactions but also upon the particular accounting principles and practices employed by a firm. In exactly the same circumstances, different procedures for handling a particular type of cost may result in materially different figures for expired and unexpired costs. The professional accountant must become familiar with the various alternative procedures and, more importantly, must learn to evaluate them critically in light of specific facts and conditions. While the manager need not have as complete a technical understanding of alternative accounting principles, he must have a basic knowledge of them in order for him to appreciate the significance and limitations of the accounting data with which he must work and upon which, in part, he must base his decisions.

## Future Costs

If the preoccupation of financial accounting is with historical costs, that of management accounting is more likely to be with future costs. *Future costs* may be defined as those costs which are reasonably expected to be incurred in some future period under some specific set of circumstances. Because these costs are expectations rather than accomplished facts, their actual incurrence is a forecast and their measurement, an estimate. Management is vitally concerned with future costs for the simple reason that they are the only costs over which managers can exercise any control. Historical costs can merely be observed and evaluated in retrospect. If they are regarded as excessive, management can ask only, "What went wrong?" Future costs, on the other hand, can be planned for—and planned to be reduced. If future costs are considered too high, management can ask the very important question, "What can be done about this?" If necessary, resources can be planned to meet the high costs; if feasible, plans can be made to reduce them. Despite the estimation inherent in the concept of future costs, the measurement of such costs is no less important than the measurement of historical costs. If anything, it is more important to management. The measurement of historical costs is basically a record keeping activity, an essentially passive function insofar as management is concerned. The measurement of future costs, however, is critically associated with the active management functions of planning and control.

When a future cost is not merely expected but is incorporated formally into the overall operating plans for a specific period in the future, it is referred to as a *budgeted cost*. A detailed examination of budgeting will be deferred until later chapters. For the present it is sufficient to observe that budgets are formal, comprehensive, and coordinated plans relative to operations in specific future periods. Budgeted costs are important elements in these overall plans.

## DIRECT AND INDIRECT COSTS

All costs incurred are, of course, identified with a particular enterprise. But this broad identification of costs with the firm is typically insufficient for purposes of determining periodic income and measuring asset values and for purposes of managerial analyses. For these purposes, it is necessary to associate costs with subcomponents or segments of the firm. These segments are referred to as *cost objectives* in this context. A cost objective is anything within an enterprise to which it is both significant and practical to assign costs. Both criteria of significance and of practicality are important here. For example, it might prove practical to associate certain costs with rainy days; but such association may be of no significance whatever to anyone concerned with the enterprise. Conversely, it might appear significant to identify costs with moments of imaginative thinking by executives; but no practical means of doing so may be available. Some fairly common illustrations of cost objectives are the following:

1. An individual unit of product: for example, an electric typewriter.
2. A product line: for example, women's sportswear.
3. A division of a corporation: for example, the Chevrolet Division of General Motors Corporation.
4. A department within a plant: for example, the assembly department of a major appliance manufacturer.
5. A sales territory: for example, the midwest territory.
6. A particular channel of distribution: for example, sales to wholesalers.

There are three possibilities with respect to the relationship between a particular cost and a given cost objective. Certain costs can be traced logically and practically in their entirety to a cost objective; there is a directly determinable relationship. Such costs are called *direct costs*. An example of a direct cost would be the monthly salary of a divisional manager, where the division is the cost objective under consideration. Other costs can be identified only partially with a cost objective, but not entirely. That is, they relate to the one under study; but they also relate to other cost objectives. The amount of the cost which is properly identifiable with any one cost objective cannot be determined. Such costs are termed *indirect costs*. An example would be the monthly salary of a corporation's president, where one of several divisions is the relevant cost objective. The president's services benefit each division, but the proportion of his salary assignable to one particular division cannot be determined. Indirect costs are frequently called *common costs*, that is, costs which are common to and shared by two or more cost objectives. Finally, there are some costs which bear no identifiable relationship to a particular cost objective. Continuing the example of a corporate division, we can see that the salary of the manager of division A is neither a direct nor an indirect cost of division B. Thus, the direct and indirect costs of a particular cost objective do not necessarily include all of the costs incurred by the firm. Some costs may be totally unrelated to the cost objective in question.

From the foregoing discussion, it should be clear that whether a specific cost is direct or indirect depends upon the cost objective under consideration. Certain costs may be direct with respect to one cost objective and indirect with respect to another. Hence, the concepts of direct and indirect costs are meaningless without identification, at least implicitly, of the relevant cost objective. In cost accounting, direct and indirect costs are sometimes described in such a way that the only cost objective suggested is the unit of product. To be sure, this is a very important cost objective in a business and one for which direct and indirect costs are usually ascertained. However, these concepts are useful in connection with many other cost objectives also and will be used in their broader context throughout this book.

## COST ELEMENTS IN A MANUFACTURING ENTERPRISE

### Manufacturing Costs

At one time, the study of cost accounting was concerned almost exclusively with the subject of manufacturing costs. While recent years have seen much greater attention devoted to nonmanufacturing costs, the costs of manufacturing remain a major concern of both students and practicing cost accountants. There are two chief reasons for this emphasis on manufacturing costs. The first is the traditional practice of including only the costs incurred to manufacture goods in the valuation of the inventories thereof. The importance of accurate inventory valuation in financial accounting necessitates considerable detail in the development and classification of factory costs. The second reason is the fact that the processes of manufacture are more standardized and routinized than those of distribution, research, and administration. The greater uniformity of operations permits a higher degree of structure and classification of manufacturing costs. The manufacture of a large and diverse line of products, typical of so many modern corporations, involves the use of a wide variety of goods and services. For accounting purposes, however, each of these items is classified as one of three manufacturing cost elements: *materials, labor,* or *manufacturing overhead*.

*Materials.* Materials include a wide range of physical commodities that go into the making of a product. These are commonly described as raw materials. This term is by no means limited to basic natural resources. The raw material of one firm may be the finished product of another. For example, automobile tires are a finished product of a rubber company but a raw material of an automobile manufacturer.

For purposes of the accounting record-keeping function, the most important classification of materials cost is the distinction between direct and indirect materials, where the product is the relevant cost objective. *Direct materials* are those which can be identified, logically and practically, with the product. Only direct materials are classified as "materials." *Indirect materials*, those which cannot be traced directly to the product, are included in the classification of manufacturing overhead.

The line between direct and indirect materials is not always an easy one to draw. To begin with, different cost accounting systems may result in different treatments of the same item. (Cost accounting systems will be discussed in Chapter 4.) Further, the direct identification of some materials with the product may be possible only at a prohibitively high cost. Hence, the distinction is commonly drawn on pragmatic as well as theoretic grounds. For example, in the manufacture of wooden chairs, the cost of the wood may be the only recognized direct material. Such materials as glue and screws, while logically traceable to the finished chair, may be treated as indirect simply because the expense of direct identification with the product would exceed the value to the firm of the added informational precision. This illustration points out a cardinal rule of accounting systems design. The benefit derived from an accounting technique must always at least equal the cost of that technique. A procedure that saves costs of $10,000 annually but itself costs $12,000 annually is clearly not justifiable on financial grounds.

**Labor.**    Like materials, the cost element "labor" includes only *direct labor*, that which can be identified directly with the product. *Indirect labor* is treated as a part of manufacturing overhead. A simple illustration may assist in explaining the distinction here. A punch-press operator works directly on the product. He spends, on the average, a certain amount of time on each piece. His efforts can be logically traced to and reasonably measured in terms of units of product. Hence, his wages are accounted for as direct labor. Other workers in the same plant, such as foremen, janitors, and watchmen, do not work directly with the product. While their services are essential to production, there is no reasonable basis for measuring their efforts in terms of units of product. Hence, their wages and salaries are regarded as indirect labor cost, a part of manufacturing overhead. In practice, there is considerable diversity with respect to the classification of direct labor. These variations, however, are problems of practical application, not of basic concepts. Thus, the simplified presentation of labor cost accounting employed in this text will in no way limit the student's knowledge of the basic concepts involved.

**Manufacturing Overhead.**    In general usage, the term "overhead" is used to describe any indirect costs necessary for the conduct of operations. Thus, overhead is incurred in manufacturing plants, in retail stores, in administrative offices, in financial institutions, and in every other type of operation. At this point, however, we are concerned only with the overhead incurred in the manufacturing process. For practical purposes, the cost classification of *manufacturing overhead* may be defined simply as including all manufacturing costs other than direct materials and direct labor. Alternatively, it may be defined as indirect manufacturing costs. Among the items commonly included in manufacturing overhead are indirect materials, factory supplies, indirect labor, electric power and other utilities, depreciation on factory equipment, insurance on factory equipment, and factory repairs and maintenance.

One unfortunate feature of manufacturing overhead is the great diversity of terms which have been used to describe the concept. *Manufacturing expense, factory expense, burden, factory burden, loading, indirect expense,* and simply *overhead* have all been used to denote exactly the same concept. The term "manufacturing overhead" will be used consistently in this book. The student should be aware, however, of some of the different terms used and should recognize them when they are encountered.

For certain purposes, it is useful to group materials and labor costs together and to identify this combination by a single term, *prime costs.* Similarly, labor and manufacturing overhead costs together are commonly referred to as *conversion costs.* This latter term stems from the fact that labor and manufacturing overhead costs are incurred in the process of converting raw materials into finished products.

**Nonmanufacturing Costs**

Despite their traditional preoccupation with manufacturing costs, cost accountants have come to devote more attention and effort to the nonmanufacturing costs incurred by business firms. One of the chief reasons for this change has been the recognition of the fact that nonmanufacturing costs account for the largest portion of every dollar spent by consumers. In other words, the sheer magnitude of the items involved makes it impossible to treat them casually. As more and more dollars are channeled into nonmanufacturing activities, business managers are becoming increasingly aware of the need for efficient planning and control of such costs and, hence, for more complete and analytical cost data concerning them.

The subclassifications of nonmanufacturing costs are not as well defined as those of manufacturing costs. For purposes of discussion in this text, four such functional classifications are here proposed.

1. *Distribution costs* are those incurred in the performance of a wide range of activities generally categorized as marketing. These include

selling, shipping, advertising, sales salaries, salesmen's travel expenses, and so forth.

2. *Administrative costs* include both executive and clerical costs which do not fit logically into some other classification (such as manufacturing or distribution). Examples are the salaries of top managers, directors' fees, general accounting costs, and public relations costs.

3. *Research and development costs* are incurred in the search for new knowledge or new products and in testing and improving established products. These costs generally reflect scientific and engineering activities rather than production or distribution.

4. *Financial costs* consist primarily of interest costs of various types. Also included in this classification are the costs of issuing securities (i.e., stocks and bonds), bank service fees, and purchase discounts lost because of late payments. With the exception of interest expense, these costs have commonly been included in the category of administrative expenses; but separate classification seems desirable.

The main focus of attention in Part One of this volume will be on manufacturing costs. However, special consideration will be given to nonmanufacturing items throughout the text as appropriate and especially in Chapter 11. Many of the concepts and techniques widely applied to manufacturing costs are applicable also to nonmanufacturing costs with little modification.

## THE BEHAVIOR OF COSTS WITH CHANGES IN VOLUME

One of the most commonly employed and useful of cost classifications is that on the basis of cost behavior with respect to changes in the volume of business activity. As volume changes, costs may either change with it or remain constant. Further, those costs which do change with volume may do so in different ways. Thus, classification of costs according to their behavior patterns with respect to changes in volume greatly facilitates the managerial functions of planning, controlling, and decision making. In this connection, costs are classified as *variable, fixed,* or *semivariable.*

### Strict Definitions of Cost-Volume Relationships

In accounting literature, the three cost classifications relative to volume changes are typically defined as follows:

1. *Variable costs* are those costs which vary in total in direct proportion to changes in volume. Successive increases in units of volume result in parallel and proportionate increases in variable costs. Similarly, decreases in volume produce proportionate cost decreases. As an illustration,

observe the following relationship between the cost of raw materials and the units of a particular product:

| Units of Product | Raw Materials Cost |
|---|---|
| 1 | $    2.50 |
| 10 | 25.00 |
| 100 | 250.00 |
| 500 | 1,250.00 |
| 842 | 2,105.00 |
| 2,400 | 6,000.00 |

Each change of one unit of product causes a change of $2.50 of materials cost. Materials cost in the illustration—and variable costs in general—change in direct proportion to volume. Expressed mathematically, there is a linear relationship between volume and cost.[2] As is apparent in the foregoing example, the directly proportional relationship between total materials cost and volume means that each additional unit of product has the same cost per unit as all other units. Thus, *variable costs vary in total in direct proportion to volume and, consequently, are constant per unit of volume.*

2. *Fixed costs* remain constant in total regardless of changes in volume. They are unaffected by volume changes. For example, the monthly rent on a computer installation may be $24,000 regardless of how many hours the equipment is used per month. Volume of operation may vary from no use at all to maximum monthly volume without altering the rental cost by one cent. Because it is fixed in total for the rental period, the rental cost of the equipment per hour of use decreases as the number of operating hours increases. This is apparent in the following comparison of several alternative monthly volumes of computer operation:

| Total Monthly Rental | Hours Operated per Month | Average Cost per Hour |
|---|---|---|
| $24,000 | 176 | $136.36 |
| 24,000 | 352 | 68.18 |
| 24,000 | 480 | 50.00 |
| 24,000 | 720 | 33.33 |

There is an inverse relationship between volume and fixed cost per unit of volume. Hence, *fixed costs are constant in total as volume changes but vary per unit of volume inversely with volume.*

---

[2] It is entirely possible that some costs might actually be a nonlinear function of volume. At present, accounting treats such costs as semivariable. There is no reason why the definition of a variable cost could not be altered to include any cost that bears some known functional relationship to volume, whether that relationship is linear or not. As a practical matter, the linear relationship is an easy one to work with and appears to be valid in a very large number of cases.

3. *Semivariable costs* are simply all costs which are neither perfectly variable nor absolutely fixed with respect to volume changes. Semivariable costs change in the same direction as volume but not in direct proportion thereto. They may remain constant over relatively small ranges of volume but increase as volume increases beyond these limited ranges. Hence, they might be called semifixed costs. (Some prefer to call them mixed costs.) The term "semivariable" is more widely used, however, and will be employed consistently here.

These three cost concepts are depicted graphically in Figure 2–1. Volume is measured on the horizontal axis of the chart; and dollars of cost

### FIGURE 2–1
#### Cost-Volume Relationships: Perfect

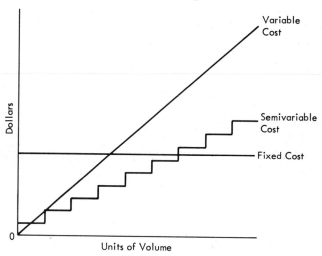

on the vertical axis. Variable costs increase with volume in a steady, linear pattern. Fixed costs are totally unaffected by volume changes; they are the same at maximum volume as at none at all. (This, of course, assumes that the firm will continue to exist while not operating. All costs may be eliminated by going out of business.) Semivariable costs increase with volume but not in the same regular manner as the variable costs. The stair-step progression of these costs in Figure 2–1 is not necessarily typical. The various steps might be of less regular length and/or height, or the overall pattern of a particular semivariable cost might be better depicted by a nonlinear curve.

*Relevant Concepts of Volume.* In the foregoing discussion of cost-volume relationships, the term volume has been used in a general sense to denote business activity of some kind. It is readily apparent that the same concept of volume is not applicable to every cost item. Thus, raw materials cost was viewed as variable with respect to the volume of goods produced. Computer equipment rental was regarded as fixed with respect to the volume of use of the equipment. This rental charge would also be fixed with respect to the volume of goods produced, but such a relationship might not be considered relevant. Materials cost could hardly be regarded as either fixed or variable with respect to computer hours. There simply is no significant relationship between the two quantities. Costs can be identified as variable, semivariable, or fixed only with reference to the volume of some activity to which those costs are pertinent. Manufacturing costs are typically evaluated in this connection in the light of the volume of goods produced. Selling costs are appraised with reference to the volume of goods sold. Administrative costs are usually viewed in relation to some relevant measure of work, such as the number of lines in letters typed or the number of payroll checks prepared. Throughout this text, *when applied to manufacturing costs,* the terms "variable" and "fixed" will have reference to cost behavior with respect to changes in the volume of units of product manufactured, unless otherwise indicated.

## Cost-Volume Relationships in Practice

The definitions of variable and fixed costs in the previous section are very rigid. Any cost that is neither perfectly variable nor absolutely fixed would be classified as semivariable. As will be evident in subsequent discussions, these rigid definitions are necessary for the analytical employment of the concepts. However, in practice, it is likely that there are comparatively few costs which would be perfectly variable or absolutely fixed over *all* ranges of volume. Hence, the preponderance of costs in real business firms might well fall into the semivariable class. Because of the indefinite nature of this category, however, such classification of most business costs would greatly impair the analytical usefulness of cost-volume relations. Hence, in practice, many costs are classified as either variable or fixed despite the fact that they meet the strict definition of neither.

Raw materials cost is commonly treated as a variable cost. As a matter of fact, as the volume of production expands, it may be possible to obtain significant quantity discounts on the purchase of materials in large lots. Thus, materials cost per unit of product might decrease as volume reaches certain critical levels. Further volume increases may ultimately result in increased unit materials cost due to diseconomies of excessive size. Such a cost pattern is depicted by the variable cost curve in Figure 2–2. In a somewhat similar fashion, certain fixed costs may remain constant in total over significant ranges of volume. Again, however, there may be critical points beyond which additional costs may have to be incurred. This may be illustrated by the cost of supervision in a factory. There are critical points of operating volume at which it becomes necessary to employ additional supervisors to assure adequate control over expanding production. Such cost behavior is shown by the fixed cost curve in Figure 2–2.

Lest it appear that the variable and fixed cost classifications have no practical validity, it must be pointed out that, while a particular cost may not fit the strict definition of either classification, it may be both useful and operationally valid to treat it as variable or fixed, whichever is more nearly the case, for purposes of managerial analysis. First of all, identification of costs as either variable or fixed is useful. It permits anal-

### FIGURE 2–2

#### Cost-Volume Relationships: Imperfect

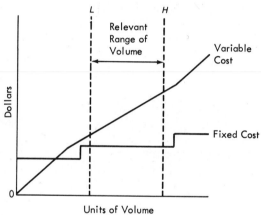

Units of Volume

yses which otherwise would not be feasible. Second, such identification may be valid for analytical purposes within limited ranges of volume. Notice that the cost curves in Figure 2–2, while not conforming to the strict definitions of variable and fixed over the entire range of volume, do so conform over significant ranges. It is quite possible that most cost items will prove to be very nearly perfectly variable or absolutely fixed over the *relevant range of volume* within which the firm is most likely to operate. Thus, in Figure 2–2, if the firm could reasonably expect that its volume of production would be no less than that indicated by the point $L$ and no greater than that indicated by the point $H$, it is apparent that the costs whose behavior is charted would conform to the strict definitions of variable and fixed over the relevant range of activity. To be sure, Figure 2–2 is constructed deliberately to make this so; it could well be that the breaks in either or both cost curves would occur within the relevant range of volume. Nevertheless, this chart serves to illustrate an important point, namely, that cost behavior in the extreme ranges of activity may not be relevant for purposes of management analysis. Within the bounds of the minimum and maximum practical levels of output, many more cost items may prove to be either variable or fixed than would be so over the full range of technically possible (but practically improbable) operations.

The semivariable cost classification presents some peculiar problems. Certain costs fail to meet the criteria of either variable or fixed costs over any significant range of activity. Treating them as semivariable, however, does not admit of any definite analysis of their behavior in response to volume changes. But it is this very analysis that makes cost classifications with respect to volume changes so important to management. Thus, as a practical matter, many costs which actually appear to be genuinely semivariable are treated as though they were either variable or fixed, whichever they more nearly approximate, or as though they were made up of separable variable and fixed components. In other words, to meet the needs of management in analyzing cost behavior, the semivariable cost classification is not uncommonly completely eliminated. The procedures to accomplish this end will be discussed in Chapter 8, along with some consideration of the limitations which such practice places upon subsequent analyses.

## COST CONCEPTS FOR CONTROL AND DECISION MAKING

### Responsibility Costing

Historically, accounting was concerned largely with the reporting of economic facts relevant to an entire enterprise. Recent years have seen increased interest in the subdivision of the enterprise along responsibility lines for purposes of reporting to management. More and more management reports are emphasizing the association of economic data with the persons responsible therefor. This involves both the reporting of information to the executive responsible for the particular area of a business and also reporting to higher management the results of operations in such a manner as to identify them with the responsible subordinates. This development has commonly been referred to as *responsibility accounting*. In cost accounting, it has resulted in the classification of costs along responsibility lines. Cost data are accumulated and reported according to areas of responsibility within a firm. These areas are commonly referred to as *responsibility centers*. Thus, reports indicate not only what costs have been incurred but also who is responsible for them. This specific subdevelopment of responsibility accounting may be termed *responsibility costing* and is one of the most important cost classification schemes as far as business management is concerned. Responsibility costing facilitates greatly the practical implementation of management's cost control objective. It permits the translation of the basic objective into a program of action centered around people, and, after all, only people can make cost control a reality.

*Controllable Costs.* The concept of responsibility costing leads directly to the classification of costs as controllable or uncontrollable. Obviously, the controllability of a cost depends upon the level of responsibility under consideration. A *controllable cost* may be defined as one which is reasonably subject to regulation by the executive with whose responsibility that cost is being identified. Thus, a cost which is uncontrollable at one level of responsibility may be regarded as controllable at some other, usually higher, level. For example, the cost of factory maintenance may be uncontrollable at the level of the department supervisor, even though it may appear reasonable to trace some portion of that cost to the individual departments. At the level of the factory manager, on the other hand, maintenance costs may be viewed as controllable.

The controllability of certain costs may be shared by two or more executives. Thus, raw materials cost is generally considered to be a controllable cost. However, there are two distinct factors involved in materials cost. One is the price paid for the materials and the other is the usage of those materials. The responsibilities for these two factors may not be coincidental. The responsibility for prices may rest with the purchasing agent, while that for usage, with the production department supervisors.

It is important that cost controllability be understood in the proper sense. It does not involve eliminating costs, but, rather, keeping costs as close as possible to some desirable and reasonably attainable levels, or standards.

### Costs Relevant to Alternative Choices

Business managers are frequently faced with decisions among two or more alternatives. These decisions may be fairly complex in terms of numbers of possible choices—for example, choosing among alternatives A, B, C, D, and E, all of which are mutually exclusive. Other decisions may involve simply the alternatives of accepting or rejecting a single proposal. Regardless of the degree of complexity of a particular decision, management must obtain all of the information relevant to the alternatives. This information will include, very importantly, cost data. It will likely also include other financial data, such as revenues, and many other facts that cannot be expressed quantitatively. For example, the impact of a decision upon employee relations or upon the corporate image is a crucial factor but is not normally subject to quantitative measurement. Thus, it must be kept in mind that, while financial data are important to a business decision, they are still only part of the basis for the final decision; they do not make the decision by themselves.

As is already apparent from the limited discussion in this chapter, there is a great variety of cost data available within a business firm. Not all of these data are likely to be relevant to the alternatives in a specific decision and, hence, not all should be reported to management for decision-making purposes. A surfeit of irrelevant information can be just as useless and misleading as a lack of significant facts. Accountants, therefore, must be able to develop those cost data which are relevant to the particular decision at hand and to report them to management in a manner which will facilitate analysis of the alternatives and formulation of a decision.

*Relevant and Irrelevant Costs.* A *relevant cost* is one which will be affected by a decision among alternatives. Hence, it is relevant to the analysis of that decision. The term *differential cost* is often used for the same concept because a relevant cost will be different in amount depending upon which alternative is chosen. An *irrelevant cost,* of course, is just the opposite of a relevant cost. It will be unaffected by a decision; it will be the same regardless of the choice that is made. Consequently, it has no relevance to the analysis for decision making. It can and should be ignored.

To illustrate these concepts, consider a decision to purchase or to rent a computer—given that the decision to acquire a computer has already been made. The rental contract would include installation, servicing, and maintenance by the manufacturer. The purchase price would include only the cost of the equipment delivered to the purchaser's plant. For the sake of simplicity, let us assume that all costs associated with the computer can be classified as one of the following:

1. Acquisition cost, including installation and debugging.
2. Service and maintenance cost.
3. Operating cost (includes labor, power, paper, and cards).
4. Space occupancy cost (depreciation, insurance, taxes, and so forth, on the portion of the plant in which the computer will be housed).

From the information given, it is apparent that acquisition costs will differ as between the two alternatives. Under the rental contract, the only acquisition costs would be the periodic rent payments. Under the purchase agreement, the acquisition costs would include the price of the equipment, installation charges, and debugging expenses. Service and maintenance cost would exist as a separate item only if the computer is purchased; the rent payments would include this item. The operating costs and the space occupancy costs would be the same regardless of the alternative chosen. The decision is, in essence, how to finance the acquisition of the computer. This decision will have no effect on the costs of housing and operating the equipment. Thus, the acquisition and the service and maintenance costs are relevant costs, while the operating and the space occupancy costs are irrelevant to the decision.

The reader should avoid the mistake of thinking of relevant costs as equivalent to variable costs and irrelevant costs as equivalent to fixed costs. In the computer illustration above, observe that the monthly rental charge, a typical fixed cost, is a relevant cost in the decision-making analysis. Conversely, the operating costs, which are likely to be largely variable with the volume of computer usage, are irrelevant costs in the analysis.

**Incremental Cost.**   The *incremental cost* of any one alternative in a decision-making situation is simply the additional cost that will be incurred if and only if that alternative is chosen. Since incremental cost is the added cost associated with a single alternative, it obviously derives from the concept of a relevant cost. In fact, it might be thought of as the net aggregation of all of the relevant costs peculiar to an alternative. The amount of the incremental cost in any case depends upon the reference point of the analysis. For example, suppose that the total output of a factory is now 100,000 units per year and the total annual cost in that factory is $500,000. A proposal has been made to increase annual output to 150,000 units and total annual cost to $650,000. The additional 50,000 units of output is the alternative that has been proposed—an alternative to no change in the present volume of production. The incremental cost of this alternative is the additional $150,000 of annual cost. The reference point for this analysis is the present production volume. Suppose, however, that management had already decided that output must be increased by 50,000 units annually and that the alternatives now being considered are different ways of accomplishing this objective. Alternative A would increase total annual costs by $150,000, while alternative B would increase them by $190,000. With respect to present operations, these two amounts represent the incremental costs of the alternatives. However, with respect to alternative A, the less costly of the two, the incremental cost of choosing alternative B is $40,000.

If an incremental cost is associated with an alternative course of action which management may or may not adopt, it is a cost that may or may not be incurred. If the alternative is rejected, the incremental cost will be avoided. Similarly, if the proposed alternative is to eliminate some existing course of action rather than to add a new one, there would be certain existing costs that could be avoided. These are referred to as *avoidable costs*. For example, a proposal to reduce output would entail the avoidance of some costs. Actually, an avoidable cost is simply a different way of looking at an incremental cost. Indeed, it might be defined as an incremental cost saving. The parallel concepts of incremental cost and avoidable cost are extremely important in decision making, for they are the cost effects of alternatives that might be chosen in the decision process.

**Marginal Cost.**   Literally, marginal cost and incremental cost are synonymous terms. Marginal cost has such a specific definition in economics, however, that it would be inaccurate and undesirable to use the terms interchangeably. In economics, marginal cost is the cost incurred in order to obtain one additional unit of output. This meaning is similar but not identical to that of incremental cost. In the preceding section, there was an example of an incremental cost of $150,000 associated with an increase of 50,000 units of output from a plant. This could not be called the marginal cost also. Marginal cost in this illustration would be the additional cost of producing each successive one of those 50,000 units. In this text, the additional costs associated with a particular alternative in a decision-making problem will consistently be referred to as incremental costs.

**Out-of-Pocket Cost.**  An *out-of-pocket cost* is one which requires a current or future outlay of cash. Hence, it is susceptible to change by a current or future management decision. For example, the decision to exploit a mineral deposit presently owned by the company will result in certain costs such as wages and supplies which will require cash outlays. The same decision also results in the incurrence of the cost item depletion, the cost of the mineral resources exhausted as a result of mining operations. This cost, however, does not involve current cash expenditures. The cash payment (or at least the commitment to make a cash payment) for the mineral deposit was made earlier, at the time of acquisition of the property. Once the property has been obtained, such costs as depletion and depreciation are not out-of-pocket costs. Prior to purchase, however, the cost of the property does constitute an out-of-pocket cost of the decision to purchase. This particular cost concept is especially useful in analyses of future cash flows related to proposed investments.

**Sunk Cost.**  In the mineral deposit example in the preceding paragraph, the cost of depletion is a sunk cost. A *sunk cost* is one which is incurred simply as a consequence of a prior investment of capital; it requires no current outlay. Thus, it is essentially the opposite of an out-of-pocket cost. Depreciation, depletion, and amortization of intangibles are the principal examples of sunk costs. Despite the somewhat negative implications of the word "sunk," especially in maritime activities, a sunk cost should not be thought of as something bad or as a mistake of the past. Rather, it is the current evidence of a commitment made in the past. As such, it is an irrelevant cost for purposes of decision making.

## MISCELLANEOUS COST CONCEPTS

### Replacement Cost

When an asset is acquired, its historical cost is presumably equal to its market value on the date of acquisition. At some later time, however, the market value of that asset may have changed significantly. For certain analytical purposes, the current market value of the asset may be more relevant to management than its historical cost. Management may need to know what it would cost to acquire the asset currently. The *replacement cost* of an asset is what the firm would have to spend currently to obtain the services provided by that asset. In general, this amount is the current market value of the asset. Replacement cost is easily and objectively determinable for assets with well established and active markets (e.g., basic raw materials such as steel or copper). Determining the replacement cost of more specialized assets (e.g., custom-made production machinery) may necessitate a fairly subjective estimate. Nevertheless, the concept is valid and useful. In financial accounting, the most familiar use of replacement cost is in connection with the valuation of inventories at "the lower of cost or market," where "market" is current replacement cost.

## Opportunity Cost

In economic analysis, the word cost most commonly means opportunity cost. The *opportunity cost* of an economic good or service is the maximum amount which that good or service could yield if applied to some other purpose. Hence, opportunity cost is frequently defined as the net cash receipts foregone in the most advantageous alternative use of capital as a consequence of employing it in its present use. So long as transactions take place in a basically free market, it is reasonable to assume that the actual cost (in the accounting sense of the term) of an asset is equal to its opportunity cost at the moment of acquisition. However, as economic conditions change, the cost of that asset as reported on the balance sheet at some future date (i.e., actual cost minus accumulated depreciation to date) is not necessarily equal to the opportunity cost of retaining it. Rather, the current fair market value, or replacement cost, of the asset may be taken as its opportunity cost then.

Obviously, the concept of opportunity cost is extremely important and useful to management in making decisions among alternatives. As a practical matter, however, it is normally impossible to identify with certainty the most advantageous alternative use of capital and, hence, impossible to determine opportunity cost, as such, quantitatively. Thus, practical business analyses must rely on such concepts as replacement cost and incremental cost to indicate the most advantageous uses of capital.

*Imputed costs* are particular types of opportunity cost. They are costs not actually incurred in an exchange transaction but still relevant to a particular business operation. For example, the use of cash already held in the company bank account to purchase additional inventory results in certain actual costs, measured in exchange transactions. The price of the goods, the freight charges on them, and the rental of additional warehouse space for them are examples. Since cash was not borrowed to finance the inventory buildup, no actual interest payments will be made. However, if the cash on hand had been invested in some other way, it could have resulted in the receipt of interest revenue. This interest foregone on an alternative investment is referred to as imputed interest and is one of the most familiar illustrations of an imputed cost. An imputed cost is a real cost, even though current accounting practice would not record it in the accounts; and management must not ignore it in making decisions.

## MULTIPLE COST CLASSIFICATION IN THE RECORDS

The discussions in this chapter should make it very clear that various schemes of cost classification are useful for various objectives. This is sometimes referred to as the concept of "different costs for different purposes." It is a very useful concept, and it should be incorporated in the design of the accounting system to the extent that it is feasible to do so. That is, the initial recording of a cost should seek to identify every class to which that cost might reasonably and usefully be assigned. The following is a purely illustrative listing of the classes to which a single cost item, the wages of a factory maintenance crew, might be assigned:

1. Cost item: wages and salaries, factory maintenance.
2. Functional classification: manufacturing overhead, indirect labor.
3. Volume relationship: variable.
4. Responsibility: controllable by plant foreman.
5. Relationship to units produced: indirect.

Such a multiple classification system is obviously very useful for a great many purposes. It permits quick answers to questions such as this: "What variable manufacturing overhead costs are controllable by the plant foreman?" Each cost item must bear an identification key for each classification to which it is assigned. Thus, the maintenance crew's wages in the illustration above must be accessible in the records according to any single classification or any combination thereof, as in the question suggested. Such detail in the accounting records cannot be attained at no cost. The more different classifications desired, the more costly will the accounting system be. Thus, management should require cost classifications that are called for with sufficient frequency to justify the cost of providing them. Information about costs that is needed only occasionally may be extracted from the records and underlying documents by special analysis. Of course, such an approach to information is not very efficient. However, it may be far less expensive than having readily available a great deal of information that is not likely to be used. A computer with random-access data storage greatly improves the practicality of multiple cost classifications. Such schemes will become increasingly practical as new storage devices with greater capacities and lower costs per record stored become available.

The reader will note that the illustrative listing above did not include any classification of the cost item as relevant or irrelevant. This omission was inevitable. It would be impossible to make such a classification without specifying the decision that was to be made. For example, the maintenance crew's wages might well be an irrelevant cost with respect to a decision to change the mix of products made in the factory; whereas it would be a relevant cost with respect to a decision to shut the factory down entirely.

## QUESTIONS FOR DISCUSSION

1. "Management is vitally concerned with future costs for the simple reason that they are the only costs over which managers can exercise any control. Hence, historical costs are of no interest to management except to the extent that they may be useful in predicting future costs." Do you agree or disagree with this statement? Explain your position.

2. What is a cost objective? Give several examples.

3. Define the concepts of direct and indirect costs. Can all of the costs incurred by a business enterprise be classified as either direct or indirect?

4. What is the difference between a cost and an expense? Is this a difference that is customarily recognized in common conversation as opposed to technical accounting discussions?

5. The Upsilon Corporation manufactures three products, Alpha, Beta, and Gamma, in its factory. Indicate whether you would expect each of the following cost items to be direct, indirect, or unrelated to product Beta, where Beta is the cost objective in question:
   a. Raw materials used to manufacture Beta
   b. Depreciation of factory and equipment
   c. Salary of factory manager
   d. Companywide advertising
   e. Wages of workers who package Beta
   f. Raw materials used to manufacture Gamma
   g. Federal income tax

6. For each cost item listed below, state whether you would expect it to be (1) variable in relation to production volume, (2) variable in relation to sales volume, (3) semivariable in relation to production volume, (4) semivariable in relation to sales volume, or (5) fixed. Briefly explain your reasoning in each case.
   a. Factory supervision
   b. Maintenance of office equipment
   c. Wages of production machine operators
   d. Bad debts

e. Depreciation on factory equipment

f. Freight on raw materials used

g. Janitors' wages

7. "Both variable and fixed costs may be either controllable or uncontrollable costs." Do you agree or disagree with this statement? Explain your position and use examples if you feel they will help support your answer.

8. What are the basic requisites of effective responsibility costing?

9. The following production costs are expected to be incurred at the indicated monthly production volumes (measured in units of output):

| Monthly Volume | Factory Wages | Maintenance | Supervision |
|---|---|---|---|
| 10,000 | $ 30,000 | $10,000 | $ 8,000 |
| 20,000 | 40,000 | 10,000 | 8,000 |
| 30,000 | 50,000 | 15,000 | 16,000 |
| 40,000 | 65,000 | 15,000 | 16,000 |
| 50,000 | 75,000 | 25,000 | 24,000 |
| 60,000 | 90,000 | 25,000 | 24,000 |
| 70,000 | 105,000 | 25,000 | 32,000 |
| 80,000 | 120,000 | 25,000 | 32,000 |
| 90,000 | 135,000 | 25,000 | 40,000 |
| 100,000 | 155,000 | 35,000 | 40,000 |

Barring some unusual occurrence, such as a strike, monthly production volume can be expected to fall somewhere between 60,000 and 90,000 units of product. As a practical matter, how would you recommend that each of these three cost items be classified—as variable, as fixed, or as semivariable? Why?

10. Jane Stewart is considering trading her sedan for a new sports car. She bought the sedan three years ago for $3,500 and still owes $400 on it. The sports car would cost $5,600. Jane could trade or sell her sedan for $1,200. With respect to Jane's decision, which costs are relevant and which are irrelevant? What would be the incremental cost (or cost saving) of a decision to buy the sports car in place of her sedan? Suppose that, if Jane does buy the sports car, she would have to abandon her plans to spend $1,500 on a European vacation this summer. How, if at all, would this fact affect your analysis of the costs relevant to her decision?

11. Michael Renzik has invented an automatic pancake turner. He plans to go into the business of making and selling this device, which he has patented. He estimates that each turner will cost $1.25 for materials. He anticipates no direct labor cost, for he plans to do all of the work himself. To this end, he will quit his present job, at which he earns $600 per month. He will rent a vacant garage as his workshop at a monthly rental of $90. He has already purchased all of the tools he needs for $150. To buy the same tools now, Renzik would have to pay $180.

In the foregoing paragraph, identify one or more examples of each of the following types of costs. (A single cost item may, of course, be identified as more than one type of cost.)

a. Historical cost      f. Out-of-pocket cost
b. Future cost         g. Sunk cost
c. Variable cost       h. Opportunity cost
d. Fixed cost          i. Replacement cost
e. Relevant cost       j. Unexpired cost

12. "All out-of-pocket costs are avoidable costs." Discuss the validity of this statement.

13. "In the long run, all costs are variable." Is this true? If so, why? If not, why not?

14. Economists generally define "cost" as opportunity cost. Why don't accountants do the same?

15. If all of a firm's costs are either perfectly variable or absolutely fixed and if its selling price remains constant no matter how many units of product are sold, will the firm's profit before tax (a) decrease as volume increases, (b) increase at a slower rate than volume, (c) increase in direct proportion to volume, or (d) increase at a faster rate than volume? Explain your answer.

16. What does it cost a manufacturing firm to make one unit of product?

# chapter 3

# The Cost Accounting Cycle

$T$HIS CHAPTER and the following one are concerned with the basic mechanics of recording and processing manufacturing cost data. These mechanics relate primarily to the financial accounting aspects of cost accounting—specifically, the valuation of inventories and the measurement of income in a manufacturing enterprise. At the same time, however, the manner of recording and classifying costs provides the key to effective cost control. Hence, cost accounting systems must be constructed with two important objectives in mind—accurate financial reports and effective cost control.

## THE FLOW OF COSTS IN MANUFACTURING

At the moment of their incurrence, all costs may be regarded as essentially identical. They are all unexpired costs, incurred in the expectation that they will contribute to the production of revenue. What happens to costs after their incurrence depends upon their natures and also upon the particular accounting practices employed by the firm. With a very few exceptions (e.g., the cost of land), all costs ultimately expire, or become expenses. The exact manner of their expiration, however, is determined by a number of factors, some of which are considered in the paragraphs that follow.

## Cost Expiration in General

*Long-Lived Assets.* Some costs are incurred in order to acquire assets which can be expected to contribute to the production of revenues over fairly long periods of time. The cost of a factory building is an example. The objective of income measurement requires that an appropriate portion of the cost of that building be charged to or matched with each dollar of revenue stemming from the sale of goods produced within its walls. Thus, only a portion of the building's cost will be matched with revenue in any one accounting period. The amount of such cost matched with revenue during any one period is the amount of the cost that expires during the period, that is, the amount which ceases to be an asset and becomes an expense. The process of periodically charging part of the cost of a long-lived asset to revenue is called *amortization*. The amortization of the cost of physical plant and equipment—buildings, machinery, vehicles, furniture, fixtures, and so forth—is called *depreciation*.

*Current Operating Expenses.* Certain other costs follow a path almost diametrically opposed to that taken by long-lived assets. Such costs as salesmen's commissions and delivery costs are normally assumed to have contributed to the creation of revenue at the moment of their incurrence. Hence, they are charged immediately to expense accounts without their ever being classified as assets. Many costs are typically accorded this same treatment, even though their direct relationship to current revenues is not as obvious as in the case of salesmen's commissions. Thus, such cost items as advertising, executives' salaries, and product development are generally treated as expenses in the period in which they are incurred, even though a careful examination of their natures might suggest that they will enhance revenues in future periods as well as in the current one. Such treatment is a matter of practical expediency in most cases, because the future revenue-generating potential would be difficult to measure or document. Whatever the reason, a great many costs are expensed as soon as they are incurred.

## Expiration of Manufacturing Costs

*Cost Transformations.* In manufacturing accounting, it is a generally accepted principle that the costs of manufacturing a product are treated as an asset—inventory—until the product is sold, at which time those costs are matched with the revenue from the sale in the process of measuring income. This means that certain costs, such as materials and plant property, which are initially recorded as separate assets, are transformed into a new type of asset before they ultimately become expenses. The process by which an asset's cost is transferred to another asset category, the cost of manufactured goods, is referred to as *cost transformation*. This amounts to a temporary change of asset classification pending the sale of the product. For example, the amortization of the cost of long-lived manufacturing facilities involves an intermediate cost transformation prior to ultimate cost expiration when the manufactured product is sold.

The concept that the costs incurred in the manufacture of a product are combined in a new asset and expire only when that product is sold (or in some way damaged or otherwise rendered unsalable) is commonly stated as the principle that *costs attach.* Under this principle, elements of cost which could not be stored in an asset account in and of themselves —such as labor cost—may become parts of the asset representing the cost of the manufactured product. Thus, manufacturing inventory accounts contain elements of cost which are not inventoriable separately. Labor cannot be stored as a commodity awaiting employment, but the cost of labor already employed can be seen in the form of a manufactured product and treated as part of the total cost of that product.

**Product and Period Costs.**  The foregoing paragraphs have explained how some costs in a manufacturing firm are included in the cost of the manufactured product, while others are treated as expenses of the accounting period in which they are incurred. The former type of cost is called a *product cost;* the latter is a *period cost.* It has already been observed that manufacturing costs are generally accepted as product costs. Nonmanufacturing costs, on the other hand, are treated as period costs. This distinction is generally accepted in current accounting practice, but it has not gone unchallenged. In recent years there has developed a significant movement away from this traditional approach to the product/period cost distinction and toward an approach which treats as product costs only those manufacturing costs that vary in proportion to the volume of goods produced. In this newer approach, fixed manufacturing costs, along with nonmanufacturing costs, are treated as period costs.

**Absorption Costing.**  The traditional method of accounting for manufacturing costs has included all of them as costs of the product, regardless of their behavior with respect to changes in volume. This method is called *absorption costing* or *full costing;* for the product "absorbs" the full amount of manufacturing costs. Fixed and variable factory costs are handled in essentially the same manner. The distinction between product and period costs is made only on the basis of the different functional areas of business activity; manufacturing costs being product costs and distribution, administrative, research, and financial costs being period costs. (Of course, certain nonmanufacturing costs, while not included as part of the cost of the product, may be deferred to future periods as assets rather than being treated as expenses of the current period. Costs of office furniture and of unexpired insurance on office buildings are examples.)

**Variable Costing.**  In many manufacturing enterprises, the traditional absorption costing technique has been replaced by the more recent innovation, *variable costing*. Under the variable costing method, only those manufacturing costs which vary with output are included in the cost of the product; fixed manufacturing costs are accounted for as period costs. Thus, this method distinguishes between product and period costs on the basis of cost-volume relationships as well as on the basis of the functional areas of business operations. Variable nonmanufacturing costs, it must be understood, are treated as period costs under variable costing, just as they are under absorption costing. In practice, direct materials and direct labor are almost always treated as variable costs. Hence, the actual distinction between absorption and variable costing lies in the accounting treatment of manufacturing overhead and, specifically, fixed manufacturing overhead. Variable manufacturing overhead, like materials and labor, is treated as a product cost under both methods. Fixed manufacturing overhead is treated as a product cost in absorption costing but as a period cost in variable costing.

In this chapter, the methodologies of both absorption and variable costing will be illustrated. A critical comparison of the two will be presented in the following chapter.

## Manufacturing Inventory Accounts

In a merchandising enterprise, a single inventory account for all merchandise on hand is typical. This single account in the general ledger is supported by detailed records for stocks of individual items in inventory. But only one general ledger account is needed for merchandise inventory from the time it is purchased until it is sold. In a manufacturing firm, however, a single inventory account is not suitable. The function that distinguishes manufacturing from merchandising is the conversion of the materials purchased by the manufacturer into a new product. Thus, pig iron is converted to sheet steel; sheet steel, to automobile fenders; and so forth. At any one time, a manufacturing enterprise is likely to have on hand raw materials as yet unprocessed, goods in the process of manufacture but not yet completed, and finished products awaiting sale. Each of these stages of goods is normally accounted for in a separate inventory account. Raw materials are reported in a Materials Inventory account; uncompleted production, in a Work in Process account; and completed production, in a Finished Product account. Each of these is an inventory account and an asset. Each is a part of the sequential flow of manufacturing costs. Materials, as such, appear when they are purchased from suppliers. They become part of Work in Process at the time they are issued from the storeroom to the factory for use. Work in Process becomes Finished Product when the process of manufacture is completed. Finally, Finished Product is transferred to the Cost of Goods Sold account at the point of sale of the items in inventory. Sale is the point at which manufacturing costs expire (excepting fixed manufacturing costs under the variable costing method); hence, Cost of Goods Sold is an expense account.

This flow of manufacturing costs in the absorption costing method is presented diagrammatically in Figure 3–1. Notice that labor and manu-

FIGURE 3–1

Flow of Manufacturing Costs in Absorption Costing

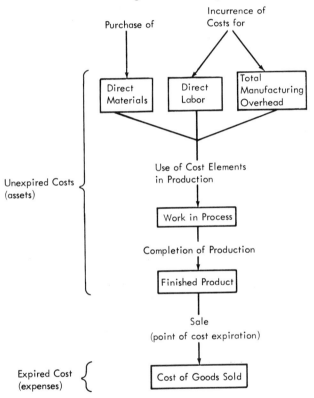

facturing overhead are included in this diagram in a position parallel to that of materials. While these two cost elements cannot be stored in inventory themselves, as can materials, they are costs of the product and are stored in the inventories of Work in Process and Finished Product. All three manufacturing cost elements finally become expenses as part of Cost of Goods Sold. Figure 3–2 repeats this cost flow diagram for variable costing. The only difference between the two is in the handling of fixed manufacturing overhead.

FIGURE 3–2

Flow of Manufacturing Costs in Variable Costing

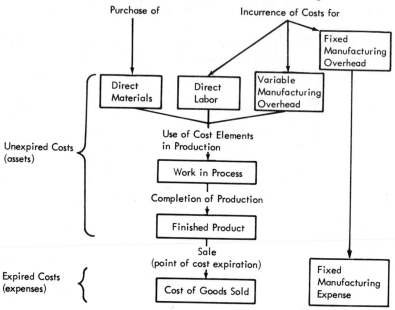

## ACCOUNTING FOR MANUFACTURING COSTS

### Recording Costs by Responsibility

One of management's major objectives in accounting for costs is to produce information that will be useful for purposes of controlling those costs. This objective can be accomplished only if costs are traced to the managers responsible for controlling them. Hence, the cost accounting system should be designed with a view toward the responsibility accounting concept discussed in the preceding chapter. Cost data should be collected and reported according to the various responsibility centers. The actual process of tracing costs to responsibility centers may vary among firms. It would be possible, for example, to have separate accounts for each cost element (i.e., materials, labor, and manufacturing overhead) in each cost center. In a large, decentralized manufacturing company, such accounting detail is very desirable. Most of the illustrations in this text will include only one set of accounts, as though there were only a single responsibility center in the firm. This is done simply to keep the sizes of the illustrations small. Of course, exactly the same accounting procedures could be extended to a large number of similar accounts.

## Accounting for Materials

*Purchase.* Accounting for materials begins when a need for a particular material is determined at some level of responsibility within the firm and a formal request is made that such material be purchased in the required amount. This formal request is commonly made on a standard form called a *purchase requisition.* This is an internal document, submitted by the department requesting the material to the purchasing department. A requisition may be initiated by one of the production departments which uses the item in question. More commonly, however, the requisition would be initiated by the materials storeroom when existing stocks of a material reach a preestablished minimum level which serves as a signal to reorder. No formal journal entry is prepared to record the issuance of a purchase requisition. However, the requisition sets into motion the activities which will ultimately result in the journalizing of a purchase.

If the purchase requisition is approved, the purchasing department will select the most advantageous supplier of the material needed and will issue a *purchase order* for the item. A purchase order is a document sent by the purchasing department to the supplier. It includes materials specifications, quantities ordered, and the date the items are needed. The supplier fills this order by shipping the materials requested and bills the purchaser for them by sending an invoice, which details the items purchased, the quantities shipped, and the prices. After the actual shipment has been compared with the invoice, called a *purchase invoice* in the hands of the purchaser, the invoice becomes the basis for the preparation of a journal entry to record the purchase, the invoice price (including freight charges, and so forth, where applicable) being the measured cost of the materials purchased. Such an entry follows:[1]

```
Materials Inventory.....................................  xxx
    Vouchers Payable....................................         xxx
```

In this entry and in similar ones throughout this text, it is assumed that a voucher system is used to control cash disbursements and, hence, that all obligations incurred in the purchase of goods or services are credited to an account titled Vouchers Payable.

*Usage.* As materials are needed in the factory, the production departments issue *materials requisitions* (not to be confused with purchase requisitions) to the materials storeroom for the required quantities of the particular items. These materials requisitions, indicating the department

---

[1] In this entry and in those on the following pages, no dollar amounts are used. Only the accounts debited and credited are indicated. A later comprehensive illustration will repeat these entries with specific dollar amounts.

requesting the items, are the bases for tracing materials costs to responsibility centers within the plant. The issuance of the materials to the factory by the storeroom signals a change in the inventory classification of those items. They now cease to be materials, as such, and become a part of the product in the process of manufacture. This results in a cost transformation from Materials Inventory to Work in Process. The following entry is made:

```
Work in Process..............................................  xxx
        Materials Inventory...................................       xxx
```

The foregoing entry assumes that the materials requisitioned are direct materials. This is not always the case. Both direct and indirect materials may be included in the Materials Inventory account when they are purchased. When issued, however, indirect materials are not charged directly to the Work in Process account. To be sure, they will ultimately be charged to that account; but they are first accumulated along with other indirect manufacturing costs in an account for manufacturing overhead costs in general. Thus, the requisition of indirect materials would be recorded as follows:

```
Manufacturing Overhead Control..........................  xxx
        Materials Inventory...................................       xxx
```

At this point, the Manufacturing Overhead Control account may be taken simply as a temporary account for the accumulation of all indirect factory costs.

## Accounting for Labor

For purposes of discussion, problems of accounting for labor may be classified in two categories: *Labor cost accounting* is concerned with the accounts and amounts to be charged (debited) for labor costs. *Payroll accounting* is concerned with the accounts and amounts to be credited in the recording and paying of obligations to employees for labor services. In large firms, it is economically feasible to departmentalize many different activities and to accomplish considerable division of work. In such a firm, labor cost accounting may be handled by a factory accounting department and payroll accounting, by a payroll department. In such cases, some account common to both departments is needed so that the two separate accounting operations may be tied together and reconciled, to the extent that they both deal with the same basic data. This account may have different titles in different companies. In this text, it will be referred to as the Payroll Summary account. This is the account credited by the factory accounting department for the total of amounts debited to the various manufacturing cost accounts affected and the account debited by the payroll department for the total of credits representing obligations to employees and other parties entitled to some portion of the employees' earnings (e.g., the federal government). Obviously, except for lags or errors in bookkeeping procedures in the two departments, the debits and credits to the Payroll Summary account for any period of time will be equal.

*Labor Cost Accounting.* The proper charging of labor costs to manufacturing cost accounts requires that distinctions be made between direct and indirect labor costs and between labor costs incurred in different responsibility centers. The former distinction is largely a matter of definition; the latter, a matter of accurate record keeping. The maintenance of records which show the amounts of time worked by employees in various centers and the availability of hourly wage rate data permit the charging of factory labor costs by areas of responsibility. As mentioned above, for the sake of simplicity, the discussions and illustrations in this chapter will assume that there is only one responsibility center—the entire factory—in the plant under study. This assumption does not alter the basic concepts involved or the mechanics of recording labor costs; it merely reduces the number of accounts to be handled.

As stated in Chapter 2, direct labor is that labor which can be traced logically and practically to the product. All other factory labor costs are regarded as indirect and are included in manufacturing overhead. The wages of foremen, janitors, watchmen, factory clerks, and others whose work is not concerned directly with the product are usually treated as indirect costs. In addition, a number of payments made to direct laborers are commonly included in manufacturing overhead rather than in direct labor. Wages paid to direct laborers while they are not actually performing productive work are usually accounted for as manufacturing overhead. Examples of such wages are vacation pay, holiday pay, and idle time pay. The reason for treating as manufacturing overhead such payments to workers whose labor is normally regarded as direct is that these payments cannot be traced directly to units of product. Vacation pay and idle time pay could hardly be charged directly to particular units of product, as no units are produced during the periods for which those costs are incurred. Premiums paid to direct laborers for overtime and for night shift work are normally included in manufacturing overhead. If such premiums were charged directly to the units produced during overtime or night shifts, those units would have higher costs than those produced during the regular 40-hour week. Yet, the overtime and night shift work is usually necessitated by a generally high level of production, not by specific units or jobs. Hence, it would not be meaningful to report units manufactured during overtime or night hours as more costly than their counterparts produced during the regular 8-hour day. Rather, overtime and night shift premiums should be viewed as costs incurred because total production exceeds the capacity of the plant during a straight 40-hour week. As such, these costs are applicable to all units produced but directly traceable to none.[2]

The following journal entry illustrates the distribution of factory labor costs to the appropriate manufacturing cost accounts:

```
Work in Process............................................  xxx
Manufacturing Overhead Control............................  xxx
    Payroll Summary.......................................         xxx
```

The debit to Work in Process is to charge the direct labor cost to the product. Manufacturing Overhead Control is debited for indirect labor costs, overtime premiums, vacation pay, and so forth. The detail supporting this entry would be accumulated and classified on a labor cost distribution sheet.

*Labor-Related Costs.*  In addition to wage and salary payments made to workers, employers incur a number of costs incidental to the employment of workers. These include such items as the employer's share of social security taxes, unemployment compensation taxes, insurance premiums, contributions to pension funds, and supplementary unemployment benefits. These are *labor-related costs* or *fringe benefits*. They are commonly treated as part of manufacturing overhead, to the extent that they relate to manufacturing workers. Labor-related costs are incurred in connection with nonmanufacturing workers also. These, logically, are charged to nonmanufacturing expense accounts rather than to manufacturing overhead. The entry to record labor-related costs applicable to factory employees is illustrated below:

```
Manufacturing Overhead Control...........................  xxx
    Social Security Taxes Payable.........................         xxx
    Unemployment Compensation Taxes Payable...............         xxx
    Health Insurance Premiums Payable.....................         xxx
    Other similar liabilities.............................         xxx
```

There is no credit to the Payroll Summary account in this entry, for the labor-related costs do not involve direct payments to workers or withholdings from workers' earnings. Thus, labor-related costs are not involved in the payroll accounting process.

Some firms include labor-related costs in the classification of direct labor. This is accomplished by estimating the total average labor-related cost per direct labor hour and adding that average to the hourly wage rate to determine the total direct labor charge per hour. For example,

---

[2] An exception to this treatment of overtime premiums as manufacturing overhead occurs when the overtime is necessitated solely in order to accelerate the completion of a specific job. For example, a ship owner may want to have his ship completed and put back into service faster than the shipyard's normal schedule would allow. Thus, he may require overtime simply to meet his own time schedule. In such a case, the overtime premium should be included in the direct labor costs charged to that specific job. Presumably, that customer would also have to pay a higher price to compensate the shipyard for the overtime pay.

assume that the direct labor wage rate in a plant is $4.00 per hour and that the average total labor-related cost is estimated to be $1.20 per hour. Direct labor is then charged at a rate of $5.20 per hour. Since the $1.20 portion of this charge is an estimate, it is likely that the total actual labor-related costs incurred would be somewhat more or less than the total charged to Work in Process. Such a difference would be disposed of by an adjustment at the end of the accounting period.[3] Including the labor-related costs applicable to direct labor wages in the classification of direct labor cost is unquestionably valid, and many accountants argue that it is distinctly preferable to including them in manufacturing overhead. Nevertheless, most firms continue to treat labor-related costs as part of manufacturing overhead; and they will consistently be included in manufacturing overhead in this text.

Regardless of how labor-related costs are classified for cost accounting purposes, their nature remains the same. The same procedures for controlling these costs would be employed no matter how they were classified in the accounts, and their significance in decision making is unaffected by their classification. Any decision that will have a direct impact upon direct labor cost will have a similar impact upon labor-related costs, and the latter are pertinent to that decision, whether they are classified as direct labor or as manufacturing overhead.

***Evolving Problems of Labor Cost Accounting.*** Traditionally, labor has been regarded as a direct cost, incurred specifically because of the units of product manufactured. Likewise, it has generally been considered to be a variable cost, fluctuating in direct proportion to the volume of production. Where labor cost is incurred on a piece rate basis—so much per unit of product manufactured—it clearly is both direct and variable with respect to production. Even where direct laborers are paid on an hourly basis, labor cost is essentially direct and variable if the workers are laid off when no production work is being done. However, if workers are regularly paid for a full 40-hour week, regardless of the amount of production, then labor cost would appear to be a fixed cost directly traceable to the firm's being in operation. It would not then vary with the volume of production nor would it be directly traceable to units of product.

At the time of this writing, it would not be accurate to say that labor has truly become a fixed cost in American industry. There is some movement in that direction, however. Supplementary unemployment benefit payments and other wage continuation plans require employers to pay workers for time when they are not working. The demands for a

---

[3] The manner of disposing of the difference between actual and estimated labor-related costs would be essentially the same as that illustrated later in this chapter for disposing of differences between actual manufacturing overhead costs and normal manufacturing overhead costs charged to production.

guaranteed annual wage, or annual salary for production workers, recur in many labor contract negotiations. It is possible that these demands will one day be met. Nor is this movement caused entirely by bargaining demands. Many employers have found numerous advantages in having a stable work force, even if it necessitates paying employees for nonproductive time.

The ultimate accounting for direct labor cost in absorption costing would be basically the same, whether the cost is variable or fixed. In variable costing, however, direct labor would be charged to the cost of the product (i.e., to Work in Process) only if it were a variable cost. If it were a fixed cost, it would be treated as an expense of the period. Throughout this text, discussions and illustrations will assume that direct labor is a variable cost. Hence, it will always be treated as a product cost. This assumption is consistent with reality in most American manufacturing firms.

*Payroll Accounting.* The mechanics of payroll accounting are common to all enterprises which employ a significant number of workers. The payroll department handles the pay records of all employees, whether they receive hourly wages or weekly salaries, whether they are employed in production or in some nonmanufacturing activity. Basically, the payroll department's task is to determine who is to receive what amount of each employee's gross earnings and to prepare payroll checks. The federal government receives a portion of each worker's earnings in the form of income tax withheld from the worker's pay and also in the form of social security[4] tax withheld. In some states, income tax is also withheld for the account of the state government. Union dues are frequently "checked," or withheld by the employer for the union. There may be withholdings for insurance programs to which employees contribute, United Fund and similar donations pledged by the employees, and investment programs such as the bond-a-month plan for the purchase of U.S. savings bonds. Finally, after all withholdings, the balance is paid to the employee; this in his "take-home" pay. Following is a general journal entry to record the payment of a payroll in accordance with the foregoing discussion:

| | | |
|---|---|---|
| Payroll Summary | xxx | |
| Federal Income Tax Withheld | | xxx |
| Social Security Taxes Payable | | xxx |
| Union Dues Withheld | | xxx |
| United Fund Contributions Withheld | | xxx |
| Vouchers Payable | | xxx |

The credit to Vouchers Payable is for the amount of the employees' net "take-home" pay. This liability will be discharged when the payroll checks are drawn and disbursed. The liabilities for the amounts withheld

---

[4] The social security tax is also referred to as the OASI (Old Age and Survivors' Insurance) tax and as the FICA (Federal Insurance Contributions Act) tax.

will be discharged when remittances are made to the government, the union, the United Fund, etc.

## Accounting for Manufacturing Overhead

Thus far, we have observed the recording of three items of manufacturing overhead cost—indirect materials, indirect labor, and labor-related costs. There are many other items in the manufacturing overhead classification, all of which must be accounted for as have these three. It is also necessary to charge manufacturing overhead costs to the product, that is, to Work in Process. In this section, we shall examine first the accumulation and classification of manufacturing overhead cost items and then the charging of these costs to the manufactured product.

*Recording Variable and Fixed Manufacturing Overhead Costs.* In the entries already illustrated, the three manufacturing overhead items encountered were charged to a single account, Manufacturing Overhead Control. As already mentioned, it is desirable to accumulate these costs according to responsibility. Hence, each distinct responsibility center ought to have its own accounts. Again, for simplicity, we shall assume that there is only one responsibility center in the plant under study. There is still a further classification of manufacturing overhead costs which should be observed, however. Traditionally, all manufacturing overhead costs have been included in one account for each responsibility center. In recent years, however, management has become increasingly interested in having manufacturing cost data identified and recorded in the accounts as variable or fixed with respect to changes in the volume of output. Since direct materials and labor are almost universally regarded as variable costs, as a practical matter only manufacturing overhead costs must be segregated into variable and fixed classifications. This can be accomplished by having two manufacturing overhead control accounts for each responsibility center—Variable Manufacturing Overhead Control and Fixed Manufacturing Overhead Control. This separate recording of variable and fixed manufacturing overhead can and should be effected under either an absorption costing or a variable costing system. For the requirements of financial accounting, separate recording is essential only in variable costing. For purposes of management, however, it is equally desirable under both methods.

There is still the very important problem of identifying those costs which are variable and those which are fixed. In a practical situation, this distinction may present some very perplexing problems. Nevertheless, as mentioned in the previous chapter, the distinction is so useful to management that it should be made even if it involves a number of approximations. For purposes of illustration in this chapter, we shall consider only eight manufacturing overhead cost items, including the three already encountered in connection with accounting for materials and labor. These eight items are listed below and classified as variable or fixed. *The classifications of the individual cost items here are for illustrative purposes and do not purport to be applicable in manufacturing enterprises generally.*

|  Variable Costs  |  Fixed Costs  |
|---|---|
| Indirect materials | Indirect labor |
| Labor-related costs | Labor-related costs |
| Power and light | Depreciation |
|  | Insurance |
|  | Property taxes |
|  | Repairs and maintenance |

Labor-related costs are unique in this listing, as they are included both as variable and as fixed. To the extent that they relate to direct labor, a variable cost here, they are variable. To the extent that they relate to indirect labor, a fixed cost here, they are fixed.

We must now retrace our steps and reconstruct some of the entries prepared earlier so that all manufacturing overhead items will be identified and recorded as variable or fixed. The entry for the requisition of indirect materials now appears as follows:

```
Variable Manufacturing Overhead Control.....................  xxx
    Materials Inventory......................................          xxx
```

The entry to record the distribution of labor costs, including indirect labor, is now prepared thus:

```
Work in Process...........................................  xxx
Fixed Manufacturing Overhead Control......................  xxx
    Payroll Summary.......................................          xxx
```

The labor-related costs are now recorded as follows:

```
Variable Manufacturing Overhead Control...................  xxx
Fixed Manufacturing Overhead Control......................  xxx
    Social Security Taxes Payable.........................          xxx
    Unemployment Compensation Taxes Payable...............          xxx
    Health Insurance Premiums Payable.....................          xxx
    Other similar liabilities.............................          xxx
```

Note that the only change in each of the three entries above is in the title(s) of the manufacturing overhead account(s) debited. The remaining manufacturing overhead items in our lists may be recorded by the following entries:

```
Variable Manufacturing Overhead Control...................  xxx
    Vouchers Payable (power and light bills)..............          xxx

Fixed Manufacturing Overhead Control......................  xxx
    Accumulated Depreciation—Plant and Equipment.........          xxx
    Unexpired Insurance...................................          xxx
    Accrued Property Taxes Payable........................          xxx
    Vouchers Payable (repair and maintenance bills).......          xxx
```

These two entries assume that power and light and repair and maintenance bills are paid currently, that insurance has been paid for in advance, and that property taxes are accrued and paid subsequently.

*Charging Actual Manufacturing Overhead Costs to Production.* Because manufacturing overhead is indirect and in total is not perfectly
variable with output, it is not possible to charge manufacturing overhead
costs to production in the same way as materials and labor. The materials and labor costs associated with a particular product or batch of
production are determinable when the materials are used and the labor
time recorded. The manufacturing overhead costs associated with a particular product, however, can be determined only by some allocation
scheme, the total manufacturing overhead costs being allocated among
the units produced in some manner which appears reasonable. Total actual manufacturing overhead cost, of course, cannot be determined until
the end of the accounting period and, hence, cannot be allocated to the
products until then. If there is no objection to such a delay in charging
manufacturing overhead costs, an entry can be prepared as of the end of
each period to charge that period's production with its manufacturing
overhead costs. The entry depends upon the costing method employed in
the firm—absorption costing or variable costing. Under absorption costing, both variable and fixed manufacturing overhead are charged to
production.

| | | |
|---|---|---|
| Work in Process......................................... | xxx | |
|     Variable Manufacturing Overhead Control............... | | xxx |
|     Fixed Manufacturing Overhead Control................. | | xxx |

Under variable costing, only the variable manufacturing overhead is
treated as a product cost.

| | | |
|---|---|---|
| Work in Process......................................... | xxx | |
|     Variable Manufacturing Overhead Control............... | | xxx |

Fixed manufacturing overhead is treated as an expense of the current
period under variable costing and, hence, would not be transferred to
Work in Process. Fixed Manufacturing Overhead Control, like other current expense accounts, would be closed at the end of the period to the
Revenue and Expense Summary account.

*Charging Manufacturing Overhead to Production at Normal Rates.*
The practice of charging actual manufacturing overhead to production
after the end of the accounting period involves a number of difficulties.
These stem from the facts that manufacturing overhead is indirect and
is composed, in part at least, of fixed costs. If all manufacturing overhead were directly traceable to and perfectly variable with output, it
could be charged to production in the same way as materials and labor.
It is a fact, however, that manufacturing overhead is partly fixed. As
more automation is introduced into manufacturing processes, it is reasonable to expect that the fixed-cost component of total manufacturing

overhead will become increasingly larger. Variable manufacturing overhead is not readily traceable to individual products either, even though it does vary in proportion to total output. For example, the usage of indirect materials is commonly a function of the volume of production; but the usage of specific indirect materials cannot ordinarily be traced to specific products. Two of the most notable difficulties attendant upon the charging of actual manufacturing overhead to production are discussed in the paragraphs which follow.

If a manufacturer contracts to produce special equipment or some other specialized product for a customer and to sell that special product at production cost plus some stipulated profit margin, no billing can be made until the total production cost of the order is determined. If actual manufacturing overhead is charged to production, the total production cost of any order will be unknown until after the end of the period in which it is produced. This is clearly an intolerable situation if actual manufacturing overhead were charged to production only at the end of each year. Even if it were charged monthly, the delay would only be reduced, not eliminated. Quite obviously, the customer would want to know as soon as the order was finished what he was going to have to pay for it. Similarly, the manufacturer would hardly care to wait until the end of the year before he could bill his customers. Hence, it is essential to have some regular method of determining the manufacturing overhead applicable to an order or to any other batch of output as soon as the production process is finished. It is true, of course, that most production is sold at established list prices. However, there are enough sales at cost plus a profit margin to make this consideration a real one. For example, many defense contracts for new or custom-designed items provide for a price equal to cost plus some predetermined profit margin. While the number of such contracts is not very large, the dollar amounts involved are usually substantial.

Another disadvantage of charging actual manufacturing overhead cost to production may be seen from an examination of a firm that experiences significant seasonal variations in the volume of its production. Such a situation is depicted in Table 3–1. For purposes of this illustration, all variable costs—materials, labor, and variable manufacturing overhead—are included in a single figure *per unit of output;* it is the same each month. Fixed manufacturing overhead, on the other hand, is the same *in total* each month. Therefore, it varies, per unit of output, inversely with the volume of production. In months of low production, unit fixed cost and, consequently, total unit cost are relatively high. Conversely, in months of high production, unit cost is relatively low. Thus, marked differences in the unit cost of the product appear from month to month even though the product remains unchanged; only the quantities in which it is produced change. These variations in unit cost are likely

TABLE 3–1

Impact of Seasonal Output on Unit Cost

| Month | Units of Output Produced | Fixed Cost in Total | Fixed Cost per Unit | Variable Cost per Unit | Total Cost per Unit of Output |
|---|---|---|---|---|---|
| January | 1,000 | $ 8,000 | $8.00 | $6.00 | $14.00 |
| February | 2,000 | 8,000 | 4.00 | 6.00 | 10.00 |
| March | 2,500 | 8,000 | 3.20 | 6.00 | 9.20 |
| April | 4,000 | 8,000 | 2.00 | 6.00 | 8.00 |
| May | 6,000 | 8,000 | 1.33 | 6.00 | 7.33 |
| June | 8,000 | 8,000 | 1.00 | 6.00 | 7.00 |
| July | 8,000 | 8,000 | 1.00 | 6.00 | 7.00 |
| August | 6,000 | 8,000 | 1.33 | 6.00 | 7.33 |
| September | 4,000 | 8,000 | 2.00 | 6.00 | 8.00 |
| October | 3,500 | 8,000 | 2.29 | 6.00 | 8.29 |
| November | 2,000 | 8,000 | 4.00 | 6.00 | 10.00 |
| December | 1,000 | 8,000 | 8.00 | 6.00 | 14.00 |
| | 48,000 | $96,000 | | | |

to be misleading and to result in meaningless fluctuations in income from month to month, for selling price is not likely to change as unit cost changes. While the extent of the fluctuations in monthly output in Table 3–1 is admittedly extreme, it serves to illustrate the problem of charging actual manufacturing overhead costs to production when output varies seasonally.

The reader should by now have recognized that the problem of unit cost fluctuating with seasonal variations in output exists only under absorption costing. Under variable costing, since no fixed costs are charged to the product, unit cost will be unaffected by volume fluctuations. The problem discussed with reference to the cost-plus-profit contract, however, is common to both absorption and variable costing.

If some manufacturing overhead cost per unit that would be valid over the whole year could be determined in advance, it would solve the two problems described above. First, it would permit the charging of manufacturing overhead cost to products as soon as they are completed. Hence, the cost-plus-profit contract could be billed as soon as the work is finished. Second, it would eliminate the seasonal fluctuations in unit cost due to the seasonal variations in output. For example, in Table 3–1, if the firm's accountant could have foreseen that a total of 48,000 units of product would have been produced during the year and that a total of $96,000 in fixed costs would have been incurred in that year, he could have predetermined that the fixed cost of producing each unit would be $2 as an average for the entire year. Therefore, the total unit cost would be $8 in each month. But can annual output and fixed costs be known in advance? While they cannot be predicted with certainty, they typically can be estimated in advance with reasonable confidence. As a matter of fact, if management is to plan business operations for a year, such estimates must be made. When these estimates are formalized, they are generally called budgets. For the present, we are concerned only with budgets for output and for fixed manufacturing overhead. Given these two budgeted data, we can determine by simple division the budgeted unit fixed cost of the product for a period. When this budgeted unit cost is used in charging fixed manufacturing overhead to production, it is referred to as a *normal fixed manufacturing overhead rate.*

A *normal variable manufacturing overhead rate* may be determined quite readily from observations of the variable manufacturing overhead costs incurred per unit of product in the past, with adjustments for changing prices and circumstances. By virtue of the fact that it is variable, the variable manufacturing overhead rate would be budgeted directly as an amount per unit of product. Budgeted output would not be needed here. The variable manufacturing overhead rate would be the same at any level of output, whereas the fixed manufacturing overhead rate would decline as higher levels of output were budgeted.

It must be understood that the use of normal manufacturing overhead rates derived from budgeted data does not mean that the budget itself is recorded in the accounts. The manufacturing overhead charged to production in this case is the normal manufacturing overhead rate(s) multiplied by the actual output for the period. Budgeted output is used only to determine the normal fixed manufacturing overhead rate, not to charge manufacturing overhead to production. The normal manufacturing overhead rates are, in effect, estimates of what actual manufacturing overhead per unit of output will be. Thus, the manufacturing overhead cost actually charged to Work in Process is a function of the normal manufacturing overhead rates and the actual output for the period.

Charging manufacturing overhead costs to production at normal rates means that the Work in Process account will not consist entirely of literally *actual* costs. The normal cost element will carry through to the Finished Product and Cost of Goods Sold accounts. (Refer to Figures 3–1 and 3–2 to see why this must be so.) This minor deviation from actual cost is widely accepted in industry and, as a matter of fact, is typical of cost accounting systems. Because the use of normal manufacturing overhead rates results in the charging to Work in Process of something other than actual manufacturing overhead costs incurred, it is general practice to make the offsetting credits for that charge to accounts other than the manufacturing overhead control accounts. These credits are made to accounts titled Variable Manufacturing Overhead Applied and, under absorption costing only, Fixed Manufacturing Overhead Applied. Journal entries to record the charging (or the application) of manufacturing overhead at normal rates are illustrated below. Under absorption costing, both variable and fixed manufacturing overhead are charged to the product.

| | | |
|---|---|---|
| Work in Process................................................ | xxx | |
|     Variable Manufacturing Overhead Applied................ | | xxx |
|     Fixed Manufacturing Overhead Applied.................. | | xxx |

Under variable costing, only variable costs enter into the cost of the manufactured product.

| | | |
|---|---|---|
| Work in Process................................................ | xxx | |
|     Variable Manufacturing Overhead Applied................ | | xxx |

The Fixed Manufacturing Overhead Control account would again be closed directly to the Revenue and Expense Summary account, just as any other current expense.

As a result of the procedure described in the previous paragraph, there will be two accounts for variable manufacturing overhead and, under absorption costing, two accounts for fixed manufacturing overhead in the general ledger—the manufacturing overhead control accounts with debit balances representing the actual costs incurred and the manufacturing overhead applied accounts with credit balances representing the manufacturing overhead cost charged to the product for the period. The balances in the two accounts for variable costs and, when appropriate, in the two accounts for fixed costs will be equal and offsetting only if the budgeted cost and output data prove to be exactly equal to the comparable actual data. Obviously, it is very unlikely that the budgeted and actual data will be identical. They may be very close to each other, but some discrepancy is virtually inevitable. Consequently, there will almost always be some differences between the debit balances in the manufacturing overhead control accounts and the respective credit balances in the manufacturing overhead applied accounts. These differences are termed *underapplied manufacturing overhead* when actual costs exceed the costs applied and *overapplied manufacturing overhead* when the costs applied are greater than the actual costs incurred. While there are alternative methods of disposing of under- or overapplied manufacturing overhead, at this point we shall simply observe that it may be closed directly to the Revenue and Expense Summary account. This would be accomplished by closing both the manufacturing overhead control accounts and the manufacturing overhead applied accounts to Revenue and Expense Summary at the end of the fiscal year. The reporting of under- or overapplied manufacturing overhead in financial statements is illustrated later in this chapter.

## COMPREHENSIVE ILLUSTRATION

At this point, it may be helpful in understanding the basic cost accounting cycle (that is, the flow of manufacturing costs through the successive accounts) to study an illustration with specific production and cost data. These data pertain to the Wedgewood Products Company for the year 1976. Both absorption and variable costing are presented in this illustration.

The company has estimated that each unit of product will involve the incurrence of $1.50 of variable manufacturing overhead costs. Hence, variable manufacturing overhead will be applied to production at a normal rate of $1.50 per unit. Fixed manufacturing overhead costs are budgeted at $750,000 for the year, and output is estimated at 300,000 units. Thus, under absorption costing only, fixed manufacturing overhead will be applied to production at a normal rate of $2.50 per unit. The variable and fixed manufacturing overhead cost items in this illustration will be those listed and classified earlier and repeated in Table 3–2.

<table>
<tr><td colspan="2">TABLE 3–2</td><td colspan="3">TABLE 3–3</td></tr>
<tr><td>*Variable Costs*</td><td>*Fixed Costs*</td><td></td><td>*Absorption Costing*</td><td>*Variable Costing*</td></tr>
<tr><td>Indirect materials</td><td>Indirect labor<br>Labor-related costs</td><td>Materials</td><td></td><td></td></tr>
<tr><td>Labor-related costs</td><td>Depreciation<br>Insurance</td><td>inventory......<br>Work in</td><td>$ 80,000</td><td>$ 80,000</td></tr>
<tr><td>Power and light</td><td>Property taxes<br>Repairs and</td><td>process........<br>Finished</td><td>200,000</td><td>150,000</td></tr>
<tr><td></td><td>maintenance</td><td>product.......</td><td>300,000</td><td>225,000</td></tr>
</table>

The inventory balances at the beginning of the year are the starting point of the illustration. These balances, taken from the balance sheet as of December 31, 1975, are shown in Table 3–3. The inventory balances for Work in Process and Finished Product are greater under absorption costing than under variable costing, of course, for the former method includes fixed manufacturing overhead in inventory while the latter method does not.

## Journal Entries

Following are the transactions relevant to the Wedgewood Products Company's manufacturing operations during 1976 and the general journal entries to record them:

1.  Raw materials costing $800,000 were purchased on account.

(1)

Materials Inventory.................................. 800,000
    Vouchers Payable...............................          800,000

2.  Materials costing $760,000 were issued to the factory for use. Of these, $680,000 were direct materials and $80,000 were indirect materials.

(2)

| | | |
|---|---:|---:|
| Work in Process...................................... | 680,000 | |
| Variable Manufacturing Overhead Control.............. | 80,000 | |
|     Materials Inventory............................ | | 760,000 |

While detailed subsidiary records of cost items would also be maintained, all variable manufacturing overhead items will be debited here to a single account, Variable Manufacturing Overhead Control, in the general ledger.

3.  The factory payroll for 1976 totaled $1,400,000, of which $1,000,000 were the cost of direct labor and the balance was indirect labor.

(3)

| | | |
|---|---:|---:|
| Work in Process.................................. | 1,000,000 | |
| Fixed Manufacturing Overhead Control............. | 400,000 | |
|     Payroll Summary............................ | | 1,400,000 |

4.  Labor-related costs amount to 20% of the total payroll cost. To keep the illustration very simple, we shall not be concerned with the exact natures of these items. Rather, we shall credit the entire amount to a single liability account for fringe benefits. Labor-related costs associated with direct labor (20% of $1,000,000) are variable manufacturing overhead, while those associated with indirect labor (20% of $400,000) are fixed manufacturing overhead. The classification of labor-related costs as fixed or variable depends upon the classification of the labor costs to which they relate.

(4)

| | | |
|---|---:|---:|
| Variable Manufacturing Overhead Control............. | 200,000 | |
| Fixed Manufacturing Overhead Control................ | 80,000 | |
|     Liability for Fringe Benefits...................... | | 280,000 |

Inasmuch as the payroll accounting procedures are not actually part of the cost accounting cycle, they are not included in this illustration. They would be handled in the manner illustrated previously.

5.  The remaining manufacturing overhead cost items are summarized as follows:

| | |
|---|---:|
| Variable costs: | |
|     Power and light.................................... | $130,000 |
| Fixed costs: | |
|     Depreciation on plant............................. | 200,000 |
|     Insurance on plant................................ | 20,000 |
|     Property taxes on plant........................... | 10,000 |
|     Repairs and maintenance of plant.................. | 70,000 |

These items are recorded below, with both power and light bills and repairs and maintenance being credited to Vouchers Payable.

(5.1)

| | | |
|---|---|---|
| Variable Manufacturing Overhead Control............. | 130,000 | |
| Vouchers Payable................................ | | 130,000 |

(5.2)

| | | |
|---|---|---|
| Fixed Manufacturing Overhead Control................ | 300,000 | |
| Accumulated Depreciation—Plant................ | | 200,000 |
| Unexpired Insurance.............................. | | 20,000 |
| Accrued Property Taxes Payable.................. | | 10,000 |
| Vouchers Payable................................ | | 70,000 |

To this point in the illustration, all entries are identical under both absorption costing and variable costing. The remaining entries, however, deal with the application of manufacturing overhead costs to production and with subsequent accounting for the full cost of the product. Hence, they will be different under the alternative costing methods. Entries for absorption costing will be keyed with the letter "A," and those for variable costing, with the letter "V."

6.   Actual output for 1976 (i.e., the total production work actually performed during that year, whether the units were completed or not)[5] totaled 280,000 units of product. Manufacturing overhead is applied to production at normal rates of $1.50 per unit for variable costs and, under absorption costing only, $2.50 per unit for fixed costs. Thus, the entry for absorption costing is as follows:

(6A)

| | | |
|---|---|---|
| Work in Process................................... | 1,120,000 | |
| Variable Manufacturing Overhead Applied........ | | 420,000 |
| Fixed Manufacturing Overhead Applied.......... | | 700,000 |

Under variable costing, only the variable manufacturing overhead is applied to production. Note that this results in a substantially lower cost in Work in Process.

(6V)

| | | |
|---|---|---|
| Work in Process................................... | 420,000 | |
| Variable Manufacturing Overhead Applied........ | | 420,000 |

7.   The total cost of production completed during a period is normally computed by determining the unit cost of goods produced in the period and multiplying that unit cost by the number of units completed. The methods of determining unit cost will be discussed and illustrated in Chapter 4. Thus, at this point, we shall simply assert that the unit cost in the Wedgewood Products Company for 1976 is $10 under absorption costing. Included in this figure, of course, is $2.50 of fixed manufacturing overhead. Under variable costing, no fixed manufacturing overhead is applied to production; hence, the unit cost would be $7.50. A total of

---

[5] The distinction between production work done and units completed will be explained fully in the next chapter.

260,000 units of product were completed in 1976. Under absorption costing, the following entry would be made to record the completion of 260,000 units at a cost of $10 each:

(7A)

| | | |
|---|---:|---:|
| Finished Product | 2,600,000 | |
| Work in Process | | 2,600,000 |

Under variable costing, the same 260,000 units would be costed at only $7.50 per unit.

(7V)

| | | |
|---|---:|---:|
| Finished Product | 1,950,000 | |
| Work in Process | | 1,950,000 |

8.  During 1976, a total of 250,000 units of product were sold on account for $16 each. The unit costs of the goods sold were $10 under absorption costing and $7.50 under variable costing. Two entries must be made to record these sales. The first records the sales revenue and is the same regardless of the costing method used.

(8.1)

| | | |
|---|---:|---:|
| Accounts Receivable | 4,000,000 | |
| Sales | | 4,000,000 |

The second entry records the expiration of the cost of the goods sold. It records the transfer of production costs from the classification of asset to that of expense. This entry will be different under the alternative costing methods. Under absorption costing, the cost per unit of the 250,000 units sold is $10.

(8.2A)

| | | |
|---|---:|---:|
| Cost of Goods Sold | 2,500,000 | |
| Finished Product | | 2,500,000 |

Under variable costing, the unit cost is only $7.50.

(8.2V)

| | | |
|---|---:|---:|
| Cost of Goods Sold | 1,875,000 | |
| Finished Product | | 1,875,000 |

The transfer of the cost of goods sold from asset to expense effectively concludes the cost accounting cycle. All manufacturing costs now appear in accounts that are consistent with the manner in which they will be reported in the financial statements.

## Ledger Accounts

Postings of the journal entries in the preceding sections are shown in Figures 3–3 and 3–4. They are keyed by numbers and letters to the entries. Only those accounts that deal directly with the costs of manufacturing are included in these exhibits. Figure 3–3 depicts the flow of manu-

## FIGURE 3–3

### Manufacturing Cost Accounts under Absorption Costing

#### Materials Inventory

| | | | |
|---|---|---|---|
| Bal. | 80,000 | (2) | 760,000 |
| (1) | 800,000 | | |
| Bal. | 120,000 | | |

#### Work in Process

| | | | |
|---|---|---|---|
| Bal. | 200,000 | (7A) | 2,600,000 |
| (2) | 680,000 | | |
| (3) | 1,000,000 | | |
| (6A) | 1,120,000 | | |
| Bal. | 400,000 | | |

#### Finished Product

| | | | |
|---|---|---|---|
| Bal. | 300,000 | (8.2A) | 2,500,000 |
| (7A) | 2,600,000 | | |
| Bal. | 400,000 | | |

#### Cost of Goods Sold

| | | |
|---|---|---|
| (8.2A) | 2,500,000 | |

#### Payroll Summary

| | | | |
|---|---|---|---|
| | | (3) | 1,400,000 |

#### Variable Manufacturing Overhead Control

| | | |
|---|---|---|
| (2) | 80,000 | |
| (4) | 200,000 | |
| (5.1) | 130,000 | |
| Bal. | 410,000 | |

FIGURE 3–3 (*continued*)

Fixed Manufacturing Overhead Control

| | | | |
|---|---|---|---|
| (3) | 400,000 | | |
| (4) | 80,000 | | |
| (5.2) | 300,000 | | |
| Bal. | 780,000 | | |

Variable Manufacturing Overhead Applied

| | | | |
|---|---|---|---|
| | | (6A) | 420,000 |

Fixed Manufacturing Overhead Applied

| | | | |
|---|---|---|---|
| | | (6A) | 700,000 |

FIGURE 3–4

Manufacturing Cost Accounts
under Variable Costing

Materials Inventory

| | | | |
|---|---|---|---|
| Bal. | 80,000 | (2) | 760,000 |
| (1) | 800,000 | | |
| Bal. | 120,000 | | |

Work in Process

| | | | |
|---|---|---|---|
| Bal. | 150,000 | (7V) | 1,950,000 |
| (2) | 680,000 | | |
| (3) | 1,000,000 | | |
| (6V) | 420,000 | | |
| Bal. | 300,000 | | |

Finished Product

| | | | |
|---|---|---|---|
| Bal. | 225,000 | (8.2V) | 1,875,000 |
| (7V) | 1,950,000 | | |
| Bal. | 300,000 | | |

## FIGURE 3–4 (*continued*)

### Cost of Goods Sold

| | | | |
|---|---|---|---|
| (8.2V) | 1,875,000 | | |

### Payroll Summary

| | | | |
|---|---|---|---|
| | | (3) | 1,400,000 |

### Variable Manufacturing Overhead Control

| | | | |
|---|---|---|---|
| (2) | 80,000 | | |
| (4) | 200,000 | | |
| (5.1) | 130,000 | | |
| Bal. | 410,000 | | |

### Fixed Manufacturing Overhead Control

| | | | |
|---|---|---|---|
| (3) | 400,000 | | |
| (4) | 80,000 | | |
| (5.2) | 300,000 | | |
| Bal. | 780,000 | | |

### Variable Manufacturing Overhead Applied

| | | | |
|---|---|---|---|
| | | (6V) | 420,000 |

facturing costs through the accounts under the absorption costing method. Figure 3–4 repeats this illustration under variable costing. The only difference in the latter exhibit is the absence of a Fixed Manufacturing Overhead Applied account and, consequently, lower total costs in Work in Process, Finished Product, and Cost of Goods Sold. These two figures show exactly the same cost flows that are presented in Figures 3–1 and 3–2, except that ledger accounts are used instead of block diagrams. An inspection of the manufacturing overhead accounts in Figure 3–3 shows that variable manufacturing overhead was overapplied by $10,000 and that fixed manufacturing was underapplied by $80,000. The same $10,000 of overapplied variable manufacturing overhead appears in Figure 3–4 under variable costing. However, under this method, there is no underapplied fixed manufacturing overhead because fixed manufacturing overhead is not applied to production at all.

## OPERATING STATEMENTS FOR A MANUFACTURING ENTERPRISE

In a manufacturing concern, as in almost all business firms, the principal operating report is the income statement. However, in manufacturing, the development of the cost of goods sold figure is so involved that the income statement is usually supported by a detailed *statement of cost of goods manufactured and sold*. This latter statement summarizes the results of manufacturing operations for the period. It is a formal summary of the data processed through the cost accounting cycle. This supporting statement and the income statement of the Wedgewood Products Company for 1976 are illustrated below under both alternatives of absorption costing and variable costing. The data are taken from the comprehensive illustration in the preceding section.

### Operating Statements under Absorption Costing

Table 3–4 is a statement of cost of goods manufactured and sold prepared in accordance with the absorption costing method. Table 3–5 is the income statement prepared under the same method. The formats of the statements presented here are not suggested as standard or as ideal. There is a considerable variety of forms used in practice. Those illustrated in this chapter are very widely used, however.

In Table 3–4, the cost of goods manufactured is equal to the cost of

**TABLE 3–4**

WEDGEWOOD PRODUCTS COMPANY
Statement of Cost of Goods Manufactured and Sold
For the Year Ended December 31, 1976

| | | | |
|---|---:|---:|---:|
| Direct materials used: | | | |
| Inventory, January 1, 1976............ | | $ 80,000 | |
| Purchases......................... | | 800,000 | |
| Available for use................... | | $880,000 | |
| Deduct: | | | |
| Inventory, December 31, 1976....... | $120,000 | | |
| Used as indirect materials.......... | 80,000 | 200,000 | $ 680,000 |
| Direct labor........................ | | | 1,000,000 |
| Variable manufacturing overhead applied. | | | 420,000 |
| Fixed manufacturing overhead applied... | | | 700,000 |
| Total current production costs......... | | | $2,800,000 |
| Deduct increase in work in process: | | | |
| Inventory, December 31, 1976........ | $400,000 | | |
| Inventory, January 1, 1976.......... | 200,000 | | 200,000 |
| Cost of goods manufactured............ | | | $2,600,000 |
| Deduct increase in finished product: | | | |
| Inventory, December 31, 1976........ | $400,000 | | |
| Inventory, January 1, 1976.......... | 300,000 | | 100,000 |
| Cost of goods sold.................... | | | $2,500,000 |

the goods that were completed and transferred from Work in Process to Finished Product (cf. entry 7A in the previous section). The final figure in Table 3–4, the cost of goods sold, is the amount transferred from Finished Product to Cost of Goods Sold (cf. entry 8.2A). In the calculation of the cost of direct materials used, it is necessary to deduct those items used as indirect materials, for they will be included in the total of variable manufacturing overhead applied to production.

The income statement in Table 3–5 is prepared in the conventional format used under absorption costing. The only new data in this report are the nonmanufacturing expenses and the income taxes. In this and other illustrations throughout the book, we shall assume that the applicable income tax rate is 40%.[6] The net underapplied manufacturing

### TABLE 3–5

WEDGEWOOD PRODUCTS COMPANY
Income Statement
For the Year Ended December 31, 1976

| | | |
|---|---:|---:|
| Sales............................................ | | $4,000,000 |
| Cost of goods sold (cf. Table 3–4)................ | $2,500,000 | |
| Add net underapplied manufacturing overhead..... | 70,000 | 2,570,000 |
| Gross margin..................................... | | $1,430,000 |
| Nonmanufacturing expenses....................... | | 780,000 |
| Income before tax................................ | | $ 650,000 |
| Income taxes (40%)............................... | | 260,000 |
| Net income...................................... | | $ 390,000 |

overhead ($80,000 underapplied fixed manufacturing overhead minus $10,000 overapplied variable manufacturing overhead) is shown in the income statement as an addition to the cost of goods sold. It might just as well have been added at the end of the statement of cost of goods manufactured and sold instead. Either way, the underapplied manufacturing overhead (an element of manufacturing cost) is associated with the expired manufacturing costs of the period (i.e., with cost of

---

[6] The assumption of a 40% income tax rate is arbitrary and not really representative of the effective tax rate paid by most corporations. At present, the federal corporate income tax rate is 22% of the first $25,000 of income plus 48% of all income in excess of that amount. If the corporation is subject to state income tax also, its total effective income tax rate is likely to be greater than 50%, unless it is a small company. The assumed rate of 40% is used here for simplicity and for clarity in illustrations. It tends to produce "round numbers" for after-tax amounts, and it avoids possible confusion between the amount of tax and the after-tax amount. (Many writers have used 50% as the assumed tax rate. While this produces "round numbers" as well, it results in the tax amount and the after-tax amount being equal to each other. In certain types of problems, this equality might possibly confuse a student just learning concepts in the illustration.)

goods sold). This is the conventional method of disposing of under- or overapplied manufacturing overhead at the end of the fiscal year. If the amount of under- or overapplied manufacturing overhead is very material, treating it simply as an adjustment to the cost of goods sold might distort reported income for the period. In such a case, the under- or overapplied amount should be allocated among Work in Process, Finished Product, and Cost of Goods Sold in proper proportions. The effect of this allocation would be the same as if actual manufacturing overhead had been applied to production. The procedure for this allocation will be illustrated in Chapter 10.

## Operating Statements under Variable Costing

The statement of cost of goods manufactured and sold under variable costing is nearly identical to that prepared under absorption costing. The only difference is that no fixed manufacturing overhead is included in any of the data in the statement. Table 3–6 illustrates such a statement with the data under variable costing in the comprehensive illustration.

The income statement for variable costing is presented in Table 3–7. It differs significantly from the one used in absorption costing. Not only are different data involved in the determination of cost of goods sold and not only is fixed manufacturing overhead reported differently, net income is different in amount. Moreover, the entire format of the statement is

**TABLE 3–6**

WEDGEWOOD PRODUCTS COMPANY
Statement of Cost of Goods Manufactured and Sold
For the Year Ended December 31, 1976

| Direct materials used: | | | |
|---|---|---|---|
| Inventory, January 1, 1976........... | | $ 80,000 | |
| Purchases........................ | | 800,000 | |
| Available for use.................. | | $880,000 | |
| Deduct: | | | |
| Inventory, December 31, 1976....... | $120,000 | | |
| Used as indirect materials.......... | 80,000 | 200,000 | $ 680,000 |
| Direct labor.......................... | | | 1,000,000 |
| Variable manufacturing overhead applied. | | | 420,000 |
| Total current variable production costs... | | | $2,100,000 |
| Deduct increase in work in process: | | | |
| Inventory, December 31, 1976........ | | $300,000 | |
| Inventory, January 1, 1976.......... | | 150,000 | 150,000 |
| Cost of goods manufactured............. | | | $1,950,000 |
| Deduct increase in finished product: | | | |
| Inventory, December 31, 1976........ | | $300,000 | |
| Inventory, January 1, 1976.......... | | 225,000 | 75,000 |
| Cost of goods sold.................... | | | $1,875,000 |

different. In absorption costing, the principal internal division of expenses is between manufacturing and nonmanufacturing expense items. The major intermediate measure of income is the gross margin, which is the excess of revenue over total manufacturing expense. In variable costing, expenses are separated in the income statement according to their behavior with respect to changes in volume. Variable and fixed expenses are separated, but no major distinction between manufacturing and nonmanufacturing expenses is recognized. The major intermediate income figure is called *variable profit,* the difference between sales revenue and variable expenses. (The terms "contribution margin" and "marginal contribution" are often used for the concept here called variable profit.

### TABLE 3–7

WEDGEWOOD PRODUCTS COMPANY
Income Statement
For the Year Ended December 31, 1976

| | | |
|---|---:|---:|
| Sales.................................................... | | $4,000,000 |
| Variable expenses: | | |
| Cost of goods sold (cf. Table 3–6)............... | $1,875,000 | |
| Less overapplied variable manufacturing overhead. | 10,000 | |
| | $1,865,000 | |
| Variable nonmanufacturing expenses............ | 280,000 | 2,145,000 |
| Variable profit...................................... | | $1,855,000 |
| Fixed expenses: | | |
| Fixed manufacturing overhead.................. | $ 780,000 | |
| Fixed nonmanufacturing expenses............... | 500,000 | 1,280,000 |
| Income before tax............................... | | $ 575,000 |
| Income taxes (40%)............................. | | 230,000 |
| Net income....................................... | | $ 345,000 |

This latter term is more accurately descriptive of the profit measure in question, however, and will be used throughout this book.) Since both sales revenue and variable expenses are direct functions of sales volume, so is the variable profit.[7] Thus, variable profit tends to be a very useful figure for managerial analysis. The only new data refinement in Table 3–7 is a separation of the total nonmanufacturing expenses of $780,000 into a variable component of $280,000 and a fixed component of $500,000. Perhaps the most important quantitative difference in the variable costing income statement is the fact that net income is $45,000 less than it was under absorption costing. This is attributable to the fact that all of

---

[7] A minor exception to this statement is caused by the fact that the overapplied variable manufacturing overhead is not a direct function of sales volume. The quantitative effect of this item, however, is usually immaterial.

the fixed manufacturing overhead costs actually incurred during the year are reported as expenses under variable costing. Under absorption costing, however, a portion of fixed manufacturing overhead remains in the inventory accounts for Work in Process and Finished Product, both of which increased during the year.

The discussions of absorption costing and variable costing in this chapter have been limited to the basic accounting procedures employed and the accounting difference between the two methods. A critical comparison of the two methods will be made in the next chapter.

## QUESTIONS FOR DISCUSSION

1. What is meant by the concept that *costs attach?* Which costs attach in absorption costing? Which costs attach in variable costing?

2. What is the difference between a product cost and a period cost? How does each type of cost become an expense?

3. Which accounts in the general ledger of a manufacturing firm may be expected to be different under variable costing as contrasted with absorption costing?

4. Several different schemes of classification of costs have been discussed in this chapter and in the preceding one. It is often desirable that the different classifications be incorporated in the recording of costs in the accounts. Identify these various cost classifications and state the purpose(s) of recording costs according to each.

5. Should labor-related costs be included as part of direct labor cost or should they be accounted for as part of manufacturing overhead? Explain your answer.

6. If the direct labor costs of production were true fixed costs of the period, how would they be accounted for? How would these procedures differ, if at all, from current practice with respect to labor cost accounting?

7. What are the advantages of using normal manufacturing overhead rates instead of actual rates? What are the disadvantages? On balance, do you believe the advantages outweigh the disadvantages or vice versa? Why?

8. "The use of a normal fixed manufacturing overhead rate results in an artificial smoothing of unit production costs over the course of a year in which there occur significant seasonal fluctuations in output." To what does this allegation refer? How would you respond to it?

9. "Variable costing is preferable to absorption costing in that it results in lower inventory values and, therefore, lower inventory carrying costs (i.e., imputed interest on the investment in inventory)." Comment on this statement.

10. How would you explain the under- or overapplied manufacturing overhead as a separate item appearing in the income statement?

11. What is the relationship between a statement of cost of goods manufactured and sold and the block diagrams of manufacturing cost flows in Figures 3–1 and 3–2?

12. What is a cost transformation? What is its significance in cost accounting? Give several examples.

13. Explain the difference between the gross margin reported in the income statement under absorption costing and the variable profit reported under variable costing.

14. "Absorption costing is clearly invalid. Since fixed manufacturing overhead is charged to the inventory of manufactured products at a rate based on the number of units expected to be produced, the value of that inventory will be greater if the firm expects to produce fewer units. In other words, the fewer units a firm expects to produce and does produce, the more valuable each individual unit becomes. This is nonsense." Discuss this criticism of absorption costing.

15. "Variable costing is obviously invalid. Since only variable costs are charged to production, the more costs that are fixed, the lower will be the value of the inventory. Thus, if all costs were fixed, the inventory would be without value. That is ridiculous." Evaluate this criticism of variable costing.

## PROBLEMS

3–1. The following data summarize the manufacturing operations of the Half Moon Company during its first year of operations:

| | |
|---|---:|
| Raw materials purchased.................... | $180,000 |
| Direct materials used...................... | 165,000 |
| Direct labor cost incurred.................. | 270,000 |
| Variable manufacturing overhead incurred....... | 110,000 |
| Fixed manufacturing overhead incurred......... | 150,000 |
| Variable manufacturing overhead applied........ | 95,000 |
| Fixed manufacturing overhead applied.......... | 140,000 |
| Total cost of products completed.............. | 630,000 |
| Total cost of products sold................... | 560,000 |

The company has adopted the absorption costing method.

*Required:*

a. Show the manufacturing costs summarized above as postings to general ledger accounts.

b. Determine the total amount of manufacturing costs charged to expense during this first year of operations.

3–2. Complete the requirements of Problem 3–1 under the assumption that the company has adopted the variable costing method. Of course, no fixed manufacturing overhead would be applied. Change the total cost of products completed to $500,000 and the total cost of products sold to $440,000.

3-3. The total factory labor cost of the Coos Bay Milling Company for the two-week period ended August 20, 1976, is $150,000. Of this amount, $120,000 is direct labor cost. The balance is indirect labor and is a fixed cost. The payroll department withholds a total of $22,000 for the employees' federal income taxes. The entire payroll is subject to the social security withholding rate of 6%. The only other item withheld is the employees' contribution to a pension fund; this amounts to 5% of the payroll. The company must match the employees' social security tax payments and makes a pension fund contribution equal to 8% of the payroll. The company also pays the unemployment compensation tax of 3% of the payroll.

*Required:*

Prepare general journal entries to record (*a*) the charging of labor costs to manufacturing cost accounts in the cost accounting department and (*b*) the distribution of the payroll in the payroll department.

3-4. The Winona Manufacturing Company charges manufacturing overhead to production at normal rates and employs the absorption costing method. Past experience, adjusted for anticipated price changes, indicated that variable manufacturing overhead would average $3 per unit of product in 1976. Fixed manufacturing overhead for that year had been budgeted at $10,000,000, and output was budgeted at 2,000,000 units of product. Actual output for 1976 proved to be only 1,800,000 units. Actual manufacturing overhead for that year included variable costs of $5,600,000 and fixed costs of $9,800,000.

*Required:*

Compute the under- or overapplied manufacturing overhead for variable and fixed costs separately. State briefly what factors appear to have caused these under- or overapplied amounts.

3-5. The Naugatuck Products Corporation charges manufacturing overhead to production at a normal rate and uses the variable costing method. Budgeted variable manufacturing overhead for 1976 was $1.25 per unit of product. Budgeted fixed manufacturing overhead was $1,800,000, and budgeted output for the year was set at 900,000 units of product. Actual output for 1976 totaled 980,000 units. Actual variable manufacturing overhead amounted to $1,250,000 and actual fixed manufacturing overhead, to $1,850,000.

*Required:*

Show the balances in all manufacturing overhead control and applied accounts at the end of 1976. Compute the amount of under- or overapplied manufacturing overhead for the year.

3–6.  The operations of the Raritan Corporation for the year ended December 31, 1976, are summarized below. The corporation uses absorption costing.

Inventory balances, January 1, 1976:
Materials inventory........................ $ 30,000
Work in process........................... 40,000
Finished product.......................... 50,000
Purchases of materials...................... 300,000
Direct materials used....................... 270,000
Direct labor cost........................... 220,000
Manufacturing overhead costs incurred (Make credit to "various accounts."):
Variable.................................. 75,000
Fixed..................................... 150,000
Cost of completed production................. 710,000
Cost of goods sold.......................... 700,000
Revenue from sales on account................ 960,000

Variable manufacturing overhead is applied to production at a normal rate of $2 per unit of product. Fixed manufacturing overhead is applied at a normal rate of $4 per unit. During 1976, a total of 40,000 units of product were manufactured.

*Required:*

a.  Prepare general journal entries to record the corporation's operations for 1976.
b.  Compute the ending balances in the three inventory accounts at December 31, 1976.
c.  Compute the under- or overapplied manufacturing overhead for the year.

3–7.  The Bonham Manufacturing Company uses variable costing in accounting for its production costs. Following is a summary of the company's operations for the year ended December 31, 1976:

Inventories, January 1, 1976:
Materials................................ $   20,000
Work in process........................... 0
Finished product.......................... 40,000
Purchases of materials...................... 600,000
Direct materials used....................... 550,000
Direct labor.............................. 200,000
Actual manufacturing overhead (Make credit to "various accounts."):
Variable.................................. 160,000
Fixed..................................... 300,000
Cost of goods completed..................... 860,000
Sales revenue............................. 1,200,000
Cost of goods sold.......................... 880,000

During 1976, 300,000 units of product were manufactured. Variable manufacturing overhead is applied to production at a normal rate of $.50 per unit produced.

*Required:*

a. Prepare general journal entries to record operations for 1976.
b. Compute the ending balances in the inventory accounts as of December 31, 1976.
c. Compute the under- or overapplied manufacturing overhead for the year.

3–8. The Wachusett Corporation manufactures ceramic ash trays. The variable costing method is used. The company began operations in January, 1976. Budgeted output for 1976 called for production of 10,000,000 ash trays. The budget projected fixed manufacturing overhead of $200,000 for the year and variable manufacturing overhead of $.04 per ash tray. Actual production data for 1976 are summarized below.

1. Raw materials in the amount of 12,000,000 pounds were purchased at an average cost of $.05 per pound. Of this quantity, 11,200,000 pounds were issued for use in production.

2. The total factory payroll for the year amounted to $500,000. Of this total, $400,000 was direct labor and the balance was indirect labor. Indirect labor cost varies in proportion to the volume of production. Federal income taxes withheld totaled $90,000. The entire payroll is subject to a 6% social security tax; both the employees and the corporation must contribute this percentage. In addition, the corporation alone is liable for a 3% unemployment compensation tax.

3. Other actual variable manufacturing overhead costs incurred during 1976 were as follows:

Factory supplies purchased and used.............. $75,000
Electric power and water bills paid.............. 25,000

4. Actual fixed manufacturing overhead costs incurred during the year included the following items:

Depreciation on plant and equipment............ $100,000
Property taxes on plant and equipment.......... 20,000
    (Half of these taxes have already been paid.
    The balance is payable on or before
    March 20, 1977.)
Insurance on plant and equipment............... 10,000
    (This is the current year's portion of a
    premium for a three-year insurance policy
    purchased on January 2, 1976.)
Repair and maintenance (All paid currently.)..... 60,000

5. A total of 8,000,000 ash trays were produced in 1976. No uncompleted work remained in process at the end of the year. Of the completed units, 7,500,000 were shipped to customers and billed at a selling price of $.25 per ash tray.

*Required:*

a. Prepare general journal entries to record the operations of the Wachusett Corporation for 1976. (Note that the cost of the ash trays sold is not given directly, but it can be computed from the records.)
b. Compute the under- or overapplied manufacturing overhead for 1976.

3-9. The Klamath Cabinet Works manufactures wooden cabinets for television sets. Absorption costing is used. Budgeted production for 1976 was set at 80,000 cabinets. Fixed manufacturing overhead was budgeted at $2,400,000 for the year, and variable manufacturing overhead was budgeted at $5 per cabinet. Actual operating data for 1976 are summarized below:

1. The cost of raw materials purchased during 1976 totaled $1,600,000. The cost of direct materials issued to the factory totaled $1,500,000.
2. The factory payroll for the year included $2,800,000 of direct labor and $800,000 of indirect labor, which is a fixed cost of production. Federal income taxes withheld totaled $420,000. The company also withholds payroll taxes equal to 6% of the employees' earnings. It must pay, in addition, 10% of the total payroll as its share of payroll taxes.
3. Indirect materials used cost $100,000 and were drawn from the inventory of raw materials. They are classified as variable costs.
4. Additional actual fixed manufacturing overhead costs included the following items:

| | |
|---|---:|
| Depreciation on factory facilities............... | $700,000 |
| Heat, light, and power (All paid currently.)....... | 150,000 |
| Property taxes (All payable in 1977.)............ | 120,000 |
| Maintenance (All paid currently.).............. | 500,000 |

5. A total of 70,000 cabinets were produced during 1976. There was no inventory of work in process at either the beginning or the end of the year. All cabinets completed were shipped immediately to customers. The selling price was $130 per cabinet.

*Required:*

a. Prepare general journal entries to record all of the operating transactions of 1976.
b. Compute the amount of under- or overapplied manufacturing overhead for the year.

3-10.  The following data are taken from the accounting records of the Campbell Corporation for the year ended December 31, 1976:

| | |
|---|---:|
| Inventories, January 1: | |
|   Raw materials............................ | $ 15,000 |
|   Work in process.......................... | 8,000 |
|   Finished products........................ | 35,000 |
| Sales......................................... | 360,000 |
| Purchases of raw materials................... | 100,000 |
| Materials issued to the factory: | |
|   As direct materials....................... | 85,000 |
|   As indirect materials (variable cost).......... | 8,000 |
| Payroll: | |
|   Direct labor............................. | 90,000 |
|   Indirect labor (variable cost)................ | 25,000 |
|   Salesmen's salaries (fixed cost)............. | 45,000 |
| Factory power and utilities (fixed cost).......... | 20,000 |
| Advertising (fixed cost)...................... | 15,000 |
| Depreciation on factory (fixed cost)............ | 25,000 |
| Inventories, December 31: | |
|   Raw materials............................ | ? |
|   Work in process.......................... | 10,000 |
|   Finished products........................ | 30,000 |

Manufacturing overhead is applied to production at normal rates of $.60 per unit of product for variable costs and $.90 per unit of product for fixed costs. The actual output of 1976 totaled 50,000 units of product. The applicable federal income tax rate is 40%.

*Required:*

Prepare an income statement and a supporting statement of cost of goods manufactured and sold for the year ended December 31, 1976.

3-11.  The data below are a summarization of the operations of the Alert Automotive Company for the year 1976.

| | |
|---|---:|
| Sales................................... | $968,000 |
| Purchases of materials.................. | 180,000 |
| Payroll: | |
|   Direct labor......................... | 240,000 |
|   Indirect labor (fixed cost).............. | 60,000 |
|   Office and sales force (fixed cost)........ | 120,000 |
| Depreciation (fixed cost): | |
|   On factory equipment.................. | 72,000 |
|   On office furnishings and equipment..... | 18,000 |
| Maintenance (fixed cost): | |
|   Of factory equipment.................. | 30,000 |
|   Of office equipment................... | 12,000 |
| Supplies used (variable cost): | |
|   In factory........................... | 26,000 |
|   In office............................. | 6,000 |
| Labor-related costs..................... | 10% of payroll |

Output for 1976 totaled 240,000 units of product. Variable manufacturing overhead is applied to production at a normal rate of $.20 per unit. Fixed manufacturing overhead is accounted for as a period expense. Inventories at the beginning and the end of the year were as follows:

|  | January 1 | December 31 |
|---|---|---|
| Materials............................. | $24,000 | $12,000 |
| Work in process....................... | 6,000 | 12,000 |
| Finished product...................... | 48,000 | 60,000 |

The applicable income tax rate is 40%.

*Required:*

Prepare an income statement and a supporting statement of cost of goods manufactured and sold for the year 1976.

3–12. Below is the statement of cost of goods manufactured and sold for the Travis Company for the year 1976.

### TRAVIS COMPANY
#### Statement of Cost of Goods Manufactured and Sold
#### For the year ended December 31, 1976

| | | | |
|---|---|---|---|
| Direct materials: | | | |
| Inventory, January 1...................... | | $ 16,000 | |
| Purchases............................... | | 120,000 | |
| Available for use........................ | | $136,000 | |
| Deduct: Inventory, December 31........... | | $ 20,000 | |
| Used as indirect materials............... | | 4,000 | |
| | | $ 24,000 | $112,000 |
| Direct labor............................. | | | 140,000 |
| Variable manufacturing overhead applied...... | | | 56,000 |
| Fixed manufacturing overhead applied........ | | | 84,000 |
| Total current production costs............... | | | $392,000 |
| Add decrease in work in process: | | | |
| Inventory, January 1...................... | | $ 18,000 | |
| Inventory, December 31................... | | 12,000 | 6,000 |
| Cost of goods manufactured................. | | | $398,000 |
| Deduct increase in finished product: | | | |
| Inventory, December 31................... | | $ 36,000 | |
| Inventory, January 1..................... | | 22,000 | 14,000 |
| Cost of goods sold........................ | | | $384,000 |
| Add underapplied fixed manufacturing overhead. | $ 12,000 | | |
| Deduct overapplied variable manufacturing | | | |
| overhead............................... | 6,000 | | 6,000 |
| Net cost of goods sold..................... | | | $390,000 |

*Required:*

Reconstruct the ledger accounts for manufacturing costs in the Travis Company for the year 1976.

3-13. Following is the adjusted trial balance of the Yeaton Manufacturing Corporation as of December 31, 1976:

|  | Thousands of Dollars | |
|  | Debit | Credit |
|---|---|---|
| Cash. | $ 54 |  |
| Accounts receivable. | 78 |  |
| Materials inventory. | 90 |  |
| Work in process. | 36 |  |
| Finished product. | 132 |  |
| Land. | 360 |  |
| Plant property and equipment. | 1,140 |  |
| Accumulated depreciation–plant property and equipment. |  | $ 180 |
| Patents. | 63 |  |
| Vouchers payable. |  | 90 |
| Accrued expenses. |  | 75 |
| Mortgage bonds payable. |  | 450 |
| Common stock. |  | 600 |
| Retained earnings. |  | 510 |
| Sales. |  | 1,380 |
| Cost of goods sold. | 864 |  |
| Variable manufacturing overhead control. | 108 |  |
| Fixed manufacturing overhead control. | 129 |  |
| Selling expenses. | 150 |  |
| General and administrative expenses. | 240 |  |
| Variable manufacturing overhead applied. |  | 117 |
| Fixed manufacturing overhead applied. |  | 126 |
| Interest expense. | 30 |  |
| Federal income tax. | 54 |  |
|  | $3,528 | $3,528 |

In addition, the cost records show that materials costing $360,000 were purchased during 1976 and that direct labor cost during the year totaled $348,000. Inventory balances at January 1, 1976, had been as follows:

| Materials inventory. | $60,000 |
|---|---|
| Work in process. | 15,000 |
| Finished product. | 96,000 |

*Required:*

Prepare an income statement and a statement of cost of goods manufactured and sold for the year ended December 31, 1976.

3-14. The adjusted trial balance of the Taney Milling Company as of December 31, 1976, appears as follows:

|  | Debit | Credit |
|---|---|---|
| Cash..................................... | $   5,000 | |
| Accounts receivable...................... | 17,000 | |
| Materials inventory...................... | 24,000 | |
| Work in process......................... | 6,000 | |
| Finished product........................ | 12,000 | |
| Land.................................... | 30,000 | |
| Buildings............................... | 66,000 | |
| Accumulated depreciation—buildings......... | | $ 33,000 |
| Machinery and equipment................. | 120,000 | |
| Accumulated depreciation—machinery and equipment.............................. | | 55,000 |
| Accounts payable........................ | | 10,000 |
| Accrued expenses........................ | | 2,000 |
| Bank note payable....................... | | 15,000 |
| Common stock........................... | | 200,000 |
| Retained earnings....................... | 12,000 | |
| Sales................................... | | 400,000 |
| Cost of goods sold....................... | 245,000 | |
| Variable manufacturing overhead control..... | 40,000 | |
| Fixed manufacturing overhead control........ | 85,000 | |
| Variable marketing expenses................ | 16,000 | |
| Fixed marketing expenses.................. | 30,000 | |
| Fixed administrative expenses.............. | 48,000 | |
| Variable manufacturing overhead applied..... | | 42,000 |
| Interest expense......................... | 1,000 | |
| | $757,000 | $757,000 |

Materials were purchased at a total cost of $135,000 during 1976. The direct labor charges for the year were $56,000. Inventories at January 1, 1976, had been as follows:

| | |
|---|---|
| Materials inventory............................. | $28,000 |
| Work in process................................ | 16,000 |
| Finished product............................... | 10,000 |

*Required:*

Prepare an income statement and a statement of cost of goods manufactured and sold for the year ended December 31, 1976.

3–15.   At December 31, 1976, the Inventory of Manufacturing account of the Mackinaw Corporation contained the following summarized data:

### Inventory of Manufacturing

| | | | |
|---|---|---|---|
| Balance, Jan. 1, 1976 | 204,000 | Cost of goods sold | 2,165,862 |
| Materials purchased | 680,000 | | |
| Factory payroll | 500,000 | | |
| Budgeted manufacturing overhead | 900,000 | | |
| Balance, Dec. 31, 1976 | 118,138 | | |

Unfortunately, the company's bookkeeper had withdrawn from his one and only accounting course in college after getting a grade of 13 (out of 100) on his first examination. The general manager had instructed him to use the absorption costing method and to apply manufacturing overhead to production at normal rates. The account above represents his efforts to comply with this instruction. He calculated the cost of goods sold by summing all of the debits to the account, dividing that sum by the total number of units available for sale during the year, and then multiplying the resultant unit cost by the number of units sold.

You have conducted an independent examination of the records and have determined that all debits in the account are correct in amount, although incorrectly handled. You have discovered that the general manager had budgeted production for 1976 at 50,000 units of product. Variable manufacturing overhead had been budgeted at $6 per unit and fixed manufacturing overhead, at $600,000 for the year.

Actual production during 1976 totaled 55,000 units. Actual production costs other than for direct materials were as follows:

| | |
|---|---:|
| Direct labor............................... | $440,000 |
| Indirect labor (fixed cost)....................... | 60,000 |
| Other fixed manufacturing overhead............ | 560,000 |
| Variable manufacturing overhead............... | 320,000 |

The inventory balance at January 1 included the following specific items:

| | |
|---|---:|
| Raw materials.............................. | $ 90,000 |
| Finished product (3,000 units)................. | 114,000 |

The inventory of raw materials at December 31, 1976, was counted and found to have a cost of $110,000. Because of the short production process, there is never any inventory of work in process at the end of a period.

The goods sold during the year consisted of the 3,000 units in finished product inventory at the start of the year plus 52,000 of the 55,000 units produced during the year.

*Required:*

Determine the correct balances in the Materials Inventory, Work in Process, Finished Product, and Cost of Goods Sold accounts as of December 31, 1976.

3–16.  The Hawthorn Metal Products Corporation manufactures a variety of small machined parts. Output is measured in pounds of finished product. The absorption costing method is used.

The budgeted output for 1976 was set at 600,000 pounds. The budget for manufacturing overhead costs for the year was prepared as shown below.

Variable costs per pound:

Indirect materials and supplies................ $.11
Indirect labor............................. .25
Labor-related costs........................ .18
Power and light........................... .06
$.60

Fixed costs per year:

Depreciation.............................. $440,000
Plant supervisors' salaries.................... 80,000
Labor-related costs........................ 8,000
Maintenance.............................. 150,000
Property taxes............................ 30,000
Property insurance........................ 12,000
$720,000

The following inventory balances appeared in the firm's balance sheet at December 31, 1975:

Materials.................................... $125,000
Work in process............................ 80,000
Finished product........................... 350,000

Raw materials purchases for the year 1976 totaled $875,000. A summary of storeroom issue slips for the year shows that $900,000 of direct materials and $60,000 of indirect materials and supplies were issued from the materials inventory to the factory.

The corporation's payroll for 1976 is summarized below:

Direct labor................................ $ 700,000
Indirect labor.............................. 150,000
Plant supervisors' salaries.................... 80,000
Salesmen's commissions...................... 200,000
Administrative salaries...................... 300,000
$1,430,000

Federal income taxes in the amount of $230,000 were withheld from employees' earnings. Social security taxes were withheld at a rate of 6% of the total payroll. The company matches the employees' social security tax payments and also pays an unemployment compensation tax equal to 4% of the total payroll.

The following additional costs were paid in cash during 1976:

Power and light............................ $ 35,000
Maintenance............................... 160,000
Property taxes for 1976...................... 20,000
Property insurance premium on a three-year
  policy covering 1976, 1977, and 1978.......... 33,000
Advertising bills............................ 120,000
Miscellaneous administrative expenses.......... 70,000
Interest on long-term notes payable............. 10,000

Depreciation on the factory and on the office furnishings were recorded in the amounts of $475,000 and $50,000, respectively.

Production records showed that 520,000 pounds of products were actually produced during 1976. The total cost of completed production was $2,510,000. The cost of goods shipped and billed to customers was $2,452,000. These goods were billed at selling prices totaling $3,900,000. The income tax rate is 40%.

*Required:*

a. Prepare general journal entries to record the operations of Hawthorn Metal Products Corporation for 1976.

b. Prepare an income statement and a supporting statement of cost of goods manufactured and sold for the year 1976.

c. Calculate the under- or overapplied manufacturing overhead for 1976 and explain as best you can what caused this amount.

3-17. The Gresham Company produces concrete septic tanks. Only variable production costs are charged to the inventories of goods produced.

Budgeted sales and production volumes for 1976 were both set at 200,000 units of product. Costs for the year were budgeted as follows:

| | |
|---|---|
| Direct materials.................. | $15 per unit produced |
| Direct labor..................... | $5.60 per unit produced |
| Indirect labor................... | $1.40 per unit produced |
| Indirect materials............... | $.90 per unit produced |
| Shipping and billing expenses...... | $.40 per unit sold |
| Salesmen's commissions........... | 10% of sales revenue |
| Administrative salaries............ | $300,000 |
| General office expenses............ | $100,000 |
| Depreciation on factory........... | $200,000 |
| Depreciation on office............. | $100,000 |
| Labor-related costs............... | 10% of all payrolls |

During 1976, a total of 240,000 units were produced and 250,000 units were sold. The selling price was $40 per unit.

Inventory balances at the beginning and the end of the year were as follows:

| | Dec. 31, 1975 | Dec. 31, 1976 |
|---|---|---|
| Materials............................ | $250,000 | $350,000 |
| Work in process...................... | 180,000 | 100,000 |
| Finished product..................... | 500,000 | 250,000 |

Direct materials used during 1976 cost $3,700,000, and indirect materials used cost $200,000. Both were drawn from the same materials inventory account.

The following items were paid in cash during the year:

| | |
|---|---|
| Payrolls: | |
| Direct labor...................................... | $1,500,000 |
| Indirect labor.................................... | 350,000 |
| Administrative salaries............................ | 320,000 |
| Salesmen's commissions............................ | 10% of sales |
| Shipping and billing expenses....................... | $ 110,000 |
| General office expenses............................. | 103,000 |

All payrolls are subject to social security tax payments of 6% by both the employees and the company. In addition, the company withheld $480,000 in income taxes from employees' earnings. The company itself is also required to pay unemployment compensation tax equal to 4% of the payrolls.

Depreciation charges for 1976 were recorded as follows:

On the factory................................. $200,000
On the office..................................  120,000

The applicable income tax rate is 40%.

*Required:*

a. Prepare general journal entries to record the operations of the Gresham Company for 1976.
b. Prepare an income statement and a statement of cost of goods manufactured and sold for the year ended December 31, 1976.
c. Compute the under- or overapplied manufacturing overhead for 1976.

# chapter 4

# Cost
# Accounting Systems

Aɴʏ ᴄᴏꜱᴛ ᴀᴄᴄᴏᴜɴᴛɪɴɢ system involves the basic cost accounting cycle described in the preceding chapter. However, the system must provide certain specific data and procedures in order that the cycle can be completed. Remember in the comprehensive illustration in Chapter 3 that it was necessary to assume the unit cost of the product in order to determine the cost of the finished product and the cost of goods sold. The cost accounting system provides the information necessary to compute this unit cost. Basically, all cost accounting systems provide for the accumulation of data about production costs and about the physical volume of units produced. Since all accounting systems produce periodic financial reports, these cost and unit data must be identified with specific accounting periods. Further, if the system is to provide useful information for purposes of control, the cost and unit statistics must also be identified with responsibility centers. The exact manner of accumulating these data differ somewhat among cost accounting systems. What type of system is used depends largely upon the nature of the production process. Cost accounting systems may be classified according to two general types—*job order systems* and *process systems*. In both types, cost data are collected and reported so as to provide useful information for management and to provide the necessary basis for determining periodic income and inventory values. Either absorption costing or variable costing may be used in conjunction with either type of cost accounting system. A single firm may employ both types of cost accounting systems. Perhaps different systems would be used for different types of products or at different stages in the production process. Finally, individual companies may adopt unique variations on a system to suit their own particular needs. Nevertheless, all cost accounting systems can be classified as one or the other of the two basic types described in this chapter.

## JOB ORDER COST ACCOUNTING SYSTEMS

A *job order cost accounting system* is a system in which production is viewed and accounted for as a series of separate and distinct lots, batches, or jobs. Costs are accumulated for each individual job, and a unit cost is computed for each job. Job order costing is normally used where production is undertaken to fill specific customers' orders—such as in construction, printing, and shipbuilding. Such a system permits the manufacturer to match the revenue from an order with the costs incurred to produce it. Job order cost systems are by no means limited to instances of production to customers' orders, however. They are implemented in many industries where production is for inventory (to be sold subsequently to as yet undetermined buyers) but is accomplished in a discontinuous series of jobs. For example, in a furniture factory, the productive facilities of the plant may be employed serially for the manufacture of a lot of 100 maple bedsteads, then a lot of 100 maple dressers, then 500 walnut chairs, then 200 oak tables, and finally 100 upholstered couches. Obviously, it is not reasonable to say that 1,000 units of a homogeneous product have been produced. There are significant differences among these various products and the costs of producing them. Simply to identify a certain amount as the total cost of manufacturing these five jobs would not be particularly meaningful. And to divide such a total cost by 1,000 units of product would result in a wholly spurious figure for unit cost. Hence, cost data are developed for and charged to each job order individually. Even where several jobs for the same item are completed during one accounting period, the element of discontinuity of production (time lapses between the several jobs) makes it necessary to accumulate costs by jobs separately. Each job has its own unit cost, the total cost of the job divided by the number of units produced for it. Different job orders for the same product will very likely have slightly different unit costs, for the human element in production and price changes over time will have some effect upon costs.

### Job Order Cost Sheets

The cost objective in a job order cost system is the individual job. Direct manufacturing costs, therefore, are those which can be traced logically and practically to the units manufactured on a particular job order. Direct materials costs are traced to individual jobs by indicating job order numbers on materials requisitions issued by the plant to the materials storeroom. Direct labor charges to the several jobs are determined by the preparation of labor time tickets which indicate the amount of time spent by a worker on a particular job and his hourly wage rate. Manufacturing overhead is typically applied at normal rates when the job is completed. It must also be applied to incomplete jobs at the end of a fiscal year in order to avoid an erroneous underapplication of manufacturing overhead for that period.

All manufacturing costs, direct and indirect, are accumulated for each job order on a *job order cost sheet*. This sheet indicates an identifying number for the job so that it may readily be traced, the product being produced, the number of units of product to be manufactured for the job, the purpose for which the job is undertaken (i.e., for customer's order or for inventory), the date by which completion is necessary, and all of the costs incurred in the production of the job. All costs charged to production during any given period must appear on some job cost sheet. Hence, the total charges to Work in Process during the period will be equal to the total of all charges to job order cost sheets in that period. Similarly, the credits to Work in Process and corresponding debits to Finished Product will represent the sum of all costs charged to job cost sheets for completed jobs. Then, the ending balance in Work in Process will be equal to the sum of all costs accumulated to date on open cost sheets (i.e., sheets for uncompleted jobs) as of the end of the period. The file of job order cost sheets is, in effect, a subsidiary ledger supporting the general ledger account, Work in Process. Unit costs are determined only for completed jobs, and a job may be started in one period and completed in a subsequent one. Consequently, the calculation of unit cost on any one job may involve cost data spanning two or more accounting periods. The only constraint on this calculation is the job.

The necessity for maintaining numerous job order cost sheets and the necessary supporting documents, such as labor time tickets, means that the clerical work involved in a job order cost system is likely to be substantially greater than that required for a process cost system. This does not mean, of course, that a process system is always preferable. In many industries, only the job order system is feasible, regardless of the greater cost of implementing it.

### Manufacturing Overhead Costs in Job Order Systems

The use of normal manufacturing overhead rates, predetermined on the bases of budgeted costs and budgeted production volume, is essential to the smooth functioning of a job order cost system. Normal manufacturing overhead rates permit the determination of the total cost and, hence, the unit cost of a job as soon as it is completed. Actual manufacturing overhead rates could not be applied until the end of the accounting period. As explained in Chapter 3, such a delay is simply not practical.

Where several materially different products are manufactured in the same plant, it is not valid to charge manufacturing overhead to all of these products by means of a single set of manufacturing overhead rates *per unit of product*. One product may require considerably more processing for each unit than another product. Obviously, the former should be charged with proportionately more manufacturing overhead than the latter. In other words, the unit of product may not be a suitable "common denominator" of production for purposes of applying manufacturing overhead to products in a multiproduct firm. In such a case, the volume of production must be stated in terms of some unit which is common to all products.

In current accounting practice, some measure of the volume of input, or production effort, is most commonly selected as the volume to be used in computing manufacturing overhead rates and applying those rates to inventories of manufactured products. The most widely used input volume measures are direct labor cost and direct labor hours. Their popularity implies that most firms tend to regard manufacturing overhead cost incurrence as some function of labor time and effort. Less frequently used are such other input volume measures as total prime cost (materials plus labor), materials cost alone, and machine hours. Logically, the volume measure chosen should be the one that is most closely related to the pattern of manufacturing overhead cost incurrence in the particular production situation.

Whatever volume measure is selected, the accounting procedures followed are essentially the same as those described in the preceding chapter, where the volume of output was used. The normal variable manufacturing overhead rate is budgeted directly as an amount per unit of volume. In order to determine a normal fixed manufacturing overhead rate, the total budgeted fixed manufacturing overhead and the total budgeted input volume for the period must be determined. This total cost is then divided by the budgeted volume to obtain the normal fixed rate. During the period, the actual input volume will be multiplied by the normal variable and fixed manufacturing overhead rates to determine the amount of manufacturing overhead applied to production. Of course, this discussion assumes that absorption costing is being used. Under variable costing, there would be no normal fixed manufacturing overhead rate. Only variable manufacturing overhead would be applied to production.

## Job Order Costing and Responsibility Costing

The fact that cost data are accumulated for job orders does not mean that they are not also accumulated for each responsibility center in the plant. The choice of a cost accounting system does not change the need for the development of cost data along responsibility lines. Thus, there may be as many charges for labor and manufacturing overhead on a job order cost sheet as there are responsibility centers involved in the production of the job. Each center would distribute its own costs to the jobs worked on in that center during the period. Since materials are not necessarily added to production in each center, there may be fewer charges for materials than there are responsibility centers.

## Job Order Cost Sheet Illustrated

Table 4–1 is an illustration of a job order cost sheet for a manufacturer of paper novelty products. Among the company's products are jigsaw puzzles. The heading of the job cost sheet identifies the job, the product, and other pertinent information. Each job has a distinctive number. In this illustration, the number partially identifies the product.

**TABLE 4–1**

SHERMAN MANUFACTURING COMPANY
Job Order Cost Sheet

| | | |
|---|---|---|
| *Job No.*  P750–69 | *Product*  Series 808 jigsaw puzzle | |
| *Date started*  8/15/76 | *Units required*  1,200 | |
| *Date required*  8/25/76 | *Purpose*  for inventory | |
| *Date completed*  8/24/76 | *Job authorized*  J.F.C. | |

Job Costs

| | *Requisition number* | *Cost* | |
|---|---|---|---|
| Raw materials: | | | |
| Picture prints...................... | 3607 | $180.00 | |
| Cardboard backing.................. | 3608 | 74.00 | |
| Boxes............................ | 3612 | 35.00 | |
| Box labels........................ | 3612 | 48.00 | $337.00 |
| Direct labor: | | | |
| Cutting department–25 hrs @ $3.60.............. | | $ 90.00 | |
| Boxing department–40 hrs @ $2.75.............. | | 110.00 | 200.00 |
| Variable manufacturing overhead: | | | |
| Cutting department–25 hrs @ $ .60.............. | | $ 15.00 | |
| Boxing department–40 hrs @ $ .75.............. | | 30.00 | 45.00 |
| Fixed manufacturing overhead: | | | |
| Cutting department–25 hrs @ $1.60.............. | | $ 40.00 | |
| Boxing department–40 hrs @ $1.25.............. | | 50.00 | 90.00 |
| Total job costs............................ | | | $672.00 |
| Unit cost................................. | | | $   .56 |
| | | Inspected and approved R. W. E. | |

The "P" shows that the job is for puzzles, and the "750" indicates the number of pieces in the puzzles. The final two digits of the job number simply show that this is the 69th job for 750-piece puzzles. The heading also describes the product and indicates how many units are required for the job. This particular job is being produced for inventory. Others may be produced to a specific customer's order. The production manager initials the cost sheet to authorize production of 1,200 units of this particular product. The date on which the finished units are required is entered along with the date on which the job is started.

All costs incurred in connection with this job are reported on the job order cost sheet. Raw materials costs are traced to the job by means of materials requisitions. Each requisition identifies not only the items being issued and their costs but also the job number for which they were issued. A summary of requisitions for Job No. P750–69 is entered on the cost sheet. Direct labor time is accumulated in each production department on labor time tickets. These tickets indicate the amount of time spent on a particular job. All tickets for a job are then summarized in each department and the departmental time totals entered on the job cost sheet, along with the departmental wage rates. Variable and fixed manufacturing overhead are applied on the basis of normal rates per direct labor hour in each department. These normal rates are predetermined at the start of the fiscal year. The actual labor hours to which they are applied are taken from the summary of labor time tickets. (The illustration assumes that the Sherman Manufacturing Company uses absorption costing.) When production is completed, the date is entered in the heading and the factory inspector initials the cost sheet to indicate that the job has been approved and the units transferred to the finished product storeroom.

## PROCESS COST ACCOUNTING SYSTEMS

*Process cost accounting systems* regard production as a continuous flow rather than as a series of identifiable lots. Hence, this type of system is employed in industries where production processes are of a continuous and repetitive nature. Examples of such industries are basic steel, cement, flour milling, and petroleum refining. The simplest illustration of a process cost system is in a firm producing a single product or a single line of homogeneous products. However, process costing may be used effectively in a firm which produces a variety of products so long as the overall production process can be broken down into suboperations of a continuous, repetitive nature. For example, the spray-paint shop in a major appliance manufacturer's plant may perform essentially the same operations regardless of whether ranges, refrigerators, or washers are being painted. These suboperations are commonly referred to as *proc-*

*esses,* or *departments* in process costing. For purposes of the present discussion, these may be identified with responsibility centers. Hence, the accumulation of cost data by responsibility will also provide the necessary cost information for the process cost accounting system.

In a process cost accounting system, the cost objective is the production in a particular department, or responsibility center, during a specified period of time, commonly one month. Thus, direct manufacturing costs are those which can be traced entirely to the department. Consequently, certain costs that would be indirect in a job order system may be direct under process costing. For example, the wages of a maintenance man whose work is confined to one department would be treated as part of the direct labor in that department in a process cost system, even though the man does not actually work on the product. The important point is that he works directly in the department.

### Determination of Unit Cost

The unit cost under process costing is the quotient of the manufacturing costs incurred in a given department during a given period of time divided by the units of product manufactured in that same department during the same time period. Thus, the calculation is subject to two constraints, the department and the time period. The basic formula for unit cost computation is very simple.

$$\text{Unit cost} = \frac{\text{Total costs in department during period}}{\text{Units produced in department during period}}$$

While this basic formula is always valid, the determination of the units produced may be somewhat complicated.

### Equivalent Units of Production

Since one of the constraints upon the unit cost computation is the time period, the units produced during a particular period must be identified. If there is an inventory of unfinished production (i.e., Work in Process) at the beginning and/or at the end of the period, the determination of units produced involves some additional computations. Obviously, the total number of units of potential finished product in the inventory at the end of the month may not be included among the units produced during that month, for such inclusion would imply that they were completed when this clearly is not so. Similarly, the total number of units in beginning inventory cannot be treated as part of current production; to do so would be to ignore the fact that those units were partially completed during the previous month. Thus, some unit is needed to measure the amount of productive work actually done during one period. The unit of measure for this purpose is the *equivalent unit of production.*

Equivalent units of production measure the amount of work accomplished during a given period. They are units of product, but not necessarily whole units. For example, assume that the drill press department of the Coppelius Manufacturing Company finished 50,000 units of product during the month of March 1976. The inventory of Work in Process in the department at the beginning of March consisted of 10,000 units that were then half completed. The inventory of Work in Process at the end of March comprised 8,000 units that were three-fourths complete. The 50,000 units completed during the month do not include any part of the ending inventory, but that inventory was partially manufactured during the month. On the other hand, the 50,000 finished units do include the 10,000 units in beginning inventory; but half of the work on those units was completed in the previous month. Hence, the work done (the equivalent units) during March consists of the units finished during that month plus the work done on the ending inventory minus the work done in February on the beginning inventory. *Equivalent units produced, then, are equal to* (1) *the total units completed during a period plus* (2) *the total units in the ending inventory of Work in Process times the fraction that the inventory is completed and minus* (3) *the total units in the beginning inventory of Work in Process times the fraction that they were already complete at the start of the period.* Using the data from the example above, the equivalent units produced in the drill press department during March would be computed as follows:

| | |
|---|---:|
| Units completed during March............................. | 50,000 |
| + Units in ending inventory times fraction completed | |
| (8,000 × ¾)......................................... | 6,000 |
| | 56,000 |
| − Units in beginning inventory times fraction completed | |
| (10,000 × ½)........................................ | 5,000 |
| = Equivalent units produced............................. | 51,000 |

The problem of equivalent units may be complicated further by the fact that not all of the elements of production cost are the same fraction complete in a given inventory of Work in Process. For example, all of the materials may be put into the production process at its inception; whereas the labor and manufacturing overhead are added throughout the process. Hence, any inventory of Work in Process would be fully complete with respect to materials but might be any fraction completed with respect to labor and manufacturing overhead. In such a case, no single figure for equivalent production would be valid. Rather, there would have to be one such figure for materials and a different one for labor and manufacturing overhead. It should be noted here that labor and manufacturing overhead are not necessarily always at the same stage of completion in an inventory. If they were not, there would have to be three separate figures for equivalent units. For purposes of the discussion and illustrations in this chapter, we shall assume that labor and manufacturing overhead are at the same stage of completion. Obviously, this would be the case whenever manufacturing overhead is applied to production on the basis of direct labor cost or hours. Thus, a single figure for equivalent units and a single unit cost could be used for the combination of labor and manufacturing overhead, commonly referred to as conversion costs. Refer again to the drill press department example in the preceding paragraph. Assume now that all materials are put into process

### TABLE 4–2

COPPELIUS MANUFACTURING COMPANY
Drill Press Department
Equivalent Units of Production
March 1976

|  | Materials | Conversion Costs |
|---|---|---|
| Units completed during March............................ | 50,000 | 50,000 |
| + Units in ending inventory times fraction complete: | | |
| Materials (8,000 × 1)................................. | 8,000 | |
| Conversion costs (8,000 × ¾)......................... | | 6,000 |
|  | 58,000 | 56,000 |
| − Units in beginning inventory times fraction complete: | | |
| Materials (10,000 × 1)................................ | 10,000 | |
| Conversion costs (10,000 × ½)........................ | | 5,000 |
| = Equivalent units produced............................ | 48,000 | 51,000 |

at the start of production (and, hence, are 100 percent complete in any inventory) and that the fractions of completion indicated above apply only to conversion costs. The calculation of equivalent units would then appear as shown in Table 4–2. As a general rule, the concept of equivalent units must be related to a particular element of cost in order for it to be operationally meaningful. Consequently, unit costs typically can be computed only for each cost element separately. Total unit cost is then the sum of the unit costs for the individual cost elements.

### Inventory Cost Flow Assumptions

For the first month of production operations in a department or in any other month in which there is no beginning inventory in process, unit cost in a process costing system may be determined simply, with no alternative assumptions to be considered. The total cost incurred during the month is divided by the sum of the units completed plus the equivalent units in the ending inventory to determine unit cost. However, if there is also an inventory in process at the beginning of the month, some assumption must be made regarding the disposition of that inventory in order to determine unit cost for the month. Three alternative assumptions might be made. They are the same three that may be applied to any other type of inventory for financial accounting purposes. The first assumes that the beginning inventory is the first group of units to be processed and completed during the current month; this is the first-in, first-out (Fifo) method. The second assumption is that the beginning inventory is inextricably merged with the new units started into production during the period and can no longer be identified separately; this is the weighted average cost method. Finally, one might assume that the beginning inventory is ignored and all production effort is devoted to units started into production currently; this is the last-in, first-out (Lifo) method. Either of the first two assumptions might reflect the physical reality of the production process, and both of them are used in costing inventories of Work in Process in process cost accounting systems. It would be difficult to imagine a production operation in which the Lifo assumption reflected the physical flow of goods in process. Moreover, the Lifo method is almost always applied on a periodic basis at the end of the year, not on a month-by-month basis. Thus, as a practical matter, Lifo is not used in process costing and will not be considered further here.

Both the Fifo and the average cost methods are illustrated below by use of the same set of data for the drill press department of the Coppelius Manufacturing Company. The equivalent units of production for this department during March 1976 were developed in the preceding section and appear in Table 4–2. The pertinent production cost data are as follows:

Costs in beginning inventory of work in process:
| | |
|---|---|
| Direct materials..................................... | $ 45,200 |
| Conversion costs (direct labor plus manufacturing overhead applied to production).................... | 57,450 |
| | $102,650 |

Costs charged to production during March, 1976:
| | |
|---|---|
| Direct materials.................................... | $244,800 |
| Conversion costs................................... | 614,550 |
| | $859,350 |
| Total costs to be accounted for during March............ | $962,000 |

Note that the relevant manufacturing overhead cost is the amount applied to production, not the actual manufacturing overhead incurred. Since it is the applied manufacturing overhead that is charged to products, that must be the manufacturing overhead used in determining the unit costs of those products. Here, manufacturing overhead is applied on the basis of direct labor hours. Hence, a single unit cost for total conversion costs may legitimately be computed.

## Average Cost Method

Since it is the more widely used alternative, the average cost method is illustrated first. Mechanically, it is the simpler of the two; for the beginning inventory of work in process need not be kept separate in the computation of unit costs. In effect, this method assumes that all of the units worked on during a period, regardless of when they were started, are so intermingled that they can only be regarded as one homogeneous group. Thus, all costs associated with the production of those units in the current period and in the preceding period are combined also. (Of course, separate analysis of both equivalent units and costs by cost elements—materials and conversion costs in our illustration—is still necessary.) Because the beginning inventory of work in process is being combined with production started currently, the fact that those units were partially finished in the preceding month is of no consequence. Thus, the equivalent units of production computed in Table 4–2 are not appropriate when the average cost method is used. The computation must stop before deduction of the beginning inventory under this method. Hence, the equivalent units to be used in this first illustration are as follows:

|  | Materials | Conversion Costs |
|---|---|---|
| Units completed during March.............................. | 50,000 | 50,000 |
| + Units in ending inventory times fraction complete: | | |
| Materials (8,000 × 1)...................................... | 8,000 | |
| Conversion costs (8,000 × ¾)............................ | | 6,000 |
| = Equivalent units for average cost method................. | 58,000 | 56,000 |

The computation of unit costs in the drill press department for the month of March and the use of those unit costs in determining the cost of finished production and the cost of the ending inventory of work in process are illustrated in Table 4–3. This is a production cost report for the department for the month. The format is not standard; different companies may choose different forms. This particular format is quite useful, however, as it shows how all costs incurred and all units worked on have been accounted for as of the end of the month. Moreover, it shows how the unit costs are computed from total costs and equivalent units and then how those unit costs are applied to the same total number of equivalent units to determine inventory costs. The first section of the production cost report shows the total costs incurred and the computation of unit costs. This computation proceeds from left to right thus: total cost divided by equivalent units equals unit cost. Because the

## TABLE 4–3

### COPPELIUS MANUFACTURING COMPANY
Drill Press Department
Production Cost Report
March 1976
(average cost method)

|  | Total Costs | Equivalent Units | Unit Cost |
|---|---|---|---|
| *Costs incurred* | | | |
| Direct materials: | | | |
| Beginning inventory.................. | $ 45,200 | | |
| Current charges.................... | 244,800 | | |
| | $290,000 | 58,000 | $ 5 |
| Conversion costs: | | | |
| Beginning inventory.................. | $ 57,450 | | |
| Current charges.................... | 614,550 | | |
| | $672,000 | 56,000 | 12 |
| Total costs incurred............. | $962,000 | | $17 |
| *Costs accounted for* | | | |
| Completed and transferred out.......... | $850,000 | 50,000 | $17 |
| Ending inventory in process: | | | |
| Direct materials.................... | $ 40,000 | 8,000 | 5 |
| Conversion costs................... | 72,000 | 6,000 | 12 |
| | $112,000 | | |
| Total costs accounted for........ | $962,000 | | |

average cost method is being used, the costs in the beginning inventory and the costs newly incurred during March are combined into single totals for both direct materials and conversion costs. Note that there is no single quantity of equivalent units that was used to calculate the total unit cost of $17. This can be determined only by adding the separately computed unit costs for materials and conversion costs.

The second section of the report shows how the total costs are finally accounted for. There are only two possible dispositions of the costs charged to a department during a period. Either they are transferred out of the department as the cost of finished production or they remain in the department as the cost of the ending inventory of work in process. The computations of these amounts proceed from right to left thus: unit cost multiplied by equivalent units equals total cost. Since all of the units completed and transferred out are at the same stage of completion (100 percent) with respect to all cost elements, they may be multiplied by the total unit cost of $17. As the ending inventory is at different stages of completion with respect to materials and conversion costs, that inventory cost must be computed by materials and conversion costs separately. Notice that the same number of equivalent units for each cost element are used in the second section as were used above in the first section to compute unit cost (i.e., 58,000 for direct materials and 56,000 for conversion costs). This re'flects the fact that all equivalent units must be accounted for and they can be only in the group of units completed and transferred out or in the group still in process at the end of the month. If any units started into production are spoiled or otherwise lost in production, they are simply omitted entirely from the equivalent units. The costs of production must be borne by the good units only.

## Fifo Method

Procedurally, the Fifo method is slightly more complex than the average cost method, because both the equivalent units and the costs in the beginning inventory of work in process must be kept separate from units and costs entered during the current month. Thus, the unit costs for materials and conversion costs are computed only from the equivalent units actually produced during the current month and the costs newly incurred during this month. The appropriate equivalent units are those calculated earlier in Table 4–2. These are truly the equivalent production of the month of March alone. All work already done during February is excluded. The production cost report for the Fifo method is shown in Table 4–4. It is in the same basic format as the report for the average cost method (Table 4–3), but the beginning inventory is handled separately in both sections. In the first section, unit costs are again computed from left to right; but they are based only on costs incurred and work done during March. The costs in the beginning inventory are noted, because they are still charged to the drill press department's inventory and must be accounted for; but they have no effect on the current unit cost calculations.

The second section of the report is considerably more complicated than in the average cost method. To begin with, consistently with the first-in, first-out assumption, the beginning inventory is accounted for as completed. The costs in the beginning inventory carried forward from February are the first part of the cost of completed production. Since the beginning inventory was unfinished, the conversion costs necessary to complete it are added next. As there were 10,000 units of potential finished product in the opening inventory and they were half complete, they were also half *incomplete* at the start of the month. Thus, 5,000 equivalent units (half of 10,000) with respect to conversion costs had to be added in order to finish the beginning inventory. A total of 50,000 units were completed during March. Ten thousand of these were from the beginning inventory; so, 40,000 units started currently were also completed. As these 40,000 units were all worked on exclusively during March, the total unit cost for this month may be applied to them. As in the case of the average cost method, the total cost of the ending in-

**TABLE 4–4**

COPPELIUS MANUFACTURING COMPANY
Drill Press Department
Production Cost Report
March 1976
(Fifo method)

|  | Total Costs | Equivalent Units | Unit Cost |
|---|---|---|---|
| Costs incurred |  |  |  |
| Beginning inventory........................ | $102,650 |  |  |
| Current charges: |  |  |  |
| Direct materials........................... | $244,800 | 48,000 | $ 5.10 |
| Conversion costs.......................... | 614,550 | 51,000 | 12.05 |
|  | $859,350 |  | $17.15 |
| Total costs incurred.................. | $962,000 |  |  |
|  |  |  |  |
| Costs accounted for |  |  |  |
| Completed and transferred out: |  |  |  |
| Beginning inventory: |  |  |  |
| Costs incurred in previous month........... | $102,650 |  |  |
| Cost to complete inventory |  |  |  |
| (conversion costs)...................... | 60,250 | 5,000 | $12.05 |
|  | $162,900 | 10,000 |  |
| Production started currently................. | 686,000 | 40,000 | 17.15 |
| Total completed production........... | $848,900 | 50,000 |  |
| Ending inventory in process: |  |  |  |
| Direct materials.......................... | $ 40,800 | 8,000 | 5.10 |
| Conversion costs......................... | 72,300 | 6,000 | 12.05 |
|  | $113,100 |  |  |
| Total costs accounted for.............. | $962,000 |  |  |

ventory must be computed separately for direct materials and conversion costs.

The unit costs, the cost of completed production, and the cost of the ending inventory in process are all different under Fifo from the parallel amounts under average cost. Apparently, unit production costs have risen. The average unit costs, partially weighted by costs and production in February, are lower than the Fifo unit costs computed only on the basis of current costs and production. The same total costs were accounted for in both methods, but they are allocated in different amounts between completed production and ending inventory. Specifically, $1,100 more would be transferred from the Work in Process account to Finished Product under the average cost method ($850,000) than under Fifo ($848,900).

## Processing in Subsequent Departments

The illustration in the preceding sections involved only a single production department, or process. Goods were started and completed in the drill press department and were then transferred to finished product inventory to await sale. In many production operations, there are two or more successive processes. The goods completed in the first department are transferred to a second department for further processing and thence, perhaps, to a third and a fourth department. When the work is completed in the final process, the costs are transferred to Finished Product. There are as many Work in Process accounts as there are processes, or departments. Each department has its own production cost report, its own unit costs, its own inventory, and its own "completed" production. The "completed" products of one department become the raw materials of the next one. Both total costs and unit costs cumulate as the goods move through the various departments. There may be some substantial changes in unit costs from department to department, however. For example, if department 1 accounts for its output in gallons and department 2 accounts for its output of the same basic product in pints, the output of the second department is immediately increased by a factor of 8. Thus, the unit cost for the materials of department 2, which are the "completed" production of department 1, will be about one-eighth the amount of the unit cost in the first department. Then, too, there may be additional changes affecting unit costs in subsequent departments. Units produced earlier may be lost in later departments. New raw materials may be added in subsequent departments so as to increase the total volume of units produced. The procedures for dealing with these various complications are explained and illustrated in most cost accounting texts.[1]

## ABSORPTION AND VARIABLE COSTING COMPARED

### The Development of Variable Costing

Absorption costing is generally accepted in current accounting practice as *the* way of accounting for manufacturing costs and, specifically, fixed manufacturing overhead costs. For many years, in fact, there was not even any significant suggestion of an alternative. During the 1930s, however, the method we know here as variable costing was proposed and given some small notice. But the growth of variable costing was slow in coming. The urgency of World War II caused a great many less critical considerations to be pushed out of men's minds, and the virtual pandemonium of the immediate postwar years was hardly conducive to careful consideration of something so technical as a method of accounting for fixed costs. Thus, the real development of the variable costing technique did not occur until the decade of the 1950s.

To begin with, we must observe that variable costing is not widely

---

[1] A detailed presentation of many of the complications of process cost accounting may be found in John J. W. Neuner, *Cost Accounting: Principles and Practices,* 8th ed. (Homewood, Ill.: Richard D. Irwin, Inc., 1973), chapters 4 and 5.

known by that name at all. Rather, the concept has developed and is most popularly known today as *direct costing*. This has been an unfortunate choice of terminology, however; for the distinction which is at the heart of the method is not that between direct and indirect costs, but that between variable and fixed costs. "Variable costing," although not so widely employed, is a much more descriptive term and will be used throughout this volume. The same concept is known as *marginal costing* in Great Britain. Again, the selection of the term seems to be unsatisfactory. Variable costs cannot necessarily be identified with marginal costs, and, as already pointed out, marginal costs has so explicit a meaning in economic theory that the author prefers to avoid its use altogether in accounting.

## Arguments for and against Variable Costing

The development of variable costing has progressed significantly since 1950. Advocates of the method have raised a number of points in its favor, and critics have advanced some alleged disadvantages of the method. Some of these arguments for and against variable costing are considered in the paragraphs that follow.

*Separate Accounting for Variable and Fixed Costs.*   One argument offered in support of variable costing is that it causes separate identification and recording of variable and fixed costs *in the accounts* and, hence, stimulates greater realization on the parts of accountants and managers of the importance of volume in the determination of costs. There can be little question that the separate recording of variable and fixed costs is useful to management. As has been demonstrated in Chapter 3, this separate recording *can* be effected just as well under absorption costing as under variable costing. The fact is, however, that a clear distinction between variable and fixed costs *has been* made less frequently in the accounts of firms employing absorption costing. Of course, these firms are able to make the distinction between variable and fixed costs by special analyses.

*Emphasis on Cost-Volume Relationships.*   Perhaps the most important and unassailable argument in favor of variable costing is that it emphasizes the distinction between variable and fixed costs in reports to management and to others. A comparison of Tables 3–5 and 3–7 in Chapter 3 will testify to the validity of this point. Under absorption costing, the principal intermediate profit figure on the income statement is the gross margin, a residual after the deduction from revenue of both variable and fixed costs of manufacturing. The principal intermediate figure on the variable costing income statement is the variable profit, the difference between the revenue (which, of course, varies with sales volume) and those costs which vary with the volume of sales (variable cost of goods sold, variable selling expenses, and so forth). Thus, variable profit itself bears a direct relationship to volume. No such relationship exists between gross margin and volume. This undeniable emphasis upon cost-volume relationships is particularly useful to management, which has the power (not without limit, of course) to effect changes in costs and/or in volume. Whether the same emphasis is equally useful to others, such as stockholders and creditors, is problematic.

Some opponents of the variable costing method have pointed out that, by excluding fixed costs from the cost of the product, the method emphasizes variable costs to the prejudice of fixed costs and that fixed costs are likely to be ignored or, at least, minimized in importance by management. This argument is particularly unsatisfactory, however; for it seems to rest upon the unattractive premise that managers are not very bright.

***Effect of Inventory Changes on Reported Net Income.*** Under absorption costing, an increase in finished product inventory levels (i.e., ending inventory greater than the beginning balance) in a year of declining sales can have the effect of mitigating a decline in income, because fixed manufacturing costs incurred during the period are partially deferred in inventory until some subsequent period when the goods are sold. Conversely, a reduction in inventory levels (i.e., ending inventory less than the beginning) has the effect of charging to the revenues of that period fixed manufacturing costs incurred in some previous period. In other words, changes in inventory balances from the beginning to the end of a period have an identifiable impact upon income under absorption costing. Advocates of variable costing have argued that such an effect is artificial and may be misleading. They point out that variable costing avoids any income effect resulting from inventory increases or decreases.[2]

The substance of this particular argument can best be seen from a simple illustration. Table 4–5 compares reported incomes under absorption costing and variable costing for the same company for three years. In the first year, more units are manufactured than sold; inventory is increased. In the second year, manufacturing volume and sales volume are identical; inventory balances remain unchanged. Finally, in the third year, sales volume exceeds the volume of production; inventory is decreased. The sales volume is the same (60,000 units) in each year, and the selling price remains stable at $4 per unit. The variable manufacturing costs total $2.50 per unit in each year, and the fixed manufacturing costs total $60,000 each year. No nonmanufacturing costs are included in the illustration because, since they are treated in the same way under

---

[2] This feature of variable costing, in contrast with absorption costing, was the central point in the earliest published article that advocated use of variable costing in reports to management. See Jonathan N. Harris, "What Did We Earn Last Month?" *N.A.C.A. Bulletin,* vol. 17 (January 15, 1936), pp. 501–22.

**TABLE 4–5**

Comparative Income Measurements
(all amounts in thousands)

|  | First Year | | Second Year | | Third Year | |
|---|---|---|---|---|---|---|
|  | Absorption Costing | Variable Costing | Absorption Costing | Variable Costing | Absorption Costing | Variable Costing |
| Unit sales volume.............. | 60 | 60 | 60 | 60 | 60.0 | 60 |
| Unit production volume......... | 75 | 75 | 60 | 60 | 48.0 | 48 |
| Sales revenue.................. | $240 | $240 | $240 | $240 | $240.0 | $240 |
| Costs charged to revenue: | | | | | | |
| Variable.................... | $150 | $150 | $150 | $150 | $150.0 | $150 |
| Fixed...................... | 48 | 60 | 60 | 60 | 69.6 | 60 |
| Total costs............. | $198 | $210 | $210 | $210 | $219.6 | $210 |
| Net income.................... | $ 42 | $ 30 | $ 30 | $ 30 | $ 20.4 | $ 30 |

both absorption and variable costing, they would have no effect upon the comparison.

Certain technical aspects of Table 4–5 must be seen clearly in order to understand fully the comparison being made. Under both costing methods, the variable costs charged to the revenue of the period are $150,000 (the 60,000 units sold each year at the unit variable cost rate of $2.50). Under variable costing, the fixed cost charged to revenue in each year is simply the total fixed costs incurred in that year—$60,000. Under absorption costing, however, the fixed costs charged to revenue are the fixed costs of the goods sold and may be more or less than the $60,000 of fixed costs incurred in each year. In the first year, the fixed costs averaged $.80 per unit ($60,000 ÷ 75,000 units produced). Thus, the fixed cost of goods sold is $48,000 (60,000 units sold at a fixed cost rate of $.80 each). In the second year under absorption costing, fixed costs average $1 per unit ($60,000 ÷ 60,000 units produced); and the fixed cost of goods sold is $60,000 (60,000 units sold @ $1). Finally, tht fixed costs per unit in the third year amount to $1.25 ($60,000 ÷ 48,000 units produced). The fixed costs of goods sold in the third year includes the fixed cost incurred in the third year (48,000 units sold × $1.25 = $60,000) plus some of the fixed costs incurred in the first year and deferred in inventory (12,000 units sold × $.80 = $9,600). This is a total of $69,600. In each year, the first fixed costs charged to revenue are those applicable to the current production. This means that the inventory is accounted for in accordance with the Lifo cost flow assumption. Year-to-year fluctuations in income under absorption costing would appear with either the Fifo or the average cost flow assumption also; only the amounts of the fluctuations would be different.

Table 4–5 implicitly assumes that budgeted and actual fixed manufacturing overheads are equal each year and also that budgeted and actual production volumes are the same each year. The effect of these assumptions is that there is no under- or overapplied manufacturing overhead in any year. These assumptions are not necessary for the illustration; they merely keep it simple.

The basic point of the illustration can now be seen quite simply. During the three year period shown, there were no changes in sales volume, selling prices, variable costs per unit, or total fixed costs. The only change was in the volume of production and, consequently, in the levels of inventory. Under variable costing, changes in inventory levels have no effect upon income. Under absorption costing, on the other hand, income is different in each of the three years as a result of the changes in inventory levels. The proponents of variable costing argue that these fluctuations in income are meaningless and potentially misleading and, hence, that variable costing is superior to absorption costing insofar as each is concerned with the measurement of periodic net income.

The validity of this particular argument in favor of variable costing rests upon the validity of the basic premise of the method, namely, that fixed manufacturing costs are period costs and not product costs. Supporters of variable costing contend that such is indeed the case, that fixed manufacturing overhead is the cost of providing productive capacity, of making production possible during a particular period, but not a part of the cost of the units actually produced in that period. Advocates of absorption costing, on the other hand, argue that the fixed costs of manufacturing are just as much costs of the product as are variable costs. They argue that the utilization of factory facilities, as represented by the cost item depreciation, is just as essential to the product as are direct materials and labor. Which of these positions is the correct one has been argued frequently and vehemently. As mentioned earlier, absorption costing is generally accepted in current accounting practice, while variable costing is not. This fact does not necessarily demonstrate the theoretic superiority of absorption costing, however. It could be interpreted simply as a reflection of the facts that absorption costing has long been entrenched in accounting practice and that accounting practices are not changed overnight.

It is important that the reader understand that the fluctuations in income shown in Table 4–5 under absorption costing are correct and proper if fixed manufacturing overhead is truly a product cost as absorption costing suggests. As a matter of fact, if fixed manufacturing overhead is properly treated as a product cost, then the use of variable costing would result in an *artificial* equalization of income over time; and such practice is generally agreed to be improper. Whether income fluctuations caused by changes in inventory levels are valid or not depends upon whether fixed manufacturing overhead is a product cost or a period cost. At this writing, it is fair to say that the latter question remains a disputed point.

## Internal and External Accounting Reports

The development of variable costing has centered around its usefulness in reports to management. Only recently has interest arisen in its use also in reports to stockholders, creditors, and other outside parties. With respect to internal reports submitted to management, the decision as to the use of variable costing is a simple one. The criteria which should guide the selection of accounting techniques in reports to management are utility and effectiveness. If variable costing proves to be useful and effective in management reports, then, by all means, it should be used. Variable costing is good management accounting if it facilitates management's achievement of its basic objectives. The popularity of the method in practice is evidence of its usefulness.

Where external reports to stockholders and others are concerned, the criteria determining the selection of accounting practices are *generally accepted accounting principles*. These consist of various concepts, rules, and practices which have attained acceptance in business. At the time of this writing, variable costing has not attained the status of a generally accepted accounting principle. It is not considered acceptable in external financial reports.

A firm which wishes to employ variable costing in its internal reporting system but must adhere to absorption costing for its external reports is not condemned to maintaining two separate sets of books. Costs may be accumulated in the accounts and internal reports may be prepared in accordance with the variable costing technique. When external reports are prepared, a simple adjustment may be made to add to inventory a proportionate share of the fixed manufacturing overhead of the period and to remove such amount from the current fixed manufacturing overhead expense account. For example, if the Fixed Manufacturing Overhead Control account had a balance of $750,000 at the end of a year and it was determined that, under absorption costing, 10 percent of that total should be deferred in inventory, a simple adjustment would transfer $75,000 of the fixed manufacturing overhead to the appropriate inventory accounts—Work in Process and/or Finished Product. The remaining $675,000 would be reported as part of the cost of goods sold on the absorption costing income statement. This adjustment would be made only in the external financial statements, of course, not in the ledger accounts, which would be maintained consistently in accordance with variable costing.

## QUESTIONS FOR DISCUSSION

1. What are the comparative merits of using normal manufacturing overhead rates rather than actual rates in job order cost systems and in process cost systems?

2. What type of industry would you expect to use job order cost accounting? What type would more likely use process costing? Give several examples of each type.

3. Describe the various functions that are served by job order cost sheets.

4. Why are equivalent units of production essential to an accurate determination of unit cost in a process cost accounting system but not in a job order system?

5. Is process costing more compatible with the objective of responsibility accounting than is job order costing? Explain.

6. Under what condition would the current unit cost in a process cost accounting system be greater under the Fifo method than under the average cost method? Under what condition would unit cost be greater under the average cost method than under Fifo?

7. Why is the Lifo method not normally used in process costing systems?

8. Refer to Table 4–4 in this chapter. Locate in the second (lower) section of the report all of the equivalent units that were used in the first (upper) section to compute unit costs.

9. What circumstances might cause the unit cost of products to decrease as those products moved through successive departments, or processes, in a process cost accounting system?

10. Of what value is an accounting system that records and reports fixed and variable costs separately?

11. Why might the income of a firm during a single period be reported differently under absorption costing as compared with variable costing?

12. You have been engaged as a consultant to a medium-sized manufacturer. The president has asked you to study his operations and to recommend a basic cost accounting method—either absorption costing or variable costing. Production costs during the most recent year totaled $50 million, about 60 percent of which were variable costs and the remainder, fixed. Which method would you recommend? Why? If you would want any additional information before making your recommendation, specify what that information would be.

13. The sales of the Pickwick Company in 1975 were somewhat disappointing in light of recent years' experience. However, a substantial inventory of finished products was accumulated during that year in anticipation of much improved sales in 1976. Actual sales in 1976 proved to be even greater than expected. All of the current output and most of the inventory accumulated in 1975 were sold. Still, when the financial statements for the year were prepared, net income was less than it had been in 1975. The president was unhappy with this report and demanded an explanation

from the controller. The controller explained that, under the absorption costing method long used in the firm, a major liquidation of an inventory of finished products, such as occurred in 1976, tended to depress income. After further discussion, the controller suggested that they prepare and examine revised income statements for 1975 and 1976 under the variable costing method. These revised statements showed a lower income for 1975 and a substantially higher income for 1976. The president was so pleased with this result that he directed that the company adopt variable costing forthwith.

In 1977, sales again declined sharply. This decline was believed to be only temporary, however. Upon the recommendation of the sales manager, production was maintained at the same level as in the two preceding years. It was agreed that any inventory accumulated in 1977 would be sold the following year. When the variable costing income statement was prepared at the end of 1977, it showed a net loss. When the president asked for an explanation of this loss, the controller said that it was simply a normal consequence of the variable costing method in such a year. He mentioned casually that a profit would have been reported for 1977 under the old absorption costing method. At this, the president glowered at the controller and snapped, "Dave, at the board meeting next week I'm going to have to explain this loss; and all this cost accounting mumbo jumbo has got me confused. So, you had better come up with an explanation of what's been going on in the past couple of years' incomes; and it had better be good. I told the board that this switch to variable costing was a good idea last year, and I don't want to look foolish up there next week."

As the controller of the Pickwick Company, prepare a satisfactory explanation for the president to present to the board of directors.

## PROBLEMS

4-1. The Mycroft Company uses a job order cost accounting system and absorption costing. The schedule below shows the number of units produced on each job order during the first month of the firm's operations, the number of labor hours worked on each job, and the direct costs charged to each job.

|  | *Job Number* | | | |
|---|---|---|---|---|
|  | *1* | *2* | *3* | *4* |
| Units of product............... | 1,000 | 1,500 | 1,300 | 1,400 |
| Direct labor hours............. | 800 | 1,500 | 1,200 | 400 |
| Direct materials cost........... | $6,840 | $9,660 | $7,780 | $4,650 |
| Direct labor cost.............. | 4,000 | 7,500 | 6,000 | 2,000 |

Manufacturing overhead is applied to production at predetermined rates per direct labor hour. These rates are as follows:

Variable......................... $ .80
Fixed........................... 2.40

Jobs 1, 2, and 3 were completed during the month. Job 4 is less than half complete.

*Required:*

a. Compute the amount of manufacturing overhead charged to each job.
b. Compute the unit cost of each complete job.
c. Prepare the journal entry to record the transfer of the completed jobs to Finished Product.
d. Determine the balance in Work in Process at the end of the month.

4–2. At April 1, 1976, the inventory balances of the Baskerville Company were as follows:

| | | |
|---|---:|---:|
| Materials........................................ | | $20,000 |
| Work in process (Job 1028): | | |
| Direct materials............................. | $2,000 | |
| Direct labor................................. | 1,000 | |
| Variable manufacturing overhead.............. | 300 | |
| Fixed manufacturing overhead................. | 600 | 3,900 |
| Finished product............................. | | 45,000 |

The job order cost sheets that were active during the month appeared as follows on April 30:

| Job order number................... | *1028* | *1029* | *1030* | *1031* |
|---|---:|---:|---:|---:|
| Direct materials.................... | $ 8,000 | $10,000 | $ 7,000 | $5,000 |
| Direct labor........................ | 5,000 | 6,000 | 4,000 | 2,000 |
| Variable manufacturing overhead..... | 1,500 | 1,800 | 1,200 | 600 |
| Fixed manufacturing overhead........ | 3,000 | 3,600 | 2,400 | 1,200 |
| Total cost......................... | $17,500 | $21,400 | $14,600 | $8,800 |
| Status as of April 30.............. | complete | complete | complete | open |

Other information about operations during April is summarized below.

| | |
|---|---:|
| Materials purchased................... | $24,000 |
| Actual manufacturing overhead: | |
| Variable........................... | 5,000 |
| Fixed.............................. | 10,000 |
| Cost of goods sold.................... | 50,000 |

*Required:*

a. Determine the inventory balances at April 30, 1976.
b. Compute the under- or overapplied manufacturing overhead for the month of April.

4–3. The Watson Tool Corporation, which commenced operations on August 1, 1976, employs a job order cost system. Manufacturing overhead is charged to production at normal rates per direct labor hour, as follows:

| | |
|---|---:|
| Variable rate..................... | $1.20 |
| Fixed rate....................... | 1.80 |

Actual operations for the month of August 1976 are summarized below.

1. Purchases of raw materials: 100,000 pieces @ $3.
2. Units produced and prime costs charged to jobs:

| Job No. | Units | Materials | Direct Labor Cost | Direct Labor Hours |
|---------|-------|-----------|-------------------|--------------------|
| 101............... | 500 | $15,000 | $ 8,000 | 2,000 |
| 102............... | 800 | 18,400 | 9,600 | 2,400 |
| 103.............. | 1,500 | 28,800 | 14,400 | 3,600 |
| 104.............. | 500 | 14,000 | 6,000 | 1,500 |
| 105.............. | 1,000 | 19,200 | 3,200 | 800 |

3. Actual manufacturing overhead costs incurred (Credit "miscellaneous accounts."):

> Variable....................... $12,600
> Fixed......................... 20,000

4. Completed jobs: nos. 101, 102, 103, and 104.
5. Sales: All units produced on jobs 101, 102, and 103 and 200 of the units produced on job 104 were sold.

*Required:*

a. Prepare general journal entries to record the operations of August 1976.
b. Compute the unit cost of each completed job.
c. Compute the balance in Work in Process at August 31. Prove the accuracy of this balance by showing its composition (i.e., materials, labor and manufacturing overhead by jobs).

4-4. The Holmes Products Company uses a job order cost accounting system and variable costing. Variable manufacturing overhead is charged to production at a normal rate of $.50 per direct labor dollar. The inventories on May 1, 1976, were as follows:

Materials................................................................. $35,000
Work in process:

| Job | Materials | Labor | Manufacturing Overhead | |
|-----|-----------|-------|------------------------|---|
| 327 | $ 6,650 | $ 8,000 | $4,000 | |
| 329 | 4,440 | 4,000 | 2,000 | |
| 330 | 1,935 | 1,000 | 500 | |
| | $13,025 | $13,000 | $6,500 | 32,525 |

Finished product (20,000 units).................................... 60,000

Operations for the month of May 1976 are summarized below.
1. Materials costing $18,000 were purchased on account.
2. A summary of materials requisitions shows the following charges to jobs:

| Job | Materials Cost |
|-----|----------------|
| 330..................... | $ 2,550 |
| 331..................... | 7,100 |
| 332..................... | 10,080 |
| 333..................... | 5,870 |
| 334..................... | 2,400 |

3. The payroll for the month of May was distributed as follows:

Direct labor:

| | |
|---|---:|
| Job 327 | $ 1,000 |
| Job 329 | 2,000 |
| Job 330 | 6,000 |
| Job 331 | 10,000 |
| Job 332 | 14,400 |
| Job 333 | 6,000 |
| Job 334 | 2,000 |
| Variable indirect labor | 15,000 |

4. Labor-related costs amount to 10% of the payroll.
5. Actual fixed manufacturing overhead totaled $25,000. (Credit "miscellaneous accounts.")
6. The following jobs and units of product were completed during May in the order in which they are listed:

| Job | Units |
|---|---|
| 327 | 6,500 |
| 329 | 4,200 |
| 330 | 4,500 |
| 331 | 6,800 |
| 332 | 9,600 |

7. Forty thousand units of product were sold during May. The company accounts for the inventory of finished product by the first-in, first-out (Fifo) method.

*Required:*

a. Prepare general journal entries to record the operations of the month of May.
b. Compute the unit cost of each completed job.
c. Compute the balance in Work in Process at May 31 and show its composition (i.e., materials, labor, and manufacturing overhead by jobs).

4-5. The Moriarty Manufacturing Company produces a variety of power garden tools. A job order cost system is used. On June 1, 1976, the factory ledger showed the following inventory balances:

| | |
|---|---:|
| Materials | $175,000 |
| Work in process | 210,000 |
| Finished product | 400,000 |

Open job order cost sheets on June 1 contained the following total charges:

| | |
|---|---:|
| Job M–1015 | $120,000 |
| Job C–908 | 50,000 |
| Job T–750 | 40,000 |

Transactions for the month of June are summarized below.

1. Materials were purchased at a cost of $700,000.
2. A summary of materials issues is as follows:

| | |
|---|---|
| Job C–908. . . . . . . . . . . . . . . . . . . . . . . . . . . . | $100,000 |
| Job T–750. . . . . . . . . . . . . . . . . . . . . . . . . . . . | 60,000 |
| Job M–1016. . . . . . . . . . . . . . . . . . . . . . . . . . | 220,000 |
| Job T–751. . . . . . . . . . . . . . . . . . . . . . . . . . . . | 125,000 |
| Job M–1017. . . . . . . . . . . . . . . . . . . . . . . . . . | 150,000 |
| Indirect materials (a variable cost). . . . . . . | 95,000 |
| | $750,000 |

3.  Factory labor costs were distributed as follows:

| | |
|---|---|
| Job M–1015. . . . . . . . . . . . . . . . . . . . . . . . . . | $ 35,000 |
| Job C–908. . . . . . . . . . . . . . . . . . . . . . . . . . . . | 25,000 |
| Job T–750. . . . . . . . . . . . . . . . . . . . . . . . . . . . | 10,000 |
| Job M–1016. . . . . . . . . . . . . . . . . . . . . . . . . . | 60,000 |
| Job T–751. . . . . . . . . . . . . . . . . . . . . . . . . . . . | 5,000 |
| Job M–1017. . . . . . . . . . . . . . . . . . . . . . . . . . | 15,000 |
| Indirect labor (a variable cost). . . . . . . . . . | 50,000 |
| | $200,000 |

4.  Labor-related costs included the following items.

| | |
|---|---|
| Social security tax. . . . . . . . . . . . . . . . . . . . . | $12,000 |
| Unemployment compensation tax. . . . . . . . . | 6,000 |

5.  The payroll department reported the following summary distribution of payroll credits:

| | |
|---|---|
| Payroll checks disbursed. . . . . . . . . . . . . . . . | $150,000 |
| Federal income tax withheld. . . . . . . . . . . . . | 28,000 |
| Social security tax withheld. . . . . . . . . . . . . | 12,000 |
| Insurance premiums withheld. . . . . . . . . . . . | 10,000 |

6.  The actual fixed manufacturing overhead costs incurred during June included the following items:

| | |
|---|---|
| Depreciation on plant and equipment. . . . . . | $60,000 |
| Property taxes and insurance. . . . . . . . . . . . | 20,000 |
| Maintenance. . . . . . . . . . . . . . . . . . . . . . . . . | 30,000 |

7.  Variable manufacturing overhead is applied to production at a normal rate of 100% of direct labor cost. Fixed manufacturing overhead is applied at a normal rate of 80% of direct labor cost.
8.  Jobs M–1015, C–908, T–750, and M–1016 were completed during June.
9.  Goods were sold for $850,000.
10.  The balance in Finished Product on June 30 was $524,000.

*Required:*

a.  Prepare general journal entries to record the transactions for the month of June.

b.  Prepare a statement of cost of goods manufactured and sold for the month ended June 30, 1976.

4–6.  The Lestrade Company manufactures two products, A and B. A job order cost system is employed. The letter prefix to the job number identifies the product being produced on that job. Work in process is

accounted for by individual job orders. Raw materials and finished prod-
duct accounts are costed under the last-in, first-out (Lifo) assumption.
A perpetual inventory system is used.

On January 31, 1976, the company's inventory accounts showed the
following balances:

| | | |
|---|---:|---:|
| Raw materials (50,000 lbs. @ $.60).......... | | $30,000 |
| Work in process: | | |
| Job A–29 (3,000 units).................. | $25,000 | |
| Job B–63 (5,000 units).................. | 9,000 | 34,000 |
| | | |
| Finished product: | | |
| Product A (2,000 units @ $11)........... | $22,000 | |
| Product B (3,000 units @ $2.80).......... | 8,400 | 30,400 |

The following raw materials purchases were made during the month
of February:

> February 10—40,000 lbs. @ $.62
> February 20—50,000 lbs. @ $.64       $5000$

Materials were issued during the month as follows:

> February 15—35,000 lbs. for Job A–30    $21\,700$
> February 25—45,000 lbs. for Job B–64

Direct labor costs during February were charged to the following
jobs:

| Job | Hours | Cost |
|---|---:|---:|
| A–29..................... | 1,500 | $ 6,000 |
| A–30..................... | 3,500 | 14,000 |
| B–63..................... | 1,000 | 4,000 |
| B–64..................... | 2,500 | 10,000 |

Actual manufacturing overhead for the month included $18,000 of
variable costs and $40,000 of fixed costs. Variable manufacturing over-
head is applied to production at a normal rate of $2 per direct labor
hour. Fixed manufacturing overhead is accounted for as a period expense.

Jobs A–29 and B–63 were completed on February 14 and February
24, respectively. On February 28, 2,500 units of Product A and 6,000
units of Product B were sold to customers.

*Required:*

Prepare analyses of the ledger accounts for Raw Materials, Work
in Process, Finished Product, and Cost of Goods Sold for the month of
February 1976. Show all debits and credits to each account and the ending balance in each. Include any supporting schedules or computations
that may be necessary.

4–7.  The Spalanzani Steel Corporation uses a process cost accounting system.
During the second quarter of 1976, 500,000 tons of steel were completed.
On April 1, there were 80,000 tons in process; these were complete with

respect to materials but only half complete with respect to labor and manufacturing overhead. The inventory in process on June 30 consisted of 100,000 tons, 75% complete with respect to materials and 25% complete with respect to labor and manufacturing overhead.

*Required:*

Compute the equivalent units produced during the second quarter. These are the equivalent units that would be used under the Fifo method of inventory costing.

4–8.  On November 1, 1976, the Antonia Products Co. had 3,000 units of product in process. They were half complete with respect to raw materials but only one-third complete with respect to direct labor and manufacturing overhead. By the end of November, 6,000 units had been completed and transferred to the warehouse. On November 30, there were 2,000 units in process. These were fully complete with respect to raw materials but only three-fourths complete with respect to direct labor and manufacturing overhead.

*Required:*

Compute the equivalent units of production during November under the Fifo method.

4–9.  Olympia Products, Inc., employs a process cost accounting system. During the month of August, 1976, the firm completed 5,000,000 pounds of product. On August 1, the inventory of work in process had included 1,500,000 pounds of product; they were one-half complete with respect to materials and one-third complete with respect to conversion costs. On August 31, there were 1,000,000 pounds in process; they were one-fourth complete with respect to materials and one-fifth complete with respect to conversion costs.

*Required:*

a.  Compute equivalent units of production under the average cost method.
b.  Compute equivalent units of production under the FIFO method.
c.  Explain why the equivalent units used under these two methods are not the same.

4–10.  The Frantz Foundry finished 45,000 pounds of output during October 1976. The inventories in process at the beginning and end of the month were as follows:

|  | Oct. 1 | Oct. 31 |
|---|---|---|
| Total units | 5,000 | 12,000 |
| Percentage of completion: | | |
| Materials | 80% | 50% |
| Conversion costs | 40% | 25% |

*Required:*

a.  Compute the equivalent units produced during October under the average cost method.

b.  Compute the equivalent units produced during October under the Fifo method.

 4–11. The Lindorf Corporation manufactures a single product in one production process. The company completed a total of 720,000 units of this product during July 1976. Production costs during July included materials charges of $264,000 and labor and manufacturing overhead charges totaling $110,400. At the end of the month, there were 80,000 units still in process, complete with respect to materials and half complete with respect to labor and manufacturing overhead.

On July 1, there had been 100,000 units in process, one-half complete with respect to materials and one-fourth complete with respect to labor and manufacturing overhead. This inventory had a total cost of $19,600, consisting of $16,000 for materials and $3,600 for labor and manufacturing overhead.

The corporation uses a process cost accounting system and the average cost method.

*Required:*

a.  Compute the equivalent units produced during July for purposes of the average cost method.

b.  Compute the average unit costs of production for the month.

c.  Determine the cost of goods completed during July and the cost of the inventory in process at the end of the month.

4–12. Stella Products, Inc., manufactures surf boards in one continuous production process. Process costing and the average cost method are used in accounting for work in process. Sixty-nine thousand boards were finished during September 1976. The inventories or work in process at the beginning and the end of the month were as follows:

|  | *Sept. 1* | *Sept. 30* |
|---|---|---|
| Units of product.......................... | 20,000 | 10,000 |
| Percentage of completion: |  |  |
| Materials............................ | 60% | 30% |
| Conversion costs...................... | 40% | 20% |

The direct costs charged to the beginning inventory in process and to production during September were as follows:

|  | *Beginning Inventory* | *Current Production* |
|---|---|---|
| Materials.................... | $96,000 | $480,000 |
| Labor....................... | 46,000 | 380,000 |

Manufacturing overhead is applied to production at normal rates of 40% of direct labor cost for variable cost items and 60% of direct labor cost for fixed cost items.

*Required:*

a. Compute the equivalent units of production for September under the average cost method.

b. Compute the average unit costs of production for September.

c. Determine the total costs of completed production during the month and of the ending balance in Work in Process.

4–13. The Nicklausse Corporation produces liquid soap in a single continuous process. A process cost accounting system is employed, and all inventories are costed under the first-in, first-out (Fifo) assumption. At February 29, 1976, the corporation had an inventory of 6,000 gallons of soap in process. All materials required for these 6,000 gallons were already in process, and the inventory was estimated to be two-thirds complete with respect to labor and manufacturing overhead. The costs in this inventory were as follows:

| | |
|---|---:|
| Materials................................. | $4,000 |
| Labor..................................... | 2,300 |
| Manufacturing overhead..................... | 1,100 |

During March 1976, 64,000 gallons of soap were completed and transferred to the finished stock warehouse. On March 31, there were 8,000 gallons in process. They were complete with respect to materials but only one-fourth complete with respect to conversion costs. Charges to Work in Process during the month of March were as follows:

| | |
|---|---:|
| Materials................................. | $52,800 |
| Labor..................................... | 24,800 |
| Manufacturing overhead..................... | 12,400 |

*Required:*

a. Compute the equivalent units produced during the month of March.

b. Compute the unit costs of production for the month.

c. Compute the costs of the soap completed during March and of the inventory in process on March 31.

4–14. The Hoffman Manufacturing Company produces a single product in one continuous production operation. A process cost accounting system and the first-in, first-out (Fifo) method are used. Both variable and fixed manufacturing overhead are charged to production at normal rates per direct labor hour of $2 and $3, respectively.

Physical production statistics for April 1976 are summarized below.

Work in process, April 1: 1,500 units, complete with respect to materials and 40% complete with respect to labor and manufacturing overhead.

Started into process during April: 9,700.

Work in process, April 30: 2,400 units, complete with respect to materials and one-third complete with respect to labor and manufacturing overhead.

No units are lost or spoiled in the production process.

Production costs in the inventory of work in process on April 1 totaled \$121,500. Current actual manufacturing costs included the following:

Materials used in production.............. \$533,500
Direct labor............................     75,000 hours @ \$5.20
Variable manufacturing overhead.......... \$160,000
Fixed manufacturing overhead............     230,000

*Required:*

a. Compute the equivalent units produced during April 1976.
b. Compute the unit costs of production for April.
c. Determine the cost of production completed during April and the cost of the unfinished production in process on April 30.

4–15. The Miracle Shortening Corporation produces a liquid cooking oil in two successive production processes, blending and bottling. Only variable manufacturing costs are charged to products in the company's process cost accounting system. Inventories are costed under the average cost method. The following cost data are taken from the records of the two production processes for the month of August 1976:

|  | Blending | Bottling |
|---|---|---|
| Direct materials used............................. | \$90,000 | \$ 9,900* |
| Direct labor....................................... | 75,900 | 26,400 |
| Actual variable manufacturing overhead.............. | 48,800 | 17,000 |
| Variable manufacturing overhead applied............. | 50,600 | 16,500 |
| Actual fixed manufacturing overhead................. | 71,400 | 98,000 |

\* The cost of goods completed in the blending process and transferred to bottling is also accounted for as a direct material cost here. It is not included in this \$9,900, which represents only the costs of bottles, caps, and labels.

Production statistics (in gallons) for the two processes are as follows:

|  | Blending | Bottling |
|---|---|---|
| Inventory, August 1.................... | 10,000 | 0 |
| Completed during August.............. | 66,000 | 66,000 |
| Inventory, August 31................. | 4,000 | 0 |

Both the beginning and the ending inventories in the blending process were complete with respect to direct materials and one-half complete with respect to direct labor and manufacturing overhead. The balance in Work in Process—Blending on August 1 included materials cost of \$15,000, labor cost of \$5,700, and applied variable manufacturing overhead of \$3,800.

The inventory of finished product on August 1 included 33,000 gallons at an average unit cost of \$4.24. During August, 70,000 gallons were sold at a net selling price of \$10 each. Variable selling expenses average \$.40 per gallon sold. Fixed selling and administrative expenses totaled \$75,000 for the month. The income tax rate is 40%.

*Required:*

a. Prepare a production report for the blending process for August 1976. This report should include computations of equivalent units, unit production costs, and total costs of completed production and work in process at the end of the month.

b. Prepare an income statement and a supporting statement of cost of goods manufactured and sold for the month of August.

4–16. The Crespel Company manufacturers an antiseptic powder in two successive production departments, compounding and packaging. A process cost accounting system and absorption costing are used. The inventory of Work in Process—Compounding is costed by the average cost method. Work in Process—Packaging is costed by the first-in, first-out (Fifo) method. The Finished Product inventory account is costed under the last-in, first-out (Lifo) assumption.

At December 31, 1975, the company's inventory balances were as follows:

| | | |
|---|---:|---:|
| Raw materials................................ | | $300,000 |
| Work in process—compounding: | | |
| Raw materials............................ | $108,000 | |
| Conversion costs......................... | 66,000 | 174,000 |
| Work in process—packaging: | | |
| Raw materials............................ | $220,000 | |
| Conversion costs......................... | 30,000 | 250,000 |
| Finished product (80,000 lbs.)............... | | 556,000 |

In the compounding department, the first production process, the inventory consisted of 60,000 pounds of product, two-thirds complete with respect to materials and half complete with respect to labor and manufacturing overhead. In the packaging department, the beginning inventory consisted of 40,000 pounds, complete with respect to materials and half complete with respect to labor and manufacturing overhead.

During 1976, raw materials purchases totaled $2,400,000. Raw materials were issued to the two production departments in the following amounts:

> Compounding.............. $2,160,000
> Packaging.................. 320,000

In addition, the completed output of the compounding department is accounted for as part of the raw materials in the packaging department.

Direct labor costs in the two departments were as follows:

> Compounding................ 200,000 hrs. @ $5
> Packaging.................... 146,000 hrs. @ $4

Actual manufacturing overhead costs incurred in each department during 1976 were as follows:

| | *Compounding* | *Packaging* |
|---|---:|---:|
| Fixed...................... | $480,000 | $420,000 |
| Variable................... | 160,000 | 75,000 |

Manufacturing overhead is applied to production at the following normal rates per direct labor hour:

|              | Compounding | Packaging |
|--------------|-------------|-----------|
| Fixed........................ | $2.50 | $3.00 |
| Variable..................... | .75 | .50 |

During 1976, a total of 750,000 pounds of product were completed in the compounding department and transferred to packaging. At the end of the year, 75,000 pounds remained in process in compounding. This inventory was 80% complete with respect to materials and 40% complete with respect to conversion costs. In the packaging department, a total of 720,000 pounds of product were completed and transferred to the warehouse for finished product. The inventory in the packaging process at the end of the year comprised 60,000 pounds, complete as to materials and half complete as to conversion costs.

During the year, 700,000 pounds of product were sold.

*Required:*

a. Prepare journal entries to record all of the manufacturing operations of the Crespel Company for 1976. Present any necessary supporting schedules or computations.

b. Prepare a statement of cost of goods manufactured and sold for the year ended December 31, 1976. Any net under- or overapplied manufacturing overhead should be added or deducted at the end of this statement.

4–17. The Darnay Company uses the absorption costing method. During 1976, 120,000 units were produced and 105,000 units were sold. The following data were extracted from the company's adjusted trial balance at December 31, 1976:

|                                               | Debit | Credit |
|-----------------------------------------------|-------|--------|
| Sales...................................... |  | $1,045,000 |
| Cost of goods sold......................... | $720,000 |  |
| Variable manufacturing overhead control..... | 63,000 |  |
| Fixed manufacturing overhead control....... | 350,000 |  |
| Variable selling expenses.................. | 60,000 |  |
| Fixed selling expenses..................... | 90,000 |  |
| Fixed administrative expenses.............. | 50,000 |  |
| Variable manufacturing overhead applied..... |  | 60,000 |
| Fixed manufacturing overhead applied....... |  | 360,000 |
| Income tax expense......................... | 52,000 |  |

Manufacturing overhead is applied to production at normal rates per unit of product. The same rates have been used since the company was founded.

*Required:*

a. Compute the net income for 1976 under absorption costing. A formal income statement is not required.

b. Compute the net income for 1976 under variable costing. A formal income statement is not required. (The income tax expense will be the same as under absorption costing.)

c. Reconcile the incomes under these two costing methods if they are not the same.

4-18. A. Manette & Co., Inc., commenced operations on January 1, 1974. Following is a summary of its operations during the first three years of the company's existence:

|  | 1974 | 1975 | 1976 |
|---|---|---|---|
| Volume in units: |  |  |  |
| Sales.......................... | 50,000 | 60,000 | 40,000 |
| Production.................... | 60,000 | 70,000 | 25,000 |
| Selling price per unit.............. | $10 | $10 | $10 |
| Variable costs per unit: |  |  |  |
| Selling........................ | 1 | 1 | 1 |
| Manufacturing................. | 4 | 4 | 4 |
| Fixed costs per year: |  |  |  |
| Selling........................ | $ 70,000 | $ 70,000 | $ 70,000 |
| Manufacturing................. | 130,000 | 130,000 | 130,000 |

Under the absorption costing method, fixed manufacturing overhead would be applied to production at a normal rate of $2 per unit of product in each of the three years.

*Required:*

a. Compute net income before tax in each of the three years under both absorption costing and variable costing.

b. Explain any differences in incomes under these alternative costing methods for each year individually and for the three-year period in total.

c. Which costing alternative do you believe presents the more useful statement of the company's income? Why?

4-19. Following is the income statement of the Carton Products Company for 1976:

CARTON PRODUCTS COMPANY
Income Statement
For Year Ended December 31, 1976

| | | |
|---|---|---|
| Sales.................................... | | $575,000 |
| Cost of goods sold: | | |
| Finished product, January 1 | | |
| (12,000 units)........................ | $ 48,000 | |
| Cost of goods manufactured during 1976 | | |
| (90,000 units)....................... | 360,000 | |
| | $408,000 | |
| Finished product, December 31 | | |
| (2,000 units)........................ | 8,000 | |
| | $400,000 | |
| Less overapplied fixed manufacturing | | |
| overhead............................ | 15,000 | 385,000 |
| Gross margin............................ | | $190,000 |
| Selling and administrative expenses.......... | | 140,000 |
| Net operating income...................... | | $ 50,000 |
| Income taxes............................. | | 20,000 |
| Net income.............................. | | $ 30,000 |

The company's president, Sidney Carton, expressed disappointment at this report; for it reflects a decline in income from the previous year despite an increase in sales volume.

An examination of the cost records shows that variable manufacturing overhead has been applied at a rate of $.50 per unit of product and that fixed manufacturing overhead has been applied at a rate of $1 per unit. Variable selling and administrative expenses average $.50 per unit sold. All of these rates have been in effect since the company was founded.

*Required:*

a. Prepare an income statement for Carton Products Company for 1976 in accordance with the variable costing method. This method will not be allowed for income tax purposes, however.

b. Explain with appropriate computations and comments any difference between the income as originally reported and the income under variable costing.

4-20. Jerry Cruncher started manufacturing operations in a small plant early in 1976. At the end of the year, his accountant prepared the following income statement for him:

CRUNCHER CRACKER COMPANY
Income Statement
For Year Ended December 31, 1976

| | | |
|---|---:|---:|
| Sales (100,000 units)............................. | | $120,000 |
| Variable expenses: | | |
|   Cost of goods sold.......................... | $60,000 | |
|   Marketing expenses........................ | 15,000 | 75,000 |
| Variable profit................................ | | $45,000 |
| Fixed expenses: | | |
|   Manufacturing overhead..................... | $45,000 | |
|   Administrative expenses..................... | 10,000 | 55,000 |
| Net loss........................................ | | $(10,000) |

As the company is unincorporated, income taxes need not be considered in its financial statements.

Cruncher was discouraged with the results of his first year of operations. A well meaning friend suggested that his mistake was in adopting variable costing. He contended that a switch to absorption costing would be a profitable move for Cruncher.

Production during 1976 totaled 150,000 units of product.

*Required:*

a. Determine the company's income for 1976 under absorption costing. Was Cruncher's friend right in his contention? Explain.

b. Assume that Cruncher again produces 150,000 units in 1977 but sells 200,000 units. Assume also that all costs and expenses adhere to exactly the same pattern of behavior with respect to volume as in

1976. Which costing method would result in the higher net income in 1977? Support your answer with appropriate computations.

4–21. This problem has been adapted from an article entitled "Try This on Your Class, Professor," by Raymond P. Marple in *The Accounting Review* for July 1956, page 492.

The Defarge Company purifies and bottles rain water for sale directly from its plant. Hence, its raw material is free and it incurs only production costs. As the plant is fully automated, all production costs are fixed in the amount of $400,000 per year. The water is sold at a price of $20 per barrel.

Consider two alternative cases for the firm's operations during its first two years in business:

Case 1.   Business is slow.

|  | 1971 | 1972 |
|---|---|---|
| Barrels produced | 50,000 | 0 |
| Barrels sold | 25,000 | 25,000 |

Case 2.   Business is booming.

|  | 1971 | 1972 |
|---|---|---|
| Barrels produced | 50,000 | 50,000 |
| Barrels sold | 25,000 | 75,000 |

*Required:*

a. Compute income before tax both in dollars and as a percentage of sales revenue for each year under both absorption costing and variable costing first for Case 1 and then for Case 2.
b. Which costing method should this company adopt? Why?
c. Are you sufficiently curious about the point in Marple's article to go over to the library and read it?

4–22. The Two Cities Steel Company maintains its ledger and prepares all internal reports in conformity to the variable costing method. For its annual report to stockholders, however, the company's independent auditors insist that it use absorption costing. The conversion from variable to absorption costing is made by debiting or crediting, as appropriate, an account titled "Fixed Manufacturing Overhead in Inventory" in an adjusting entry made at the end of each year. No other entry is ever made to this account. This account is then included along with Work in Process and Finished Product, which contain only variable costs, in the published balance sheet. Any under- or over-applied fixed manufacturing overhead which appears as a result of the conversion to absorption costing is debited or credited to "Under/ Overapplied Manufacturing Overhead," an account that is closed at the end of each year. For purposes of the conversion to absorption costing, a normal fixed manufacturing overhead rate is determined in the customary way. All inventories are costed under the first-in, first-out (Fifo) method.

The following pertinent data were taken from the internal reports for the first three years of the company's operations:

|  | *1974* | *1975* | *1976* |
|---|---|---|---|
| Tons of steel: |  |  |  |
| Sold.......................... | 120,000 | 210,000 | 300,000 |
| Actual production.............. | 150,000 | 220,000 | 275,000 |
| Budgeted production........... | 150,000 | 220,000 | 300,000 |
| Fixed manufacturing overhead: |  |  |  |
| Actual...................... | $600,000 | $640,000 | $700,000 |
| Budgeted.................... | 600,000 | 660,000 | 720,000 |

*Required:*

Prepare the necessary adjusting entry at the end of each of the three years of operations to convert the company's accounts from variable costing to absorption costing. Present appropriate computations in support of each entry.

4–23. Put your pencil and your calculator away! This short case requires no computations at all—just careful thought and sound reasoning.

Late in 1975, the Lon-Par Oil Company completed construction of a major oil refinery at Smog Harbor, California. The total cost of the refinery was $110,000,000, and the facilities are expected to have an economic life of 20 years. The maximum productive capacity of the new refinery is 15 million barrels of crude oil per year. However, during 1976, the first year of operations, it was estimated that actual production would be only two-thirds of capacity.

Refinery operations will be largely automated. Hourly employees for the first year of operations have been planned as follows:

| *Position* | *Number* | *Hourly Wage* |
|---|---|---|
| Refinery operator........................... | 250 | $4.80 |
| Maintenance man.......................... | 80 | 4.25 |
| Watchman................................ | 40 | 3.25 |
| Shipping-dock worker...................... | 75 | 3.75 |
| Boat crewman............................. | 12 | 4.50 |

Refinery operators run the refining machinery; most of this work involves monitoring instruments that reflect the status of computer controlled machine operations. Maintenance men perform routine repair and maintenance work on buildings and equipment. Shipping-dock workers load tank trucks which carry finished products to Lon-Par Oil Company's bulk stations for further distribution. Boat crews assist tankers delivering crude oil to the refinery and tend the subsurface pipeline from the offshore tanker anchorage to the crude oil storage tanks. In addition to hourly wages, the following monthly salaries are anticipated:

| | |
|---|---|
| Administration................................. | $90,000 |
| Refinery foremen.............................. | 25,000 |
| Shipping-dock foremen......................... | 3,000 |
| Boat captains................................. | 6,000 |

Normally there will be 255 16-hour working days in each year.

The only significant raw material used by the refinery will be crude oil. It is expected to have an average cost of $11.40 per barrel, delivered.

On the basis of its experience with other refineries, the company has estimated that other operating expenses will be as follows:

Variable manufacturing overhead . . . . . . . . . . $.30 per bbl. of crude oil
Fixed manufacturing overhead (not
　including depreciation) . . . . . . . . . . . . . . . . $300,000 per mo.
Miscellaneous administrative expense . . . . . . $120,000 per mo.

Although the refinery is a "modern" one with pollution control equipment installed, emission of air pollutants from time to time is virtually inevitable. A county ordinance requires that the refinery be shut down after any four-hour period of excessive pollutant emission until the situation has been corrected. The company's labor agreement requires that all hourly employees be paid in full if they are on the premises during such shut-down periods.

*Required:*

a. Should Lon-Par Oil Company use a job order or a process cost accounting system for this refinery? Explain.
b. Should the output of the refinery be costed by the absorption costing method or by the variable costing method? Explain.
c. Should the wages of the shipping-dock workers be accounted for as direct labor? Explain. If not as direct labor, how should they be classified?
d. How should the wages and salaries of the boat crewmen and captains be accounted for? Why?
e. During 1976, the refinery was shut down because of air pollutant emission for a total of 18 working days. How should employees' wages paid for these 18 days be reported in the company's financial statements? Explain.

# chapter 5

# Allocation of
# Indirect Costs

IN GENERAL, *allocation* is the process of distributing or spreading some financial quantity over one or more cost objectives or time periods. Although quantities other than costs may be allocated, we are here concerned only with allocations of costs. Costs may be allocated among cost objectives. For example, the rent on a building may be allocated among the departments housed in it; or the cost of maintaining production equipment may be allocated among the products manufactured with that equipment. Costs may also be allocated among time periods. Depreciation, for example, is essentially the process of allocating the cost of an asset over the several periods of its useful life. Cost allocations present some of the most substantial and troublesome problems of financial accounting and of cost accounting, in particular.

In its broadest definition, allocation includes the tracing of a direct cost to a single cost objective as well as the distribution of an indirect cost to two or more cost objectives or periods. In this chapter, however, we will focus only on the allocation of indirect costs to cost objectives. This particular allocation can involve some very difficult and, possibly, arbitrary choices. The basic nature of an indirect cost is that it is not directly traceable to any single cost objective. It is truly common to two or more objectives. Nevertheless, accounting principles often require that some reasonable allocation be made. Moreover, it is entirely possible that a single cost item will be allocated and reallocated several times before its final impact on cost objectives has been determined.

## OBJECTIVES OF INDIRECT COST ALLOCATIONS

Whether a particular indirect cost is allocated or not and how it is allocated, if at all, depend upon the objectives of the specific accounting system or upon the context of a particular situation. The same cost item may be allocated for one purpose but not for another. Further, it may be allocated in different ways for different purposes. In considering the objectives of allocations, it is useful to distinguish between financial accounting and management accounting applications.

### Financial Accounting

Most allocations of indirect costs are for purposes of financial accounting. A major requirement of financial accounting is that all of the costs of manufacturing a product be charged to that product. Since many of the costs of manufacturing are indirect with respect to a single product, only by some allocation can each product be charged with a share of those indirect costs. Ideally, the share of indirect costs assigned to any single product will be reasonable in view of the apparent relationship between that product and the costs. If no relationship of any sort is apparent and, yet, allocation is still considered necessary, the share of costs assigned to the product will be essentially arbitrary—but not capricious. Inasmuch as most manufacturing costs are allocated to products via the several responsibility centers in the factory, certain indirect costs may have to be allocated first to these centers and then to the products. Thus, there may be successive stages of allocation.

Allocations play an important role in the typical cost accounting system. In Chapter 3 we saw that direct manufacturing costs (materials and labor) are traced directly to the products but that indirect manufacturing costs (manufacturing overhead) must be allocated among the products by means of normal rates. Even though manufacturing overhead cost is not directly traceable to individual products, it is necessary if any products are to be produced. Hence, a reasonable share of it is allocated to each product. Once all manufacturing costs have been assigned to all products, unit costs are computed according to the procedures described in Chapter 4. These unit costs become the basis for allocating those manufacturing costs to the incomes of successive accounting periods. That is, the unit costs are applied to the quantities of goods sold during a period to determine the current cost of goods sold. Similarly, the same unit costs are used to determine the cost of the ending inventories of manufactured products. These inventories are assets, and they will be charged to the incomes of subsequent periods in which they are sold.

**Management Accounting**

As a general rule, allocations of indirect costs are neither useful nor appropriate for management accounting purposes. Cost control, for example, is not facilitated by allocations of indirect costs. A cost must be controlled at its source. Any allocation of the cost away from its source to other cost objectives will be of no value at all in the cost control process. Indeed, if someone attempts to control a cost at the cost objective to which it has been allocated, the allocation will have resulted only in confusion.

Ideally, the planning of indirect costs would be done at their sources also. If this can be done effectively, allocations would again serve no useful purpose. However, in some cases, past allocations may be helpful in planning future costs. Some manufacturing overhead costs, for example, are roughly variable with the volume of production even though they cannot be traced directly to individual products. In such a case, predicting the volume of production leads to the planning of the indirect costs. Not all allocations can be used in this way to plan future costs, however. If an allocation made for financial accounting purposes is purely arbitrary, it will be of no use in cost planning.

Indirect cost allocations are generally not useful for purposes of decision making. The relevant costs for decision making are those that are directly traceable to a particular decision alternative and would not be incurred if that alternative were rejected. Thus, allocation, as opposed to direct tracing, of costs is inappropriate. There is one significant exception to this general rule. Pricing is certainly a decision making problem. Setting the price for special goods produced to a customer's order is often done on the basis of total costs plus a negotiated profit margin. In such a case, there is no market price because there is no regular market for the products. Major weapon systems and space vehicles are examples of such nonmarketable products. In these cases, pricing is more a problem of equity between the two parties than a question of economics. The costs of producing such items are frequently unpredictable. Hence, the customer agrees to compensate the producer for his actual costs. Since the special products are part of the total output of the producer's firm, it is felt to be equitable that the customer compensate the producer for a reasonable share of the indirect costs that are common to all of the output but directly traceable to no single portion of it. Thus, allocations of indirect costs are used in determining prices under these special circumstances.[1] Although cost-based pricing of nonmarketable products may appear to be a very specialized case, it is a fairly important one, particularly in the area of government procurement. In fact,

---

[1] This subject will be discussed further in Chapter 15.

there is a special federal agency whose responsibility is to establish cost accounting practices to be used for this purpose. This agency is the Cost Accounting Standards Board.

## COST ACCOUNTING STANDARDS BOARD

The Cost Accounting Standards Board was created by an act of Congress in 1970. It is an agency of the Congress, not a part of the Executive Branch of the government. Its statutory responsibility is to promulgate Cost Accounting Standards to be used by all defense contractors in costing products manufactured under negotiated defense procurement contracts in excess of $100,000. For this purpose, "defense" is construed to include not only the Department of Defense but also the Energy Research and Development Administration (formerly the Atomic Energy Commission) and the National Aeronautics and Space Administration. Further, by an administrative ruling, the General Services Administration has extended the applicability of these standards to negotiated contracts under its jurisdiction. Other governmental agencies, state as well as federal, are likely to adopt them also. While the legal scope of the Cost Accounting Standards Board's authority is limited to government procurements, its actual influence may prove to be much broader. If contractors are compelled to use certain cost accounting practices for their government contracts and if they find these practices to be reasonable and generally feasible, they may elect to use them in costing all of their products. In that case, these practices would attain the status of generally accepted accounting principles and would likely be adopted by other manufacturing companies that had no negotiated defense contracts at all.

The allocation of indirect costs has been the subject of much of the Cost Accounting Standards Board's concern. It has addressed the questions of allocating manufacturing overhead to products, allocating home office expenses to the operating segments of a corporation, and allocating the administrative expenses of operating segments to production contracts. In each case, the basic premise of cost-based pricing requires that truly common costs be assigned to individual products and contracts. Thus, the Cost Accounting Standards Board has already been the source of potentially useful techniques for indirect cost allocations, and it is likely to do more in this area.

## THE ALLOCATION PROCESS

The process of allocating indirect costs requires first that the costs to be allocated be clearly identified and then that the base by which they will be allocated to cost objectives be determined. Given both the costs and the allocation base, one may compute the allocation rate thus:

$$\text{Allocation Rate} = \frac{\text{Costs}}{\text{Base}}$$

This rate is then used to allocate the costs to the appropriate cost objectives. Each step in the process is considered below.

## Indirect Cost Pools

There are many different indirect costs in the typical company, and there is likely to be no practical way that all of them can be allocated to appropriate cost objectives by a single rate. To begin with, certain costs may be regarded as irrelevant to certain cost objectives. For example, the manufacturing overhead incurred in one responsibility center would not be allocated to products that were not worked on in that center. Further, not all indirect costs are related to a single cost objective in the same way. For example, certain indirect costs may appear to be related to labor effort, while others may be associated with materials input or machine time. These different types of costs should be allocated separately in order to make the total allocations as reasonable as possible. Thus, the costs to be allocated by a single allocation rate must be identified separately. Groupings of indirect costs to be allocated by one rate to two or more cost objectives are called *indirect cost pools*. A firm may recognize as many or as few of these pools as it feels are appropriate to its situation and its costing requirements. In the illustrations in this chapter, we shall see indirect cost pools which group costs by their basic nature (e.g., labor-related costs) and by responsibility centers.

## Allocation Bases

Ideally, the base used to allocate indirect costs to cost objectives should be one which identifies a causal or beneficial relationship between the cost objectives and the costs. We have already seen manufacturing overhead allocated to production on the base of units of output in a single-product company and on some input base, such as direct labor cost or hours, in a multiproduct firm. In the single-product firm, it is fairly easy to sustain the argument that manufacturing overhead is incurred because of and for the benefit of the units of the product manufactured during a period. In a multiproduct firm, we observed that units of various products cannot usually be taken as a common denominator of output. Hence, some input measure is usually chosen as the allocation base instead. If manufacturing overhead is incurred basically in proportion to the labor effort expended in production, it would seem reasonable to argue that a causal relationship runs from the incurrence of labor cost or the expenditure of laborers' time to the incurrence of the manufacturing overhead costs. Thus, labor cost or hours would appear to be rational bases for the allocation of manufacturing overhead to production.

Different allocation bases may be appropriate for different types of costs. However, most bases may be classified as one of the following types:

1. A measure of input, or activity, in the responsibility center in which the cost is incurred and from which it will be allocated (e.g., hours of processing time in a computer center or man-hours in a repair shop).
2. A measure of the output of the responsibility center in which the cost is incurred and from which it will be allocated (e.g., pages of printed output from a computer center or number of completed repair orders in a repair shop).
3. A measure of activity in the center to which the indirect cost will be allocated. (For example, machine hours in production departments may be used as the base for allocating the indirect costs incurred in a repair shop. The implicit assumption is that greater repair cost is incurred as machines are used for longer periods of time.)

The Cost Accounting Standards Board has expressed a preference for allocation bases in the order listed above. An example of each of these three types of allocation bases is included in the illustration of manufacturing overhead allocation in the next section.

In some instances no reasonable allocation base may appear. For example, the costs of the corporate executive office may appear to benefit all operations of the company, but in a vague and general way. No allocation base seems to define the beneficial relationship. In such a case, if allocation is necessary, an arbitrary allocation base must be used. One such base is the total sales revenue of the operating divisions, where these divisions are the cost objectives to which the allocation is to be made. Perhaps the most common justification for selecting such a base is that it indicates the divisions' abilities to bear the allocated costs in their profit reports. However, one might argue that more executive time and effort is likely to be directed to those divisions with the smallest sales revenues on the grounds that these are the divisions in which problems exist. Another arbitrary allocation base often used is the total of all other costs already assigned to a cost objective. This is really nothing more than a measure of the size of the cost objective, and its use suggests that more indirect costs should be allocated to larger cost objectives.

## Allocation Rates

The costs to be allocated by a particular allocation rate may be either actual costs or budgeted costs. Similarly, the allocation base used may be either actual volume or budgeted volume of activity. Hence, the allocation rate may be deriv,ed from any one of the following four combinations:

*1.  Actual Cost/Actual Volume.*  This is the type of rate that would be used if actual costs were being allocated after the end of an accounting period. We saw in Chapter 3 that such a rate might be used for allocating manufacturing overhead costs to production but that it generally would not be considered suitable for that purpose. In some cases, waiting until the end of the period would be inconsistent with the purpose for which the allocation was intended. Hence, although feasible, this type of allocation rate would seldom be used.

*2.  Budgeted Cost/Budgeted Volume.*  In general, this is how an allocation rate would be computed initially. Normal fixed manufacturing overhead rates, for example, are based on budgeted fixed costs and budgeted production volumes. If a rate is to be determined in advance of actual operations, this is the only practicable method.

*3.  Budgeted Cost/Actual Volume.*  Since such a rate could be computed only at the end of a period, it could be used only for allocations that could be deferred that long. In such a case, the first type of rate described above would probably be used. If management believes that allocations of indirect costs are appropriate for purposes of measuring performance in responsibility centers,[2] this type of allocation rate might be considered desirable. The actual volume of service to or benefit in the responsibility centers to which the allocation is made might be considered the appropriate allocation base. However, management might feel that only budgeted costs of the center from which the allocation is made should be distributed to other centers. In this way, any difference between actual and budgeted costs will remain in the center which incurred the costs and may be presumed responsible for controlling them.

*4.  Actual Cost/Budgeted Volume.*  This type of rate could be computed only after the end of a period. It is difficult to think of a practical application that would be served effectively by the use of such a rate.

## ALLOCATION OF MANUFACTURING OVERHEAD COSTS TO PRODUCTION

In Chapters 3 and 4, we saw manufacturing overhead cost allocations as a fairly simple process of setting normal rates and then applying them to actual volume as production occurred. In many firms, particularly those with large and complex organization structures, that may be only the final step in a more complex allocation process. Some indirect costs may be incurred initially for the firm as a whole and may not be directly

---

[2] As a matter of fact, many accountants and managers would contend that such a belief was misguided. The question of allocating indirect costs for purposes of management's evaluation of performance in separate responsibility centers will be discussed further in Chapter 12.

traceable to any single responsibility center. These costs must be allocated among all of the responsibility centers that are presumed to benefit from their incurrence. Some of these responsibility centers may not work directly on the production of manufactured products. Such centers are commonly referred to as *service centers*. They render essential services that support the production process, but they do not deal directly with products. Consequently, their costs must be allocated to *production centers* which actually work on the manufactured products. Only after all production costs have been assigned to production centers can the final allocation of manufacturing overhead to products be made. Thus, the total process of allocating manufacturing overhead to production depends upon three successive allocation stages.

1. Primary allocation of common costs among all responsibility centers receiving some benefit from those costs.
2. Secondary allocation of costs of service centers to production centers. This stage may involve several steps. The costs of one service center may first be allocated to other service centers and only then to production centers.
3. Final allocation of production centers' manufacturing overhead to products.

Each of these stages of the total manufacturing overhead allocation process is demonstrated below as part of a single illustration. The Hoosier Manufacturing Company has a factory whose operations are subdivided into six departments, three service centers and three production centers. Most of the manufacturing overhead costs are incurred in one or the other of these six departments. However, certain costs are incurred initially on a factory-wide basis. These include depreciation, property taxes, insurance, and maintenance on the factory building plus the salary of the factory superintendent. Collectively, these common costs will be referred to here as *factory occupancy costs*. The total of all manufacturing overhead costs budgeted for this factory for 1977 are as follows:

| | |
|---|---:|
| Factory occupancy costs..................... | $ 500,000 |
| Service center costs: | |
|    Maintenance department.................... | 600,000 |
|    Power plant.............................. | 400,000 |
|    Safety department....................... | 200,000 |
| Production center costs: | |
|    Production department A................... | 750,000 |
|    Production department B.................. | 900,000 |
|    Production department C.................. | 500,000 |
| | $3,850,000 |

Before normal manufacturing overhead rates can be established, all of the costs must be allocated to the three production departments only. The three stages of allocation are presented below.

## Primary Allocation

The first allocation to be made will distribute the factory occupancy costs to the six responsibility centers. A widely used allocation base for this purpose is the square feet of floor space occupied by the various departments. Basically, this is an arbitrary allocation base; for it assumes that the benefits of plant occupancy are proportional to departments' physical sizes. This would be difficult to document, but it certainly is not intuitively unreasonable. If a better base could be demonstrated in a particular situation, of course, it should be used. Square feet of floor space in the Hoosier Manufacturing Company's plant are utilized as follows:

Service centers:
Maintenance department...................... 10,000 sq. ft.
Power plant.................................. 15,000 sq. ft.
Safety department............................ 5,000 sq. ft.
Production centers:
Production department A....................... 20,000 sq. ft.
Production department B....................... 30,000 sq. ft.
Production department C....................... 20,000 sq. ft.
                                             —————————————
                                             100,000 sq. ft.

The allocation rate is then computed as follows:

$$\text{Rate} = \frac{\text{Costs}}{\text{Base}} = \frac{\$500,000}{100,000 \text{ sq. ft.}} = \$5 \text{ per sq. ft.}$$

This rate is then multiplied by the number of square feet in each center to determine its allocated share of the factory occupancy costs. The results of this primary allocation are shown in the second row in Table 5–1.

## Secondary Allocation of Service Center Costs

If the service centers rendered their services to the production centers only, the secondary allocation process would be simple and direct. Each service center's costs, independently, would be allocated among the production departments according to the appropriate base. However, if the service centers provide services to one another as well as to production centers, the allocation process may be more complicated. Service center costs may be allocated to other service centers as well as to production centers. Thus, some portions of total manufacturing overhead costs may pass through two or more centers before they are finally charged to production. If service center costs are allocated to other service centers, the allocation may be done either sequentially or simultaneously.

*Sequential Allocation.* One way of dealing with the situation of interdependent service centers is to allocate each service center's costs in sequence to the production departments and to the other service centers whose costs have not yet been allocated. Thus, the first service center

## TABLE 5–1

### HOOSIER MANUFACTURING COMPANY
Allocation of Budgeted Manufacturing Overhead
1977

| | Allocation Rate | Factory Occupancy | Safety Department |
|---|---|---|---|
| Direct departmental costs.............. | | $500,000 | $200,000 |
| Primary allocation of factory occupancy costs........................... | $5 per sq. ft. | (500,000) | 25,000 |
| | | | $225,000 |
| Secondary allocation of service departments: | | | |
| Safety department............... | $562.50 per person | | (225,000) |
| Maintenance department........... | $67.25 per maintenance hour | | |
| Power plant..................... | $1.149537 per kilowatt hour | | |
| Budgeted direct labor hours.................................................... | | | |
| Normal manufacturing overhead rate.......................................... | | | |

whose costs were allocated could have no other service center's costs distributed to it, even though it might receive some benefit from that other service center. If sequential allocation is chosen, the first service center whose costs are allocated should be that one which is least served by the others. The second one allocated should be the one that is next least served by others, and so forth. In the Hoosier Manufacturing Company, the safety department is the one least affected by the efforts of the other two service departments and will be the first one whose costs are allocated. It receives only a modest amount of electricity from the power plant and no assistance from the maintenance department. Next to be allocated is the maintenance department, which receives limited services from both the safety department and the power plant. Finally, the power plant costs will be distributed to the three production centers only.

The costs of the safety department will be allocated on the base of the number of personnel in the departments that it serves. This base is a measure of the activity in the centers to which the costs will be allocated. Maintenance department costs will be allocated on the base of the number of hours spent by maintenance crews in the other departments. This is a measure of the activity, or input, in the center from which the costs will be allocated. Finally, the costs of the power plant will be

**TABLE 5–1** (*continued*)

| Maintenance Department | Power Plant | Production Departments | | | Totals |
| | | A | B | C | |
|---|---|---|---|---|---|
| $600,000 | $400,000 | $ 750,000 | $ 900,000 | $500,000 | $3,850,000 |
| 50,000 | 75,000 | 100,000 | 150,000 | 100,000 | |
| $650,000 | $475,000 | $ 850,000 | $1,050,000 | $600,000 | |
| 22,500 | 11,250 | 33,750 | 67,500 | 90,000 | |
| $672,500 | | | | | |
| (672,500) | 134,500 | 201,750 | 269,000 | 67,250 | |
| | $620,750 | | | | |
| | (620,750) | 206,917 | 275,889 | 137,944 | |
| | | $1,292,417 | $1,662,389 | $895,194 | $3,850,000 |
| | | 120,000 | 240,000 | 300,000 | |
| | | $ 10.77 | $ 6.9266 | $ 2.984 | |

allocated on the base of the number of kilowatt hours of electricity used in the departments served. This is a measure of the output of the center from which the costs will be allocated. Budgeted statistics for each of these allocation bases are as follows:

| | Personnel | Maintenance Hours | Kilowatt Hours |
|---|---|---|---|
| Maintenance department............. | 40 | | 48,000 |
| Power plant........................ | 20 | 2,000 | |
| Safety department.................. | | | 12,000 |
| Production department A............. | 60 | 3,000 | 180,000 |
| Production department B............. | 120 | 4,000 | 240,000 |
| Production department C............. | 160 | 1,000 | 120,000 |
| | 400 | 10,000 | 600,000 |

Note that no amounts are shown for the department whose costs are to be allocated by a particular base. Obviously, the costs of a service center cannot be allocated to itself. It must also be observed that, when sequential allocation is employed, the quantities used in the allocation base are only those for the departments that have not yet been allocated. Four hundred personnel would be used as the allocation base for the safety department, as it is the first to be distributed. Ten thousand maintenance hours would be the base used for allocation of the maintenance department, because it renders no services to the safety department. However, only 540,000 kilowatt hours would be used as the allocation base for the power plant, because its costs will be charged only to the three production departments.

The primary allocation of the factory occupancy costs and the sequential secondary allocation of the service center costs are shown in Table 5–1. It shows how all of the manufacturing overhead costs incurred in the factory are ultimately allocated to the three production centers, from which they will finally be allocated to production. This final allocation will be made by means of the normal overhead rates explained in Chapter 3 and illustrated at the bottom of Table 5–1. Manufacturing overhead in all three departments is applied on the basis of direct labor hours. For the sake of simplicity, the illustration deals only with total manufacturing overhead, with no separate identification of variable and fixed costs. Consequently, only one normal rate can be computed. As we have noted before, separate recording of variable and fixed manufacturing overhead and two separate normal rates are highly desirable for purposes of management.

**Simultaneous Allocation.**   Although sequential secondary allocation is usually considered acceptable, it does have the disadvantage that the service centers whose costs are allocated first receive no share of the allocated costs of those that are distributed later. For example, in Table 5–1, neither the safety department nor the maintenance department was charged with any portion of the power plant's costs, although both of them did use electric power. This disadvantage can be corrected by simultaneous allocation of the costs of all service centers. The amounts to be allocated are determined by solving a system of simultaneous equations. Instead of computing an allocation rate, the allocation base for each service department is converted to fractions or percentages for the other service departments and production departments to which its costs will be distributed. This conversion is shown below for the three allocation bases used in the secondary allocation of manufacturing overhead in the Hoosier Manufacturing Company.

|  | Personnel | Maintenance Hours | Kilowatt Hours |
|---|---|---|---|
| Maintenance department | .10 |  | .08 |
| Power plant | .05 | .20 |  |
| Safety department |  |  | .02 |
| Production department A | .15 | .30 | .30 |
| Production department B | .30 | .40 | .40 |
| Production department C | .40 | .10 | .20 |
|  | 1.00 | 1.00 | 1.00 |

Now each department's total cost, both its direct costs and its allocated share of other departments' costs, is expressed as an algebraic equation. These equations for the Hoosier Manufacturing Company are shown below. The maintenance department is represented as $M$, the power plant, as $P$; and the safety department, as $S$. Each production department is represented by its letter designation as above.

$$M = \$650{,}000 + .08P + .10S$$
$$P = \$475{,}000 + .20M + .05S$$
$$S = \$225{,}000 + .02P$$
$$A = \$850{,}000 + .30M + .30P + .15S$$
$$B = \$1{,}050{,}000 + .40M + .40P + .30S$$
$$C = \$600{,}000 + .10M + .20P + .40S$$

The constant dollar amount in each equation is the sum of the direct costs originally charged to the department plus its share of the primary allocation of the factory occupancy costs. The equations are now rearranged into the conventional format for simultaneous equations.

$$
\begin{aligned}
M - .08P - .10S & & & = \$650{,}000 \\
-.20M + P - .05S & & & = \$475{,}000 \\
-.02P + S & & & = \$225{,}000 \\
-.30M - .30P - .15S + A & & & = \$850{,}000 \\
-.40M - .40P - .30S & + B & & = \$1{,}050{,}000 \\
-.10M - .20P - .40S & & + C & = \$600{,}000
\end{aligned}
$$

Now all six equations may be solved simultaneously. Alternatively, only the first three equations need be solved simultaneously; and the last three may then be solved by substituting in them the computed values of $M$, $P$, and $S$. Either way, the ultimate secondary allocation of the total $3,850,000 of manufacturing overhead is as follows:[3]

$$A = \$1{,}292{,}459$$
$$B = \$1{,}663{,}708$$
$$C = \$893{,}833$$

Notice that these amounts are not greatly different from the parallel amounts in Table 5–1. While simultaneous secondary allocation is conceptually superior, sequental allocation will often produce acceptable results. However, it must be remembered that the final results in sequential allocation depend upon the allocation sequence chosen. There could be circumstances under which sequential and simultaneous allocations would produce significantly different results. In such circumstances, simultaneous allocation should be employed.

[3] The solutions to the first three equations are as follows: $M = \$724{,}303$; $P = \$631{,}742$; and $S = \$237{,}635$. These amounts are of no particular significance themselves. When substituted in the last three equations, they provide the allocations of the service centers' costs to the three production centers.

## ALLOCATION OF COMMON PRODUCTION COSTS

In some manufacturing enterprises, two or more different products emerge from a single, common production process and a single raw material. A familiar example is the variety of petroleum products derived from the refining of crude oil. Such products present some peculiar and important problems to cost accountants and to managers. They are identifiable as separate products only at the conclusion of the common processing. This point of separation is commonly referred to as the *split-off point*. The costs incurred up to the split-off point are true common costs; they cannot be traced to the separate products in any direct or logical manner. For inventory costing purposes, however, it is necessary that all production costs be charged to products and, more particularly here, to separate products. Thus, common production costs must be allocated among the products manufactured jointly in order that inventory values and income may be determined in accordance with generally accepted accounting principles.

### Joint Products

Where two or more products are derived from a common production process and a single raw material and each is regarded as a major product of the company, they are usually referred to as *joint products* or as *coproducts*. For purposes of inventory valuation and income determination, the common costs of producing joint products are allocated among them according to some reasonable scheme. The most widely accepted basis for this allocation is the relative sales values of the several joint products at the split-off point. This may be illustrated by a simple example. Products A, B, and C are obtained from a single raw material. Each product is salable as it comes from the common processing; that is, each has a readily determinable market value at the split-off point. The common production costs—including raw materials, direct labor, and all manufacturing overhead—total $600,000 for a given period. The unit output and market value of each product is indicated below, along with the allocation of the common production costs in proportion to the relative market values of the products at the split-off point:

| Product | Unit Output | Market Value at Split-off | Allocation of Common Cost |
|---|---|---|---|
| A | 20,000 | $ 600,000 | $300,000 |
| B | 25,000 | 200,000 | 100,000 |
| C | 15,000 | 400,000 | 200,000 |
| | 60,000 | $1,200,000 | $600,000 |

This illustration assumes the absorption costing approach. Under variable costing, fixed manufacturing overhead would be excluded from the cost of the coproducts; but the same allocation problem would remain for the common variable costs.

It has sometimes been suggested that the common costs be allocated among joint products in proportion to the number of units produced. If such an allocation scheme were applied to the three products above, their respective costs would be as follows:

Product A............... $200,000
Product B...............  250,000
Product C...............  150,000

Since the cost allocated to product B under this scheme is greater than its sales value, product B would appear to be unprofitable. Of course, its lack of profitability in that case could be traced directly to the cost allocation method employed. Hence, the common cost allocation is usually made on the basis of relative sales values. This is a neutral method insofar as individual product profitability is concerned. Allocation by relative sales values assures that each product will have the same gross margin ratio at the split-off point. In the illustration above, each product has a gross margin ratio of 50 percent of sales value.

If a product is not readily salable at the split-off point, its market value at that point may be approximated by subtracting from its ultimate sales value the further costs of processing it separately. Thus, if product C above could be sold at a final price of $500,000 but only after further processing costs of $80,000, its market value at the split-off point would be estimated to be $420,000. Obviously, such an approach assumes that no profit attaches to the product beyond the split-off point; sales value added beyond that point is presumed to be exactly equal to the separate processing costs. Although this assumption is artificial, it should not be seriously objectionable, particularly if the separate processing costs are not substantial in relation to the common costs.

## By-Products

If one of the products emerging from a common material and production process is regarded as relatively unimportant in the overall product line of the company, it is described as a *by-product*. A by-product is usually regarded as produced incidentally to the manufacture of a principal product, or main product. Generally speaking, a by-product is identified as such if its revenue is not considered a significant portion of total revenue and if little special effort is required in its manufacture and distribution. No portion of the common production costs is allocated to a by-product. Rather, all of the common costs are charged to the principal product(s). The net realizable value (final sales value minus any separate costs of processing and selling) of the by-product is then credited to the total cost of manufacturing the principal product(s). This may be illustrated by a very simple example. A corporation produces two products, Mapo and Bypo; the former is the principal product and the latter, a by-product. Output, cost, and sales data for a year are as follows:

|  | *Mapo* | *Bypo* |
|---|---|---|
| Units produced.................. | 100,000 | 8,000 |
| Unit selling price............... | $5.00 | $.40 |
| Common production costs........ | $300,000 | |
| Separate costs.................. | $ 60,000 | $1,200 |

The cost of the principal product would then be determined thus:

| | | |
|---|---|---|
| Common costs............................... | | $300,000 |
| Separate costs.............................. | | 60,000 |
| | | 360,000 |
| Less net realizable value of Bypo: | | |
| Sales value........................... | $3,200 | |
| Less separate costs.................... | 1,200 | 2,000 |
| Total cost of Mapo........................ | | $358,000 |
| Units produced............................ | | 100,000 |
| Unit cost................................. | | $3.58 |

If all of the by-product is sold in the period in which it is produced, its full net realizable value is realized; there is no inventory of by-product. If there remains an inventory of by-product, it must be valued at its net realizable value in order that the full amount of the net realizable value of by-product produced during a period may be credited to the cost of the principal product manufactured in the same period. This deviation from the customary practice of valuing inventories at cost is generally accepted and, in view of the relative insignificance of by-products, is not likely to have a material effect upon total asset valuation or upon reported income.

There are no set rules for distinguishing between joint products and by-products. The distinction is a matter of judgment to be made in each individual situation. Similarly, the distinction between by-products and scrap is a question of judgment. Salable scrap is accounted for in substantially the same way as by-products. Unsalable scrap, of course, requires no accounting, except to the extent that costs are incurred in order to dispose of it.

## QUESTIONS FOR DISCUSSION

1. Define the term allocation as it is used in cost accounting. What kinds of costs are allocated?
2. For what reason(s) should allocations of indirect costs be made?
3. When should allocations of indirect costs *not* be made? Why not?
4. Why should the Cost Accounting Standards Board be particularly interested in the subject of indirect cost allocations?
5. Define an indirect cost pool. Give several examples.
6. What is an allocation base? How should a particular allocation base be selected?
7. The Cost Accounting Standards Board has proposed a priority ranking of three basic types of allocation bases. What is the Board's ranking? Can you think of any reasons to support this particular priority ranking?
8. Distinguish between primary and secondary allocation of manufacturing overhead costs.
9. What is the effect of using sequential secondary allocation instead of simultaneous secondary allocation?
10. What is the difference between joint products and by-products? What is the difference between by-products and scrap? Are these differences important to accounting? Explain.
11. "The most logical way to allocate common production costs among joint products is in proportion to their weights or volumes. It is obvious that more costs are incurred to obtain the heavier or bulkier products." Comment on this proposition.

## PROBLEMS

5-1. The Alexander Corporation is a small manufacturer of specialized electric lighting equipment. Its products include traffic signals, emergency lights for buildings, flashing lights for navigational buoys, and high-reliability portable lamps. The firm is organized in five departments, whose functions are described below.

*Accounting department.* This department maintains the general accounting records of the corporation and prepares both periodic financial statements and the annual tax returns. Its functions include the maintenance of accounts payable and receivable, payroll, and cost accounting.

*Maintenance department.* This department performs all routine maintenance work in all other departments and in all parts of the firm's building.

*Manufacturing department.* All of the products are made in this department in accordance with the specifications of customers' orders. Finished products are packed and shipped as soon as production is completed.

*Marketing department.* This group consists chiefly of a sales force that solicits orders and maintains periodic contacts with potential customers.

*Personnel department.* This department recruits and hires employees for all of the other departments and the corporate office. It maintains employee records and is responsible for programs of employee training and development.

Most of the corporation's costs are incurred initially in one of these five departments. There are certain costs that are not identified with the departments but are incurred on a corporate-wide basis. They include the following items:

1. Salaries of top management and directors' fees.
2. Clerical salaries in the corporate office.
3. Depreciation on the building which houses all departments, as well as the corporate office.
4. Property taxes and insurance on the building.
5. Fees paid to attorneys, public accountants, and consultants.
6. Interest on borrowed capital.

Corporate management has decided that the company might profitably compete for certain government cost-based contracts. For purposes of such contracts, all of the indirect costs of the company, excepting interest expense, must be allocated to customers' orders, which are the ultimate cost objectives in the firm.

*Required:*

a. What indirect cost pools would you recommend the Alexander Corporation establish? Explain your reasons.
b. What allocation base would you expect to be most appropriate for each of these indirect cost pools? Why?

5–2. Brown Bros. & Co. accumulates indirect costs in the eight cost pools listed below. With the exception of the first two pools, all are organized as departments of the company. Certain significant data for these cost pools are shown in the following tabulation:

| | Square Feet of Floor Space | Employees | Mainte- nance Hours | Materials and Supplies | Total Direct Costs |
|---|---|---|---|---|---|
| Plant occupancy... | | | 800 | | $ 2,000,000 |
| General admin- istration........ | 20,000 | 20 | 400 | $ 250,000 | 1,000,000 |
| Personnel......... | 10,000 | 10 | 200 | 50,000 | 200,000 |
| Maintenance...... | 10,000 | 15 | | 250,000 | 500,000 |
| Public relations.... | 5,000 | 5 | 100 | 50,000 | 200,000 |
| Purchasing........ | 5,000 | 10 | 200 | 20,000 | 100,000 |
| Sales.............. | 50,000 | 50 | 500 | 400,000 | 3,000,000 |
| Production........ | 150,000 | 300 | 1,800 | 4,000,000 | 14,000,000 |
| | 250,000 | 410 | 4,000 | $5,020,000 | $21,000,000 |

For various purposes, it is necessary to allocate the indirect costs of all of these cost pools, with the exceptions of sales and production. The allocation bases used for the costs pools that are allocated are as follows:

Plant occupancy—square feet of floor space
General administration—total direct costs
Personnel—number of employees
Maintenance—number of maintenance hours
Public relations—total direct costs
Purchasing—cost of materials and supplies used

*Required:*

Compute the allocation rate to be used for each of the six cost pools whose indirect costs are to be allocated.

5–3.   The Dean Systems Division of the Gashouse Aircraft Corporation is a major defense contractor. Actual indirect costs accumulated in service centers are allocated to contracts at the end of each quarter. The actual costs and the allocation bases for these service centers during the second quarter of 1976 were as follows:

|  | Cost | Allocation Base |
|---|---|---|
| General administration | $500,200 | Total contract costs |
| Engineering | 300,000 | Engineering hours |
| Personnel | 13,500 | Total productive hours |
| Accounting and data processing | 187,500 | Direct contract costs |
| Research and development | 450,000 | Contract R&D costs |

Pertinent statistics for the five contracts that were in process during the second quarter of 1976 are as follows:

| Contract | Engineering Hours | Direct Labor Hours | Direct Costs | Contract R&D Cost |
|---|---|---|---|---|
| AF–6012 | 1,200 | 12,000 | $  240,000 | $  60,000 |
| AF–7180 | 2,000 | 20,000 | 640,000 | 90,000 |
| N–1065 | 1,500 | 10,000 | 280,000 | 75,000 |
| E–880 | 800 | 6,000 | 90,000 | 25,000 |
| S–2492 | 500 | | | 50,000 |
| | 6,000 | 48,000 | $1,250,000 | $300,000 |

Total contract costs include both the direct costs and the contract R&D costs traced to the contracts and also the allocated portions of indirect costs other than general administrative expense. Direct labor hours include only production work; productive engineering hours are accumulated separately. In total, the division spent $750,000 on research and development. Of this total, $300,000 was directly chargeable to contracts; and the balance was incurred in order to maintain the division's general level of technical expertise.

*Required:*

Determine the amounts of indirect costs allocated to the five contracts during the second quarter of 1976.

5–4. The Feller Metalcraft Corporation records manufacturing overhead costs initially in three service centers and three production departments and in one nondepartmental plant-wide cost pool. All manufacturing overhead is ultimately assigned to the three production departments, through which it is charged to manufactured products.

Budgeted manufacturing overhead and other pertinent data for 1977 are as follows:

|  | Manufacturing Overhead | Floor Space | Workers | Materials Cost | Machine Hours |
|---|---|---|---|---|---|
| Plant occupancy...... | $ 630,000 |  |  |  |  |
| Service centers: |  |  |  |  |  |
| Personnel.......... | 65,200 | 10,000 | 20 | $ 20,000 | 100 |
| Maintenance....... | 96,000 | 20,000 | 40 | 80,000 | 200 |
| Materials storage |  |  |  |  |  |
| and handling....... | 130,216 | 150,000 | 30 | 10,000 | 1,200 |
| Production depts: |  |  |  |  |  |
| Molding........... | 700,000 | 80,000 | 160 | 360,000 | 4,000 |
| Welding........... | 328,000 | 70,000 | 90 | 60,000 | 2,000 |
| Assembly......... | 850,000 | 120,000 | 230 | 230,000 | 800 |
|  | $2,799,416 | 450,000 | 570 | $760,000 | 8,300 |

Plant occupancy and service center costs are allocated to the production departments and the service centers not already allocated in the following sequence and according to the allocation bases indicated:

1. Plant occupancy on the basis of floor space.
2. Personnel center on the basis of numbers of workers.
3. Maintenance center on the basis of machine hours.
4. Materials storage and handling center on the basis of materials cost.

*Required:*

Determine the primary and secondary allocation of manufacturing overhead costs to the three production departments.

5–5. The Ford Manufacturing Co., Inc., charges variable manufacturing overhead to production at normal rates per direct labor hour in each of its three manufacturing processes. These variable costs are incurred initially in three service centers and in a general plant administration cost pool. They must then be reallocated to the manufacturing processes before normal manufacturing overhead rates are computed. Fixed costs are accounted for as period expenses and are not charged to products.

Variable manufacturing overhead costs and other relevant statistics have been budgeted as follows for 1977:

| | Variable Manufacturing Overhead | Value Added in Production | Materials Cost | Personnel | Floor Space |
|---|---|---|---|---|---|
| Plant administration..... | $120,000 | | | | |
| Service centers: | | | | | |
| Plant services......... | 60,800 | | | 25 | 2,000 |
| Quality control........ | 16,444 | | $ 10,000 | 12 | 500 |
| Storeroom............ | 22,492 | | 20,000 | 16 | 20,000 |
| Manufacturing processes: | | | | | |
| Cutting.............. | 52,068 | $ 500,000 | 350,000 | 64 | 12,500 |
| Stitching............. | 87,580 | 400,000 | 200,000 | 90 | 16,000 |
| Finishing............. | 60,116 | 200,000 | 50,000 | 43 | 9,000 |
| | $419,500 | $1,100,000 | $630,000 | 250 | 60,000 |

Plant administration costs are allocated on the basis of square feet of floor space. Plant services are allocated on the basis of the number of personnel in the responsibility centers to which they are distributed. Quality control costs are allocated on the basis of total value added in production. Variable manufacturing overhead in the storeroom is allocated on the basis of materials cost in the responsibility centers served.

The following direct labor hours have been budgeted for the three manufacturing processes for 1977:

Cutting...................................... 24,000
Stitching.................................... 27,000
Finishing.................................... 20,000

*Required:*

a. In what sequence should the costs of the three service centers be allocated? Why?

b. Compute the normal rates that should be used to charge variable manufacturing overhead to production in the three manufacturing processes during 1977. Show all necessary computations and analyses.

 5-6. Manufacturing overhead costs in the Gomez Company are accumulated in two service departments and three production departments. Since each of the service departments renders service to the others as well as to the production departments, management has decided to reallocate the manufacturing overhead incurred in the service departments simultaneously. The general services department's costs are allocated on the basis of square feet of floor space. Personnel department costs are allocated on the basis of the numbers of employees.

The following data were extracted from the budget for 1977:

|  | Manufacturing Overhead | Floor Space | Employees |
|---|---|---|---|
| Service departments: | | | |
| General services......... | $ 2,000,000 | | 300 |
| Personnel............... | 500,000 | 9,000 | |
| Production departments: | | | |
| A..................... | 3,000,000 | 48,000 | 360 |
| B..................... | 2,500,000 | 30,000 | 180 |
| C..................... | 2,000,000 | 45,000 | 240 |
| D..................... | 1,000,000 | 18,000 | 120 |
| | $11,000,000 | 150,000 | 1,200 |

*Required:*

Complete a simultaneous secondary allocation of the manufacturing overhead budgeted for the service departments in 1977.

5-7. Grove Industries, Inc., makes a simultaneous allocation of service center costs among the other service centers and the manufacturing processes. Departmental cost and allocation base data for 1976 were as follows:

|  | Manufacturing Overhead | S Personnel | M Facilities Investment | P Kilowatt Hours |
|---|---|---|---|---|
| Service centers: | | | | |
| Health and safety....... | $ 200,000 | 50 | $ 400,000 | 2,000 |
| Maintenance............ | 600,000 | 100 | 1,800,000 | 7,500 |
| Power and light......... | 400,000 | 60 | 2,500,000 | 5,000 |
| Manufacturing processes: | | | | |
| Agglomerating.......... | 500,000 | 80 | 4,700,000 | 22,500 |
| Packaging.............. | 300,000 | 160 | 2,400,000 | 18,000 |
| | $2,000,000 | 450 | $11,800,000 | 55,000 |

Allocation bases for the service centers are as follows:

Health and safety.................. numbers of personnel
Maintenance...................... investment in facilities
Power and light.................. kilowatt hours

*Required:*

Make a simultaneous allocation of the service center costs for 1976.

5-8. The Hubbell Corporation produces five joint products from a common raw material and common processing. The budgeted annual outputs of these products and their unit market values at the completion of the common processing are as follows:

| Product | Units Produced | Market Value |
|---|---|---|
| A...................... | 5,000 | $ 4.00 |
| B...................... | 15,000 | 3.00 |
| C. .................... | 2,000 | 12.00 |
| D...................... | 20,000 | 1.00 |
| E...................... | 10,000 | 2.10 |

The basic raw material cost for a year is $36,000. Labor and manufacturing overhead incurred in the common processing total $55,000 annually.

*Required:*

Allocate the common production costs among the five joint products.

5–9. The Johnson Company produces a main product, M, and a by-product, B. During 1976, the company's first year of operations, common production costs totaled $560,000. Output consisted of 90,000 units of M and 10,000 units of B. Separate processing costs amounted to $360,000 for M and $30,000 for B. Sales during the year included 80,000 units of M at $12 apiece and 8,000 units of B at $5 each. Nonmanufacturing costs totaled $360,000 during 1976.

*Required:*

a. Compute the values of the inventories of M and B on hand at December 31, 1976.
b. Determine the income before tax to be reported for 1976.

5–10. The Matthewson Corporation manufacturers two products, Curv and Slid. Under present operations, raw materials are processed in Department A; and the two products are separated at the end of this processing. For every unit of Curv, three units of Slid are obtained. Curv is then finished in Department B and Slid, in Department C. Actual operating data for 1976 were as follows:

|  | *Departments* | | |
|---|---|---|---|
|  | *A* | *B* | *C* |
| Units produced: |  |  |  |
| Curv.............................. | 25,000 | 25,000 |  |
| Slid............................... | 75,000 |  | 75,000 |
| Costs incurred: |  |  |  |
| Direct materials...................... | $150,000 |  |  |
| Direct labor......................... | 80,000 | $30,000 | $40,000 |
| Variable manufacturing overhead......... | 20,000 | 10,000 | 20,000 |
| Fixed manufacturing overhead........... | 90,000 | 25,000 | 35,000 |

At present, Curv is sold for $10 and Slid for $5 per unit. Both products are also readily marketable at the completion of processing in Department A—Curv for $8 per unit and Slid for $3 per unit.

*Required:*

Under an absorption costing system, what were the average unit costs of Curv and Slid during 1976? Show appropriate supporting computations.

5–11. The Paige Corporation manufactures three different products from a single raw material. A summary of operating data for 1976 is presented below. The production costs identified with the individual products are only the separate costs incurred after the split-off point.

| | *Products* | | | |
| | A | B | C | *Totals* |
|---|---|---|---|---|
| Output in pounds............... | 90,000 | 60,000 | 30,000 | 180,000 |
| Selling price per pound........... | $1.10 | $2.20 | $3.30 | |
| Production costs: | | | | |
| Direct materials.............. | | | | $100,000 |
| Direct labor.................. | $ 8,000 | $12,000 | $10,000 | 80,000 |
| Variable manufacturing overhead. | 4,000 | 6,000 | 4,000 | 30,000 |
| Fixed manufacturing overhead... | 6,000 | 10,000 | 8,000 | 56,000 |

*Required:*

Allocate the common production costs among the three joint products in some appropriate manner.

5-12.   The Spahn Packing Company prepares and packs a variety of meat products. Bones are cleaned of all usable meat and then are ground into meal, which is packed at once in 50-pound sacks and then sold to fertilizer manufacturers. The company's output and sales in 1976 were as follows:

| | *Meat* | *Bone Meal* |
|---|---|---|
| Production (in pounds)................ | 800,000 | 75,000 |
| Sales (in pounds)..................... | 760,000 | 60,000 |
| Sales revenue realized................ | $820,000 | $48,000 |

Total operating costs for 1976 were as follows:

| | |
|---|---|
| Raw materials used........................... | $325,000 |
| Direct labor................................... | 105,000 |
| Variable manufacturing overhead applied......... | 84,000 |
| Fixed manufacturing overhead applied........... | 126,000 |
| Selling and administrative expenses............. | 125,000 |
| Underapplied manufacturing overhead........... | 15,000 |

Variable and fixed manufacturing overhead are applied at normal rates per dollar of direct labor cost. The direct labor cost of grinding and packing bone meal was $5,000 during 1976; this amount is included in the $105,000 above. Bone meal is accounted for as a by-product.

All inventories are accounted for by the average cost method. The inventory of finished meat products at December 31, 1975, had consisted of 50,000 pounds of products at a total cost of $57,500. There was no inventory of unsold bone meal at December 31, 1975. There were no inventories of work in process at the beginning or at the end of the year 1976.

The income tax rate is 40%.

*Required:*

Prepare an income statement and a supporting statement of cost of goods manufactured and sold for 1976.

5-13.  The basic processing of raw materials in the Waddell Chemical Corporation's plant yields three semifinished products, Worlon, Nantron, and Extron. The budgeted cost of the basic processing for 1977 is $3,110,000. Budgeted production, price, and separate processing cost data for the three products are as follows:

|  | *Worlon* | *Nantron* | *Extron* |
|---|---|---|---|
| Output in units................ | 600,000 | 300,000 | 80,000 |
| Selling price per unit............ | $5 | $12 | $1.50 |
| Separate processing costs: |  |  |  |
| Variable cost per unit.......... | $1 | $1.20 | $.60 |
| Fixed cost per year............ | $300,000 | $240,000 | $22,000 |

Worlon and Nantron are accounted for as joint products. Extron is treated as a by-product.

*Required:*

Compute the budgeted unit cost of each of the joint products for 1977 under the absorption costing method. Show any supporting computations.

5-14.  C. Young & Sons, Inc., derives eight different items from a single common production process. Four of these items are regarded as the company's principal products; two are treated as by-products; and two are considered to be scrap. One of the scrap items can be sold, but the other must be hauled away as garbage. During the month of November 1976, the company incurred common production costs of $387,000. The following tabulation summarizes production and sales data for November:

|  | *Units Produced* | *Units Sold* | *Unit Selling Price* | *Costs of Separate Processing or Disposal* | |
|---|---|---|---|---|---|
|  |  |  |  | *Variable per Unit* | *Fixed Costs* |
| Main products: |  |  |  |  |  |
| A.................. | 200,000 | 180,000 | $ .75 | $.10 | $10,000 |
| B.................. | 100,000 | 90,000 | 1.00 | .12 | 8,000 |
| C.................. | 150,000 | 140,000 | 1.60 | .08 | 18,000 |
| D.................. | 50,000 | 50,000 | 2.00 | .10 | 5,000 |
| By-products: |  |  |  |  |  |
| M.................. | 40,000 | 30,000 | .30 | .05 | 2,500 |
| N.................. | 20,000 | 20,000 | .25 |  | 1,000 |
| Scrap: |  |  |  |  |  |
| Y.................. | 30,000 | 30,000 | .06 | .02 | 200 |
| Z.................. | 10,000 | 10,000* |  | .05* |  |

* All 10,000 units of Z were scrapped. The company had to pay $.05 per unit to have them hauled away and dumped.

*Required:*

a.  Compute the unit costs of the products for the month of November.
b.  Compute the aggregate gross margin for the company for the month.

# part two

## ANALYSIS FOR PLANNING AND CONTROL

# chapter 6

# Budgets: Tools of Planning and Control

**B**UDGETS are probably the most familiar devices for financial planning and control in organizations of all types. Business enterprises, nonprofit institutions, government agencies, and households all use budgets. There is, of course, a very wide range of the degree of formality and detail applied to budgets. A large corporation or a government agency will likely have an intricately detailed and documented budget covering all phases of its operations. A household's budget may be nothing more than a housewife's reminder to herself that she can afford to spend no more than $35 each week on groceries. The more formal budgets are important tools of management, but they are only parts of much broader systems of planning and control. These larger systems are difficult to define precisely, but they have certain general characteristics that may be observed. First, in any organization some basic objectives, or strategic goals, are established. These objectives define the fundamental purposes of the organization and the general directions in which it is to proceed. Next, specific programs of action are approved to enable the organization to pursue its goals. Finally, these programs are translated into explicit periodic budgets. The budgets contain the expected financial implications of the approved programs during short periods of time, typically single years.

## PLANNING, PROGRAMMING, AND BUDGETING

### Planning

In the hierarchy of planning and control systems, the first stage is commonly referred to simply as planning. *Planning* entails the specification of the basic objectives that the organization will pursue and the fundamental policies that will guide it. For example, identification of the lines of business in which a company will engage is a basic policy. Growth in established markets or diversification into new markets are examples of objectives that might be defined at the planning stage. Obviously, planning is essential when a new organizaticn is formed. Its purpose for existence must be clearly specified. However, the need for this type of planning does not cease once the organization begins operations. From time to time, new opportunities and new challenges confront the organization. It may be compelled to rethink some of its basic objectives. It may decide to proceed in new and different directions. Major events, such as the international oil crisis in 1973 and 1974, often force management to reconsider policies and objectives. Even without such external pressures, periodic reviews of basic plans are appropriate.

It might be possible for planning to be done on a company wide basis, for all policies and objectives to be reviewed and reassessed at one time. More commonly, however, it would be done for only one segment of the firm or one area of operations. Thus, basic policies regarding the markets in which a firm will sell its products or new lines of business to be pursued may be established without changing other basic policies regarding existing operations.

Since planning deals with fundamental policies and objectives, it must be done by top management. In a decentralized organization, responsibility for planning will be shared to some extent with divisional management. In government, planning is sometimes thought to be the special province of the legislature. The laws enacted are viewed as the basic policies that will guide the government's courses of action. However, when major legislative proposals originate in the executive branch of the government, that branch is clearly participating in, if not leading, the planning function.

### Programming

*Programming* is the function of developing and implementing specific courses of action intended to meet basic objectives. It is one of the most important decision-making functions in any organization. Generally, various alternative possible programs are considered as means of achieving basic goals. Choosing one and rejecting others involves major commitments of resources, often for substantial periods of time. Programs are of many different types. The introduction of a major new product line (e.g., compact cars in an automobile manufacturer) is one example. A concerted effort to develop and test a particular pollution control device for automobiles would be an example of a research and development program. Marketing programs might include a major advertising campaign or the opening of a new international sales division. A program of hiring and training members of disadvantaged minority groups would be a course of action consistent with an equal employment opportunity policy.

The relationship between planning and programming may best be explained by an illustration. An American manufacturer of farm equipment may have determined that the most rapidly growing market for its products is in foreign countries, while it has long adhered to a policy of domestic marketing only. Thus, it might define a new strategic objective for itself—to compete effectively in the international farm equipment market. This decision would complete the planning phase. The plan might be implemented in a variety of ways. The company could set up its own foreign sales force, which would market American-manufactured equipment abroad. On the other hand, it might enter into agreements with foreign marketing organizations to sell its products abroad. Further, it might build its own manufacturing plants in foreign countries and sell locally produced equipment there. Finally, it might enter into a joint venture with a foreign company that has the necessary manufacturing and/or marketing expertise. Each of these four alternatives constitutes a program that might be undertaken in pursuit of the new strategic objective. Each has its own advantages and risks. Each would involve a different level of resource commitment on the part of the American manufacturer. Only one can be implemented, and the company may be committed to its choice for many years. The importance of good program decisions could hardly be exaggerated.

## Budgeting

Basically, *budgeting* is the periodic financial planning to implement all approved programs during a particular fiscal period, usually one year. It translates programs, which are specific courses of action over many years, into annual operating plans. The relationship between programming and budgeting may best be explained by a graphic illustration. Figure 6–1 is a schematic representation of the interface between programming and budgeting. Programs are represented by the horizontal bars and budgets, by the vertical division of time into years. Some programs continue across all of the budget periods in the graph. Others begin or end in one of those periods. If the future could be predicted with

FIGURE 6–1

Relationship between Programming and Budgeting

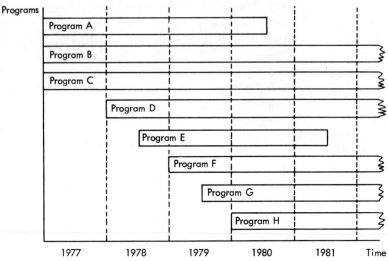

certainty, budgeting would be a fairly trivial task of summing the approved programs for a period and expressing them in terms of their financial effects within that period. Realistically, of course, programs are initially approved under conditions of uncertainty. Hence, successive budgeting efforts require reviews and revisions of programs. Such reviews may be as extensive or as limited as the situations require. Annual budgeting will be far more effective, however, if management recognizes that plans for the coming year are not made in a vacuum but are only one step in an indefinite succession of integrated steps. Plans for the coming period are influenced by program decisions made in the past and have implications for programs that will continue into future periods.

The remainder of this chapter and the next chapter deal with the subject of periodic budgeting. The reader should keep in mind, however, that budgets are parts of a larger system. It would be impossible to budget in the absence of basic objectives; and budgeting would be a very disjointed activity in the absence of programs.

## THE PERIODIC BUDGET

### Definition of a Budget

A budget is a comprehensive and coordinated plan, expressed in financial terms, for the operations and resources of an enterprise for some specified period in the future. It is not suggested that the student memorize this definition verbatim but that he understand the essential elements of it. These elements are discussed in some detail below.

*Comprehensive.* A budget is comprehensive in that it takes into account all of the many facets and activities of the enterprise. It is a plan for the firm as a whole rather than for only one segment of the firm. It is true that we very commonly encounter such things as departmental budgets and advertising budgets. This terminology is perfectly correct, but implicit in it is the assumption that a departmental or advertising budget is but one component of a total budget for the firm. Clearly, one segment of a company cannot have any very significant plan of its own unless that plan is a part of a total plan for the entire enterprise. The total plan is frequently referred to as the *master budget;* it is supported by numerous integrated component budgets.

*Coordinated.* If a comprehensive plan for an even moderately complex organization is to be useful, it must consider all segments of that organization and recognize the situation and problems of each segment. The plans for the various segments of the firm must be prepared jointly and in harmony with one another. If these component plans are not coordinated logically and practically, the whole will not be equal to the sum of the parts and the master plan will evoke only confusion.

*Plan.* In the foregoing paragraphs, the word "plan" has been used without amplification. While it is a word the meaning of which is commonly understood, it has some very specific connotations when used in connection with budgeting. A housewife plans a menu, something which is totally within her discretion. She also plans for winter, the occurrence of which is completely beyond her control. Planning the menus is a matter of active intent; planning for winter is one of passive expectation. A business budget also involves both of these two notions of planning. Some of the factors which will determine a firm's future operations are entirely within its own discretion and control—such as promotional programs, manufacturing processes, and executives' bonuses. Other determinants of future activities are wholly beyond the control of the firm—general business conditions, governmental regulatory policies, and shifts in population age groups, for examples. Thus, a business budget is an expression partly of what the firm's management expects will happen and partly of what management intends to make happen. This does not suggest that mere wishing can make something come true, but careful planning and preparation can bring about a result that would not otherwise be achieved. In other words, good budgeting can not only suggest what will happen but can also make things happen.

*Financial Terms.* Business budgets are stated in terms of the monetary unit (the dollar in the United States). This is essential if a budget is to be comprehensive, for the monetary unit serves as the common denominator of business activities. A materials budget, for example, may deal with tons of steel; and a labor budget will involve men and man-hours. But tons and man-hours cannot be summed to any significant quantity. Similarly, the advertising budget may deal with such quantities as hours of network television time, pages of national magazine space, and thousands of direct mail brochures; but some common denominator is needed to express a total amount of planned advertising effort. A wide variety of quantities are likely to be involved in the basic development of a budget, but the final budget must express business plans in terms of money.

*Operations.*   One of the fundamental objectives of a budget is the quantification of the revenues that will be realized and the expenses that will be incurred in the future. This information must be provided in detail. Revenues should be related to particular products sold or services rendered. Expenses should be identified with specific goods and services employed in the production of those revenues. The development of budgets for operations is discussed in detail in Chapter 7.

*Resources.*   It is not sufficient simply to plan revenues and expenses for the future. The enterprise must also plan the resources necessary for the operating plans to be realized. Basically, the planning of financial resources involves planning for the various types of assets (cash, inventory, plant property, and so forth) in the proper amounts for the efficient operation of the firm and planning the sources of the capital to be invested in these assets. Various aspects of planning for capital resources will be discussed in Chapter 7 and also in Chapters 16 and 17.

*Specified Future Period.*   A budget is meaningless unless it is related to a particular period of time. It is not helpful for management to know that $10 million of sales will be made unless it also knows *when* these sales will be made.

## Purposes of Budgets

As the title of this chapter implies, budgets are intended to facilitate the managerial functions of planning and control.[1] Good managers do not enter into new periods blindly. They plan, as carefully as possible, the normal operations of the period, as well as the unusual occurrences to the extent that these can be foreseen. Good budgets compel manage-

---

[1] The terms "planning" and "control" are used here in fairly well-understood contexts. However, the subject of management planning and control has been considered in much greater depth by many writers. Unfortunately, they are not all in agreement. While an exploration of the subject is beyond the scope of this text, interested readers will find it a very worthwhile area to investigate. A good reference is Robert N. Anthony, *Planning and Control Systems: A Framework for Analysis* (Boston: Division of Research, Graduate School of Business Administration, Harvard University, 1965). In addition to presenting his own framework, Anthony makes numerous references to other writers' conceptions of planning and control.

ment to plan in a comprehensive and coherent manner and to plan specifics, not vague generalities. Planning improved profits is of no value unless the planning involves the specific production, distribution, and financial programs necessary to yield higher profits.

The control implications of budgeting are inextricably linked with the planning aspects. For example, to plan delivery costs of $60,000 during the first quarter of the next year when such costs are viewed as reasonable and consistent with planned sales is to afford, simultaneously, a basis for evaluating the propriety of actual delivery costs. Of course, changes in sales as compared with the budget may reasonably necessitate changes in delivery costs. Perhaps a more useful approach to the budgeting of delivery costs would be to plan them in relation to units of sales volume so that changes in delivery costs may be anticipated and handled efficiently as actual sales volume is seen to deviate from the budgeted volume. This latter approach to the budgeting of costs and expenses is commonly referred to as *flexible budgeting* and will be discussed in detail in Chapter 8.

As a tool of control, the budget gives the responsible manager a guide to the conduct of operations and a basis for evaluating actual results. Actual revenues and expenses can be judged satisfactory or unsatisfactory in light of the relevant budgeted data and also in light of changes in conditions since the budget was prepared. The last portion of the preceding sentence is very important. The budget should not be regarded as a rigid requirement of performance. As already observed, many of the factors upon which a budget must be based are beyond the control of the firm's management; and all of them are subject to some degree of uncertainty. The budget is a plan, not an immutable commitment to performance; it is a means of control, but not a straitjacket on operations. Blind compliance with a budget may be worse than having no budget at all.

Another important aspect of budgetary planning and control is the efficient (i.e., profitable) allocation of the capital available to the enterprise. All expenditures require capital, in one form or another; and capital is a scarce resource. Not unusually, the sum of all desirable expenditures exceeds the total amount of available capital. Where such is the case, there must be some procedure and some person in the budget system to weigh the alternative uses of capital and to select those uses which offer the greatest profit potential for the firm. Thus, one of the functions of the budget is to plan the most efficient possible allocation of the capital resources of the firm.

As a final note here, it is important to remember that a business budget is a tool of management to be employed appropriately in the pursuit of management's basic objective, the optimum long-run profit of the firm. Like all tools, budgets are costly; and the more detailed and carefully prepared a budget is, the more it will cost. In any firm, the cost of the budget should be justified in terms of the additional revenues and/or cost savings it produces. Not the same degree of budget sophistication is appropriate for all firms. The discussions of budgeting in this text assume a relatively large company which finds it economically expedient to employ a complete and carefully detailed budget. The concepts illustrated here, however, may be adapted with more or less modification to suit the needs and means of a firm of any size.

## FRAMEWORK FOR BUDGETING

### The Budget Period

In order to be operationally meaningful, a budget must be related to a specific time period, called the budget period. A detailed budget for all segments and activities of an enterprise is normally prepared for relatively short periods of time only, typically no longer than one year. A fully detailed budget would include all expected revenues, expenses, receipts, disbursements, and other financial activities for each segment (e.g., division) of the firm for each significant time interval (e.g., a month) in the budget period. For example, an operating budget for one year may include a complete breakdown of revenues and expenses for each of the 12 months of the year. Alternatively, it might provide monthly detail for the first half of the year only, with the budgeted data for the second six months given by quarters or in total only. Long-range plans looking further than one year into the future may be developed for those segments of the business in which they are considered useful. Detailed long-range planning for the enterprise as a whole is seldom practicable. However, in certain segments of the firm it is highly desirable, if not absolutely necessary. As examples, long-range planning is essential in the areas of product development, equipment replacement, plant expansion, and the procurement of long-term capital.

In a fully developed budget system, there may be two or more budget periods planned simultaneously, the differences among such periods being the relative amounts of detail in which they are planned. Following is a description of such a budget system for a hypothetical corporation: By December 15, 1976, the operating budget for 1977 is finalized. This budget is fully detailed, by months, for all phases of operations for the first half of 1977. It includes details of budgeted revenues, expenses, receipts, and disbursements by divisions of the corporation and by product lines. For the second half of 1977, estimated data for the entire company are summarized by quarters only. No detail is given for the several divisions or for the individual product lines. By June 15, 1977, a new budget will be prepared. This will provide full details for the second half of 1977 and summarized quarterly estimates for the first half of 1978. This procedure is repeated every six months. Thus, the budget system is constantly moving forward into the future but is able to build its short-range detailed budget partly upon the basis of an earlier semi-detailed plan. In addition to this formalized annual budget, the corporation prepares annually an intermediate-range sales forecast for the next three years. Finally, long-term capital procurement and investment needs are planned in general terms five year ahead.[2]

Thus, there are three different time periods in the future for which financial plans are formulated. Each of these might be regarded as a unique budget period. Within the framework of the definition of a budget posited earlier, however, only the operating plan for the next year would qualify as a true budget. Even within that year, there are two subperiods of differing budget detail. While the terminology of budgeting is not so standardized that definitive conclusions can be stated here, there is a useful distinction to be made between budgeting, as such, and long-range planning. For purposes of discussion in this text, we shall regard any plans that are not comprehensive and coordinated for the entire enterprise and that extend further into the future than the normal detailed budget period as falling into the category of long-range planning.

### Environmental Factors

Once the budget period has been established, management must attempt to predict the nature of the external, or environmental, conditions that may be expected to occur during that period. The environment here includes all of the factors outside the firm that will influence its operations during the budget period but will not be controllable by the firm's management. Environmental factors include a wide variety of social, economic, and political conditions; and they are subject to a wide range of degrees of predictability. Yet, collectively, they define some of the most important opportunities and constraints that the firm will face during the period. The market for a firm's products, for example, is determined largely by factors outside of its control.

Among the most significant of the environmental factors are changes in the composition or the behavior of the population as a whole. Such changes as a decrease in the birth rate and an increase in the proportion of the population over 65 years of age have substantial impacts on the demands for specific goods and services. The nature of the demand for housing, for example, may be materially altered. Recent years have seen a significant increase in the construction of multiple-family dwellings.

---

[2] Long-range planning is not limited to five years in the future, of course. It may be carried forward as far as is considered practical in the individual firm. Generally speaking, however, the longer the planning period the less certain the plans will be.

Such social movements as the growing concern for ecology and changing definitions of "the quality of life" may have major effects on the operations of many business and nonbusiness enterprises. Economic conditions, such as inflation and recession are extremely important determinants of events during a budget period. Yet, they are essentially beyond the control of the individual firm. The worldwide oil shortage, first widely recognized in 1973, sparked a major shift in automobile demand from large to small cars. In general, American automobile manufacturers had not anticipated this shift when they prepared their budgets; and this failure was dramatically reflected in reduced sales and profits in 1974. Governmental actions and policies may have great impacts on budgeting. An expected change in the tax law may have a considerable effect on a firm's budgeted profit and cash flow from operations. A change in federal antitrust policy may induce a firm to alter its programs drastically. Government policies designed to bolster or to restrain the economy may have important influences on management decisions. Increases in government spending designed to counter a recession may greatly enhance a firm's sales prospects for the budget period. Conversely, restrictive monetary policies by the Federal Reserve Board may cause management to reduce or to defer the implementation of new programs requiring additional capital.

Budgetary planning of environmental conditions is essentially a matter of passive expectation. Management's objective is to predict what these conditions will be, regardless of whether they will be favorable or adverse to the firm's best interests. However, management's plans in response to these conditions are very much a matter of active intent. Indeed, the short-term success or failure of a company may be largely dependent upon how well its management responds to some uncontrollable external force.

### Company Policies

In addition to the environmental factors, there are many internal conditions and policies that must be taken into account in the preparation of a budget. For example, a firm may have the policy of limiting itself to the production of a high quality, high-priced commodity. If such a policy is to be continued, then a number of additional avenues for distribution of the product must be regarded as closed. A family corporation may adhere to a policy of operating only within one region of the country because expansion into the national market would not permit the family to retain effective control over the corporation. While management may believe that entry into the national market would be highly profitable, it must exclude any such profits from its planning because of the policy imposed by the family owners of the firm. At this point we need not be concerned with whether such policies are wise. We merely note that they sometimes exist and form a part of the framework within which the budget must be developed.

## HUMAN IMPLICATIONS OF BUDGETING

Thus far, we have discussed budgeting in an impersonal manner and have used the term management as an impersonal singular noun. But management is an aggregation of people, and these people must prepare and implement the budget. Insofar as the actual workings of a budget are concerned, the most important aspects are the effects of people upon the budget and, conversely, the effects of the budget upon people.

### Personnel Involved in Budget Preparation

There is no standardized organization of people for budget preparation. Different firms use different procedures, but there are certain basic guidelines which are applicable in all cases and should be given proper recognition. These basic guidelines may be stated as follows:

1.  The budget must be prepared and used in such a way that it helps the enterprise as a whole attain its basic objectives. In an organization with many separate responsibility centers, of course, the budget must also aid the managers of those centers in the attainment of their specific objectives. Consequently, the budget should be so devised as to facilitate the simultaneous achievement of both responsibility centers' goals and the entire firm's goals. That is, the budget should foster *goal congruence;* the goals of each segment of the organization should be congruent with those of the entity as a whole.

2.  The budget must logically and effectively coordinate all segments and functions of the enterprise. Since the operations of one segment or function (e.g., manufacturing) inevitably interact with those of other segments or functions (e.g., marketing), personnel involved in budget preparation in one segment must work harmoniously with those in other areas. The development of a sound budget must be a cooperative venture.

3.  The budget must be understood and accepted by those who will actually work with it and under it. Thus, these people should be involved in the budgetary process from the outset. They should want to make the budget work well. If they chafe under the budget and work against it, the results will inevitably be unsatisfactory.

*The Budget Director.*    In every organization, one executive should be assigned responsibility for the overall coordination and the final compilation of the budget. The budget director should supervise the process of preparing the budget but should not personally prepare it. That is, the director's responsibility for the budget should be limited to the *system* of budgeting; he or she should not determine the substance of the budget prepared within that system. The ideal budget director would be a person with no other responsibilities. However, this ideal could be attained only in a very large organization in which budgeting was a continuous process. In most enterprises, the budget director must be an executive with other duties. In many cases, this responsibility is assigned to the controller, whose duties are generally the design and supervision of systems for accounting and control. He or she has no functional operating authority, except for the management of his or her own staff. Alternatively, the budget director may be a member of the controller's staff.

**The Budget Committee.**  In order to ensure that all segments of the firm are properly coordinated in the final budget, all major segments should be represented on a committee of executives that compiles the budget in its final form. This committee would be chaired by the budget director and would include representatives of all major functional divisions of the firm—including manufacturing, distribution, finance, research, and any other distinct functions recognized in the firm's organization. If not already serving as the budget director, the controller would also be a member of this committee. The composition of the budget committee would differ among firms, but the purpose would be the same in all cases—effective coordination of planning for the firm. The budget committee should not prepare the budget from the start but should compile it in its final form, after satisfactorily reconciling all initial conflicts in the various components.

**Initial Budget Preparation.**  The initial development of budgetary data ordinarily should come from the managers who will be responsible for performance under the budget. The preparation of the budget should be a "bottom-up" process. That is, budget data should be originated at the lowest levels of operating management and should be refined and coordinated at higher levels. This practice is commonly referred to as the *participative approach* to budgeting. It is designed to get everyone who will have to operate under the budget involved in its original preparation. If a manager has participated in the budgeting process, that person is more likely to be in sympathy with the final budget, and consequently, will be motivated to meet budget goals. This approach might well be described as "before-the-fact responsibility accounting." In contrast is the *authoritarian approach* to budgeting. Here top management sets budget goals and passes these down as directives to operating managers. The authoritarian approach may be quite effective in some cases, particularly where lower level managers have little initiative or discretion in the conduct of their operations.

In the participative approach to budgeting, an operating manager still needs some general guidelines in the preparation of a budget. A sales manager, for example, should be provided with market forecasts and predictions of economic conditions before undertaking to plan sales in his or her territory or sales of certain product lines. A production manager could hardly plan manufacturing operations without some preliminary information about projected sales of products. Moreover, the initial budget submission by an operating manager may require considerable modification to make it compatible with other conditions, constraints, and plans that are beyond the manager's knowledge or control. For example, a plant manager may budget for equipment replacements that the company will simply be unable to afford during the budget period. One product line manager may plan an expansion of the sales of that product while another product line manager is planning to introduce a new and directly competitive product. Top management must identify such inconsistencies and call them to the attention of the responsible lower managers. Any changes to the initial budget estimates should be made first by the responsible manager, however. Thus, the budget may have to be recycled from the bottom to the top a second time and, perhaps, again. The objective of this repeated "bottom-up" budget preparation is complete acceptance of the final budget at all levels of management. Complete acceptance is unlikely unless all managers really believe that the budget against which their performance will be evaluated is truly *their* budget.

**The Final Budget.** Once all internal inconsistencies and conflicts have been resolved and the various operating managers have submitted budgets which are in harmony with each other, with the goals of the enterprise, and with the realities of the environment of the budget period, a final master budget is compiled by the budget director with the assistance of the budget committee. This budget is submitted to top management, the president and/or the board of directors, for final approval. Once approved at this level, the budget is published to all responsible management personnel. However, even in this final form, the budget is still only a plan, not a hard-and-fast commitment. The budget is a powerful tool of management, but it does not eliminate the need for informed and intelligent management action as actual operations progress throughout the budget period.

## Budgets and Human Behavior

The interrelationships between management and the behavioral sciences are extensive and very important. They go far beyond the scope of this discussion, however. Hence, the comments in this section will be both brief and nontechnical. However, it is important for the student to have at least a general appreciation of the potential impacts of budgets on human behavior. If a budget is prepared realistically by a department supervisor and revised with his or her aid and approval, it may evoke a favorable response and serve as a stimulus to efficient and profitable performance. If it is prepared by someone else without the aid or approval of the supervisor, it may generate hostility and act as a deterrent to intelligent thinking and, ultimately, may reduce efficiency and profits. However the budget is prepared, people will react to it. Their reactions will be either positive or negative, depending upon whether they feel the budget is reasonable and whether they were involved in its preparation. (Totally neutral reaction to a budget is conceivable but highly unlikely.) Thus, the budget is as much a tool of good human relations as of financial planning and control. The latter objectives will not be well served if the former is not carefully incorporated in the preparation and implementation of the budget.

Budget systems may include rewards and punishments for good and bad performances under the budget. Rewards might take the form of additional monetary compensation, faster advancement within the firm, public recognition, and/or other means. Punishment might involve simply the loss of additional compensation, promotion, or recognition; or it might take the form of positive unfavorable action such as demotion or dismissal. Where rewards and/or punishments are involved in a budget, it is extremely important that they be meted out in light of actual conditions during the budget period and not be based wholly upon the predetermined budget data. The rewards should be so conceived as to be given for performance which is in the overall best interests of the firm. A department supervisor may be able to minimize operating costs and, hence, maximize his or her own reward by employing operating procedures that do not serve the best interests of the entire firm. Punishment for failure to meet reasonable budgeted achievement should be designed in such a way as to avoid fear and the blunting of initiative on the parts of responsible supervisors. Slavish adherence to budgets should not be the aim of budget reward and punishment schemes. Budgets must walk a narrow line between encouragement and discouragement, between motivation and fear. Specifically how this is to be accomplished is beyond the scope of this volume, but it is a critical importance to the success of a budget system.[3]

## CONSTRUCTION OF THE BUDGET

The mechanics of budget preparation are the subject of the following chapter. At this point, however, it is appropriate to consider three general aspects of budget preparation.

---

[3] There is a considerable body of literature on the behavioral implications of budgeting. Reports of empirical studies in this area may be found in Chris Argyris, *The Impact of Budgets on People* (New York: The Controllership Foundation, Inc., 1952); G. H. Hofstede, *The Game of Budget Control* (London: Tavistock Publications Limited, 1968); and Andrew Stedry, *Budget Control and Cost Behavior* (Englewood Cliffs, N.J.: Prentice-Hall, Inc., 1960).

## Limiting Factor on Operations

In every enterprise there is some factor which effectively restricts the total magnitude of operating activity during a given period. In the majority of industrial firms in the United States, this limiting factor is sales demand. Most of these firms find that the reasonably expected sales of their products determine the overall scope and size of their operations. In other firms, production capacity may be the limiting factor on operations. An oil company might be unable to meet full demand because its refinery capacity cannot be expanded during the budget period. A farm can produce no more than the available land will yield in a good harvest season. In some firms the limiting factor is capital. No matter how great the demand for its product and irrespective of available production facilities, a firm must have capital in order to operate. Firms with histories of financial difficulties often find that they are unable to obtain the necessary funds to produce and sell at a volume that would cure their financial ills.

Whatever the limiting factor for a firm may be, it is the element which determines the size of total operations and, hence, the point at which the planning process should begin. There is no sense in planning production greatly in excess of forecasted sales unless some profitable use of the resultant inventory accumulation can be foreseen in the more distant future. It may happen that, as a budget is developed from one limiting factor, a different one is discovered. For example, the preparation of a budget may begin with a sales forecast on the assumption that sales demand is the limiting factor on operations; but the planning may reveal production limitations which cannot be exceeded and which require a reduction in the planned sales volume. Alternatively, it may be found that additional capital would be needed to operate at the level called for in the sales forecast and that none is available.

## Setting Budget Allowances

There is no one way in which the appropriate quantity for a particular budget item is determined. All budget data are, of course, estimates; but they are influenced strongly by past experience. After all, the only basis management has for judging the future is the past. This does not mean that budgeting simply presumes that what happened in the past will happen again. Changes in future conditions must be taken into account in applying the lessons of the past to the future. But even expectations of changes are necessarily conditioned by experience. Nevertheless, planning is essentially a future-looking activity. Actual data of the past are useful in budgeting only to the extent that they help to develop estimates of future data. Budget data must be drawn primarily from studies of the future.

One possible way to estimate future data is to extend the actual data of the past by means of an average rate of growth or decline in a particular quantity that has persisted over some significant period of time. Seasonal variations in historical data should also be considered. Thus, March of 1976 may be a useful basis for planning for March of 1977. Further, the relationship between March of 1976 and the fourth quarter of 1975 may be of some help in estimating data for March of 1977 when the data for the fourth quarter of 1976 are known.

## The Budget Base

In addition to all other considerations, there must be some base, or starting point, for the budget of any organization or activity. One common and fairly easy starting point is the actual level of operations during the current period. From this base, the budget seeks to identify only the changes that are expected or intended during the budget period. This approach is called *incremental budgeting*. The budget process is concerned directly only with the increment in operations during the budget period. In some cases, incremental budgeting may be entirely appropriate. A sales budget for a product that enjoys a secure position in a stable market might be prepared in this way. The salary budget for a corporate executive office is another example in which only changes might require attention. The principal disadvantage of incremental budgeting is that it presumes that the current level of operations is appropriate. A sales budget prepared in this way may ignore opportunities to penetrate into new market areas. An expense budget developed by the incremental approach may perpetuate existing inefficiency in a department.

The major alternative to incremental budgeting is referred to as *zero-base budgeting*. In this approach, the budget is developed from a starting point of no operations at all. A zero-base sales budget would be developed by examining the market potential for a product and would not necessarily be constrained by current sales operations. A departmental expense budget would be developed by determining the operational requirements of that department. The current scope and size of operations would not be assumed to be proper. Obviously, the zero-base approach is likely to be more difficult and time-consuming than the incremental approach; for it raises more questions. Logically, it may be preferable because it is less dependent upon the past.

In practice, both approaches may be used quite effectively. A zero-base budget might be prepared for a particular operation only occasionally, perhaps every fourth year. Intervening years' budgets would be developed by the incremental approach. In this way, most annual budgets would be prepared by the simpler incremental method. However, periodically, a more fundamental examination of the appropriate level of operations would be made. Thus, inefficiencies or unduly restrictive practices would be less likely to be perpetuated indefinitely.

## BUDGETARY REVIEW

Once the budget period has begun, the budget process must not cease to function until it is time to prepare the next period's budget. If the budget is to be an effective tool of control and an aid to dynamic planning, it must be reviewed periodically with views to both the past and the future. As regards the past, budgetary review is concerned with a comparison of actual operating performance with budgeted performance for a given period of time. As regards the future, budgetary review provides a basis for revising and/or extending future plans.

Budgetary review is commonly accomplished by preparation of periodic reports and holding periodic meetings of the budget committee to evaluate actual performance and to reappraise future plans. While there is no standard frequency for these formal reports and meetings, monthly review is found in many business firms. Probably budgetary review should be undertaken in a formal manner at least quarterly. Waiting until the end of an annual budget period before a careful comparison of actual and budgeted performances is made leaves no room for corrective action during that period. Only the next budget period can benefit from such review.

The comparison of actual and budget data is designed to afford a basis for controlling current and future operations. It is always possible that the conclusion from the comparison of actual and budgeted operating data will be that the budget was unrealistic to begin with or that actual conditions during the budget period are so different from those anticipated that the budget data are no longer valid. In any event, the causes of deviations of actual performance from the budget should be sought and, where appropriate, corrected. The mere fact that actual operating data differ from the budget and are so reported is only the prelude to managerial control. Identification of causes and corrective action are the essence of control.

In addition to evaluating past performance in light of the budget, the budget committee should review and reappraise the budget data for the remainder of the current budget period. Changes in actual conditions from those originally expected normally require parallel changes in operating plans. When such changes in the budget are deemed appropriate, they should be made and approved by all responsible managers. This revised budget, brought up to date by a discriminating budgetary review policy, then becomes the formal statement of operating plans for the remaining portion of the budget period. Further, in this process of reviewing conditions and prospects for the current budget period are the seeds of the budget for the subsequent period. Thus, budgeting can and should be a continuous, dynamic process.

## QUESTIONS FOR DISCUSSION

1.  What are the practical distinctions between the functions of planning, programming, and budgeting? Can these three functions really be clearly distinguished from one another? Discuss.

2.  "Programming is nothing more than long-range planning (or budgeting). As such, it is undoubtedly useful; but it is hardly a distinct managerial activity." Discuss this statement.

3.  "Budgets may actually prove detrimental to effective managerial control. They provide preconceived plans as the criteria for evaluating actual operations. Thus, any errors in the planning process may be compounded in the control process." Comment on this criticism of budgets.

4.  What are the essential elements of good budgeting?

5.  Is it possible that the establishment of a formal budget period may impose arbitrary and potentially harmful limitations on management's planning function? Discuss.

6.  What social, economic, and political conditions existing currently and/or anticipated within the year would you expect to have the most significant identifiable impacts upon the budgeted operations of (*a*) an automobile manufacturer, (*b*) a county welfare department, and (*c*) a private university?

7.  You have recently been hired as budget director and systems analyst for a medium-sized manufacturer of industrial machinery. The firm has been in business for many years and has a history of steady growth, satisfactory profit margins, and work force stability. It has never made any formal use of budgets. The president has asked you to design and install a budgetary system as soon as practicable. After several months on the job, you have developed a basic outline of the budget system you believe is right for this company. The president has called a meeting of middle managers and factory supervisors to hear your initial presentation of this proposed budget system. He has asked you to describe the objectives of the system and, basically, how it will work. How will you begin your presentation at this meeting?

8.  Inasmuch as the accounting department works closely with cost and expense data for an entire company, isn't it the logical unit to develop expense budgets for the several operating departments? Explain your position.

9.  The Galena Company employs a merit system in compensating its supervisory personnel. In addition to a basic salary, each department supervisor receives a bonus based upon the relationship between his department's actual performance and its budget for the period. For most departments, this involves comparisons of actual and budgeted costs. An excess of actual costs over budgeted costs results in negative points. An excess of budget over actual costs produces positive points. The points are then added

algebraically. Net negative points are ignored. Net positive points are multiplied by a predetermined bonus rate to determine the supervisor's merit compensation. Evaluate this bonus plan.

10. What benefits should a firm derive from the periodic meetings of its budget committee?

11. "Realistically, sales demand is the only limiting factor on the volume of a business firm's operations. Sales demand will inevitably generate the necessary capital and productive capacity to fill that demand." Discuss this assertion.

12. Define "goal congruence." Why is it important in budgeting?

13. How can a firm reconcile the notion of "bottom-up" budget development with top management's inescapable responsibility for planning the total operations of the firm?

14. "Do you know," said the president of the Streator Corporation, with a satisfied puff on his cigar, "Our budget system has saved us a half a million dollars since we began it three years ago." How would you expect such a financial saving to be measured? Is it important that such a saving be measured? Discuss.

15. How might statistical analysis be used to advantage in a budget system?

16. "Quite obviously, zero-base budgeting is inherently preferable to incremental budgeting because it considers the entire operation and not just the next step, or increment, in operations. Therefore, management would be well advised to employ zero-base budgeting exclusively." Comment on this argument.

17. Read at least the first chapter of Robert N. Anthony's *Planning and Control Systems: A Framework for Analysis* (Boston: Harvard University, 1965). If this book is not available, substantially the same framework is summarized in the first chapter of Anthony, Dearden, and Vancil's textbook, *Management Control Systems*, rev. ed. (Homewood, Ill.: Richard D. Irwin, Inc., 1972). How does budgeting relate to Anthony's framework of planning and control?

18. There has been considerable debate as to the merits of employee participation in budgeting. Some argue that employees work best when they have been involved directly in the budgetary process. Others suggest that at least some employees function best under an authoritarian budget system. An interesting discussion of these points of view appeared in an article by Selwyn Becker and David Green, Jr., "Budgeting and Employee Behavior" in the *Journal of Business* for October, 1962. A reply to this article by Andrew C. Stedry was published in the April, 1964, *Journal of Business* along with a rejoinder by Becker and Green. (All three of these items are reproduced in William J. Bruns, Jr., and Don T. DeCoster, *Accounting and Its Behavioral Implications* (New York: McGraw-Hill Book Co., 1969) and also in L. S. Rosen, *Topics in Managerial Accounting*, 2d ed. (Toronto: McGraw-Hill Ryerson Limited, 1974). Read this article and the subsequent discussions of it. If you were responsible for the decision, would you have your employees participate in the budget process? Explain your decision.

# chapter 7

# Budgeting Operations and Financial Resources

THE PRECEDING CHAPTER discussed the basic concepts and purposes of budgeting. This chapter addresses the procedures for preparing a comprehensive periodic budget. Necessarily, the presentation of budgeting procedures here will be quite general. The specific process of budget preparation depends upon the circumstances in the particular organization and in the budget period. The discussion will deal first with the budget of operations, the revenues and expenses expected to be recognized during the budget period. Then we shall address the budgeting of financial resources, the capital necessary to finance the conduct of operations. Obviously, operations and financial resources cannot be planned independently of one another. Operations are usually the source of much of the capital generated during a period, and the availability of capital is one of the most important factors supporting or constraining the level of operations. Moreover, the operations of the various segments and activities of an enterprise all interact with each other. Sales and production clearly cannot be planned independently. Thus, the separate discussions of various facets of budget preparation in this chapter are intended only to focus on each facet in sequence. The interdependencies will be evident, however.

Throughout this chapter, a single, integrated illustration of budget preparation will be used. It depicts the development of the 1977 annual budget of the Mission Electric Corporation, a manufacturer of a variety of electrical products which are marketed throughout the world. The level of detail presented in this illustration will be much less than a real firm of this size would require. A truly realistic illustration would fill many pages with detailed budgets analyzed by various classification schemes. Here, both the details and the variety of classifications will be greatly reduced. For example, the annual budget will be broken down into quarterly estimates only. For many purposes, at least monthly estimates would be necessary. Monthly analysis would only triple the size of the illustration, however; it would not present fundamentally different concepts or procedures. Numerous additional refinements and complications will be mentioned in the text but will not be illustrated in the tables presented.

The Mission Electric Corporation is organized functionally. The two major functional divisions are production and marketing. The production division manufactures the following three product lines: small appliances, electrical parts, and industrial control units. There are numerous individual products in each product line. Each product line is produced in a separate production department, comprising one or more plants. Thus, analysis of data by product line coincides with analysis by major responsibility centers. The marketing division has five distinct sales territories: northeastern, midwestern, southern, western, and international. All products are sold in each sales territory. Sales are made in substantial quantities to retailers, to wholesalers, and to industrial users. Each of these classifications is a potential basis for budgetary planning.

## THE SALES FORECAST

The limiting factor on the operations of the Mission Electric Corporation is sales demand. Hence, the logical starting point in the development of the annual budget is the sales forecast. Sales forecasting is partly a passive assessment of market conditions and the market potential for a firm's products during a budget period. However, it also involves an important element of active planning. Management may plan positive actions designed to stimulate total demand for its products or to increase its share of the total market.

### Factors Determining Sales

*The Environment.* The importance of the various social, economic, and political factors that make up the environment within which a firm operates was discussed in the preceding chapter. An assessment of these environmental factors is particularly critical in the preparation of the sales forecast, for sales constitute one of the principal points of contact between a firm and its environment. Insofar as sales are concerned, the environment may be identified with the markets for the firm's products.

Markets are enormously complex and defy precise definition. Yet, management must not only arrive at an operational definition of its markets but must also predict behavior in those markets during specific future periods. The task of making such a prediction is difficult, and the cost of making a bad prediction may be high, as witnessed by the large number of business failures every year.

For purposes of the Mission Electric Corporation illustration, we shall assume that 1977 is expected to be a year of general prosperity in the world economy. Domestic sales demand is expected to grow to record high levels, and foreign demand is anticipated to be growing even more rapidly. No major shifts in U.S. governmental policy are anticipated, although the identity of the new president would not be known when the sales forecast is begun. Concern for energy conservation has resulted in demand for more efficient electric motors that will accomplish a particular job with less power consumption. Mission Electric Corporation plans to introduce new and more efficient motors in several of its industrial products in 1977. While management has high hopes that this innovation will improve its share of that market, it also recognizes that buyers may be cautious in trying something new and may wait until these motors have been proved in use. Thus, there is a greater degree of uncertainty associated with the forecast of sales of industrial control units than with the sales of the other two product lines.

*Competition.*    Each firm's share of a market is determined largely by competition among firms. In economic theory, competition implies that there are many firms selling a product in a particular market and that, as a consequence, the individual seller's discretion in setting prices is limited. In common terms, competition denotes rivalry. In this latter sense, competition among firms may take many forms. Most competition can be related to prices, product quality, customer services, or sales promotion programs. Competitive initiatives by one firm may be successful in capturing a larger share of the market than that firm would otherwise have enjoyed. Of course, that firm may expect its competitors to react to its initiatives. Part of the sales forecasting process involves predictions of what competitors will do during the budget period and how they will react to initiatives taken by the firm preparing the budget. Mission Electric Corporation is a relatively small company competing in markets dominated by such giants as General Electric Company, Westinghouse Electric Corporation and, in foreign markets, Philips Industries of the Netherlands. It maintains profitable operations by competing effectively in only selected segments of the electrical products market. It must be highly sensitive to the plans and actions of its much larger competitors.

*Company Policies and Programs.*    Sales forecasting is not entirely a matter of looking outside the firm, of course. Management may undertake a variety of programs intended to generate sales, and the prospective effects of these programs during the budget period must be considered carefully. Prices may be raised or lowered. New products may be introduced, or new sales outlets may be opened. The firm may attempt to penetrate new markets, or it may change basic marketing strategies. Different methods of sales promotion may be planned. Whatever the action planned, management must predict the effect that it will have on sales volume during the budget period. Of course, it must also recognize that competitors may be planning new programs themselves.

## Detailed Development of the Sales Forecast

There are many different classification schemes by which a sales forecast might be developed. Sales might be classified by individual products, by product lines, by sales territories, by channels of distribution, by sizes of customers, by responsibility centers that manufacture the products, or by the centers that market the products. In the typical business firm, the sales forecast will be detailed according to more than one of these schemes. For production planning, the breakdowns by products and by production centers would be important. For sales planning, breakdowns by product lines, by sales territories, by channels of distribution, and by marketing centers would probably be emphasized. For the Mission Electric Corporation, only two basic sales breakdowns will be illustrated. Many more would be appropriate and can be visualized quite easily.

*Sales Forecast by Product Lines.* Table 7–1 is a summary sales forecast of Mission Electric Corporation's product lines for 1977. Sales are detailed by quarters only. As noted before, monthly breakdowns would be more common; but they would only lengthen the illustration, not change it substantively. This summary forecast would be supported by more detailed sales projections for each different product in each of the

**TABLE 7–1**

MISSION ELECTRIC CORPORATION
Sales Forecast by Product Lines
1977
(in thousands of dollars)

| Product Lines | Quarter | | | | Totals for Year |
|---|---|---|---|---|---|
| | First | Second | Third | Fourth | |
| Small appliances............. | $10,000 | $ 8,000 | $12,000 | $20,000 | $50,000 |
| Electrical parts.............. | 5,000 | 7,000 | 8,000 | 5,000 | 25,000 |
| Industrial control units....... | 3,000 | 4,000 | 4,000 | 4,000 | 15,000 |
| Total sales............ | $18,000 | $19,000 | $24,000 | $29,000 | $90,000 |

three product lines. Thus, a separate sales forecast for small appliances would show detailed sales of mixers, blenders, toasters, irons, coffee pots, and so forth. Similarly, the budgeted sales of electrical parts would be broken down by such items as switches, fuses, plugs, sockets, brushes, and coils. Industrial control units include some standard products, but most of these items are manufactured to a specific customer's order. In such a case, a breakdown by individual products may not be feasible. The summary sales forecast in Table 7–1 is presented in terms of dollar sales volume only. More detailed product forecasts might show both physical sales volumes and unit prices. Physical volumes are essential inputs to production planning. Finally, it should be noted that there are

**TABLE 7–2**

MISSION ELECTRIC CORPORATION
Sales Forecast by Sales Territories
1977
(in thousands of dollars)

| Sales Territories | Quarter | | | | Totals for Year |
| | First | Second | Third | Fourth | |
|---|---|---|---|---|---|
| Northeastern............... | $ 5,400 | $ 5,600 | $ 7,400 | $ 8,800 | $27,200 |
| Midwestern................ | 4,500 | 4,800 | 5,900 | 7,300 | 22,500 |
| Southern................... | 2,700 | 2,900 | 3,600 | 4,300 | 13,500 |
| Western................... | 3,600 | 3,700 | 4,800 | 5,800 | 17,900 |
| International............... | 1,800 | 2,000 | 2,300 | 2,800 | 8,900 |
| Total sales........... | $18,000 | $19,000 | $24,000 | $29,000 | $90,000 |

seasonal patterns to the expected sales of small appliances and electrical parts. Such patterns are extremely important in the budget process. It is not sufficient to plan a particular annual sales volume. The timing of the planned sales is also essential. A seasonal sales pattern will have significant implications for the production budget, operating expense budgets, the working capital budget, and the cash budget.

*Sales Forecast by Sales Territories.* The forecast of sales by product lines coincides with a sales budget by major production responsibility centers, that is, the three production departments. A similar forecast by marketing responsibility centers would show projected sales by quarters in the five sales territories. Such a sales forecast is presented in Table 7–2. The total sales by quarters are, of course, the same as in the product line forecast in Table 7–1. Both summaries were developed from the same basic budget data. Indeed, the forecasts by territories could not have been prepared initially in total amounts. They had to have been developed by products expected to be sold in the territories. Further breakdowns by channels of distribution (i.e., sales to retailers, to wholesalers, and to industrial users) or by sizes of customers (i.e., by dollar amounts of annual sales to customers) might also be made. These breakdowns would be integrally coordinated with those by product lines and by sales territories. It would be impossible to plan sales by one classification without considering the others at the same time. Management cannot plan what will be sold without simultaneous attention to when, where, and to whom it will be sold.

## Budgeting Sales in Total Only

The discussion in the preceding section indicated that the sales forecast was developed by estimating unit sales volume for each product in each sales territory and then multiplying those volumes by selling prices to obtain the total budgeted sales revenues. This approach is entirely logical and feasible for companies which do not have a very large number of different products and whose products are known in advance. Other companies may handle thousands of different items and the composition of those items may change quickly in response to market conditions. Examples of such companies are large department stores, mail-order houses, and drug wholesalers. For these firms, forecasting sales by units of individual products would not be practicable. Instead, they develop their sales forecasts initially in terms of dollars of sales revenue. Breakdowns by sales territories, channels of distribution, and responsibility centers may still be possible; but a complete breakdown by products is not. The sales forecast reflects management's assessment of the total market for the general class of products which the firm sells and of the firm's likely share of that market. While this approach may appear to be less precise than one based on individual products, it is not necessarily less useful. It may provide the best possible projection of sales in the terms in which management is accustomed to dealing. If so, it is as useful for purposes of planning and control as any budget can be.

## Long-Range Sales Forecasts

The annual sales forecast described above is sufficient for purposes of preparing the comprehensive annual budget. Any longer-range sales projection would be beyond the requirements of budgeting. However, sales volume over time is such an important variable to the business firm that most companies attempt to plan it for a longer period than just the annual budget period. Future plant capacity and capital requirements are partly dependent upon future sales, and planning for these items normally involves a longer lead time than a single year. There is no unique period for which long-range sales forecasting is appropriate, but many companies attempt to do it for periods of three to five years. Some firms, such as public utilities, may prepare rough sales forecasts for much longer periods.


## PRODUCTION BUDGETS

In a manufacturing company, the budgeting of production in units and of production costs is one of the most important and detailed parts of the total budget process. Production budgets must be prepared in detail for individual products or groups of related products, for production departments, for plants, and for the many components of manufacturing cost.


### Factors Determining Production Volume

*Sales.* In most cases, the major determinant of production volume is the forecasted volume of sales. Thus, most of current output is intended to fill expected current sales demand. The timing of sales as well as the total sales volume is important in planning production during the budget period. Goods must flow from the factories on a schedule that enables the firm to fill sales orders as they are received or within a reasonable time thereafter. Production scheduling is easiest when all goods are produced to customers' orders and there is a long lead time between receipt of an order and delivery of goods. It is most difficult when a firm produces a large variety of items and customers' orders are unpredictable in terms of both their timing and the specific goods ordered. In such a case, the manufacturer must carry a fairly substantial "safety stock" of all goods or risk the loss of sales because he is out of stock of certain items when orders are received.

When there is a significant degree of seasonal variation in sales demand during a period, production may be scheduled to vary with sales or it may be planned at a stable level despite the variations in demand. In the first instance, where output is scheduled to fluctuate with sales, the firm must plan to expand operations, including its work force, during or immediately prior to periods of peak demand and to reduce operations and lay workers off during the slack season. In the second instance, where output is stabilized despite demand fluctuations, the company must plan to build up inventories of finished products during the slack period and to reduce those stocks during the peak sales season. Of course, there is also the opposite situation, in which production is subject to seasonal variations but sales are not. Canning and other raw food processing companies often experience such conditions. In these companies, there is little alternative to periods of peak and low (if any) production, along with substantial inventory buildups and reductions.

*Inventory Plans.*  While production normally is determined chiefly by budgeted sales, it should be planned with inventory requirements in mind also. For example, if a firm anticipates that future sales demand will continue to rise, it may conclude that its inventories of finished products must be greater at the end of the budget period than at the beginning. Obviously, the only way that inventory levels can be increased is by producing more than is expected to be sold. On the other hand, management may believe the company has been carrying excessive inventory quantities and may plan a reduction in stocks as of the end of the period as compared with the beginning. In this case, planned production volume will be lower than budgeted sales volume. Although planning inventory levels a year or more in advance may be quite difficult, some plan for the ending inventory must be incorporated in the production budget.

*Capacity.*  Finally, production is necessarily limited by the productive capacity of the firm's plants. Capacity, however, does not admit of any simple practical definition. It is not merely a matter of plant size. Capacity may be expanded by construction of new plant facilities or by purchase of new equipment. Construction, of course, normally requires a long planning time, frequently more than a year. Capacity may also be expanded in the short run by working additional shifts, by working overtime and on weekends, and by contracting with other companies to produce some of the necessary output. Such schemes increase operating costs, of course. Night shifts and overtime work command wage premiums in excess of the regular straight-time pay for a day shift. Goods produced under contract by another firm will cost more because the other manufacturer will add a profit margin to his cost. Thus, capacity is established by managerial decisions as well as by physical plant limitations. However it is defined, capacity places an upper limit on output. It may be a somewhat flexible limit, but it cannot be stretched indefinitely in the short run.

## Summary Production Budgets

Total output and total production costs will be summarized in the final master budget. The first line of cost planning and control is at the level of the manufacturing responsibility centers, however. Hence, production costs must be budgeted initially for individual production departments and plants. Further, production schedules for individual products or classes of products are necessary. These component production budgets are then compiled into a summary budget. Table 7–3 is a summary production cost budget for one of the four plants of the Mission Electric Corporation. This is the Bridgeport plant, which produces about half the total output of small appliances. Production costs are detailed here by direct materials, direct labor, and variable and fixed manufac-

**TABLE 7–3**

MISSION ELECTRIC CORPORATION
Bridgeport Plant
Production Cost Budget
1977
(in thousands of dollars)

| | Quarter | | | | Totals |
| Cost Elements | First | Second | Third | Fourth | for Year |
|---|---|---|---|---|---|
| Direct materials................. | $1,500 | $1,800 | $2,100 | $ 2,400 | $ 7,800 |
| Direct labor..................... | 2,500 | 3,000 | 3,500 | 4,000 | 13,000 |
| Variable manufacturing overhead... | 1,000 | 1,200 | 1,400 | 1,600 | 5,200 |
| Fixed manufacturing overhead..... | 2,000 | 2,000 | 2,000 | 2,000 | 8,000 |
| Total costs............... | $7,000 | $8,000 | $9,000 | $10,000 | $34,000 |

turing overhead. More detailed cost budgets by types of material, classes of labor, and specific indirect cost items would be prepared for the various responsibility centers in the plant. Note that the three variable production costs are planned to increase quarter by quarter. This pattern indicates that the volume of production in the plant is expected to grow during 1977. Fixed manufacturing overhead, however, is planned at the same amount each quarter. This reflects the fairly typical practice of budgeting total fixed costs for the year and then dividing this total by four to obtain quarterly budgets. Thus, the budgeted fixed manufacturing overhead shown is the amount expected to be incurred in each quarter, not necessarily the amount expected to be applied to production. The normal fixed manufacturing overhead rate would be set at an amount designed to apply total costs over the entire year. Thus, in the Bridgeport plant, we would expect fixed manufacturing overhead to be underapplied during the first two quarters and overapplied by a compensating amount during the last two quarters.

Budgets of production costs alone are not sufficient for planning purposes. Schedules of the projected production of each product or group of products are also needed. Table 7–4 is a unit production schedule for electric mixers, only one of the several products of the small appliance department of the Mission Electric Corporation. In this department, the individual products are sufficiently different from one another that production planning by product groups is not practical. In the electrical parts department, on the other hand, unit production schedules are prepared for product types, such as fuses and brushes of all sizes and styles. Note in Table 7–4 that the production schedule for mixers shows a seasonal pattern that leads the seasonal sales pattern by a quarter. As a consequence, the inventory of finished mixers will be increased during the first three quarters of the year. There will also be a net increase in

## TABLE 7–4

MISSION ELECTRIC CORPORATION
Bridgeport Plant
Unit Production Schedule—Mixers
1977
(in units of output)

| | Quarter | | | | Totals for Year |
| --- | --- | --- | --- | --- | --- |
| | First | Second | Third | Fourth | |
| Inventory at beginning of period.... | 20,000 | 21,000 | 40,000 | 45,000 | 20,000 |
| Current production................ | 35,000 | 45,000 | 55,000 | 45,000 | 180,000 |
| | 55,000 | 66,000 | 95,000 | 90,000 | 200,000 |
| Current shipments................ | 34,000 | 26,000 | 50,000 | 56,000 | 166,000 |
| Inventory at end of period......... | 21,000 | 40,000 | 45,000 | 34,000 | 34,000 |

inventory over the course of the year (from 20,000 to 34,000 units). This increase reflects management's expectation that sales of mixers will continue to grow in 1978.

### Labor Budget

Where the maximum practical output of a plant is not required to meet projected sales demand, there is a degree of flexibility for management in the scheduling of production. Within this range of flexibility, production may be planned so as to minimize the total costs of manufacturing. This objective may be accomplished in different ways in different firms. In many firms, it can best be achieved by making maximum use of a stable work force. Work force stability may be reflected in a constant work force or in one that is growing at a stable rate, as in the Bridgeport plant of the Mission Electric Corporation (cf. budgeted direct labor amounts in Table 7–3). A stable work force with minimum turnover is likely to enhance employees' morale and efficiency and also to minimize employment and training costs. If there are significant seasonal variations in total sales volume, a stable work force requires seasonal buildups and liquidations of inventory. There are, of course, additional costs associated with inventory buildups—costs of financing and storing the larger inventory. These costs may partially offset the savings associated with work force stability, or they may even override those savings. In the latter case, it would be more economical to minimize inventory costs and accept the disadvantages of a fluctuating work force.

If work force stability is management's objective, it will be a major determinant of the production schedule for each manufacturing responsibility center. The labor cost budget then follows from the production schedule. Mechanically, the development of the labor budget is quite simple. Planned production in units during each time period is multiplied by the amount of time that each class of worker must spend on those units and then by the hourly wage rate for that class of worker. The total labor cost budget for the period is then the summation of these individual amounts. The time required by each class of worker for each product is usually determined by engineering studies.[1]

## Materials Budget

While both direct labor and direct materials are normally variable costs of production, the variability of labor cost within very short time periods is somewhat limited by practical considerations. Workers cannot be laid off as easily as materials can be returned to the storeroom if they are not needed. Thus, planning for reasonable work force stability is a logical approach to the labor budget in most companies; and work force stability then becomes a significant determinant of the production schedule. Materials cost, on the other hand, usually is completely variable, even within very short periods. Materials can be stored and withdrawn from storage as needed in production. Thus, the materials budget can follow the production schedule in most cases. There are, however, some instances in which the availability of materials is the principal determinant of the production schedule. Food processing is a good example. Generally, fresh vegetables must be packed as soon as they are harvested; and management cannot control the time of harvest. Salmon must be canned in season. In these cases, the materials budget may be the inescapable starting point in production planning.

*Purchase Planning.* The fact that the usage of raw materials is quite flexible does not necessarily mean that they may be purchased according to a schedule dictated simply by fluctuations in production. There are many factors which determine materials purchasing policies. Ideally, materials would be purchased just before they are needed for use in production. In this way, capital required for inventory stocks and for storage facilities would be minimized. There are many cogent reasons for purchasing more than will be needed immediately for production, however. To begin with, some "safety stocks" must be maintained to protect against the uncertainties of both delivery schedules and materials usage. Stock-outs are far too disruptive and costly; they can force the shutdown of an entire production operation. Then, purchases in quantities larger than required immediately may entitle the purchaser to significant quantity discounts. These tend to reduce the total cost of materials. Larger purchases may also be made to build up stocks in anticipation of a price

---

[1] The setting of standard labor times for production operations is discussed more extensively in Chapter 9.

increase or a shortage in supply, perhaps due to an expected strike in suppliers' plants. Two important variables in the determination of materials purchasing policies are the timing of orders and the quantity ordered. Obviously, they are interrelated variables; for larger quantities would be consistent with less frequent orders, and vice versa.

*Inventory Reorder Points.*  Most companies have well defined inventory control systems that include specific rules for the timing of purchase orders. Materials and other goods that are regularly stocked are usually reordered when the inventory balance reaches some predetermined level, called a *reorder point.* This reorder point is determined largely by the normal time lag, or lead-time, between the placement of an order and the delivery of the goods and by the expected volume of usage of the materials during that time lag. Since both the delivery lead time and the usage during that period are uncertain, the reorder point should allow for some safety stock. A major advantage of predetermined reorder points is that the decision analysis for inventory ordering need not be repeated for every purchase order. Management makes the reorder decision and then clerical employees can implement it on signal when the reorder point is reached. Of course, conditions change over time; and reorder points must be reexamined and changed from time to time. Nevertheless, formal management attention need be given to the reorder decision only occasionally, with considerable savings in time and cost as a consequence.

*Economic Order Quantities.*  As noted before, the timing of purchase orders depends partly upon the quantities purchased at each order. Certain factors tend to favor large purchases. Discounts are frequently available for purchases of large quantities. Large orders mean fewer orders, with an accompanying saving of the costs of processing purchase orders, receipts, and vouchers for payments to suppliers. Other factors tend to favor purchases in small quantities. Small purchases lead to small inventories and low inventory carrying costs, including both storage costs and interest on the investment in inventory. Purchasing in small lots leaves a firm more flexible as regards possible changes in products or in production schedules. Of course, the volume of usage of the materials is also a major determinant of the quantity in which they are ordered. Management must weigh all of these factors, some of which are conflicting, and determine the most advantageous size for purchase orders.

The order size that results in the minimization of the total costs of buying, storing, and using materials is referred to as the *economic order quantity,* or EOQ. The economic order quantity may be computed by a formula such as the following one:

$$EOQ = \sqrt{\frac{2CS}{UI + A}}$$

where

$C$ = cost of placing one order for materials,
$S$ = number of units required for use in one year,
$U$ = unit cost of the material,
$I$ = interest rate that the firm pays for its capital, and
$A$ = cost of carrying one unit in stock for one year.[2]

This formula will produce very useful results if the five independent variables are estimated with reasonable accuracy. Some of them may be fairly easy to measure, but others are not. The cost of placing an order $(C)$ is usually quite difficult to measure. It should include only the variable costs of processing one order; the fixed costs of order processing, which are unaffected by the number of orders placed, should not be included. The annual usage requirements for a particular material $(S)$ can be estimated with the same degree of reliability as the production budget for those products that use that material. The unit cost of the material $(U)$ is probably the easiest quantity to measure, particularly where it is a standard commodity sold at published list prices. The interest paid for capital $(I)$ may be fairly difficult to determine exactly, but a reasonable approximation can usually be made. The method of computing a firm's interest cost, or cost of capital, is presented in Chapter 16. Finally, the annual carrying cost of materials inventory $(A)$ may be quite difficult to measure. It should include only the variable costs of storing and handling the particular material in question. Fixed storage costs which are common to all materials should not be considered here. Thus, the economic order quantity formula may be expected to yield a reasonable indication of the optimal purchase quantity. Like all budget estimates, of course, it is subject to some degree of uncertainty and potential inaccuracy. Nevertheless, when used intelligently, it can be a very constructive aid to management's planning and control of materials cost.

*Materials Purchase Schedule.*   As part of the total production budget, there should be a schedule of the purchases of each raw material or class of materials used in manufacturing operations. This schedule should identify the material, its principal uses, the major suppliers, and the planned orders, purchases (or receipts), usage, and inventory balances during the budget period. Table 7–5 is an illustration of such a schedule. It covers purchases of the steel housing used in the assembly of mixers in the Bridgeport plant of the Mission Electric Corporation. Since the suppliers must manufacture these housings to Mission's specifications, there is a three-month lead time for orders. Thus, housings are ordered in one quarter and received in the following quarter. They are, of course, not

---

[2] Adapted from Robert I. Dickey (ed.) *Accountants' Cost Handbook,* 2nd ed. (New York: The Ronald Press Company, 1960), p. 5.16. In some variations of this *EOQ* formula, $A$ is expressed as a percentage of $U$. Then $A$ and $I$ are summed and treated as a single factor to be multiplied by $U$.

**TABLE 7–5**

MISSION ELECTRIC CORPORATION
Bridgeport Plant
Materials Purchase Schedule
1977

| Item    mixer housing | Suppliers | Renfrew Tool & Die Co. |
|---|---|---|
| Stock no.    8072 | | Grace Stamping Division |
| Uses    all electric mixers | | Intel, Inc. |

| | Quarter | | | | Totals for Year |
|---|---|---|---|---|---|
| | *First* | *Second* | *Third* | *Fourth* | |
| Orders......................... | 50,000 | 50,000 | 45,000 | 50,000 | 195,000 |
| Inventory at beginning of period.... | 15,000 | 19,650 | 24,200 | 18,650 | 15,000 |
| Purchases (receipts)............... | 40,000 | 50,000 | 50,000 | 45,000 | 185,000 |
| | 55,000 | 69,650 | 74,200 | 63,650 | 200,000 |
| Usage......................... | 35,350 | 45,450 | 55,550 | 45,450 | 181,800 |
| Inventory at end of period......... | 19,650 | 24,200 | 18,650 | 18,200 | 18,200 |

recorded as purchases until they are received. Because of the set-up costs in the suppliers' plants, it is more economical for the corporation to purchase a full quarter's requirements of these housings on one order. A safety stock equal to at least one third of the following quarter's budgeted usage is planned for the end of each period. Note that budgeted usage in each quarter is 1 percent greater than budgeted production of mixers in that quarter (cf. Table 7–4). This excess allows for unavoidable damage to housings and defective housings discovered in the assembly process.

## Manufacturing Overhead Budgets

Indirect manufacturing costs should be budgeted initially by the departments, or responsibility centers, in which they will be incurred. The exact methodology for estimating these costs will vary somewhat with the natures of the different cost items. In general, of course, variable manufacturing overhead will be planned in relation to production volume; and fixed manufacturing overhead is planned independently of volume. More extensive discussion of the budgeting of manufacturing overhead will be found in Chapter 8.

## BUDGETS OF NONMANUFACTURING COSTS

Budgets for distribution, administrative, and research and development costs are typically prepared in essentially the same way as budgets for manufacturing overhead. They are normally developed on departmental bases appropriate in the particular firm. To the extent practical, they also should be subclassified into variable and fixed costs. Of course, the volume base for cost variability is not likely to be production volume in the case of nonmanufacturing costs. Whatever volume measure is determined to cause the incurrence of variable costs should be selected. Sales volume might be appropriate in a selling department; clerical work volume might be used in an administrative department. Of course, it is entirely possible that some departments will have only fixed costs in their budgets. In such a case, no volume measure need be considered in preparing the budget. Specific problems and approaches to the planning and control of nonmanufacturing costs are discussed in Chapter 11.

## WORKING CAPITAL BUDGET

The preceding sections have dealt with the operating budget, the planned revenues and expenses during the budget period. The master budget must also provide plans for the flows of capital necessary for the firm's continuing operations. Roughly, capital may be subclassified into long-term and short-term capital. Long-term capital consists of those financial resources that are invested in the firm for long or indefinite periods of time; it is often referred to as the capital structure of the firm. Short-term capital is that pool of resources that regularly flow into and out of the firm in connection with ongoing operations. The distinction between long-term and short-term capital is not always a clear one, but it is useful for purposes of discussion.

Short-term financial resources are usually identified with working capital, the excess of current assets over current liabilities. By definition, current assets are those that are in the form of cash or are expected to be converted into cash or consumed in operations during the normal operating cycle of the firm. They typically consist of cash, short-term marketable securities, receivables, inventories, and prepaid expenses. Current liabilities are those obligations that are expected to be paid out of current assets during the normal operating cycle. They usually include accounts and notes payable, accrued liabilities, and current maturities of long-term debts. Since working capital is the excess of current assets over current liabilities, it reflects an investment of long-term capital in the net short-term assets required for operations.

The annual working capital budget is essentially a schedule of expected inflows (or sources) and outflows (or uses) of working capital during the budget period. Both inflows and outflows are classified according to their natures. Typically, most inflows and outflows are associated with normal operations. Working capital is received from sales of products and services and is used in the purchase of the materials and services required to produce and sell products and to sustain other operations. Working capital may also be obtained from nonoperating sources, such as new long-term borrowing, new capital investments by owners, and sales of noncurrent assets (e.g., unused facilities). Nonoperating uses of working capital include such transactions as purchases of noncurrent assets, retirement of long-term debt, and payment of dividends to owners. The working capital budget, thus, is essentially a budgeted statement of changes in financial position.

The working capital budget for the Mission Electric Corporation is presented in Table 7–6. Its format is that of the typical statement of changes in financial position. The net amount of working capital expected to be generated from normal operations is shown first, and then nonoperating sources and uses of working capital follow. The major operating source of working capital is sales, and the major operating uses are current operating out-of-pocket costs. Thus, the budgeted net change in working capital as a result of operations is the same as budgeted net income from operations, except for such expenses as depreciation which are not out-of-pocket costs and entail no current use of working capital. Table 7–6 shows the development of the net working capital from operations by subtracting out-of-pocket operating costs from sales revenue. An alternative approach that is more often seen in end-of-year statements of changes in financial position is to begin with net income and

**TABLE 7–6**

MISSION ELECTRIC CORPORATION
Working Capital Budget
1977
(in thousands of dollars)

| | Quarter | | | | Totals for Year |
|---|---|---|---|---|---|
| | First | Second | Third | Fourth | |
| *Sources of working capital* | | | | | |
| Operations: | | | | | |
| Sales.................. | $18,000 | $19,000 | $24,000 | $29,000 | $90,000 |
| Out-of-pocket costs........ | 16,664 | 17,412 | 21,152 | 24,892 | 80,120 |
| | $ 1,336 | $ 1,588 | $ 2,848 | $ 4,108 | $ 9,880 |
| Sale of land............... | 1,500 | | | | 1,500 |
| Long-term borrowing........ | | | 8,000 | | 8,000 |
| Total sources.......... | $ 2,836 | $ 1,588 | $10,848 | $ 4,108 | $19,380 |
| *Uses of working capital* | | | | | |
| Dividends................. | $ 750 | $ 750 | $ 750 | $ 750 | $ 3,000 |
| Purchase of warehouse....... | | | 10,000 | | 10,000 |
| Retirement of bonds........ | | 2,000 | | | 2,000 |
| Total uses............. | $ 750 | $ 2,750 | $10,750 | $ 750 | $15,000 |
| Net increase (decrease) in working capital............ | $ 2,086 | $(1,162) | $ 98 | $ 3,358 | $ 4,380 |

add back depreciation for the period. The net flow of working capital from operations is the same by either approach, of course. The Mission Electric Corporation plans to sell land which it no longer needs for operating purposes early in the year. This sale will produce additional working capital. In the third quarter, the corporation plans to take possession of a new warehouse for sales in the western territory. The warehouse will cost $10 million, of which the company will pay $2 million from internally general funds and will borrow the remaining $8 million on a long-term mortgage note. These nonoperating working capital flows are both projected in the third quarter. A serial instalment of bonds becomes due and payable at the end of June, and this nonoperating outflow of working capital is budgeted in the second quarter. Finally, the regular quarterly dividend is budgeted for each quarter.

## Cash Budget

One particular current asset is of such great importance to an organization that considerable management attention is devoted to it alone, and it is typically planned with great care and in great detail. This asset is cash. Cash is a critical asset in every firm. Ultimately, virtually every transaction involves a receipt or a payment of cash. Cash is uniquely convertible into any other type of asset, and it is uniquely required for the settlement of almost all liabilities. A firm must have the right amount of cash, and it must have it at the right time. Both too little and too much cash are undesirable from the point of view of good financial management. A certain amount of cash is necessary in order to carry on normal day-to-day operations. Payrolls and other current obligations must be met on time. However, cash is not an earning asset. No revenue derives from holding cash itself, whereas revenue does derive from such other assets as inventory, plant facilities, and investments in securities. Thus, too little cash endangers the liquidity of a company and too much cash tends to restrict profitability. The basic objective of cash budgeting is to plan cash profitably, that is, to plan for sufficient cash at all times to meet the needs of current operations and of such long-term projects as will require cash during the budget period but for no more cash than is reasonably necessary for these purposes. Of course, cash planning, like all budgeting, is subject to uncertainty. Hence, the cash budget must provide for more cash than the minimum amount required in order to allow some margin for error in planning. Further, management should always be prepared to obtain additional cash in the event that the planned sources fail to provide the needed cash on time. Established lines of credit at banks typically provide this additional cash availability.

Table 7–7 is a cash budget for the Mission Electric Corporation for 1977. Cash flows associated with normal operations are shown separately

**TABLE 7–7**

MISSION ELECTRIC CORPORATION
Cash Budget
1977
(in thousands of dollars)

| | Quarter | | | | Totals for Year |
| --- | --- | --- | --- | --- | --- |
| | *First* | *Second* | *Third* | *Fourth* | |
| Operating receipts: | | | | | |
| Collections on account: | | | | | |
| Current quarter's sales.... | $ 7,200 | $ 7,600 | $ 9,600 | $11,600 | $36,000 |
| Prior quarter's sales...... | 10,350 | 8,100 | 8,550 | 10,800 | 37,800 |
| Second prior quarter's sales................. | 2,600 | 2,990 | 2,340 | 2,470 | 10,400 |
| | $20,150 | $18,690 | $20,490 | $24,870 | $84,200 |
| Operating outlays: | | | | | |
| Payrolls.................. | $ 7,400 | $ 8,450 | $ 9,700 | $ 9,950 | $35,500 |
| Payments to suppliers...... | 2,800 | 3,400 | 3,900 | 3,900 | 14,000 |
| Manufacturing overhead.... | 4,140 | 4,340 | 4,550 | 4,550 | 17,580 |
| Selling expenses........... | 1,240 | 1,270 | 1,420 | 1,570 | 5,500 |
| Administrative expenses..... | 600 | 600 | 600 | 600 | 2,400 |
| Research and development expenses................ | 300 | 300 | 300 | 300 | 1,200 |
| Interest expense........... | | 280 | | 240 | 520 |
| Income taxes............. | | 1,960 | 980 | 980 | 3,920 |
| | $16,480 | $20,600 | $21,450 | $22,090 | $80,620 |
| Net cash flow from operations.. | $ 3,670 | $(1,910) | $( 960) | $ 2,780 | $ 3,580 |
| Nonoperating receipts: | | | | | |
| Sale of land............... | $ 1,500 | | | | $ 1,500 |
| Long-term borrowing....... | | | $ 8,000 | | 8,000 |
| | $ 1,500 | | $ 8,000 | | $ 9,500 |
| Gross cash inflow (outflow).... | $ 5,170 | $(1,910) | $ 7,040 | $ 2,780 | $13,080 |
| Nonoperating outlays: | | | | | |
| Dividends................. | $   750 | $    750 | $    750 | $    750 | $ 3,000 |
| Purchase of warehouse...... | | | 10,000 | | 10,000 |
| Retirement of bonds........ | | 2,000 | | | 2,000 |
| | $   750 | $ 2,750 | $10,750 | $    750 | $15,000 |
| Net cash inflow (outflow)...... | $ 4,420 | $(4,660) | $(3,710) | $ 2,030 | $(1,920) |
| Beginning cash balance....... | 3,200 | 7,620 | 2,960 | 2,500 | 3,200 |
| Total cash available (shortage)................ | $ 7,620 | $ 2,960 | $( 750) | $ 4,530 | $ 1,280 |
| Required short-term borrowing................ | | | 3,250 | | 3,250 |
| Repayment of short-term borrowing................ | | | | (2,030) | (2,030) |
| Ending cash balance.......... | $ 7,620 | $ 2,960 | $ 2,500 | $ 2,500 | $ 2,500 |

from nonoperating flows. The only operating receipts planned are cash collections from customers. All sales are made on account. The firm's experience indicates that collections on account will be made according to the following time schedule: 40 percent of the accounts will be collected during the quarter in which the sale takes place; 45 percent will be collected in the quarter following sale; and 13 percent will be collected in the second quarter after the sale. Two percent of accounts receivable are expected to prove uncollectible. In order to prepare the projection of cash collections, we must know the sales of the last two quarters of 1976 as well as budgeted sales for 1977. Actual sales during the third quarter of 1976 were $20 million, and budgeted sales during the fourth quarter of 1976 are $23 million. (Total actual sales for the last quarter of 1976 would not be known when this cash budget is prepared, as the budget must be completed before the end of the prior year.) Operating cash outlays are broken down into whatever details management finds useful. All payrolls are summarized here in one total, including direct and indirect labor plus selling, administrative, and research salaries. Thus, the budgeted outlays for manufacturing overhead and for nonmanufacturing expenses are out-of-pocket costs other than wages and salaries. Note that the net cash flow from operations is significantly different from the net working capital provided by operations (cf. Table 7–6). There are various reasons for the difference. Sales generate working capital immediately but produce no cash until the accounts receivable are collected. Materials cost is part of the reduction in working capital only when the manufactured products are sold, but a cash outlay is incurred as soon as the suppliers of those materials are paid. Similarly, the out-of-pocket costs in manufacturing overhead reduce working capital as part of the cost of goods sold; but they reduce cash when they are incurred and paid for. Income taxes are reductions of working capital in the quarters in which they are charged to expense. They are cash outlays in the quarters in which they must be remitted to the Department of Treasury under the provisions of the Internal Revenue Code.

Nonoperating cash receipts and outlays are the same nonoperating transactions reflected in the working capital budget (Table 7–6). The net cash inflow (or outflow) during the period is the consequence of both operating and nonoperating cash flows. To this amount is added the cash balance at the beginning of the period. The resulting total is the amount of cash available during the period or the cash shortage in that period. Short-term borrowing is planned to make up any cash shortage. In addition, borrowing may be necessary in order to maintain the minimum required cash balance. No company can tolerate a zero cash balance. The management of the Mission Electric Corporation has established the minimum required balance at $2.5 million. Thus, in the third quarter, the company plans to borrow enough cash to offset the cash shortage and to restore the ending balance to that minimum amount. In the fourth quarter, sufficient cash is expected to be received that most of the short-term borrowing can be repaid and still leave the minimum cash balance considered necessary.

*Profitable Cash Management.* The cash budget in Table 7–7 is adequate to give management a general notion of the projected cash flows and cash requirements for the year. It is not nearly detailed enough to be a basis for management of the cash balance, however. For this purpose, daily cash projections are necessary. In most cases, daily projections are made for only short periods at a time (e.g., one week in advance). On a day-by-day basis, financial management must plan the company's cash receipts and outlays and its cash balance. If the balance is in excess of current operating needs, the excess should be invested in short-term marketable securities to provide some revenue from what would otherwise be idle cash. Presumably, the management of the Mission Electric Corporation would plan to make such short-term investments during the first quarter of 1977. If the cash balance is deficient, management must plan for short-term borrowing. This borrowing would be undertaken only when actually needed, however. For example, the Mission Electric Corporation would not plan to borrow at the beginning of the third quarter if the cash shortage would not appear until the latter part of August. And the company would plan to repay portions of that borrowing as early in the fourth quarter as cash flows permitted. Generally, financial management seeks to maintain the cash balance just about at the established minimum. That minimum, however, may vary from time to time over the course of the budget period. Greater cash balances may be necessary at times of peak operations than when operating activity is at a low level.

## LONG-TERM CAPITAL PLANNING

In addition to planning the flows of short-term capital into and out of the firm during the budget period, management must plan for changes in its long-term capital. Such changes during the budget period must be included specifically in the organization's financial resource budget for that period. For example, in the working capital budget of the Mission Electric Corporation (Table 7–6), we saw plans for a long-term investment of $10 million in a new warehouse and for new long-term borrowing of $8 million to finance it. Also, retirement of $2 million of outstanding long-term debt was projected. The budget must consider such long-term capital transactions more explicitly to ensure that the amounts and the timing are proper. Moreover, financial management must determine that long-term borrowing is the appropriate means of financing the new warehouse.

The cash and working capital budgets are usually restricted to the immediate budget period, no more than one year in the future. Continued profitable operations require more extensive planning of long-term capital resources, however. There is no logical limit on the number of future periods for which long-term capital should be planned. In general, these resources should be planned as far ahead as is practicable. Planning long-term capital resources involves consideration of two related problems, or decisions. One is the source from which that capital will be obtained, and the other is the use to which that capital will be put. Obviously, sources and uses of capital are closely related. Firms sometimes seek capital with a specific use in mind. A firm that has demonstrated its ability to make profitable use of the capital it obtains will typically find more sources of additional capital open to it. Conversely, persistently unprofitable uses of capital will have the effect of closing off new sources. Nevertheless, obtaining capital and using capital are distinct activities and they entail separate decisions. The decision to obtain capital and the selection of sources of capital is commonly referred to as the *financing decision*. Uses of capital are determined in the *investment decision*. Financing decisions are discussed extensively in business finance texts. They will not be considered directly here. Investment decisions are the subject of Chapters 16 and 17.

## UNCERTAINTY OF BUDGET ESTIMATES

Budgeting involves making estimates of the future value of many different financial quantities. These estimates are, of course, uncertain. Different items are subject to different degrees of uncertainty. For example, the sales forecast is generally subject to a high degree of uncertainty; for it entails projections of external variables as well as of management's actions. An administrative salary budget, on the other hand, would involve a lesser degree of uncertainty; but some unanticipated changes in personnel or in salaries may occur. Most organizations deal implicitly with the problem of uncertainty by simply recognizing that budget estimates are only approximations, albeit the best that can be made at the time. Thus, single values are estimated for all financial quantities; but those single values are admitted to be estimates that may actually prove to be wrong. Obviously, an intelligently chosen single estimate is preferable to no planning at all.

Some accountants and managers have proposed that uncertainty be incorporated explicitly in budgets. This might be accomplished by budgeting all financial quantities as probability distributions rather than as single estimates. For example, sales management might estimate that the sales of a particular product might vary all the way from no units to 100,000 units during the budget period. Of course, sales might assume any value from zero to 100,000; but it would be very cumbersome for management to work with 100,001 alternative possible values. Hence, as a practical expedient, management might select ten representative values and estimate the probability of each of these values occurring. For example, the range from zero to 100,000 might be divided into ten 10,000-unit subranges; and the midpoint of each of these subranges might then be chosen as the representative value. This approach would produce a probability distribution such as the following:

| Sales in Units | Probability |
|---|---|
| 5,000 | .01 |
| 15,000 | .02 |
| 25,000 | .05 |
| 35,000 | .08 |
| 45,000 | .10 |
| 55,000 | .20 |
| 65,000 | .35 |
| 75,000 | .15 |
| 85,000 | .03 |
| 95,000 | .01 |
| | 1.00 |

As always, the sum of the probabilities of all possible alternative events is 1.00. Now, this probability distribution might be accepted as the sales forecast. Similar probability distributions would then be prepared for budgets of sales revenue and of all costs that vary in proportion to the volume of sales of this product. Alternatively, management might use the probability distribution to derive a single value for the sales budget. If this were done, the single value chosen would most likely be the expected value of the sales volume. The *expected value* of a variable is the sum of all possible alternative values, weighted by the probabilities of their occurrence. That is, each alternative sales volume would be multiplied by its probability; and these ten products would then be added to obtain the expected value of the sales in units. In this illustration, the expected value is 57,400 units, computed as follows:

| Sales in Units | × Probability | = Weighted Value |
|---|---|---|
| 5,000 | .01 | 50 |
| 15,000 | .02 | 300 |
| 25,000 | .05 | 1,250 |
| 35,000 | .08 | 2,800 |
| 45,000 | .10 | 4,500 |
| 55,000 | .20 | 11,000 |
| 65,000 | .35 | 22,750 |
| 75,000 | .15 | 11,250 |
| 85,000 | .03 | 2,550 |
| 95,000 | .01 | 950 |
| Expected value | | 57,400 |

The advantage of an expected value is that it is a single value and much easier to work with than a probability distribution itself. Its principal disadvantage is that it depends upon management's estimates of probabilities. These are inevitably subjective probabilities, and management may doubt its ability to assign probabilities to all of the alternative possible values for a particular variable. Nevertheless, the effort of thinking about probabilities of alternative outcomes may be beneficial to management, even if the resultant expected value is not viewed with a great deal of confidence.

## BUDGETED FINANCIAL STATEMENTS

The comprehensive master budget frequently includes budgeted statements comparable to the actual financial statements that will be prepared at the end of the period. These budgeted statements will probably be prepared for the same time intervals that actual statements will later be prepared (e.g., quarterly). The operating budget is typically summarized in the form of a budgeted income statement. A budgeted balance sheet may also be included, although this is less likely. One study of budget practices showed that 98 percent of the firms observed prepared budgeted income statements, whereas only 56 percent of them prepared budgeted balance sheets.[3] A budgeted statement of changes in financial position is normally included in the form of the working capital budget (Table 7–6).

## BUDGET REVIEW REPORTS

The importance of budgetary review was mentioned in Chapter 6. Budget review usually involves a comparison of actual data with the parallel budget data. Any difference is identified as a variance from the budget. Since budgeting is an uncertain art, some variance from the budget is always expected. Fairly large variances may be taken as signals to operating managers that plans are not being realized. If the variance is in a direction that is unfavorable to the firm's economic interests (e.g., sales below or expenses above expectations), corrective action may be taken. There is no uniform format in which budget review reports should be prepared. The one in Table 7–8 is quite frequently used, however. It is simple to understand and it focuses attention on variances. It compares actual and budgeted sales volumes of small appliances in the midwestern sales territory of the Mission Electric Corporation for the third quarter of 1977 and also for the year to date (i.e., the first nine

---

[3] Burnard H. Sord and Glenn A. Welsch, *Business Budgeting: A Survey of Management Planning and Control Practices* (New York: Controllership Foundation, Inc., 1958), pp. 277 and 280.

months of 1977). Favorable variances from the budget (actual sales greater than budgeted) are shown as positive numbers, and unfavorable variances (actual sales less than budgeted) are shown in parentheses as negative amounts. This sales report is prepared in physical units. A similar report might be prepared in dollar sales volume. Such a report must be used carefully, however; for it would not immediately distinguish variances due to changes in volume of sales from variances due to changes in selling prices. Note that no totals are shown in Table 7-8, for they would not be meaningful to management. Sales performances of the individual products are important to sales management if this report is

**TABLE 7-8**

MISSION ELECTRIC CORPORATION
Midwestern Sales Territory
Sales Report—Small Appliances
For the Quarter Ended September 30, 1977

| | *Sales in Units* | | | | | |
|---|---|---|---|---|---|---|
| | *Third Quarter* | | | *Year to Date* | | |
| | *Actual* | *Budget* | *Variance* | *Actual* | *Budget* | *Variance* |
| Mixers............. | 13,200 | 12,500 | 700 | 33,400 | 32,000 | 1,400 |
| Blenders........... | 18,800 | 17,500 | 1,300 | 45,500 | 42,500 | 3,000 |
| Toasters........... | 16,600 | 18,000 | (1,400) | 41,200 | 44,000 | (2,800) |
| Irons.............. | 22,800 | 24,000 | (1,200) | 54,500 | 60,000 | (5,500) |
| Coffee pots......... | 16,600 | 16,000 | 600 | 39,000 | 37,500 | 1,500 |
| Waffle irons......... | 9,900 | 11,000 | (1,100) | 28,400 | 27,000 | 1,400 |
| Heating pads....... | 6,200 | 6,000 | 200 | 15,800 | 17,000 | (1,200) |

to be the basis for any action. For example, sales of toasters and irons are consistently below expectations for the quarter and for the year to date. This shortcoming should not be ignored simply because sales of mixers and blenders are better than planned.

Knowing the amounts of the variances of actual data from the budget is only the beginning of control, of course. The really important step is the next one, attempting to determine exactly *why* these variances occurred. Causes of favorable variances are as important as causes of unfavorable variances. If management can ascertain why mixers and blenders are selling so well, it may be able to take positive action to reinforce and extend the sales improvement. On the other hand, the causes of the lower demand for the company's toasters and irons should be sought and, if possible, corrected.

Similar reports would be prepared for other product lines and other sales territories. Essentially the same report format might be used for various types of expenses. Expense reports will be illustrated in the next chapter.

## QUESTIONS FOR DISCUSSION

1.  Given the budgeted sales volume for a period, a planned inventory balance at the end of the period, and the prospect of adequate capital to finance operations, with which element of production cost (materials, labor, or manufacturing overhead) would you begin the preparation of a production cost budget? Why?

2.  If you were the budget director of a large manufacturing company with sales outlets in ten different sales territories and several hundred salesmen, how would you go about preparing the initial draft of a sales forecast?

3.  Some companies determine the compensation of their salesmen partly on the basis of sales in excess of predetermined sales quotas. Should all sales quotas be equal to budgeted sales for the period? If so, why? If not, why not and what should be the relationship between the sales budget and sales quotas?

4.  What alternatives with respect to the timing of production are available to a firm that experiences significant seasonal variations in the volume of its sales? Discuss the advantages and disadvantages of each of these alternatives.

5.  Under what conditions would you advise a firm to budget sales in total dollar volume only, without specific plans for sales of individual products in units?

6.  It has been suggested that the planned level of inventory of finished product at the end of a budget period should be a partial determinant of the physical production volume budgeted for that period. How would management decide what the level of the ending inventory should be?

7.  List all of the factors that you would take into consideration in preparing a materials purchase schedule, and list them in what you believe to be the order of their relative importance.

8.  How would the five independent variables in the economic order quantity formula be measured in practice? Which ones would you expect to be the easiest to measure? Which ones would you expect to be most difficult to measure? Why?

9.  How would the budgeting of each of the following operating costs be different from the budgeting of the others:
    *a.* Direct materials?
    *b.* Repair and maintenance of production equipment?
    *c.* Research and development?
    *d.* Depreciation?

10. Distinguish between short-term and long-term capital. Of what significance to management is this distinction?

11. What basic rules should be observed in effective cash planning?

12. Cash budgeting has sometimes been described as the process of reconciling conflicting objectives regarding cash in the most satisfactory possible compromise. To what conflicting objectives does this description refer? Is the conflict real or imagined?

13. How might alternative accounting standards affect a budget? Give some examples.

14. What is the difference between a financing decision and an investment decision?

15. Why do you suppose that more business firms prepared budgeted income statements than prepare budgeted balance sheets? Do you believe these reasons are valid?

16. What is the expected value of a budgeted financial quantity? What are the alternatives to expected values? Which alternative do you feel would normally be most useful to management in budgeting?

17. "The operating budget must be prepared before the financial budgets, for the latter are dependent upon the former, particularly as regards cash and working capital generated by operations. The operating budget is independent of financial budgets, however, and may be completed without regard to them." Discuss the validity of these statements.

## PROBLEMS

7-1. The Java Boat Corporation manufactures fiberglas boat hulls. Actual sales data for 1976 are summarized below.

| | |
|---|---:|
| First quarter............................... | $ 6,000,000 |
| Second quarter............................. | 8,000,000 |
| Third quarter.............................. | 4,000,000 |
| Fourth quarter............................. | 2,000,000 |
| | $20,000,000 |

The seasonal sales pattern experienced in 1976 is typical of the company's operations. For the past several years, the company has realized a steady growth in sales volume of 10% per year. This growth rate is expected to continue through 1977. In view of generally rising prices, the company plans to increase all selling prices by 8% effective on January 1, 1977. This price increase is not expected to affect the trend of growth in sales volume.

*Required:*

a. Prepare a sales forecast by quarters for 1977.

b. Revise this sales forecast to reflect the assumption that the planned price increase will not only halt the growth in sales volume but will actually cause a 5% reduction in volume in 1977.

7-2. Honshu Motor Company, Ltd., of Japan sells three models of cars in three different markets. The domestic market represents sales to Japanese dealers; the commercial market is the sales to Japanese fleet buyers, chiefly leasing companies and large industrial corporations; and the export market reflects sales to foreign dealers. Budgeted sales of the three models in units for 1977 are shown below along with the projected distributions of these sales among the three markets.

| Model | Unit Sales | Market | | |
|---|---|---|---|---|
| | | Domestic | Commercial | Export |
| Deluxe......... | 200,000 | 30% | 10% | 60% |
| Superior....... | 400,000 | 30% | 20% | 50% |
| Standard....... | 800,000 | 50% | 30% | 20% |

Retail list prices of the three models are as follows:

Deluxe................................... 850,000 yen
Superior................................. 680,000 yen
Standard................................ 570,000 yen

Honshu, however, sells the cars to domestic dealers at a 25% discount, to foreign dealers at a 20% discount, and to commercial fleet buyers at a 10% discount.

The expected distribution of sales of all three models by quarters during 1977 is as follows:

First quarter............................ 40%
Second quarter.......................... 30%
Third quarter............................ 20%
Fourth quarter.......................... 10%

*Required:*

a.  Prepare a quarterly sales budget, in yen, by car models.
b.  Prepare a quarterly sales budget, in yen, by markets.

7–3.  Oahu Company, Inc., produces and sells a single product. The 1977 sales forecast in units of product is as follows:

First quarter................................... 15,000
Second quarter................................ 18,000
Third quarter.................................. 24,000
Fourth quarter................................ 21,000

The inventory of finished product on January 1, 1977, is expected to contain 5,000 units. The planned inventory at the end of 1977 is 7,000 units.

Production is customarily scheduled to provide for two thirds of the current quarter's sales demand plus one third of the following quarter's demand. Thus, production anticipates sales volume by about one month.

The average variable costs per unit of product are as follows:

Materials (10 lbs. @ $.80)........................ $8.00
Direct labor (1½ hrs. @ $4)...................... 6.00
Manufacturing overhead (1½ hrs. @ $.80).......... 1.20

Fixed manufacturing overhead has been budgeted at $234,000 for 1977. In accordance with the absorption costing method, manufacturing overhead is applied to production at normal rates per direct labor hour.

*Required:*

a. Prepare a production budget by quarters. Show the number of units produced and the total costs for materials, direct labor, and manufacturing overhead.

b. Explain the way you included fixed manufacturing overhead in this production budget. Did you include any under- or overapplied manufacturing overhead? Why?

7–4. The Kauai Company uses 80,000 gallons of a chemical acid each year. This acid costs $25 per gallon, and the annual cost of carrying one gallon in inventory is $1.50. The company estimates that each purchase order, including all processing and handling, costs $100. The average interest paid by the company is 10%.

*Required:*

Compute the economic order quantity for purchases of this chemical acid.

7–5. The Maui Corporation wishes to purchase its raw materials in the most economical lot sizes. In order to achieve this objective, it applies the following economic order quantity formula to each of the various raw materials that it uses:

$$Q = \sqrt{\frac{2CS}{UI + A}}$$

For one of the company's raw materials, the cost of placing an order $(C)$ is estimated to be $360. The annual usage $(S)$ of this material is approximately 1,500,000 units. The unit cost $(U)$ of the item is $.28. The company's interest cost $(I)$ is 10%. The annual cost of carrying one unit in stock $(A)$ averages $.02.

*Required:*

a. Compute the economic order quantity $(Q)$ in which this material should be purchased.

b. How would you expect each of the five variables under the radical to be measured? Which would you expect to be the most difficult ones to measure?

c. What additional factors, if any, not included in the formula might be considered in determining the lot size in which this material should be ordered?

d. If each of the five variables, in turn, were increased by 20% with no change in any of the others, which increase(s) would have the greatest effect on the economic order quantity? In other words, to which variable(s) is the economic order quantity most sensitive?

7–6. The Hawaii Machine Tool Company manufactures precision instruments in its Ewa plant. There is no notable seasonal pattern to the sales of these instruments. The total production time for the instruments averages one and one-half months from start to finish. On December 31, 1976, there is an inventory of 4,500 finished units on hand. Unit sales for 1977 have been forecast as follows:

| | | | |
|---|---|---|---|
| January | 2,200 | July | 3,200 |
| February | 2,400 | August | 3,300 |
| March | 2,500 | September | 3,500 |
| April | 2,600 | October | 3,600 |
| May | 2,800 | November | 3,800 |
| June | 3,000 | December | 3,900 |

The maximum productive capacity of the plant at present is 4,000 units of output per month.

*Required:*

a. Prepare a monthly production schedule in units for 1977. This schedule should show units produced (i.e., finished), units shipped to customers, and finished units in stock at the end of the month. (You may assume that enough units are in process at the beginning of the year to attain whatever output you budget for the first month and a half of the year.)
b. Explain the inventory balance that you plan for December 31, 1977.
c. On the basis of your production schedule, have you any further observations about the company's operations?

7-7. The Molokai Steel Corporation converts scrap steel into usable ingots. This conversion process requires just one working day. Finished ingots are shipped to customers as soon as possible after completion. For every ton of scrap put into process, there is a yield of .75 ton of usable ingot steel. In carload lots of 500 tons, scrap steel is purchased for $120 per ton. Freight charges for one carload are $2,000. In lots smaller than a carload, the price of scrap steel is $140 per ton; and freight charges on odd lot purchases average $8 per ton.

Ordinarily, orders for scrap steel must be placed one month in advance of the date on which the materials are needed. The company's storage facilities can accommodate a maximum of 15,000 tons of scrap at one time. At December 31, 1976, the inventory of scrap consists of 2,000 tons. In addition, 8,000 tons are on order and are due to arrive on January 1, 1977.

The sales forecast for the year 1977 is as follows:

| Month | Ingot Tons | Month | Ingot Tons |
|---|---|---|---|
| January | 6,000 | July | 9,300 |
| February | 7,200 | August | 8,850 |
| March | 8,100 | September | 8,400 |
| April | 8,700 | October | 7,800 |
| May | 9,000 | November | 7,500 |
| June | 9,600 | December | 7,200 |

Preliminary estimates indicate that about 7,500 ingot tons will be sold in January 1978.

As a matter of company policy, all orders for scrap steel are placed on the first day of a month. Hence, shipments may be expected to arrive on the first day of the following month. It is also company policy that the inventory of scrap steel should not be allowed to fall below 2,000 tons at any time.

*Required:*

Prepare a schedule, by months, of budgeted scrap steel orders, purchases (i.e., receipts of orders), usage, and ending inventory balances in tons. This schedule should conform to production and inventory requirements as stipulated and should seek to minimize materials purchase costs.

7–8. The Bali Machine Company sells light machinery to manufacturers. Sales orders are obtained in two ways. Most are obtained by the company's salesmen when they call on customers. Others, called catalog orders, are placed directly by the customers, usually by mail. The salesmen leave catalogs with all of their customers for this purpose. Salesmen receive commissions of 5% of sales that they obtain personally and 3% of catalog orders received from their territories.

Budgeted sales for 1977 are as follows:

| Quarter | Total Sales | Salesmen's Orders | Catalog Orders |
|---|---|---|---|
| First.................. | $ 8,000,000 | 80% | 20% |
| Second.............. | 12,000,000 | 75% | 25% |
| Third................ | 15,000,000 | 60% | 40% |
| Fourth.............. | 10,000,000 | 80% | 20% |

Shipping and billing expenses average 4% of sales revenue, regardless of the source of the order. Fixed selling expenses for 1977 have been budgeted as follows:

| | |
|---|---|
| Sales salaries............................. | $ 500,000 |
| Advertising............................... | 2,000,000 |
| Travel.................................... | 600,000 |

Sales salaries and travel expenses are paid in a fairly steady flow throughout the year. Advertising expenditures, however, are made at irregular intervals in varying amounts. Their exact timing is difficult to predict, as it depends upon receipts of bills from advertising agencies.

*Required:*

a. Prepare a budget of selling expenses, by quarters, for 1977.
b. Explain your allocation of fixed selling expenses to the several quarters.

7–9. The Pitcairn Corporation manufactures two products, Bli and Bou. As of January 1, 1977, the inventory of finished products will include an estimated 20,000 units of Bli and 30,000 units of Bou. The sales forecast in units for 1977 is as follows:

| Quarter | Bli | Bou |
|---|---|---|
| First............................... | 60,000 | 40,000 |
| Second............................. | 40,000 | 40,000 |
| Third............................... | 50,000 | 50,000 |
| Fourth............................. | 70,000 | 60,000 |

The unit selling prices of Bli and Bou are $12 and $20, respectively.

Both products are manufactured from a single raw material, the expected price of which is $1.20 per pound. Production of Bli requires 3 pounds of this material and production of Bou, 4 pounds. As of January 1, 1977, it has been estimated that the inventory of raw material will contain 140,000 pounds and that an additional 250,000 pounds will be on order. Delivery of materials is regularly made about one month after the order is placed. Present storage facilities will hold no more than 400,000 pounds of raw material. The minimum "safety stock" of raw material at any given time is 100,000 pounds. Purchases must be made in lots of 10,000 pounds.

The factory wage rate is $4 per hour. Regular production times are one man-hour for Bli and two man-hours for Bou. The normal variable manufacturing overhead rate has been set at $.90 per man-hour. The maximum productive capacity of the factory is 150,000 man-hours per quarter, and this limit cannot be exceeded during 1977.

Variable selling expenses average 10% of selling prices. Budgeted fixed expenses for 1977 are as follows:

| | |
|---|---|
| Manufacturing................................ | $600,000 |
| Selling......................................... | 200,000 |
| Administration................................ | 300,000 |

The applicable income tax rate is 40%.

Planned inventory balances at December 31, 1977, have been established as follows:

| | |
|---|---|
| Raw material........................... | 150,000 pounds |
| Finished product—Bli.................... | 30,000 units |
| Finished product—Bou................... | 25,000 units |

The finished product warehouse will accommodate a maximum of 75,000 units of product—Bli and/or Bou. Any inventory in excess of that quantity must be stored in public warehouses at a cost of $2 per unit per quarter or fraction thereof in storage. The company's production process is such that there is never any work in process at the end of the day.

*Required:*

Prepare the budget schedules listed below for the Pitcairn Corporation for the year 1977. Each schedule should show details by quarters. Where alternatives appear feasible, select the ones that will tend to minimize costs.

a. Unit production schedule by products.
b. Production cost budget.
c. Materials purchase schedule.
d. Budgeted income statement in accordance with variable costing.

7–10. The Kodiak Corporation manufactures and sells a single product. All sales are for cash at a standard price of $30 per unit. All out-of-pocket costs are paid in cash at the time they are incurred. This includes the cost of raw materials, which are purchased locally every other day as they are required in production. Goods are produced only to customers' orders; there are no inventories.

The sales forecast in units of product for 1977 is as follows:

| | |
|---|---:|
| First quarter.................................... | 10,000 |
| Second quarter................................. | 14,000 |
| Third quarter.................................. | 20,000 |
| Fourth quarter................................. | 16,000 |

Budgeted variable production costs per unit appear below.

| | |
|---|---:|
| Raw materials (10 lbs. @ $.50)...................... | $5 |
| Direct labor (2 hrs. @ $4).......................... | 8 |
| Manufacturing overhead (2 hrs. @ $1.50)............. | 3 |

Fixed manufacturing overhead was budgeted at $400,000 for the year; this amount includes depreciation of $160,000. Production volume has been budgeted at 120,000 labor hours for the year.

Variable selling expenses amount to $.50 per unit sold. Fixed selling expenses are expected to average $50,000 per quarter; included in this total is $20,000 of depreciation expense.

*Required:*

Prepare a budget of cash generated by operations, by quarters, during 1977.

7–11. The Adak Steel Products Company's operating budget for 1977 includes the following revenues and expenses involving cash receipts and disbursements:

| | Quarter | | | |
|---|---:|---:|---:|---:|
| | *First* | *Second* | *Third* | *Fourth* |
| Sales on account...... | $2,500,000 | $2,000,000 | $2,200,000 | $2,800,000 |
| Purchases of materials on account......... | 500,000 | 500,000 | 600,000 | 700,000 |
| Payrolls............. | 800,000 | 800,000 | 900,000 | 1,000,000 |
| Miscellaneous expenses | 400,000 | 400,000 | 400,000 | 400,000 |

The company's experience indicates that 70% of accounts receivable are collected in the quarter in which the sales are made; 20% are collected in the following quarter; 6% are collected in the second following quarter; and 4% prove to be uncollectible. Sales in the third and fourth quarters of 1976 were $1,800,000 and $2,400,000, respectively.

Half of the materials purchased during a quarter are paid for in that quarter, and the other half are paid for in the following quarter. Purchases during the fourth quarter of 1976 totaled $600,000. Payrolls and miscellaneous expenses are paid for in the quarter in which they are incurred.

Nonoperating cash outlays call for dividend payments of $90,000 on the last day of each quarter. In addition, bond interest in the amount of $60,000 is payable on June 30; and $40,000 is payable on December 31. Further, serial bonds in the principal amount of $1,000,000 will mature on June 30, 1977, and must be paid out of the regular cash account.

The cash balance on January 1, 1977, will be $120,000. The minimum cash balance considered necessary is $100,000.

*Required:*

Prepare a cash budget, by quarters, for 1977. If borrowing is necessary at any time during the year, include it in this budget. Assume that any borrowing will be for a period of one quarter (but may be refinanced by new loans for additional periods of one quarter) and will bear interest at 8% per annum.

7–12.  The Malta Power & Light Company has completed its operating budget for 1977 and has prepared the following monthly analysis of budgeted cash provided by (or consumed in) operations:

| | | | |
|---|---:|---|---:|
| January............ | $ 80,000 | July............... | $( 60,000) |
| February........... | 60,000 | August............. | ( 30,000) |
| March............. | 25,000 | September.......... | 20,000 |
| April.............. | ( 10,000) | October............ | 50,000 |
| May............... | ( 75,000) | November.......... | 90,000 |
| June.............. | (100,000) | December.......... | 100,000 |

The company adheres to a strict policy of cash management that is designed to provide adequate cash balances at all times and to avoid excessive balances. If the cash balance is between $50,000 and $100,000, the cash position is regarded as satisfactory and no specific action is taken. If the balance exceeds $100,000, the excess is invested in short-term marketable securities. These securities will be purchased and, when necessary, resold in even multiples of $1,000. They will earn interest at an annual rate of 6%, collectible when the securities are resold. For planning purposes, no gain or loss is anticipated on resale of marketable securities.

If the cash balance falls below $50,000, any short-term securities held will be sold. If the proceeds from such sales are not sufficient to restore the balance to $50,000, cash will be borrowed in even multiples of $1,000 at an annual interest rate of 10%, payable when the loans are repaid. As soon as the cash position permits, these short-term loans will be repaid in $1,000 blocks.

As of January 1, 1977, the cash balance is expected to be $70,000. There will be no marketable securities on hand and no outstanding loans payable.

*Required:*

Prepare a cash budget, by months, showing (a) cash balances, (b) cash provided by or consumed in operations, (c) amounts to be invested in short-term securities, (d) resales of short-term securities, (e) short-term borrowing, and (f) repayments of short-term loans. For simplicity, it may be assumed that all cash transactions occur on the last day of the month. Apply a first-in, first-out assumption when short-term securities are resold and when loans are repaid.

7–13. The Truk Corporation is in the midst of a major expansion program. Its new plant building is scheduled for completion on September 30, 1977. Construction contract payments must be made as the work progresses, in accordance with the following fixed schedule:

| | |
|---|---:|
| February 1, 1977 | $ 200,000 |
| April 1, 1977 | 200,000 |
| June 1, 1977 | 250,000 |
| August 1, 1977 | 400,000 |
| September 30, 1977 | 550,000 |
| | $1,600,000 |

As of January 1, 1977, the corporation has a sinking fund for plant expansion that consisted of marketable securities with a total market value of $800,000. This market value is not expected to change during the first nine months of 1977. The sinking fund securities yield a rate of return of 5% per annum. All sinking fund earnings through December 31, 1976, have already been collected. Earnings in 1977 will be collected as the securities are sold to meet contract payments. The sinking fund can be used only for payments to the construction contractor.

The cash balance on January 1, 1977, is $50,000. Cash provided by (or consumed in) operations during 1977 is budgeted as follows:

| | | | |
|---|---:|---|---:|
| January | $ 40,000 | July | $30,000 |
| February | 50,000 | August | 60,000 |
| March | 20,000 | September | 80,000 |
| April | (30,000) | October | 50,000 |
| May | (70,000) | November | 40,000 |
| June | (10,000) | December | 20,000 |

A minimum cash balance of $50,000 is considered necessary. Balances in excess of that amount will be held as cash rather than being invested, however.

Any construction contract payments that cannot be met from operating sources or from the liquidation of sinking fund securities will be financed by borrowing at 8%. Any such borrowing will be repaid as soon as possible. Loan repayments will include accrued interest on the amounts repaid.

*Required:*

Prepare a monthly budget showing (*a*) cash flow from operations, (*b*) cash realized on sales of sinking fund securities, (*c*) cash borrowed, (*d*) construction contract payments, (*e*) loan repayments, and (*f*) cash balances. Assume that securities will be sold and that loans will be made and repaid in even multiples of $1,000 (exclusive of interest).

7–14.  The Catalina Appliance Store plans to begin operations on January 1, 1977. Estimated sales, in units, for the first six months of that year are as follows:

| | |
|---|---:|
| January.......................................... | 100 |
| February......................................... | 160 |
| March............................................ | 180 |
| April............................................ | 220 |
| May.............................................. | 380 |
| June............................................. | 360 |

Each appliance will be sold at a list price of $200. It is anticipated that 25% of sales will be for cash and the remainder on installment contracts. The installment contract will require a down payment of 10% of the price and 10 monthly payments of $20 each, including all finance charges.

The store will purchase appliances for $125 each. Purchases will be financed by paying 20% down and giving a noninterest bearing note for the balance. This balance must be paid at the end of the month in which the appliance is sold. An average inventory of 200 units is to be kept in stock.

The store plans to use the installment contracts as collateral for bank loans equal to 60% of the unpaid balance on all new installment contracts obtained each month. These loans must be repaid monthly in an amount equal to 60% of the installment collections for the month. The interest charge on these bank loans will be 6% per annum on the balance of loans outstanding at the end of the preceding month. Interest will be paid monthly.

Salesmen will receive a commission of $20 on each appliance sold. The commission is payable in the month of sale. Other variable out-of-pocket expenses will be $30 per unit sold. Fixed out-of-pocket expenses are expected to average $1,200 per month.

Receipt of the bank loans and repayments thereof will be effected on the last day of the month.

*Required:*

Prepare a cash budget, by months, for the first half of 1977. Include any appropriate supporting schedules. It will be the company's policy to maintain a minimum cash balance of $5,000. Any deficiency of cash provided from the business will be made up by additional investments by the owner of the store.

(Adapted from CPA Examination)

7-15.   The Tahiti Beverage Company plans to introduce a new soft drink, called Polynesian Punch, in 1977. Forecasted sales volumes, in cases, for the company's five sales territories during 1977 are as follows:

| Month | East | South | Midwest | West | Foreign |
|---|---|---|---|---|---|
| January.......... | 6,000 | 8,000 | 7,000 | 10,000 | 4,000 |
| February......... | 8,000 | 9,000 | 8,000 | 14,000 | 5,000 |
| March.......... | 10,000 | 10,000 | 8,000 | 16,000 | 6,000 |
| April........... | 12,000 | 12,000 | 9,000 | 18,000 | 6,000 |
| May............ | 15,000 | 14,000 | 10,000 | 20,000 | 7,000 |
| June........... | 18,000 | 17,000 | 12,000 | 24,000 | 8,000 |
| July............ | 22,000 | 23,000 | 15,000 | 27,000 | 8,000 |
| August.......... | 27,000 | 28,000 | 18,000 | 30,000 | 8,000 |
| September....... | 24,000 | 26,000 | 16,000 | 28,000 | 8,000 |
| October......... | 20,000 | 23,000 | 14,000 | 25,000 | 8,000 |
| November....... | 18,000 | 21,000 | 13,000 | 22,000 | 8,000 |
| December....... | 15,000 | 20,000 | 13,000 | 20,000 | 8,000 |

Actual sales data for the first six months of 1977 show the following numbers of cases sold in the five territories:

| Month | East | South | Midwest | West | Foreign |
|---|---|---|---|---|---|
| January.......... | 6,750 | 4,500 | 5,770 | 9,500 | 5,500 |
| February......... | 8,200 | 5,800 | 6,820 | 12,640 | 7,250 |
| March.......... | 11,480 | 7,250 | 7,250 | 12,380 | 4,860 |
| April........... | 12,550 | 9,660 | 8,800 | 13,650 | 5,300 |
| May............ | 13,800 | 11,250 | 10,500 | 12,620 | 3,920 |
| June........... | 15,740 | 12,980 | 14,430 | 12,200 | 6,660 |

All domestic sales were made at the standard list price of $2.40 per case. Foreign sales were made at a standard export price of $2.70 per case.

*Required:*

a.  Prepare a sales report that will be useful for purposes of budget review.

b.  On the basis of this report, can you draw any generalizations about the original sales forecast for Polynesian Punch?

7-16.   The Prince Edward Doll Company makes five different dolls. All sales are to toy wholesalers and large retailers at the same prices. The budgeted sales volume in units and the list prices planned for the month of December 1976 were as follows:

| Doll | Budgeted Units | List Price |
|---|---|---|
| Dancing Dolores................... | 9,000 | $10.00 |
| Raggedy Randy................... | 10,000 | 4.50 |
| Sleepy Sally...................... | 7,500 | 8.00 |
| Sophisticated Suzette.............. | 6,000 | 15.00 |
| Talking Tommy................... | 12,000 | 12.00 |

Actual sales in units and in total dollars of revenue for December were reported as follows:

| Doll | Units | Dollars |
|---|---|---|
| Dancing Dolores................... | 9,900 | $ 97,020 |
| Raggedy Randy................... | 8,200 | 29,520 |
| Sleepy Sally...................... | 8,100 | 64,800 |
| Sophisticated Suzette.............. | 6,300 | 102,060 |
| Talking Tommy................... | 10,200 | 116,280 |
| | | $409,680 |

*Required:*

a. Prepare a sales report for the month of December to compare actual and budgeted sales in whatever manner you believe would be most useful to management.

b. What differences between actual and budgeted sales volumes would you consider worthy of special attention by management? Why?

c. What additional information might be helpful to management in evaluating the sales report for December?

7–17. Isle Royale Airlines wishes to develop a sales forecast that reflects the uncertainties that exist in its market. Accordingly, it has budgeted total passenger revenue for 1977 at five alternative levels and has made subjective assessments of the probabilities of these alternatives occurring. The results of these projections are shown below.

| | Passenger Revenue | Probability |
|---|---|---|
| Most optimistic volume................ | $36,000,000 | .05 |
| High volume......................... | 30,000,000 | .15 |
| Most likely volume................... | 25,000,000 | .40 |
| Conservative volume.................. | 20,000,000 | .25 |
| Pessimistic volume................... | 12,000,000 | .15 |

Variable operating expenses average 20% of passenger revenue. Fixed operating expenses are budgeted at $17,500,000 for 1977.

*Required:*

a. Compute the expected value of passenger revenue for 1977.

b. What would be the effect on budgeted profit before tax of using the expected value instead of the most likely volume as the basis of the operating budget?

7–18. Hispaniola Mines, Ltd., annually produces 1,500,000 tons of bauxite. Because of its favorable geographic location, Hispaniola Mines' annual production is assured. World-wide production, however, fluctuates widely from year to year in an unpredictable manner. Hence, the selling price of bauxite varies significantly in inverse proportion to total world output. In a normal year, the price will be $500 per ton. In a good year (i.e., one of high world output), this price will be 25% lower. In a poor production year, on the other hand, the price will be 25% higher than normal.

Hispaniola Mines' management has estimated the following probabilities of good, normal, and poor production years:

Good...................................... .3
Normal.................................... .5
Poor...................................... .2

The world market forecast for 1977 generally anticipates a good year. This prediction, however, is subject to revision as weather and economic prospects become clearer.

*Required:*

a. Compute the expected value of sales revenue for Hispaniola Mines, Ltd.

b. For 1977, what selling price should be used in sales forecasting? Why?

c. For long range sales forecasting, what selling price should be used? Why?

# chapter 8

# Flexible Budgets

W<sub>E HAVE</sub> already seen that the operating budget for an enterprise includes budgets of operating costs and expenses in all of the various departments within the firm. Among manufacturing costs, those that are directly traceable to the product and that vary in direct proportion to the volume of production—direct materials and labor costs—are relatively easy to budget. They are direct functions of the volume of production. If the actual volume of production deviates from the planned volume, planned materials and labor costs can be adjusted quite readily to conform to the new volume. For indirect manufacturing costs, however, this direct functional relationship does not obtain. Manufacturing overhead costs are, of course, incurred because of production; but the direct input-output relationship existing between materials and labor costs and production volume is lacking. Even those manufacturing overhead costs which vary with the volume of production typically do so in a vaguely defined manner. For example, experience may indicate that indirect materials cost varies quite nearly in direct proportion to output; but it may be impossible to identify any specific indirect materials input per unit of output. Fixed manufacturing costs, of course, are incurred in amounts unrelated to variations in output.

What is true of manufacturing overhead in this context is largely true of nonmanufacturing costs also. These latter costs usually vary, in part, with the volume of activity to which they are logically related. Thus, selling costs may vary with the volume of sales; clerical costs, with the volume of clerical work done; and so forth. However, as in the case of manufacturing overhead, there is usually no direct relationship between the amount of a particular nonmanufacturing cost and the volume of activity. (Sales commissions are the classic exception here.) Certain nonmanufacturing costs are fixed in amount, regardless of the volume of activity. In summary, then, there is some degree of variation of manufacturing overhead and of most nonmanufacturing costs with appropriate measures of volume; but the variation is partial and the total costs cannot readily be expressed as a certain amount per unit of volume.

If indirect costs are budgeted simply at a given amount for the budget period, with no indication as to how those costs would behave if volume were to deviate from the planned level, such a budget would be of limited usefulness to management. If, however, the budget is developed in some way that indicates what the manufacturing overhead or nonmanufacturing costs may be expected to be at various levels of volume, its utility for purposes of cost planning and control is greatly enhanced. Budgets of indirect costs at a single volume only, with no basis for determining the impact of a change in volume on the budgeted costs, are called *fixed budgets* or *static budgets*. Budgets which do provide a basis for determining the costs anticipated at various levels of operating activity are referred to as *flexible budgets, variable budgets,* or *sliding budgets.* The first term seems most descriptive of the essential character of these budgets and will be used consistently throughout this book.

## CONSTRUCTION OF A FLEXIBLE BUDGET

### Departmentalization of Costs

In any firm large enough to have significant departmental distinctions for operating purposes, a separate flexible budget should be prepared for the indirect costs of each department, whether it be a manufacturing, administrative, selling, or other type of department. The development and construction of flexible budgets are the same, whether they pertain to manufacturing or nonmanufacturing operations. Flexible budgets for indirect manufacturing costs may have more uses than nonmanufacturing cost budgets, however. For example, a flexible budget for manufacturing overhead is ordinarily used to establish normal manufacturing overhead rates. Since nonmanufacturing costs are treated as period costs and, thus, are not applied to production, normal rates would not be determined. The illustrations in this chapter will focus on indirect manufacturing costs, but the same basic concepts are equally applicable to nonmanufacturing costs. The latter subject will be given specific attention in Chapter 11.

An illustration of a flexible manufacturing overhead budget is pre-

**TABLE 8–1**

M-G STANLEY CORPORATION
Monthly Expense Budget
1977

*Department* Light machinery                                          *Approved* 12/10/76
*Supervisor* W. S. Gilbert

| | Variable Rate per Hour | Fixed Cost per Month | Volume in Labor Hours | | | |
|---|---|---|---|---|---|---|
| | | | 15,000 | 18,000 | 21,000 | 24,000 |
| Controllable costs: | | | | | | |
| Indirect labor.......... | $ .90 | | $13,500 | $16,200 | $18,900 | $21,600 |
| Labor-related costs..... | .20 | $   800 | 3,800 | 4,400 | 5,000 | 5,600 |
| Indirect materials....... | .50 | | 7,500 | 9,000 | 10,500 | 12,000 |
| Fuel and power......... | .08 | 2,000 | 3,200 | 3,440 | 3,680 | 3,920 |
| Repairs and | | | | | | |
| maintenance......... | .10 | 4,000 | 5,500 | 5,800 | 6,100 | 6,400 |
| | | | $33,500 | $38,840 | $44,180 | $49,520 |
| | | | | | | |
| Noncontrollable costs: | | | | | | |
| Supervision............ | | 3,200 | $ 3,200 | $ 3,200 | $ 3,200 | $ 3,200 |
| Taxes and insurance.... | | 800 | 800 | 800 | 800 | 800 |
| Depreciation.......... | | 25,000 | 25,000 | 25,000 | 25,000 | 25,000 |
| | | | $29,000 | $29,000 | $29,000 | $29,000 |
| Total costs......... | $1.78 | $35,800 | $62,500 | $67,840 | $73,180 | $78,520 |

sented in Table 8–1. This budget is for the light machinery department of the M-G Stanley Corporation. Similar budgets would be prepared for the other manufacturing departments and for the various nonmanufacturing departments. Because the M-G Stanley Corporation prepares monthly operating reports for its management and wishes to analyze and evaluate its operating costs monthly, the budgeted manufacturing overhead data in this illustration are for one month. Obviously, the data in the flexible budget can be expressed in terms of any period of time—a month, a quarter, a year. As a practical matter, the flexible budget would rarely, if ever, apply to more than one year.

## The Measure of Volume

The essence of a flexible budget is the presentation of estimated cost data in such a manner that permits their determination at various levels of volume. As a practical matter, this means that all costs must be identified as to how they behave with changes in volume—whether they vary or remain fixed. In order to identify the behavior of the various cost items in a department, it is necessary first to define volume in the most meaningful way. For a department which is engaged in the production of several substantially different products (e.g., refrigerators, clothes dryers, and ranges), units of output would not be an appropriate measure of volume, for the various units are not alike. In such a case, volume is typically expressed in terms of some unit of input, such as direct labor hours, direct labor cost, or machine-hours. The volume measure selected for any given department should be that quantity which displays the greatest degree of correlation with those costs of the department that do vary with the level of operating activity. This quantity may be determined by a logical examination of the causal or beneficial relationships between costs and alternative measures of volume. It might also be determined by statistical tests of correlation. That measure which shows the highest degree of correlation with the variable costs would then be chosen as the volume indicator for the department.[1]

Different departments are likely to use different measures of volume. The light machinery department in Table 8–1 uses direct labor hours as its volume measure, presumably because observations and studies have shown that the variable cost items tend to vary more nearly in proportion to the labor hours worked in the department than to any other possible indicator of departmental activity. In the same firm's heavy machinery department, it might be found that machine-hours afford the best indication of cost behavior. There is no reason why the same volume measure should be used in all departments within a single firm. One might even raise the question as to whether it is necessary that only one measure be employed in each department. Correlation analyses might show that some costs in a department vary in proportion to labor hours, while others vary in proportion to machine hours. Should both measures of volume be used for the department, or should only one be selected? In theory, there would be no objection to two or more volume indicators being used in a single department. In practice, this would require two or more flexible budgets for the department. Whether the additional precision would be worth the additional clerical cost involved in such a plan is dubious. In the discussion in this chapter, a single measure of volume for each department will be assumed.

## Budget Cost Allowances

*Cost Variability.* Once the measure of volume has been selected, the next step in the development of the flexible budget is the determination of the behavior of each cost item with respect to that volume indicator. In the illustration in Table 8–1, this means that each cost item had to be studied in conjunction with direct labor hours to determine how it behaved as the hours increased and decreased. The first two money

---

[1] The student is referred to any basic statistics text for the specific technique to be employed for this correlation analysis.

columns in this budget schedule depict the behavior of each cost item with respect to labor hours worked in the department. Fixed costs are budgeted as total amounts. Variable costs are budgeted as amounts per labor hour. Some of the cost items—labor-related costs, fuel and power, and repairs and maintenance—comprise both variable and fixed components. In total, therefore, these are semivariable costs. For reasons to be explained shortly, semivariable costs restrict the usefulness of the flexible budget. Hence, in practice, they are most frequently treated as wholly variable, as absolutely fixed, or as consisting of separable variable and fixed components.

These first two columns, showing the variability and/or fixedness of the departmental cost items, are the essence of the flexible budget. In fact, if we were not interested in the individual cost items but only in the total departmental costs, the final figures in these two columns would be all we would need. The entire flexible budget could be reduced to a simple statement that variable costs in the department are incurred at the rate of $1.78 per direct labor hour and fixed costs are $35,800 per month.[2] With this information we could estimate total departmental cost at any volume. Even where the details of the several cost items are of interest, the first two columns provide an adequate statement of the flexible budget. With the information in these columns, we can provide budget estimates for any volume. (To demonstrate this, the student should use the data in those first two columns to calculate the budget cost allowances for 16,000 and for 19,245 hours.)

***Cost Controllability.*** As a part of the overall plan of cost control, the flexible budget is commonly developed in such a way as to distinguish between those costs which are regarded as controllable by the department supervisor and those which are not. The noncontrollable costs in Table 8–1 include the supervisor's own salary and those of the assistant foremen in the department, for these are set by the plant manager. Taxes, insurance, and depreciation on departmental equipment are also regarded as beyond the control of the supervisor, as they derive from decisions made at higher levels of management. It must be understood that the noncontrollable costs in Table 8–1 are such only at the level of responsibility of the departmental supervisor. At some higher level of responsibility, they also would be controllable. All costs in a firm should be controllable at some level of responsibility.

Cost controllability must always be evaluated critically and cautiously. Not all of the items listed as controllable costs are necessarily completely subject to the discretion of the department supervisor. A certain amount of maintenance cost, for example, is inevitably incurred as a

---

[2] Of course, this flexible budget might just as well be expressed as a fixed cost of $35,800 per month plus a variable rate of $1.78 multiplied by the production volume of the period. In this arrangement, it is easily recognizable as a specific application of the general form of a linear equation (i.e., $y = a + bx$).

consequence of the decision to acquire and use equipment. If this decision is not made by the department supervisor, it is doubtful that this basic maintenance cost can be said to be truly controllable by him. Nevertheless, the identification of controllable and noncontrollable costs at the several levels of responsibility is so important to effective cost control that a practical distinction between the two is needed. That distinction must then be interpreted reasonably.

## ESTABLISHING BUDGET ALLOWANCES

As with so many things in life, the most important step in the development of a flexible budget is the most difficult. A flexible budget is only as good as the cost allowances included in it and the separation of these costs into variable and fixed components. At the outset, we must recognize that no flexible budget can be perfect, because the composite budgeted cost allowances cannot be perfect. In a practical situation, it is unlikely that there will be any perfectly variable costs that vary in direct proportion to volume over the full range of possible operating volumes. Likewise, there will probably be few absolutely fixed costs that do not change at all over the entire range of possible operations. Nevertheless, the concepts of variable and fixed costs are so useful to effective planning and control that it is better to make a reasonable assumption regarding the variability or fixedness of a cost than to throw up one's hands in frustration at a fruitless search for perfection.

### Variable Costs

Despite the fact that there may be no costs which are perfectly variable over all ranges of volume, there may be a substantial number of cost items which come fairly close to being so. In addition, there may be cost items which approach perfect variability over the relevant range of volume, that is, the range within which the department is almost certain to operate. For example, if a particular department regularly operates between 60% and 90% of capacity, there is little merit in the accountant's being concerned with the behavior of departmental costs at 20% or 30% of capacity. In such a case, the flexible budget may be entirely valid over the range of activity which may reasonably be expected. The fact that it is not valid at some operating level which would be reached only under highly unusual circumstances—such as a strike—is then of little practical consequence. Thus, many cost items which do not meet the strict definition of a variable cost are commonly treated as variable costs for purposes of establishing flexible budget allowances and for subsequent analyses. The attendant degree of imprecision is greatly outweighed by the utility of the flexible budget to management.

## Fixed Costs

For purposes of planning and control, it is useful to distinguish between two types of fixed costs. First, there are some costs that are fixed in amount and that must be incurred each period as a consequence of a decision made at some time in the past. These are referred to as *committed costs*. The most familiar examples of committed fixed costs are those that derive from an earlier decision to acquire and use plant property. Depreciation, property taxes, and property insurance are examples of committed costs. It is true that management has some discretion as to the amount of periodic depreciation by virtue of its choice of a depreciation method. However, this choice affects only the timing of depreciation charges; and it is available only once, when the asset is acquired. The second type of fixed cost is fixed in amount as a result of a current management decision. Such costs are called *discretionary costs*, *managed costs*, or *programmed costs*. Implicit in the concept of a discretionary cost is periodic management discretion as to the amount of the cost in the ensuing period. Perhaps the best examples of discretionary costs are in the area of nonmanufacturing costs.[3] Certain elements of manufacturing overhead also tend to fit the category, however. The amount budgeted for supervision is usually determined by a management judgment as to the optimal ratio of supervisory to operating employees. As technology and other conditions change, that judgment may change. Fixed maintenance costs are partially committed in that the earlier decision to acquire plant facilities necessitates some current expenditures to maintain them. However, management usually has some discretion as to the amount of fixed maintenance costs. To some extent, there is a trade-off between the amount spent on maintenance and the frequency of replacement of machinery. Thus, the distinction between committed and discretionary costs is not always a clear one; but it is a useful one for planning and control purposes.

Some fixed costs may meet the strict definition of the concept. Such items as depreciation, property taxes, and insurance are likely to be the same at full capacity as they would be if the plant were temporarily shut down. Others, such as supervision, are more likely to remain fixed only over certain ranges of volume. Perhaps one supervisor can handle operations in a department up to 30% of capacity; a second becomes necessary when operations exceed 30%; a third must be added when volume reaches 60%; and a fourth is required at 90% of capacity. Obviously, supervision cost in this case does not qualify as a true fixed cost. However, if the department's operations are almost certain to fall somewhere between 60% and 90% of capacity, supervision may validly be treated as a fixed cost. Changes in the cost outside the relevant range of opera-

---

[3] Cf. Chapter 11.

tions are irrelevant. As in the case of variable costs, utility is a much more significant criterion than perfection.

## Semivariable Costs

*Step Budgeting.* Unfortunately, not all costs are so nearly variable or fixed that they may be treated as one or the other without further study. Many cost items do vary with volume even within fairly small ranges, but they do not do so in a manner even close to direct proportionality. One possible method of dealing with such costs is to budget them at each of the several levels of volume which are to be tabulated in the formal flexible budget, without reference to how they might behave at nontabulated levels. This method is usually described as *step budgeting.* While this solution to the problem would permit the preparation of a formal budget schedule, it would limit the flexibility of the budget. Step budgets do not provide for any direct determination of the budgeted cost at some volume not tabulated. This amount might be estimated by interpolation between tabulated amounts. However, interpolation implies a linear relationship between the cost and volume; whereas the use of step budgeting denies the existence of such a relationship. In any event, it is important that management be able to determine the budgeted cost at any given volume; and step budgets are of limited value for this purpose. The alternative to step budgeting is to eliminate semivariable costs from the budget by treating them as variable, as fixed, or as a combination of the two.

*Classification by Dominant Characteristics.* The simplest and, unfortunately, the least precise method of disposing of semivariable cost items is to treat them as either variable or fixed according to their dominant characteristics. Thus, if observation shows that a particular semivariable cost is closer to being variable than fixed, it is treated as variable and an average rate of variability is established on the basis of past experience, as adjusted for expected changes in conditions. If inspection indicates that the item is closer to being fixed, it is treated as such in an amount which would be expected to be incurred at the most likely level of operations. Obviously, this solution to the problem of semivariable costs introduces a considerable degree of imprecision into subsequent analyses based upon the flexible budget allowances. In a study of practices in 58 firms, the National Association of Accountants found that identification of variable and fixed costs on the basis of their dominant characteristics was a common, if not the commonest, practice.[4]

---

[4] NAA, "Separating and Using Costs as Fixed and Variable," *N.A.A. Bulletin,* Accounting Practice Report 10, vol. 41 (June 1960), sec. 3, p. 15.

*Least Squares Regression Method.* This method is based upon the assumption that a semivariable cost can be separated into fixed and variable components. This separation is usually based upon an analysis of past experience, adjusted appropriately for expected changes in costs or in other conditions. Several actual costs and the volumes at which they occurred are analyzed to determine a general trend of cost in relation to volume. For example, assume that a production department measures its operating volume in machine hours and management believes that its maintenance costs are partially related to the number of machine hours worked. Actual experience with volume in machine hours and maintenance cost during the most recent year is shown in Table 8–2.

TABLE 8–2

|  | Machine Hours | Maintenance Cost |
|---|---|---|
| January..................... | 120,000 | $90,000 |
| February.................... | 130,000 | 91,000 |
| March...................... | 115,000 | 84,000 |
| April...................... | 105,000 | 85,000 |
| May....................... | 90,000 | 82,000 |
| June....................... | 80,000 | 73,000 |
| July....................... | 70,000 | 72,000 |
| August..................... | 80,000 | 78,000 |
| September.................. | 95,000 | 75,000 |
| October.................... | 110,000 | 89,000 |
| November.................. | 125,000 | 95,000 |
| December.................. | 140,000 | 93,000 |

If we may assume that there will be no change in maintenance operations or in prices during the coming budget period, these data may be used directly to determine the separate variable and fixed portions of maintenance cost. On the other hand, if there is reason to anticipate some change, this should be reflected in the data first. For example, if the prices of maintenance services were expected to rise by 5%, all of the amounts in the second column of Table 8–2 would be multiplied by 105% before proceeding further with the analysis.

In our illustration, we shall assume that no change to the previous year's data is necessary. The variable and fixed components of the semivariable maintenance cost are computed by solving the following equations:

$$b = \frac{n \Sigma XY - \Sigma X \Sigma Y}{n \Sigma X^2 - (\Sigma X)^2}$$

$$a = \frac{\Sigma Y}{n} - b\left(\frac{\Sigma X}{n}\right)$$

where

$n$ = the number of observations used (12 months' data in this case),

$X$ = value of the independent variable (machine hours here),

$Y$ = value of the dependent variable (maintenance cost),

$b$ = variable cost rate per unit of volume (per machine hour),

$a$ = fixed cost per period (per month).

From the data in our illustration, we find that $a = \$49,110$ and $b = \$.3315$. In other words, maintenance cost is budgeted at $\$49,110$ per month plus $\$.3315$ per machine hour worked.[5] In practice, these figures might be rounded for convenience. Total budgeted maintenance cost at any given volume may now be found by solving the following equation:

$$Y = a + bX$$

where all of the symbols have the same meanings as in the previous equations.

The least squares method of analysis of semivariable costs is commonly accompanied by a graphic depiction of the relationship between cost and volume. Figure 8–1 is a graph of the maintenance cost illustra-

---

[5] This solution to the least squares regression analysis is presented below. The student who is not familiar with this technique is referred to any standard textbook on statistics.

| Months (n = 12) | Machine Hours (X) | Maintenance Cost (Y) | XY | X² |
|---|---|---|---|---|
| January | 120,000 | $ 90,000 | 10,800,000,000 | 14,400,000,000 |
| February | 130,000 | 91,000 | 11,830,000,000 | 16,900,000,000 |
| March | 115,000 | 84,000 | 9,660,000,000 | 13,225,000,000 |
| April | 105,000 | 85,000 | 8,925,000,000 | 11,025,000,000 |
| May | 90,000 | 82,000 | 7,380,000,000 | 8,100,000,000 |
| June | 80,000 | 73,000 | 5,840,000,000 | 6,400,000,000 |
| July | 70,000 | 72,000 | 5,040,000,000 | 4,900,000,000 |
| August | 80,000 | 78,000 | 6,240,000,000 | 6,400,000,000 |
| September | 95,000 | 75,000 | 7,125,000,000 | 9,025,000,000 |
| October | 110,000 | 89,000 | 9,790,000,000 | 12,100,000,000 |
| November | 125,000 | 95,000 | 11,875,000,000 | 15,625,000,000 |
| December | 140,000 | 93,000 | 13,920,000,000 | 19,600,000,000 |
| Σ | 1,260,000 | $1,007,000 | 107,525,000,000 | 137,700,000,000 |

Then

$$b = \frac{n\Sigma XY - \Sigma X \Sigma Y}{n\Sigma X^2 - (\Sigma X)^2} = \frac{12(107,525,000,000) - 1,260,000(1,007,000)}{12(137,700,000,000) - 1,260,000^2} = .3315$$

and

$$a = \frac{\Sigma Y}{n} - b\left(\frac{\Sigma X}{n}\right) = \frac{1,007,000}{12} - .3315\left(\frac{1,260,000}{12}\right) = 49,110$$

tion. It shows a scattergraph of actual maintenance costs incurred in the recent year (i.e., a plot of the maintenance cost incurred at the volume worked in each month). A least squares regression line is then drawn on the basis of computed values of $a$ and $b$.[6] This line shows the budgeted total maintenance cost at any volume. The slope of the line is the variable rate per unit of volume. The total monthly fixed cost is found at the point where the regression line intersects the vertical axis. The graph, of course, is not essential to effective use of the least squares

**FIGURE 8–1**

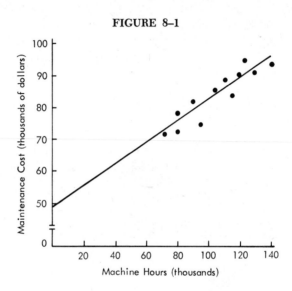

Machine Hours (thousands)

method. The least squares computations, however, are necessary if the line on the graph is to depict cost behavior accurately.

The study by the National Association of Accountants referred to earlier found that most of the firms whose practices were observed and who did separate semivariable costs into fixed and variable components used the least squares method to do so.[7] One final note of caution is appropriate here. The reader should not be mesmerized by the mathemati-

---

[6] This line is drawn by computing and plotting cost at two different volumes and then connecting those two points by a straight line. Thus, we might compute budgeted maintenance cost ($Y$) at 120,000 machine-hours and at 60,000 machine hours by twice solving the equation $Y = a + bX$, where $X$ has successive values of 120,000 and 60,000. This produces the following results:

$$Y_{120,000} = \$49,110 + \$.3315(120,000) = \$88,890$$
$$Y_{60,000} = \$49,110 + \$.3315(60,000) = \$69,000$$

Of course, the same line will be obtained by connecting any two points computed from this equation; and any solution to the equation will represent a point that lies on the line.

[7] NAA, "Separating and Using Costs," p. 11.

cal precision of the least squares method. The mathematics are precise, but they are applied in the development of an approximation of actual cost behavior. The separation of a semivariable cost into variable and fixed components is made because it is useful and it is a reasonable approximation of reality.

**High-Low Method.** Another method of separating semivariable costs into variable and fixed components is the *high-low method*. This method is based upon only two observations of actual cost behavior, one at a high volume of activity and a second at a low volume. Logically, the high and low volumes used should be the upper and lower limits of the relevant range within which actual volume is most likely to fall. Because it uses only two sets of data, the high-low method is much simpler to use than the least squares method. For the same reason, however, it is also less precise. Suppose, for example, that a production department determined that at a high production volume of 24,000 direct labor hours per month its fuel and power cost was $3,920. At a low volume of 15,000 direct labor hours, fuel and power cost was $3,200. With these data only, variable and fixed elements of fuel and power cost may be computed. The change in cost between the high and low volumes is assumed to reflect the pattern of cost variability. Thus, the variable rate per labor hour is computed as follows:

|  | Labor Hours | Fuel and Power Cost |
|---|---|---|
| High volume.............. | 24,000 | $3,920 |
| Low volume.............. | 15,000 | 3,200 |
| Differences.............. | 9,000 | $ 720 |

As volume changed by 9,000 hours, cost changed by $720. Thus, fuel and power cost is assumed to include a variable component equal to $.08 per direct labor hour ($720 ÷ 9,000 hours). With this variable rate, we can compute the fixed cost component at either the high or the low volume or at both. The fixed cost is simply the difference between the total cost at either volume and the newly found variable cost component.

|  | High Volume | Low Volume |
|---|---|---|
| Total cost.............. | $3,920 | $3,200 |
| Variable cost: |  |  |
| 24,000 hrs. @ $.08...... | 1,920 |  |
| 15,000 hrs. @ $.08...... |  | 1,200 |
| Fixed cost.............. | $2,000 | $2,000 |

Thus, we have determined that fuel and power cost should be budgeted at $2,000 per month plus $.08 per direct labor hour.

The high-low method is an acceptable way of approximating cost behavior when no better data are available. It is likely to be less accurate than the least squares method, however. The latter method is based upon numerous data, perhaps representative of various points in the relevant range of volume. The high-low method uses only data drawn from the extreme ends of that range.[8]

## DEPARTMENTAL EXPENSE REPORTS

### Report Form

Table 8–3 is a departmental expense report for one month. It reports the actual expenses incurred in the light machinery department of the M-G Stanley Corporation for the month of April 1977. Actual expenses are compared with the budgeted expenses as presented in the departmental flexible budget, Table 8–1 in this chapter. Differences between the actual and budgeted cost data are identified as variances and provide the focal point from which the process of cost control proceeds. Table 8–3 is not offered as a standard report form, but it is representative of the type of information usually contained in such expense reports. Inclusion of data for the year to date as well as for the month just ended is not essential to the basic nature of the report, but it does afford management a basis for appraising the department's cost performance over a series of months and for evaluating the effectiveness of cost control efforts suggested by prior months' reports. The various components of this report will be discussed in the paragraphs that follow.

### Adjusting the Budget to Actual Volume

If the M-G Stanley Corporation used fixed departmental budgets instead of flexible budgets, there would be only one level of budgeted costs against which actual costs could be compared. Assume that the corporation had originally estimated that operating volume in the light machinery department would be 18,000 direct labor hours per month during the budget period under consideration. A fixed budget would present only the costs budgeted for that volume, with no indication of cost variability or fixedness. While this would afford some basis for evaluating actual costs, it would not permit management to distinguish between those variances which arise because actual operating volume has differed from that originally anticipated and those variances attributable

---

[8] To illustrate the difference in results under these two methods, assume that the high-low method were to be applied to the maintenance cost and machine-hour data used in connection with the least squares illustration. The high volume was 140,000 machine-hours, with a cost of $93,000. The low volume was 70,000 hours, with a cost of $72,000. Using the high-low method with these data, we would compute a variable cost rate of $.30 per hour (instead of $.3315) and a fixed cost of $51,000 per month (instead of $49,110).

**TABLE 8–3**

M-G STANLEY CORPORATION
Monthly Expense Report

*Department*  Light machinery                                    *Month of* April, 1977
*Supervisor*  W. S. Gilbert

| | Current Month | | | Year to Date | | |
|---|---|---|---|---|---|---|
| | *Actual Cost* | *Budgeted Cost* | *Spending Variance* | *Actual Cost* | *Budgeted Cost* | *Spending Variance* |
| Direct labor hours........ | 19,150 | 19,150 | | 72,600 | 72,600 | |
| Controllable costs: | | | | | | |
| Indirect labor.......... | $17,880 | $17,235 | $( 645) | $ 68,465 | $ 65,340 | $(3,125) |
| Labor related costs..... | 4,675 | 4,630 | ( 45) | 17,982 | 17,720 | ( 262) |
| Indirect materials...... | 9,318 | 9,575 | 257 | 36,394 | 36,300 | ( 94) |
| Fuel and power........ | 4,120 | 3,532 | ( 588) | 15,820 | 13,808 | (2,012) |
| Repairs and maintenance......... | 5,200 | 5,915 | 715 | 21,640 | 23,260 | 1,620 |
| Total............ | $41,193 | $40,887 | $( 306) | $160,301 | $156,428 | $(3,873) |
| Noncontrollable costs: | | | | | | |
| Supervision............ | $ 3,360 | $ 3,200 | $( 160) | $ 13,120 | $ 12,800 | $( 320) |
| Taxes and insurance.... | 800 | 800 | | 3,200 | 3,200 | |
| Depreciation.......... | 26,500 | 25,000 | (1,500) | 101,500 | 100,000 | (1,500) |
| Total............ | $30,660 | $29,000 | $(1,660) | $117,820 | $116,000 | $(1,820) |
| Total costs............. | $71,853 | $69,887 | $(1,966) | $278,121 | $272,428 | $(5,693) |

to spending more or less than the budget calls for. A flexible budget enables management to distinguish between these two types of variances, for it allows the determination of budgeted costs at any volume.

In order to appraise departmental spending during a given period, management wishes to compare actual costs with the costs which the budget indicates should have been incurred at the operating volume actually achieved during the period. Thus, the budgeted costs tabulated in Table 8–3 are budgeted costs for 19,150 direct labor hours, the actual volume for April. To the extent that costs are variable (cf., Table 8–1), budget allowances for the actual volume are simply the products of 19,150 hours multiplied by the several variable cost rates per hour. To the extent that costs are fixed, they are the same dollar amount at any volume. Repairs and maintenance costs, for example, are budgeted at 19,150 hours by multiplying 19,150 by $.10, the variable rate per hour, and then by adding $4,000, the fixed amount per month. Similar computations are made to determine budgeted costs for the actual volume of the year to date. In this instance, the actual labor hours used (72,600) are the total actual hours worked in the department during the first four months of 1977.

## Spending Variances

The difference between actual costs incurred and budgeted costs for the actual volume is referred to as the *spending variance*. It is shown as a positive amount when the variance is favorable (i.e., actual cost is less than budgeted) and in parentheses as a negative amount when the variance is unfavorable (i.e., actual cost is greater than budgeted). The spending variance is uniquely associated with a flexible budget and cannot be identified if a static budget is used. For example, Table 8–3 shows that the flexible budget allows spending of $17,235 on indirect labor, a variable cost, when a volume of 19,150 direct labor hours is attained. The department actually spent $645 more than the amount allowed, however. Why this excess spending occurred is a question for the department supervisor to investigate, but he will be starting with the appropriate amount. If the actual indirect labor cost were compared with the budget allowance in a static budget established at 18,000 direct labor hours per month, the resultant variance would be much greater than $645. However, we would expect a variable cost to increase if volume increases. Consequently, the variance from the static budget would not be a useful figure for management to use in its efforts to evaluate performance and to control costs. The spending variance from a flexible budget reflects only that variance that would not be expected at the actual volume worked. The expected increase attendant upon an increase in volume from the original budget is properly handled by adjusting the budget to the actual volume.

Technically, depreciation does not involve current spending. Rather, it is a periodic allocation of an amount spent earlier when the assets were acquired. However, a spending variance may appear for depreciation, as is the case in Table 8–3. The explanation must be either that a new depreciable asset was acquired after the budget was prepared or that the remaining useful lives of the existing assets have been revised and are now estimated to be shorter than originally expected.

## QUESTIONS FOR DISCUSSION

1. Why is a flexible budget a better technique for planning and controlling costs than a static budget?

2. "As long as the separation of manufacturing overhead or of any other cost into variable and fixed components is inexact, the resultant flexible budget is inexact. When this budget is then applied to actual cost data for purpose of cost control, the comparisons produced will also be inexact. Consequently, they may produce confusion, ill feelings, and possibly even inappropriate managerial action." Discuss this allegation.

3. The flexible budget illustrated in Table 8–1 and the expense report in Table 8–3 in this chapter both could have been completed without identification

of cost items as controllable and noncontrollable. Why then should this distinction be included in these exhibits?

4. Discuss the advantages and disadvantages of step budgeting of semivariable costs. What are the principal alternatives to step budgeting?

5. Discuss the relative advantages and disadvantages of the least squares regression method and the high-low method of separating semivariable costs into variable and fixed components.

6. For purposes of planning and control, what is (are) the essential difference(s) between committed and discretionary fixed costs?

7. What is the significance of the spending variance from budgeted costs?

8. The controller of the Alpine Corporation is impressed with the success of flexible budgets for manufacturing overhead in the corporation's manufacturing departments. He would like to use them also in the departments under his direct supervision—payroll, billing, and general accounting. What are the requirements for the establishment of useful flexible budgets in nonproduction departments such as these?

9. Flexible budgets involve, fundamentally, the distinction between variable and fixed costs. Are they, then, as useful in variable costing systems, where only variable costs are charged to production, as they are in absorption costing systems, where both variable and fixed costs are charged to production? Discuss.

10. Discuss the potential application of flexible budgets to the planning and control of (a) direct material cost, (b) factory managers' salaries, and (c) factory repair and maintenance costs.

## PROBLEMS

8-1. The Amador Frozen Food Company packages all of its products in its packing department. The budgeted costs for the operation of this department in 1977 have been established as follows:

Variable costs:
| | |
|---|---|
| Direct materials | $1,800,000 |
| Direct labor | 1,000,000 |
| Packing supplies | 150,000 |
| Indirect labor | 200,000 |
| Labor-related costs | 80,000 |
| | $3,230,000 |

Fixed costs:
| | |
|---|---|
| Maintenance | $ 90,000 |
| Heat, light, and power | 120,000 |
| Taxes and insurance | 40,000 |
| Depreciation | 150,000 |
| | $ 400,000 |
| Total budgeted costs | $3,630,000 |

Management wishes to have flexible budgets prepared for all operating departments. Operating volume in the packing department is best measured in direct labor hours. Direct labor cost in this department has been budgeted at a rate of $4 per hour.

*Required:*

a. Prepare, in its most basic format, a flexible budget of manufacturing overhead costs for 1977 in the packing department.
b. Compute the normal variable and fixed manufacturing overhead rates for this department for 1977.

8-2. The following manufacturing overhead costs may reasonably be expected to be incurred in the assembly department of the Plumas Office Furniture Company:

| | |
|---|---|
| Indirect materials............... | $.35 per labor hour |
| Indirect labor.................... | $20,000 per month plus $.20 per labor hour |
| Supervision...................... | $32,000 per month |
| Repairs and maintenance.......... | $5,000 per month |
| Depreciation..................... | $21,000 per month |
| Cleaning supplies................ | $.15 per labor hour |
| Heat, light, and power........... | $8,000 per month plus $.40 per labor hour |
| Insurance and taxes.............. | $2,200 per month |

All of these cost items, excepting supervision, depreciation, and insurance and taxes, are regarded as controllable by the department foreman.

*Required:*

a. Prepare a tabular flexible budget for manufacturing overhead in the assembly department at each of the following monthly levels of production volume: 80,000, 90,000 and 100,000 labor hours.
b. Assuming that the company uses absorption costing and that it budgets production volume at 90,000 labor hours per month, compute the normal manufacturing overhead rates for the asssembly department.

8-3. You have recently been appointed budget director of the Inyo Machine Corporation. One of your objectives is to establish flexible budgets of manufacturing overhead in all production departments. For this purpose, you asked each department supervisor to submit a report of his monthy costs. The following report was received from Charles Kumishiro, the supervisor of the stamping department:

"My biggest cost item, of course, is labor. There are 10 machines in the department. Each one needs an operator, a materials handler, and an assistant. Operators get $6 an hour; handlers, $4 an hour; and assistants, $3.40 an hour. Now, I have 11 operators. Ten are regularly assigned to machines. The 11th relieves the regular operators when they take their breaks and at other times when they need relief. Then there is the janitor; he gets $750 per month. My own salary is $1,400 a month, incidentally.

"When the machines are running the full eight-hour day, our monthly maintenance charges run about $21,500. Even when we were shut down for three months during the strike last year, though, routine maintenance cost $15,340 each month. Power is metered at each machine, and each one uses about 120 kilowatt-hours for each hour that it is in operation. Supplies seem to depend on how much we use the machines. For a full eight-hour day, we use about $124 worth of supplies. If the machines are working less, the supplies usage goes down accordingly. I know there are other costs charged to the department, but I don't know how the amounts are arrived at."

Further investigation reveals that monthly depreciation on the machinery in the stamping department is $12,500. Insurance and taxes total $36,000 for a year. The corporation pays the commercial rate of $.0275 per kilowatt-hour for electric power. From the payroll department, you learn that fringe benefits average 10% of gross wages and salaries.

Each month may be assumed to consist of 22 eight-hour working days.

*Required:*

a. What measure of, operating volume would you use for the stamping department's flexible budget? Why?

b. Construct a flexible budget of manufacturing overhead in the stamping department for one month. Include budget allowances at 75% and at 100% of full operating capacity.

8-4. The Modoc Corporation is developing flexible budgets for the first time. It appears that the indirect labor in the light machining department is a semivariable cost. Volume in this department is measured in dollars of direct labor cost. Management believes that it is entirely reasonable to expect that this department will operate at a direct labor cost of no more than $400,000 per month and no less than $240,000 per month. Indirect labor cost has been budgeted at $140,000 for a volume of $400,000 direct labor cost and at $101,600 for a volume of $240,000 direct labor cost.

*Required:*

By use of the high-low method, resolve the budgeted indirect labor cost into a variable rate per dollar of direct labor cost and a fixed cost per month.

8-5. The Sonoma Electric Company wishes to set flexible budgets for each of its various departments. A separate maintenance department performs all major and routine repair work on the company's equipment and facilities. It has been determined that maintenance cost is primarily a function of machine hours worked in the various production departments. Total actual machine hours worked and maintenance costs incurred during 1976 were as follows:

| Month | Machine Hours | Maintenance Cost |
|---|---|---|
| January.................... | 140,000 | $330,000 |
| February.................. | 125,000 | 300,000 |
| March..................... | 120,000 | 298,000 |
| April...................... | 105,000 | 275,000 |
| May....................... | 90,000 | 252,000 |
| June...................... | 80,000 | 235,000 |
| July....................... | 100,000 | 270,000 |
| August.................... | 110,000 | 283,000 |
| September................. | 125,000 | 299,000 |
| October................... | 30,000 | 215,000 |
| November................. | 140,000 | 312,000 |
| December................. | 150,000 | 340,000 |

The company's plant was shut down by a strike for three and a half weeks during October 1976. The plant superintendent used this opportunity to accomplish some deferred maintenance on the equipment.

*Required:*

a. Assuming that maintenance costs are expected to be 10% higher in 1977 than they were in 1976, compute the variable cost per machine hour and the fixed cost per month by use of the high-low method.

b. If the company wished to allocate maintenance costs to production departments at a normal rate, how would such a rate be established? How, then, should the company account for any differences between actual maintenance costs incurred and maintenance costs allocated to the production departments by means of this normal rate?

 8-6. The cost of heat, light, and power in the Tulare Valve Company tends to vary with the volume of direct labor hours worked in the factory but not in direct proportion thereto. Budgeted heat, light, and power costs in 1977, by quarters, have been estimated as follows:

| Quarter | Cost | Labor Hours |
|---|---|---|
| First......................... | $ 73,000 | 20,000 |
| Second...................... | 79,500 | 30,000 |
| Third....................... | 110,500 | 50,000 |
| Fourth...................... | 92,000 | 40,000 |

*Required:*

a. By means of the least squares regression method, compute budgeted heat, light, and power cost as a variable rate per labor hour and a fixed cost per quarter.

b. Using the cost data computed in (a), calculate total budgeted cost at 20,000 and at 50,000 labor hours.

c. With the foregoing data, plot a least squares regression line on a graph of heat, light, and power cost.

8–7. The Placer Plastics Company is preparing a flexible budget of manufacturing overhead costs in its extrusion department. Volume in this department is measured in machine hours. Budgeted volume and budgeted power costs for the year 1977 have been projected as follows:

| Month | Machine Hours | Power Costs |
|---|---|---|
| January......................... | 2,000 | $ 6,000 |
| February....................... | 2,500 | 6,500 |
| March.......................... | 3,000 | 6,700 |
| April.......................... | 3,300 | 6,800 |
| May........................... | 4,000 | 7,100 |
| June........................... | 5,000 | 7,800 |
| July........................... | 6,000 | 8,600 |
| August......................... | 5,000 | 7,700 |
| September...................... | 4,500 | 7,500 |
| October........................ | 4,000 | 7,200 |
| November...................... | 3,500 | 7,000 |
| December...................... | 3,000 | 6,600 |
| | 45,800 | $85,500 |

Required:

a. Construct a graph of the projected relationship between machine hours and power costs for 1977.
b. By the least squares regression method, compute the budgeted power cost allowances at 3,000 and 6,000 machine hours. Draw the regression line on the graph prepared in a.

8–8. The San Benito Explosives Corporation has prepared the following quarterly budget of conversion costs in its Hollister Plant:

| | Quarter 1 | Quarter 2 | Quarter 3 | Quarter 4 |
|---|---|---|---|---|
| Direct labor................ | $ 600,000 | $ 750,000 | $ 800,000 | $ 700,000 |
| Indirect materials........... | 72,000 | 90,000 | 96,000 | 84,000 |
| Indirect labor.............. | 120,000 | 120,000 | 120,000 | 120,000 |
| Repair and maintenance..... | 225,000 | 262,500 | 275,000 | 250,000 |
| Depreciation............... | 300,000 | 300,000 | 300,000 | 300,000 |
| Supervision................ | 40,000 | 40,000 | 40,000 | 40,000 |
| Power and light............ | 184,000 | 220,000 | 232,000 | 208,000 |
| Labor-related costs.......... | 136,000 | 164,500 | 174,000 | 155,000 |
| | $1,677,000 | $1,947,000 | $2,037,000 | $1,857,000 |

Required:

Using direct labor cost as the measure of volume, prepare a flexible budget of manufacturing overhead in good form for the Hollister plant.

8-9.  The monthly flexible budget for manufacturing overhead in department 44 of the Humboldt Manufacturing Company is as follows:

| Cost Item | Variable Rate per Hour | Fixed Costs | 40,000 Labor Hours | 50,000 Labor Hours | 60,000 Labor Hours |
|---|---|---|---|---|---|
| Indirect labor.............. | $ .60 | $ 33,000 | $ 57,000 | $ 63,000 | $ 69,000 |
| Supervision................ | | 44,000 | 44,000 | 44,000 | 44,000 |
| Labor-related costs......... | .28 | 6,000 | 17,200 | 20,000 | 22,800 |
| Indirect materials.......... | .24 | | 9,600 | 12,000 | 14,400 |
| Power and light............ | .12 | 9,000 | 13,800 | 15,000 | 16,200 |
| Maintenance............... | .36 | 12,000 | 26,400 | 30,000 | 33,600 |
| Depreciation............... | | 48,000 | 48,000 | 48,000 | 48,000 |
| Miscellaneous.............. | | 18,000 | 18,000 | 18,000 | 18,000 |
| | $1.60 | $170,000 | $234,000 | $250,000 | $266,000 |

The volume of operations in department 44 was expected to average 50,000 labor hours per month during 1977. For the month of August, actual operations in the department totaled 55,000 labor hours. The actual manufacturing overhead costs incurred during August were as follows:

| | |
|---|---|
| Indirect labor......................... | $ 68,500 |
| Supervision........................... | 39,500 |
| Labor-related costs.................... | 22,200 |
| Indirect materials..................... | 12,500 |
| Power and light....................... | 15,300 |
| Maintenance.......................... | 33,000 |
| Depreciation.......................... | 49,800 |
| Miscellaneous......................... | 17,700 |
| | $258,500 |

*Required:*

a.  Prepare an expense report for department 44 for the month of August 1977. Show the variances of actual costs from budgeted costs in whatever manner you feel would be most useful to management.

b.  Under absorption costing, what would the normal variable and fixed manufacturing overhead rates be in department 44 for 1977?

8-10.  The flexible manufacturing overhead budget for the packing department of the Imperial Drug Company allows $300,000 per month plus $2.50 per man hour worked in the department. Actual cost data for the first quarter of 1977 are summarized below:

| Month | Variable Costs | Fixed Costs | Man Hours |
|---|---|---|---|
| January........... | $198,000 | $320,000 | 82,000 |
| February.......... | 188,000 | 310,000 | 76,000 |
| March............ | 166,000 | 295,000 | 64,000 |

Operating volume in this department for 1977 has been budgeted at 75,000 man hours per month.

*Required:*

a. Prepare a report showing the spending variance from the budget for each month and for the quarter in total.

b. What inferences about packing department costs may be drawn from an examination of the variances in this report?

 **8-11.** Following is the manufacturing overhead budget for the shearing department of the Contra Costa Swimwear Company for one month:

| Direct labor hours...... | 20,000 | 30,000 | 40,000 | 50,000 |
|---|---|---|---|---|
| Indirect labor......... | $18,000 | $23,000 | $28,000 | $33,000 |
| Supplies.............. | 6,000 | 9,000 | 12,000 | 15,000 |
| Space occupancy....... | 25,000 | 25,000 | 25,000 | 25,000 |
| Total manufacturing overhead............ | $49,000 | $57,000 | $65,000 | $73,000 |

Volume for 1977 had been budgeted at 40,000 direct labor hours per month. During September 1977, the department worked a total of 32,000 direct labor hours and incurred the following manufacturing overhead costs:

| | |
|---|---|
| Indirect labor......................... | $25,000 |
| Supplies.............................. | 9,000 |
| Space occupancy...................... | 23,500 |
| Total................................ | $57,500 |

*Required:*

a. Identify each cost item in this budget as variable, fixed, or semi-variable.

b. Convert the budget shown above into the basic format of a flexible budget.

c. Prepare an expense report for September 1977.

8-12. The flexible budget for the smelting department of the Kern Copper Corporation appears as follows:

| Cost Item | Variable Rate per Machine Hour | Fixed Cost per Quarter |
|---|---|---|
| Indirect materials..................... | $ 2.50 | |
| Indirect labor........................ | 6.00 | $ 45,000 |
| Power and water...................... | 1.20 | 20,000 |
| Maintenance.......................... | 12.00 | 150,000 |
| Taxes and insurance................... | | 5,500 |
| Depreciation.......................... | | 225,000 |
| Labor-related costs.................... | 3.30 | 4,500 |
| | $25.00 | $450,000 |

Production volume in this department had been budgeted at 15,000 machine hours per quarter for the year 1977. During the third quarter of 1977, actual production volume was only 12,000 machine hours. The following actual manufacturing overhead costs were incurred in the smelting department during the third quarter:

| | |
|---|---|
| Indirect materials............................ | $ 32,750 |
| Indirect labor............................... | 112,500 |
| Power and water............................ | 36,800 |
| Maintenance............................... | 278,000 |
| Taxes and insurance........................ | 6,000 |
| Depreciation............................... | 212,500 |
| Labor-related costs......................... | 47,250 |
| | $725,800 |

*Required:*

a. Prepare an expense report for the smelting department for the third quarter of 1977. Show variances of actual costs from the budget in the most appropriate way.
b. How could there be a variance for a committed fixed cost like depreciation?

8–13. Solano Corporation uses fixed budgets for manufacturing overhead. For 1976, a total of $450,000 was budgeted for the assembly department. This total was divided by 12 to obtain monthly budget allowances, which were then used to compute the monthly variances shown in the table below. Also included in this table are the actual labor hours worked in the assembly department during 1976. Management believes that manufacturing overhead costs are affected more by the number of labor hours worked than by any other factor.

| Month | Variance from Budget | Labor Hours |
|---|---|---|
| January..................... | $ 7,500 | 5,000 |
| February.................... | 5,500 | 6,000 |
| March...................... | 3,500 | 7,000 |
| April....................... | 1,500 | 8,000 |
| May........................ | ( 2,500) | 10,000 |
| June........................ | ( 6,500) | 12,000 |
| July........................ | (12,500) | 15,000 |
| August...................... | ( 8,500) | 13,000 |
| September................... | ( 2,500) | 10,000 |
| October..................... | 1,500 | 8,000 |
| November................... | 5,500 | 6,000 |
| December................... | 7,500 | 5,000 |
| | $      0 | 105,000 |

*Required:*

Determine more useful monthly variances from the budget for 1976.

8-14. You have been engaged as a management consultant to the Calaveras Manufacturing Corporation. The firm is not large, and its entire factory is treated as a single responsibility center for purposes of charging manufacturing overhead to production. The corporation manufactures three products: Dese, Dem, and Dose. Normal production times for these three products are two labor hours, eight labor hours, and three labor hours, respectively.

You have learned that budgeted output for 1976 called for production of 100,000 units of Dese, 20,000 units of Dem, and 70,000 units of Dose. Manufacturing overhead for the year was budgeted at $1,140,000 for variable costs and $1,710,000 for fixed costs. Variable manufacturing overhead varies in relation to labor hours. You are satisfied that the budgeted cost allowances were reasonable and that the classifications of costs as fixed and variable are proper.

The corporation's chief accountant established normal manufacturing overhead rates per unit of product by means of the average labor time per unit of budgeted output. This average labor time was computed as shown below.

| Product | Budgeted Units | Labor Hours per Unit | Total Labor Hours |
|---------|---------------|----------------------|-------------------|
| Dese............... | 100,000 | 2 | 200,000 |
| Dem............... | 20,000 | 8 | 160,000 |
| Dose............... | 70,000 | 3 | 210,000 |
|  | 190,000 |  | 570,000 |

Average labor time per unit of output = 570,000 hours ÷ 190,000 units = 3 hours per unit.

The normal manufacturing overhead rates used for product cost accounting were then determined as follows:

| | Total Costs | ÷ Total Hours | = Normal Rate per Hour | × Average Hours per Unit | = Normal Rate per Unit |
|---|-----------|---------------|------------------------|--------------------------|------------------------|
| Variable costs....... | $1,140,000 | 570,000 | $2 | 3 | $ 6 |
| Fixed costs......... | 1,710,000 | 570,000 | 3 | 3 | 9 |
| Totals............ | $2,850,000 |  |  |  | $15 |

Actual output for 1976 consisted of 80,000 units of Dese, 40,000 units of Dem, and 40,000 units of Dose. The normal production times for the three products were met exactly throughout the year. Actual variable manufacturing overhead for the year totaled $1,150,000 and actual fixed manufacturing overhead, $1,750,000. The chief accountant submitted the following analysis of underapplied manufacturing overhead to the factory manager at the end of the year:

Actual manufacturing overhead costs incurred . . . . . . . . . . $2,900,000
Manufacturing overhead applied to production
   (160,000 units @ $15) . . . . . . . . . . . . . . . . . . . . . . . . . . . . .   2,400,000
Net underapplied manufacturing overhead . . . . . . . . . . . . .  $ 500,000

The factory manager expressed surprise upon receiving this analysis. He said that he had been under the impression that the factory was operating at a level even greater than originally planned, and he could not understand how more than 17% of total manufacturing overhead could have been unabsorbed by production. He has asked you to review the cost and production records and submit a report to him.

*Required:*

a. Evaluate the manufacturing overhead costing procedure developed by the chief accountant.
b. Prepare for the factory manager a report showing what you feel is the most useful comparison of actual and planned manufacturing overhead costs for 1976.
c. The inventory of finished product at December 31, 1976, consists of 3,000 units of Dese, 2,000 units of Dem, and 1,500 units of Dose. There is no inventory of work in process at the end of the year. Finished product is costed by the first-in, first-out cost flow assumption. As a consequence of the costing procedure used by the chief accountant, are the Finished Product and Cost of Goods Sold accounts correctly stated as of December 31, 1976? If not, what adjusting entry or entries should be made to correct them? Support any adjustments with appropriate computations. (Assume that the inventory of finished product at January 1, 1976, had been costed correctly.)

# chapter 9

# Standards and Standard Costs

$\mathrm{T}$HE DISCUSSION of cost accounting in Chapters 3 and 4 focused on historical costs, the costs that *actually were incurred*. In Chapter 7, the focus was on budgeted costs, those that management expects *will be incurred* in the future. In this chapter and the next one, we will turn our attention to accounting procedures that deal with the costs that *should be incurred*. Planning and control are active management functions that depend upon the availability of relevant information. Financial information and cost data, in particular, are important parts of that set of relevant information. In order to plan and control costs most effectively, management needs to know not only what costs have been and what they may be expected to be but also what they ought to be. In other words, management needs criteria for determining the "right amount" of costs. These criteria are found in standards and standard costs.

## STANDARDS

In general, *standards* may be defined as measured quantities which *should be* attained in connection with some particular operation or activity. The amount which should be attained is determined by management in accordance with its best judgment. Standards are not determined according to unquestioned and immutable natural laws. They are set by human judgment and, consequently, are subject to the same fallibility which attends all human activity. In the paragraphs that follow, we shall consider some of the quantities for which standards are frequently established in manufacturing enterprises and also the degrees of accuracy and precision implicit in standards.

## Price Standards

*Materials Price Standards.* In most manufacturing operations, one of the most important cost elements is the cost of purchased raw materials. Management is interested in keeping this cost as low as possible, consistent with the need to maintain product quality. Part of the control of materials cost depends upon efficient purchasing and obtaining the most favorable possible price for the materials needed. A *materials price standard* is the price which should be paid for a particular raw material under the most favorable possible conditions. "The most favorable possible conditions" must be interpreted in light of the individual firm. The best price for one firm for a particular material may be either lower or higher than the best price for another firm for the identical item. In most cases, materials price standards can be set only for the firm, not for the industry as a whole.

Included in the standard materials price are all components of the amount which must be expended in order to acquire a particular material. Different suppliers may sell the same materials at different list prices. Assuming no differences in the qualities of the goods or in the services rendered by the various suppliers, the supplier offering the lowest price would be selected; and the materials price standard would be established on that basis. Differences in quality or in service may justify the selection of a higher-price supplier, however. Thus, a supplier who cannot be relied upon to deliver materials when needed ought not be chosen simply because he sells materials at lower prices than his more dependable competitors. To the extent that his lower prices are reflected in unsatisfactory service, they are false savings to the buyer.

Freight charges are part of the purchase cost of materials, and they normally vary with the distance between the supplier and the purchaser. Thus, in setting materials price standards, a firm should look to the closest reliable sources of supply (presuming that all other factors are equal). Where materials are purchased from foreign suppliers, there may be import duties involved. These should be included as part of acquisition costs and incorporated in price standards.

Where discounts are available to the purchaser of materials, they should be included in the determination of price standards. *Quantity discounts* are granted for purchases of materials in relatively large lots. For example, the price per unit of an item may be lower when it is purchased in carloads than when it is purchased in smaller quantities. To the extent that quantity discounts are reasonable in the circumstances of the individual purchaser, they should be included in the calculation of the standard materials price. Obviously, it would be unreasonable for a firm to set materials price standards on the basis of carload discounts when carload quantities would represent supplies for excessively long periods of time and would involve undue materials storage and handling costs.

*Cash discounts* are granted for prompt payment of invoices, typically within 10 to 15 days. For example, the terms "2/10, n/30" on an invoice mean that the purchaser may deduct a 2% discount from the billed price if he pays within 10 days and that, in any event, the amount billed is due within 30 days. In the past, the materials cost in such a case was generally considered to be the gross amount billed, and the 2% discount, if taken by the purchaser, was treated as an adjustment to the cost of goods sold for the period. More recently, accountants have come to view the actual price of such materials as the net invoice price after deduction of the discount. This would be 98% of the gross amount billed in the example above. This view assumes that all cash discounts will be taken by a profit motivated firm. Any discounts not taken (accounts not paid within the allowed discount period) are then regarded as financial costs attributable to a lack of proper planning of cash resources and not to improper purchasing practices. In our discussion, we shall accept this latter view of cash discounts and shall incorporate them in price standards.

Let us now consider a simple illustration of the setting of a materials price standard. The Rackstraw Marine Corporation uses only one raw material, steel, in the manufacture of its product. It has investigated alternative sources of supply and has determined that the Bobstay Company is the most advantageous supplier. Bobstay's regular list price for steel is $182 per ton, f.o.b. shipping point (i.e., the purchaser pays the freight charges). However, there is a $7 quantity discount per ton for carload orders of 20 tons. The volume of Rackstraw's business is sufficient to make it economical for the corporation to purchase steel in carload lots. Hence, Rackstraw would base its price standard on the carload price. The Bobstay Company also allows a 2% cash discount for payment within 15 days. Finally, there is a freight charge of $170 per carload; this is paid directly to the carrier and is not eligible for any cash discount. Rackstraw's computation of its standard materials price is as follows:

| | |
|---|---:|
| Carload price ($182 − $7) | $175.00 |
| Less cash discount (2% × $175) | 3.50 |
| | $171.50 |
| Add freight charges ($170 ÷ 20 tons) | 8.50 |
| Standard price per ton | $180.00 |

This standard price provides a basis for planning future materials costs and for controlling current costs by providing a criterion against which actual prices paid for materials may be evaluated.

*Labor Rate Standards.*  The price paid for labor is usually stated as a wage rate per hour or per piece of production or as a weekly or monthly salary. While it is possible to conceive of a standard weekly or monthly salary, such labor costs are normally not stated in terms of standards. Salaries are typically controlled by means of budgets rather than standards. Thus, labor price standards may be thought of as *wage rate standards* only. The rate may be either an hourly rate or a piece rate.

Wage rate standards are normally either a matter of company policy or the result of negotiations between management and a union. In either case, the accountant simply incorporates the rate established, however it may have been determined, in his work as appropriate. Deviations from established wage rates are unlikely to occur without foreknowledge on the part of management. A contractual wage increase due to a rise in the consumer price level, for example, may be predicted and planned for by observation of the trend of the Consumer Price Index.

In most manufacturing firms there will be several different wage rates. Rates will vary depending upon the degree of skill necessary for a particular job, the element of danger (if any) involved in a specific task, workers' seniority, and other characteristics of the various workers. Both hourly rates and piece rates may be paid in the same plant. Thus, there is typically a series of standard wage rates rather than a single rate. In most of the illustrations in this text, however, only one or two rates will be used for the sake of simplicity and brevity.

In the Rackstraw Marine Corporation (the illustration begun in the preceding section) there are two production departments. In the first, the molding department, the current standard wage rate is $4.80 per hour. In the second, the grinding department, the standard wage rate is $5.00 per hour. The difference between these two rates reflects a higher level of skill required of workers in the grinding department.

## Quantity Standards

*Materials Usage Standards.*  The cost of materials used by a manufacturer is a function of two factors, the price paid for the materials and the quantity of the materials used. Materials price standards have already been discussed. The quantity of materials used for the production of a particular product can also be subjected to standardization. Of course, there will be different quantity standards for different materials; and different standards may apply to the usage of a single material in different products or in different departments. *Materials quantity standards,* or *materials usage standards,* are established on the basis of necessary input-output relationships between materials and products and also upon observations of actual experience. For example, it may be a simple fact that a two-pound hammerhead requires two pounds of steel.

It may also be a fact that the firm's experience shows that a two-pound hammerhead can be manufactured only by using slightly more than two pounds of steel in order to allow for weight losses due to scraping and smoothing. Both of these facts should be incorporated in the materials usage standard for hammerheads. These standards do not represent the minimum possible use of materials in production but the minimum efficient use after due allowances for materials shrinkage and loss. Any time that a liquid is boiled, for example, there will be some quantity loss due to evaporation. It would be clearly unrealistic and useless in such a case to set a materials quantity standard that did not allow for the evaporation loss.

The Rackstraw Marine Corporation produces a single product, capstan heads. As indicated before, the only raw material used in the manufacture of this product is steel. Each finished head weighs 40 pounds. However, in the grinding department, part of the steel that comes out of the molds is removed as the heads are ground and smoothed. Thus, it is necessary to use more than 40 pounds of steel in order to get a 40-pound finished product. Past experience coupled with careful engineering studies has shown that a steel input equal to 105% of the desired output is proper if the grinding process is performed efficiently. Thus, the standard materials usage per unit of product is as follows:

| | |
|---|---:|
| Weight of finished product | 40 lbs. |
| Allowance for normal loss in grinding (5% × 40) | 2 lbs. |
| Standard materials usage | 42 lbs. |

This standard quantity does not provide for loss of materials due to careless handling, damage to units in process, or other undesirable circumstances. Indeed, these are the types of materials losses that use of the standard is intended to help eliminate.

*Labor Time Standards.* Labor quantities are measured in units of time, generally the time required to complete a particular operation. Thus, *labor time standards* are the amounts of time which particular productive operations should take. The labor time standard for a product is the sum of the time standards for all operations necessary to the completion of the product. Labor time standards are normally established on the basis of observations of actual operations and a critical evaluation of whether or not those operations are being performed as efficiently as is feasible. Labor time standards typically include provisions for a reasonable amount of time lost simply because human beings are not mechanical devices and cannot utilize every second on the job for actual production. However, labor time standards ought not provide for prolonged periods of idleness or for incompetence. If such time losses were incorporated in them, the standards would be of little value to management for purposes of cost control.

Labor time standards are commonly set on the basis of engineering studies of how long it should take an efficient worker to perform a particular task. A fairly familiar example of this process is a time and motion study. In this study, an engineer observes many workers performing a particular task many times. Through these observations, he determines what is the most efficient way to perform each step in the total operation. For example, if the worker must turn from a machine to pick up a piece of material, the time and motion study might determine when the worker should turn, in which direction he should turn, and where the stack of materials should be located so as to minimize his total time and effort. The final time standard is then the sum of the times required for each step in the operation. To some extent, time standards usually reflect an average of numerous actual observations. That is, if one worker was once able to complete an operation in a very short time, this single observation might not be a realistic and useful basis for setting the standard. Although labor time standards deal directly with workers' time, they may be affected by factors other than the workers themselves. If a worker performs an operation with a machine or a hand tool, the labor time standard for that operation will be controlled partly by the performance characteristics of the machine or the tool. For example, a laser can cut steel faster than an acetylene torch can. Thus, technical features of equipment are also relevant to setting the standard.

Engineering studies in the Rackstraw Marine Corporation have shown that each capstan head should be produced in one fourth of an hour in the molding department and one half of an hour in the grinding department. Each of these standards is the summation of times required for individual operations. For example, in the molding department, steel is first melted in caldrons. The molten metal is then poured into molds. When a mold has cooled, it is opened and the molded head is removed. The head is then washed with a mild acid solution and placed on a conveyor belt that takes it to the grinding department. Each operation in this process was studied and a standard time determined. The sum of those standard times is the quarter-hour time standard. A similar procedure was required to set the time standard in the grinding department.

*Rework Costs.*  In many production operations, a portion of the goods manufactured are spoiled or damaged during the process. Such goods may have to be discarded or sold as scrap. Alternatively, they may be salvageable if they are reworked. Whatever the case, there will be costs incurred in the production of units which never become finished products or are finished only after extra work is done on them. To the extent that spoilage is unavoidable, such costs should be incorporated in the standard cost of the good units produced. If some of the units produced have to be scrapped, the costs incurred to produce them may simply be allocated equally among the good units that are completed. If rework is necessary on some units, the normal amount of rework should be charged equally to all units produced. In other words, there should be a standard rework charge. If rework also involves the use of additional materials, this materials cost should be allocated among the good units produced.

In the Rackstraw Marine Corporation, an average of 1 out of every 20 capstan heads removed from molds is spoiled. This may be caused by cracking when the mold is opened or by air pockets formed during the cooling process. These spoiled heads are simply thrown back into the caldron to be remelted and poured again. Hence, there is no loss of materials associated with the spoilage; but there is rework time. The time required to put a defective head back into the caldron is the same as the time required to rinse a good head and load it onto the conveyor belt. Thus, it is necessary to work one fourth of an hour in the molding department 21 times in order to produce 20 good heads. So long as this rate of spoilage is considered unavoidable, the additional time should be included in the determination of the standard cost. One way to do this is to compute the standard labor cost in the molding department in two steps. The first step computes the cost of one fourth of an hour at the standard wage of $4.80 per hour. The second step adds a standard rework charge equal to one twentieth of this cost. Thus, the final standard labor cost per head would be as follows:

Basic labor cost ($\frac{1}{4}$ hr. $\times$ $4.80) . . . . . . . . . . . . . . . . . . . . . . $1.20
Plus rework charge (1/20 $\times$ $1.20) . . . . . . . . . . . . . . . . . . . .06
$1.26

Alternatively, the rework time could be included directly in the labor time standard. Thus, the initial standard time would be one fourth of an hour. This would then be increased by one twentieth of one fourth. The resultant standard labor cost would be exactly the same as that computed under the first method.

$$\frac{1}{4} \text{ hour} + (\frac{1}{4} \text{ hr.} \times 1/20) = 21/80 \text{ hour}$$
$$21/80 \text{ hour} \times \$4.80 = \$1.26$$

This latter method will be used in subsequent considerations of this same illustration throughout the chapter.

## Degree of Precision in Standards

The discussion of quantity standards in the preceding paragraphs has suggested that these standards be set in light of reasonable circumstances and not in accordance with some determination of perfect performance. Most standards, in practice, do provide for reasonable amounts of excess quantities. Such standards are described as *current attainable standards*. They reflect quantities which can reasonably be attained under current conditions. They provide for lost time and materials due to circumstances which cannot reasonably be corrected. This does not mean that they are based simply upon what is actually done presently, but rather, upon what can be done by efficient performance of tasks. For example, a labor time standard may be set according to the conclusions drawn from a time and motion study as to the length of time required for a competent and experienced worker to perform an operation, with due allowances for normal lost time. If the firm has several inexperienced workers performing this operation at a particular time, it is highly improbable that the time standard will be met. This does not invalidate the standard, nor does it necessarily mean that these workers' performance is bad. The workers' inexperience serves to explain a temporary deviation from the standard. It may be expected that these deviations will diminish and ultimately disappear as the workers reach the standard level of experience.

The principal alternatives to current attainable standards are *perfection standards*, which allow only those quantities of materials or time which are absolutely essential to the accomplishment of a job. For example, it may be mathematically possible to obtain 324 brass disks of a 2-inch diameter from 1 square yard of sheet brass. The shortcomings of both humans and machines are such, however, that it is extremely unlikely that so many could actually be obtained. Nevertheless, a perfection standard would ignore this fact and would be based upon the maximum possible yield of disks. A current attainable standard, on the other hand, would allow for additional lost materials in light of what can be ascertained to be reasonable. The perfection standard, it should be observed, does allow for materials loss in this illustration, but only that loss which is technologically unavoidable. Obviously, not all of the brass in a sheet can actually be used in the cutting out of round pieces.

Some businessmen have contended that perfection standards are preferable to attainable standards because they provide a stimulus, or incentive, to workers to achieve the best possible performance. While this may prove true in some instances, it is more likely that a perfection standard, never attained, will result only in discouragement and resentment on the part of workers and, thus, defeat its own avowed purpose. A better incentive may be provided by an attainable standard which is set as "tight" as appears to be reasonable. Thus, while it may not be met often, it at least offers the workers a goal which they feel can be reached. Urging a runner to a four-minute mile may stimulate his competitive spirit; urging him to a three-minute mile may only frustrate him.

## Review and Revision of Standards

A standard set at one moment of time may be reasonably attainable and may be a suitable criterion for the evaluation of actual performance at that moment. At some later time, however, the standard may no longer be attainable; or it may be so easily bettered that it is useless for purposes of planning and control. As market conditions change, prices change. A materials usage standard and/or a labor time standard may be rendered obsolete by technological innovations. Hence, standards must not be regarded as static quantities. As conditions change, relevant standards must change with them in order to remain useful. This means that all standards must be reexamined frequently and, when necessary, altered to conform to new circumstances. It is not necessary that standards be altered every time there is some slight change in the factors which bear upon them. If this were attempted, a company might find that its principal products were standards and that a technique originally adopted to control costs had become excessively costly itself. While minor changes in conditions do invalidate standards slightly, such minor changes can be compensated for in management's evaluation of actual performance against standards. Temporary changes in conditions, even if material in their effects, should not cause changes in standards. For example, a temporary shortage of a particular commodity may increase its price substantially, but not permanently. Many firms which employ standards adhere to a practice of frequent (perhaps quarterly) review of standards but revision of standards only as of the beginning of a new fiscal year, except where a substantial and permanent change in circumstances makes earlier revision appear desirable.

## STANDARD COSTS

### Materials and Labor

In line with the foregoing discussion of standards, *standard costs* may be defined as costs that reasonably should be incurred in the manufacture of a product. Thus, standard costs are quantities associated with units of output (i.e., products), whereas standards are measures associated with units of input (i.e., materials and labor). The standard direct materials cost and the standard direct labor cost of a product are based upon price and quantity standards. They are computed by multiplying price standards by quantity standards. Standard materials and labor costs are shown below for the continuing illustration of the Rackstraw Marine Corporation.

We have seen previously that the standard price paid for steel by Rackstraw is $180 per ton. The standard usage of steel is 42 pounds per finished unit of product. Obviously, these two standards are not directly compatible. The price standard must first be reduced to an amount per pound of steel before it can be used to determine the standard materials cost. The standard price per pound is $.09 ($180 ÷ 2,000 lbs.). Thus, the standard materials cost for one unit of product is $3.78 (42 lbs. of steel @ $.09).

Standard labor costs are computed in the same way. Standard wage rates are multiplied by standard labor times. In the Rackstraw Marine Corporation, there are two separate production departments, each with its own standard wage rate and standard labor time. Thus, the standard labor cost per unit of product must be calculated in two steps. First, in the molding department, the standard wage rate is $4.80 per hour. The standard labor time is one fourth of an hour plus an additional one twentieth of that time for unavoidable rework. This makes a total of 21/80 of an hour in the department. The standard labor cost in the molding department, then, is $1.26 per unit (21/80 hr. @ $4.80). In the grinding department, the standard wage rate is $5.00 per hour and the standard labor time is one-half hour per unit. Thus, the standard labor cost is $2.50 per unit of product (½ hr. @ $5.00). The total standard labor cost, then, is the sum of these two departmental costs.

### Manufacturing Overhead

The standard materials and labor costs of a product are based upon price and quantity standards. This is possible because there is a functional relationship between the number of units of a product produced and the quantities of materials and labor required and because each material has its standard price and each worker, his standard wage rate. No such functional relationship exists between the units produded and total manufacturing overhead, however. Even that portion of manufacturing overhead which varies with the volume of production cannot be directly related to production as can direct materials and labor. As a consequence, standard costs for manufacturing overhead are based upon budgets, not upon standards. Again, a proper understanding of the distinction between standards and standard costs is important. Standard costs can be established without standards, and they are in the case of manufacturing overhead.

Mechanically, standard manufacturing overhead rates are determined in essentially the same way as normal manufacturing overhead rates, which were explained in Chapter 3. Separate rates for variable and fixed costs are essential if the standard manufacturing overhead costs are to be useful for purposes of planning and control. Consequently, these rates must be derived from flexible budgets. The volume measure used in the flexible budget is the basis for the standard rates. Most commonly, this volume measure is some measure of input, such as direct labor cost or hours. The standard variable manufacturing overhead rate is set directly per unit of volume, just as a normal variable rate. The only difference between standard and normal fixed manufacturing overhead rates lies in the volume at which they are set. Normal fixed rates are set at the budgeted volume for the budget period, as shown in Chapter 3. Standard fixed rates, however, are usually set at some volume representative of the company's operations over a longer period than a single budget year.

*Normal Volume.* The volume level most commonly selected for setting standard fixed manufacturing overhead rates is *normal volume*. Normal volume is usually defined in either of two ways, which may or may not prove to be equivalent in any given situation. The first definition of normal volume is the preferred rate of operating capacity in a firm's manufacturing facilities. Each firm identifies a particular rate, or level of capacity at which it would most like to operate its plant. Logically, this is that level at which the mix of productive inputs is optimized and, hence, total manufacturing cost per unit of product is minimized. It is easy to see that such a concept of normal volume would be consistent with the notion of standard cost—the cost that should be incurred under efficient operating conditions. In many firms, the preferred rate of operating capacity is at or near 90 percent of full capacity.

The second definition of normal volume is the average level of production activity over a complete business cycle. This is a difficult concept to quantify because business cycles are not always easily defined and because, in most firms, there is a long-term growth trend underlying cyclical fluctuations. Thus, this long-term average level of operations would usually be an upward moving average. While management might wish that the average production volume would be equal to the preferred rate of capacity, it is more likely that it would be lower. The preferred rate is more likely to be achieved only during periods of economic prosperity.

However it is defined, normal volume will not necessarily be equal to budgeted production volume for any given period. While the standard fixed manufacturing overhead rate is properly based on normal volume, the operating budget should be predicated upon the best estimate of what volume actually will be during the budget period.

*Standard Manufacturing Overhead Rates.* In the Rackstraw Marine Corporation, direct labor hours are the volume measures in the flexible budgets of both departments and, hence, the basis on which manufacturing overhead is applied to production. Variable manufacturing overhead is budgeted at $1.60 per direct labor hour in the molding department. Fixed manufacturing overhead in that department is budgeted at a total of $160,000 per year, and normal production volume has been established at 40,000 direct labor hours per year. Hence, the standard fixed manufacturing overhead rate is $4 per hour. Standard labor time in the molding department is 21/80 hour per unit produced. Multiplication of this time standard by the standard manufacturing overhead rates produces standard manufacturing overhead costs per unit of output of $.42 for variable manufacturing overhead (21/80 hr. × $1.60) and $1.05 for fixed manufacturing overhead (21/80 hr. × $4). In the grinding department, variable manufacturing overhead is budgeted at $1 per direct labor hour and fixed manufacturing overhead, at $120,000 per year. Normal production volume is 80,000 labor hours per year. The standard fixed manufacturing overhead rate, then, is $1.50 per labor hour. Standard labor time is one-half hour per unit of output. Thus, the standard variable manufacturing overhead cost per unit is $.50 (½ hr. × $1); and the standard fixed manufacturing overhead cost per unit is $.75 (½ hr. × $1.50). Obviously, Rackstraw Marine Corporation is using absorption costing. If variable costing were used, there would be no standard fixed manufacturing overhead costs.

## Standard Cost Sheet

The total standard cost of a product is usually summarized on a *standard cost sheet* or *standard cost card*. This is simply a listing of the various raw materials, classes of labor, and departmental manufacturing overhead charges that make up the total standard cost of the product. It is illustrated for the Rackstraw Marine Corporation in Table 9–1.

### TABLE 9–1
#### RACKSTRAW MARINE CORPORATION
Standard Cost Sheet
One Capstan Head

| | | |
|---|---:|---:|
| Direct materials: | | |
| Steel (42 lbs. @ $.09)............................... | | $ 3.78 |
| Direct labor: | | |
| Molding department (21/80 hr. @ $4.80)............... | $1.26 | |
| Grinding department (½ hr. @ $5.00)................. | 2.50 | 3.76 |
| Variable manufacturing overhead: | | |
| Molding department (21/80 hr. @ $1.60)............... | $ .42 | |
| Grinding department (½ hr. @ $1.00)................. | .50 | .92 |
| Fixed manufacturing overhead: | | |
| Molding department (21/80 hr. @ $4.00)............... | $1.05 | |
| Grinding department (½ hr. @ $1.50)................. | .75 | 1.80 |
| | | $10.26 |

In this particular illustration, standard cost is determined for an individual unit of product. This need not always be the case. Especially where each unit is small and inexpensive, standard production cost may be expressed in terms of some group of units (e.g., one gross, one case, one thousand, and so forth).

## Nonmanufacturing Operations

Historically, standards and standard costs have been related almost exclusively to manufacturing. In recent years, considerable interest has been demonstrated in methods of setting and using standards for non-manufacturing operations. Obviously, standards can be established only for routine, repetitive operations. Certain nonmanufacturing activities do not lend themselves to standardization. It would be impossible to establish a useful standard cost for the retail sale of one automobile, for example. No two customers and, hence, no two sales are exactly the same. It may not be impossible to set standards for certain automobile servicing functions, however, or for the routine processing of customers' accounts. Conceivably, the cost of certain nonmanufacturing supplies may be controllable by the use of price and quantity standards, much in the same way as are materials. Some administrative work may lend itself to the establishment of wage rate and labor time standards. More often, however, administrative employees receive weekly or monthly salaries that do not vary with the amount of work done. Thus, while some standard costs for nonmanufacturing operations may be feasible on the basis of price and quantity standards, most commonly such standard costs would have to be based upon budgets in a manner similar to the setting of standard manufacturing overhead costs. A more expansive treatment of this subject will be deferred until Chapter 11. The reader should be aware, however, that standards and standard costs are not necessarily restricted to manufacturing costs, even though the majority of their applications has been in that area.

## STANDARDS AS TOOLS OF PLANNING AND CONTROL

At the beginning of this chapter, we noted that standards and standard costs are used as criteria for management in the planning and control of costs. Current attainable standards can be very useful bases for planning future costs. If standard costs for materials and labor and standard variable manufacturing overhead rates are available, an estimate of future production volume can be converted into an estimate of variable manufacturing costs by simple multiplication. Materials usage standards, along with volume forecasts, can provide the basis for purchase planning. Work force requirements can be determined by coupling volume estimates with labor time standards. Thus, standard variable costs may be used as budgeted variable costs. However, they need not always be the same. Budgeted costs should reflect management's best judgment of what may be expected to occur. For certain periods, management may expect that standard costs will not be met because of uncontrollable circumstances. In such cases, the standard costs should not be used as budgeted costs. Nevertheless, if the special circumstances are expected to be only temporary, the standards and standard costs should be left unchanged. Consequently, the budget will include planned variances from established standard costs.

Standards are useful in controlling costs because they provide targets for performance and references against which actual performance may be evaluated. Variances of actual data from standards are signals to management of conditions that may require attention and corrective action. These variances are the subject of the following chapter.

## QUESTIONS FOR DISCUSSION

1.  What is the difference between a standard and a standard cost?
2.  Why might a standard cost differ from the corresponding actual cost?
3.  What is the nature of the fundamental difference between standard costs for direct materials and labor and standard manufacturing overhead costs? What causes it?
4.  How do standards and standard costs facilitate the managerial functions of planning and control?
5.  "If standard costs are to be useful techniques for improving cost performance and for tightening cost control, they must be based upon perfection standards. Anything less will only encourage inefficiency." Do you agree with this statement? Explain your position.
6.  What is normal production volume? How is it determined? What function does it serve in connection with standards and standard costs?
7.  If reasonable standards are carefully established, why should it ever be necessary to change them? How often, if ever, should standards be changed?
8.  What factors should be considered in setting a materials price standard? A materials usage standard?
9.  In a large manufacturing firm, whom would you expect to be responsible for setting price and quantity standards for direct materials and labor?
10. Are standards and standard costs applicable to nonmanufacturing activities? Discuss.

## PROBLEMS

9–1.  The Domingo Corporation manufactures ornamental brass lamp bases in a single production process. The only raw material is brass, which is purchased in truckloads at a price of $.60 per pound. Four pounds are used in the manufacture of each lamp base. The production process requires 2 hours for each lamp base by workers who are paid an hourly wage rate of $4.20. Variable manufacturing overhead is applied to production at a rate of $.90 per labor hour, and fixed manufacturing overhead is applied at a rate of $1.80 per labor hour.

*Required:*

Prepare a standard cost sheet for one lamp base.

9–2.  Stewart Enterprises produces a high-strength adhesive for use in the installation of linoleum and floor tiles. It is a mixture of powder and oil that is heated and stirred until it forms a thick but pliant paste. Each can of this adhesive requires 4 pounds of powder and 12 ounces of oil. The production process takes 4 hours of work by a crew of six laborers and results in the production of 200 cans of adhesive. Manufacturing overhead is applied to production at standard rates per labor hour.

The standard cost sheet for one can of adhesive is as follows:

| | | | |
|---|---|---:|---:|
| Materials: | | | |
| | Powder............................... | $3.00 | |
| | Oil................................... | 4.20 | |
| | Can and label........................ | .15 | $7.35 |
| Direct labor............................. | | | .57 |
| Manufacturing overhead: | | | |
| | Variable............................. | $ .18 | |
| | Fixed................................ | .30 | .48 |
| | | | $8.40 |

*Required:*

Compute (*a*) the standard price per pound of powder, (*b*) the standard price per ounce of oil, (*c*) the standard wage rate per hour, (*d*) the standard variable manufacturing overhead rate per hour, and (*e*) the standard fixed manufacturing overhead rate per hour.

9–3. The Tucker Company manufactures a sealant from a single raw material. This material is regularly purchased in half-carload lots of 600 drums. Each drum contains 50 gallons. The most favorable supplier's list price for this material is $1.75 per gallon. He allows a discount of 2% for payment of invoices within 10 days of receipt. In addition, the purchaser is billed $15 for each drum shipped; this is a deposit on the drum itself. The purchaser receives full credit of $15 for each drum returned to the supplier. On the basis of long experience, it is reasonable to anticipate that 8% of the drums received will unavoidably not be returned for credit. No discount is allowed on drum deposits forfeited. The freight for a half-carload is $1,230.

The sealant is produced in standard lots of 72 gallons of finished product. Experience has shown that 10% of the materials put into the production process are unavoidably lost due to evaporation.

*Required:*

Compute the standard price per gallon of raw material, the standard usage of raw material per 72-gallon production lot, and the standard materials cost per gallon of finished product.

9–4. The Sills Manufacturing Company produces Product A from an input of two raw materials, X and Y. Material X is purchased in 50-pound bags at a list price of $120 per bag on credit terms of 1/15,n/30. Freight charges average $880 per truckload of 400 bags. Material Y is imported from Central America. Its list price is $9 per gallon. Import duties of $.60 per gallon must be paid by the purchaser. The average freight cost for a shipment of 1,000 gallons is $300.

Product A is manufactured in standard batches of one gross of pint jars. (One gross equals 144.) Jars are purchased in cases of 250 at a standard price of $16.10 per case. Eight percent of the jars received are broken before they can be filled; this breakage is regarded as normal. For each batch of Product A, 20 pounds of Material X and 16 gallons of Material Y are required.

*Required:*

Compute the standard materials cost per pint of finished product.

9–5. The Shirley Office Furniture Company manufactures 5-shelf steel bookcases in four successive production processes. These processes and their respective labor time and wage rate standards are as follows:

Frame forming: ⅓ hr. per frame @ $4.20 per hr.
Shelf cutting: ⅒ hr. per shelf @ $4.00 per hr.
Assembling: ¼ hr. per bookcase @ $4.80 per hr.
Painting: 1½ hrs. per rack @ $3.60 per hr.

In the assembling process, five shelves are welded to a frame. The completed bookcase is then hung on a large rack. When 20 bookcases have been placed on a rack, that rack is wheeled into the paint shop where all of the bookcases on it are spray-painted and then baked dry. The finished units are then transferred to the warehouse pending shipment to customers.

*Required:*

Compute the standard labor cost per finished bookcase.

9–6. The Milnes Company produces a liquid sweetener in three successive production departments: blending, cooking, and bottling. The operations of each department have been studied, and the time-study report reveals the following data for the completion of a standard 100-gallon batch of the sweetener:

|  | *Blending* | *Cooking* | *Bottling* |
|---|---|---|---|
| Minimum possible time............ | 2.00 hrs. | 3.75 hrs. | .50 hrs. |
| Normal time by trained and experienced personnel............ | 2.20 hrs. | 4.00 hrs. | .56 hrs. |
| Average time recently............. | 2.10 hrs. | 4.25 hrs. | .60 hrs. |
| Standard hourly wage rate.......... | $4.50 | $3.90 | $3.75 |

On the basis of past experience and an evaluation of future production requirements, it has been estimated that overtime work will be required in each department. Planned overtime will average 20 percent of the total time worked in each department. Each hour of overtime is paid at one and one-half times the regular standard hourly wage rate.

*Required:*

Compute the total standard labor cost of one batch of the liquid sweetener. If you felt that there were any alternatives in the computation of this standard labor cost, explain why you chose the alternative(s) you did.

9–7. The flexible budget of the Diaz Corporation for 1977 allows \$.60 per dollar of direct labor cost plus \$540,000 per quarter for manufacturing overhead costs. At budgeted direct labor wage rates, the total direct labor cost at 100% of operating capacity would be \$750,000 in 1977. The corporation's preferred rate of operating capacity is 90%. However, throughout the company's history, actual operations have averaged only 80% of capacity. During 1977, operations are budgeted at only 60% of capacity because of industry-wide excess capacity coupled with an expected severe contraction in total demand.

*Required:*

a. Compute the standard fixed manufacturing overhead rate under each of the alternative definitions of normal volume.

b. In an actual cost system, what would the predetermined fixed manufacturing overhead rate be in 1977?

c. Which fixed manufacturing overhead rate do you feel would be most useful in a standard cost accounting system? Why?

d. How will the choice of a fixed rate affect the spending variance from the flexible budget?

9–8. The Dooley Tool Corporation manufactures hammers in three production processes. Each finished hammer consists of a steel head weighing exactly one pound and a wooden handle. The standard purchase prices of the raw materials are as follows:

Steel........................... \$260 per ton
Lumber........................ \$.45 per board foot

In the process of cleaning the molded hammer heads, approximately .05 pounds of steel are necessarily scraped away. Ten handles are cut from one board foot of lumber, and 10% of the handles cut are broken or otherwise spoiled before they are finished. This loss is considered unavoidable.

The direct labor times and rates in the three production processes are as follows:

| Process | Time | Hourly Rate |
|---|---|---|
| Head molding: | | |
| Mold pouring................ | .08 hrs. per head | \$3.75 |
| Mold cleaning............... | .25 hrs. per head | 4.40 |
| Handle shaping: | | |
| Cutting.................... | .18 hrs. per handle | 4.50 |
| Finishing.................. | .15 hrs. per handle | 4.20 |
| Assembly................... | .05 hrs. per hammer | 4.60 |

Both variable and fixed manufacturing overhead costs are charged to production at standard rates per direct labor hour. The budgeted manufacturing overhead costs and the normal volumes in labor hours, by processes, are as follows:

|                                              | Head<br>Molding | Handle<br>Shaping | Assembly |
|----------------------------------------------|-----------------|-------------------|----------|
| Variable manufacturing overhead<br>per hour................................ | $   .95 | $   .80 | $  1.40 |
| Fixed manufacturing overhead per year.... | $264,000 | $224,000 | $48,000 |
| Normal volume in labor hours per year.... | 132,000 | 140,000 | 20,000 |

*Required:*

Prepare a standard cost sheet for one hammer.

9–9.  The Price Beauty Products Company makes a mild astringent for cosmetic use. It is sold to distributors in cases of one dozen 5-ounce bottles. The company uses variable costing in its production accounting system.

The principal raw material is a special chemical purchased in 50-gallon drums at a list price of $12 per gallon. The supplier allows a 2% discount off the list price for payment of invoices within 10 days. Freight charges average $7 per drum.

Bottles cost $3.42 per gross. Five percent of the bottles purchased are broken in handling. This breakage is considered normal.

The astringent is manufactured in standard batches of 75 gallons of finished product. One sixteenth of the material put into process is unavoidably lost because of spillage and evaporation.

Direct labor costs are incurred as follows:

    Distilling:   8 hours @ $5 per 75-gallon batch

    Bottling:   ¼ hour @ $4.80 per case

Budgeted manufacturing overhead costs are as follows:

    Distilling:   $1.50 per labor hour plus $15,000 per month

    Bottling:   $.90 per labor hour plus $45,000 per month

Direct labor hours are budgeted at 5,000 per month in distilling and 25,000 per month in bottling.

*Required:*

Compute the standard cost per case of finished product.

9–10.  A new product of the Elias Toiletries Corporation is Lan-O-Lov Skin Lotion, to be marketed in 4-ounce bottles at a suggested retail price of $.69 per bottle. Cost and production studies have resulted in the following estimated costs:

**Raw Materials**

| Item | Cost | Comment |
|------|------|---------|
| Container: | | |
|     4-oz. bottle.......... | $8.50 per gross | Allow additional 2% for breakage. |
|     Label............... | $5 per 1,000 | Allow additional 3% for waste. |
| Ingredients: | | |
|     Compound HX107... | $80 per 100 lbs. | 70 lbs. used per 125-gallon batch. |
|     Alcohol and glycerine. | $40 per 100 gals. | 80 gals. used per 125-gallon batch. |
|     Perfume oil.......... | See below. | 5 lbs. used per 125-gallon batch. |

Perfume oil is produced in 90-pound batches by another division of the corporation. The standard cost of one such batch is $1,296.

An allowance for lost ingredients due to overfilling, waste, and bottle breakage must be made in the amount of 5% of the total ingredients cost before consideration of this loss.

### Direct Labor per Gross

Compounding department..................... 1½ hours @ $4.20
Bottling and packing department............... 1 hour @ $3.95

### Manufacturing Overhead

| | Rate per Standard Labor Hour |
|---|---|
| Variable costs: | |
| Compounding department................... | $2.50 |
| Bottling and packing department............. | 1.80 |
| Fixed costs: | |
| Compounding department................... | 2.00 |
| Bottling and packing department............. | 3.00 |

*Required:*

Prepare a standard cost sheet for one gross of 4-ounce bottles of Lan-O-Lov Skin Lotion.

(Adapted from CPA Examination)

9–11.  Vickers, Ltd., manufactures steel automobile jacks in three successive production departments. In the stamping department, parts are stamped out on large presses. In the parts finishing department, these parts are ground and smoothed. In the assembly department, the parts are assembled into completed jacks, which are then tested and, if accepted, packed for shipping.

Following are the standard prices of materials and the standard labor and manufacturing overhead rates per hour in the three departments:

| | Stamping | Parts Finishing | Assembly |
|---|---|---|---|
| Steel......................... | $300 per ton | | |
| Packing materials.............. | | | $ .25 per jack |
| Direct labor.................. | $4.20 per hr. | $4.50 per hr. | $4.80 per hr. |
| Manufacturing overhead: | | | |
| Variable.................... | .90 per hr. | 1.00 per hr. | 1.60 per hr. |
| Fixed...................... | 2.10 per hr. | 1.50 per hr. | .60 per hr. |

Each finished jack contains 8 pounds of steel. In the parts finishing department, another pound per jack is unavoidably lost in the process.

After assembly, each jack is tested. If it does not function properly, it is rejected. The defective part is identified and thrown into a scrap bin. The good parts are returned to the beginning of the assembly process and reused. Experience has shown that about 5% of the total quantity of jack parts, by weight, is defective and must be scrapped.

Jacks that are tested and accepted are then packed and transferred to a warehouse.

Both the steel lost in the parts finishing department and the defective parts identified in the assembly department are accumulated and sold to scrap dealers for $140 per ton.

Standard production times by departments are as follows:

Stamping............................... 1/30 hr. per lb. of steel
Parts finishing.......................... 1/10 hr. per lb. of steel
Assembly:
   To assemble and test.................... ¼ hr. per jack
   To pack............................. 1/20 hr. per jack

*Required:*

Prepare a standard cost sheet for one finished jack. Show all necessary supporting computations.

chapter **10**

# Analysis of Variances from Standard Costs

$\mathbf{T}$HE PRECEDING CHAPTER introduced the concepts of standards and standard costs and explained how such measures are established for manufacturing cost elements. In this chapter, we will turn to the uses of standards and standard costs. There are two major applications of these concepts in a manufacturing firm. The principal purpose is to facilitate the planning and control of costs. Cost control is approached by comparing actual costs against established standards and then seeking the reasons for any variances. The secondary application is the use of standard costs in lieu of actual costs in the manufacturing cost accounts. Most of this chapter focuses on the analysis of variances from standard costs. Standard cost accounting is illustrated at the end of the chapter.

## VARIANCES

Differences between actual costs and standard costs are called *variances*. If actual cost is greater than standard cost, the variance is unfavorable. If actual cost is less than standard, the variance is favorable. The words "favorable" and "unfavorable" are used here in a specialized sense to denote simply the direction of the variance from standard cost. They are not intended to imply that the variance is necessarily good or bad in terms of the firm's best interest. Such a qualitative evaluation can be made only after the underlying cause of the variance has been determined. In this text, variances are computed by subtracting actual costs from standard costs. Thus, favorable variances will appear as positive quantities and unfavorable variances, as negative amounts (indicated by enclosing them in parentheses). Obviously, the opposite arithmetic approach could be taken to arrive at exactly the same variances. The approach used here was selected simply because it seems intuitively appealing to show favorable variances as positive and unfavorable variances as negative numbers.

By definition, a variance indicates the amount by which actual cost differs from standard cost, the cost that should have been incurred. Thus, variances are particularly useful tools in the implementation of the concept of *management by exception.* This concept is founded on the very simple and logical premises that the limited time of business executives should be employed as productively as possible and that their time may most productively be spent in dealing with conditions which are not as they should be. In other words, the basic rule of management by exception is to concentrate on operations and segments of an enterprise that deviate from target performance and not to spend much time reviewing satisfactory performances. Variances are just as useful to management for purposes of cost control as the standards from which they are derived are valid. If truly current and attainable standards are used, variances should be good indications of exceptions requiring management attention. Both favorable and unfavorable variances deserve attention. An unfavorable variance suggests a condition that may require correction. A favorable variance may suggest an opportunity that management can exploit.

The following sections describe both the mechanics of computing variances and the possible causes of those variances. Determining the causes of variances is the more important step insofar as management is concerned, but computation must precede causal analysis. Moreover, one cannot investigate causes until he understands exactly what variables enter into the computation of a variance. Variance computation might be learned by simply committing to memory a series of variance formulas. Such an approach, however, cannot relate the mathematical procedure to the ultimate managerial objective. Hence, the discussion of each variance below will begin with a description of the fundamental meaning of that variance. If one understands what a variance is intended to depict and what the pertinent variables really mean, he ought to be able to deduce the variance formula logically.

All of the variances are illustrated for a hypothetical company, Cather Creations, Inc. One of its products is an ornamental brass dish manufactured in a single department. The standard cost sheet for one of these brass dishes is as follows:

Direct materials (12 pounds @ $1.50)............................. $18
Direct labor (10 hours @ $4.20)..................................   42
Variable manufacturing overhead (10 hours @ $1.20).................   12
Fixed manufacturing overhead (10 hours @ $2.40)...................   24
                                                                    ----
                                                                    $96

Manufacturing overhead is applied to production on the basis of direct labor hours. The flexible budget for manufacturing overhead allows $1.20 per labor hour plus $120,000 per month. Normal production volume for this product has been established at 50,000 direct labor hours per month. The company uses absorption costing.

## MATERIALS VARIANCES

The cost of materials in a manufactured product is determined by two basic factors, the price paid for materials and the quantity of materials used in production. The time of purchase and the time of usage are not necessarily the same. Materials may be purchased in one period and used in a subsequent period. To the extent that a materials cost variance arises from purchasing, it should be associated with the period in which the purchase was made. To the extent that it arises from usage, it should be associated with the period in which the materials were used in production. Thus, a single net materials variance, comprising both price and usage elements, cannot be computed directly. Of course, a single variance can be computed as the algebraic sum of the separate price and usage variances. It is doubtful that such a net variance would be useful to management, however.

## MATERIALS PRICE VARIANCE

*Computation.* When materials are purchased, they may be bought either at the established standard price or at some price above or below standard. In the latter instance, a variance will arise because of the price differential from standard. This is the *materials price variance*. While this variance is not necessarily attributable to good or bad purchasing practices, it does arise at the time of purchase and, logically, should be identified at that point. Obviously, the total amount of the variance will be greater the more units of material are purchased. Thus, the materials price variance is a function of the difference between the standard and actual prices per unit of material and the quantity of material purchased. The formula then follows logically:

The materials price variance is equal to the difference between the standard price and the actual price per unit of material multiplied by the quantity of materials purchased.

or

$$MPV = (SP - AP) \times QP \qquad (1)$$

During the month of July 1976, Cather Creations, Inc., purchased 55,000 pounds of brass at a unit price of $1.60 per pound. The standard price is $1.50 per pound. Thus, the materials price variance is computed as follows:

$$MPV = (\$1.50 - \$1.60) \times 55{,}000 \text{ pounds} = (\$5{,}500)$$

Since the actual price was greater than the standard price, the variance is unfavorable and is enclosed in parentheses to indicate a negative number.

*Causal Analysis.*    The materials price variance is the difference between actual and standard purchase prices. As it arises at the point of purchase, one might be inclined to take it as an indicator of the efficiency or inefficiency of the purchasing function in a firm. Such a conclusion would be tenuous at best, however, and might prove to be completely erroneous. For example, if the actual price exceeded the standard price because of a marked shift in market conditions, whether temporary or permanent, the resulting price variance might be wholly beyond the control of the purchasing department or, for that matter, of anyone in the firm. If the average market price for a particular material has increased by 5% from the level implicit in the firm's price standard and the firm's price variance for the period is 4% in excess of standard, the situation seems to reflect unusually efficient purchasing practices. Here a nominally unfavorable variance would be traceable ultimately to a combination of uncontrollable circumstances and exceptionally good performance. On the other hand, an unfavorable price variance may reflect the purchasing department's negligence in failing to seek the most advantageous sources of supply. A favorable price variance might be achieved by purchasing from an unreliable supplier, but consequent delivery delays may precipitate a partial shutdown of production facilities and delays in filling customers' orders, if not the actual loss of orders. Such a favorable variance, obviously, is favorable in name only; it is clearly adverse in effect.

A particular price variance or some portion thereof may be attributable to a department other than purchasing. For example, if the foreman of a production department fails to notify purchasing of a shortage of materials on hand, an emergency order may become necessary at a price above standard—perhaps because special handling and airfreight charges must be incurred in order to obtain delivery in time to avert a production stoppage. In this example, a price variance is caused by inefficiency in a materials using department.

In an actual situation, it is likely that several different causes will combine to produce a net price variance. To begin with, variances of different directions and various causes may occur in connection with purchases of different raw materials. Different types of variances may be encountered in connection with successive purchases of a single material. In such a case, the net materials price variance may not be very useful to management. A net variance of $800, for example, may appear negligible when compared with total purchases of $4,000,000. But that net variance may be the algebraic sum of very substantial offsetting favorable and unfavorable variances. Obviously, the apparently negligible net variance here masks significant component variances; and the latter are important to effective cost control.

## Materials Usage Variance

*Computation.* The *materials usage variance,* or *materials quantity variance,* seeks to identify the difference between actual and standard materials costs attributable to the use of more or less materials in production than the standard quantity. The actual usage of materials is determined from a summary of materials issue reports during the period under study. The standard quantity of materials in production depends upon two factors, the standard quantity of materials required for each unit of product and the number of units produced during the period.

If the materials usage variance is to do what it is intended to do, namely, to measure the cost variance attributable to usage of materials only, it must abstract from the problem of price differences. As the difference between actual and standard price (if any) is determined at the time of purchase of materials, the usage variance ignores such difference and translates physical quantities to costs by means of the standard price only. Thus, the materials usage variance is a function of the difference between the standard and actual materials input quantities and the standard materials price. The formula is as follows:

The material usage variance is equal to the difference between the standard quantity of materials in production and the actual quantity used multiplied by the standard materials price.

or

$$MUV = (SQ - AQ) \times SP \qquad (2)$$

During July 1976, Cather Creations, Inc., produced a total of 4,400 ornamental brass dishes and used a total of 54,000 pounds of material in production. The materials usage standard calls for 12 pounds of material for each dish produced. Thus, during July, the company should have used 52,800 pounds (4,400 dishes × 12 pounds per dish). It actually used 1,200 pounds more than this standard quantity. This excess usage resulted in the following unfavorable materials usage variance:

$$MUV = (52,800 \text{ pounds} - 54,000 \text{ pounds}) \times \$1.50 = (\$1,800)$$

*Causal Analysis.* A materials usage variance may be traced to a great variety of causes. Excessive usage may be caused by careless handling of materials by production personnel, by inefficient or poorly adjusted machinery, by pilferage, by a tightening of quality control requirements, or by an almost endless list of other possible circumstances and events. Changes in product specifications may cause either favorable or unfavorable usage variances for which the only solution is to alter materials usage standards. Purchasing of substandard materials may result in excessive materials consumption. This may or may not be desirable, depending upon the net impact on total cost. For example, a firm's price and usage standards for copper tubing may be based upon purchases of precut pieces of uniform length. The purchasing department may learn that it can effect substantial savings by buying random mill lengths instead, but use of these random length pieces will result in greater amounts of scrap in the factory. The consequent unfavorable materials usage variance may be more than offset by a favorable price variance. If so, the unfavorable usage variance is actually a reflection of a profitable change in policy and will ultimately be eliminated by a change in the materials usage standard to conform to the new policy.

Separate materials usage variances should be determined for each type of material used and for each production center. Tracing variances to cost centers is at least the beginning of an answer to the question, "Who is responsible for the variances?" Responsibility must be determined before control can be effected.

*Materials Mix Variance.* In some production processes, two or more different raw materials are combined in a standard formula to produce a product. In such a situation, it may be possible to vary the mix of materials used (i.e., to change the quantities of certain materials relative to the quantities of others) and still produce a satisfactory product. Such variations in the standard materials mix could be reflected simply in the materials usage variance. Thus, an unfavorable usage variance for one material might be offset by a favorable variance for another. However, the net effect of these two variances is not likely to be zero. If the material whose usage was increased is more expensive than that whose usage was reduced, the net financial effect of the two variances will be unfavorable. Thus, substituting one raw material for another, even though the total input quantity of all materials does not exceed the standard amount, can cause a special type of materials usage variance. This is usually referred to as a *materials mix variance.* It is a consequence of materials usage, but a consequence of relative rather than absolute differentials in usage. Hence, where it can be identified separately, it is useful to do so. Substantial deviations from the standard product mix may not only cause variances from standard cost; they may also impair product quality, possibly to the point that the output is useless.

## LABOR VARIANCES

Unlike materials, labor cannot be stored. Thus, the purchase and usage of labor services are effectively simultaneous. Hence, a single net labor variance for a given period can be computed. It is the difference between the standard labor costs and the actual labor costs of the period. It is, however, both feasible and useful to break this net variance down into components attributable to price and quantity differences. Unlike the two materials variances described above, these two labor variances do sum to a single significant variance.

### Labor Rate Variance

*Computation.* The difference between standard and actual labor costs attributable to a difference between the standard and actual hourly wage rates is identified as the *labor rate variance*, or *wage rate variance*. In order to isolate the effect of wage rate differentials, the labor rate variance ignores the question of whether the number of labor hours worked during the period was above or below the standard number that should have been worked. It is concerned only with the number of hours that actually were worked and, hence, that were paid at the actual wage rate and should have been paid at the standard rate. The labor rate variance, thus, is a function of the difference between the standard and actual wage rates and the actual labor hours worked.[1] The formula is as follows:

The labor rate variance is equal to the difference between the standard wage rate per hour and the actual wage rate multiplied by the actual number of hours worked.

or

$$LRV = (SR - AR) \times AH \qquad (3)$$

During July 1976, Cather Creations, Inc., payroll records showed that a total of 43,000 direct labor hours were worked in the department that produces ornamental brass dishes at an average wage rate of \$4.40 per hour. The standard wage rate is \$4.20 per hour. The following labor rate variance results:

$$LRV = (\$4.20 - \$4.40) \times 43,000 \text{ hours} = (\$8,600)$$

As the actual hourly rate is greater than the standard rate, this variance is unfavorable.

*Causal Analysis.* A difference between the actual and standard wage rates may be attributed simply to a negotiated wage increase not yet re-

---

[1] Less frequently today, the standard labor rate is a rate per piece of production rather than per hour worked. In this case, the labor rate variance would be equal to the difference between the standard piece rate and the actual piece rate multiplied by the actual units produced during a period.

flected in the standard wage rate. While management may not be pleased about the wage increase, the resultant wage rate variance, as such, is a normal and proper consequence of the change in the rate. Of course, the net labor rate variance should be analyzed according to different classes of laborers. A wage increase may not be uniform among all classes of workers, and variances in different classes may have significantly different causes.

Part of a labor rate variance may be caused by the assignment of higher paid workers to jobs regularly performed by lower paid employees. Such practice is not desirable but sometimes is unavoidable. For example, a temporary reassignment of highly paid workers may be necessary to reduce a production bottleneck. During a period of reduced demand and output, the company may prefer to lay off the lower paid employees and reassign the higher paid ones in order to retain the more highly skilled (and, hence, more highly paid) members of its work force. This particular type of labor rate variance is sometimes reported separately as a *labor substitution variance*.

Of the variances considered here, the labor rate variance is probably the least susceptible to direct control by management. This does not mean that its causes are of no interest, however. Knowing the causes of variances assists management in planning future costs as well as in controlling current costs.

## Labor Efficiency Variance

*Computation.* The quantity of labor used in a period is measured in units of time, usually man-hours. The time required for production is commonly thought of as an indication of the efficiency of the labor force. Hence, the variance which seeks to identify the impact of working more or less hours than the standard hours in production is called the *labor efficiency variance*, or *labor time variance*. It abstracts from problems of rate differences, which have already been identified in the labor rate variance, and is concerned only with the standard wage rate. The actual hours worked are determined from payroll summary sheets. The standard hours in production are determined by the established standard hours required for the production of one unit of product and the number of units produced during the period. Thus, the labor efficiency variance is a function of the difference between the standard and actual labor hours worked and the standard wage rate.[2] The formula is as follows:

---

[2] If direct laborers were compensated by a piece rate instead of an hourly rate, there would be no labor efficiency variance as described here. Under a pure piece-rate system, direct labor cost (after allowance for any labor rate variance) would be a direct function of output. However, as a practical matter, workers in a piece-rate

The labor efficiency variance is equal to the difference between the standard and the actual labor hours worked during a period multiplied by the standard wage rate per hour.

or

$$LEV = (SH - AH) \times SR \qquad (4)$$

The standard cost sheet of Cather Creations, Inc., calls for ten man-hours of direct labor for each brass dish manufactured. Since 4,400 dishes were produced during July, there were a total of 44,000 standard labor hours in production that month. However, only 43,000 actual hours were worked. Thus, there would be a favorable labor efficiency variance, as follows:

$$LEV = (44,000 \text{ hours} - 43,000 \text{ hours}) \times \$4.20 = \$4,200$$

***Causal Analysis.*** The root causes of a labor efficiency variance may be personal to the workers and/or inherent in the work situation. The first type of cause is the more difficult for management to deal with. A worker's personal efficiency may be affected by his health, family or financial problems, a real or imagined grievance against management, fear of a layoff, imminent retirement, and the World Series. There is usually little, if anything, management can do directly about such matters. However, there is also little likelihood that all workers will be affected by the same personal problems at the same time. Management, of course, is primarily interested in the average efficiency of the labor force. Concern for an individual worker's inefficiency is usually restricted to his immediate supervisor and then only if his inefficiency is persistent. To combat personal causes of labor inefficiency and to foster efficiency in general, the most management can do ordinarily is to provide a work environment conducive to satisfying the workers' personal needs and goals.

The second type of cause of a labor efficiency variance—that inherent in the work situation—is of more general concern to management. Examples of such causes are the introduction of new equipment or tools in a factory, a failure to maintain machinery in proper working condition, use of substandard raw materials, production bottlenecks, and changes in production processes. These situations can cause general efficiency or inefficiency in an entire department or, perhaps, throughout a plant. Thus,

---

system must still be paid at least a minimum hourly wage. Thus, an inefficient worker whose output was insufficient to make his piece-rate compensation at least equal to the minimum hourly wage would receive an additional amount so that his total earnings equaled the minimum wage for the number of hours he worked. Such additional payment is referred to as a "makeup to minimum" and amounts to a labor efficiency variance. This type of variance, of course, could only be unfavorable.

their potential impact upon production costs and profits is greater than that of purely personal problems. At the same time, these situations are likely to be more readily identifiable and more amenable to managerial action.

The mere existence of a labor efficiency variance does not necessarily indicate good or bad performance by workers. The variance might be caused by poor planning on the part of management. It might reflect changes in the factory layout, in production equipment, or in quality control standards. Finally, the labor efficiency variance may be affected by the firm's manner of accounting for idle time. If all idle time is recorded and charged to manufacturing overhead rather than to direct labor, a significant unfavorable labor efficiency variance may be avoided—but only by an increase in the manufacturing overhead spending variance. On the other hand, during a period of temporarily reduced output, workers may be assigned make-work tasks to avoid temporary layoffs. This could cause a substantial unfavorable efficiency variance that reflected a conscious managerial decision and not the quality of labor performance at all.

## MANUFACTURING OVERHEAD VARIANCES IN GENERAL

As explained in Chapter 9, standard costs for manufacturing overhead are based upon budgets rather than standards. Unlike direct materials and labor, manufacturing overhead is not entirely variable with production volume. Thus, variances from standard manufacturing overhead cost are significantly different from the variances for materials and labor. The distinction between variable and fixed manufacturing overhead costs is very important in the analysis of manufacturing overhead variances. Consequently, measures of volume play an important role in that analysis.

### Volume Measures

An understanding of standard manufacturing overhead costs and variances depends upon a prior understanding of several concepts of production volume. One of these is normal volume. Normal volume was explained in the preceding chapter as that volume at which the standard fixed manufacturing overhead rate is established. This is the only role that normal volume plays, insofar as standard costs are concerned; but it is a very important role in determining one of the variances from standard manufacturing overhead cost. In Cather Creations, Inc., normal volume has been set at 50,000 direct labor hours per month in the department that makes ornamental brass dishes.

***Actual Output Volume.*** *Actual output volume* is simply the number of units of product actually produced during a given period.[3] Output measures the results of production. Thus, it may be regarded as good or bad, adequate or inadequate, in relation to plans for output. There is no such concept as "standard output volume," however. As the term is used here, "standard" refers only to inputs. During July 1976, the actual output of brass dishes in Cather Creations, Inc., totaled 4,400 units. As we have already seen, this actual output is used to determine standard materials usage and standard labor time.

***Standard Input Volume.*** Production volume may also be measured in units of input. For example, direct labor hours are used as the production volume measure in Cather Creations, Inc. *Standard input volume* is the total quantity of some input measure (labor hours in Cather Creations, Inc.) that the pertinent standard (the labor time standard here) indicates should be used to produce the actual output of the period. Thus, standard input volume and actual output volume are equivalent measures of the level of operations. There is a direct functional relationship between the two volumes. For Cather Creations, Inc., in July, standard input volume is computed by multiplying the actual output of 4,400 units by the standard labor time of 10 hours per unit. The result is 44,000 hours, the standard labor hours in production that were determined earlier.

***Actual Input Volume.*** The *actual input volume* is simply the actual quantity of input during a period. Where volume is measured in labor hours, actual input volume is the total actual labor hours worked during the period. It may differ from standard input volume. During July, Cather Creations, Inc., worked only 43,000 direct labor hours to produce the output that the labor time standard indicates should have required 44,000 hours. That time saving, of course, is the source of the favorable labor efficiency variance computed earlier.

## Net Manufacturing Overhead Variance

As in the case of direct labor, a single variance for manufacturing overhead may be determined. This is the net difference between the standard manufacturing overhead cost of production for a period and the actual manufacturing overhead costs incurred during that period. Where volume is measured in units of output, standard manufacturing overhead

---

[3] Throughout this chapter, actual output is given as a simple quantity of goods manufactured. The same quantity is assumed to be started and completed during the period. As we saw in Chapter 4, there may be units in process at the beginning and/or at the end of the period. In that case, the actual output of the period must be measured in terms of equivalent units of production. The equivalent units used for this purpose would be those shown in Table 4–2 in Chapter 4 and used in process costing under the Fifo method.

cost is computed by multiplying the actual units produced by the standard variable and fixed manufacturing overhead costs per unit of product. Where volume is measured in units of input, standard manufacturing overhead cost is computed by multiplying the standard input volume by the standard variable and fixed manufacturing overhead rates per unit of input. This discussion presumes that absorption costing is used. In variable costing, there would be no standard fixed manufacturing overhead rate. Since absorption costing is the more inclusive alternative, it will be used for illustrative purposes in this chapter.

The flexible budget for manufacturing overhead in the department that makes ornamental brass dishes for Cather Creations, Inc., allows variable manufacturing overhead of $1.20 per direct labor hour plus $120,000 of fixed costs per month. Normal volume is 50,000 labor hours per month. Hence, the standard fixed manufacturing overhead rate is $2.40 per hour ($120,000 ÷ 50,000 hours). The total standard manufacturing overhead cost in production for the month of July is computed by multiplying the standard input volume of 44,000 hours by these standard rates, thus:

| | |
|---|---:|
| Standard variable manufacturing overhead (44,000 hrs. × $1.20)... | $ 52,800 |
| Standard fixed manufacturing overhead (44,000 hrs. × $2.40)...... | 105,600 |
| Total standard manufacturing overhead cost..................... | $158,400 |

The actual manufacturing overhead costs incurred during July totaled $180,000, including $55,000 of variable costs and $125,000 of fixed costs. The net manufacturing overhead variance, then, is the difference between the total standard and actual manufacturing overhead costs.

| | |
|---|---:|
| Total standard manufacturing overhead cost............ | $158,400 |
| Total actual manufacturing overhead cost.............. | 180,000 |
| Net manufacturing overhead variance.................. | ($ 21,600) |

As the actual costs are greater than the standard costs, the net variance is unfavorable.

This net variance is the result of several substantially different factors. Thus, by itself, it is not very useful to management for evaluating performance or controlling costs. Consequently, two or three component variances for manufacturing overhead are usually computed. These component variances are explained below. Of course, they always sum algebraically to the net variance.

## THREE-VARIANCE PLAN FOR MANUFACTURING OVERHEAD

Where volume is measured in units of input, the net manufacturing overhead variance can be broken down into three component variances. Each is significant because each has a very different source.

## Manufacturing Overhead Spending Variance

*Computation.* The *manufacturing overhead spending variance* seeks to identify and isolate that portion of the net variance that is attributable to differences between actual and budgeted spending on manufacturing overhead cost items. It ignores any differences between actual and standard input volumes or between standard input volume and normal volume. It takes actual input volume as it is and measures the difference between the budgeted manufacturing overhead costs for the actual input volume and the actual manufacturing overhead costs incurred. Flexible manufacturing overhead budgets are essential for the computation of this variance, for the budget must be adjusted to the actual input volume of the period. Thus, this variance is identical to the spending variance computed from a flexible budget in Chapter 8. The variance formula is as follows:

> The manufacturing overhead spending variance is equal to the difference between the budgeted manufacturing overhead costs for the actual input volume and the actual manufacturing overhead costs incurred.

or

$$MOSV = BCAIV - AC \qquad (5)$$

For the month of July 1976, the actual input volume of Cather Creations, Inc., was 43,000 direct labor hours. The flexible budget allows $1.20 for each of these hours plus $120,000 for the month. The manufacturing overhead spending variance is then computed as follows:

| | | |
|---|---:|---:|
| Budgeted costs for actual input volume: | | |
| Variable costs (43,000 hours × $1.20)............. | | $ 51,600 |
| Fixed costs................................. | | 120,000 |
| | | $171,600 |
| | | |
| Actual costs: | | |
| Variable costs.............................. | $ 55,000 | |
| Fixed costs................................. | 125,000 | 180,000 |
| Spending variance............................ | | ($ 8,400) |

As the actual costs exceed the budget allowance at the actual hours, the variance is unfavorable.

The spending variance includes both variable and fixed costs, because both differed from the amounts budgeted. As a general rule, the spending variance should always cover both types of cost, regardless of whether absorption costing or variable costing is being used. Even though no fixed manufacturing overhead is charged to production under variable costing, any difference between budgeted and actual fixed costs is still of interest to management for purposes of control. Hence, any such difference should always be a part of the spending variance. Of course, for effective cost control, the spending variance should be determined separately for each item of manufacturing overhead cost, as was done in Table 8–3 in Chapter 8. The single-figure variance computed here is used purely for simplicity.

*Causal Analysis.* There are at least as many possible causes of the manufacturing overhead spending variance as there are distinct cost items. The flexible budget provides a specified amount per unit of volume for each variable cost item and a certain amount per period for each fixed cost item. These budgeted amounts are based upon expected prices, consumption rates for the variable cost items, and a variety of other operating conditions. Any one or combination of these budget spending expectations may prove to be inaccurate. For example, if indirect materials cost is greater than budgeted, the excess may be caused by an increase in the price of indirect materials or by an increase in the rate of usage of these items or by a combination of both. Such price and usage differences may ultimately be traced to the same types of causes mentioned earlier in connection with direct materials. Similarly, variable indirect labor may differ from the budget because of wage rate and/or time differences. Fixed indirect labor cost, on the other hand, would differ from the budget because of salary adjustments or because of changes in the number of personnel employed in such categories. Power costs and other utilities might change because of rate changes or variations in consumption. Property tax rates might change and/or the assessed valuation of the firm's taxable property might be changed. Repairs and maintenance might vary from the budget because of wage rate changes, price changes for parts and supplies, conscious alterations in maintenance schedules, or unexpected equipment failures. Thus, any meaningful causal analysis of the spending variance must focus on each individual cost item.

## Manufacturing Overhead Efficiency Variance

*Computation.* This variance can be identified only when volume is measured in units of input. The *manufacturing overhead efficiency variance* measures the excess cost incurred or the cost saving due to the fact that actual input volume is more or less, respectively, than standard input volume. Logically, this variance relates only to variable manufacturing overhead costs; for only variable costs are affected by changes in volume. The formula for the efficiency variance is as follows:

> The manufacturing overhead efficiency variance is equal to the difference between the standard input volume and the actual input volume multiplied by the standard variable manufacturing overhead rate.

or

$$MOEV = (SIV - AIV) \times SVMOR \qquad (6)$$

Where labor hours are the measure of input volume, the manufacturing overhead efficiency variance is caused directly by labor efficiency. Thus, some have argued that the manufacturing overhead efficiency variance should be regarded as a part of the labor efficiency variance. Certainly, in this case, the two variances have the same cause and must be in the same direction; but there is no objection to these two efficiency variances being stated separately.

For Cather Creations, Inc., in July 1976, the standard input volume was 44,000 direct labor hours; and the actual input volume was 43,000 hours. The standard variable manufacturing overhead rate is $1.20 per hour. Thus, the manufacturing overhead efficiency variance is computed as follows:

$$MOEV = (44{,}000 \text{ hours} - 43{,}000 \text{ hours}) \times \$1.20 = \$1{,}200$$

Since the actual input volume is less than the standard input volume, variable manufacturing overhead costs have been saved and the variance is favorable. Whenever volume is measured in direct labor hours, the labor efficiency variance and the manufacturing overhead efficiency variance will always be in the same direction.

*Causal Analysis.* This variance is caused by whatever causes the efficiency or inefficiency in the volume of input to which variable manufacturing overhead costs are related. If this volume is direct labor hours, the causes of the labor efficiency variance noted earlier are also applicable here. If volume is measured in direct labor cost, the manufacturing overhead efficiency variance could be caused by either changes in wage rates or differences in labor time. Where machine hours are the volume measure used, the efficiency variance may ultimately be attributable to anything that could cause variations in machine utilization. Perhaps machine operators are unskilled or careless; if so, the ultimate cause is labor inefficiency. Possibly, maintenance schedules for the machines have not been observed and, as a consequence, the machines are not properly adjusted to their planned operating efficiency. In this case, the root cause is the failure of the responsible supervisor to adhere to established maintenance policies.

## Manufacturing Overhead Volume Variance

*Computation.* The *manufacturing overhead volume variance* is traceable to the difference between the standard input volume and normal volume. Specifically, it arises because a standard fixed manufacturing overhead rate is computed at normal volume and then applied to production at standard input volume. Strictly, a fixed manufacturing overhead rate per unit of volume is valid only at the volume at which the rate is computed. This is so because fixed manufacturing overhead costs are constant in total and, hence, are different per unit at each different level of volume. Nevertheless, in a standard cost system, a fixed manufacturing overhead rate computed at normal volume is charged to production at standard input volume, which is most likely different from normal volume. Thus, this practice almost invariably causes a variance. The standard fixed manufacturing overhead rate is strictly conceived to absorb total budgeted fixed manufacturing overhead only at normal volume. If used at any other volume, the fixed manufacturing overhead rate will result in either more or less than the total budgeted fixed manufacturing overhead being absorbed by production. Inasmuch as fixed manufacturing overhead is charged to production only under absorption costing, the volume variance can occur only under that method. The formula for the volume variance is as follows:

> The manufacturing overhead volume variance is equal to the difference between the standard fixed manufacturing overhead cost charged to production and the budgeted fixed manufacturing overhead cost.[4]

or

$$MOVV = SFMOC - BFMOC \qquad (7)$$

For Cather Creations, Inc., the standard fixed manufacturing overhead charged to production during July 1976 was $105,600 (44,000 standard labor hours × $2.40 per hour). The budgeted fixed manufacturing overhead was given as $120,000 per month. The volume variance, then, is computed as follows:

$$MOVV = \$105,600 - \$120,000 = (\$14,400)$$

The variance is unfavorable because the standard input volume is not sufficient to absorb all of the budgeted fixed manufacturing overhead costs at the standard fixed manufacturing overhead rate of $2.40 per hour. Any time that a fixed manufacturing overhead rate is applied at a volume lower than the normal volume at which it was computed (as is the case here), the standard fixed manufacturing overhead cost will be less than the budgeted cost and the volume variance will be unfavorable. Conversely, if a fixed manufacturing overhead rate is applied at a volume higher than normal volume, the volume variance will invariably be favorable.

---

[4] An alternative method of calculating the manufacturing overhead volume variance is to multiply the difference between the standard input volume and the normal volume by the standard fixed manufacturing overhead rate. Actually, this is not a different formula but a different arrangement of the same formula.

*Causal Analysis.* The manufacturing overhead volume variance is unique among the variances from standard cost in that it is caused by the mechanics of the cost accounting system itself. It is attributable solely to the fact that a standard fixed manufacturing overhead rate is computed at normal volume and is then applied to production at some other volume. The fundamental nature of fixed costs, of course, is that they are some specified amount per period of time, regardless of operating volume. Thus, while a fixed manufacturing overhead rate per unit of volume may be required for cost accounting purposes, it abstracts from the true nature of fixed costs. The volume variance is, in other words, a "man-made" variance. As such, it is of no significance to management for purposes of planning and control. If budgeted production volume were not equal to normal volume (and it often would not be), a volume variance would be anticipated at the start of the period. Hence, it would signal no exception requiring management's attention. Any difference between budgeted volume and the standard input volume determined at the end of the period may be of concern to management, but such a difference can be observed directly in physical production volume statistics. It is not necessary to compute a dollar variance to see the difference. Changes in production volume from the amount budgeted may be caused by shifts in demand for products, labor disputes, materials shortages, working capital deficiencies, ineffectual marketing tactics, poor product quality, or any one or combination of numerous other factors. Some of these factors may be controllable by management, while others are not.

## Summary of Three-Variance Plan

We have now observed the computation of three separate component variances from standard manufacturing overhead cost. As noted earlier, their algebraic sum must be equal to the net variance between standard and actual costs. That such is the case may be demonstrated very simply.

| | |
|---|---:|
| Manufacturing overhead spending variance............. | ($ 8,400) |
| Manufacturing overhead efficiency variance............. | 1,200 |
| Manufacturing overhead volume variance.............. | ( 14,400) |
| Net manufacturing overhead variance................. | ($21,600) |

The spending variance relates to both variable and fixed manufacturing overhead costs. The efficiency variance relates exclusively to variable costs. The volume variance is based entirely on fixed costs.

## TWO-VARIANCE PLAN FOR MANUFACTURING OVERHEAD

When production volume is measured in units of output rather than input, only two separate manufacturing overhead variances can be computed. As Cather Creations, Inc., uses an input measure of volume, we must construct a different illustration for the two-variance plan. Assume that the following budgeted and actual data are taken from the records of the Lovecraft Company for the month of December 1976:

| | |
|---|---|
| Normal volume. . . . . . . . . . . . . . . . . . . . . . . . . . . . . . . . . . . . | 15,000 units of output |
| Budgeted variable manufacturing overhead. . . . . . . . . | $.60 per unit of output |
| Budgeted fixed manufacturing overhead. . . . . . . . . . . | $13,500 per month |
| Actual output volume. . . . . . . . . . . . . . . . . . . . . . . . . . | 16,000 units of output |
| Actual variable manufacturing overhead. . . . . . . . . . . | $9,500 |
| Actual fixed manufacturing overhead. . . . . . . . . . . . . . | $13,900 |

The standard fixed manufacturing overhead rate is $.90 per unit ($13,500 ÷ 15,000 units at normal volume). The net manufacturing overhead variance is then computed as follows:

| | | |
|---|---|---|
| Total standard manufacturing overhead cost: | | |
| Variable cost (16,000 units × $.60). . . . . . . . . . . . . . . . | | $ 9,600 |
| Fixed cost (16,000 units × $.90). . . . . . . . . . . . . . . . . . | | 14,400 |
| | | $24,000 |
| | | |
| Total actual manufacturing overhead cost: | | |
| Variable cost. . . . . . . . . . . . . . . . . . . . . . . . . . . . . . . . . | $ 9,500 | |
| Fixed cost. . . . . . . . . . . . . . . . . . . . . . . . . . . . . . . . . . . | 13,900 | 23,400 |
| Net manufacturing overhead variance. . . . . . . . . . . . . . | | $    600 |

This net variance is favorable.

## Manufacturing Overhead Budget Variance

Where manufacturing overhead is charged to production on the basis of output rather than input, there is no basis for measuring manufacturing overhead efficiency and, hence, no efficiency variance. Thus, the two-variance plan identifies variances attributable to spending and volume differences only. The *manufacturing overhead budget variance* in the two-variance plan is fundamentally similar to the spending variance in the three-variance plan. The use of a different name for the variance in the two-variance plan is common practice and is helpful in distinguishing the two plans. Further, the budget variance is not identical to the spending variance. The budget variance is the difference between the costs that the flexible budget indicates should be incurred at actual *output* volume and the actual costs of the period. The formula is as follows:

The manufacturing overhead budget variance is equal to the difference between the budgeted manufacturing overhead cost at the actual output volume and the actual manufacturing overhead cost incurred.

or

$$MOBV = BCAOV - AC \qquad (8)$$

For cost control purposes, the budget variance should be determined separately for each distinct manufacturing overhead cost item.

For the Lovecraft Company for the month of December 1976, the manufacturing overhead budget variance is the difference between the budgeted costs for the actual output volume of 16,000 units of product and the actual costs incurred. It is computed thus:

| | | |
|---|---:|---:|
| Budgeted cost at actual output volume: | | |
| Variable costs (16,000 units × $.60).............. | | $ 9,600 |
| Fixed costs..................................... | | 13,500 |
| | | $23,100 |
| Actual cost: | | |
| Variable costs................................. | $ 9,500 | |
| Fixed costs.................................... | 13,900 | 23,400 |
| Budget variance................................ | | ($ 300) |

As the actual costs exceed the budget allowance for the actual volume, the variance is unfavorable.

The budget variance can also be employed in firms which use an input measure of volume. In such firms, it is simply the algebraic sum of the spending variance and the efficiency variance of the three-variance plan. It may be computed directly as the difference between the budgeted cost for the standard input volume and the actual cost. Because of the basically different sources of the spending and efficiency variances, however, the three-variance plan is normally more useful to management where it can be used.

The causal analysis of the budget variance is essentially the same as that for the spending variance under the three-variance plan. Hence, no separate discussion is necessary here.

## Manufacturing Overhead Volume Variance

The volume variance is the same under the two-variance plan as it is in the three-variance plan. It is the difference between the standard fixed manufacturing overhead cost charged to production and the budgeted fixed manufacturing overhead cost. Since volume is now measured in units of output, standard fixed manufacturing overhead cost is determined by multiplying the standard fixed rate by the actual output volume. For the Lovecraft Company, the volume variance for December 1976 is computed as follows:

| | |
|---|---:|
| Standard fixed manufacturing overhead cost | |
| (16,000 units × $.90 per unit)....................... | $14,400 |
| Budgeted fixed manufacturing overhead cost.............. | 13,500 |
| Volume variance...................................... | $ 900 |

The variance is favorable because actual output volume (16,000 units) is greater than normal volume (15,000 units).

### Summary of Two-Variance Plan

The algebraic sum of the manufacturing overhead budget and volume variances computed for the Lovecraft Company should be equal to the net manufacturing overhead variance of $600 computed earlier. That this is so is shown below:

Manufacturing overhead budget variance.................. ($300)
Manufacturing overhead volume variance................. 900
Net manufacturing overhead variance..................... $600

The budget variance pertains to both variable and fixed costs, while the volume variance relates exclusively to fixed costs.

## SUMMARY OF VARIANCE FORMULAS

For the sake of ease in studying and reviewing variances, the formulas for the eight variances discussed in the foregoing sections are summarized below. In each case, the formula is so arranged that a positive variance is favorable and a negative variance, unfavorable.

### Materials and Labor:

(1)  Materials price variance = (standard price per unit of material − actual price) × quantity of materials purchased.

(2)  Materials usage variance = (standard quantity of materials in production − actual quantity used) × standard price per unit.

(3)  Labor rate variance = (standard wage rate per hour − actual wage rate) × actual labor hours worked.

(4)  Labor efficiency variance = (standard labor hours in production − actual hours worked) × standard wage rate per hour.

### Manufacturing Overhead—Three-Variance Plan:

(5)  Manufacturing overhead spending variance = budgeted manufacturing overhead costs for actual input volume − actual manufacturing overhead costs.

(6)  Manufacturing overhead efficiency variance = (standard input volume − actual input volume) × standard variable manufacturing overhead rate.

(7)  Manufacturing overhead volume variance = standard fixed manufacturing overhead cost in production − budgeted fixed manufacturing overhead cost.

### Manufacturing Overhead—Two-Variance Plan:

(8)  Manufacturing overhead budget variance = budgeted manufacturing overhead cost for actual output volume − actual manufacturing overhead cost.

(7)  Manufacturing overhead volume variance is the same as under the three-variance plan.

## SIGNIFICANCE OF VARIANCES

As one may easily conclude from the discussions in the preceding sections, determining the cause(s) of a variance from standard cost can be a difficult, time consuming, and, hence, expensive task. Management's goal of cost control will hardly be furthered if the firm spends more in uncovering the causes of variances than the variances are likely to amount to in the future. Thus, variance analysis is customarily restricted to those variances that are considered significant. The significance of a variance is a function of both its amount and its recurrence. That is, the larger a variance is in relation to standard cost, the more significant it will be considered by management. Even more importantly, the more likely a variance is to recur, the greater significance management will accord it. Obviously, the significance of a variance is heightened if it is both large in amount and persistent in occurrence.

How large a variance must be in order to be considered significant is a difficult problem that must be resolved largely on the basis of managerial judgment. Probably no one would disagree that a variance equal to 25 percent of standard cost was material in amount or that a 1 percent variance was immaterial. Where the line separating materiality from immateriality lies, however, would be less easily agreed upon. Is a 5 percent variance material? Some firms do use this particular figure as a threshold for materiality of variances. The significance of a variance of a particular size depends partly upon the tightness of the underlying standard. The tighter a standard is, the larger an unfavorable variance from it may be expected to be. Consequently, management ought to set a higher significance threshold for an unfavorable variance from a tight standard than for one from an easily attained standard. An unfavorable variance is specified here because a variance is more likely to be unfavorable as the standard is set tighter. Also, most managers are predisposed to be more concerned about unfavorable variances. As we have observed before, however, favorable variances should not be ignored. An investigation of their causes may lead the way to long-run cost reductions.

The size of a variance, of course, is known when it is computed. Thus, a decision as to its significance on that basis may be made as soon as the variance has been calculated. Unfortunately, the same is not true of a variance's likelihood of recurrence. Until one has made a determination of the cause(s) of a variance, he can hardly decide how likely it is to occur again. Thus, some preliminary investigation of substantial variances is necessary in order to determine whether they are the results of nonrecurring circumstances or of continuing conditions. Obviously, the latter situation is of greater concern to management. Once a variance has been determined to have been caused by circumstances that may be expected to persist, a more extensive study of the problem and of possible solutions should be made.

## REPORTING VARIANCES BY RESPONSIBILITY

Determining the cause of a variance will usually entail the fixing of reponsibility for it at the same time. Additionally, in many cases it is possible to fix responsibility without ascertaining the precise cause of a variance. For example, a labor efficiency variance may be traced to a particular production department fairly readily if cost data are departmentalized. Fixing responsibility for the variance upon an individual department supervisor does not, of course, assure effective control; but it does set the problem at the level at which it may be controllable. Hence, one of the most important facets of a standard cost system is the variance reporting mechanism. This mechanism must be so structured as to get the right information to the right people at the right time and in the most useful manner.

### Timing of Reports

Reports are expensive. There are costs involved in their preparation, their transmittal, their reading, and their storage. These costs, like all costs in a business enterprise, should be justifiable in terms of basic objectives. Too many reports can be just as bad as too few. It might be possible to report daily all manufacturing variances to all supervisory personnel in a plant. If this were done, however, it is quite likely that the surfeit of information would only confuse the readers of the reports and obscure the truly relevant facts. A much more practicable and useful practice might be to report daily *some* variances to *some* supervisors. Other variances might be reported less frequently and only to selected persons.

Daily reports are most useful in connection with those variances which may arise and, hence, may be controlled from day to day. This is likely to be particularly true of the materials usage and the labor efficiency variances. It may be true of the manufacturing overhead spending variance, at least as regards some components of it. The latter is such a conglomerate variance, however, that day-to-day control might be prohibitively expensive. Where manufacturing overhead is applied to production on the basis of labor hours, control of the manufacturing overhead efficiency variance should be regarded as part of the control of labor efficiency. Even if some materials are purchased each day, it is unlikely that the same materials would be purchased daily. Hence, daily reports of the materials price variance would not appear to be desirable. In some industries, however, daily purchases of the same materials may be common; if so, daily price variance reports may be very useful. The labor rate variance is not likely to lend itself to day-to-day control efforts and, consequently, seems an unlikely candidate for daily reporting. Finally, daily reports of the manufacturing overhead volume variance would almost certainly be both useless and meaningless. For those variances where daily reporting and control are inapplicable, monthly reports may be adequate. It is not possible to state general rules for the frequency of reporting specific variances. It is pertinent to observe, however, that once a frequency has been established, reports should be disseminated as promptly as possible. Late reports are of as little value as last week's newspaper.

## Distribution of Reports

As a general rule, variance reports should be directed only to those persons in the organization who may reasonably be held responsible for the variances. Thus, a departmental foreman should probably receive reports of materials usage and labor efficiency. If materials prices and labor rates are beyond his scope of authority, there would seem to be little value in reporting price and rate variances to him. While his conduct may on occasion be the cause of price variances (as when he delays requesting a reorder of materials until the stock is so low that an emergency purchase must be made at an unfavorable price), his responsibility in such instance can be fixed without furnishing him copies of all price variance reports. The plant manager should receive reports of all manufacturing variances, with the possible exception of the volume variance, for which he may not be responsible. Reports to him would usually be less detailed than those submitted to the department foremen; the only breakdown may be by departments. If an individual is not responsible for a variance, the only valid reason for reporting it to him would be to broaden his perspective of the enterprise's operating problems. In such case, the report would seem to be a training rather than an operating device. Variance reports to top corporate management are typically submitted in summary form on a monthly basis. Even if certain variances are reported to immediate supervisors daily, it is unlikely that they would be made available to top management so frequently.

## Format of Reports

It is not possible to formulate a standard variance report which might be used by any firm. However, certain fundamental ideas should be considered. Where variances are analyzed by causes in the report, some effort should be made to distinguish between amounts which are and which are not controllable at the level of responsibility to which the report is directed. Controllability is quite often a very difficult concept to identify operationally, but some effort in that direction is likely to be beneficial to management. Comparison of current variances with those of some prior period and/or with those of the year to date is often helpful in establishing a frame of reference within which the current data can be appraised. Variances may be stated as percentages of standard costs, particularly where comparative data are presented. Percentages often afford a more meaningful basis for comparison than do absolute figures. Materials usage and labor efficiency variances may be reported to departmental foremen in terms of physical quantities only. If a foreman knows that his time is excessive on certain operations, it is questionable whether his capacity to control the excess would be improved by his knowing the dollar impact of the excess time.

Finally, variance reports should be prepared in accordance with the principle of exceptions. That is, significant variances should be highlighted and separated from immaterial ones. This is often accomplished by presenting the variance report in a tabular format with four columns for standard cost, actual cost, variances, and those variances that exceed the established significance threshold (e.g., 5 percent of standard cost). The fourth column, then, would be the one to which the managerial reader's attention would be most directed, for it would indicate the exceptions from established levels of acceptable performance. The same analysis might very effectively be presented in a graphic format.

Relationships between two quantities, such as standard cost and actual cost, may often be shown more clearly and vividly by lines on a graph than by a comparison of tabulated dollar amounts. Graphs also lend themselves particularly well to presentation of data trends over time. Figure 10–1 is an illustration of a graphic report of the materials usage variance in a production department over a period of three months. It is a continuing report, one that is updated daily. This continuing feature facilitates evaluation of the department's performance over time and of the results of efforts to correct prior variances. The report in Figure 10–1 shows variances as percentages of standard usage rather than as physical quantities or as dollar amounts. The center line represents standard materials usage per unit of output. On either side of this line is a line indicating the boundary of the range of tolerable variances (the shaded area). Notice that the tolerable excess usage (2% of standard) is greater than the tolerable variance below standard (1%). This may reflect the need to maintain product quality. If materials usage falls below the minimum, product quality may be so impaired that the units produced that day must be rejected.

Graphic reports, of course, are not necessarily preferable to those in

**FIGURE 10–1**

**TRYON MANUFACTURING COMPANY**
Materials Usage Variance Report

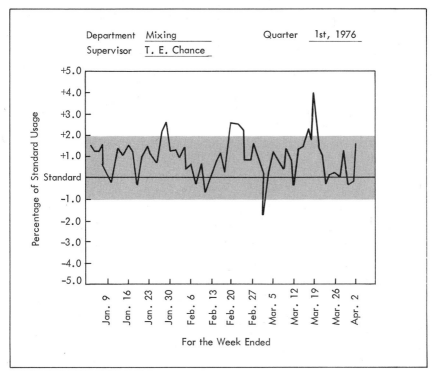

tabular form. Indeed, current reporting practices would seem to suggest just the opposite. Graphs tend to be less precise than tabulations. Further, they become increasingly difficult to read as more and more data are reported in them. Probably their greatest advantage is that they enable the reader to grasp broad relationships or patterns quickly.

## VARIANCES FROM BUDGETED COSTS

Thus far in this chapter, we have been concerned with computing and analyzing variances from standard costs. While such variances are generally useful in the managerial process of cost control, they are not necessarily the most significant bases for control. Occasionally, particular variances will be expected during a future period and will be incorporated in the operating budget for that period. For example, a materials price variance may be budgeted in the anticipation of a temporary market shortage of raw materials. If an unusually large number of trainees will be on the job during a budget period, it would be reasonable to budget an unfavorable labor efficiency variance. And as long as fixed manufacturing overhead is charged to production (under absorption costing) at a rate established at normal volume, it is quite likely that a volume variance may be budgeted each year, for no one year is likely to be the average year implicit in the concept of normal volume.

Where variances are included in the budgeted manufacturing costs for a period, the more significant variances are those not budgeted, that is, those which reflect deviations of actual costs from budgeted levels. For example, a substantial favorable volume variance may be budgeted in a period of peak business activity. If the actual volume variance is favorable, as compared with standard cost, but is not as great as the budgeted variance, the indication is that actual volume, while still above the normal level, was not as high as originally planned for the period. Thus, there may be an unfavorable variance from the budget included in a favorable variance from standard. (Remember that the terms favorable and unfavorable are used in this context to indicate the direction of a variance, not a qualitative evaluation of it.) Once variances have been included in the formal operating plan for the year, management will be better served by concentrating upon any additional, unplanned variances. A budgeted variance is a part of the operating plan rather than a deviation therefrom. Of course, changing conditions during the budget period may require adjustments to any of the budgeted data, including budgeted variances. As long as the budget is considered a valid basis for planning and control, however, budgeted variances should be considered as parts of the base from which operating deviations are measured rather than as parts of the deviations.

## DETERMINATION OF VARIANCES BY STATISTICAL SAMPLING

In all of our discussions of variances thus far, we have implicitly assumed that separate variances are computed for each different raw material, each class of labor, and each production department. This is not always practicable, however, particularly in cases of materials and labor variances that are to be reported frequently. A factory or even a single department may use so many different materials or classes of labor that regular determination of price and usage variances for each would be prohibitively expensive. As an alternative, variances might be computed for only a sample of the materials or labor classes. If this were a statistically valid random sample, the average variances determined for the sample could be extended to the entire population by statistical inference. For example, suppose that the average materials usage variance found in a sample were 4% of standard materials cost in the sample. It might then be inferred that the average usage variance for all materials was within a specified range on either side of 4% of standard cost. Further, the probability that this sample result fairly represented the entire population could be quantified. To illustrate this procedure, it might be said that, on the basis of the sample results, there is a 95% probability that the total materials usage variance was between 3.2% and 4.8% of total standard materials cost. (In statistical terminology, it would be said that there was a 1.6 percentage point confidence interval about the sample mean of 4% at the 95% confidence level.) Then, if the materials usage variance were taken to be 4% of standard cost, management would have to recognize that this figure is only an estimate and that the actual variance might be as low as 3.2% or as high as 4.8% without violating the statistical requirements specified in computing it. Further, there still remains a 5% probability that the variance is yet lower or higher than the limits specified. When variances are computed by sample procedures, management should determine that the resultant variances are statistically significant and not merely a consequence of the limitations of the sampling process.

Computer-based standard cost accounting systems make computation of all variances for all items more feasible than manual accounting systems. Sampling procedures are usually employed to avoid the excessive time and cost requirements of a complete survey. If all of the necessary data are already stored in computer-accessible memory devices, it may be quite simple and economical to obtain variances based upon data for the entire population rather than only a sample.

## STANDARD COST ACCOUNTING

While standard costs are used primarily for purposes of planning and control, they also are used quite commonly in lieu of actual costs in the cost accounting records. As long as standard costs are already available, incorporating them in the accounts is likely to save clerical time and accounting costs. For example, if an inventory of finished product is valued at standard cost, the inventory records may be maintained in terms of physical quantities only. The cost of the inventory may then be determined at any time simply by multiplying the quantity on hand by the standard cost per unit. This use of standard cost in the inventory accounts avoids the necessity of dealing with an inventory cost flow assumption such as first-in, first-out; last-in, first-out; or average cost. So long as the standard costs used are current and attainable, they are acceptable bases for reporting inventories and cost of goods sold in published financial statements. In other words, standard costs are allowed within the framework of generally accepted accounting principles.

There is no uniform system whereby standard costs are incorporated in the cost accounting cycle. The differences are merely procedural, however. The resultant inventory valuations and incomes are the same in all methods, and the same variances would be recognized in all cases. In this chapter, we shall consider the *single plan* of standard cost accounting, wherein all manufacturing inventory accounts are debited and credited only for standard costs. Differences between standard and actual costs are debited or credited to variance accounts. Favorable variances appear as credit balances, for they represent cost reductions or savings as compared with standard costs. Unfavorable variances appear as debit balances, for they are additional costs in excess of standard.

The cost accounting cycle for Cather Creations, Inc., for the month of July 1976 will be illustrated here. Basically, the entries are the same as those presented in Chapter 3 for an actual cost system. The variances recorded in the accounts are those computed earlier in this chapter and will not be explained further here.

**1. Purchase of Materials.** Fifty-five thousand pounds of raw materials were purchased at a price of $1.60 per pound. The standard price is $1.50 per pound.

| | | |
|---|---|---|
| Materials Inventory................................. | 82,500 | |
| Materials Price Variance........................... | 5,500 | |
|     Vouchers Payable............................... | | 88,000 |

The inventory account is debited for the standard price of the units purchased. The liability to the supplier, of course, is recorded at the actual price; for this is the amount that will have to be paid.

**2. Usage of Materials.** Fifty-four thousand pounds of materials were actually used. The standard input is 12 pounds per brass dish produced. As 4,400 dishes were manufactured during the month, standard materials usage amounts to 52,800 pounds.

| | | |
|---|---|---|
| Work in Process...................................... | 79,200 | |
| Materials Usage Variance........................... | 1,800 | |
|     Materials Inventory............................. | | 81,000 |

Work in Process is debited for the standard quantity of materials at the standard price ($1.50 per pound). Materials Inventory is credited for the actual quantity used at the standard price.

**3. Manufacturing Payroll.** The actual hours worked by direct laborers totaled 43,000 for the month. The standard hours in production amounted to 44,000. The actual wage rate paid was $4.40 per hour, as compared with a standard rate of $4.20 per hour.

| | | |
|---|---|---|
| Work in Process.................................... | 184,800 | |
| Labor Rate Variance............................... | 8,600 | |
|     Labor Efficiency Variance....................... | | 4,200 |
|     Payroll Summary............................... | | 189,200 |

Work in Process is debited for the standard hours in production at the standard wage rate. Payroll Summary is credited for the actual direct labor cost of the month (the actual hours at the actual rate). Indirect labor costs are ignored here for the sake of simplicity. They, of course, would be accounted for as part of manufacturing overhead. The entry for payment of the payroll is no different from the same entry under the actual cost system. The payroll department is concerned only with actual labor cost data.

   **4.  Actual Manufacturing Overhead Costs.**  The actual manufacturing overhead costs are recorded in the same way under a standard cost system as in an actual cost system. The credit in the entry below is purely a convenience to represent the many different accounts that would actually be credited.

```
Variable Manufacturing Overhead Control.............   55,000
Fixed Manufacturing Overhead Control..............  125,000
     Various accounts.............................               180,000
```

   **5.  Application of Manufacturing Overhead to Production.**  Work in Process is debited for the standard manufacturing overhead cost of the units produced during the month. Under absorption costing, this will be the sum of the standard variable cost rate ($1.20 per labor hour) and the standard fixed cost rate ($2.40 per labor hour), each multiplied by the standard labor hours in production for the month (44,000 hours).

```
Work in Process....................................  158,400
     Variable Manufacturing Overhead Applied........                52,800
     Fixed Manufacturing Overhead Applied...........               105,600
```

Under variable costing, of course, only the variable manufacturing overhead would be applied to the product. Only absorption costing is illustrated in this and the following entries.

   **6.  Recording Manufacturing Overhead Variances.**  The entries in paragraphs 4 and 5 above do not show the manufacturing overhead variances directly. Rather, they leave the net manufacturing overhead variance as the difference between the debit balances in the Manufacturing Overhead Control accounts and the credit balances in the Manufacturing Overhead Applied accounts. This may be an entirely satisfactory method of accounting for these variances. If, however, management wishes to have them recorded in individual variance accounts, the Manufacturing Overhead Control and Applied accounts may be closed and the desired variance accounts established as a consequence. This procedure is illustrated below for absorption costing and the three-variance plan.

```
Variable Manufacturing Overhead Applied..............   52,800
Fixed Manufacturing Overhead Applied.................  105,600
Manufacturing Overhead Spending Variance.............    8,400
Manufacturing Overhead Volume Variance...............   14,400
     Manufacturing Overhead Efficiency Variance.........                 1,200
     Variable Manufacturing Overhead Control...........                55,000
     Fixed Manufacturing Overhead Control.............               125,000
```

**7.  Completion of Production.**  The standard cost sheet shows that the total standard cost of one ornamental brass dish is $96. Since Work in Process has been debited for the standard costs of production only, it will be the standard cost of the completed units that is transferred from that account to Finished Product. The entry to record the completion of 4,400 dishes is as follows:

| | | |
|---|---|---|
| Finished Product..................................... | 422,400 | |
| Work in Process.................................. | | 422,400 |

As there was no beginning or ending inventory of Work in Process, that account now shows no balance.

**8.  Sales.**  During July 1976, Cather Creations, Inc., sold 4,000 brass dishes at a unit price of $140. The entry to record the sales revenue is the usual one.

| | | |
|---|---|---|
| Accounts Receivable.................................. | 560,000 | |
| Sales........................................... | | 560,000 |

The cost of the goods sold would be the product of the 4,000 dishes sold multiplied by the standard unit cost of $96.

| | | |
|---|---|---|
| Cost of Goods Sold................................... | 384,000 | |
| Finished Product.................................. | | 384,000 |

## DISPOSITION OF VARIANCES

### Debit or Credit to Current Period's Income

Once the variances have been computed and have been debited or credited to individual variance accounts, the question arises as to what should be their final disposition. In most cases, as a practical matter, variance accounts are debited (unfavorable variances) or credited (favorable variances) to the income of the current period. This may be accomplished by closing the variance accounts either to the Revenue and Expense Summary account or to the Cost of Goods Sold account. Net income, of course, would be the same under either alternative. In the income statement, the net total of all the variances is treated as an adjustment to the cost of goods sold figure. If the net variance is favorable, it is deducted from cost of goods sold; if the net variance is unfavorable, it is added to cost of goods sold.[5] Showing each variance in detail would seem unnecessary in a summarized report such as the income statement. Individual variances should, of course, be reported to appropriate levels of management for action.

---

[5] This is essentially the same method of reporting as suggested in Chapter 3 for net under- or overapplied manufacturing overhead.

So long as standards are current and attainable and so long as flexible budgets for manufacturing overhead are based upon reasonable current cost estimates, debiting or crediting manufacturing variances to current income appears to be a theoretically sound and practically satisfactory method of disposing of them—with one possible exception to be noted shortly. If, on the other hand, standards and budgets are not current and attainable, standard cost is not a satisfactory measure of current production costs; and, hence, the variances are not valid indicators of departures from cost levels that should have been attained. In such instance, it would be better to dispose of the variances by adjusting the several manufacturing cost accounts from the invalid standard cost to the actual cost of the period.

## Allocation of Variances to Manufacturing Cost Accounts

If standards and budgets do not reflect current attainable cost levels, debiting or crediting variances to income may result in an overstatement or understatement of inventories and cost of goods sold. In such a case, it is better to adjust the inventory and cost of goods sold accounts to .actual costs by allocating the manufacturing variances among them. Variances would be allocated among the several accounts to which the standard manufacturing costs had been charged—Work in Process, Finished Product, and Cost of Goods Sold. The amount allocated to each of these accounts would be determined by the amount of the relevant standard cost in each account as of the end of the period relative to the total amount of that standard cost charged to production during the period. For example, labor variances would be allocated on the basis of standard labor cost of the period. Assume that a total of $600,000 of standard labor cost had been charged to Work in Process during a given period. Of that total, $540,000 had been transferred to Finished Product and $420,000 had been further transferred from Finished Product to Cost of Goods Sold. At the end of the period, the standard labor cost of the period in each of these accounts would be as follows:

| | |
|---|---|
| Work in Process......................... | $ 60,000 |
| Finished Product....................... | 120,000 |
| Cost of Goods Sold..................... | 420,000 |
| | $600,000 |

The net labor variance would then be allocated as follows: one tenth to Work in Process, two tenths to Finished Product, and seven tenths to Cost of Goods Sold. Allocation of materials and manufacturing overhead variances would be accomplished in a similar manner; standard materials cost and standard manufacturing overhead cost, respectively, being used as the bases for allocations. It should be noted that the materials price variance would likely be allocated partly to Materials Inventory as well as to the three accounts listed above.

## Special Problem of the Volume Variance

The discussions in the preceding two sections is sufficient for all of the variances from standard cost except one, the manufacturing overhead volume variance. Even if the flexible budget contains current attainable fixed cost estimates, the standard fixed manufacturing overhead rate may not provide for a reasonable assignment of current fixed manufacturing overhead to production. This fixed rate is computed on the basis of normal volume, which, as explained earlier, may deviate substantially from the budgeted and/or from the actual volume in any single period. Thus, a substantial volume variance could actually be anticipated in most periods. If normal volume is the average level of operations expected over the course of the business cycle, one would expect that favorable and unfavorable volume variances would tend to offset one another over a complete cycle. If normal volume is defined as the company's preferred rate of operating capacity, however, and if that rate is not always reached and almost never exceeded, the volume variance over long periods of time would be unfavorable.

Where the amount of the volume variance is not very material in relation to total inventory cost or to net income for the period, it may safely be treated as an adjustment to cost of goods sold along with the other variances. If the amount is very material, it would have to be allocated among the accounts affected. However, it should be noted that in most cases, most of the volume variance would be debited or credited to Cost of Goods Sold even if it is allocated among the several accounts. This is a result of the fact that most of the goods produced currently are also sold currently. Thus, the volume variance would be unlikely to have a substantial effect on income except in cases of substantial changes in the level of inventories of manufactured products at the end of a period as compared with the beginning of that period.

If it is expected that favorable and unfavorable volume variances will offset each other over time, a firm might wish to defer the volume variance at the end of each period. It would be a deferred credit (a liability) if favorable and a deferred charge (an asset) if unfavorable. This practice is usually restricted to monthly financial reporting. Annual financial statements almost invariably provide for a final disposition of the volume variance. Where there are significant monthly variations in production volume, deferral of the volume variance at the end of each month seems appropriate. Deferral at the end of a fiscal year, however, seems questionable. The volume variance derives from the practical exigencies of an absorption costing system. It is not so much a consequence of operations as it is a consequence of how operations are accounted for. Further, a deferred volume variance would be a dubious asset or liability in any event.[6]

## QUESTIONS FOR DISCUSSION

1. Explain the essential source of each of the variances listed below. That is, from what conditions or factors do they derive?
    a. Materials price variance
    b. Labor rate variance
    c. Materials usage variance
    d. Labor efficiency variance
    e. Manufacturing overhead efficiency variance
    f. Manufacturing overhead spending variance
    g. Manufacturing overhead volume variance
2. Which of the variances listed in Question 1, if any, would be different under variable costing as compared with absorption costing? What would cause these differences?
3. Can any of the variances in Question 1 be computed without knowledge of the actual volume of output during the period? If so, which ones and why?
4. Why is it generally invalid to sum the materials price and usage variances and to describe the total as a significant net materials variance for the period?
5. Define each of the following terms: (a) normal volume, (b) actual output volume, (c) standard input volume, and (d) actual input volume. What is the role of each of these four concepts of volume in the determination of three manufacturing overhead variances for a company that charges manufacturing overhead to production on the basis of direct labor hours?
6. What is the basic difference between the two-variance plan and the three-variance plan for analyzing manufacturing overhead costs? Under what circumstances may only one of these plans be used? Under what circumstances may either be used? When either may be used, which one would be preferable and why?
7. What does a materials mix variance disclose that the materials usage variance does not?
8. The production manager of a manufacturing company notices that the usage of a particular raw material has consistently exceeded the standard for several weeks. A review of production techniques and quality control practices indicates that the materials quantity standard for this item is still reasonable and attainable. How might the production manager go about determining the specific cause(s) of this materials usage variance and identifying the person(s) responsible for it?

---

[6] The proponent of variable costing in published financial statements may smile at this point and observe that, if people would only listen to him, there would be no volume variance to worry about at all.

9. The prices of some commodities are established in very organized competitive markets and may fluctuate from day to day. Agricultural products are typical examples of such commodities. Are materials price standards and price variances practicable control techniques for firms that use such commodities as raw materials? Explain.

10. Is the manufacturing overhead volume variance controllable? If so, by whom? If not, why not?

11. The management of a manufacturing firm has noticed that the variable cost portion of its manufacturing overhead spending variance is almost invariably favorable when production volume exceeds normal and unfavorable when operations fall below normal volume. Conversely, the fixed cost portion of the spending variance is favorable when operations are below normal and unfavorable at volumes above normal. Without further information, what condition(s) might this situation suggest?

12. In a company that charges manufacturing overhead to production at standard rates per direct labor hour, how frequently should each of the three variances from standard manufacturing overhead be reported to management?

13. "Inasmuch as standard costs reflect costs that should have been incurred rather than costs that actually were incurred, they are useful only for purposes of cost analysis and control. They may not be used in the valuation of inventories or in the measurement of income. If standard costs were used for the latter purposes, the financial statements would reflect, in part, the operating goals of the company rather than its operating results." Comment on this statement.

14. How do standard costs and variances relate to the concept of management by exception?

15. Is fixing responsibility for a variance equivalent to ascertaining its cause? Explain.

16. In a standard cost system, is "variance control" the same thing as "cost control"? In other words, can management effectively control costs by focusing attention only on variances and their control? Discuss.

17. What criteria should be used by management to determine whether a variance is significant and requires special action?

18. What is the difference between variances from standard costs and variances from budgeted costs? In a firm that uses both budgets and standard costs, might these variances prove to be different in amount? If so, which variances would be more useful to management for purposes of cost control—variances from standard costs or variances from the budget? Explain.

19. How may variances be disposed of in the accounts and reported in the financial statements? If there are alternatives, which is most appropriate and why?

20. A corporation uses approximately 1,500 different materials in the manufacture of its various products. It would like to have daily reports of materials usage and the usage variance, but it does not want to incur the cost of determining the actual and standard usages of each material every day.

Can you suggest a procedure that would yield acceptably accurate and complete daily materials usage reports without analyzing each item every day?

## PROBLEMS

 The Roberts Corporation manufactures ceramic ash trays. A standard cost system is used to account for production. The standard cost sheet for one ash tray is as follows:

Raw materials:
| | |
|---|---|
| Clay (1½ lbs. @ $.60)......................... | $ .90 |
| Pigment (5 oz. @ $.80)......................... | 4.00 |
| Direct labor (¼ hr. @ $4.20)..................... | 1.05 |
| Manufacturing overhead: | |
| Variable....................................... | .42 |
| Fixed......................................... | .63 |
| | $7.00 |

During the month of October 1976, actual production totaled 20,000 ash trays. Actual production cost data for that month are summarized below.

Materials purchases: 35,000 lbs. of clay @ $.56 and 90,000 oz. of pigment @ $.84
Materials usage: 32,000 lbs. of clay and 102,500 oz. of pigment
Direct labor: 4,800 hrs. @ $4.30
Variable manufacturing overhead: $8,500
Fixed manufacturing overhead: $13,000

There was no inventory of work in process at the beginning or at the end of October. Sales for the month totaled 18,500 ash trays.

*Required:*
Compute the following quantities and show all computations.
a. Standard materials, labor, and manufacturing overhead costs in production for the month of October 1976.
b. Standard cost of finished production.
c. Standard cost of goods sold.
d. Materials price and usage variances.
e. Labor rate and efficiency variances.

10-2. The Buck Manufacturing Company makes widgets and employs a standard cost accounting system. The standard cost of one widget is as follows:

| | |
|---|---|
| Materials (3 units @ $2.50)....................... | $ 7.50 |
| Labor (2 hrs. @ $4.75).......................... | 9.50 |
| Manufacturing overhead: | |
| Variable (2 hrs. @ $2)......................... | 4.00 |
| Fixed (2 hrs. @ $3)........................... | 6.00 |
| | $27.00 |

During the year 1976, actual output amounted to 80,000 finished widgets. Materials purchases for the year totaled 300,000 units at a price of $2.44 each. The total materials usage for the year was 250,000 units. The factory payroll for the year included a total of 163,000 direct labor hours at an average wage rate of $4.65 per hour.

*Required:*

Compute all variances from standard direct materials and labor costs. Show all computations.

10–3. The Fitzgerald Corporation manufactures a variety of children's clothing. All products require some work in the stitching department. Normal production volume in that department is 60,000 direct labor hours per month. The budgeted monthly manufacturing overhead cost for the stitching department is $150,000 plus $.90 per direct labor hour. The company uses absorption costing.

During June 1976, the stitching department recorded a total of 67,500 labor hours, 1,500 of which were in excess of the standard hours allowed for the department's output that month. Actual manufacturing overhead for the month included $156,000 of fixed costs and $62,000 of variable costs.

*Required:*

Compute three variances from standard manufacturing overhead cost for the month of June 1976. Show all computations.

10–4. Following is the flexible budget of manufacturing overhead for the Crane Company for one month:

| Percent of full capacity... | 70% | 80% | 90% | 100% |
|---|---|---|---|---|
| Standard machine-hours.. | 42,000 | 48,000 | 54,000 | 60,000 |
| Variable costs........... | $ 52,500 | $ 60,000 | $ 67,500 | $ 75,000 |
| Semivariable costs....... | 42,200 | 44,300 | 46,400 | 48,500 |
| Fixed costs............. | 107,500 | 107,500 | 107,500 | 107,500 |

Management believes that the range of volume tabulated in this budget encompasses any volume that might reasonably be expected to occur. Normal volume has been set at 90% of capacity. Both variable and fixed manufacturing overhead costs, including variable and fixed components of the semivariable costs, are charged to production at standard rates per machine-hour.

Actual operating data for the month of April 1976 are as follows:

| | |
|---|---|
| Actual machine-hours..................... | 51,600 |
| Standard machine-hours.................... | 50,000 |
| Variable manufacturing overhead........... | $ 63,800 |
| Semivariable manufacturing overhead........ | 45,700 |
| Fixed manufacturing overhead............. | 105,000 |

*Required:*

a. Separate the semivariable costs in the budget into variable and fixed components. Then compute standard variable and fixed manufacturing overhead rates per machine-hour.

    *b.* Calculate three variances from standard manufacturing overhead cost for the month of April 1976.

    *c.* Explain briefly the essential meaning of each of these three variances.

10–5. The Ferber Products Company uses a standard cost system and variable costing. Manufacturing overhead is applied to production on the basis of standard direct labor cost. The flexible budget for the company's manufacturing overhead allows $150,000 per month plus $.60 per direct labor dollar. Budgeted direct labor costs for the month of October 1976 were $200,000. Actual operations for October are summarized below.

| | |
|---|---|
| Actual direct labor cost..................... | $225,000 |
| Standard direct labor cost.................. | 210,000 |
| Actual variable manufacturing overhead...... | 140,000 |
| Actual fixed manufacturing overhead......... | 148,000 |

*Required:*

    *a.* Compute the standard manufacturing overhead cost of production for the month of October 1976.

    *b.* Compute as many variances from standard manufacturing overhead cost for October as you can.

10–6. The Melville Company produces a single product. Both variable and fixed manufacturing overhead costs are charged to production at standard rates per unit of product. The flexible budget for manufacturing overhead allows $4 per unit of product plus $60,000 per month. Normal volume is 12,000 units per month. During the month of July 1976, a total of 9,500 units were produced. Actual variable manufacturing overhead totaled $36,000 and actual fixed manufacturing overhead, $57,500.

*Required:*

    *a.* Compute the standard manufacturing overhead cost of production for July 1976.

    *b.* Compute as many variances from standard manufacturing overhead cost as you can.

10–7. The Jackson Manufacturing Company processes its three products in three separate production departments. Product A is processed in Department 10. Manufacturing overhead is charged to production in this department at standard rates per unit of Product A. The standard variable manufacturing overhead rate is $1.20; the standard fixed manufacturing overhead rate is $2. Normal production volume is 750,000 units of Product A annually.

    During 1976, a total of 800,000 units of Product A were manufactured. Actual manufacturing overhead for 1976 included variable costs of $985,000 and fixed costs of $1,515,000.

*Required:*

Compute as many variances from standard manufacturing overhead cost in Department 10 during 1976 as you can.

10–8.  The Gardner Chemical Corporation manufactures an automobile oil additive from three basic raw materials. Standard materials cost for a batch of 25 gallons of this additive is as follows:

Material X (50 qts. @ $3)................ $150
Material Y (30 qts. @ $5)................  150
Material Z (20 qts. @ $12)...............  240
                                          ‾‾‾‾‾
                                          $540
                                          ‾‾‾‾‾

During 1976, 8,000 batches of the additive were produced. Actual materials usage for this output is summarized below:

|  | *Quarts* |
|---|---|
| Material X........................ | 360,000 |
| Material Y........................ | 225,000 |
| Material Z........................ | 215,000 |

*Required:*

a.  Compute the materials usage variance for 1976 in quarts only.
b.  Compute the materials usage variance for 1976 in dollars.
c.  Explain any notable difference between the two variances computed in (*a*) and (*b*).

10–9.  The Bloch Frozen Foods Company prepared the following graphic analysis of its labor cost for August 1976:

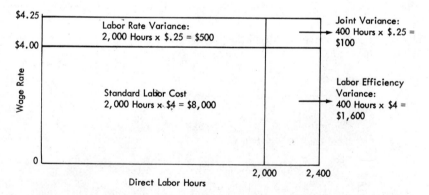

The area of the largest rectangle represents total actual labor cost for the month. The areas of the four smaller, internal rectangles are labeled on the graph. (These are not drawn accurately to scale.)

*Required:*

Comment on the usefulness of this graphic variance analysis to management.

10-10.  The Hemingway Corporation manufactures a single product. Production is costed at standard variable cost. The standard cost sheet for one unit of product is as follows:

> Materials (10 pcs. @ $.70).....................$ 7
> Labor (3 hrs. @ $4)............................. 12
> Variable manufacturing overhead (3 hrs. @ $2).... __6__
> $25

The flexible budget for manufacturing overhead allows $2 per direct labor hour plus $400,000 per year.

Actual production data for 1976 are summarized below.

> Unit output: 150,000 units of product
> Materials purchases: 1,400,000 pcs. @ $.66
> Materials usage: 1,488,000 pcs.
> Direct labor hours: 475,000
> Direct labor cost: $1,957,000
> Variable manufacturing overhead: $920,000
> Fixed manufacturing overhead: $420,000

*Required:*

Compute as many variances from standard cost for 1976 as you can.

10-11.  The Mitchell Frock Company manufactures women's clothing. Work in Process is charged with standard manufacturing costs, including both variable and fixed manufacturing overhead. The Kismet nightgown is the sole product of the sheer department and is produced in standard lots of 250 units. The relevant standards and budget data are as follows:

> Direct materials:
>   Silk: 1,200 yards per lot @ $5 per yard        30 lots
>   Lace: 400 yards per lot @ $8.75 per yard            #5
> Direct labor: 100 hours per lot @ $4.50 per hour
> Manufacturing overhead: $1.80 per direct labor hour plus $15,000 per month

Normal production volume has been set at 24 lots per month.

The actual operations in the sheer department for the month of December 1976 are summarized below.

> Purchases of materials:
>   Silk: 40,000 yards @ $5.05
>   Lace: 12,500 yards @ $8.80
> Usage of materials:
>   Silk: 37,500 yards
>   Lace: 12,400 yards

Direct labor: 3,120 hours @ $4.40
Manufacturing overhead:
  Variable: $5,500
  Fixed: $14,895
Output: 30 lots of Kismet nightgowns

*Required:*

Compute as many variances from standard cost for the month of December as you can.

10–12. The Faulkner Company uses the single plan of standard cost accounting and absorption costing in its production records. The standard cost sheet for one of its principal products is as follows:

*Product W*

| | | |
|---|---:|---:|
| Materials (4½ lbs. of Material J @ $1.20)...... | | $ 5.40 |
| Labor (½ hr. @ $4.80)...................... | | 2.40 |
| Manufacturing overhead: | | |
|   Variable (½ hr. @ $2.20)................. | $1.10 | |
|   Fixed (½ hr. @ $5)...................... | 2.50 | 3.60 |
| | | $11.40 |

Normal production volume for Product W has been set at 12,000 labor hours per month.

Actual operations for the month of March 1976 are summarized below.

1. Purchased 110,000 pounds of Material J at $1.25 each.
2. Used 99,000 pounds of Material J in production.
3. The payroll included 10,800 hours of direct labor time on Product W at an average rate of $4.90 per hour.
4. Actual variable manufacturing overhead applicable to Product W amounted to $26,000. Applicable fixed manufacturing overhead totaled $61,000.
5. During March, 21,600 units of Product W were completed and transferred to finished stock. On March 1, there were 1,600 units in process; they were complete with respect to materials and half complete with respect to labor and manufacturing overhead. At the end of March, 2,400 units remained in process, complete as to materials and half complete as to conversion costs.

*Required:*

a. Prepare a schedule showing all postings to Work in Process— Product W for the month of March 1976, including the opening and closing balances.
b. Compute as many variances from standard production cost for March as you can.

10–13. The Updike Products Company produces a single product. Absorption costing and the single plan of standard cost accounting are used in the valuation of inventories and the measurement of periodic income. The standard cost sheet for the company's product appears as follows:

| | |
|---|---|
| Materials (4 lbs. @ $.75)..................... | $ 3.00 |
| Direct labor (1.6 hrs. @ $4.25)............... | 6.80 |
| Manufacturing overhead..................... | 4.00 |
| | $13.80 |

The flexible budget for manufacturing overhead allows $1.50 per unit of product plus $30,000 per month. Normal production volume is measured in units of output, and manufacturing overhead is applied to production on the same basis.

Transactions for the month of January 1976, the first month of the company's operations, are as follows:

Materials purchased: 60,000 lbs. @ $.72
Materials used: 57,800 lbs.
Direct labor: 22,000 hrs. @ $4.33
Variable manufacturing overhead: $22,200
Fixed manufacturing overhead: $30,800
Production: 14,000 units of product

*Required:*

Compute as many variances from standard cost for January 1976 as you can.

10–14.   The Cooper Boat Corporation produces a single product, concrete boat hulls. Absorption costing and standard cost accounting are employed. The standard direct production costs of one unit of product are as follows:

| | |
|---|---|
| Materials: | |
| 600 lbs. of cement @ $.15.................... | $ 90 |
| 45 yards of wire mesh @ $2.40............... | 108 |
| | $198 |
| Labor (20 hours @ $5)....................... | 100 |
| | $298 |

The flexible budget for manufacturing overhead allows variable costs of $1.75 per direct labor hour and fixed costs of $2.25 per labor hour, based upon a normal volume of 160,000 hours per year.

Actual operations during 1976 were as follows:

1. Seven thousand and two hundred concrete hulls were completed. Two hundred hulls were in process at the end of the year; they were complete as to materials and half complete as to conversion costs. There was no work in process at the start of the year.

2. Two thousand and five hundred tons of cement were purchased at an average price of $.15½ per pound. Three hundred and fifty thousand yards of wire mesh were purchased for $2.50 per yard.

3. The factory used 4,500,000 pounds of cement and 345,000 yards of wire mesh during the year.

4. The factory payroll included 142,000 direct labor hours at an average wage rate of $4.90 per hour.

5. Variable manufacturing overhead costs totaled $275,000, and fixed manufacturing overhead amounted to $375,000.

6. Seven thousand finished hulls were sold at a price of $550 each.

*Required:*

a. Compute as many variances from standard cost as you can.

b. Prepare journal entries to record the operations of 1976.

10–15. The Salinger Rubber Company manufactures rubber washers and employs a standard cost system with absorption costing. Standards have been set for production lots of 1,000 washers. Materials standards call for 7½ kilograms of rubber per lot at a standard price of $.80 per kilogram. Labor standards call for 2.4 hours per lot at a standard wage rate of $3.75 per hour. The flexible budget for manufacturing overhead for one month is as follows:

| Output (in lots)............. | 12,000 | 15,000 | 18,000 |
|---|---|---|---|
| Machine-hours............... | 36,000 | 45,000 | 54,000 |
| Variable costs............... | $ 43,200 | $ 54,000 | $ 64,800 |
| Fixed costs................. | 108,000 | 108,000 | 108,000 |

Manufacturing overhead is applied to production on the basis of machine-hours. Normal production volume has been established at 15,000 lots of washers per month.

Operations for October 1976 are summarized below.

Rubber purchases: 120,000 kg. @ $.82
Rubber usage: 127,500 kg.
Direct labor: 40,400 hrs. @ $3.88
Variable manufacturing overhead: $59,600
Fixed manufacturing overhead: $104,000
Machine-hours worked: 48,500
Output: 16,600 lots
Sales: 17,000 lots

*Required:*

Prepare journal entries to record operations for October 1976. Show variance computations to support these entries.

10–16. Grey Electric Products, Inc., manufactures condensers in Department 101. Standard costing and absorption costing are used to account for production. The standard cost sheet for one condenser is as follows:

| Materials: | |
|---|---|
| Part no. 98736 (1 unit @ $4.08)............ | $ 4.08 |
| Part no. 6485 (2 units @ $2.27)............ | 4.54 |
| Labor (.8 hour @ $4.50).................... | 3.60 |
| Manufacturing overhead: | |
| Variable (.8 hour @ $.80)................. | .64 |
| Fixed (.8 hour @ $1.80).................. | 1.44 |
| | $14.30 |

The flexible budget for Department 101 allows variable manufacturing overhead of $.80 per labor hour and fixed manufacturing overhead of $720,000 per year.

During 1976, a total of 420,000 condensers were produced. The average prices paid for parts no. 98736 and no. 6485 were $3.99 and $2.35, respectively. Four hundred thousand units of part no. 98736 and 900,000 units of part no. 6485 were purchased. The total direct labor cost in Department 101 during 1976 was $1,513,000; total labor time was 340,000 hours. A summary of materials requisitions shows that 425,000 units of part no. 98736 and 848,000 units of part no. 6485 were used during the year. Variable manufacturing overhead for the year totaled $260,000; fixed manufacturing overhead totaled $722,000.

During 1976, 400,000 condensers were sold at an average price of $21 apiece.

*Required:*

Prepare journal entries to record the operations of 1976. Present variance computations to support these entries.

10–17.  The Tarkington Company manufactures turnbuckles in lots of 250. A single plan standard cost accounting system is used. The standard cost of one lot of production is as follows:

| | | |
|---|---:|---:|
| Materials (400 lbs. @ $.25)............ | | $100.00 |
| Labor (14 hrs. @ $4.25)............... | | 59.50 |
| Manufacturing overhead: | | |
| Variable (14 hrs. @ $1.75)........... | $24.50 | |
| Fixed (14 hrs. @ $3)............... | 42.00 | 66.50 |
| | | $226.00 |

Normal production volume has been established at 60,000 direct labor hours per month.

Actual operating data for the month of February 1976 are summarized below.

Output: 4,400 lots
Materials purchases: 1,800,000 lbs. @ $.27
Materials usage: 1,750,000 lbs.
Labor: 63,000 hrs. @ $4.28
Variable manufacturing overhead: $122,000
Fixed manufacturing overhead: $192,000
Sales: 1,000,000 turnbuckles @ $1.45
Selling and administrative expenses:
  Variable: $145,000
  Fixed: $275,000
The applicable income tax rate is 40%.

*Required:*

a.  Compute as many variances from standard cost as you can.
b.  Prepare an income statement for the month of February 1976.

10–18.  The Wharton Engine Company produces engine blocks in its forging department. Blocks are charged with the standard variable costs incurred in production. The standard cost sheet for one engine block is as follows:

| | | |
|---|---:|---:|
| Materials (60 lbs. @ $.40)..................... | | $24.00 |
| Direct labor: | | |
| Machine operators (2¼ hrs. @ $5.60).......... | $12.60 | |
| Handlers (½ hr. @ $4.00)................... | 2.00 | 14.60 |
| Manufacturing overhead (2 machine-hrs. @ $3.20).. | | 6.40 |
| | | $45.00 |

The output of the forging department is budgeted at 25,000 units annually. Fixed manufacturing overhead in the department is budgeted at $400,000 per year.

During 1976, the actual output of the forging department was 20,000 engine blocks. Purchase invoices showed that 1,400,000 pounds of material were purchased at an average price of $.39 per pound. Materials usage reports showed that a total of 1,275,000 pounds were used during 1976. The cost accounting department's records indicated that machine operators worked 44,000 hours at an actual wage rate of $5.50 and that handlers worked a total of 10,600 hours at a wage rate of $4.10. Forging department cost records showed that total variable manufacturing overhead was $140,000 and total fixed manufacturing overhead was $425,000. The total actual machine-hours worked during the year amounted to 40,000.

*Required:*

a. Prepare journal entries to record the operations of the forging department during 1976. Show variance computations in support of these entries.
b. The output of the forging department in 1976 was 20% below the budgeted annual output. Can the effects of this reduced volume on costs be measured within the framework of the company's standard cost system? Explain.

10–19. The Hawthorne Company assembles power drills in two successive production departments. Actual assembly work is done in Department 10. The drills are then tested and boxed in Department 20. The company uses variable costing and a single plan standard cost accounting system. The standard cost sheet for one drill is as follows:

| | | |
|---|---:|---:|
| Materials: | | |
| Drill housing (1 @ $3.95)...................... | $3.95 | |
| Electric motor (1 @ $6.75)..................... | 6.75 | |
| Cord with plug (1 @ $.43)..................... | .43 | |
| Box (1 @ $.17)............................... | .17 | $11.30 |
| Direct labor: | | |
| Department 10 (¼ hr. @ $4.80)............... | $1.20 | |
| Department 20 (⅓ hr. @ $4.50)............... | 1.50 | 2.70 |
| Variable manufacturing overhead: | | |
| Department 10 (¼ hr. @ $2)................... | $ .50 | |
| Department 20 (⅓ hr. @ $1.50)............... | .50 | 1.00 |
| | | $15.00 |

During 1976, a total of 450,000 power drills were assembled in Department 10 and transferred to Department 20. In the latter department, 435,000 drills were tested, boxed, and transferred to the finished stock room.

Actual materials purchases during 1976 were as follows:
Drill housings: 440,000 @ $3.83
Electric motors: 425,000 @ $6.89
Cords: 480,000 @ $.45
Boxes: 500,000 @ $.15

Materials usage in 1976 is summarized below.
Drill housings: 450,800
Electric motors: 452,200
Cords: 451,500
Boxes: 448,000

The direct labor payroll for 1976 included the following charges to the two production departments:
Department 10: 116,000 hrs. @ $4.88
Department 20: 144,000 hrs. @ $4.60

Actual manufacturing overhead costs incurred during the year were as follows:

|  | Variable | Fixed |
|---|---|---|
| Department 10............ | $246,000 | $185,000 |
| Department 20........... | 204,000 | 288,000 |

*Required:*

a. Compute as many variances from standard cost as you can.
b. Prepare an analysis showing all debits and credits to the accounts for Work in Process—Department 10 and Work in Process—Department 20.

10–20. The Steinbeck Paper Company began operations in 1976. During that year, it completed production of 210,000 reams of paper and sold 150,000 reams. At the end of the year, the inventory of work in process consisted of 30,000 reams of paper, half complete with respect to all cost elements.

Materials standards called for 4 pounds of pulp per ream at a price of $.30 per pound. Actual material usage in 1976 totaled 1,500,000 pounds of pulp. A total of 1,700,000 pounds were purchased at an average price of $.39 per pound. The company's auditors have stated that they regard the materials price and usage variances as unacceptably large because the standards established were clearly not realistic. Accordingly, management has agreed to adjust the affected accounts to reflect the average cost of raw material. The single plan of standard cost accounting has been used.

*Required:*

a. Determine the proper allocations of the materials price variance and the materials usage variance to the appropriate accounts.
b. Prepare a journal entry to adjust the accounts to conform to the auditors' requirement.

10–21. The O'Hara Manufacturing Company produces a single product. The standard costs for materials and labor total $40 per unit of product. The flexible budget allows $3 per machine-hour for variable manufacturing overhead and $4,200,000 per year for fixed manufacturing overhead. Normal volume is 600,000 machine-hours per year. During 1976, the company was shut down by a strike for five months. Actual production and cost data for 1976 are as follows:

> Actual output volume: 90,000 units of product
> Actual input volume: 375,000 machine-hours
> Standard input volume: 360,000 machine-hours
> Actual variable manufacturing overhead: $1,100,000
> Actual fixed manufacturing overhead: $4,200,000
> Variable nonmanufacturing expenses: $500,000
> Fixed nonmanufacturing expenses: $1,500,000
> Sales revenue: 100,000 units of product @ $100

There were no materials or labor variances in 1976. Income taxes may be ignored.

*Required:*

a. Assuming that the company uses absorption costing, compute as many manufacturing overhead variances as you can.
b. Prepare an income statement for 1976 in the absorption costing format.
c. Now, assuming that the company has consistently used variable costing, prepare an income statement for 1976 in that format.
d. Explain why you treated the manufacturing overhead volume variance as you did in part (b). Discuss alternative presentations of this variance under absorption costing. Which alternative do you feel would be most useful to management in this case? Why? Are the same alternatives available under variable costing? Explain.

10–22. The Allen Drug Company produces a patented cough syrup in its San Jose plant. The standard cost sheet for one case of 24 5-ounce bottles is as follows:

Raw materials:

| | | |
|---|---:|---:|
| Glycerine (90 oz. @ $.16).................... | $14.40 | |
| Alcohol (15 oz. @ $.12)....................... | 1.80 | |
| Cherry flavoring (30 oz. @ $.20).............. | 6.00 | |
| Bottles (25 @ $.06)......................... | 1.50 | $23.70 |

Direct labor:

| | | |
|---|---:|---:|
| Blending department (½ hr. @ $4)............ | $ 2.00 | |
| Bottling department (¼ hr. @ $4.80)......... | 1.20 | 3.20 |

Manufacturing overhead:

| | | |
|---|---:|---:|
| Blending department: | | |
|   Variable (½ hr. @ $1.40).................. | $ .70 | |
|   Fixed (½ hr. @ $1.80).................... | .90 | |
| Bottling department: | | |
|   Variable (¼ hr. @ $2)..................... | .50 | |
|   Fixed (¼ hr. @ $4)....................... | 1.00 | 3.10 |
| | | $30.00 |

Normal volume is 10,000 labor hours per month in the blending department and 5,000 labor hours per month in the bottling department.

The glycerine, alcohol, and cherry flavoring are mixed together in 25-gallon batches in the blending department and then piped to the bottling department, where it is placed into 5-ounce bottles by machines.

During August 1976, a total of 24,000 cases of cough syrup were prepared and bottled. There were no inventories in process in either department at the beginning or at the end of the month.

Purchases and usage of raw materials during August are summarized as follows:

| | Purchases | Usage |
|---|---|---|
| Glycerine............ | 18,000 gals. @ $20.90 | 18,000 gals. |
| Alcohol.............. | 2,400 gals. @ $16.06 | 2,900 gals. |
| Cherry flavoring...... | 6,000 gals. @ $24.75 | 4,800 gals. |
| Bottles.............. | 5,000 gross @ $ 8.95 | 4,200 gross |

The actual payroll for August included 12,200 hours in the blending department at an average wage rate of $3.95 per hour and 6,300 hours in the bottling department at an average rate of $4.72 per hour. Actual manufacturing overhead costs incurred were as follows:

| | Variable | Fixed |
|---|---|---|
| Blending department......... | $16,900 | $19,000 |
| Bottling department.......... | 13,400 | 19,600 |

During August, 22,000 cases of cough syrup were sold at an average price of $45 per case. Variable selling expenses amounted to 10% of sales revenue. Fixed administrative expenses totaled $150,000. The applicable income tax rate is 40%.

*Required:*

a. Compute as many variances from standard cost for August as you can.

b. Prepare an income statement for the month of August.

10–23. The net labor efficiency variance for the stamping department of the Lewis Lamp Corporation for the month of November 1976 was computed as follows:

| | |
|---|---:|
| Standard labor hours............................ | 28,500 |
| Actual labor hours.............................. | 30,200 |
| Excess hours.................................. | (1,700) |
| Standard wage rate per hour.................... | $ 3.60 |
| Unfavorable variance........................... | $(6,120) |

The factory superintendent is responsible for all production operations. He asked the stamping department foreman to explain the reasons for the excess labor hours in his department. The foreman submitted the following analysis of excess labor time for November:

| | | |
|---|---:|---:|
| Standard hours in production...................... | | 28,500 |
| Excess hours: | | |
| Trainee operating machine........................ | 48 | |
| Experienced operator instructing trainee........... | 12 | |
| Rework time on units rejected by inspector........ | 420 | |
| Rework time on Job No. 337; original specifications had been in error............................. | 80 | |
| Raw materials received from storeroom were too thick........................................ | 75 | |
| Work done on obsolete standby equipment; regular equipment was overloaded.................... | 600 | |
| Partial lot run on Job No. 345................... | 20 | |
| Extra setup time required after machine breakdown.. | 15 | |
| Idle time; no production scheduled................ | 420 | |
| Unexplained.................................. | 450 | 2,140 |
| | | 30,640 |
| Hours saved: | | |
| New tools used................................ | 360 | |
| Consecutive jobs run for same product; no setup time required for second job...................... | 40 | |
| Assistant foreman assigned to machine operation for one week..................................... | 40 | 440 |
| Actual hours worked............................ | | 30,200 |

*Required:*

Prepare a report that classifies the various causes of the labor efficiency variance as controllable by the department foreman, controllable by the factory superintendent, or uncontrollable at the level of the factory. Indicate which causes you believe require further attention by management. Comment on any further action that might be taken with respect to the various causes of the variance.

10–24. Die casting in the Hammet Tool & Die Company is done in three separate but basically identical departments. The company's management believes that volume is too great to be handled efficiently in a single department. Monthly materials usage reports are used to compare performances in the three departments. These reports compare standard and actual usages for the current month and for the year to date. A tabular summary of the data reported in the first half of 1976 is presented below.

| | *Pounds of Metal* | |
| --- | --- | --- |
| | *Standard Usage* | *Actual Usage* |
| **Department 1:** | | |
| January | 43,500 | 46,800 |
| February | 43,100 | 45,800 |
| March | 44,700 | 47,100 |
| April | 45,800 | 47,200 |
| May | 46,800 | 47,700 |
| June | 46,500 | 46,800 |
| Year to date | 270,400 | 281,400 |
| **Department 2:** | | |
| January | 45,900 | 46,500 |
| February | 44,700 | 45,000 |
| March | 43,200 | 43,000 |
| April | 44,900 | 45,300 |
| May | 46,200 | 45,600 |
| June | 47,000 | 46,700 |
| Year to date | 271,900 | 272,100 |
| **Department 3:** | | |
| January | 44,900 | 44,000 |
| February | 44,300 | 43,800 |
| March | 45,900 | 45,700 |
| April | 46,500 | 46,500 |
| May | 47,000 | 47,300 |
| June | 47,200 | 47,800 |
| Year to date | 275,800 | 275,100 |

*Required:*

Draft a report in what you believe to be the best form for purposes of a comparative analysis of the operating performances of the three departments with respect to materials usage during the first half of 1976.

10–25.  Dreiser Creative Toys, Inc., manufactures toy metal trucks and similar items in three successive production departments. Labor time records in these departments during 1976 show the following data:

| | Standard Hours | Actual Hours | Variance |
|---|---|---|---|
| **Stamping department:** | | | |
| First quarter............. | 52,000 | 54,750 | (2,750) |
| Second quarter........... | 48,000 | 50,250 | (2,250) |
| Third quarter............ | 54,000 | 57,000 | (3,000) |
| Fourth quarter........... | 58,000 | 60,800 | (2,800) |
| | 212,000 | 222,800 | (10,800) |
| **Assembly department:** | | | |
| First quarter............. | 130,000 | 127,200 | 2,800 |
| Second quarter........... | 120,000 | 124,000 | (4,000) |
| Third quarter............ | 135,000 | 133,500 | 1,500 |
| Fourth quarter........... | 145,000 | 145,900 | (900) |
| | 530,000 | 530,600 | (600) |
| **Painting department:** | | | |
| First quarter............. | 26,000 | 24,600 | 1,400 |
| Second quarter........... | 24,000 | 23,400 | 600 |
| Third quarter............ | 27,000 | 27,500 | (500) |
| Fourth quarter........... | 29,000 | 30,100 | (1,100) |
| | 106,000 | 105,600 | 400 |

*Required:*

Draft a report in what you believe to be the best form for purposes of a comparative analysis of the labor efficiencies of the three departments during 1976.

10–26.  The James Home Appliance Corporation produces small refrigerators used primarily in small apartments and in home bars. There are five successive production departments. Steel frames and sides are manufactured in Department No. 1. The basic frame is assembled and painted in Department No. 2. Various pieces of hardware are installed in the frame, insulating fiber is inserted in the sides, some packing materials are put into place, and the frame is repainted in Department No. 3. Shelves and interior compartments are installed in Department No. 4, along with additional interior packing materials. Finally, in Department No. 5, the motor is installed, insulation fiber is placed in the motor compartment, and the last packing materials are put into place. The refrigerators are then transferred to a warehouse pending shipment to customers.

During 1976, a total of 120,000 refrigerators were manufactured and transferred to the warehouse. The following materials usage reported was submitted to management for that year:

| Material | Standard Quantity @ Standard Price | Actual Quantity @ Standard Price | Materials Usage Variance |
|---|---|---|---|
| Steel parts: | | | |
| Department 1.......... | $1,440,000 | $1,620,000 | $(180,000) |
| Department 3......... | 240,000 | 246,000 | (6,000) |
| Plastic parts: | | | |
| Department 2.......... | 150,000 | 165,000 | (15,000) |
| Department 4......... | 720,000 | 691,200 | 28,800 |
| Insulating fiber: | | | |
| Department 3......... | 180,000 | 185,400 | (5,400) |
| Department 5......... | 90,000 | 87,600 | 2,400 |
| Paint: | | | |
| Department 2......... | 60,000 | 68,000 | (8,000) |
| Department 3......... | 96,000 | 98,400 | (2,400) |
| Packing materials: | | | |
| Department 3......... | 24,000 | 25,200 | (1,200) |
| Department 4......... | 60,000 | 69,000 | (9,000) |
| Department 5......... | 12,000 | 11,700 | 300 |
| Motors: | | | |
| Department 5......... | 1,800,000 | 1,878,000 | (78,000) |
| | $4,872,000 | $5,145,500 | $(273,500) |

*Required:*

Evaluate this report critically.

10–27.  The Welty Seating Company manufactures arm chairs for classroom use. The standard manufacturing cost of one chair is as follows:

Direct materials:
Tubular steel (8 lbs. @ $.60)........... $4.80
Wood (2 bd. ft. @ $.30).............. .60
Chrome casters (4 @ $.12)............. .48     $ 5.88
Direct labor (¾ hr. @ $5.60)............     4.20
Manufacturing overhead:
Variable (¾ hr. @ $1.80)............. $1.35
Fixed (¾ hr. @ $4)................. 3.00     4.35
$14.43

The standard manufacturing overhead rates are based upon the following flexible budget:

| Cost Item | Variable Rate per Labor Hour | Fixed Cost per Year |
|---|---|---|
| Indirect labor........................ | | $1,080,000 |
| Labor-related costs.................... | $1.12 | 216,000 |
| Indirect materials...................... | .23 | |
| Power and light....................... | .10 | 480,000 |
| Depreciation.......................... | | 1,500,000 |
| Taxes and insurance................... | | 124,000 |
| Repair and maintenance................ | .35 | 600,000 |
| | $1.80 | $4,000,000 |

For the past five years, the company's sales and production have grown steadily. Actual output, in units, during this period is summarized below.

| Year | Units |
|---|---|
| 1971....................... | 1,060,000 |
| 1972....................... | 1,200,000 |
| 1973....................... | 1,340,000 |
| 1974....................... | 1,500,000 |
| 1975....................... | 1,700,000 |

This growth pattern continued during 1976, when production totaled 2,000,000 units.

A total of 8,200 tons of tubular steel was purchased during 1976 at an average price of $1,240 per ton. Materials usage reports indicate that 8,160 tons were used in production during the year. Five million board feet of wood were purchased for $.20 per foot. All of this wood was used in production during 1976. It was very green wood and proved to be quite difficult to work with. Cracking and warping in the production process was far in excess of normal. Fifty thousand hours of rework time were required for chairs on which the wood originally installed proved to be defective and had to be replaced prior to shipment. During 1976, 17,000 cases of casters were purchased; each case contains 500 casters. Twelve thousand of these cases contained the standard chrome casters and were purchased at $61.50 per case. The remaining 5,000 cases contained brass casters, which were purchased because of a temporary shortage of chrome. The brass casters, which cost $45 per case, were substantially similar to the standard item but tended to have a somewhat shorter life in service. All of the brass casters purchased and 11,040 cases of chrome casters were used in production during the year.

Production workers recorded a total of 1,560,000 direct labor hours in 1976 at an average wage rate of $5.75 per hour. As of July 1, 1976, employees were granted a $.30 per hour wage increase in accordance with a new labor agreement signed in June.

Actual manufacturing overhead costs incurred during 1976 were as follows:

|                        |              |
| ---------------------- | -----------: |
| Indirect labor         | $1,140,000   |
| Labor-related costs    | 2,022,000    |
| Indirect materials     | 375,000      |
| Power and light        | 660,000      |
| Depreciation           | 1,480,000    |
| Taxes and insurance    | 132,000      |
| Repair and maintenance | 1,211,000    |
|                        | $7,020,000   |

*Required:*

a. Analyze the variances from standard manufacturing cost for 1976 by their causes to the maximum extent possible from the information available.

b. Comment on the implications of these variances for specific action by management.

# chapter 11

# Planning and Control of Nonmanufacturing Costs

D ISCUSSIONS in the preceding three chapters have focused largely on procedures for the effective planning and control of manufacturing costs. This relative emphasis upon production costs reflects traditional business practice. Cost accounting has always been concerned primarily with manufacturing costs, and the most significant efforts toward efficiency and cost control have been directed at production operations. There is an increasing interest in extending these efforts into the area of nonmanufacturing operations, however. The costs of distributing goods and services, of administering large and complex organizations, of financing those organizations, and of conducting substantial research represent a large and an increasing share of the total costs of business enterprises and of our gross national product. In total, these costs exceed all manufacturing costs. Thus, they are too big to be ignored. They should be planned and controlled as carefully as are manufacturing costs. To the extent that they are similar in nature to production costs, similar control techniques may be used. To the extent that they are dissimilar, special techniques must be devised to control them.

The relatively high degree of controllability of manufacturing costs may be ascribed to two basic factors. First, most manufacturing costs are functionally related to manufactured products, and a fairly clear cause-and-effect relationship exists. If the cost item is variable, it is controlled in relation to units of product. If it is fixed, it is usually related to productive capacity and is incurred as a consequence thereof. The relationship of semivariable costs to production is more complex and uncertain, but it is customarily assumed to exist.[1] The second factor contributing to the controllability of manufacturing costs is the routine and repetitive nature of most manufacturing operations. Mass production has resulted in the standardization of manufacturing operations and, hence, of manufacturing costs. When a task is done the same way over and over, it becomes increasingly easy to predict and to control the cost of performing that task. While most manufacturing costs are functionally related to output and are incurred in routine, repetitive activities, not all are. Such activities as quality control, factory accounting, and value analysis involve nonstandardized operations only remotely related to specific units of product. Hence, their costs are not controllable as are most other manufacturing costs. Rather, they must be controlled in the same way as most nonmanufacturing costs.

Nonmanufacturing costs characteristically are not functionally related to units of product. Some of them, however, are related to some other measure of operating volume. Those that are may be controlled in relation to that volume, much as manufacturing costs are controlled in relation to the volume of production. Many nonmanufacturing costs are unrelated to any useful volume measure, and these must be controlled by other methods. Similarly, many nonmanufacturing activities are neither routine nor repetitive. Each successive task may be different from any previous one. Obviously, the inability to apply the lessons of experience complicates the problems of planning and control. Nevertheless, these problems may not be ignored. Positive procedures for planning and controlling these costs must be devised and implemented.

## VARIABLE COSTS

Any cost item that varies in direct proportion to some volume of activity may be planned and controlled in terms of that volume. The measure used for these purposes is the cost per unit of volume. For planning and control, this unit cost is allowed for each expected and each actual unit of volume. Material deviations from this unit cost are investigated and, hopefully, corrected if they are unfavorable. This use of a unit variable cost for managerial purposes requires that it be the *right* unit cost, that is, the amount that each unit of volume *should* cost. Determining the right unit cost is fairly easy in some cases and quite difficult in others. Shipping costs, for example, tend to vary with the volume of sales. Shipping rates may differ among the various modes of transportation, however; and they may also be affected by the total

---

[1] See Chapter 8.

quantity of goods in a single shipment. Thus, it may be necessary to use an average shipping cost per unit of sales and to expect some variation from that average. Moreover, the mere fact that a cost has been identified as variable does not mean that it is wholly controllable. For example, postage cost varies with the volume of mailings; but an increase in postal rates will cause an uncontrollable rise in postage cost.

## Flexible Budgets for Nonmanufacturing Costs

For certain nonmanufacturing operations, costs may effectively be controlled by means of departmental flexible budgets, much in the manner of manufacturing overhead costs. In order for a flexible budget to be operative, it is essential that the operations of the department be expressible in terms of some measure of volume that bears a significant relationship to the costs incurred in that department. Further, a significant amount of the total departmental costs must vary in reasonably direct proportion to the volume measure selected. A flexible budget comprising almost nothing but fixed costs would be little more useful than a static budget. The appropriate measure of volume will vary from department to department. For example, some selling expenses are likely to vary in proportion to sales volume, whether in dollars or in units. Salesmen's commissions are the classic example here, but other costs, such as credit losses and packing and shipping expense, may also be very close to perfectly variable with sales volume. Administrative costs may vary with respect to some specialized volume of administrative work done. Such specialized measures of volume are often referred to as *work units*. For example, the number of bills prepared might provide a useful basis for planning and controlling many of the costs in a billing department. The number of documents typed might be taken as a measure of the volume of work in a typing pool. A more precise measure here might be the number of lines typed. However, the time consumed in actually measuring volume (i.e., counting lines) might be considered excessive in relation to the potential benefits from the added precision.

Once a relevant volume measure has been selected for a particular nonmanufacturing department, the flexible budget is constructed in the manner described in Chapter 8. Variable costs are stated as rates per unit of volume and fixed costs, as total dollar amounts per time period. Semivariable costs are resolved into variable and/or fixed components by one of the methods discussed in Chapter 8. Actual departmental costs may then be compared with the flexible budget, adjusted to actual volume, to provide a basis for an evaluation of performance and a start for positive cost control efforts. All of this is exactly the same as the use of flexible budgets for manufacturing overhead. The only significant difference is in the measure of volume that is used.

## Standard Nonmanufacturing Costs

Only infrequently have standards been applied to nonmanufacturing operations and costs. There seem to be two reasons for this. First, standard manufacturing costs are customarily used for inventory valuation as well as for control; and nonmanufacturing costs are not charged to inventory accounts. Second, and more importantly, standard costs are applicable only to routine, repetitive operations. Rightly or wrongly, businessmen have generally concluded that most nonproduction operations are not sufficiently standardized to admit of useful standard costs. Actually, there are many nonmanufacturing activities that are standardized and for which standard costs are feasible. Thus, the infrequent use of standard costs in these areas is probably largely attributable to the fact that managers have found budgets to be satisfactory means of cost control.

Standard nonmanufacturing costs based upon price and quantity standards are feasible if there is a direct functional relationship between some readily measurable unit of volume and the cost items in question. Thus, usage of certain types of supplies (e.g., preprinted forms and packing materials) might be controlled by use of price and quantity standards, just as are direct materials used in production. Similarly, certain nonmanufacturing operations (e.g., check preparation and invoice processing) may lend themselves to the establishment of labor time and rate standards, as in the case of direct factory labor. In all likelihood, however, the aggregate amount of nonmanufacturing costs for which price and quantity standards could be set is small. The cost of a multicopy preprinted purchase order, for example, is only a small portion of the total cost of making a purchase. The work involved in purchasing is not likely to be standardized.

A greater amount of nonmanufacturing cost items could be included in flexible budgets. With such budgets and with defined normal volumes of activity, standard nonmanufacturing costs could be established in the same way as are standard manufacturing overhead costs. However, these standard costs would not be needed for inventory valuation; and they would be no better for purposes of cost control than the flexible budgets from which they were derived. For control purposes, the most significant manufacturing overhead variance is the spending variance. As seen in Chapters 8 and 10, this is exactly the same whether flexible budgets alone or standard costs based upon them are used. Inefficiency in the use of an input factor, such as labor time, can be identified and investigated without first determining an efficiency variance in dollars. Also, deviations of actual volume from expected volume do not demand the computation of a dollar variance. And deviations of actual volume from normal volume in the short run are not usually considered significant to management.

Thus, development of standard nonmanufacturing costs from flexible budgets would appear to be superfluous.

## The Importance of the Volume Measure

Both flexible budgets and standard costs depend upon the existence of a readily measurable and useful concept of volume. Measurability is obviously important, but usefulness is even more so. In manufacturing, flexible budgets and standards are usually based upon the volume of output of goods or upon the volume of some productive input that bears a direct relationship to output. As long as the goods produced can be sold, output volume can fairly easily be identified as good (sufficient to meet sales demand) or bad (insufficient). Such a qualitative appraisal of volume is very important to management. Volume must be compatible with the basic objectives of the firm. Cost control would hardly be effective simply because cost per unit of output was equal to or less than budgeted or standard cost, if the output so exceeded demand that much of it would have to be scrapped.

Making a qualitative appraisal of the volume of some activity other than sales (usually considered good because they increase revenue and income) or production (normally considered good as long as the goods can be sold) may be difficult. For example, assume that the volume of activity in a purchasing department is measured by the number of purchase orders prepared, and that variable costs are stated as a rate per purchase order. Now, variable costs may be controlled in relation to the number of actual orders processed; but such control does not necessarily mean that spending in the purchasing department is in harmony with the firm's basic goals. Perhaps too many or too few purchase orders are being prepared. Management's objective of cost control is not fully achieved if the purchasing department is very efficiently preparing an excessive quantity of purchase orders. There remains to be answered a very important question. Given more fundamental objectives, what volume of purchase orders may be considered appropriate for the period? A purchase order is a means to an end, not an end in itself. The same is true of many other items whose volumes might be used to measure activity in nonmanufacturing departments—for example, the number of paychecks prepared, credit applications processed, advertising circulars distributed, bills prepared, reports written, and miles traveled. Too few of any of these items may inhibit sales, profits, growth, and other managerial objectives. Too many of them, on the other hand, will be wasteful. Hence, management must first define the appropriate volume of nonmanufacturing activity in light of its basic goals and then seek to control costs in terms of that volume. In many instances, unfortunately, the former requirement may prove to be very difficult. Few objective standards for the "right" volume of these activities exist.

## COMMITTED FIXED COSTS

Committed fixed costs were defined in Chapter 8 as fixed costs that must be incurred in each period as a consequence of a major decision made at some time in the past. Most committed fixed costs are associated with contracts (e.g., a long-term employment contract with the corporation's president) or with the acquisition of long-lived assets (e.g., a plant or a warehouse). The identifying characteristic of a committed cost is that its amount, as well as its incurrence, is predetermined and can be altered only by another major decision to reverse or to amend the earlier commitment. There are many costs, of course, to whose incurrence management is effectively committed. One cannot visualize an organization functioning unless wages and salaries are paid, but the amounts of wages and salaries paid to specific individuals need not be predetermined. Thus, a committed cost is one whose amount is not subject to periodic control by management. Consequently, committed costs must be planned and controlled at the time that the basic commitment is made. Chapters 16 and 17 discuss the planning of major capital expenditures, such as for plant and equipment. This capital budgeting process should explicitly include consideration of the consequent committed fixed costs.

The concept of a committed fixed cost is easy to define, and its control implications are easily explained. Once a major commitment has been made, the resultant committed costs must be included at a given amount in the annual budget. Further control is not feasible. Unfortunately, determining just exactly what is a committed cost in a particular situation may not be quite so easy. For example, the decision to construct a factory commits the firm to certain costs over the factory's life. Some of these costs, such as depreciation and property taxes, are truly uncontrollable in amount each year. Other costs are equally necessary as a consequence of the construction decision, but their annual amounts are not so rigidly fixed. For example, every factory requires periodic maintenance. Therefore, the incurrence of annual maintenance costs cannot be avoided. A managerial decision to omit maintenance altogether would entail such dire consequences that it could not be seriously considered at all. However, the exact amount that must be spent on maintenance in any single year need not be fixed. To some degree, there is a tradeoff between maintenance costs and productive efficiency or between maintenance costs and factory life. Management might conceivably make this tradeoff decision differently in one year as compared with the previous year. (Obviously, the tradeoff between maintenance and factory life is not perpetually flexible. Reduced maintenance expenditures in any one year may irrevocably shorten the plant's life.) Thus, although there is probably some absolute minimum annual maintenance cost to which a firm is effectively committed, the total annual maintenance cost is most accurately described as a discretionary cost.

## DISCRETIONARY FIXED COSTS

A large number of fixed costs are fixed in amount for a given period as a result of a current management decision. Management has some significant range of discretion as to the amount of cost it will budget for the particular purpose or program in question. These are referred to variously as *discretionary costs, managed costs,* or *programmed costs.* The first term will be used consistently here. It is most descriptive of the essential character of these costs; they are subject to current management discretion. Some common examples of discretionary fixed costs are the costs of advertising, public relations, research and development, employee training, executive development, and various other types of staff assistance. A discretionary cost is fixed in amount because management has determined that that amount is all that need be, should be, or can be spent for the purpose in the current period. The amount allowed for that purpose may change significantly from period to period, however. In this respect, a discretionary cost is quite different from a committed cost. At the same time, variations in the amount spent over time may bear no meaningful relationship to any measure of volume. There is, thus, no similarity to variable costs. Herein lies the great difficulty in planning discretionary costs. If the cost is not a function of any observable volume measure and if it is not predetermined as a consequence of some earlier commitment, how does management decide on the appropriate amount to spend in any given period?

There are many ways of answering this question, and they are not necessarily mutually exclusive. One approach is to determine how much competitors are spending for the same purpose. This is a particularly useful method in dealing with items that are directly related to the firm's competitive position—such as advertising, other promotional programs, and product development and testing. Much advertising (in the cigarette market, for example) is regarded as defensive. Its goal is not so much to gain new customers as to avoid losing old customers to competitors. If management believes that its advertising budget is primarily a defensive weapon, amounts spent by competitors logically become a dominant factor in determining the current amount of this particular discretionary cost. Of course, some firms may consciously decide to behave differently from their competitors. A company that prides itself on product leadership, for example, may deliberately choose to spend substantially more than the industry average on research and development. An industry leader may feel it can safely cut its promotional outlays, whereas a new or an ambitious firm may decide it must spend more than the average on promotion.

There are many programs in any organization which are largely internal in their implications and effects. They have little direct impact upon competitors. Examples of such programs are general accounting, order processing, purchasing, and legal services. The complete absence of any of these functions might have dire competitive consequences, but the level of spending for them is not likely to have any observable short-run effect on competition. What criteria can management apply to determine appropriate spending levels for such items? Once again, average levels of spending for the same item in other firms, particularly those in the same industry, may be a useful, if rough, guide. If trade association data indicate that firms in a particular industry annually spend an average of 2% of net sales on general accounting or an average of $300 per employee on general personnel functions, these averages may be taken as presumptive guidelines for any single firm's spending. Essentially, management asks, "If others are spending this much, how can we justify spending significantly more or less?" Of course, there may be a very sound answer to that question. While management may begin by presuming it should spend about what the rest of the industry does for an item, it should be willing to accept reasons for deviating from industrial averages. For example, a firm may attribute its employees' loyalty and work force stability to relatively high expenditures for employee recruitment and training. Thus, it may justify higher than average costs in terms of better than average results.

Another possible criterion for planning discretionary costs that have primarily internal implications is a subjective notion of effectiveness. For example, management may decide that personnel administration will be more effective if some specified level of spending is allowed for that purpose. This spending level is necessarily related to some level of work performed in the personnel function. These subjective notions are difficult to justify, however; and they are likely to differ considerably among individual managers. It is ordinarily impracticable to test the effectiveness of various levels of funding for a program such as personnel administration, but it may be possible to simulate the effects of various levels of spending if a suitable model of that program's impact upon the entire firm can be constructed. Computer-based simulation may offer some significant opportunities for improved planning and control of discretionary costs. Such opportunities are largely unexplored at this time, however.

A substantial portion of discretionary costs, particularly in the area of administration, represents salaries. Thus, one way of controlling these costs is to impose personnel ceilings on departments. This is a useful device, for the efficiency of a department may often be appraised better in terms of the number of persons working in it than in terms of the dollars that it spends. Personnel and dollars are closely related, of course. A reduction in personnel entails a cost saving. Personnel ceilings are not very popular, however. Department supervisors tend to regard them as unwelcome restrictions. Other personnel may view them as potential threats to their own jobs. These adverse implications should be considered before such ceilings are imposed. Nevertheless, control of discretionary costs in many areas inevitably means control of salaried personnel.

A very pragmatic approach to planning and controlling discretionary costs is to allow spending in an amount that management believes it can afford. Some firms, for example, budget research and development costs as a percentage of expected sales. Logically, this appears to be a somewhat backward approach to the problem. One would expect sales to be determined, at least partially, by research and development programs. Budgeting for the latter on the basis of the former seems to suggest just the opposite relationship. Actually, sales are selected as the basis for the research and development budget not because of any presumed causal relationship but because they are one useful indicator of how much the firm can afford to spend for that purpose. Nevertheless, management must recognize that declining sales may be the result of insufficient product research and development. Hence, it may be appropriate to increase spending for this purpose as sales decline. Other discretionary costs are likely to be budgeted on the basis of ability to spend also. Public relations and charitable contributions are typical examples.

One writer has suggested that discretionary costs may usefully be separated further into policy costs and operating costs.[2] Policy costs are dependent almost entirely on managerial judgment and would include such items as advertising, research, and executive development. Changes in amounts budgeted for these items would be unlikely to have any direct and immediate effect on current production and sales operations. Operating costs, on the other hand, are closely tied to these current operations; and changes in spending levels might have immediately recognizable impacts on production or sales. Examples are supervision, purchasing, and quality control. While this distinction may have conceptual validity, it would be a difficult one to define in practice. A reduction in advertising, for example, may have as prompt an effect on sales volume as would a cutback on quality control inspections. Rather than using a dual classification of discretionary costs, it may be useful to think of them as a broad spectrum, ranging from close to slight relationships to current operations.

The spectrum of discretionary costs may also be visualized as com-

---

[2] Marshall K. Evans, "Profit Planning," *Harvard Business Review,* vol. 37 (July–August 1959), p. 46.

prising degrees of variability of spending levels. It might be feasible for a firm to vary its charitable contributions at will, with no effect other than on the financial positions of its beneficiaries. It might be very damaging for the firm to vary its research and development expenditures widely from year to year, however. A budget cut in this area may mean that an ongoing project, in which much has already been invested, would have to be terminated. It might mean that valuable scientific personnel would have to be laid off one year and recruited anew in some later year. While such great variations may be unavoidable in some instances, they are not conducive to stable growth in sales and profits. This illustration again highlights the essential characteristic of discretionary costs. The program for which these costs are incurred may well be indispensable, but the dollar amount spent on it in any single year is subject to considerable managerial discretion. That discretion must include adequate consideration of a wide range of factors, some of which are likely to suggest conflicting decisions. These conflicts cannot be avoided, and they must be resolved.

## PROGRAM PLANNING IN THE DEPARTMENT OF DEFENSE

The United States Department of Defense annually spends billions of dollars on what may properly be considered nonmanufacturing programs. (It also spends billions on activities essentially equivalent to manufacturing operations—notably materials procurement, shipyard work, and aircraft repairs.) It has, of course, a great need to plan and control these costs effectively and some very serious obstacles to overcome in doing so. To meet this challenge, it has developed a fairly complex system for financial planning and control. This system has also been implemented in other Federal agencies, in many state and local governments, and in numerous private organizations. The details in the application of the system may have to be varied to meet the special situation of any individual organization, but the basic ideas are generally applicable. Hence, it is worthwhile to examine this system briefly.

Prior to 1961, planning in the Department of Defense was not as systematic and comprehensive as it is now. While longer range plans were made, the formal planning process was tied very closely to the annual budget submitted to Congress. As a consequence, planning tended to follow the budgetary structure employed by the Congress and focused excessively on each year alone. Congress' consideration of the Defense budget was centered on the individual services (Army, Navy, and Air Force) and on specific spending items (e.g., wages and salaries, materials, equipment, and so forth). The emphasis on the distinction among the services was more practicable when each service had fairly clear and distinct responsibilities. During World War II, for example, the Navy was concerned almost exclusively with the war at sea. Navy planes ordinarily did not fly the same types of combat missions as did the Army Air Corps (now the Air Force). Even the types of combat missions assigned to the Marine Corps and the Army infantry were quite different, and the Marines' activities were limited almost exclusively to the Pacific theater. These mission distinctions among the services no longer exist. Carrier-based Navy planes and land-based Air Force planes flew essentially the same tactical missions in Korea and in Viet Nam. Hence, they may legitimately be thought of as interchangeable, at least partially. The nation's nuclear defense forces are manned by all three of the services. Indeed, the operational military commands are coordinated. Thus, financial planning and control along service lines has limited value today.

The budgetary emphasis on individual cost items has never been a satisfactory means of effective planning. It was intended originally to give Congress effective control over government spending, as the Constitution provides. However, if spending items are too narrowly defined, the result could be to make governmental management all but impossible. This danger was recognized very early. Thomas Jefferson had argued that Congress ought to appropriate funds for "every specific purpose susceptible of definition." In challenging this view, Alexander Hamilton raised an admittedly extreme example of the consequent danger. He observed that funds might be appropriated separately to purchase oats and hay as feed for Army horses. Should the appropriation for oats be fully expended but not that for hay and should only oats be available at a particular moment, the horses might starve and their riders with them —and all because the supply officer lacked the authority to spend hay money on oats.[3] As a matter of fact, cost items were never that narrowly defined; and, in 1951, spending categories in the Defense appropriations were consolidated into fewer, broader classes (e.g., military personnel, civilian personnel, operation and maintenance, construction, and research and development). While this consolidation is an obvious improvement, it still entails budgetary emphasis upon the items for which government funds will be expended rather than upon the goals to be achieved as a result of the expenditures.

In 1961, the Department of Defense formally inaugurated a new planning system referred to as the Planning-Programming-Budgeting System (PPBS).[4] As a matter of fact, these terms had been used since 1949, when Congress required a "performance budget" from the Department as a whole. However, prior to 1961, this approach was limited largely to the

---

[3] Arthur Smithies, *The Budgetary Process in the United States* (New York: McGraw-Hill Book Co., Inc., 1955), pp. 51–52.

[4] This system is a specific application of the basic concepts of planning, programming, and budgeting that were discussed in Chapter 6.

annual budgetary process. To be sure, long-range planning did occur; but it was not systematically related to the annual budgets and it did not coordinate the three services' plans. The essence of PPBS is both simple and logical. At the planning stage, basic objectives are formulated for American defense policy as far into the future as is considered practical and useful. These objectives are formalized in the Joint Strategic Objectives Plan, prepared by the Joint Chiefs of Staff and reviewed by the Secretary of Defense, the President, and the National Security Council. After review of these objectives, detailed planning guidance is given to the services. Specific programs are then developed to meet the objectives in accordance with official guidance; this is the programming phase. Approved programs are planned in detail for five years and are incorporated in the Five-Year Defense Program. This is both a military plan and a financial forecast. Ideally, the annual budgeting process would simply draw the financial requirements for the next year from the five-year plan and present them both in terms of programs and in terms of spending items for consideration by Congress. In recognition of the fact that conditions and estimates can change, the system formally provides for program change requests that may be submitted in advance of the annual budget to obtain changes in the approved programs contained in the five-year plan. The annual budget process does not actually function quite so easily, of course. There is much give-and-take between the Department and the Office of Management and Budget, between the Administration and the Congress, and also among the members of Congress.

In summary, then, PPBS approaches the planning process by defining first what the government wishes to achieve in the way of defense (planning), then determining what means of reaching these goals are to be used (programming), and finally providing resources to implement the chosen means (budgeting).

The Joint Strategic Objectives Plan deals with political and military assessments of potential threats to national security and with projections of force levels required to cope with them. For example, the threat of nuclear attack is evaluated and the forces necessary to deter it are determined. Deterrent forces must then be established in specific programs, such as retaliatory strike missiles (ICBMs), antimissile missiles (the Safeguard system), and civil defense. All three of these are specific program elements within a single major program titled Strategic Forces, which is only one of ten major programs. The complete list at the time of this writing is as follows:[5]

---

[5] The major programs have changed before and undoubtedly will change again. This list gives the reader a general idea of the types of distinctions that are involved, however. The programs are obviously interrelated. General Purpose Forces for use in so-called "limited wars" depend upon Transportation and Logistics if they are to fulfill their mission.

| | |
|---|---|
| Strategic Forces | Research and Development |
| General Purpose Forces | Logistics |
| Specialized Forces | Personnel Support |
| Transportation | Administration |
| Guard and Reserve Forces | Support of Other Nations |

Within each major program there are several program elements or sub-programs. Strategic Forces, for example, include the land-based Minuteman missile system, the submarine-based Poseidon and Trident missile systems, and the air-borne Strategic Air Command. These are all means of nuclear retaliation. Since an increase in any one of the three would diminish the need for the other two, given certain objectives, it is clear that financial planning for defense must focus on missions rather than on objects or on the services, as was formerly the case. With plans and programs defined, the budgeting process can be more meaningful to governmental managers. A cut in the Defense budget can be translated into a reduction in specific programs. Conversely, a call for additional Poseidon missiles, for example, can be converted to annual cost increases for the missiles, the submarines to carry them, the men to operate these craft, their training, and all of the other necessary support facilities. Further, knowledge of lead times permits each of these increased costs to be placed in a particular year's budget.

An obvious question that arises in connection with the defense planning process is, "How much is enough?" How are force levels justified? There is no convenient measure of effectiveness. Sales promotion, for example, may be justified in terms of sales volume. A new plant may be justified in relation to output. There is no similar measure of volume to support defense spending, however. The ultimate objective of our Strategic Forces, for example, is to *deter* attack. Thus, our nuclear retaliatory weapons are truly effective only if they are never used. But how can one decide how many of them are required in order to ensure that they won't be used? The answer to this question is inevitably subjective, but some measurable concepts of defense capability have been developed to support requests for specific weapons. Such measures as target coverage (i.e., number of targets that could be struck by a weapon system), flight distance, payload (commonly measured in tons of destructive force), and invulnerability to enemy attack are used as indexes of defense capability. Yet, these are only intermediate aims; the basic objective is still deterrence. Similar measurement problems arise in nondefense areas. It is easy to see that PPBS could be a valuable tool in planning water resources, urban improvements, transportation, and other national needs. Yet, how does one measure an improvement in something as complex as the urban environment? An increase in housing units is one measure, but it may be achieved in different ways, some of which might aggravate other urban problems. Transportation needs may be met by building freeways, but these often impinge on housing and recreational areas and they add to air pollution problems. Thus, not only are the objectives of any single program difficult to measure but they may also conflict with the goals of other programs.

In the final analysis, PPBS is a useful approach to the planning and control of expenditures for a wide variety of programs. In industrial firms, it would seem particularly applicable to research and development, sales promotion, training, and other programs whose payoffs are expected to be realized only sometime after the expenditures have been made. It is by no means a panacea, of course. It does not resolve the problem of defining goals; yet, it depends upon a resolution of that problem. It does not obviate the need for judgment nor avoid disagreements as to the effectiveness of specific programs (witness the heated disputes in Congress over the necessity for and even the feasibility of certain weapon systems). Finally, one cannot demonstrate that PPBS has always worked better than the earlier, less systematic methods. The Polaris missile program has often been cited as a model of good military planning and development, and it was operational before PPBS was initiated. On the other hand, some major weapons projects developed under PPBS have encountered serious problems in their operational effectiveness and/or in their costs. Among the more widely publicized of these "problem" programs are the C–5A transport, the Cheyenne helicopter, and the Mark 48 torpedo. Obviously, neither PPBS nor any other management system can compensate for bad decisions. PPBS can facilitate the making of better decisions, however.[6]

Between 1965 and 1971, PPBS was required to be used in most federal departments and agencies. In 1973, a new system called Management by Objectives (MBO) was imposed upon most of the federal government. This new system is somewhat less formalized and rigid than PPBS, but it has essentially the same basic purpose—to ensure that federal funds and the efforts of government agencies are expended in pursuit of approved national goals. The Department of Defense is required to conform to MBO, but it also uses PPBS for its internal management. The two systems are quite compatible.

## FUNCTIONAL COST CLASSIFICATIONS

One of the most familiar and widely used schemes of cost classification is by functions.[7] This classification scheme is reflected in the traditional

---

[6] The reader interested in pursuing PPBS further is referred to Stephen Enke (ed.), *Defense Management* (Englewood Cliffs, N.J.: Prentice-Hall, Inc., 1967); and to David Novick (ed.), *Program Budgeting*, 2d ed. (New York: Holt, Rinehart & Winston, Inc., 1968).

[7] Functional classifications of costs were discussed earlier in Chapter 2.

income statement. Typical functional classifications of nonmanufacturing costs include distribution or marketing costs, administrative costs, research and development costs, and financial costs. These functional categories are quite useful for certain purposes, and there is no reason why they should not be retained. However, they are less useful for purposes of planning and control than the classification of costs as variable, discretionary, and committed. Flexible budgets, for example, may be used in exactly the same way to control manufacturing, marketing, or administrative costs that are partly variable with some measurable concept of volume. Functional classification may be of some value as a very gross tool of cost control. Thus, a corporate president may compare what his firm spends on administration with amounts spent in similar companies to determine very roughly whether his firm's administrative costs seem excessive, too low, or about right. There is a very real danger in this approach. To begin with, "similar" companies are not identical. Organizational structures and administrative practices vary among companies, and there is no reason to presume that one way is necessarily better than others. Administrative efforts and costs are validated by success in the attainment of the organization's goals. If success may be achieved in a variety of ways, one may legitimately conclude that administrative standardization is neither necessary nor desirable. In addition, different firms may define administrative costs differently. One firm may treat sales executives' salaries as administrative costs, while another reports them as marketing costs. Similarly, the cost accounting department's costs might be charged either to administrative cost or to manufacturing overhead.

Whatever limitations functional cost categories may have for control purposes, they very often must be used. If a firm is organized along functional lines (manufacturing departments, sales departments, research department, and so forth), cost data will be collected and reported along the same lines. This is required for effective responsibility accounting. Hence, a brief consideration of some of these functional classifications is appropriate.

## Distribution Costs

Distribution, or marketing, encompasses a wide range of activities; and there is no clearly defined distinction between distribution and other functions. For example, are credit losses (bad debts) distribution costs or financial costs? Is the sales manager's salary a distribution cost or an administrative cost? These questions need not be answered in order to plan and control the individual cost items, but they do highlight the difficulty of broad functional cost classifications. For purposes of discussion here, we shall subclassify distribution costs into three categories: direct selling, promotion, and customer servicing.

*Direct selling costs* are those incurred in the course of making sales and attempting to make sales. They include such items as salesmen's salaries and commissions, salesmen's travel expenses, and costs of operating sales and display facilities. In the long run, of course, such costs must be related to and justified in terms of results—that is, sales. For purposes of short-run control, however, they may more effectively be related to effort than to accomplishment. Travel expenses, for example, may vary greatly among salesmen and over time insofar as they relate to sales volume. On the other hand, they may bear readily definable and logical relationships to calls made and miles traveled. In the long run, of course, sales calls and travel must be justified in terms of sales revenue. In the short run, however, the frequency and duration of calls are usually established as a matter of policy. Given such a policy, travel expenses may be largely controllable by reference to the volumes of calls and mileage. Thus, these costs may be viewed as discretionary costs for purposes of policy planning. Once the managerial decisions have been made, however, the costs vary partially with volume and may be controlled accordingly.

*Promotional costs* are intended to stimulate demand for a company's products and services. Hopefully, this demand will then be translated into actual sales. Promotion includes such things as advertising, catalogs, premium offers, and contests. It is difficult to relate these costs to actual sales, because they are intended to stimulate future sales. Even after the fact, it is seldom possible to attribute specific amounts of sales to particular promotional projects. Hence, promotional costs are unlikely to be controllable in terms of any measure of sales volume. Advertising costs may be related to some measure of volume of effort, however. Minutes of network television time, pages of national magazine space, numbers of readers reached, and numbers of direct mailings might be useful bases for appraising the efficiency of advertising expenditures; but they could not easily be translated into effectiveness, as measured by increased sales. Thus, promotional costs must be regarded essentially as discretionary costs. Possibly, over fairly long periods of time, useful measures of effectiveness might be derived from statistical analyses of actual promotional cost and sales data.

*Customer servicing costs* include activities attendant upon sales, such as billing, shipping, credit analysis, accounts receivable maintenance, and handling claims and complaints. Many of these operations, notably billing, shipping, and accounting, may be so routine and repetitive as to permit cost control by techniques similar to those used for production costs—especially flexible budgets. The important distinctive feature of customer servicing is that it involves activities primarily internal to the firm. So long as these activities are performed properly, there is no interface between the firm and its customers, as there must be in the cases of direct selling and promotion. (Such customer service activities as handling complaints and collecting overdue accounts may become exceptions to this general statement if established routine procedures fail to produce the desired results.)

### Administrative Costs

The 20th century has witnessed a significant increase in the number of white-collar, or administrative, workers relative to blue-collar, or production, workers. Since most administrative personnel are paid weekly or monthly salaries and are laid off only in unusual circumstances, administrative labor costs are largely fixed. And salaries normally constitute the majority of all administrative costs. Such nonlabor costs as office rent, depreciation, and maintenance are also largely fixed. Hence, the bulk of administrative costs are typically discretionary or committed fixed charges. Some, however, are likely to vary with the volume of work done. For example, the payroll department might be considered part of the administrative structure of a firm. Some part of the cost of preparing and distributing paychecks and maintaining pay records is likely to vary in direct proportion to the number of checks prepared. Similarly, stenographic costs may be controllable, at least partially, on the basis of the number of documents typed.

### Research and Development Costs

The problems of planning and controlling these costs have been discussed before in the section on discretionary costs. Research and development is an excellent example of an activity in an industrial firm that may be viewed as a major program, designed to meet the objective of long-term growth and expansion, and comprising many subprograms (individual research projects). Thus, the planning-programming-budgeting procedures used in the Department of Defense might prove very useful for cost planning and control in this area. Research may be considered essential to future sales, but there is no practical way of relating current research outlays to future revenues—except long after it is too late to control those outlays. Moreover, it is an unhappy reality that research will often entail fairly expensive projects that must ultimately be abandoned as fruitless. Regrettably, investigation of several blind alleys is frequently unavoidable if any significant accomplishments are to be made. This is similar to drilling for oil, where many dry wells may have to be drilled in order to get one producing well. Perhaps the best control that can be exercised over research costs is to ensure that all costs directly traceable to a particular project are charged to it. In this way, management will have an idea of how much is being spent on fruitful projects and how much on projects that yield no return at all. The performance of research administrators may be evaluated to some extent by reference to project cost analysis. Finally, management must recognize that much spending on research and development actually constitutes capital investments made in anticipation of benefits in the future. Analysis of such investments is the subject of Chapters 16 and 17.

## Financial Costs

Financial costs include interest, costs of issuing securities, bank service charges, and other costs incurred in the process of obtaining and holding capital. Control of these costs is in the province of financial managers, such as the corporate treasurer. This aspect of capital management is beyond the scope of this text. The primary contribution that management accounting can make in this area is to provide information that will facilitate profitable operations, given some actual or target sales volume, with the lowest practicable investment in assets. Reductions in assets mean reduced interest cost on invested capital. While reduction of assets is always a secondary goal after more important objectives, such as growth, profits, and stability, it should not be ignored.

## QUESTIONS FOR DISCUSSION

1. Discuss the problems associated with the establishment of useful standard costs for nonmanufacturing operations.
2. "As a general rule, variable costs are more easily controllable than fixed costs, simply because the former have some defined relationship to a measurable volume of operating activity." Do you agree with this statement? Explain your position.
3. How would you go about establishing a flexible budget for the cost accounting department in a manufacturing company? Compare this process with that of establishing a flexible budget for one of the company's production departments.
4. Suggest work units that would be practicable measures of operating volumes in the nonmanufacturing departments listed below. Explain briefly why you chose each work unit suggested. If you believe no practicable measure of volume is available for a particular department, give your reasons.
   a. Customer billing department
   b. Purchasing department

    *c.* Legal department

    *d.* Shipping department

    *e.* Factory first-aid station

5. The sales promotion department of the Wilkes Publishing Company promotes sales of encyclopedias by magazine advertising and by direct mail solicitations. Advertising costs are budgeted and controlled in relation to the number of magazine readers reached, as determined by the magazine publishers' circulation statistics. Mailing costs are budgeted and controlled in relation to the number of promotional brochures mailed. Evaluate these bases for planning and controlling promotional costs.

6. "It would be hard to imagine a cost to which management is more committed than income tax. Of course, income tax is not fixed; it varies with the firm's taxable income. So, I have discovered a new cost concept—the committed variable cost." Comment on this assertion.

7. What are the basic principles of planning and controlling discretionary costs ?

8. Suggest some useful criteria for the planning and control of research and development costs in a manufacturing corporation. Rank these criteria in what you believe to be the order of their importance. Justify your choice of the most important criterion.

9. While sipping coffee in the Student Union after a particularly trying managerial accounting class, three students were discussing the controllability of faculty salaries. "Basically, they're variable costs," said the first; "because the number of faculty members depends on the student enrollment." "No," argued the second student, "faculty salaries are discretionary costs; they are set by the Board of Regents and voted by the legislature." The third student smiled and replied, "You're both wrong! Most of those professors have tenure; so, their salaries are committed costs." What kind of cost are faculty salaries?

10. "If the Planning-Programming-Budgeting System is such a wonderful thing, how can the Department of Defense keep coming up with such tremendous cost overruns and production delays on programs like the C-5A transport and the Mark 48 torpedo?" Can you answer this question?

11. How can we measure the effectiveness of such social programs as public education and recreation? Is it necessary that their effectiveness be measured? If not, how can we decide how much money to spend on them?

12. "Technical advances in business information systems and data processing will ultimately provide the same degree of control over nonmanufacturing costs as over manufacturing costs." Do you agree or disagree with this prediction? Why?

13. Outline a planning-programming-budgeting system that you believe would be effective for governmental planning and control of costs incurred to achieve some nondefense social objective, such as mass transportation, solid waste disposal, or air pollution abatement. Describe what would be involved in each phase of the system. Keep in mind that such a system might involve various levels of government, as well as private enterprise.

## PROBLEMS

11-1.  The O'Hara Company has established standard costs for the operation of its payroll department. The standard time allowed for the preparation of one paycheck and related documents and records is one quarter of an hour. The department's costs have been budgeted at $6 per hour plus $12,000 per month. Normal volume in the department has been set at 8,000 paychecks per month, as the company's work force of 4,000 people is regularly paid twice each month. During May 1976, a total of 7,200 paychecks were prepared and distributed. Timekeeping records show that the payroll department worked 1,900 hours during May. Actual variable costs for the month were $12,000, and actual fixed costs amounted to $12,500.

*Required:*

Compute as many variances from standard cost in the payroll department for the month of May as you can.

11-2.  Hamilton Shoe Co., Inc., has established standard costs for its invoicing department. These standard costs are as follows:

Variable cost per invoice prepared............... $.60
Variable cost per invoice line typed.............. .04
Fixed cost per invoice prepared.................. .40

Normal annual volume is 80,000 invoices. During 1976, a total of 87,500 invoices were prepared. A random sample of 650 invoices showed that the average number of lines on an invoice was 12. The total fixed cost incurred in the department during 1976 was $33,500. The total variable costs were $90,000.

*Required:*

Compute as many variances from standard invoicing cost for 1976 as you can.

11-3.  The management of the Benteen Corporation believes that its planning and control of nonmanufacturing costs have been less effective than the procedures used for manufacturing costs. Accordingly, it is seeking to establish flexible departmental budgets for most of its nonmanufacturing operations. The facts outlined below were developed from a study of the costs incurred in the purchasing department.

The purchasing department supervisor receives a monthly salary of $1,500. Her secretary receives $750 per month. There are five purchasing clerks who are paid an hourly wage of $6. Typists are paid $4 per hour. The standard 8-part purchase order form used costs $.40 per form, and one form is required for each purchase order. However, experience indicates that approximately 10% more forms are spoiled and must be discarded. Typing supplies are estimated to cost $.88 per hour of typing time. Rent on the office space occupied by the purchasing

322    *Accounting for Managerial Analysis*

department is charged on the basis of floor space; this charge amounts to $900 per month. Property taxes and insurance on this portion of the building are $840 per year. Labor-related costs average 20% of hourly wages and 16% of monthly salaries. During a normal month, about 3,000 purchase orders are issued. It takes a purchasing clerk about one quarter of an hour to process an order and give it to a typist with the necessary instructions. Typists can type approximately 120 lines per hour. The average purchase order contains 15 lines. When not working on purchase orders, purchasing clerks update vendors' files and review vendors' catalogs. Typists are reassigned to the typing pool when not needed in the purchasing department.

*Required:*

Prepare a flexible expense budget for the purchasing department for one month. Include budgeted cost allowances for the normal monthly volume of 3,000 purchase orders.

11–4.  During the month of November 1976, the purchasing department of the Benteen Corporation (cf. Problem 11–3 above) processed a total of 2,500 purchase orders. The actual costs recorded in the department for the month were as follows:

> Labor costs:
> Supervisor............................... $ 1,500
> Secretary................................ 775
> Purchasing clerks........................ 3,900
> Typists.................................. 1,375
> Labor-related costs...................... 1,419
> Supplies:
> Purchase order forms used................ 1,220
> Typing supplies used..................... 250
> Space occupancy charges:
> Rent..................................... 900
> Taxes and insurance...................... 76
>                                          $11,415

*Required:*

Prepare an expense report for the purchasing department for the month of November. Compare actual costs with budgeted costs.

11–5.  The marketing division of the Butler Corporation is responsible for promotion, sales, and delivery of the company's products. It comprises five sales territories, all of which are served by two regional warehouses. These warehouses were substantially expanded in 1975 and are expected to meet the corporation's requirements for the storage of finished products for at least five more years.

A summary of the operating statistics for the marketing division for the preceding five years is presented below. All dollar amounts in this summary are stated in terms of constant 1976 dollars. The general price level has risen an average of 8% per year over this 5-year period.

|  | *1976* | *1975* | *1974* | *1973* | *1972* |
|---|---|---|---|---|---|
| Number of shipments........ | 15,400 | 13,800 | 15,200 | 14,000 | 12,500 |
| Sales revenue |  |  |  |  |  |
| (in thousands)............ | $107,000 | $93,000 | $99,000 | $87,000 | $75,000 |
| Costs (in thousands): |  |  |  |  |  |
| Advertising............... | $ 9,000 | $ 8,500 | $ 9,000 | $ 8,000 | $ 7,000 |
| Salesmen's travel.......... | 3,000 | 2,600 | 2,900 | 2,700 | 2,500 |
| Salesmen's commissions.... | 5,350 | 4,650 | 4,950 | 4,350 | 3,750 |
| Order processing........... | 616 | 552 | 608 | 560 | 500 |
| Executives' salaries........ | 1,480 | 1,400 | 1,350 | 1,260 | 1,200 |
| Warehousemen's wages..... | 1,284 | 1,209 | 1,188 | 957 | 900 |
| Depreciation.............. | 2,500 | 2,500 | 1,500 | 1,500 | 1,500 |
| Labor-related costs........ | 1,623 | 1,452 | 1,498 | 1,313 | 1,170 |
| Total costs............. | $ 24,853 | $22,863 | $22,994 | $20,640 | $18,520 |

The general business prosperity of the early 1970s continued throughout 1973 and early 1974. Business slowed in the second half of 1974, and the country plunged into the most severe postwar recession in 1975. The recovery in 1976 was rapid.

*Required:*

a. Classify each of the marketing division's costs as variable, discretionary, or committed. Propose guidelines for budgeting each cost in 1977. The preliminary sales forecast for 1977 is for about 17,000 shipments and total sales revenue of $122,000,000.
b. How would your analysis of these costs have been affected if the comparative data for the preceding five years had not been adjusted for general price-level change?

11-6. The research division of Pittypat Petrochemicals, Inc., has recently been reorganized and expanded. It is directed by a vice president for research and development who has overall administrative responsibility for the division. The chief of research is Dr. Amahl Hussan, who is responsible for the technical direction of the division. He is assisted by a research staff of 24 graduate scientists and 60 laboratory technicians. The personnel complement of the division is completed by secretaries, maintenance personnel, janitors, and watchmen. The division occupies its own facilities in Houston.

The work of the division is carried on in a series of distinct research projects of varying lives. Each project is assigned to the immediate supervision of one of the 24 staff scientists, each of whom is ordinarily responsible for two or more projects at any one time. Dr. Hussan, of course, has general responsibility for all research projects.

Most projects involve the testing of materials for desired properties and efforts to develop new materials with desired characteristics. Some projects require the use of special equipment which cannot be reused within the division and must be sold at nominal prices to universities or for scrap. All equipment and material used in the research division are procured through the corporation's central purchasing department in Dallas.

When a project culminates in the development of a new and valuable product, a patent is obtained and the new product is produced and marketed. Other projects result in significant improvements to existing products. Many projects, however, produce no useful result at all and must be abandoned without benefit to the firm.

In the past, the total costs of the research division have been reported annually to management in a single figure. The same figure has been reported as part of general and administrative expenses in the corporation's published income statement. Management is not sure that this method of reporting provides the appropriate information about these costs. For budgeting purposes, the research division has usually been allowed the amount spent in the previous year plus an additional factor for inflation. If Dr. Hussan has requested an amount substantially greater than this allowance, it has usually been approved only if management feels it can afford the extra spending without cutting expenditures elsewhere in the company. Management is also concerned that treating all research and development costs as current expenses may be understating the value of the company's patents and technical processes.

*Required:*

a. How would you recommend that research division costs be analyzed and reported to management for purposes of budgetary planning and control?

b. How should research and development costs be reported in the annual published financial statements? (Remember that external reporting practices are governed by generally accepted standards and are not wholly at the discretion of management.)

11–7. On January 2, 1975, the U.S. Air Force entered into a contract with the Belle-Watling Aerospace Corporation to produce the new F-22 "Sherman" fighter plane. The contract calls for the production and delivery of 300 aircraft over the next five years at a total price of $2.64 billion. This price represents the contractor's estimated total cost plus a profit margin of 10% of that cost. The contract provides that the contractor and the Air Force may negotiate later adjustments to the contract to allow for inflationary cost increases. It also provides an·option for the Air Force to order a "second buy" of 150 additional aircraft at a total price of $990 million plus an allowance for inflation. This "second buy" price was determined in the same way as the price of the "first buy" of 300 planes.

On February 4, 1977, the first "Sherman" fighter was delivered to the Air Force. The corporation has advised the Air Force project manager that its total costs on the "first buy" of 300 aircraft will be approximately $3.8 billion. Accordingly, it is requesting an adjustment to the contract to a new total price of $4.18 billion, with provision for proportional increase in the price of the "second buy." The general price level rose at an annual rate of 6% during both 1975 and 1976.

*Required:*

How would you explain the pattern of cost behavior implicit in the original contract? How might that explanation affect your assessment of the contractor's request for a contract adjustment in 1977? Discuss fully.

11-8.    For many years, one of the most controversial portions of the Federal budget has been the annual appropriation for military procurement. This appropriation includes the purchase of new weapon systems and of additional units of existing systems. It typically is a very substantial amount of money—an estimated $24 billion for fiscal year 1976. It has been a perennial target for opponents of defense policy. However, it is also a prime target for budget cutters generally for the simple reason that it is vulnerable. It is one of the few major areas in which the budget *can* be cut significantly, because it is one of the few areas in which Congress has any real spending discretion.

It is generally recognized that Congress is effectively committed to spending most of the money requested in the budget. More than one-third of the 1976 budget, for example, involves funds that may be spent without any explicit action by Congress. This category includes such items as Social Security benefits, Civil Service pension benefits, and interest on the Federal debt. In addition, there are many items in the budget which have already been authorized by existing legislation. Income security payments, funds for Federally financed public housing, and revenue sharing payments to state and local governments are examples. Finally, many other budget items could be cut only at the risk of the viability of established government programs. For example, the appropriation for military pay and allowances could not be cut greatly without undermining approved military programs. Moreover, even if the number of personnel on active duty in the armed services is reduced, increases in military pay rates are likely to offset any potential budget saving.

Thus, a comparatively small portion of the total Federal budget is regarded as truly discretionary. Naturally, most Congressional attention is focused on that portion. Discretionary spending in many areas (e.g., Department of State) is so small that even drastic cuts would provide little reduction in the overall budget. Consequently, the fairly substantial military procurement budget is an obvious target. Moreover, cutting the procurement appropriation does not necessarily mean eliminating programs; it may simply require reducing program size or deferring program implementation. Billions of dollars may be saved currently by reducing the number of squadrons of a new tactical fighter or by delaying the date on which a new submarine will become operational.

*Required:*

Analyze and discuss the situation of discretionary and committed spending in the Federal budget in the light of the concepts of variable, discretionary, and committed costs discussed in this chapter.

# chapter 12

# Divisional Performance Measurement

$A$s BUSINESS enterprises and other organizations grow larger in size, more complex in structure, and more diverse in operations, they are typically subdivided into several segments or divisions. Each division is a separately identifiable center of operating activity and of managerial responsibility. The degree of autonomy enjoyed by divisions varies widely. Some operate within the constraints of narrowly defined policies dictated by top management. Others may be charged broadly with the task of operating efficiently or profitably. Whatever the situation may be, top management clearly retains a very positive concern for the operations of all divisions. Consequently, top management wishes to establish and maintain a dependable method of measuring performance in each division and a regular system of performance reporting. Of course, divisional managers also are interested in having reports on their own divisions' performances.

It should be noted that the term "division" is being used here in a very general sense to describe any logical segment or subcomponent of an organization. That segment may be a distinct organizational subcomponent and may be formally designated as a division (e.g., the Chevrolet Division of General Motors Corporation). It may also be designated as a department, a branch office, a district, a service center, or any of a variety of other titles. It need not be a separate organizational entity at all, however. A product line, a channel of distribution, or a class of customers might be regarded as a "division" of a firm for purposes of this

327

discussion. The important characteristic of a division here is that its operating performance is separately identifiable and measurable in some way that is of practical significance to management.

The methods of divisional performance measurement discussed in this chapter all involve financial data. Thus, they are essentially measures of financial performance. While this emphasis is entirely appropriate in this book, the reader should be aware that there are many other very useful measures of performance that do not employ financial data. A division might be evaluated on such nonfinancial matters as employee attitudes, customer relations, innovative technology, maintenance of equipment, and delivery schedules. While all of these matters may be expected to have financial implications, at least over a long term, their direct measurement would likely be in nonfinancial quantities. Such measures are important to management, but they will not be considered directly here.

## OBJECTIVES OF DIVISIONAL PERFORMANCE MEASUREMENT

Any system of divisional performance measurement and appraisal must begin with a clear statement of its objective(s). If it doesn't, the system may measure the wrong things; management may draw the wrong inferences from these measures; and the wrong action may be taken as a consequence. In a specific situation, the objective(s) must be very explicitly defined. In general, however, such objectives may be classified into three basic categories, as follows:

1.  To determine the contribution that a division, as an entity, makes to the total organization.
2.  To provide a basis for evaluating the quality of the divisional manager's performance.
3.  To motivate the divisional manager to operate his division in a manner consistent with the basic goals of the total organization.

These are by no means mutually exclusive objectives of a divisional performance measurement, and a single measure might serve all three. There are certain measures of divisional performance, however, which are not appropriate for one or more of these objectives. If such a measure is used improperly, it may do serious harm to the organization and may impede the attainment of basic goals.

If management wishes to evaluate the contribution of a division as a distinct entity, it must be careful that the measure chosen includes all factors directly traceable to that division and excludes all others. Only the incremental data directly pertinent to the division in question are properly included in the measure. If management wishes to evaluate the division manager's performance, it must select a measure that deals only with factors subject to that manager's control. Thus, the relevant data must fall within the scope of the division manager's responsibility. At first thought, it may seem artificial, if not impossible, to distinguish between the performance of a division and that of the division's manager. It is true that, in the long run, the two performances might be indistinguishable. The long run is made up of many short periods, however. In the short run, a very useful and, perhaps, necessary distinction may be made. It is conceivable, for example, that a manager could do a very good job of managing a highly unsuccessful division. Perhaps his job would be to liquidate the division at minimum loss to the firm. In such a case, the division could hardly be said to have made a satisfactory contribution to the company as a whole. Yet, the division manager may be judged to have discharged his responsibility very well. The distinction between the performance of a division as an entity and the personal performance of a division manager will be pointed out more specifically in subsequent sections.

Any performance measurement system may be expected to influence the behavior of the managers affected by it. In general, managers may be expected to attempt to make themselves look good. Further, if there is any potential personal benefit from the measurement (e.g., a bonus for good performance), managers will seek to attain that benefit. Such behavior is perfectly normal and should not be deplored. On the contrary, it should be turned to the firm's advantage. Top management should design the divisional performance measurement in such a way that, in seeking to achieve their own goals, the division managers will simultaneously be working toward the goals of the firm. Such a result is described as *goal congruence*. It should be foremost in the mind of anyone attempting to design a system of performance measurement and evluation.

As a final note here, it is useful to distinguish between the measurement and the evaluation of performance. Measurement seeks to determine in an objective fashion what performance actually is. Evaluation is then a somewhat subjective judgment as to whether that performance is good or bad. The former is appropriately within the province of the management accountant; he should be an expert in financial measurements for all purposes. The latter, however, is the responsibility of operating management. An evaluation of performance must be made in light of the circumstances within which the division or the manager had to perform. These circumstances may change over time, and it may be difficult to determine the extent to which they affect performance. It is not practicable to make the measurement system so sensitive and flexible that it can cope with the effects of changing circumstances directly. Rather, the necessary adjustments and allowances must be part of the evaluation process.

## EXPENSE CENTERS

For purposes of measuring financial performance, the divisions of a firm may be classified according to the types of financial data used in the measurement. Three basic classes of divisions have been identified on these grounds—expense centers, profit centers, and investment centers. Each of these is considered in some detail below.

An *expense center* may be defined as a segment or division whose financial performance is measured by comparing its actual expenses with either budgeted or standard expenses for a given period. The essential requirement for an expense center is that the costs of operating the division be directly traceable to it. This requirement is both necessary and sufficient. The performance of an expense center is measured by financial measures of inputs only. No measure of output, or accomplishment, is needed. The analysis of performance compares actual and planned (or standard) consumption of resources in the division. There is no reference to what the division achieved as a consequence of consuming those resources. Thus, the performance measured in an expense center is the efficiency of operation in that center. "Efficiency" is used here in the engineering sense of the quantity of inputs used in producing some given output. Actual inputs are compared to some predetermined level that represents efficient utilization. In an expense center, these inputs are measured in dollars. Thus, efficiency is expressed by variances from budgeted or standard costs. Whether the output of an expense center is good or bad is a question that is not addressed by this measurement.

In many cases, the output of an expense center cannot reliably be measured in financial quantities. Hence, financial efficiency is the only feasible measure of divisional performance. Examples of such centers are legal departments, public relations staffs, accounting departments, and most personnel department activities. Each of these divisions may be regarded as necessary for the effective functioning of the firm as a whole. Further, each has a conceptually identifiable output—for example, legal advice, good public relations, reliable accounting reports, and better qualified personnel. The difficulty is that these outputs cannot be expressed in terms of money. Indeed, there may be no quantitative measures of such things as good public relations. In cases such as these, the only practicable financial performance measure is one of efficiency. Such divisions can be evaluated only as expense centers. In other divisions, there may be financial measures of both inputs and outputs available. This does not mean that they must be treated as something more than expense centers, however. Management may elect to treat such a division as an expense center even though its actual inputs could be related to its outputs as well as to planned or standard inputs. For example, a production department in a factory may be regarded as an expense center for performance reporting purposes even though the goods that it produces have a readily determinable financial value. The choice of a performance measure should depend upon what management finds most useful.

If the objective of expense center analysis is to appraise the performance of the division as an entity, the relevant costs are the incremental, or avoidable costs of operating that division. These are the costs that would be avoided if the division were shut down permanently. In most instances, these incremental costs would include both variable and fixed costs. Irrelevant to this analysis are costs common to several divisions

## TABLE 12–1

### BLACK PRODUCTS CORPORATION
Monthly Expense Report

| *Department* Factory Maintenance | | *Month of* August 1976 | |
|---|---|---|---|
| *Supervisor* H. A. Cassidy | | | |
| | *Budgeted Cost* | *Actual Cost* | *Spending Variance* |
| Incremental costs of department: | | | |
| Controllable costs (measure of department manager's performance).................. | $400,000 | $420,000 | $(20,000) |
| Noncontrollable costs...................... | 250,000 | 275,000 | (25,000) |
| Total incremental costs (measure of departmental performance)............................... | $650,000 | $695,000 | $(45,000) |
| Allocated share of common costs (not a measure of any departmental performance)............ | 150,000 | 160,000 | (10,000) |
| Total costs......................... | $800,000 | $855,000 | $(55,000) |

and allocated among them on some arbitrary basis. While such allocations may be appropriate for purposes such as inventory valuation, they are misleading in analyses of performance. If the objective is to evaluate the performance of the division manager, only those incremental costs controllable by that manager are relevant. These distinctions are illustrated in Table 12–1, a simplified and summarized expense report for a division formally organized as a factory department. (The reader will note that this report is simply an abridged version of the form used in Table 8–3 in Chapter 8, with an additional distinction made between incremental and allocated common costs.) In order to be fully useful in a real situation, this report would have to show details by cost items under each of the three basic cost categories included. The variance from the budgeted controllable costs is a measure of the department manager's performance during the month. Any qualitative evaluation of his performance, however, must depend also upon an analysis of the causes of the variance. The variance from total incremental costs is a measure of the efficiency of the performance of the department as a segment of the firm. This is an impersonal measure, for it includes variances that the department manager is not responsible for.

The last line of the report includes the department's allocated share of common costs. Consequently, the variance on this line cannot be interpreted as any indication of the performance of the department as a separate entity. Managers differ in their views as to the validity of including this last line at all. Some argue that it is appropriately included, for these common costs must be incurred if all departments are to continue to operate. Hence, they should be allocated among the departments in some equitable fashion. Some claim that inclusion of these cost allocations makes the division manager more aware of the relationship of his particular division to the entire organization and, thus, helps prepare him for greater responsibilities in later years. Others contend that only those costs directly traceable to the division should be included in its report. They argue that inclusion of the allocated portion of common costs can only cause confusion and, possibly, mistrust. Actually, the most important requirement is that such cost allocations not be misunderstood. The best way to ensure that they are not misunderstood is to avoid them altogether. If management feels that it is desirable to allocate common costs among the divisions, however, at the very least they should be clearly labeled and segregated in the report. Table 12–1 shows a spending variance from the department's allocated share of budgeted common costs. Such a variance clearly has nothing to do with the performance of that division. Hence, it would be better if it did not appear in the report at all. This variance would be avoided if only budgeted common costs were allocated to divisions. In this way, the actual and budgeted common costs in the divisional reports would always be equal and there would be no variance. Variable common costs would be allocated by applying budgeted rates to actual volume in the division receiving the allocation. Fixed common costs would be allocated in a predetermined lump sum. Variances from budgeted common costs would then appear only in reports for the organizational component in which those costs are incurred, and that is exactly where they belong.

## PROFIT CENTERS

A *profit center* may be defined as a division for which separately traceable revenues and expenses are matched to determine the division's profit. Thus, it is one step above an expense center in terms of its financial data requirements. Both revenues and expenses must be identified with the division. In a profit center, there are financial measures of the outputs as well as of the inputs. Consequently, it is feasible to measure the effectiveness of the division's performance in financial terms. Of course, it is also possible to measure efficiency in terms of actual and budgeted cost data. A profit center requires all of the data needed in an expense center as well as the additional data regarding revenues. Hence, management can determine whether the division was efficient in its utilization of resources and, further, whether the division was effective in attaining its objective. This objective is, presumably, to earn a satisfactory profit. The criterion for a "satisfactory" profit may be budgeted profit, past profit performance in the division, profits of other similar divisions, profits of other companies, or some combination of two or more of these. There is considerable potential danger in comparing the profit of a division to that of a separate company, however, even if both are approximately the same size and are in the same industry. A division can rely upon corporate management for many services that a separate company must provide for itself. Allocation of the costs of such services among divisions is not likely to neutralize this difference. Consequently, one might expect a division to be more profitable per dollar of sales volume than a separate company. If this expectation proves wrong consistently, one must then question the desirability of having a large firm with many operating divisions. The usual advantage alleged for such firms is that they foster economies of operation because of their size. If these economies are not reflected in relatively higher profits, the advantage would appear to be illusory.

Profit center analysis may be used as a basis for evaluating the performance of a division as an entity or for evaluating the performance of a division manager. While one would expect that these two performances would become indistinguishable over a long period, they might diverge significantly in any single short period. Further, division managers may be transferred often enough to warrant explicit efforts to distinguish their sequential personal performances from the ongoing operations of the division itself. In evaluating the performance of a division per se, external criteria are relevant. That is, it is reasonable to assess a segment's performance in light of its performance in prior periods or in comparison with performances of other similar divisions. In evaluating the division manager's performance, however, external criteria are less applicable. They entail factors over which the manager cannot reasonably exert any control. Hence, budgeted profit would be a more realistic performance criterion. Ideally, any profit measure of a division manager's performance should be made up exclusively of revenue and expense items subject to his control. Thus, a specially constructed "responsibility profit" would be desirable. In practice, this may prove simply to be the difference between revenues and controllable expenses. Noncontrollable revenues may exist, as in the case of a division that has a sister division as a captive customer because of a directive from top management. Such revenues are usually not reported separately, however. Profit measures for the division as an impersonal entity should be based only on revenues and expenses directly traceable to the division and avoidable if the division were closed down. This concept of divisional profit is often referred to as the *profit contribution,* as it is the amount of profit contributed directly by the division. It might also be described as an *incremental profit,* the additional profit earned solely as a result of the operations of the division. Incremental profit is a very useful concept for purposes of decision analyses, and we shall refer to it again.[1]

Divisional profit may be measured either before or after income taxes. Since income taxes are assessed on the basis of the income of the entire company, they might be regarded as similar to common costs and excluded from the calculation of divisional profit. This is certainly the easier alternative, and it is entirely suitable for purposes of measuring divisional performance. Of course, income taxes could be allocated among divisions by applying the effective tax rate to divisional profits. Since this allocation would simply reduce all divisional profits by a proportionate amount, it would make no substantial difference in one's evaluation of those profits. Income taxes will be ignored in discussions of divisional profit in this chapter.

## Natural and Constructive Profit Centers

In general, a profit center is visualized as buying resources in one market (the input market) and selling goods and services in another (the output market). Thus, its revenues are measured by output market prices and its expenses, by input market prices. To this extent, the profit center is much like an independent firm. A profit center that deals directly in both input and output markets is called a *natural profit center.* This is the most familiar type of profit center. A product division is the classic example. There is also a second type of profit center that may be identified and that may be very useful to management. For want of a better term, let us call it a *constructive profit center.* It is not naturally a profit center, but it may be made to appear as one. An example is the computer center or data processing department in a corporation. It purchases the resources that it requires in input markets, but it does not sell its product. Rather, it performs computing services for other divisions at no charge to them. On the face of it, the computer center would appear to be a logical expense center. So it might be. However, management might wish to know whether it is better to own and operate its own computer or to purchase computer time from a data processing service

---

[1] See Chapter 14.

bureau. In order to answer this type of question, the computer center may be treated as a constructive profit center.

Assume, for example, that computing time may be purchased from an independent service bureau at a price of $250 per hour of processing time. Assume further that the corporation operates its own computer center at a monthly fixed cost of $20,000 plus variable costs of $150 per hour of processing time.[2] If the company-owned computer is used for 400 hours of processing during a given month, the following constructive profit statement may be prepared for the computer center for that month:

| | | |
|---|---:|---:|
| Revenue (400 hrs. @ $250)................. | | $100,000 |
| Expenses: | | |
| Variable (400 hrs. @ $150)................ | $60,000 | |
| Fixed................................. | 20,000 | 80,000 |
| Divisional profit........................... | | $ 20,000 |

The "revenue" in this case is not actual revenue in the customary sense. Rather, it is an alternative cost avoided. Thus, this constructive profit analysis shows that the corporation saved $20,000 during the month by operating its own computer rather than buying computer time from a service bureau. Implicit in this analysis is the assumption that all 400 hours of processing time would have been used regardless of where the data processing was done. This assumption is not always valid. It may be economical for a firm to perform certain jobs on its own machine but not on the service bureau's machine. This would be the case in our illustration if the value of a job to the firm were more than $150 but less than $250 per hour.

The illustration above is based on the premise that the firm already has its own computer. It would also be valid if the company were considering renting a computer on a contract that could be canceled at short notice. If the decision were to purchase a computer or to rent one on a long-term lease contract, however, it would have to be analyzed as a capital investment decision. Such decisions are explained and illustrated in Chapters 16 and 17.

Divisional profit data may be used to evaluate the performance of the division per se or of the division manager in the case of a natural profit center. In the case of a constructive profit center, however, profit analysis

---

[2] An adjustment to a common denominator of processing time may be necessary here if a valid analysis is to be made. A large computer may be able to process jobs in considerably less time than a smaller one. In that case, an hour of processing time on the large machine is obviously not equivalent to an hour on the smaller one. Thus, the hourly cost rates of the two machines could be compared only after adjusting them for the difference in the speed of processing. For example, in the illustration above, if the service bureau's computer could complete any job in half the time the company's computer would take and the service bureau charged $500 per hour for processing, the appropriate comparison would be $250 per hour and $150 per hour (as indicated above) or, equivalently, $500 per hour and $300 per hour.

can be used only to appraise the performance or contribution of the division as an entity. Thus, the computer center in our example made a contribution of $20,000 to the corporation's profit before taxes during the month studied. Corporate profit would have been $20,000 less if computing services had been purchased from an independent service bureau. This profit cannot be attributed to the computer center manager, however. Presumably he is responsible for his division's costs, but he cannot control his revenue. If he is required to perform all services requested by sister divisions but is not allowed to sell any services to external customers, he cannot control his "sales" volume. Moreover, he has no responsibility for or control over his "selling price" of $250. Hence, the division manager's performance might best be appraised by comparing the actual and budgeted costs of operating the computer center. It is quite possible for the division to show a constructive profit (a favorable performance measure) but an unfavorable spending variance from budgeted cost (an adverse performance measure).

### Divisional Profit and Corporate Profit

From the discussion to this point it is possible to infer an important point. The sum of the profits of all divisions is not necessarily equal to the profit of the corporation as a whole. Divisional profits are incremental profits. Costs not directly traceable to any single division are intentionally excluded from consideration in the computation of the profit of any division. Yet, they must be considered in determining corporate profit. This nonadditivity of divisional profit to corporate profit reflects the fact that these are two conceptually different measures. Divisional profit does not sum to corporate profit because it was never intended to do so. Divisional profit is a unique concept, designed to serve specific managerial needs. This is especially true in the case of a constructive profit center where the "revenue" is not recognized as revenue to the corporation at all.

### Divisional Profit Reporting in Diversified Companies

The published income statements of business corporations have traditionally disclosed only summary data on revenues and expenses for a period. In recent years this practice has been reexamined, particularly in the cases of diversified companies, or conglomerates. In 1969, the Securities and Exchange Commission initiated a requirement that all corporations subject to its jurisdiction must report revenues and income by major "lines of business." Companies whose annual sales exceed $50 million must disclose revenues and income for each line of business that accounts for 10 percent or more of total revenue or of total income before tax. Smaller companies need disclose this information only for lines of business representing at least 15 percent of their total revenue or income.

To date, the SEC has allowed companies considerable latitude in their interpretation of this divisional reporting requirement. A line of business may be defined, at management's discretion, as an organizational division, a product line, a market, or any other logical segment of the individual firm's operations. Divisional revenues and incomes may be reported either in dollar amounts or as percentages of company totals. The income for a line of business may be its incremental profit, or it may be calculated after an allocation of common costs among all lines of business.[3] At the time of this writing, these divisional reporting requirements have not been applied to firms not subject to the jurisdiction of the SEC. There is considerable likelihood that they will, however. Even before the SEC's action, the Accounting Principles Board of the American Institute of Certified Public Accountants urged diversified companies to consider voluntary disclosure of divisional operating data.[4]

## INVESTMENT CENTERS

An *investment center* is essentially a profit center in which profit is related to the investment in the assets used in the division. The basic premise of this additional information is that profit is most meaningful when stated in terms of the capital investment required to produce it. Investment center analysis permits an assessment of the efficiency (in the economic sense of returns on resources used) with which division management has utilized the assets entrusted to its care. This analysis may be used as a basis for evaluating the contribution of the division as an entity and also the performance of the division manager. In both cases, however, it must be used very carefully. Misuse of this analysis may cause a serious lack of goal congruence between the division and the company as a whole.

### Rate of Return on Investment

Unquestionably, the most common device for reporting performance in an investment center is the rate of return on investment in assets, or

---

[3] For additional discussion of these requirements and examples of several companies' actual reports in compliance with them, see Paul A. Pacter, "Line-of-Business Earnings Disclosures in Recent SEC Filings," *The Journal of Accountancy,* vol. 130 (October 1970), pp. 52–63.

[4] "Statement of the Accounting Principles Board: Disclosure of Supplemental Financial Information by Diversified Companies," September, 1967, p. 4. At the time of this writing, the Financial Accounting Standards Board was considering the publication of a standard dealing with financial reporting for the segments of a business enterprise.

simply return on investment (ROI). The rate of return on investment is the ratio of net income to total assets. It may be computed directly as follows:

$$\text{ROI} = \frac{\text{Income}}{\text{Total assets}}$$

Frequently, however, the same result is attained by means of two intermediate calculations. The first is the ratio of income to sales revenue.

$$\text{Rate of income on sales} = \frac{\text{Income}}{\text{Sales}}$$

Then the ratio of sales to total assets is computed; this is called the asset turnover.

$$\text{Asset turnover} = \frac{\text{Sales}}{\text{Total assets}}$$

The rate of return on investment is then computed as the product of the rate of income on sales and the asset turnover, thus:

$$\text{ROI} = \text{Rate of income on sales} \times \text{Asset turnover}$$

$$\text{ROI} = \frac{\text{Income}}{\text{Sales}} \times \frac{\text{Sales}}{\text{Total Assets}} = \frac{\text{Income}}{\text{Total Assets}}$$

Clearly, this three-step method of computing the rate of return can be collapsed to the direct computation shown initially. The three-step method is sometimes preferred because it shows more detailed information that may be particularly significant in individual industries. For example, financial performance in the retail grocery business is characterized by a low rate of income on sales (or a low markup) and a high (rapid) asset turnover. Conversely, the petroleum refining industry has a fairly high rate of income on sales but a much lower asset turnover. A knowledgeable person analyzing the performance of a company or a division in one or the other of these industries might well consider himself better informed in an important way if he knew all three of these statistics instead of the return on investment only.

As noted earlier, the rate of return on investment must be used very carefully to avoid serious misunderstandings and erroneous actions. To begin with, a rate of return is a useful index of performance only if there is some reasonable criterion available for comparison. That criterion may be the rate of return in the same division in prior periods, the rate in other divisions, the rate in independent companies, or some target rate of return. Independent companies are not likely to be good bases for comparison, however, for the same reasons mentioned in connection with profit center analysis. Corporate headquarters would relieve its divisions of substantial asset investments and operating expenses that would have to be borne directly by an independent company.

*Danger of Unprofitable Behavior by Division Manager.* A danger in the rate of return on investment is that a division manager may feel compelled to maximize a ratio rather than the financial welfare of his division and the firm as a whole. For example, assume that a division holds assets valued at $500,000 and earns income of $100,000 per year. Its annual rate of return on investment is 20% ($100,000 ÷ $500,000). The company's average cost of capital is 10%. The division manager has an opportunity to purchase for $100,000 an asset that would increase his division's income by $15,000; and the corporate treasury has the necessary $100,000 available in surplus cash that might otherwise be invested in marketable securities yielding 6%. From the point of view of the corporation, the new asset would yield a rate of return of 15%, which is higher than the cost of capital and vastly better than the return on marketable securities. Yet, the investment would reduce the division's rate of return to 19% ($115,000 ÷ $600,000). If the division manager understood that his performance would be measured only by the *rate* of return on his assets, with no attention to the absolute amount of his division's income, he would be tempted to forego the new asset. Conversely, if he held an asset valued at $100,000 that could be disposed of with a consequent reduction in divisional income of less than $20,000, he might be inclined to dispose of the asset and thus increase his rate of return. The fact that cash recovered from the sale of the asset might then be invested in marketable securities yielding only 6% would not appear to be his problem. One way of averting this danger is to evaluate the divisional manager's performance by several different measures and to impress upon him that the rate of return on investment is only one of the measures that should concern him.

*Problems of Measuring Investment in Assets.* Perhaps the most difficult problem of all is the appropriate measurement of a division's assets for purposes of the rate of return computation. The most readily available measure in most cases is the book value of the assets, the amount at which they are recorded in the company's accounts. This may also be the least useful measure, unfortunately. Assuming that some significant portion of the division's assets are depreciable, using book value as the basis for the investment in assets would tend to produce a rate of return that increased over time as the assets aged and were increasingly depreciated. Thus, so long as divisional income did not decline as rapidly as the book value of the division's assets, the divisional rate of return would rise as the assets became more worn and obsolete. A very popular way of correcting for this tendency is to use the gross book value of assets, that is, the original cost without any deduction for depreciation.

While this does avoid the problem of a meaningless rise in the rate of return as time passes, it still is not a measure of the current economic value of the assets involved. For purposes of rate of return computations, valuation of assets at their current replacement cost[5] would be the most generally appropriate solution to the problem. Although replacement cost data are not found in the accounts, they may usually be determined quite easily for a large number of assets. The replacement costs of inventories and of equipment for which an active market exists may be obtained directly from quoted market prices. Replacement costs of buildings may be approximated by periodic appraisals or by applying a construction price index to the original costs. Appraised values for land are usually reliable estimates of replacement costs. Special equipment and intangible assets may present more difficult problems, but some estimate of replacement cost is normally possible, even if it is no more than an adjustment of original cost for change in the general price level.

The assets included in the investment base for a division should be only those assets used exclusively in that division. Allocations of portions of the values of assets controlled by corporate headquarters and used for the general benefit of all divisions are not appropriate. Some firms have excluded from a division's investment base any assets that are currently idle (e.g., standby equipment). The resultant rate of return is said to be the return on invested capital *employed* rather than on the total available invested capital. This approach would tend to raise the rate of return, for idle assets presumably generate no income. Yet, this practice would seem to defeat one of the objectives of the measure—the determination of how efficiently assets have been used. The presence of idle assets suggests inefficient utilization of resources. If this is the case, it should be reflected in the rate of return on investment and not artificially excluded from that measure.

*Problems of Measuring Divisional Income.* All of the problems of profit center analysis are encountered also in investment centers. There are also some special problems of income measurement when a rate of return is to be computed. If assets are valued at replacement cost for this purpose—and they should be—depreciation expense should also be based upon replacement cost. The rate of return on investment for a company is customarily computed by reference to income after tax. A division pays no tax, however. Its incremental income is normally determined without regard to taxes. Consequently, any attempt to compare a division's rate of return with that of a company will probably encounter a very fundamental inconsistency. It is possible to compute divisional income after tax by applying the income tax rate to the division's incremental income. This is seldom done, however.

---

[5] Replacement cost was defined in Chapter 2.

**Residual Profit**

There is an alternative measure of financial performance in an investment center that avoids some (but not all) of the problems associated with the rate of return on investment because it is not expressed as a ratio. *Residual profit* is the incremental profit of a division minus an interest charge based on the division's investment in assets. The interest rate used for this computation would normally be the company's average cost of capital. Residual profit is computed below for the division whose rate of return was 20% in the illustration in the preceding section. This division had income of $100,000 and assets of $500,000. The company's cost of capital was 10%. It's residual profit is determined as follows:

| | |
|---|---:|
| Incremental profit...................................... | $100,000 |
| Interest on invested capital (10% × $500,000)........... | 50,000 |
| Residual profit........................................ | $ 50,000 |

While the form of this measure is like that used in a profit center, the effect of a costly investment in assets is reflected in the final figure. Now, when the division in the example has the opportunity of purchasing a new asset for $100,000 in order to increase income by $15,000, the division manager would be induced to do so. Incremental profit would rise to $115,000. The interest charge also would increase to $60,000 (10% × $600,000). But the residual profit would increase, too—from $50,000 to $55,000.

Residual profit is not as widely used in investment center analyses as is the rate of return on investment. Actually, either measure is equally useful to management if it is properly interpreted and if the division manager's performance is intelligently evaluated. The problems and dangers associated with the rate of return are not inherent in that method. Rather, they reflect potential misuses of the method. Residual profit could also be misused, of course. Whichever method is used, it should be used correctly; and all parties concerned should understand clearly what it means and how it relates to top management's assessment of their performances.

## INTERDIVISIONAL TRANSFER PRICING

Systems of measuring profit or return on investment in separate divisions are inevitably complicated when two or more divisions in the same company trade with each other. A division that purchases goods or services from independent suppliers and sells its products to independent customers has been described as a natural profit center. (If its investment in assets is clearly defined, it might also be referred to as a natural investment center.) This status is not appreciably changed if the division also purchases from a sister division and/or sells to a sister division *and if it deals with such sister divisions essentially as it does with independent companies.* If the latter condition is not met, the buyer-seller relationship between sister divisions is not the natural, or arm's length, bargaining situation. As a consequence, profit responsibility may become blurred and divisional profit measurements may be tenuous, at best. Hence, we may distinguish between two basic situations. In the first, each division manager is free to trade with sister divisions or not as he chooses. This is the simpler—and the rarer—situation. Where it exists, divisional performance measures should not be complicated by the interdivisional trading that does occur. In the second situation, divisions are required to trade with each other by a top-management policy decision. While this decision may be entirely appropriate from the point of view of top management, it causes potential problems in measuring the performance of any one division. These problems are critical in the selection of the interdivisional transfer price.

A *transfer price* is the price at which goods or services are exchanged between sister divisions of the same company. This price may be set either by the division managers involved or by top management. If the divisions are free to decide whether or not to trade with each other, it is logical that the division managers should also set the transfer price for goods they actually agree to exchange. In that case, the transfer price would be equivalent to a price for goods exchanged between two independent firms. Consequently, the factors determining the transfer price would be the same as those that determine prices in general.[6] On the other hand, if the divisions are required to trade with each other, it is reasonable to expect top management to establish the price at which the exchanges will take place. Hence, part of the determination of the revenue of the selling division and the costs of the buying division is beyond the control of the respective division managers. Evaluation of division managers' performance in terms of any of the financial measures discussed earlier in this chapter would then be more difficult and would be potentially disruptive of harmonious relations among divisions and between individual divisions and top management.

A considerable variety of transfer prices has been proposed and used. Many of these are merely minor variations of a single method, however. In the sections that follow, we shall consider five basic types of transfer prices:

1. Cost.
2. Cost plus a normal markup.
3. Market price.

---

[6] Some of these factors will be discussed in Chapter 15.

4. Incremental cost.
5. Negotiated price.

It is possible that more than one of these types would be used in the same company and even for the same transfer. Any or all of the first four may be used when top management requires that the divisions trade with each other. A negotiated transfer price, on the other hand, is appropriate only when the divisions are free to deal with each other or not, according to their own determinations of their own best interests.

## Cost

Perhaps the simplest method of transfer pricing is cost, usually defined as the selling division's unit cost to produce and ship the product. This information is routinely collected in the cost accounting system in any event. Further, unit cost is the basis of inventory valuation in corporate accounting records. Thus, no unique information is required for purposes of transfer pricing. If it is management's intent to evaluate both the selling and the buying divisions as expense centers, pricing transfers at cost is appropriate. If standard cost data are available, the transfer price should be standard rather than actual cost. In this way, efficiencies and inefficiencies (as reflected in variances from standard cost) will be reported in the selling division, where they presumably originate. Cost would be an inappropriate transfer price for purposes of profit center or investment center analysis, however. It would tend to reduce profit in the selling division, for there would be no profit margin on goods sold to a sister division. Conversely, it would inflate the profit of the buying division, for that division's purchase costs would be artificially low.

## Cost Plus a Normal Markup

Some firms have attempted to take advantage of the simplicity of cost-based transfer prices and, yet, derive divisional profit data from them. The means of doing this is to set transfer prices at cost (actual or standard) plus some predetermined profit margin or normal markup. In this way, the selling division apparently realizes a profit on the interdivisional sale. That profit, however, is an artificial margin dictated by policy rather than one generated by market forces. Its validity as a basis for evaluating the performance of the division as an entity or of the division manager is questionable, at best, and may be very misleading. If the profit margin is a target profit set by management or is computed so as to ensure that the selling and buying divisions will share equally in the total profit realized by the company upon sale of the final product to an outside customer, it provides management no useful information for purposes of performance appraisal. If, on the other hand, the normal markup is equivalent to the profit margin that a competing firm might reasonably be expected to realize, then the total transfer price begins to approximate a market value. As such, it might be useful for managerial analyses. Its usefulness tends to be a function of the closeness to which it approaches a true market price. A transfer price based on cost plus a normal markup has no unique value of its own, however.

## Market Price

If there is an active market for the goods or services transferred between divisions and there are readily determinable market prices, these prices are logical values for the interdivisional transfers. Market prices reflect the collective values of many buyers and sellers; they are neither arbitrary nor artificial. Most importantly, market prices represent the divisions' alternatives. The selling division could sell its goods to independent customers at market prices. Similarly, the buying division would have to pay an independent supplier market prices for its materials. Market prices may require adjustments in some instances, and these are appropriate as long as they are consistent with market conditions. For example, the buying division may purchase materials in such a large quantity that it could obtain a discount from any independent supplier. If so, the same discount is properly allowed on internal transfers.

To a large degree, internal transfers at market prices leave the divisions in the same situations they would be in if they dealt with each other at arm's length. Of course, there are still some advantages of their corporate relationship. For example, the selling division bears no risk of bad debts on sales to sister divisions. In most corporations, payment is made regularly by a transfer from the Cash account of the buyer to the Cash account of the seller in the books of the corporation. Also, if the internal transfer is required by management policy, the selling division incurs no direct promotional expenses on a sale to a sister division. The buying division also derives some special benefits from the internal transfer. Ordinarily, a sister division is regarded by the seller as a preferred customer. Hence, the buying division can usually rely on delivery schedules and full customer services.

Obviously, market prices exist only for standard products or specialized products that are made up of standard components. For example, there may be a readily determined market price for a specially equipped forklift if it is built entirely of standard parts, each of which has its own market price. In the case of custom-designed products, however, there are usually no easily identified market prices. In such situations, cost plus a normal profit margin is often suggested as a reasonable approximation of what the market price ought to be. As noted in the preceding section, this method may be acceptable if the profit margin is comparable to what a competitor might realize. A market price for a custom made product may also be established by requesting bids from several different manufacturers. The low bid may then be taken as the market price and used for internal transfer pricing. While this approach may generate a useful market price, it is not without disadvantages. If outside bidders come to realize that their only function is to provide the bid requester with an internal transfer price and that they have no real chance of obtaining the order, they will quickly discontinue submitting bids or might even submit wholly spurious bids. This would clearly be an undesirable situation. No firm wishes to make enemies.

### Incremental Cost

If internal transfers are required as a matter of policy and if the principal objective of the transfer price is to provide useful information for top management decision making, the best transfer price is the incremental cost in the selling division. In most cases, incremental cost would include all variable costs of producing and shipping the goods in question plus any fixed costs directly and exclusively traceable to the internal transfer. Transfer pricing at incremental cost is incompatible with the objective of measuring divisional profit. If top management wishes to have incremental cost data for its own purposes but still wants to evaluate the divisions as profit or investment centers, at least two different transfer prices will have to be used for these two distinct objectives. There is no reason why more than one transfer price should not be used for the same internal transfer, except for the added clerical cost of preparing and reporting the duplicative information.

In the preceding paragraph, we noted that incremental cost is equal to the directly traceable costs of production and shipping in the selling division "in most cases." This is the case when the selling division has adequate capacity to produce all goods demanded by both sister divisions and independent customers or when there are no outside customers for the goods in question. However, if there are outside customers and if the selling division lacks sufficient capacity to meet the full demand for its products, the situation is very materially changed. In this case, the incremental cost to the selling division and to the company as a whole is the revenue lost on sales to outside customers that must be foregone in order to make the internal transfer to a sister division. Thus, incremental cost would be equal to the market price for those goods. Of course, if the selling division filled all orders from independent customers first and, hence, was unable to meet the buying division's demand, the buying division would have to fill its requirements by paying the market price to an outsider supplier. In such a situation, it is entirely reasonable that top management might prefer to decide whether the two divisions should deal with each other or not. Incremental cost data are still the appropriate bases for that decision, but they are now equal to the market price and not to the internal production costs.

### Negotiated Price

Division managers should be allowed to negotiate with each other on transfer prices only if they also have the discretion to trade with one another or with independent parties. If internal transfers are required by top management, transfer price negotiations would be a useless and probably damaging exercise in gamesmanship. Neither party would have the normal bargaining leverage of taking his business elsewhere. The division managers would simply be arguing about the sharing of a predetermined total amount. At best, the result of such negotiations would be meaningless. At worst, the result would be damaging internal conflicts.

Where the selling division does have a choice of customers and the buying division, a choice of suppliers, however, negotiated transfer prices should work well. If there is a well-established market price, the negotiations should promptly settle upon that as the transfer price. In the absence of a firm market price, the selling division should be willing to agree to some price greater than its incremental cost; and the buying division should be happy to agree to a price no higher than it could expect to pay to an independent supplier. (Remember that the selling division's incremental cost is equal to the revenue it would have to forego on some other sale if it is already producing at full capacity.) If the buying division could purchase the goods outside at a price below the selling division's incremental cost, it would be to the advantage of both divisions and the company for it to do so. Otherwise, the negotiations should result in a transfer price mutually advantageous to both divisions and to the company as a whole.

### QUESTIONS FOR DISCUSSION

1. How can one really distinguish between the performance of a division and the performance of that division's manager?
2. What kind of performance is measured in an expense center? What are the criteria for evaluating that performance?
3. What kind of performance is measured in a profit center? What are the criteria for evaluating that performance?

4. Distinguish between a natural profit center and a constructive profit center. Can the same performance analyses be made in both?

5. How do performance measures in investment centers differ from those in profit centers?

6. May divisional profits and divisional rates of return on investment be compared to the profits and rates of return of independent companies in the same industry? Explain.

7. What are the principal alternative bases for measuring a division's investment in assets? What are some of the problems involved in using each?

8. Should common costs be allocated among divisions for purposes of divisional performance measurements? Discuss.

9. What is a division's residual profit? What are its advantages as a measure of divisional performance?

10. What is a transfer price? Is it a true price in the same sense as the prices of goods exchanged between firms in normal markets?

11. How, if at all, is the selection of a transfer price dependent upon the identification of the divisions involved as expense centers or as profit centers?

12. Under what circumstances are incremental costs appropriate and useful transfer prices?

13. Under what circumstances are negotiated transfer prices appropriate and useful?

14. "It is meaningless to say that all of a company's divisions are profitable but that the company itself is not. A company is the sum of its divisions, and its profits inevitably depend upon theirs." Comment on this statement.

## PROBLEMS

12-1. The maintenance department of the Wildman Corporation performs all routine maintenance work in the corporation's factory, as well as much of the major repair work. This department is evaluated as an expense center. Its flexible budget for one year's operations appears as follows:

|  | *Variable Rate per Machine-Hour* | *Fixed Cost per Year* |
|---|---|---|
| Indirect materials..................... | $1.10 | |
| Indirect labor......................... | 2.40 | $ 21,000 |
| Supervision........................... | | 40,000 |
| Labor-related costs.................... | .48 | 12,200 |
| Power and light....................... | .72 | 18,000 |
| Depreciation.......................... | | 33,000 |
| Plant occupancy costs................. | | 35,400 |
| | $4.70 | $159,600 |

Indirect materials, indirect labor, and power and light are cost items regarded as controllable by the maintenance department supervisor. Plant occupancy costs are allocated among all of the departments occupying space in the factory on the basis of square feet of floor space. They include such things as depreciation, taxes, and insurance on the factory building.

During 1976, a total of 90,000 machine-hours were worked in the factory. The actual costs charged to the maintenance department during this year were as follows:

| | |
|---|---|
| Indirect materials............................ | $ 92,500 |
| Indirect labor............................... | 248,000 |
| Supervision................................. | 37,500 |
| Labor-related costs.......................... | 57,100 |
| Power and light............................. | 85,200 |
| Depreciation................................ | 33,800 |
| Plant occupancy costs....................... | 36,900 |
| | $591,000 |

*Required:*

Prepare an expense report for the maintenance department that will be useful to management in evaluating both the department supervisor's performance and the performance of the department as an entity.

12–2.  The Elwell Company has three distinct sales divisions, each of which is evaluated as a profit center. The company's budgeted income statement for 1976, in thousands of dollars, appeared as follows:

| | *Sales* | | | |
|---|---|---|---|---|
| | *Indus-trial* | *Whole-sale* | *Govern-ment* | *Total Company* |
| Sales........................ | $30,000 | $40,000 | $20,000 | $90,000 |
| Expenses: | | | | |
| Standard production costs.... | $15,000 | $20,000 | $10,000 | $45,000 |
| Sales commissions........... | 2,400 | 3,200 | 1,600 | 7,200 |
| Sales promotion............. | 2,000 | 2,500 | 1,000 | 5,500 |
| Other selling costs.......... | 1,500 | 2,000 | 1,000 | 4,500 |
| Divisional administration..... | 2,500 | 2,500 | 1,800 | 6,800 |
| General corporate costs...... | 4,500 | 6,000 | 3,000 | 13,500 |
| | $27,900 | $36,200 | $18,400 | $82,500 |
| Earnings before tax........... | $ 2,100 | $ 3,800 | $ 1,600 | $ 7,500 |

Actual operations for the year 1976 are summarized below, again in thousands of dollars:

| | Sales | | | |
| | Indus-trial | Whole-sale | Govern-ment | Total Company |
|---|---|---|---|---|
| Sales........................ | $44,000 | $32,000 | $14,000 | $90,000 |
| Expenses: | | | | |
| Standard production costs.... | $22,000 | $16,000 | $ 7,000 | $45,000 |
| Production cost variances.... | 880 | 640 | 280 | 1,800 |
| Sales commissions........... | 3,520 | 2,560 | 1,120 | 7,200 |
| Sales promotion............. | 2,200 | 2,500 | 1,200 | 5,900 |
| Other selling costs........... | 2,200 | 1,600 | 700 | 4,500 |
| Divisional administration..... | 2,600 | 2,600 | 1,800 | 7,000 |
| General corporate costs...... | 7,480 | 5,440 | 2,380 | 15,300 |
| | $40,880 | $31,340 | $14,480 | $86,700 |
| Earnings before tax........... | $ 3,120 | $   660 | $  (480) | $ 3,300 |

General corporate costs include all of the company's costs that are not incurred directly in one of the sales divisions nor included as part of production costs. They are allocated among the three sales divisions on the basis of sales volumes.

*Required:*

Evaluate the Elwell Company's practices regarding the measurement of performances in the sales divisions. What specific changes, if any, would you recommend? Why?

12–3.  The power plant of the Hatfield Company produced a total of 6,000,000 kilowatt-hours of electricity in 1976. The variable operating costs of the power plant were $180,000 for one year, and the fixed costs directly traceable to it were $450,000. Additional fixed costs of $150,000 were allocated to the power plant as its share of general corporate expenses. The rate for electricity from the local power and light company is $.11 per kilowatt-hour.

In the past, the company has always evaluated the performance of the power plant by comparing its actual costs with budgeted costs. The company's new president, however, wants all operating segments of the company to be evaluated as profit centers, if possible.

*Required:*

Can the power plant be evaluated as a profit center? If so, present an analysis of its profit performance in 1976. If not, explain why not?

12–4.  The transportation department of the Scovill Distributing Corporation maintains a fleet of 80 automobiles for use by authorized company personnel. The departmental budget allows $.12 per mile of vehicle operation plus $160,000 per year for general maintenance. During 1976, the 80 cars were operated an average of 40,000 miles each. Total cost in the transportation department in 1976 was $576,000. The rental charge for similar cars would have been $60 per month per car plus $.17 per mile.

*Required:*

a.  Evaluate the operations of the transportation department in 1976 as though it were an expense center.

b.  Evaluate the operations of the transportation department in 1976 as though it were a profit center.

 **12-5.** Following are the budgeted and actual income statements for the household products division of the Madden Rubber Company for the year 1976:

|  | Budgeted | Actual |
|---|---|---|
| Sales................................ | $7,500,000 | $7,800,000 |
| Variable expenses...................... | $3,000,000 | $3,250,000 |
| Fixed expenses........................ | 3,600,000 | 3,750,000 |
| Total expenses......................... | $6,600,000 | $7,000,000 |
| Income before tax..................... | $ 900,000 | $ 800,000 |
| Total assets........................... | $3,750,000 | $4,000,000 |

Actual selling prices were exactly equal to those planned in the budget.

*Required:*

a.  Evaluate the performance of the household products division during 1976 first as a profit center, then as an expense center, and finally as an investment center.

b.  Compute the effect that the increase in sales volume alone had on actual income as compared with budgeted income. What were the causes of the remaining difference between actual and budgeted incomes?

 **12-6.** The small appliance division of the Rittenhouse Electric Company reports the following assets on its divisional balance sheet:

| | |
|---|---|
| Original cost......................... | $18,000,000 |
| Accumulated depreciation.............. | 7,500,000 |
| Book value........................... | $10,500,000 |

These assets have an estimated current replacement cost of $21,000,000. The division's income statement for 1976 is summarized below.

| | |
|---|---|
| Sales............................... | $25,000,000 |
| Avoidable expenses of division........... | $21,000,000 |
| Allocated share of corporate expenses..... | 2,500,000 |
| | $23,500,000 |
| Income before taxes.................... | $ 1,500,000 |

*Required:*

a. Compute the rate of return on investment in the division's assets, valued at (1) book value, (2) gross original cost, and (3) replacement cost.

b. Which of these three rates of return would be most useful for purposes of comparing the performance of this division with other divisions? Explain.

12-7. The McKinsey Corporation has eight major product divisions. The financial statements of the turbine division at the end of 1976 appeared as follows:

McKINSEY TURBINE DIVISION
Balance Sheet
December 31, 1976

| | | | |
|---|---|---|---|
| Current assets....... | $ 7,000,000 | Current liabilities.... | $ 4,000,000 |
| Plant property....... | 21,000,000 | Long-term debt...... | 7,000,000 |
| Accumulated depre- | | Stockholders' equity.. | 12,000,000 |
| ciation........... | ( 7,000,000) | | |
| Intangibles......... | 2,000,000 | | |
| | $23,000,000 | | $23,000,000 |

McKINSEY TURBINE DIVISION
Income Statement
For Year Ended Dec. 31, 1976

| | |
|---|---|
| Sales..................................... | $30,000,000 |
| Cost of goods sold......................... | 21,000,000 |
| Gross margin.............................. | $ 9,000,000 |
| Selling and administrative expenses........... | 5,000,000 |
| Income before tax.......................... | $ 4,000,000 |
| Income tax (40%)......................... | 1,600,000 |
| Net income................................ | $ 2,400,000 |

All expenses are incurred directly in the division, except for $1,000,000 of selling and administrative expenses that are allocated from the general corporate expenses.

The McKinsey Corporation's cost of capital is 12%.

*Required:*

a. Compute the rate of return on investment in the turbine division by the three-step method.

b. Compute the turbine division's residual profit for 1976.

12-8. The food products division of the Kester Company has assets valued at a current replacement cost of $20,000,000. The budgeted revenue of the division for 1977 is $80,000,000, and its budgeted expenses total $75,000,000. The company's cost of capital is 10%.

Early in January 1977, the division was offered the opportunity of taking over the assets and the operations of a going concern which the company had just purchased for $10,000,000. The budgeted revenue of this concern are $36,000,000 for 1977, and its budgeted expenses are $34,000,000.

*Required:*

a. Compute the budgeted rate of return on investment and the budgeted residual profit of the food products division for 1976 before consideration of the opportunity to take over the newly acquired firm.

b. If the division does take over the assets and operations of the acquired concern, how would this change affect its budgeted rate of return and residual profit computed in *a*?

c. If the division is evaluated as an investment center, would you expect the division manager to accept the offered addition of the acquired firm to his area of responsibility? Explain.

12-9. Following is a report of the operations and the assets of the Filbey Corporation, by divisions:

| | Division | | | Total Company |
|---|---|---|---|---|
| | A | B | C | |
| Sales..................... | $60,000 | $90,000 | $40,000 | $190,000 |
| Cost of goods sold.......... | $45,000 | $54,000 | $20,000 | $119,000 |
| Selling and administrative expenses................ | 9,000 | 12,000 | 6,000 | 27,000 |
| | $54,000 | $66,000 | $26,000 | $146,000 |
| Operating income........... | $ 6,000 | $24,000 | $14,000 | $ 44,000 |
| Unallocated corporate expenses................ | | | | 18,000 |
| Income before tax........... | | | | $ 26,000 |
| Income tax................ | | | | 10,400 |
| Net income............... | | | | $ 15,600 |
| Assets of divisions........... | $50,000 | $80,000 | $35,000 | $165,000 |
| Unallocated corporate assets | | | | 35,000 |
| Total assets................ | | | | $200,000 |

The corporation has an estimated cost of capital of 10%.

*Required:*

a. Compute the rate of return on investment for each division and for the corporation in total. Similarly, compute the residual profit for each division and for the company as a whole.

b. Explain the relationship between the divisional measures and the related corporate measures computed in *a*.

12–10.  The electric motor division of the Krebs Corporation manufactures a heavy-duty motor that it sells at a competitive market price of $90 per unit. The standard cost sheet for one of these motors is as follows:

| | |
|---|---:|
| Direct materials.......................... | $24 |
| Direct labor.............................. | 20 |
| Variable manufacturing overhead............ | 8 |
| Fixed manufacturing overhead............... | 12 |
| | $64 |

The furnace division of the Krebs Corporation currently purchases this type of heavy-duty motor from the Himmelblau Electric Company. Because it purchases 50,000 motors annually, it obtains a quantity discount of $5 per unit off the market price of $90. Since the electric motor division is currently producing 200,000 of these motors annually and has the capacity to produce 300,000, management is considering whether it might be more advantageous to have the furnace division purchase the motor from the electric motor division instead of from an outside supplier.

*Required:*

a.  From the point of view of corporate management, what transfer price would be most useful in helping it decide where the furnace division should purchase its motors? Why?

b.  If both divisions are to be evaluated as profit centers and the electric motor division will sell the motor to the furnace division, what would be the most appropriate transfer price? Why?

c.  Would your answer to either *a* or *b* be changed if the electric motor division was already producing at its full capacity of 300,000 motors per year and selling the entire output at the market price of $90? Explain.

12–11.  The Jackson Athletic Equipment Company manufactures trampolines in two plants. The casting plant makes tubular aluminum frames, which are then shipped to the assembly plant, where nylon nets are attached to the frames.

The company uses absorption costing in charging costs to products. The materials cost per frame in the casting plant is $27. Two labor hours at a wage rate of $4.60 per hour are required for the production of each frame. The flexible budget for manufacturing overhead in the casting plant allows $1.35 per hour plus $750,000 per year. Normal volume is 300,000 labor hours per year. Trampoline frame production represents about 20% of normal production volume.

Comparable frames could be purchased from independent manufacturers for $42 each. Finished trampolines are sold for $85 apiece. Selling and shipping costs average $9 per unit sold.

*Required:*

a.  If both plants are treated as profit centers, at what transfer price should frames be transferred from the casting plant to the assembly plant? Explain.

b. What transfer price would be most helpful to corporate management in deciding whether to continue production of its own frames or to purchase them from an independent manufacturer? Explain.

12–12. The boiler division of Rosenkampff Industries, Inc., has redesigned several of its principal products. As a consequence, it will now need 80,000 highly sensitive thermal control units each year. The corporation's controls division produces such a unit and sells it at the current market price of $55. This unit requires three hours of labor time and has a unit materials cost of $15. The controls division has a productive capacity of 1,000,000 labor hours per year. It is currently operating at 70% of capacity. Total conversion costs in that division amount to $7 per labor hour plus $2,000,000 per year.

It is the corporation's policy to permit each of its divisions to operate essentially as though it were an independent company. Division managers are free to determine their own sources of supply and to set their own prices.

*Required:*

a. What is the most the boiler division could afford to pay for the thermal control unit?
b. What is the lowest price at which the controls division could afford to sell the thermal control unit?
c. Irrespective of your answers in *a* and *b*, assume that the two divisions have negotiated a one-year exclusive supply contract for the thermal control unit at a price of $50 per unit. Is this arrangement advantageous to each division? Is it advantageous to the corporation?
d. Assume now that the boiler division has entered into an exclusive supply contract for the thermal control unit with an independent vendor for one year at a unit price of $48. Is this arrangement advantageous to each division? Is it advantageous to the corporation?

# part three

ANALYSIS FOR
DECISION MAKING

chapter 13

# Cost-Volume-Profit Relationships

As THE title of Part Three suggests, the chapters in this part of the book will be concerned chiefly with the analysis and application of financial data in specific business decision-making situations. This must not be interpreted to mean that the cost concepts and the procedures discussed in the previous parts of the book have no impact upon business decisions. A budget, for example, is a decision in itself. Cost control, however effected, requires that specific decisions be made; these decisions must be based primarily upon accumulated cost data, including actual, planned, and standard costs. The same fundamental types of costs are involved in decision-making analysis, but here they are classified and analyzed in accordance with their relationships to the specific facts of the decision at hand. A great many business decisions affect directly the revenues, the costs, and/or the operating volume of the enterprise. Thus, at the outset, it will be useful to examine the relationships among these quantities and the implications thereof for the firm's profit. At this point, before proceeding, the reader may wish to review the discussion of cost behavior in relation to volume in Chapter 2. Much of the material in this and in the following chapters assumes a full understanding of the natures of variable and fixed costs, as well as of the practical difficulties involved in attempting to identify specific costs as variable or fixed.

Costs identified as variable are assumed to vary in direct proportion to volume, however volume may be measured. Fixed costs are assumed to be absolutely fixed over the relevant range of volume. So long as these basic assumptions are reasonably valid, the behavior of an enterprise's costs with respect to changes in the volume of its operations can be predicted and analyzed quite accurately. The existence of truly semivariable costs, however, clouds the cost-volume picture. The effective elimination of such costs by one of the methods described in connection with the development of flexible budgets[1] simplifies the analysis but also renders it that much less precise. Nevertheless, the usefulness of cost-volume analysis to management justifies this simplification and overrides the degree of imprecision created thereby.

Revenues, like variable costs, are assumed to vary in direct proportion to the volume of units sold. Where sales volume is expressed in terms of sales dollars, it is definitionally equal to revenues (excluding from consideration here such nonoperating revenues as interest, dividends, and rent). As both revenues and variable costs vary directly with volume, the net difference between them—variable profit—must also vary in proportion to volume. Thus, the effects of changes in operating volume may be analyzed simply in terms of a variable profit which varies, in total, in direct proportion to changes in volume (and, hence, is constant per unit of volume) and fixed costs which are constant in total regardless of volume fluctuations. Such analysis is quite simple, but there may be some fairly complicated problems underlying it. The most appropriate measure of volume is not always obvious. In a single product firm, volume may be measured quite readily in terms of units of product. In a multiproduct firm, however, it is more likely that sales volume will be measured in terms of dollar sales and production volume in terms of some measure of input (e.g., labor hours). Further, the volumes of sales and production are not necessarily equal. Thus, no one volume measure may be a suitable common denominator for total operations. This problem will be discussed further in a subsequent section. Finally, as observed in Chapter 2, the concepts of variable and fixed costs are simple and definite; the task of classifying actual costs as one or the other may be quite difficult, however. The discussions in this and the following chapter will assume that these practical problems have been resolved satisfactorily and will be concerned only with the basic analysis.

## BREAK-EVEN ANALYSIS

The most familiar form of cost-volume profit analysis is break-even analysis. In fact, many businessmen and accountants regard these two ideas as synonymous. More precisely, though, the latter is a specific type of the former. Break-even analysis involves the study of revenues and costs in relation to volume and, specifically, the determination of that

---

[1] Cf., Chapter 8.

volume at which the firm's revenues and expenses will be exactly equal. The *break-even point* may be defined as that level of operations at which total revenue is equal to total expense and, hence, net income is equal to zero.

### Determining the Break-Even Point

*In Units of Product.* For a single product firm, the break-even point may be computed very conveniently in terms of units of product. The break-even volume for a given period is the number of units of product that must be sold in order to create enough revenue just to cover all expenses, both variable and fixed. Each unit sold will cover its own variable costs and leave a remainder, the variable profit per unit, to contribute to covering fixed costs. When enough units have been sold so that the total variable profit is equal to the total fixed expenses, the break-even point has been reached. Thus, the break-even volume in units may be expressed algebraically as follows:

$$\text{Break-even volume} = \frac{\text{Total fixed costs}}{\text{Variable profit per unit}}$$

Assume that a small manufacturing company produces a single product. The selling price is $8 per unit and the variable costs are $5 per unit. These variable costs include all items that vary in proportion to volume—both manufacturing and nonmanufacturing costs. The company's annual fixed costs total $150,000. In order to break even, the company must sell 50,000 units of product annually. This volume is computed as follows:

$$\text{Break-even volume} = \frac{\$150,000}{\$3} = 50,000 \text{ units}$$

That the company's net income is equal to zero at a volume of 50,000 units may be demonstrated quite easily.

| | |
|---|---:|
| Revenues (50,000 units @ $8) | $400,000 |
| Variable costs (50,000 units @ $5) | 250,000 |
| Variable profit | $150,000 |
| Fixed costs | 150,000 |
| Net income | $      0 |

*In Dollar Sales Volume.* Single product companies play a relatively small role in our modern industrial society, and most multiproduct firms are not able to measure volume in terms of any common unit of product. Hence, multiproduct firms typically express sales volume in terms of total dollar sales. The basic requirement of the break-even point is unchanged, however; total revenue must just cover total expense. In this situation, variable costs and variable profits are expressed as amounts per dollar of sales or, more simply, as percentages of sales. The break-even volume is then computed by equating total variable profit to total fixed costs, as before. Since the variable profit is a known ratio, or percentage, of total sales revenue, the sales volume necessary to generate sufficient variable profit just to cover fixed costs may be computed thus:

$$\text{Break-even volume} = \frac{\text{Total fixed costs}}{\text{Variable profit ratio}}$$

Assume that a medium-sized multiproduct manufacturing corporation compiles the following budgeted operating data:

| | |
|---|---:|
| Budgeted sales for one year | $20,000,000 |
| Budgeted variable costs for one year | 12,000,000 |
| Budgeted fixed costs for one year | 6,000,000 |

The variable costs can be seen to be equal to 60% of sales; hence, the variable profit ratio is 40% of sales. The break-even volume is then computed as follows:

$$\text{Break-even volume} = \frac{\$6,000,000}{.40} = \$15,000,000$$

Proof of this break-even computation is as follows:

| | |
|---|---:|
| Revenues | $15,000,000 |
| Variable costs (60% of $15,000,000) | 9,000,000 |
| Variable profit (40% of $15,000,000) | $ 6,000,000 |
| Fixed costs | 6,000,000 |
| Net income | $ 0 |

**As a Percentage of Full Capacity.** Many business managers are accustomed to thinking of their firm's operations in terms of percentages of full productive capacity. Full capacity is usually defined as the greatest volume presently attainable, given the firm's production facilities and its operating policies. This concept is sometimes termed *practical capacity*. It is not necessarily the maximum possible volume. Unusual amounts of overtime by both men and machines may stretch a firm's capacity considerably, but ordinarily only for fairly short periods of time. Whatever volume is selected as full capacity, it is established as 100% of capacity. While the break-even point as a percentage of full capacity cannot be determined by direct computation, it may easily be determined indirectly. If the operating volume at full capacity is known in terms of units or dollar sales and the break-even point has been determined in comparable terms, the latter may be stated as a percentage of the former very simply. In the illustration of the single product company above, assume that full capacity is 100,000 units of product. The break-even point, 50,000 units, is reached at 50% of capacity. If full capacity for the multiproduct corporation illustrated in the preceding paragraph is set at an annual sales volume of $25,000,000 and the break-even sales volume is $15,000,000, the break-even point is achieved at 60% of full capacity.

## Break-Even Graphs

Break-even analysis is very commonly presented in graphic form. Break-even graphs can depict the profit-volume position of the firm clearly and simply. The traditional break-even graph is illustrated in Figure 13–1. This is a graphic depiction of the break-even point com-

**FIGURE 13–1**

**Break-Even Graph**

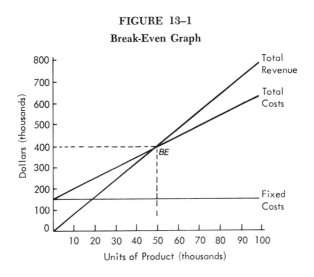

puted in units of product for the single product firm in the preceding section. Units of product are measured on the horizontal axis, and dollars (both revenues and costs) on the vertical axis. Fixed costs are shown as a constant amount, $150,000, at all levels of operation. Variable costs are then plotted over and above total fixed costs. The resultant line is the total cost line, including both variable and fixed costs. There is no variable cost line in the graph; variable costs are depicted as the vertical distance between the fixed cost and the total cost lines. The total cost at any point is the sum of the $150,000 fixed costs plus the $5 variable cost per unit of product multiplied by the number of units sold at that point. Total revenue at any point is the product of the unit price of $8 and the number of units sold. The upper limits of the graph are determined on the basis of the firm's full capacity, 100,000 units of product in this illustration. The break-even point (*BE*) occurs at the intersection of the total revenue and total cost lines. Dropping a perpendicular from the point *BE* to the horizontal axis shows the break-even point in units of product. Dropping a perpendicular from *BE* to the vertical axis shows the break-even point in dollar sales volume. Below (to the left of) point *BE*, total costs are higher than total revenue and operations are unprofitable. Above (to the right of) *BE*, total revenue exceeds total costs and operations are profitable. The amount of the profit or loss at any volume is simply the vertical distance between the total revenue and total cost lines. Thus, given budgeted sales volume, the budgeted profit may be read directly from the graph. The excess of budgeted volume over the break-even volume is commonly referred to as the *margin of safety*. If budgeted volume here were 80,000 units of product, the margin of safety would be 30,000 units.

Where the break-even point is measured in terms of dollar sales volume rather than in units, the break-even graph remains basically the same as in Figure 13–1. The only difference is that volume on the horizontal axis is measured in sales dollars. In that case, a perpendicular from the point *BE* to either axis would show the break-even dollar sales volume. The same type of graph could depict the break-even situation in relation to full capacity; in this case, the horizontal axis would measure percentages of capacity. Thus, except for the quantity on the horizontal axis, the break-even graph is the same regardless of the concept of volume used.

***Profit-Volume Graph.*** A popular variation on the traditional break-even graph is the profit-volume graph. 'This is a plot of an enterprise's profit in relation to volume. It is illustrated in Figure 13–2, using the data for the multiproduct manufacturing corporation whose break-even point was computed in dollar sales volume earlier. Total profit or loss is measured on the vertical axis—profit above the horizontal axis and loss below it. Volume is measured on the horizontal axis, which is drawn at the point of zero profit (i.e., the break-even point). Volume may be expressed in whatever terms desired by management. Here, it is stated in terms of dollar sales volume. The maximum loss, which occurs at a volume of zero, is simply the total fixed costs of the enterprise. As volume increases, a proportionate variable profit appears and increases with it. Total profit, however, is negative until the break-even point is reached. The operating loss declines and ultimately disappears at that volume at which the total variable profit is equal to total fixed costs— the break-even volume. Beyond this point, there is a positive net income. On this graph, the break-even point is measured on the horizontal axis at the point where that axis is intersected by the profit line.

In Figure 13–2, the total fixed costs and, hence, the maximum loss are equal to $6,000,000. The variable profit rate is 40% of sales. As already demonstrated, this company breaks even at a sales volume of $15,000,-

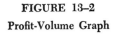

FIGURE 13–2

Profit-Volume Graph

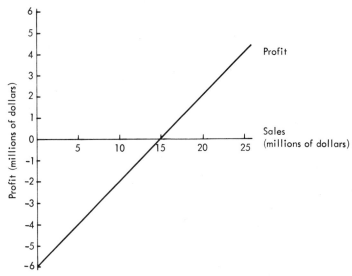

000. The graph shows the amount of profit or loss that may be expected at any level of operations. At full capacity, for example, the budgeted profit would be $4,000,000. This profit may be read from the profit-volume graph or computed by applying the variable profit rate (40%) to sales at full capacity ($25,000,000) and subtracting the fixed costs ($6,000,000).

## Divisional Break-Even Analysis

The break-even point for a division of a company, like the profit of a division, is computed from revenues and costs directly traceable to that division. Since costs common to two or more divisions would thus be excluded from all divisions' break-even computations, the total of all divisions' break-even volumes would not be equal to the break-even volume of the company. Further, if a division were evaluated as a constructive profit center,[2] the company's break-even volume would not even include the "revenues" used in that division's break-even analysis. In Chapter 12, we used an illustration of a corporate computer center that incurred monthly fixed costs of $20,000 plus variable costs of $150 per hour of processing time. The same computer service could alternatively be purchased from an independent service bureau at a price of $250 per

---

[2] Cf. Chapter 12.

hour. This alternative processing cost was used as the "revenue" of the computer center. Hence, the center's variable profit is equal to $100 per hour of processing time ($250 "revenue" minus $150 variable cost per hour). The computer center would break even when the costs avoided by not having data processing done by an outside service bureau were exactly equal to the internal costs of operating the center. The divisional break-even volume would be computed in the usual way, as follows:

$$\text{Break-even volume} = \frac{\text{Total fixed costs}}{\text{Variable profit per hour}} = \frac{\$20,000}{\$100} = 200 \text{ hours}$$

This is the same type of analysis used for a single product company, for the computer center's volume is expressed by a single measure, hours of processing time. From this break-even analysis, management may observe that it is more profitable for the company to operate its own computer center as long as monthly processing volume exceeds 200 hours. Below that volume, it would be cheaper to have the work done outside.

## Assumptions Underlying Break-Even Analysis

The validity of the break-even analysis explained and illustrated above is based upon several assumptions. Effective use of break-even analysis demands an appreciation of the significance of each of these assumptions.

*Uniform Prices.*   The assumption that all financial data are comparable underlies all of accounting, not merely break-even analysis. If dollar amounts are to be compared in any meaningful way, the dollars involved should have the same real value (i.e., the same purchasing power). In break-even analysis, the dollars of revenue and the dollars of cost should be uniform in terms of their purchasing powers. Dollars of depreciation on assets acquired in past periods should be adjusted to conform to the current price level before a break-even point is determined. Unfortunately, price-level adjustments are only infrequently made in present business practice. Hence, most break-even computations violate the uniform price assumption without even specifically recognizing it.

*Completely Predictable Cost Behavior.*   As is evident in both the formulas and the graphs in the preceding sections, conventional break-even analysis presumes that all of an enterprise's costs are either perfectly variable or absolutely fixed over all ranges of operating volume. Total variable cost is assumed to be a positive linear function of volume, and total fixed cost is assumed to be wholly unaffected by volume. As a practical matter, it is not necessary that these assumptions be valid over all ranges of volume. If they are basically true over the relevant range of volume, that range within which the firm is most likely to operate, break-even analysis is valid. Even within the relevant range of volume, it is probable that there will be some degree of imprecision in the assumptions regarding cost-volume relationships. Nevertheless, managers have found the analysis useful despite its imprecision.

***Perfectly Variable Revenue.*** A third assumption, related to the second, is that an enterprise's total revenue is perfectly variable with its physical volume. Like variable cost, revenue is assumed to be a positive linear function of volume. For some firms, this assumption may be completely valid; selling prices per unit may be the same at all volumes. For others, however, it is not valid. The same products may be sold to large customers at lower prices than to small customers. Price reductions may be necessary in order to attain high levels of sales volume. Once again, however, the assumption is generally useful and not so unrealistic as to impair the analysis seriously.

***Effect of Imperfect Cost or Revenue Behavior.*** If revenue and/or variable costs are not perfectly variable with physical volume—that is, if they are nonlinear functions of volume—and/or if fixed costs are not absolutely fixed, the revenue and/or cost lines in the break-even graph (Figure 13–1) will not be straight. If one or more of these lines is curved or kinked, it is possible that the total revenue and total cost lines will intersect at two or more points. Such a situation would imply multiple break-even points. These might be caused by a nonlinear revenue function, a nonlinear variable cost function, a fixed cost line that is other than perfectly horizontal, or by any combination of these circumstances. Figure 13–3 illustrates a graph of multiple break-even points in which each of the three possible circumstances is present. (Notice the similarity between the cost lines in this exhibit and those in Figure 2–2 in Chapter 2.)

The existence of multiple break-even points in Figure 13–3 is caused by three factors. First, total revenue is not a perfectly linear function of volume. At 90% of capacity, the revenue line is kinked. This reflects the fact that the average net selling price is expected to decrease beyond this point, presumably because of quantity discounts to large purchasers and price reductions offered to induce new customers to purchase from the company. In reality, these price discounts and reductions would more likely occur gradually as volume increases. Thus, the total revenue curve might be curved gradually rather than kinked abruptly. The second factor at work in the illustration is the change in the rate of variable costs. At 30% of capacity, the variable cost rate decreases. This decrease might be caused by materials price reductions attributable to purchasing in large quantities. Also, labor costs may be reduced by more efficient utilization of the larger work force required to handle an increasing volume. As with the price reductions, these cost decreases might well

FIGURE 13–3

Illustration of Multiple Break-Even Points

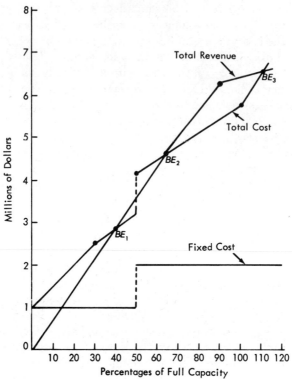

occur in stages. If so, the total cost curve would be curved, not kinked. At 100% of capacity, the variable cost rate increases because of diseconomies of operating above the preferred rate of capacity. In other words, plant capacity is used more intensively and less efficiently above 100%. The third factor causing multiple break-even points is an increase in fixed costs in a single step at 50% of capacity. This may reflect the use and maintenance of additional machinery and an increase in the supervisory staff. As a consequence, both the fixed cost line and the total cost line are discontinuous at that point. Both are pushed upward by the amount of the increase in fixed costs.

As a result of these three circumstances and their relationships to each other, there are three break-even points. The first is reached, much as in Figure 13–1, when total revenue is sufficient to cover costs; this is at point $BE_1$. Above $BE_1$, operations are profitable until the firm reaches the volume at which the fixed costs are increased. Between that point and $BE_2$, operations are again unprofitable. Between $BE_2$ and $BE_3$, profits are once more realized. Finally, beyond $BE_3$, operations are unprofitable because of a decline in revenue per unit of volume and an increase in unit variable cost. Such a graph would be enormously useful to management if cost behavior could be budgeted so precisely. Even apart from the existence of multiple break-even points, knowledge of alterations in cost behavior at critical levels of volume would be extremely useful. As a practical matter, business managers have found that break-even analysis is more feasible and still useful where the conventional assumptions about cost and revenue relationships to volume are employed. If the relevant range of volume in Figure 13–3 were between 50% and 90% of full capacity, the conventional break-even assumptions would be entirely valid.

The profit-volume graph (Figure 13–2) would be affected in much the same way as the break-even graph by nonlinear revenue and cost functions. The profit line would not be straight; it might be discontinuous; and it might intersect the horizontal axis at two or more points.

***Stable Product Mix.*** A fourth assumption underlying break-even analysis relates only to multiproduct firms. As such firms are dominant in our economy, however, this assumption is generally applicable. We have seen that, for a multiproduct firm, the break-even point is determined by dividing total fixed costs by an average ratio of variable profit to sales. If each product has the same variable profit ratio, the break-even point is unaffected by changes in the product mix. However, if, as is more likely, different products have different variable profit ratios, a shift in the product mix can cause a shift in the break-even point.

| | | | | | | | |
|---|---|---|---|---|---|---|---|
| **TABLE 13–1** | | | | **TABLE 13–2** | | | |
| Product | Budgeted Sales (in $000) | Variable Profit (in $000) | Variable Profit Ratio | Product | Actual Sales (in $000) | Variable Profit (in $000) | Variable Profit Ratio |
| X.... | $ 600 | $120 | 20% | X.... | $1,000 | $200 | 20% |
| Y.... | 900 | 315 | 35 | Y.... | 200 | 70 | 35 |
| Z.... | 500 | 125 | 25 | Z.... | 800 | 200 | 25 |
| | $2,000 | $560 | | | $2,000 | $470 | |

This is illustrated in the following example: A manufacturing corporation produces and sells three products; its annual fixed costs total $420,000. Budgeted sales and variable profits, by products, are shown in Table 13–1. The average variable profit ratio in this budget is 28% ($560,000 ÷ $2,000,000). The break-even sales volume, then, is $1,500,-000 ($420,000 ÷ .28). This break-even point is based upon a weighted average variable profit ratio computed from the budgeted product mix.

If the product mix is altered, the average variable profit ratio and the break-even point may be changed also. Assume, for example, that the actual sales and variable profit data for the budget period turn out to be as shown in Table 13–2. The average variable profit is now 23.5% ($470,000 ÷ $2,000,000), and the break-even volume is $1,787,235 ($420,000 ÷ .235). The raising of the break-even point is caused by a shift in the product mix, with no change whatever in total sales volume. In comparison with the budget, there has been an increase in the sales of products with low variable profit ratios and a decrease in the sales of the product with the high ratio. The impact of this change in product mix on income before taxes is substantial. Budgeted income was $140,-000; actual income is $50,000.

***Equality of Sales Volume and Production Volume.***  A final assumption underlying conventional break-even analysis is that the volume of sales and the volume of production are equal. Everything produced is sold; there is no significant change in the level of inventory of goods on hand. This assumption is necessary because the analysis matches total costs and total revenues for the period and relates them jointly to a single measure of volume. It is, of course, very possible that some of the costs of one period will be incurred in the production of goods to be sold in a subsequent period. This is quite a normal business occurrence, but it tends to complicate the calculation of a break-even point for one period. Where this assumption is clearly invalid (i.e., where sales and production volumes are significantly different), the break-even point may still be computed as shown above if the sales value of production is substituted for current revenue in the computation. In effect, this alternative assumes that goods produced for inventory will eventually be sold at the current selling price.

## Utility of Break-Even Analysis

Probably the best summary evaluation of break-even analysis is to say that it is a useful tool of managerial planning and decision making but not a sharp tool. Because of the several restrictive assumptions underlying the analysis, the computation of a break-even volume should be regarded as an approximation rather than as a precise measurement. Nevertheless, even if the analysis yields only an approximate break-even operating volume, this estimate is much superior to no such information at all. The break-even point is of special interest to management, for it identifies that level of operations below which the objective of profit would be missed altogether. A corollary of the profit motive is the desire to avoid losses. Some managers may feel a stronger desire to avoid a loss of a given amount than to obtain a profit of the same amount. If management places a proportionately higher value upon a situation that involves some profit (and avoids any loss) than upon one that involves an increase in an existing level of profit, then the break-even point represents the operating volume at which management's scale of values (or utility function) changes. As such, it is of unique significance.

Even if the break-even point is not considered uniquely useful, the analysis underlying it may be. Often management is more interested in the general pattern of the relationships among volume, costs, and profit than in the break-even point itself. The popularity of the profit-volume graph (Figure 13–2) attests to this interest, for that graph focuses attention upon expected profits at all levels of operations.

## ANALYSIS OF CHANGES IN PRICES, COSTS, AND VOLUME

One of the most useful and simplest applications of cost-volume-profit relationships is the analysis of changes in one or more of the basic elements—revenue, cost, and volume. This type of analysis can be employed to answer questions such as the following: What would be the impact upon profits of a price increase if that increase caused volume to decline? Can profits be improved by increasing the advertising budget and thereby boosting volume? Can prices be raised to offset the impact on profits of a wage increase? What sales volume must be achieved in order to attain some target profit? The analysis of problems of these types will be illustrated in the following paragraphs.

### Effect of Price Increase

If a price increase has no effect upon volume, the effect upon profit will be very simple. Profit before taxes will rise by the amount of the price increase multiplied by the present volume. Net income after taxes will be increased by the before-tax profit rise multipled by the complement of the applicable income tax rate (i.e., 100% minus the tax rate). As a matter of fact, however, it is likely that volume will decline in response to a price increase. The extent of the volume decline depends upon the degree of competition in the market and upon the price elasticity of demand for the product (i.e., the extent to which buyers' demand for it is influenced by its price). Assume that a manufacturer is contemplating a 5% price increase on all of its products in 1977. Its sales in 1976 totaled $6,000,000 and its variable costs, $4,800,000. The 5% price increase would raise total revenue by $300,000. However, the company expects that the sales volume of all products will be 8% lower in 1977 because of the higher prices. Since volume affects both revenue and variable costs proportionately, the impact of the volume reduction may be computed directly in terms of the variable profit. Without a change in volume, variable profit in 1977 would be $1,500,000 ($6,300,000 − $4,800,000). The volume decline, however, means that the variable profit will be 8% lower than this amount, or 92% of it. Thus, the budgeted variable profit would be $1,380,000. This is still better than the 1976 variable profit of $1,200,000. If the applicable income tax rate is 40%, the after-tax increase in profit is $108,000 (60% of $180,000, the increase in variable profit). The company's fixed costs may be ignored in this analysis, for they will be unaffected by the proposed change.[3]

## Effect of Increase in Fixed Costs

An increase in the total annual fixed costs of an enterprise may be caused either by external circumstances (e.g., an increase in property taxes) or by a managerial decision (e.g., an increase in executives' salaries). In either event, the effect is to raise the break-even point of the firm, assuming no change in the variable profit. Any increase in price or decrease in variable costs would tend to offset this effect, for either would increase the variable profit ratio. Of course, an increase in fixed costs might cause an increase in volume; while not affecting the variable profit ratio, this could increase the total variable profit. For example, assume that a small company producing and selling a single product sold 25,000 units during 1976 at a price of $80. Variable costs per unit are $60 and fixed costs total $400,000, including $50,000 of advertising costs. The company's management is dissatisfied with the present rate of income on sales volume. The market research firm engaged to study the problem suggests that a 20% increase in the advertising budget would boost sales volume by 6%. Would such a move be profitable? The question can be restated as follows: Will the additional variable profit generated by the higher volume cover the increase in fixed costs? The variable profit of $20 per unit would be obtained on an additional 1,500 units (6% of 25,000); in total, then, variable profit would be increased by $30,000. This would be three times the amount of the increase in fixed advertising

---

[3] It may be tempting to try a shortcut in working with problems of this type. If there is to be a 5% price increase and an 8% volume decrease, one might reason, won't the net effect be a 3% decrease in total revenue? Unhappily, the answer is, "No!" The base of the 5% price increase is not the same as the base of the 8% volume decrease. Hence, there is no net 3% change. First, the 5% price increase is applied to the prior year's sales of $6,000,000. This produces a tentative sales revenue of $6,300,000. The 8% volume decrease is then applied to this new figure, not to the original $6,000,000. Thus, the volume decrease will reduce sales by $504,000 (8% of $6,300,000). Total sales revenue, then, will be $5,796,000 ($6,300,000 − $504,000). Exactly the same result would be obtained if the 8% volume decrease were first applied to the original $6,000,000 sales and the 5% price increase were then applied to the amount so computed. Applying a net 3% reduction to the original $6,000,000 would indicate that sales, after both price and volume changes, should be $5,820,000. And this is not correct.

cost—$10,000 (20% of $50,000). After income tax at a rate of 40%, net profit would be greater than in 1976 by $12,000 (60% of $20,000).

This profit-volume analysis must be employed carefully; it is not always appropriate. A very different type of situation is presented by the firm that finds it is unable to meet the demand for its products because of limited production facilities. It is considering doubling its productive capacity by building a new plant. Such a move would increase annual fixed costs by $7,500,000. Present sales volume is $72,000,000 annually; annual variable costs total $48,000,000. It is expected that the additional capacity would result in a 25% increase in sales volume during the first year of operations in the new plant. This would mean a 25% increase in the current variable profit, or an increase of $6,000,000. Obviously, this additional profit does not justify a $7,500,000 increase in fixed costs. But, just as obviously, it is not valid to seek to justify an increase in productive capacity in terms of one year's sales increase alone. The new plant will last for many years, and it must be justified or defeated in light of the expected impact upon variable profit over all of those years. For reasons to be explained in Chapter 16, simple profit-volume analysis is inadequate for an evaluation of effects that will occur over a period of several years. Unlike the increase in the advertising budget, the construction of a new plant commits the enterprise's resources to a specific use for a long period of time. Its profitability must be evaluated by means of long-term investment analysis, not by any short-run profit measurement.

## Effect of Wage and Price Increases

A great deal has been written in recent years about the so-called wage-price spiral, in which wage increases trigger price increases which, in turn, cause further wage and price rises ad infinitum. If given credence at all, this spiral is usually thought of as a phenomenon of the economy as a whole. For the individual firm, the wage-price problem is unlikely to be so clear or so nearly automatic. A firm may wish to raise prices to offset the decline in profits attendant upon a wage increase. As we have already observed, however, a price increase may result in a volume decline, which tends to reduce profits also. As an example, assume that a firm had prepared a budgeted income statement in the variable costing format, as shown in the first Column of Table 13–3. Shortly after the preparation of this budget, the company learns that a wage and salary increase will cause variable costs to increase by 4% and fixed costs to increase by 2%. With no change in price or in volume, this cost increase would reduce income before tax by $1,500, as shown in the second column of Table 13–3. A 3% price increase, with no volume reduction, would just offset the cost increase and restore budgeted profit to the original $5,000.

**TABLE 13–3**

Effects of Cost, Price, and Volume Changes

|  | Original Budget | Cost Increase Only | Cost and Price Increase | Cost and Price Increase Plus Volume Decrease |
|---|---|---|---|---|
| Sales......................... | $50,000 | $50,000 | $51,500 | $49,955 |
| Variable costs................. | 30,000 | 31,200 | 31,200 | 30,264 |
| Variable profit............... | $20,000 | $18,800 | $20,300 | $19,691 |
| Fixed costs................... | 15,000 | 15,300 | 15,300 | 15,300 |
| Income before tax............ | $ 5,000 | $ 3,500 | $ 5,000 | $ 4,391 |

This effect is shown in the third column of Table 13–3. However, if the firm's competitors did not experience comparable wage and salary increases and, hence, did not plan to raise their prices, a price increase by this firm would probably cause a reduction in its sales volume. If volume decreased by 3% as a consequence of the 3% price increase, profit would again be less than in the original budget—although more than it would be without the price increase. This result is shown in the last column of Table 13–3. Of course, a larger price increase is likely to cause a greater volume decline. Given any set of assumptions, management can easily assess the impact of cost, price, and volume changes on budgeted profits.

## Volume Needed to Attain Target Profit

The basic mechanics of break-even analysis may be adapted very easily to determine the operating volume necessary for a firm to attain a specific target profit. Assume, for example, that a corporation seeks a minimum rate of return on invested capital of 8% after taxes. For a given budget period, this objective requires a net income of $2,400,000. The company's variable costs average 60% of selling prices; fixed costs total $18,000,000 per year; and the applicable income tax rate is 40%. The volume here must be sufficient to produce a total variable profit that will cover fixed costs plus the target profit. Since fixed costs are a before-tax quantity, the profit employed in the analysis must also be measured before taxes. The target profit before taxes here is $4,000,000 ($2,400,000 ÷ .60). Thus, sales volume must be sufficient so that 40% of it—the variable profit—will be equal to $22,000,000, the sum of the fixed costs and the target profit before tax. This volume is computed thus:

$$\text{Target volume} = \frac{\$22,000,000}{.40} = \$55,000,000$$

This and the other analyses illustrated in the foregoing paragraphs are but examples of the types of situations and problems that may be analyzed in terms of the relationships among revenue, cost, and volume.

## PROFIT VARIANCE ANALYSIS

Another very useful application of the relationships among revenues, costs, and volume is the analysis of the difference between budgeted and actual profits for a period. Profit is affected by at least three basic factors: sales volume, selling prices, and costs. In addition, in a multiproduct company, if not all products are equally profitable, net profit is affected by the mix of products sold. Thus, the net difference between budgeted and actual profits may be broken down into as many as four component differences, or variances: sales volume, selling price, cost, and sales mix variances. Such detailed analysis of the profit variance is far more useful to management than the net variance alone. Detailed profit variance analysis is illustrated below for three situations: (1) a single product firm, (2) a multiproduct firm for which only aggregate data are available, and (3) a multiproduct firm for which detailed data by products are available.

### Single Product Firm

Profit variance analysis is simplest in a single product firm, for there is only one selling price, one set of costs, and a unitary measure of sales volume. The following budgeted and actual data for a given period are used to illustrate this analysis:

| | | |
|---|---:|---:|
| Budget data: | | |
| Sales (100,000 units @ $6)............................ | | $600,000 |
| Variable costs (100,000 units @ $3.50).............. | $350,000 | |
| Fixed costs....................................... | 180,000 | 530,000 |
| Profit before tax................................. | | $ 70,000 |
| Actual data: | | |
| Sales (110,000 units @ $5.80)...................... | | $638,000 |
| Variable costs (110,000 units @ $3.60).............. | $396,000 | |
| Fixed costs....................................... | 190,000 | 586,000 |
| Profit before tax................................. | | $ 52,000 |
| Net profit variance............................... | | $(18,000) |

This net unfavorable profit variance can be broken down into three components: a sales volume variance, a selling price variance, and a cost (spending) variance.

Inasmuch as both sales revenue and variable costs are direct functions of sales volume, the sales volume variance can be computed in a single step by using the variable profit, the difference between sales revenue and variable costs. The sales volume variance is calculated by multiplying the change in volume by the budgeted variable profit per unit of product. This is the amount by which profit would have varied from the budget if nothing but sales volume had changed. For our illustration:

$$\text{Sales volume variance} = 10{,}000 \text{ units} \times (\$6 - \$3.50) = \$25{,}000$$

Since actual sales volume was greater than budgeted, this variance is favorable; it tends to increase profit.

The selling price variance is simply the change in unit price multiplied by the actual sales volume, thus:

$$\text{Selling price variance} = 110{,}000 \text{ units} \times (\$6 - \$5.80) = \$(22{,}000)$$

As the actual price was lower than budgeted, this variance is unfavorable; it tends to reduce profit. Some accountants prefer to show the selling price variance as the change in price multiplied by the budgeted sales volume rather than the actual volume. If this approach is taken, there is then another variance, a joint price-volume variance, that is computed by multiplying the change in price by the change in volume. Technically, this refinement is correct. However, the joint variance has no unique cause; hence, it adds nothing to management's understanding of the reasons for the profit variance. The approach presented here does not identify this joint variance; it is simply included as part of the selling price variance.

The cost variance is simply the familiar spending variance from a flexible budget and is computed exactly as shown in Chapters 8 and 10.

| | | |
|---|---:|---:|
| Actual costs: | | |
| Variable...................................... | $396,000 | |
| Fixed......................................... | 190,000 | $586,000 |
| Budgeted costs at actual sales volume: | | |
| Variable (110,000 units @ $3.50)................... | $385,000 | |
| Fixed......................................... | 180,000 | 565,000 |
| Spending variance............................... | | $ (21,000) |

Since actual costs exceed budget allowances, this variance is unfavorable.

The algebraic sum of the three component variances is equal to the net profit variance computed originally.

| | |
|---|---:|
| Sales volume variance............................. | $ 25,000 |
| Selling price variance............................. | (22,000) |
| Spending variance................................ | (21,000) |
| Net profit variance................................ | $(18,000) |

## Multiproduct Firm with Aggregate Data Only

In a multiproduct firm with a large number of products, it is easiest to perform the profit variance analysis with aggregate data only. In this case, the net variance can be resolved into the same three variances described above for a single product firm. No sales mix variance can be determined. If all products have approximately the same variable profit ratio, this method is entirely satisfactory; for there would be no significant sales mix variance anyway. This method of profit variance analysis is illustrated by use of the following budgeted and actual data:

|  | Budget | Actual |
|---|---|---|
| Sales.............................. | $400,000 | $462,000 |
| Variable costs...................... | $240,000 | $270,000 |
| Fixed costs......................... | 100,000 | 107,000 |
|  | $340,000 | $377,000 |
| Profit before tax................... | $ 60,000 | $ 85,000 |

In addition, management knows that selling prices were increased by an average of 5 percent during the period under review. With this information, we can determine the actual sales volume at the budgeted prices (i.e., what actual sales would have been in the absence of a price increase). This amount is $440,000 ($462,000 ÷ 105%). Now the sales volume variance is equal to the budgeted variable profit ratio multiplied by the difference between this actual sales volume at budgeted prices and the original budgeted sales. Since variable costs are 60 percent of sales in the budget ($240,000 ÷ $400,000), the variable profit ratio is 40 percent. The sales volume variance is then computed as follows:

Sales volume variance = 40% × ($440,000 − $400,000) = $16,000

Since volume is greater than budgeted, this variance is favorable.

The selling price variance is the difference between the actual sales and the computed actual sales volume at the budgeted prices.

Selling price variance = $462,000 − $440,000 = $22,000

We already knew that this variance was favorable, because we knew that prices had increased during the period.

The spending variance is computed in the usual way.

| Actual costs: | | |
|---|---|---|
| Variable....................................... | $270,000 | |
| Fixed......................................... | 107,000 | $377,000 |
| Budgeted costs at actual sales volume: | | |
| Variable (60% × $440,000)...................... | $264,000 | |
| Fixed......................................... | 100,000 | 364,000 |
| Spending variance (unfavorable)................... | | $(13,000) |

Note that budgeted variable costs are based upon the actual volume at the budgeted prices rather than on the actual sales of the period. This is necessary because the budgeted variable cost rate of 60 percent of sales was derived before the 5 percent price increase occurred.

The three component variances, of course, sum algebraically to the net profit variance identified at the outset.

| | |
|---|---:|
| Sales volume variance | $ 16,000 |
| Selling price variance | 22,000 |
| Spending variance | (13,000) |
| Net profit variance ($85,000 − $60,000) | $ 25,000 |

## Multiproduct Firm with Data by Products

If unit price and cost data are available for each product in a multi-product firm, it is possible to identify a fourth component of the profit variance. This is the sales mix variance, the effect on profit of selling a different proportionate mix of products than had been budgeted. This variance arises when different products have different variable profits. If there is a large number of products, this analysis may become unduly cumbersome. However, it may be possible to group products into a smaller number of classes, each of which has a uniform variable profit ratio. Then essentially the same analysis as is illustrated below can be performed by product classes. This illustration is based on the following data:

| | | |
|---|---:|---:|
| Budget data: | | |
| Sales—Product A (20,000 units @ $8) | $160,000 | |
| Product B (30,000 units @ $5) | 150,000 | |
| Product C (10,000 units @ $12) | 120,000 | $430,000 |
| Variable costs—Product A (20,000 units @ $5) | $100,000 | |
| Product B (30,000 units @ $3.50) | 105,000 | |
| Product C (10,000 units @ $10) | 100,000 | 305,000 |
| Variable profit | | $125,000 |
| Fixed costs | | 75,000 |
| Profit before tax | | $ 50,000 |
| Actual data: | | |
| Sales—Product A (28,000 units @ $7.50) | $210,000 | |
| Product B (32,000 units @ $5.25) | 168,000 | |
| Product C (6,000 units @ $12.50) | 75,000 | $453,000 |
| Variable costs—Product A (28,000 units @ $4.85) | $135,800 | |
| Product B (32,000 units @ $3.75) | 120,000 | |
| Product C (6,000 units @ $10.20) | 61,200 | 317,000 |
| Variable profit | | $136,000 |
| Fixed costs | | 72,000 |
| Profit before tax | | $ 64,000 |
| Net profit variance | | $ 14,000 |

In this illustration, physical sales volume differed from the budget in two ways. The total aggregate number of units sold was 66,000 instead of 60,000. Moreover, the mix of the three products was not proportionate to the budgeted mix. Sales of Product A increased by more than the aggregate 10 percent increase in volume. Sales of Product B increased by less than 10 percent. And sales of Product C decreased. Each of these two different types of changes in volume is reflected in a separate variance. In order to compute these variances, we need to know two additional measures of variable profit. First, we need the variable profit that would have been attained if volume had increased by 6,000 and the sales mix had remained in the same proportion as budgeted (i.e., if the sales of each product had increased by 10 percent) and the budgeted prices and variable costs had been maintained.

| | | |
|---|---|---:|
| Product A: | 22,000 units × ($8 − $5) | $ 66,000 |
| Product B: | 33,000 units × ($5 − $3.50) | 49,500 |
| Product C: | 11,000 units × ($12 − $10) | 22,000 |
| Total variable profit | | $137,500 |

Next, we need the variable profit that would have occurred at the actual sales volume and the actual mix but with the budgeted prices and variable costs.

| | | |
|---|---|---:|
| Product A: | 28,000 units × ($8 − $5) | $ 84,000 |
| Product B: | 32,000 units × ($5 − $3.50) | 48,000 |
| Product C: | 6,000 units × ($12 − $10) | 12,000 |
| Total variable profit | | $144,000 |

Now the sales volume variance is the difference between the budgeted variable profit for the actual sales volume and the budgeted sales mix and the variable profit that was budgeted originally.

$$\text{Sales volume variance} = \$137{,}500 - \$125{,}000 = \$12{,}500$$

This variance is favorable because total sales volume rose. Since aggregate volume rose by 10 percent, the variance is equal to 10 percent of the original budgeted variable profit.

The sales mix variance is the difference between the budgeted variable profit for the actual volume and the actual sales mix and the budgeted variable profit for the actual volume and the budgeted sales mix, thus:

$$\text{Sales mix variance} = \$144{,}000 - \$137{,}500 = \$6{,}500$$

This variance is favorable because the shift in the sales mix was toward Product A, which has the highest variable profit per unit.

The selling price variance is computed exactly as in the single product firm illustration, except that it consists of three price differentials.

| | | |
|---|---|---:|
| Product A: | 28,000 units × ($8 − $7.50) | $(14,000) |
| Product B: | 32,000 units × ($5 − $5.25) | 8,000 |
| Product C: | 6,000 units × ($12 − $12.50) | 3,000 |
| Net selling price variance | | $( 3,000) |

The spending variance is calculated again in the customary manner.

| | | |
|---|---:|---:|
| Actual costs: | | |
| Variable...................................... | $317,000 | |
| Fixed......................................... | 72,000 | $389,000 |
| Budgeted costs at actual sales volume: | | |
| Variable—Product A (28,000 units @ $5)........... | $140,000 | |
| Product B (32,000 units @ $3.50)........ | 112,000 | |
| Product C (6,000 units @ $10)........... | 60,000 | |
| | $312,000 | |
| Fixed........................................ | 75,000 | 387,000 |
| Spending variance............................... | | $( 2,000) |

Once again, the four component variances may be summed to the net profit variance that was observed initially.

| | |
|---|---:|
| Sales volume variance................................... | $12,500 |
| Sales mix variance..................................... | 6,500 |
| Selling price variance................................. | (3,000) |
| Spending variance..................................... | (2,000) |
| Net profit variance................................... | $14,000 |

## ADVANTAGE OF VARIABLE COSTING

Throughout the discussion in this chapter, the importance of an effective separation of variable and fixed costs and of the variable profit as a unique figure has been obvious. The distinction between variable and fixed costs and the identification of the variable profit are essential to the variable costing method and to variable costing reports. While the same data may be derived from absorption costing records, they are incidental to rather than inherent in that method. In practice, it has been observed that firms using absorption costing usually do not separate variable and fixed costs in the accounting records. Consequently, when such cost data are required for special analyses, they must be developed in a manner not characteristic of the cost accounting system in use and, hence, at extra cost. Under variable costing, on the other hand, separate reporting of variable and fixed costs is basic to the system. Hence, the distinction is always available for analysis. Further, the variable costing income statement shows directly the variable profit. Thus, without additional information, management can make analyses of the anticipated impacts of volume, price, and/or cost changes. Such analyses are ordinarily not possible from absorption costing income statements without supplementary information. Thus, variable costing appears to be clearly superior insofar as the utility of the income statement for profit-volume analysis is concerned. This does not mean, of course, that variable costing is preferable to absorption costing as a general rule; but it certainly is a point in its favor.

## QUESTIONS FOR DISCUSSION

1. Describe the effects on a company's profit of a change in sales volume only, when all other pertinent variables remain unchanged. What are the effects on profit of a change in production volume only?

2. "Since business firms seldom operate at their break-even points for any prolonged period of time, break-even analysis is of very limited use to management." Evaluate this statement.

3. What would be the impact on a firm's break-even point if there were a uniform general increase in the price level, i.e., an increase of the same proportion in all prices? Consider the case of a firm which holds a sufficient inventory of merchandise to meet all anticipated sales demand during the coming fiscal year. Effective on the first day of that period, all prices are doubled as a consequence of a devaluation of the currency. In that period, when would this firm break even—when revenues equaled the original dollar cost of the merchandise sold or when revenues equaled the current market value of the goods sold? Ignore any costs other than the cost of the goods sold.

4. Does the choice between absorption costing and variable costing have any implication for the break-even point of a firm? Explain.

5. Is it a fair generalization to say that the product with the highest variable profit ratio is the most profitable product in a company's product line? Explain.

6. If a firm's management believed that its anticipated break-even sales volume for a particular budget period were too high, what action(s) might it take to lower that break-even volume?

7. Will a firm that plans to liquidate previously accumulated inventory during a period break even at a different volume from that at which it would break even if it were planning to build up its inventory during the period? Explain.

8. If, as is typically assumed in economic analysis, there is an inverse relationship between sales volume and selling price, what is the effect on profit when selling price is increased and costs remain unchanged? Does the assumption of a linear relationship between sales volume and total revenue in break-even analysis conflict with the customary economic assumption that volume and selling price vary inversely with each other? Explain.

9. How might a profit-volume graph be used by management in the process of developing a comprehensive operating budget?

10. How should income taxes be considered in break-even computations? In cost-volume-profit analyses generally?

11. If a multiproduct firm's break-even point depends upon the product mix sold, what is the firm's true break-even point?

12. The break-even graphs in this chapter show fixed costs on the bottom, with variable costs on top of them. Why can't these graphs show variable costs on the bottom and fixed costs on top?

13. How would detailed analysis of the variance between budgeted and actual profits help management to evaluate the operations of a particular period?

## PROBLEMS

13–1. The Bellini Bell Company, which produces a single model, reports the following summarized budget data:

| | |
|---|---|
| Unit selling price.................................. | $36 |
| Unit variable costs............................... | $21 |
| Annual fixed costs................................ | $7,200,000 |
| Full productive capacity.......................... | 750,000 units |

*Required:*

Compute the company's break-even point in terms of
a. Units sold,
b. Dollar sales volume, and
c. Percentage of full capacity.

13–2. The income statement of the Bizet Cigarette Company for 1976 appeared as follows:

BIZET CIGARETTE COMPANY
Income Statement
For Year Ended Dec. 31, 1976

| | | |
|---|---|---|
| Sales..................................... | | $900,000 |
| Variable expenses: | | |
|   Cost of goods sold......................... | $540,000 | |
|   Distribution............................. | 99,000 | 639,000 |
| Variable profit............................. | | $261,000 |
| Fixed expenses: | | |
|   Production.............................. | $125,000 | |
|   Administration.......................... | 78,000 | 203,000 |
| Income before taxes........................ | | $ 58,000 |
| Income taxes............................... | | 23,200 |
| Net income................................ | | $ 34,800 |

*Required:*

a. Assuming that the data for 1976 are representative of future periods' operations, determine the company's break-even point.
b. Draft a break-even graph for the company and label all important parts of it.

13–3. The Verdi Company sells anvils for $40 apiece. Variable costs of producing and selling anvils average $27.50 per unit. Annual fixed costs of operation total $400,000. The income tax rate is 40%.

*Required:*

How many anvils must the company sell in order to earn a net income after tax of $90,000?

13–4. The Rossini Products Company is considering purchasing an old lumber mill in Roseburg, Oregon, as a plant site for the manufacture of widgets. The mill would cost $2,500,000 initially, and an additional $4,000,000 would have to be spent to convert it to a modern widget factory. The converted plant would have an estimated useful life of 25 years and an expected terminal salvage value of $1,200,000. It would have a productive capacity of 150,000 widgets per year.

Widgets sell for $16 apiece. The variable costs of one widget are as follows:

| | |
|---|---|
| Materials........................... | $3.10 |
| Labor.............................. | 4.80 |
| Manufacturing overhead............ | 1.20 |
| Distribution....................... | 1.50 |
| Franchise fee...................... | .60 |

The annual fixed out-of-pocket costs of operating the new factory would amount to $292,000.

*Required:*

a. Compute the annual break-even volume for the widget factory in terms of both units and dollar sales.
b. Draft a properly labeled break-even graph for the new plant.

13–5. The graph below depicts the conventional break-even analysis. Physical units of product are measured on the $x$ axis. Budgeted sales volume in units of product is depicted by the line segment $c \rightarrow k$.

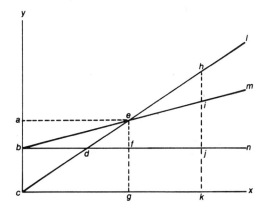

*Required:*

By the use of the letters on the graph above, identify the point, line segment, or area on the graph that represents each of the following:

    *a.*  Total revenue at any volume
    *b.*  Total variable cost at any volume
    *c.*  Fixed costs
    *d.*  Break-even point in dollar sales
    *e.*  Break-even point in units
    *f.*  Margin of safety
    *g.*  Total budgeted revenue
    *h.*  Total budgeted variable cost
    *i.*  Total budgeted costs
    *j.*  Budgeted operating profit
    *k.*  Maximum possible total loss

13–6.  The Massenet Corporation manufactures a variety of hand tools. The following summary data are taken from the operating budget for 1977:

| | |
|---|---:|
| Sales...................................... | $20,000,000 |
| Variable expenses.......................... | 11,000,000 |
| Fixed expenses............................. | 7,200,000 |

*Required:*
    *a.*  Compute the break-even point.
    *b.*  Draft a profit-volume graph for the Massenet Corporation. Show the budgeted profits before tax for sales volumes of $12,000,000 and $24,000,000.
    *c.*  What sales volume would have to be achieved to yield a net income after tax of $1,500,000? The income tax rate is 40%.
    *d.*  What are the principal assumptions underlying the break-even point computed in (*a*)?

13–7.  On the profit-volume graph below, dollar sales volume is measured on the *x* axis. The line segment *b → f* represents budgeted sales volume.

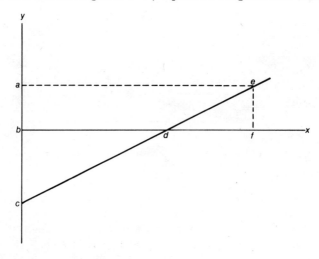

*Required:*

Identify the quantity represented on this graph by each of the following:

a.  Point *a*.
b.  Point *c*.
c.  Point *d*.
d.  Line segment $d \rightarrow f$.
e.  $\dfrac{c}{d}$

13-8.  The Denver Plant of the Moore Manufacturing Company produces control panels used on most of the company's final products. This plant and all of the equipment in it are leased; the lease is cancellable on six month's notice. Budgeted production and cost data for this plant for 1977 are as follows:

| | |
|---|---:|
| Direct materials............................. | $2,200,000 |
| Direct labor................................. | 1,400,000 |
| Variable manufacturing overhead.............. | 700,000 |
| Fixed manufacturing overhead (including rent).. | 1,000,000 |
| Variable shipping expense..................... | 200,000 |
| Fixed plant administrative expense............ | 600,000 |
| Allocated share of general corporate expenses.... | 400,000 |
| Total costs.......................... | $6,500,000 |
| | |
| Output of control panels..................... | 15,000 |

The output of the Denver plant is planned to meet the production requirements of the company's principal manufacturing plants. Recently, the company has learned that it could purchase a comparable control panel from an independent supplier at a price of $425 per panel, delivered.

*Required:*

At what volume of output does the Denver plant break even?

13-9.  The delivery department of Britten & Co., Wholesalers, operates 20 company-owned delivery trucks. During 1977, each truck will be operated an estimated 25,000 miles. The budgeted costs of this department are $.15 per mile plus $60,000 per year. Trucks could be leased for $.25 per mile.

*Required:*

a.  In 1977, would it be cheaper to own or to lease delivery trucks?
b.  At what volume of operation, if any, is it more profitable to own trucks than to lease them?

13-10.  The following summarized data are adapted from a study of one year's operation of the U.S. Post Office. This study was conducted prior to the 1971 reorganization which established the Post Office as a semi-independent corporation. Dollar amounts below are in millions.

|  | First | Second | Third | Fourth | Totals |
|---|---|---|---|---|---|
|  | | | *Class* | | |
| Revenue............. | $4,000 | $ 275 | $ 900 | $1,200 | $ 6,375 |
| Variable expenses..... | 2,240 | 605 | 450 | 800 | 4,095 |
| Variable profit margin. | $1,760 | $(330) | $ 450 | $ 400 | $ 2,280 |
| Traceable fixed expenses.......... | 1,200 | 500 | 600 | 700 | 3,000 |
| Net margin.......... | $ 560 | $(830) | $(150) | $ (300) | $( 720) |
| Common fixed expenses............ |  |  |  |  | 1,400 |
| Net operating deficit... |  |  |  |  | $(2,120) |

*Required:*

*a.* At what volume does each class of mail service break even?

*b.* At what volume would the entire Post Office break even if the mix of classes of service remains as shown above?

*c.* What percentage increase in second class postal rates would be necessary in order for that class of service to break even at its present volume?

*d.* Would it be profitable to double second class postal rates if such a rate increase would reduce the volume of second class mail by half?

13–11. The budgeted income statement of the Meyerbeer Corporation, by product lines, for 1977 is as follows:

|  | A | B | C | Totals |
|---|---|---|---|---|
|  | | *Product* | | |
| Sales................... | $400,000 | $1,000,000 | $600,000 | $2,000,000 |
| Variable expenses: |  |  |  |  |
| Cost of goods sold..... | $180,000 *45* | $ 540,000 *54* | $300,000 *50* | $1,020,000 |
| Selling............... | 60,000 *15* | 180,000 *18* | 90,000 *15* | 330,000 |
|  | $240,000 | $ 720,000 | $390,000 | $1,350,000 |
| Variable profit........... | $160,000 *40* | $ 280,000 *28* | $210,000 *35* | $ 650,000 |
| Fixed expenses: |  |  |  |  |
| Manufacturing overhead | $ 72,000 | $ 180,000 | $108,000 | $ 360,000 |
| Administrative........ | 32,000 | 80,000 | 48,000 | 160,000 |
|  | $104,000 | $ 260,000 | $156,000 | $ 520,000 |
| Income before tax........ | $ 56,000 | $ 20,000 | $ 54,000 | $ 130,000 |
| Income tax (40%)....... | 22,400 | 8,000 | 21,600 | 52,000 |
| Net income............ | $ 33,600 | $ 12,000 | $ 32,400 | $ 78,000 |

All products are manufactured in the same production facilities under common administrative control. Fixed expenses are allocated among the products in proportion to their budgeted sales volumes.

*Required:*

a. Compute the budgeted break-even point of the corporation for 1977.

b. What would be the effect on budgeted income if half of the budgeted sales volume of Product B were shifted in equal dollar amounts to Products A and C, with no change in total budgeted sales volume?

c. What would be the effect of the change in product mix suggested in (*b*) on the budgeted break-even point?

13–12. The budgeted sales of the Donizetti Company for 1977 amount to $200,000,000. Variable costs are expected to average $.60 per dollar of sales. Fixed costs are budgeted at $66,000,000 for the year.

*Required:*

a. What is the company's break-even point in 1977?

b. What sales volume would be necessary in order to earn a profit before tax equal to 10% of sales?

c. Would it be profitable for the company to increase budgeted sales volume by 20%, without changing prices, by improving product quality and increasing the variable cost rate by 20%?

13–13. The Wagner Company manufactures a single product in one continuous process. The standard cost sheet for one unit of this product is as follows:

| | |
|---|---:|
| Direct materials (7½ lbs. @ $2) | $15 |
| Direct labor (4 hrs. @ $4.25) | 17 |
| Variable manufacturing overhead (4 hrs. @ $1.50) | 6 |
| Fixed manufacturing overhead (4 hrs. @ $1.75) | 7 |
| | $45 |

Normal production volume is 1,600,000 direct labor hours per year. Sales and production for 1977 have been budgeted at 300,000 units of product. The budgeted selling price is $50 per unit. Variable selling expenses average 10% of sales. Fixed nonmanufacturing expenses are budgeted at $980,000 for the year.

*Required:*

a. What is the budgeted break-even point for 1977?

b. Would the break-even point be different if volume were budgeted at 400,000 units instead of 300,000? Explain.

c. Would it be profitable for the company to raise its selling price by 20% if such an increase would result in a 40% reduction in the volume of units sold?

d. What effect, if any, would a 20% price increase have on the break-even point?

13–14. In government, an industrial fund (or working capital fund) activity is a business-type operation that sells commercial services to other governmental units. Typical examples are printing plants, aircraft repair facilities, and shipyards. Because it is a governmental unit providing services to other governmental units, an industrial fund activity attempts to set its prices so that it will just break even. Both profits and losses are avoided.

The Cilea Naval Shipyard is an industrial fund activity. Its budgeted variable costs are $17.50 per man hour, and budgeted fixed costs are $7,500,000 per quarter. On the basis of ship repair schedules and other information, shipyard management has estimated that its volume of work in 1977 will average about 600,000 man hours per quarter.

*Required:*

a. What price should the Cilea Naval Shipyard announce for 1977?
b. What would be the impact on the Shipyard's profit or loss in 1977 if variable costs increased by 4% and volume decreased by 5%?

13–15. The Gounod Corporation manufactures and sells industrial machinery in two sales territories. Budgeted income statements for these territories and for the company as a whole for the year 1977 are presented below.

|  | Northern Territory | Southern Territory | Corporation Totals |
|---|---|---|---|
| Sales | $8,000,000 | $6,000,000 | $14,000,000 |
| Variable expenses: | | | |
| Direct materials | $2,000,000 | $1,500,000 | $ 3,500,000 |
| Direct labor | 2,400,000 | 1,800,000 | 4,200,000 |
| Manufacturing overhead | 800,000 | 600,000 | 1,400,000 |
| Selling expenses | 400,000 | 300,000 | 700,000 |
| Fixed expenses: | | | |
| Manufacturing overhead | 1,000,000 | 1,000,000 | 2,000,000 |
| Selling expenses | 360,000 | 270,000 | 630,000 |
| Administrative expenses | 400,000 | 300,000 | 700,000 |
| Total expenses | $7,360,000 | $5,770,000 | $13,130,000 |
| Income before tax | $ 640,000 | $ 230,000 | $ 870,000 |
| Income tax (40%) | 256,000 | 92,000 | 348,000 |
| Net income | $ 384,000 | $ 138,000 | $ 522,000 |

All of the fixed expenses, excepting manufacturing overhead, are incurred in the home office and are allocated between the two territories in proportion to their sales volumes. Fixed manufacturing overhead is actually traceable to the individual territories.

The vice president for sales has suggested that a price reduction of 5% in both territories would increase sales volume in both by 15%. The manager of the Southern Territory has argued that his sales volume could be increased by 20%, with no price reduction, if he were allowed to spend an additional $250,000 annually on sales promotion in his territory. The manager of the Northern Territory has countered that any expanded sales effort should be concentrated in his territory, which he points out is the more profitable of the two. He notes that the Southern Territory expects sales equal to 75% of his but a profit equal to only 36% of his. Thus, he contends, every dollar of increased sales in the Northern Territory will add more to corporate profit than another dollar of sales in the Southern Territory.

*Required:*

a. Accepting the validity of their basic assumptions, determine the profitability of the suggestions made by the vice president for sales and by the manager of the Southern Territory.

b. Evaluate the argument by the manager of the Northern Territory.

13–16. The income statement of the Strauss Steel Strapping Company for the year 1976 appeared as follows:

**STRAUSS STEEL STRAPPING COMPANY**
Income Statement
For Year Ended Dec. 31, 1976

| | | |
|---|---:|---:|
| Sales................................... | | $68,000,000 |
| Cost of goods sold at standard cost....... | $48,000,000 | |
| Manufacturing overhead volume variance.. | 3,000,000 | 51,000,000 |
| Gross margin......................... | | $17,000,000 |
| Selling and administrative expenses...... | | 14,600,000 |
| Income before tax..................... | | $ 2,400,000 |
| Income tax........................... | | 960,000 |
| Net income........................... | | $ 1,440,000 |

The company's president is very dissatisfied with the year's operating results. He considers the net income of just over 2% of sales revenue to be disgraceful, in view of the fact that the industry average for 1976 was 7½% of sales. In addition, he is concerned by the fact that the company has not been able to utilize its capacity fully.

Further study of the cost records shows that fixed manufacturing overhead of $9,000,000 was included in the standard cost of goods sold in 1976 and that $6,000,000 of fixed selling and administrative expenses were incurred in that year. Production and sales volume in 1976 were equal. The income tax rate is 40%.

*Required:*

a. If there were no changes in prices or in costs, what sales volume in 1977 would be necessary in order for Strauss Steel Strapping Company to earn a percentage profit margin equal to the current industry average?

b. Would such a target profit margin appear to be feasible for 1977? Discuss.

13–17. Sales of the Puccini Company's product have been declining for the past several years. In 1976, 600,000 units were sold. For 1977, sales volume has been budgeted initially at 500,000 units, which represent only half the company's productive capacity. Several plans have been proposed to reverse the downward sales trend.

The sales manager recommends reducing the price of the product by 10%. This, he contends, will result in a 30% increase in sales volume over the amount initially forecast for 1977.

The production engineer argues that the difficulty lies with product quality. He asserts that volume would be increased by 20% over the initial 1977 sales forecast if higher quality raw materials were used in the product. Use of higher quality materials would increase materials cost by 12%.

A management consultant has recommended that the production engineer's proposal be adopted and coupled with a 5% price increase. This action, he estimates, would increase budgeted sales volume by 10% in 1977.

In any event, the company's direct labor cost will be increased by 5% as of January 1, 1977.

Income for 1976 was reported as follows:

| | | |
|---|---:|---:|
| Sales.................................... | | $30,000,000 |
| Raw materials cost...................... | $8,100,000 | |
| Direct labor........................... | 6,000,000 | |
| Variable manufacturing overhead......... | 2,700,000 | |
| Fixed manufacturing overhead............ | 5,000,000 | |
| Variable selling expenses................ | 2,100,000 | |
| Fixed selling expenses................... | 2,700,000 | |
| Fixed administrative expenses........... | 3,200,000 | 29,800,000 |
| Net profit............................. | | $   200,000 |

*Required:*

Analyze the effects of each of the alternative operating proposals for 1977 and identify the one that would result in the greatest budgeted profit before tax. Unless something to the contrary is stated, assume that the 1976 financial data will be applicable in 1977.

13–18. Leoncavallo & Co., Inc., has a maximum productive capacity of 900,000 units per year. Normal volume is regarded as 800,000 units per year. Standard variable manufacturing costs total $5.25 per unit. Fixed manufacturing overhead is $720,000 per year. Variable selling expenses average $.75 per unit, and fixed selling and administrative expenses total $750,000 per year. The unit selling price is $9.

Operations during 1976 resulted in the production of 720,000 units and the sale of 750,000 units. There was a net unfavorable variance from standard variable manufacturing costs in the amount of $25,000. All variances are disposed of as adjustments to the cost of goods sold.

*Required:*

For *a*, *b*, and *c* below, assume no variances from standard manufacturing costs and no difference between sales and production volumes.

*a.* What is the break-even point in dollar sales?

    *b.* How many units must be sold in order to earn a net profit of $450,000 per year before tax?

    *c.* How many units must be sold in order to earn a net income before tax equal to 10% of sales?

    *d.* Compute the company's income before tax in 1976 under (1) absorption costing and (2) variable costing.

    *e.* Explain any difference between the two incomes computed in *d.*

(Adapted from CPA Examination)

13–19. The Mascagni Specialties Company is engaged in manufacturing and wholesaling two principal products. As special assistant to the president, you have been asked for your advice on sales policy for the coming year. Two different plans are under consideration by management. Management believes that either plan will (*a*) increase sales volume, (*b*) decrease unit production costs, and (*c*) reduce the ratio of selling expenses to sales. The two plans are outlined below.

*Plan 1: Premium Stamp Books*

    Each package of Product X would contain three premium stamps, and each package of Product Y would contain two premium stamps. Premium stamp books would be given to consumers. When a book was filled with 50 stamps, it would be redeemed by the award of a cash prize, the amount of which would be indicated under an unbroken seal on the cover of the book. Each batch of 5,000 books distributed would provide for cash prizes in accordance with the following schedule:

| Number of Books | Prize per Book | Total Prizes |
|---|---|---|
| 1 | $1,000 | $ 1,000 |
| 4 | 500 | 2,000 |
| 10 | 200 | 2,000 |
| 25 | 100 | 2,500 |
| 50 | 50 | 2,500 |
| 100 | 10 | 1,000 |
| 4,810 | 1 | 4,810 |
| 5,000 | | $15,810 |

    The costs of this plan would be as follows:

Books, including distribution....... $40 per 1,000 books
Stamps......................... $5.96 per 1,000 stamps
Prizes......................... per schedule above

This plan would take the place of all previous advertising expenditures. Previous selling prices would remain unchanged.

*Plan 2: Reduced Selling Prices*

    The selling price of Product X would be reduced by 6% and that of Product Y, by 8%. The rate of advertising expenditures in relation to sales would be increased by one-third.

The two plans are mutually exclusive alternatives. In addition to the foregoing facts about the two proposed plans, you have obtained the following data about operations during the preceding year and projected changes therein under the alternative plans:

|  | *Product X* | *Product Y* |
|---|---|---|
| Preceding year's operations: | | |
| Units produced and sold.................... | 120,000 | 300,000 |
| Selling price per unit...................... | $4.00 | $3.00 |
| Variable production costs per unit........... | $2.25 | $1.50 |
| Total fixed production costs................ | $90,000 | $150,000 |
| Selling expenses (one-third of which was | | |
| advertising)............................. | 18% of sales | 18% of sales |
| Administrative expenses................... | 10% of sales | 10% of sales |
| Projected changes in operations: | | |
| Increase in unit sales volume— | | |
| Under Plan 1........................... | 25% | 30% |
| Under Plan 2........................... | 35% | 40% |

Under both plans, administrative expenses would increase by 10% of the total dollar amount expended in the preceding year. Selling expenses other than advertising would be incurred at the same rate as in the preceding year. No changes are projected in production costs.

*Required:*

a. Prepare a report comparing the operations of the preceding year with those proposed for the coming year under each of the two alternative plans.

b. Is management correct in its expectations as to the three specific improvements in operations that were mentioned in the first paragraph of the problem?

(Adapted from CPA Examination)

13–20. The Gluck Beer Company had budgeted sales of 6,000,000 barrels in 1976 at an average price of $40 per barrel. Variable costs had been budgeted at $22 per barrel and fixed costs, at $90,000,000 for the year. Actual sales for 1976 totaled 5,400,000 barrels at an average price of $45 per barrel. Actual variable costs totaled $135,000,000 and actual fixed costs, $93,000,000.

*Required:*

Prepare a detailed analysis of the variation between actual and budgeted profits before tax for 1976.

13–21. The controller of the Halevy Manufacturing Corporation presented the following summary budget review report for the third quarter of 1976 to the president:

| | Budget | Actual | Variance |
|---|---|---|---|
| Sales: | | | |
| In units.................. | 90,000 | 112,000 | 22,000 |
| In dollars............... | $720,000 | $868,000 | $ 148,000 |
| Variable expenses........... | $450,000 | $571,200 | $(121,200) |
| Fixed expenses.............. | 175,000 | 180,000 | ( 5,000) |
| | $625,000 | $751,200 | $(126,200) |
| Income before taxes.......... | $ 95,000 | $116,800 | $ 21,800 |

The president expressed his pleasure that profit had exceeded plans for the quarter, but he said that he was not sure he understood why it had. Hence, he asked the controller to elaborate upon the reasons for the improvement in profit.

*Required:*

Present additional analysis of the change in third quarter profits to assist the president in understanding the reasons therefor.

13–22. E. Humperdinck & Sons is an unincorporated wholesale grocery distributor. The chief accountant prepared the following income statement for 1976:

| | |
|---|---|
| Sales..................................... | $1,652,400 |
| Variable expenses.......................... | 1,173,000 |
| Variable profit............................ | $ 479,400 |
| Fixed expenses............................ | 260,000 |
| Net income............................... | $ 219,400 |

As 1976 had been a year of many changes, Mr. Humperdinck, Sr., was interested in knowing just why income had fallen below expectations for the year. He recalled that the following budgeted income statement had been developed prior to the start of the year:

| | |
|---|---|
| Sales..................................... | $1,500,000 |
| Variable expenses.......................... | 1,000,000 |
| Variable profit............................ | $ 500,000 |
| Fixed expenses............................ | 200,000 |
| Net income............................... | $ 300,000 |

Further, he said that he knew the company had increased selling prices by an average of 8 percent during the year; and he had assumed that a price increase would result in higher profits.

*Required:*

Analyze the $80,600 decline in net income for 1976 in as much detail as is possible.

13–23. The Menotti Company sells three different models of industrial pumps. The operating budget for 1976 is summarized below:

Sales:

| | |
|---|---|
| Model 10 (80,000 @ $85)............. | $ 6,800,000 |
| Model 20 (70,000 @ $120)............ | 8,400,000 |
| Model 30 (50,000 @ $220)............ | 11,000,000 |
| | $26,200,000 |

Variable costs:

| | | |
|---|---|---|
| Model 10 (80,000 @ $60)............. | $4,800,000 | |
| Model 20 (70,000 @ $80)............. | 5,600,000 | |
| Model 30 (50,000 @ $128)............ | 6,400,000 | 16,800,000 |
| Variable profit margin................. | | $ 9,400,000 |
| Fixed costs......................... | | 7,200,000 |
| Profit before tax.................... | | $ 2,200,000 |

The actual results of operations for 1976 are shown in the following income statement:

Sales:

| | |
|---|---|
| Model 10 (88,000 @ $87.50)............ | $ 7,700,000 |
| Model 20 (86,000 @ $120)............ | 10,320,000 |
| Model 30 (66,000 @ $210)............ | 13,860,000 |
| | $31,880,000 |

Variable costs:

| | | |
|---|---|---|
| Model 10 (88,000 @ $62)............. | $5,456,000 | |
| Model 20 (86,000 @ $84)............. | 7,224,000 | |
| Model 30 (66,000 @ $130)............ | 8,580,000 | 21,260,000 |
| Variable profit margin................. | | $10,620,000 |
| Fixed costs......................... | | 7,500,000 |
| Profit before tax.................... | | $ 3,120,000 |

*Required:*

Explain in as much detail as you can why the actual profit in 1976 was $920,000 (or almost 42 percent) more than had been budgeted.

13–24. The Barber Corporation sells three lines of cosmetics: the high-price Princess Vanessa line, the medium-price Prince Anatol line, and the low-price Dame Erica line. The budgeted income statement, by product lines, for 1976 was as follows:

BARBER CORPORATION
Budgeted Income Statement
1976
(in thousands of dollars)

| | Princess Vanessa | Prince Anatol | Dame Erica | Total |
|---|---|---|---|---|
| Sales....................... | $10,000 | $16,000 | $14,000 | $40,000 |
| Variable costs............... | $ 4,000 | $ 8,000 | $ 8,400 | $20,400 |
| Fixed costs.................. | 2,500 | 4,000 | 3,500 | 10,000 |
| | $ 6,500 | $12,000 | $11,900 | $30,400 |
| Operating profit............. | $ 3,500 | $ 4,000 | $ 2,100 | $ 9,600 |

It is the company's practice to allocate fixed costs among product lines in proportion to sales volumes. As all products are produced in the same plants and sold through the same marketing organization, however, none of these fixed costs is really traceable to individual product lines.

During 1976, various cost increases made it necessary for the corporation to increase its selling prices by an average of 10 percent on the Princess Vanessa line and by 6 percent on the Dame Erica line. Intensified competition in the medium-price market, however, forced the company to cut prices on the Prince Anatol line by an average of 5 percent.

The income statement prepared at the end of 1976 showed the following actual results for the year:

BARBER CORPORATION
Income Statement
For Year Ended December 31, 1976
(in thousands of dollars)

|  | Princess Vanessa | Prince Anatol | Dame Erica | Total |
|---|---|---|---|---|
| Sales | $12,650 | $15,580 | $17,066 | $45,296 |
| Variable costs | $ 5,060 | $ 9,020 | $10,626 | $24,706 |
| Fixed costs | 3,072 | 3,784 | 4,144 | 11,000 |
|  | $ 8,132 | $12,804 | $14,770 | $35,706 |
| Operating profit | $ 4,518 | $ 2,776 | $ 2,296 | $ 9,590 |

*Required:*

a. Prepare a detailed analysis of the variance between actual and budgeted profits for 1976.

b. What impact, if any, would each of the following changes have had on the budgeted break-even volume for 1976: (1) change in volume, (2) change in sales mix, and (3) change in fixed costs?

# chapter 14

# Incremental Profit
# Analysis For
# Decision Making

$A$T ONE time, accounting data were accumulated in business firms almost solely for the purpose of reporting the results of operations after they had occurred. Accounting, consequently, was regarded primarily as a backward looking function. Accounting reports were required for investors but were of limited use to management. Recent years have witnessed a marked departure from this point of view. The importance of reports to investors has not diminished, but the uses of accounting data by management have grown to the point that they are often regarded as more important than reports to investors. Actually, accounting reports are equally important to both groups, but often in quite different ways. The types of data required by management and the manner of their presentation frequently differ greatly from the data in and form of conventional reports to investors. Investors' reports continue to emphasize historical data; this emphasis may be debated, but it remains a fact of "generally accepted accounting principles." Management, on the other hand, is not bound by the constraint of general acceptance. Managers are concerned chiefly with data pertinent to the future, and they are not satisfied with historical reports as indicators of future operations. Managers want to know very specifically what costs and profits can be and should be, not just what they were. Further, management must be concerned with the details of operating problems and prospects for individual segments or components of the enterprise. Investors, on the other hand, are ordinarily interested in the operations of the enterprise as a whole only. The accounting system should be designed so as to meet the needs of both management and investors as completely as possible.

Accounting data are generally recognized to be indispensable tools of management in the making of business decisions. These financial data alone do not make decisions, but they are essential elements to be considered in the process of deciding. For purposes of discussion in this book, business decisions will be classified as two general types, short-term operating decisions and long-term investment decisions. The distinction between these two types is one of time. Short-term decisions may be implemented and, if desired, reversed within a short period of time. (As a practical expedient, a "short period of time" is often considered as one year or less.) Long-term investment decisions affect the operating position of a firm for a sufficiently long period of time that their financial consequences must be evaluated in light of the impact of time upon them. Investment decisions involve the commitment of capital resources to some asset (e.g., a building) or to some project (e.g., a new product line) for an anticipated long period of time. Abandonment of the asset or project before the end of its expected economic life may entail a substantial loss of capital. Short-term decisions, on the other hand, do not involve long-term capital commitments. If a short-term decision proves to be unwise, it may be reversed promptly without significant loss of capital. Hence, the element of time may be ignored in the decision-making analysis. Short-term decisions will be discussed in this chapter. Long-term investment decisions will be considered in Chapters 16 and 17.

## FINANCIAL DATA FOR DECISION MAKING

### Relevant Costs

For purposes of inventory valuation and income reporting, the distinction between manufacturing and nonmanufacturing costs is an important one. In profit-volume analysis, the distinction between variable and fixed costs is most important. For purposes of making a specific decision among alternative possible courses of action, however, these distinctions are merely incidental. The essential distinction for decision making is between relevant and irrelevant costs. Any costs that will be affected by a particular decision—whether they will be increased or decreased—are relevant costs insofar as that decision is concerned. Costs that will be the same regardless of how a particular decision is made are irrelevant costs.[1] Relevant costs are always out-of-pocket costs, of

---

[1] Refer to Chapter 2 for a more extensive discussion of cost classifications for purposes of decision making.

course; they always entail future cash flows. As noted in Chapter 2, a sunk cost cannot be a relevant cost because it cannot be changed; it is a consequence of a past decision. There are no general rules for distinguishing practically between relevant and irrelevant costs. They can be determined only in the context of the circumstances surrounding a specific decision. The very same cost item may be relevant to one decision and irrelevant to another. The discussions in the following paragraphs are concerned with how to look for relevant costs.

*Variable Costs.* It would be wrong to say that variable costs are always relevant costs.[2] Of course, any cost that varies with volume will be affected by a decision that will cause a change in volume. A decision may, however, have some relationship to variable costs without affecting their amounts. For example, a decision among alternative methods of handling and storing raw materials will not affect the cost of the materials themselves; yet, raw materials cost is almost always regarded as variable. Relevant costs can be identified only in light of the particular decision at hand. By their very nature, however, variable costs are highly susceptible to change. Hence, it is probably a good rule always to scrutinize variable costs very carefully to determine whether or not they will be affected by a decision.

*Fixed Costs.* In a short-term decision-making situation, fixed costs may be either relevant or irrelevant. If a fixed cost is wholly traceable to a specific decision and will be incurred if and only if that decision is made, it is a relevant cost. For example, opening a new sales territory would likely entail the salary of a new sales manager for the territory. His salary would be a fixed cost if it were incurred, but it would be incurred only if the decision to open the new territory were made. If a fixed cost would be incurred in the same amount regardless of how a particular decision is resolved, it is an irrelevant cost. Thus, the salary of the vice president for marketing would probably be a fixed cost; and it would most likely be unaffected by the opening of a new sales territory, even though the vice president may be deeply involved in the operations of the new territory. The vice president's salary here would be an irrelevant cost, not because it is unrelated to the object of the decision at issue but because it would not be affected in amount by that decision. It is not necessary that there be relevant fixed costs in every decision situation, of course; but the possibility of their existence should always be investigated. They might be easy to overlook and, yet, quite significant in amount.

*Interest.* In strict theory, interest cost is independent of individual decisions. It is the cost of obtaining capital and, as such, is not affected

---

[2] The computer acquisition decision discussed in Chapter 2 involves irrelevant variable costs.

by decisions as to the utilization of that capital. In practice, however, sources and uses of business capital are often viewed as interdependent, particularly in connection with short-term decisions. One of the alternatives under consideration in a given case may necessitate short-term borrowing, while the other(s) do not. In such case, the interest on that borrowing may be considered a relevant cost in the decision-making process. If all of the alternative courses of action would require equal short-term borrowing, of course, the interest would be common to all of the possible choices and would be an irrelevant cost. Inclusion of short-term interest among the relevant costs of a particular alternative is appropriate only if the short-term borrowing would be undertaken if and only if that course of action were adopted.

In theory, the firm is thought of as faced with a wide range of possible sources of capital, whether short-term or long-term, not all of which alternatives would be related to one specific decision. Thus, short-term borrowing would be entered into in any event so long as there were some profitable use for the capital. As a practical matter, however, business managers usually are unable to evaluate all possible sources and uses of short-term capital in so broad a perspective. Business decisions are often made within the framework of a single problem or program. In such cases, it would be acceptable to regard short-term borrowing and the interest thereon as peculiar to one possible decision. This could be true only for short-term interest, however. In the long-run, a broad overview of all possible investment opportunities must be adopted.

***Depreciation.*** Depreciation is the periodic amortization of the cost of a long-lived asset acquired at some time in the past. As such, it necessarily derives from a long-term investment decision. Once the investment decision has been implemented and the asset purchased, the subsequent depreciation expense is determined in light of the asset's expected useful life and in accordance with one of a number of alternative depreciation methods available at the option of management. Thus, depreciation is inherently related to what we have described as a long-term decision. To include depreciation as a relevant cost in any short-term decision-making situation is erroneous and may be seriously misleading. If a particular decision would have the effect of increasing periodic depreciation, the increase could be attributed to an investment in a new asset, to a shortening of the life of an old asset, or to a change in the depreciation method used. Either of the first two causes would entail an investment decision which would have to be analyzed in relation to the relatively long period of time involved. The third possible cause would involve no substantive financial implications, except in the event that the change in depreciation charges were acceptable for income tax purposes. Any reduction in depreciation attendant upon the disposition of a long-lived asset would also be a consequence of a long-term investment decision.

Actually, in this case, it would be a disinvestment decision. Thus, depreciation should be ignored in short-term decision-making situations.

## Incremental Profit

A full analysis of the expected accounting implications of a specific decision, including both costs and revenues relevant to it, will yield the amount of profit which that decision would contribute to the enterprise as a whole. This amount is referred to as the *incremental profit* from the decision. The incremental profit is that portion of the total income of the firm which can be traced directly to a particular decision. It may be either positive or negative. It may be the net difference between incremental revenues and incremental costs generated by the decision; as such, it would be either positive or negative depending upon whether the revenues or the costs, respectively, were greater. Revenues need not be involved, of course. The incremental profit may be simply the amount of a cost reduction (positive incremental profit) or of a cost increase (negative incremental profit). A change in the method of handling materials, for example, would not be likely to affect revenues; but it could reduce or increase the materials handling costs.

It should be noted here that all business decisions need not produce positive incremental profits. In order for a decision to be profitable in the short run, the incremental profit must be positive. But short-run profits may be sacrificed in the anticipation of improved long-run profits, however vague the expectation may be. A negative incremental profit is certainly an adverse feature of a possible course of action, but it does not necessarily mean that the decision must go against that course. Financial data are indispensable parts of the decision-making process, but they do not make the decision by themselves.

Determination of the incremental profit in a given situation begins with an identification of the relevant costs and the incremental revenues that would obtain if a particular decision were made. The incremental profit may be computed as follows:

| | | |
|---|---|---|
| Additional revenues.............. | | xxx |
| Plus:  Cost saving.............. | | xxx |
| | | xxx |
| Less:  Lost revenues............ | xxx | |
| Cost increases............ | xxx | xxx |
| Incremental profit.............. | | xxx |

Any one or all but one of the items in this computation might be equal to zero, of course. If all of them were zero, the decision would appear to have no direct financial implications. Such a decision might be illustrated by the choice of a new production manager. The choice made may well have very substantial long-run and/or short-run profit implications, but it is highly unlikely that they could be quantified in advance.

*Uncertainty.* The incremental revenues, costs, and profit related to a particular decision situation are, in essence, budget data. They are management's predictions of the results of a proposed course of action. Like all budget data, they are subject to some degree of uncertainty. Probably the most common approach to dealing with this problem of uncertainty is to recognize it implicitly but to use single-value estimates of all relevant financial variables in the decision analysis. Such an approach is not necessarily inappropriate, as long as management recognizes that it is looking only at the best single estimate of the results of a decision but that the actual results may be somewhat different. Alternatively, management could construct a probability distribution of various possible results. Further, an expected value of the incremental profit from the decision could be computed from that probability distribution.[3] The examples in this chapter present only single estimates of all relevant data. These could be interpreted as expected values derived from prior assessments of probabilities.

## SHORT-TERM DECISION-MAKING PROBLEMS

In the paragraphs that follow, we shall examine and analyze several short-term decision-making situations in terms of their incremental profits. Some of the nonfinancial considerations which would be pertinent to the decisions will also be noted briefly. The nature and purposes of this text demand that the financial data be emphasized in these illustrations, but they are still only parts of the total decision-making process, albeit essential parts.

### Extent of Processing a Product

*The Facts.* The Blaine Corporation manufactures a single product which it sells to other firms who process it further for ultimate sales to clothing manufacturers. The normal monthly operating volume for the corporation is 100,000 units of product produced and sold. The unit selling price and standard unit costs under the present operations are shown on the following page.

---

[3] This procedure was explained and illustrated in Chapter 7.

| Selling price............................ | | $6.50 |
|---|---|---|
| Standard costs: | | |
| Direct materials..................... | $1.20 | |
| Direct labor........................ | 1.75 | |
| Variable manufacturing overhead....... | 1.10 | |
| Fixed manufacturing overhead.......... | .85 | |
| Variable selling expense............... | .90 | |
| Fixed selling expense.................. | .30 | 6.10 |
| Unit profit before tax.................... | | $ .40 |

The corporation's management is considering the possibility of performing the further processing necessary for the corporation itself to sell directly to clothing manufacturers. A study has shown that this further processing would require no added investment in productive facilities. After further processing, the product could be sold to clothing makers for $8 per unit. The additional costs of the further processing are estimated as follows:

| | |
|---|---|
| Direct labor................................. | $.65 per unit |
| Variable manufacturing overhead.............. | $.25 per unit |
| Variable selling expense...................... | $.10 per unit |
| Fixed manufacturing overhead................ | $15,000 per month |
| Fixed selling expense........................ | $10,00 per month |

The decision at hand is whether to process the product further or to continue selling it as is now done.

*Incremental Profit Analysis.*  Before commencing an analysis of the alternative choices here, it is well to observe the way in which fixed costs have been presented above. The current fixed costs are stated as standard amounts per unit of product. By definition, fixed costs can be expressed per unit only at one given volume. Here, that volume is 100,000 units per month. Thus, the present fixed manufacturing overhead amounts to $85,000 per month and fixed selling expense, to $30,000 per month; and *this* is how fixed costs *should* be stated. In this particular case, no change in volume is contemplated in connection with the decision; but the practice of stating fixed costs per unit of volume is potentially misleading and should be avoided.

There is no standard format in which financial analyses for decision making must be presented. The form depends upon the particular decision, the nature of the relevant data, and the preferences of management. It may be useful, however, to identify two basic types of approaches to the presentation of financial analyses for decision making. The first type is a gross comparison of the operations of the entire organization under each alternative being considered. In the Blaine Corporation illustration, such a gross comparison might take the form of comparative budgeted income statements for the two alternative methods of processing. These statements are presented below in the variable costing format:

| | Present Processing | Further Processing |
|---|---|---|
| Sales revenue | $650,000 | $800,000 |
| | | |
| Variable costs: | | |
| Direct materials | $120,000 | $120,000 |
| Direct labor | 175,000 | 240,000 |
| Manufacturing overhead | 110,000 | 135,000 |
| Selling expense | 90,000 | 100,000 |
| | $495,000 | $595,000 |
| Variable profit | $155,000 | $205,000 |
| | | |
| Fixed costs: | | |
| Manufacturing overhead | $ 85,000 | $100,000 |
| Selling expense | 30,000 | 40,000 |
| | $115,000 | $140,000 |
| Income before tax | $ 40,000 | $ 65,000 |
| Federal income tax (40%) | 16,000 | 26,000 |
| Net income | $ 24,000 | $ 39,000 |

Since further processing would result in a greater net income than the present processing, the new proposal would be more profitable. So long as the income tax rate is less than 100%, inclusion of the tax in the analysis only reduces the absolute amount by which further processing would increase profits; but the relative advantage of further processing remains. Nevertheless, it is good practice always to include income taxes in decision-making analyses. In some cases, tax implications may be controlling factors in the decisions.

The gross comparison of the alternatives is certainly a correct and a reasonable way of presenting the relevant data for decision making. Because it is a complete analysis of the firm's operations, however, it also presents irrelevant data, data that will be the same regardless of the alternative that is chosen. The second approach to presenting the financial analysis for decision making is a net analysis of the relevant data only. It presents only those revenues and costs that will be changed by the decision and highlights the resultant incremental profit. For the Blaine Corporation, such an incremental analysis would appear as follows:

| | |
|---|---|
| Incremental revenue per unit | $ 1.50 |
| Incremental variable cost per unit | 1.00 |
| Incremental variable profit per unit | $ .50 |
| Monthly volume in units | 100,000 |
| Incremental variable profit per month | $ 50,000 |
| Incremental fixed cost per month | 25,000 |
| Monthly incremental profit before tax | $ 25,000 |
| Federal income tax (40%) | 10,000 |
| Incremental profit | $ 15,000 |

This analysis, of course, shows exactly the same result as the first one. Profit after taxes will be increased by $15,000 if the company undertakes the further processing. Thus, the proposed change of operating policy would be profitable.

Which method of presentation is used—the gross comparison or the incremental analysis—is partly a matter of individual choice. The gross comparison would seem to be most useful when the alternatives being compared are all new and different from current operations. For example, if a firm were considering two or more alternative locations for one new plant, a gross comparison of operating results anticipated at each location would be logical. If the decision is to change an ongoing operation, however, as it is in the Blaine Corporation's case, the incremental analysis is more direct and concise.

***Other Considerations.*** The facts in this illustration indicate that a decision to engage in further processing would not require additional capital investment. This is a very important condition. If further capital investment were necessary, the decision would have to be evaluated as an investment proposal; incremental profit analysis as illustrated above would not be adequate. The analysis above also presumes that additional laborers could be obtained and laid off on short notice. Even if hiring new workers presents no problem, laying them off might; periodic hirings and layoffs are discouraged by the provisions of many union labor agreements. The Blaine Corporation must also question whether its production personnel have the technical knowledge and skill to perform the further processing efficiently. The decision to process further entails the marketing of the company's product in an unfamiliar channel of distribution. Establishing effective working agreements with clothing manufacturers may make new demands on the abilities of the sales force and it may take some little time. Not all of these considerations lend themselves to precise financial measurement, but they must not be ignored. Thus, the monthly incremental profit of $15,000 is an important factor in the decision-making process; but it is not the final answer in itself.

## Make or Buy

***The Facts.*** The Bonham Radio Company manufactures a variety of electronics equipment. Several of the items produced contain one or more units of a small capacitor, part No. 63812 in the company's list of standard materials. This capacitor is manufactured by the company in its own parts plant. The standard cost for one capacitor is as follows:

| | |
|---|---|
| Materials..................................... | $3.20 |
| Direct labor................................. | 2.40 |
| Variable manufacturing overhead.............. | 1.10 |
| Fixed manufacturing overhead................. | 1.40 |
| | $8.10 |

All of these costs reflect current attainable standards. Monthly usage of this part averages 60,000 units. At a budget meeting, the purchasing agent suggested that the company might save money by purchasing this part from an independent supplier. He stated that he knew it could be purchased in the quantity used by the Bonham Company for $7 per unit. Buying the part would increase clerical purchasing costs by approximately $1,000 per month. The supervisor of the stores department estimated that the additional costs of storing and handling the part, if purchased, would be about $.25 per unit. No additional facilities would be needed to store the part, nor would any production facilities be abandoned if its production were discontinued. The parts plant manager reported that the manufacture of this capacitor is not so significant a portion of his total operation that its discontinuance would have any impact upon the plant's fixed manufacturing overhead.

**Incremental Profit Analysis.** A cursory glance at the facts in this situation might suggest that a decision to buy the capacitor would indeed be a cost saving. Eighty-five cents per unit ($8.10 − $7.25) would appear to be saved, and this amounts to $51,000 per month for 60,000 units. Even after the additional clerical cost of $1,000 per month, there appears to be a $50,000 monthly cost saving (before taxes, of course). The saving is purely illusory in this case, however. Part of the standard cost of $8.10 for this part is fixed manufacturing overhead. For inventory costing purposes, it is perfectly correct to assign $1.40 of the parts plant's fixed manufacturing overhead to this capacitor, assuming that the absorption costing method is employed and that a valid cost allocation scheme is applied. However, the basic nature of these fixed costs is that they are a certain amount per period of time, not an amount per unit of volume. If the manufacture of this part is discontinued, there will be no change in the parts plant's fixed manufacturing overhead. The fixed cost now charged to part No. 63812 would either be reallocated to other parts or be charged to the volume variance. In either event, the plant's fixed manufacturing overhead would not be reduced. Thus, fixed manufacturing overhead is an irrelevant cost in respect to the decision to make or buy part No. 63812. Only the variable production costs—materials, direct labor, and variable manufacturing overhead—are relevant to the decision. The variable costs to manufacture total $6.70. Thus, there is an incremental cost of $.55 per unit ($7.25 − $6.70) inherent in the decision to purchase this part. At a monthly usage of 60,000 units, the decision to purchase the capacitor would be analyzed as follows:

| | |
|---|---:|
| Monthly purchase cost (60,000 units @ $7.25) . . . . . . . . . . . | $435,000 |
| Plus: Incremental monthly clerical cost . . . . . . . . . . . . . . . . | 1,000 |
| | $436,000 |
| Variable manufacturing costs per month (60,000 units @ $6.70) . . . . . . . . . . . . . . . . . . . . . . . . . . . . . . | 402,000 |
| Incremental cost to purchase (before taxes) . . . . . . . . . . . . . | $ 34,000 |
| Federal income tax (40%) . . . . . . . . . . . . . . . . . . . . . . . . . | 13,600 |
| Incremental cost per month to purchase part No. 63812 . . . | $ 20,400 |

Thus, an apparent incremental cost saving is actually an incremental cost. The incremental profit of the suggested change in policy is a negative $20,400 per month.

*Other Considerations.* If a decision to make a part would require an investment in new production facilities or if a decision to buy a part would permit the disposal of existing facilities, the alternatives would have to be evaluated as long-term investment decisions. The situation described here suggests that any decision made could be reappraised and reversed within one month. Other factors must also be considered. If the part were purchased, could the capacity of the parts plant thus idled be employed in some other profitable manner? The analysis above implies that the answer to this question is "No," but the question was not really raised. It should be. Perhaps other parts now being purchased could more profitably be manufactured. Possibly the capacity might be used to produce parts for sale to other manufacturers.

Would there be any difference in the quality or technical characteristics of the purchased capacitor as compared with the present part No. 63812? Would an independent supplier be as reliable as the company's own parts plant? Even if the relevant costs of purchasing the part were lower, the danger of a costly stock-out due to an unreliable source of supply might outweigh the computed cost saving. Finally, the incremental profit analysis in the preceding paragraph presumed that direct laborers could be laid off if the production of the capacitor were discontinued. Even if such a layoff were feasible, it might create long-run labor relations problems which would offset the short-run cost saving. The impact of a decision on labor relations can seldom be quantified, but it should never be ignored.

## Dropping a Product Line

*The Facts.* The Turandot Products Company produces and markets three products. It has prepared the income statement shown in Table 14-1, in the absorption costing form.[4] The company's management is considering dropping Pong from the line of products because it has consistently shown a loss.

*Incremental Profit Analysis.* A useful starting point in this analysis is to recast the income statement presented in the variable costing form and to eliminate the allocation of fixed costs among the products. However valid such an allocation may be for purposes of inventory costing and income measurement, it is not relevant to the question of the profitability of the individual products. Here we shall assume that all of the com-

---

[4] The distinction between variable and fixed costs is not ordinarily made in absorption costing statements, but it is included here to facilitate subsequent analysis. If not included in the income statement, it could be derived from the cost records.

## TABLE 14–1

TURANDOT PRODUCTS COMPANY
Conventional Income Statement

|  | *Ping* | *Pang* | *Pong* | *Total* |
|---|---|---|---|---|
| Sales...................... | $600,000 | $450,000 | $150,000 | $1,200,000 |
| *Cost of goods sold:* |  |  |  |  |
| Variable................. | $360,000 | $270,000 | $105,000 | $ 735,000 |
| Fixed................... | 120,000 | 90,000 | 30,000 | 240,000 |
|  | $480,000 | $360,000 | $135,000 | $ 975,000 |
| Gross margin.............. | $120,000 | $ 90,000 | $ 15,000 | $ 225,000 |
| *Selling expenses:* |  |  |  |  |
| Variable................. | $ 40,000 | $ 30,000 | $ 15,000 | $ 85,000 |
| Fixed................... | 30,000 | 22,500 | 7,500 | 60,000 |
|  | $ 70,000 | $ 52,500 | $ 22,500 | $ 145,000 |
| Net income before tax....... | $ 50,000 | $ 37,500 | $ (7,500) | $ 80,000 |
| Income tax (40%).......... | 20,000 | 15,000 | (3,000) | 32,000 |
| Net income................ | $ 30,000 | $ 22,500 | $ (4,500) | $ 48,000 |

pany's fixed costs are common to the three products. We also assume that the sales and production volumes for the year were equal, so that the same total amount of fixed manufacturing costs will be charged to revenue under variable costing as under absorption costing.[5] The report of profits by product lines in the variable costing form and under the assumptions postulated is as illustrated in Table 14–2. Now it is clear that each product has a positive variable profit. So long as there are no relevant fixed costs, each product also has a positive incremental profit. Here Pong's contribution to the total profit of the firm (before taxes) is $30,000. The apparent loss from its continued sale can be seen to be attributable to the allocation of a portion of the common fixed costs of the company to it. Even if relevant fixed costs were present in the analysis, Pong would have a positive incremental profit as long as its relevant fixed costs were less than $30,000. Whenever a decision is to be made on the basis of the relative profitabilities of several product lines, their respective profits should be measured by their incremental profits. Allocations of fixed costs common to all products are irrelevant and misleading.

On the basis of the information given, the incremental profit of a decision to discontinue production and distribution of Pong would be a negative $18,000 after tax ($30,000 × .60). This may be proved by subtracting all data relevant to Pong from the totals for the company in the income statement above and then recomputing the income tax accordingly.

---

[5] See Chapter 4 for a discussion of the impact of differences between sales and production volumes on reported incomes under these alternative costing methods.

## TABLE 14–2

### TURANDOT PRODUCTS COMPANY
Income Statement Showing Profits by Products

|  | *Ping* | *Pang* | *Pong* | *Total* |
|---|---|---|---|---|
| Sales...................... | $600,000 | $450,000 | $150,000 | $1,200,000 |
| *Variable costs:* |  |  |  |  |
| Production.............. | $360,000 | $270,000 | $105,000 | $ 735,000 |
| Selling.................. | 40,000 | 30,000 | 15,000 | 85,000 |
|  | $400,000 | $300,000 | $120,000 | $ 820,000 |
| Variable profit............. | $200,000 | $150,000 | $ 30,000 | $ 380,000 |
| *Fixed costs:* |  |  |  |  |
| Production.............. |  |  |  | $ 240,000 |
| Selling.................. |  |  |  | 60,000 |
|  |  |  |  | $ 300,000 |
| Net income before tax....... |  |  |  | $ 80,000 |
| Income tax (40%).......... |  |  |  | 32,000 |
| Net income............... |  |  |  | $  48,000 |

*Other Considerations.* Any decision concerning the continuation of one product in a company's line must take into account a wide range of possible implications. Product income statements can be very misleading; they may show only the apparent profitability of each product. For example, if one product is dropped from the line, there may be adverse effects on the sales of other products. If two or more products are complementary, discontinuing one is almost certain to result in reduced sales of the other(s). As an illustration, a manufacturer of machinery could reasonably expect to sell fewer machines if he stopped making and selling spare parts for the machinery. Buyers may place orders with a particular seller because they can obtain a complete line of merchandise from him. If he reduces that line, the buyers may look elsewhere for suppliers from whom they can purchase the complete line. Thus, in the case analyzed above, discontinuance of Pong might involve a negative incremental profit of more than the amount computed because of reduced sales of Ping and/or Pang. Unfortunately, such interproduct demand relationships usually cannot be measured accurately; but they can be extremely important.

The discontinuance of a product line was illustrated here as a very simple situation. Ignored was the very pertinent question of what might be done to fill the void left by the abandoned product. If a company discontinues making and selling one product, there will be some amount of idle capacity in both production facilities and the sales force. This idle capacity may be diverted to production and sales of a new product or of one or more of the other products already in the line. For example, the decision to discontinue Pong would take on new and significant dimensions if we knew that the capacity thus idled could be diverted to additional output and sales of Ping and/or Pang. Suppose that the loss of all Pong sales could be replaced with an equal dollar volume of some combination of Ping and Pang sales. The latter two products both have a variable profit ratio of 33⅓% of sales, as compared with Pong's variable profit ratio of 20%. Thus, additional sales of either or both of these products in the amount of $150,000 would add $50,000 to total variable profit. The incremental profit of the decision to discontinue Pong would then be positive, as shown below:

| | |
|---|---:|
| Increase in variable profit from Ping/Pang........... | $50,000 |
| Less: Loss of variable profit from Pong.............. | 30,000 |
| Incremental profit before taxes..................... | $20,000 |
| Incremental profit after tax ($20,000 × .60)......... | $12,000 |

Finally, there are other factors which may not lend themselves to short-run financial analysis. What will be the impact of the discontinuance of a product line on the overall company image? What will be the impact of the decision on the company's employees—specifically, their job security? What psychological effect, if any, might this decision have upon the salesmen in their subsequent promotion of the other products? The fact that these questions may be unanswerable does not mean that they must not be asked.

## Common Production Costs in Decision Making

The allocation of common production costs among joint products was discussed and illustrated in Chapter 5. The purpose of that allocation was to provide product cost data required for inventory valuation and income measurement. For decision making, allocations of common costs are inappropriate. Only if a decision concerned the production of the entire group of joint products would the common costs be relevant. To the extent that common costs would be avoided if the output of a group of products were discontinued or reduced, those common costs would be relevant to the decision. If the decision at hand involves only one product in a group, however, the common production costs are not relevant to it. Abandonment of only one of a group of joint products would not reduce the common costs at all.[6] The incremental profit of the entire group is

---

[6] This statement implicity assumes that the proportions of joint products emerging from the common process are fixed. In some instances, it is possible to alter the product proportions by varying the inputs of labor or materials. For example, the proportion of one joint product might be reduced if certain labor tasks were omitted from the common processing. Thus, a decision to abandon that product alone could possibly entail a reduction in common costs with no change in the output of the other joint product(s).

measured by the difference between the revenue obtained from all of the products and the total costs, both common and separate, directly traceable to the group. The incremental profit of an individual product in the group, however, is measured by the excess of its own revenue over its own separate costs. Any allocation of common cost to one product is irrelevant to its incremental profit. Common cost allocations can be dangerously misleading for decision-making purposes.

It may seem somewhat bothersome that the incremental profits of two joint products can be determined without regard to the very significant common costs of making those products. But incremental profit is not the same thing as net profit. Incremental profit is the amount which an individual product (or a decision) contributes to total enterprise profit, recognizing that the sum of all incremental profits from the several products (or other segments) of the enterprise must be greater than the common costs if a net profit for the firm as a whole is to be realized. The relationship of the profit contributed by one segment of an enterprise to the total enterprise profit was discussed in Chapter 12.

*Incremental Profits of Joint Products.*   The preceding paragraphs suggested that the incremental profit of an individual joint product is simply the difference between its sales value and its separate costs. This is true if "separate costs" are properly defined and measured. The relevant separate costs of a product are those which are directly traceable to it and would be avoided if the product were discontinued. Thus, if the cost accounting system allocates a portion of fixed manufacturing overhead to all operations in the plant, that portion of the separate processing costs which represents such allocations is irrelevant to the incremental profit of an individual product. The same is true of fixed selling and administrative expenses which may be allocated among the various products for some reporting purpose (not inventory valuation, of course). Only those selling and administrative expenses directly traceable to the individual product may be included in the determination of the product's incremental profit.

Everything said above concerning joint products is equally true of by-products. In the case of a principal product (as distinguished from a by-product), on the other hand, it would seem that the revenue from the sales of that main product should normally be adequate to cover not only its own separate costs but also the production costs common to it and the by-product. There are instances where this is not so and where the overall profitability of the combination of principal product and by-product is assured only by sales of the by-product. In such instance, it would appear that the by-product is such only by arbitrary definition; in a very real sense, it is a joint product.

## QUESTIONS FOR DISCUSSION

1. For purposes of decision making, what are relevant costs?

2. Is the incremental profit from a decision the same as the variable profit from the decision? Explain.

3. Distinguish clearly among the following three concepts: relevant cost, direct cost, and variable cost. Distinguish among these three concepts: fixed cost, indirect cost, and irrelevant cost.

4. Suggest an operational distinction between short-term and long-term decisions. Into which category would you expect each of the following decisions to fall:
   a. A decision to purchase a new building?
   b. A decision to rent a new building?
   c. A decision to sell products in new market areas?
   d. A decision to create a long-term planning committee of the board of directors?

5. "Since fixed costs are unaffected by a change in the volume of operations, they are always irrelevant to any business decision short of a decision to discontinue operations altogether." Evaluate this statement.

6. Is incremental profit analysis pertinent to decision making in nonprofit institutions such as schools and hospitals? Discuss.

7. The uses of cost data in income measurement and inventory valuation are not always compatible with the uses of cost data for decision making. How can a single cost accounting system provide data for both of these purposes? Would such a system include all of the cost data necessary for financial accounting purposes? Would it include all of the cost data necessary for decision making?

8. Describe the procedures that the management of a manufacturing firm might employ to identify and measure all of the costs relevant to a decision whether to make or to buy a part used in the manufacture of a product.

9. This chapter asserts that the common costs of producing two or more joint products are irrelevant to a decision regarding any one of these joint products. Yet, in Chapter 5, these same common costs were indicated to be relevant to the valuation of an inventory of a single joint product. These two positions appear to be inconsistent. If a cost is irrelevant to a particular product, how can it reasonably be included in the cost of an inventory of that product?

10. A lumber company is planning to build a new mill. It has two basic alternatives with regard to the disposition of sawdust. The sawdust can be swept up, placed in sacks, and sold; or it can be burned in an incinerator. Assuming that the incinerator will be needed for other refuse, regardless of the decision regarding the sawdust, what factors would be relevant to the decision as to how sawdust should be disposed of? Would this decision situation be changed materially if the incinerator would not be needed if the sawdust were not to be burned?

11. If depreciation on manufacturing equipment is recorded by the productive

hours method and the company is considering adding a second production shift, is depreciation a relevant cost in connection with the decision regarding the second shift? Why or why not?

12. Are income taxes relevant costs with respect to decisions that are expected to have the effect of increasing or decreasing taxable income? Could income tax considerations ever be the deciding factors in such decisions? Explain.

13. Should the incremental profits of all decisions actually made by management sum algebraically to the net income subsequently reported for the firm? Why or why not?

## PROBLEMS

14–1. The Spenser Electronics Company produces most of its own parts and components. The standard wage rate in the parts department is $4.75 per hour. Variable manufacturing overhead is applied at a standard rate of $1.20 per labor hour and fixed manufacturing overhead, at a standard rate of $3.20 per hour.

For its 1977 output, the company will require a new part that it has never used before. This part could be made in the parts department without any expansion of existing facilities. However, it would be necessary to increase the monthly cost of product testing and inspection by $1,200. Estimated labor time for the new part would be eight-tenths of an hour per unit. Raw materials cost has been estimated at $8.68 per unit. Alternatively, the part could be purchased from an independent supplier for $15.50 per unit, delivered. The company has estimated that it will use 80,000 of the new parts during 1977.

*Required:*

Would it be more economical for the company to make or to purchase this new part in 1977? Support your answer with appropriate financial analysis.

 14–2. The Dryden Company, Ltd., produces a single product in its Leeds plant. This product is manufactured in three successive production departments. Following are the budgeted annual production costs for an output of 150,000 units, which is regarded as normal volume:

|  | Department | | |
|---|---|---|---|
|  | *A* | *B* | *C* |
| Direct materials. . . . . . . . . . . . . . . . | $330,000 | $115,500 | |
| Direct labor. . . . . . . . . . . . . . . . . . . | 210,000 | 270,000 | $126,000 |
| Variable manufacturing overhead. . | 105,000 | 135,000 | 63,000 |
| Fixed manufacturing overhead. . . . | 315,000 | 405,000 | 189,000 |
|  | $960,000 | $925,500 | $378,000 |

Fixed manufacturing overhead is applied to production at a plant-wide rate of 150% of direct labor cost. None of the fixed manufacturing overhead is considered to be directly traceable to individual departments.

Recently, the company has learned that it can purchase a semifinished product, ready for work in Department B, from a Birmingham manufacturer at a unit price of $4.95, delivered. If this semifinished product were purchased instead of the basic raw material, Department A could be closed down. However, direct labor and variable manufacturing overhead costs in Department B would be increased by 10% because of changes in operations necessitated by the introduction of the semifinished product into that department.

*Required:*

a. On the basis of short-run profitability, would it be better for the company to purchase the semifinished product or to continue producing it in Department A?

b. What additional factors should the company's management consider before making the decision in this situation?

14–3. The Donne Engine Company produces most of its engine parts in its own plant. Recently, it has been weighing the merits of purchasing some finished parts instead of manufacturing them. At present, it is studying the advantages of buying part no. 66 from an outside supplier for $12.75 per unit. If this were done, monthly purchasing costs would be increased by $1,500.

Part no. 66 is now manufactured in the stamping department along with numerous other parts. The department would continue operations on a somewhat reduced basis if part no. 66 were no longer produced there. The average monthly usage of part no. 66 is 20,000 units. The direct costs of producing the part include $3.60 per unit for materials and one and one-half labor hours per unit at a wage rate of $4.80 per hour. Manufacturing overhead is applied to production in the stamping department on the basis of direct labor hours. The monthly flexible budget for manufacturing overhead in this department is as follows:

| Direct labor hours | 200,000 | 240,000 | 280,000 |
|---|---|---|---|
| Variable costs | $150,000 | $180,000 | $210,000 |
| Fixed costs | 300,000 | 300,000 | 300,000 |
| Total costs | $450,000 | $480,000 | $510,000 |

Normal production volume in the stamping department is 240,000 labor hours per month, and current actual production is at about the same level. Discontinuation of the production of part no. 66 would cause an unfavorable volume variance of about $37,500 per month in the department.

*Required:*

Would it be more profitable for the company to continue making part no. 66 or to purchase it?

14-4.  The Marvell Bakery sells two very popular specialty cakes, a Vienna creame torte and a rum butter cake. Both are baked in the same oven, which will accomodate 30 cakes at one time and can be operated for a maximum of 80 hours per week. The demand for both cakes is so great that the bakery could sell the maximum output of the oven in any combination of the two cakes, including all of one or all of the other. The only direct costs of these cakes are their respective ingredients costs. A comparison of the selling prices, ingredients costs, and oven times of the two cakes is as follows:

|  | Vienna Cream Torte | Rum Butter Cake |
|---|---|---|
| Selling price.......................... | $3.50 | $2.75 |
| Ingredients cost....................... | 1.50 | 1.10 |
| Oven time............................. | 20 min. | 15 min. |

*Required:*

What would be the most profitable sales mix of these two cakes?

14-5.  The Browning Corporation manufactures two products, Rime and Vurs. Under present operations, raw materials are processed in Department A; and the two products are separated at the end of this processing. For every unit of Rime, three units of Vurs are obtained. Rime is then finished in Department B and Vurs, in Department C. Budgeted operating data for 1977 are as follows:

|  | Department | | |
|---|---|---|---|
|  | A | B | C |
| Units produced and sold: |  |  |  |
| Rime......................... | 25,000 | 25,000 |  |
| Vurs......................... | 75,000 |  | 75,000 |
| Costs incurred: |  |  |  |
| Direct materials................ | $150,000 |  |  |
| Direct labor................... | 80,000 | $30,000 | $40,000 |
| Variable manufacturing overhead.. | 20,000 | 10,000 | 20,000 |
| Fixed manufacturing overhead.... | 90,000 | 25,000 | 35,000 |

All costs are directly traceable to the individual departments.

At present, Rime is sold for $10 per unit and Vurs for $5 per unit. Both products are also readily marketable at the completion of processing in Department A—Rime for $8 per unit and Vurs for $3 per unit.

*Required:*

From the point of view of short-run profit maximization, when should each product be sold during 1977—after final completion, as at present, or at the split-off point? Support your answer with appropriate financial analysis.

14–6. The Swinburne Corporation manufactures three different products from a single raw material and common processing. Budgeted data for 1977 are presented below. The production costs identified with the individual products are only the separate processing costs incurred after the split-off point.

| | Product | | | Common |
| | X | Y | Z | Costs |
|---|---|---|---|---|
| Output in pounds.............. | 90,000 | 60,000 | 30,000 | |
| Selling price per pound......... | $ 1.10 | $ 2.20 | $ 3.30 | |
| Production costs: | | | | |
| Direct materials............. | .098 | .20 | .333 | $100,000 |
| Direct labor................ | $ 8,000 | $12,000 | $10,000 | 50,000 |
| Variable manufacturing overhead................. | -.044 4,000 | -1 6,000 | -.133 4,000 | 16,000 |
| Fixed manufacturing overhead................. | 6,000 | 10,000 | 8,000 | 32,000 |

*Required:*

Would it be profitable to alter the output mix from the one budgeted to 60,000 pounds of Product X, 80,000 pounds of Product Y, and 40,000 pounds of Product Z at the cost of increasing total common processing costs by $40,000?

14–7. The basic processing of raw materials in the Yeats Chemical Company's plant yields three semifinished products, Worlon, Nantron, and Extron. The budgeted cost of the basic processing for 1977 is $3,110,000. Budgeted production, price, and separate processing cost data for the three products are as follows:

| | Worlon | Nantron | Extron |
|---|---|---|---|
| Output in units.................. | 600,000 | 300,000 | 80,000 |
| Selling price per unit............. | $ 5 | $ 12 | $ 1.50 |
| Separate processing costs: | | | |
| Variable cost per unit........... | $ 1 | $ 1.20 | $ .60 |
| Fixed cost per year............. | $300,000 | $240,000 | $22,000 |

Worlon and Nantron are accounted for as joint products. Extron is treated as a by-product.

*Required:*

a. Would it be profitable to spend $400,000 more on basic processing in order to alter the product mix to yield one-fifth more Nantron and one-fourth more Extron, with no change in the total number of units of output of all three products?

b. Would it be profitable to spend $450,000 more on basic processing in order to convert all production of Extron to equal quantities of Worlon and Nantron, with no increase in the total number of units of output of all three products?

c. What is the most that the company could afford to spend to convert all output of Extron to an equal quantity of Worlon?

14-8. The Milton Products Company produces Product A. This product sells for $12 per unit. Variable costs to make and sell the product are $6 per unit, and fixed costs are $5 per unit at a normal volume of 600,000 units per year. Sales volume recently has been equal to normal volume and is expected to continue at that level.

Montague Worth & Co. has offered the Milton Products Company a contract for 200,000 units of Product A each year at a price of $10 per unit. As these units would be distributed under Montague Worth's private brand name, they would not adversely affect regular sales of Product A. The company could avoid $.50 of variable selling expenses for each unit sold under this proposed contract. Fixed production costs would have to be increased by $750,000 in order to increase production volume to 800,000 units.

The production engineer has recommended a plan to improve product quality and, thereby, increase sales volume. His proposal would increase variable production costs by $.40 per unit and fixed costs by $600,000 per year. Sales volume would be increased by 150,000 units annually with no change in selling price.

The sales manager has suggested still another plan to boost sales volume. He would reduce the selling price by 10%. This price reduction would increase sales volume by 50%. This additional output could be achieved by an increase in fixed costs of $900,000 per year.

None of the three proposed changes in operations would necessitate any new capital expenditures.

*Required:*

Accepting the assumptions underlying each of the three proposals for increased sales volume and assuming that the three proposals are mutually exclusive, evaluate the profitability of the alternative courses of action open to management.

14-9. The Pope Plumbing Company manufactures a wide variety of component parts. Two of these, the Type K Valve and the Type J Elbow Joint, are currently suffering greatly reduced sales volumes because of competition from lower priced substitutes. Data relevant to these two products are as follows:

| | Type K Valve | Type J Elbow Joint |
|---|---|---|
| Units currently sold annually............. | 20,000 | 50,000 |
| Unit selling price...................... | $4.50 | $1.25 |
| Unit production costs: | | |
| Direct materials...................... | $2.09 | $ .42 |
| Direct labor......................... | .95 | .37 |
| Variable manufacturing overhead........ | .46 | :15 |
| Fixed manufacturing overhead.......... | .80 | .24 |
| Total costs...................... | $4.30 | $1.18 |

Unabsorbed fixed manufacturing overhead currently is about $22,000 per year.

The sales manager has suggested that selling prices of $3.95 for the Type K Valve and $1.20 for the Type J Elbow Joint would make these products more competitive and would restore the company's former market shares for these items—40,000 units per year of the valve and 70,000 units annually of the elbow joint.

The purchasing agent has pointed out that identical items could be purchased from Japanese manufacturers below the company's own cost and then resold to the company's customers. Such an arrangement, he claims, would partially mitigate the impact of the suggested price reductions. Type K Valves could be purchased from Japanese suppliers for $3.75 each and Type J Elbow Joints, for $.95 each. Both of these prices include all freight and import duties.

The volume of production of the two items in question here is not so great that any decision affecting them would have any impact on investments in production or distribution facilities. All selling and administrative expenses are considered fixed costs and are currently allocated among the company's products at a rate of 20% of full manufacturing costs.

*Required:*

Prepare an analysis of the profitability of the proposed reduction in selling prices and of the suggested procurement of these two parts from Japanese manufacturers. What course of action would be most profitable?

14–10. The Gray Corporation produces a single product in its plant. This product sells for $44 per unit. The standard production cost per unit is as follows:

| | |
|---|---|
| Raw materials (5 lbs. @ $3).................... | $15 |
| Direct labor (2 hrs. @ $4.50)................... | 9 |
| Variable manufacturing overhead.............. | 4 |
| Fixed manufacturing overhead................. | 8 |
| | $36 |

The plant is currently operating at full capacity of 800,000 units per year on a single shift. This output is inadequate to meet projected sales demand, and the sales manager has estimated that the firm will lose sales of 500,000 units next year if the capacity constraint is not eased.

Plant capacity could be doubled by adding a second shift. This would require additional out-of-pocket fixed manufacturing overhead costs of $5,000,000 annually. Also, a night-work wage premium equal to 10% of the standard wage rate would have to be paid during the second shift. However, if annual production volume were 1,200,000 units or more (but not less), the corporation could take advantage of a 5% quantity discount on its raw materials purchases.

*Required:*

a. Would it be profitable to add the second shift in order to obtain the additional sales volume of 500,000 units per year?

b. What would be the minimum annual increase in sales volume over the present 800,000 units necessary to justify adding the second shift?

14–11. You are the independent auditor for the Burns Company. When you had completed your audit for the preceding year, top management asked your assistance in arriving at a decision whether to continue manufacturing a part or to buy it from an outside supplier. The part, called a Faktron, is a component used in several of the company's finished products.

From your audit working papers and from further investigation, you have developed the following data relative to the company's operations:

1. The annual requirement for Faktrons is 20,000 units. The lowest list price quotation from a supplier was $27.50 per unit.

2. Faktrons are being manufactured in the precision machinery department. Following are the total costs in this department during the preceding year, when 20,000 Faktrons were produced:

| | |
|---|---:|
| Materials...................................... | $600,000 |
| Direct labor.................................. | 750,000 |
| Indirect labor................................ | 200,000 |
| Light and heat................................ | 40,000 |
| Power......................................... | 60,000 |
| Depreciation.................................. | 350,000 |
| Property taxes and insurance..................... | 35,000 |
| Payroll taxes and other fringe benefits............. | 190,000 |
| Miscellaneous................................. | 75,000 |

3. The following proportions of the variable costs in the precision machinery department could be avoided if production of Faktrons was discontinued:

| | |
|---|---:|
| Materials...................... | 35% |
| Direct labor................... | 40% |
| Power......................... | 25% |

4. If Faktrons are purchased from an outside supplier, shipping charges would average $.50 per unit. Also, indirect labor in the precision machinery department would be increased by $30,000 annually because of the receiving, inspecting, and handling of the purchased parts.

*Required:*

a. Prepare a schedule showing the relative costs of making and buying Faktrons. Which alternative would be more economical?

b. What considerations other than this cost comparison would you bring to management's attention in order to help them to arrive at a decision?

(Adapted from CPA Examination)

14–12. The Coleridge Theater has shown the motion picture *Shallow Mouth,* for the past two weeks. It has been the most successful film that has played at the theater for several years. Because of the "explicit" nature of the film, the manager of the theater has scrupulously restricted admission to adults only. The manager believes that attendance will continue to be above normal for another two weeks if the run of *Shallow Mouth* is extended. Another movie, *Tarzan Goes to Cleveland,* is booked for the next two weeks, however. Even if *Shallow Mouth* is extended, the theater will have to pay the rental for *Tarzan Goes to Cleveland* as well.

Normal attendance at the Coleridge Theater is 5,000 patrons per week, approximately 30% of whom are children under the age of 12. Attendance for *Shallow Mouth* has been 60% greater than the normal total, despite the "adults only" policy. The manager believes that there would be some tapering off during a second two weeks. He estimates that attendance would be 20% below that of the first two weeks during a third week and 30% lower than during the first two weeks during a fourth week. Attendance at *Tarzan Goes to Cleveland* would be expected to be normal throughout its run, regardless of whether it was one or two weeks.

All features at the theater are shown at the regular prices of $3 for adult admissions and $1.50 for children under 12. The rental charge for *Shallow Mouth* would be $5,000 for one more week or $9,000 for two more weeks. For *Tarzan Goes to Cleveland,* the rental is $7,500 for two weeks. All other operating costs are fixed in the amount of $15,000 per week, except for the cost of popcorn and candy, which averages 30% of its selling price. Sales of popcorn and candy regularly average $.40 per patron, regardless of age.

*Required:*

The manager of the Coleridge Theater has three courses of action open to him for the next two weeks. He can extend the run of *Shallow Mouth* for two more weeks; he can extend its run for one week and show *Tarzan Goes to Cleveland* for one week; or he can show the

Tarzan film for the full two weeks as originally booked. Which alternative would be the most profitable?

14–13. The Wordsworth Doll Company has asked your assistance in determining the most profitable sales and production mix of its products for 1977. The company manufactures a line of dolls and a doll dress sewing kit. The sales department has provided you with the following budget data:

| Product | Estimated Demand in Units in 1977 | Net Price per Unit |
|---------|---------------------------------|--------------------|
| Laurie doll.................... | 60,000 | $ 7.25 |
| Debbie doll.................... | 100,000 | 3.95 |
| Sarah doll..................... | 50,000 | 8.30 |
| Kathy doll..................... | 45,000 | 12.60 |
| Sewing kit..................... | 220,000 | 3.00 |

To promote sales of the sewing kit, as well as the dolls, there is a 20% reduction in the regular net selling price for a kit sold to a customer who purchases a doll at the same time. Based on past experience, the sales department estimates that sewing kits will be sold in conjunction with 60% of the sales of each of the four dolls.

You have developed the following additional data from the accounting files:

1. Standard direct production costs per unit are as follows:

| Product | Materials | Labor |
|---------|-----------|-------|
| Laurie........................... | $2.10 | $2.50 |
| Debbie........................... | 1.05 | 1.25 |
| Sarah............................ | 2.75 | 3.00 |
| Kathy............................ | 5.00 | 4.00 |
| Sewing kit....................... | .95 | .75 |

2. The standard wage rate of $5 per hour is expected to continue unchanged throughout 1977. The plant has an effective production capacity of 150,000 labor hours per year on a single shift. The current equipment can be used to produce any and all of the products.

3. Variable manufacturing overhead is budgeted at $1.50 per direct labor hour. Total fixed manufacturing overhead for 1977 is planned at $360,000.

4. There will be no inventories of work in process or of finished products on January 1, 1977.

*Required:*

a. Prepare a schedule showing the incremental profit of each product in whatever manner will be most useful to management in planning the product mix.

b. Is the present effective capacity on a single shift adequate to meet the estimated sales demand in 1977? If not, how would you recommend that the company alter its budgeted product mix in order to keep production within the limits of a single shift?

c. Irrespective of your answer in *b*, assume now that capacity is not sufficient to meet 1977 sales demand. How might the company expand capacity to meet that demand? Under what conditions would each method of expanding capacity be profitable in 1977?

(Adapted from CPA Examination)

14–14. Following is the budgeted income statement of the Byron Products Corporation for the year 1977:

|  | A | B | C | Totals |
|---|---|---|---|---|
|  | *Product* | | | |
| Sales................... | $500,000 | $225,000 | $300,000 | $1,025,000 |
| Cost of goods sold: | | | | |
| Direct materials......... | $ 90,000 | $ 40,500 | $ 54,000 | $ 184,500 |
| Direct labor........... | 120,000 | 54,000 | 72,000 | 246,000 |
| Variable manufacturing | | | | |
| overhead............. | 60,000 | 27,000 | 36,000 | 123,000 |
| Fixed manufacturing | | | | |
| overhead............. | 80,000 | 40,000 | 50,000 | 170,000 |
|  | $350,000 | $161,500 | $212,000 | $ 723,500 |
| Gross margin............ | $150,000 | $ 63,500 | $ 88,000 | $ 301,500 |
| Selling and administrative | | | | |
| expenses: | | | | |
| Variable............... | $ 30,000 | $ 13,500 | $ 18,000 | $ 61,500 |
| Fixed................. | 55,000 | 25,000 | 35,000 | 115,000 |
|  | $ 85,000 | $ 38,500 | $ 53,000 | $ 176,500 |
| Income before tax........ | $ 65,000 | $ 25,000 | $ 35,000 | $ 125,000 |
| Income tax (40%)........ | 26,000 | 10,000 | 14,000 | 50,000 |
| Net income.............. | $ 39,000 | $ 15,000 | $ 21,000 | $ 75,000 |
| Units produced and sold.... | 10,000 | 7,500 | 8,000 | |

The factory is expected to operate at full capacity during 1977. It takes twice as long to produce one unit of Product A as it does to produce one unit of Product B. It takes half again as long to produce one unit of Product A as it does to produce one unit of Product C.

All fixed costs are common to all three products.

*Required:*

a. Rank the three products in the order of their contributions to total corporate profit.

b. Assume that the corporation has decided to discontinue production of one product and to produce equal quantities of the remaining two products. Operations would continue at full capacity. In order to maximize profit in 1977, which two products should be produced and in what quantities?

c. What would be the incremental profit of the proposed shift in product mix determined in *b*?

14–15.  The management of the Keats Cottonseed Company has engaged you to assist in the development of information to be used for managerial decision making. The company has a capacity to process 200,000 tons of cottonseed per year. The output yield of one ton of cottonseed is as follows:

| Product | Average Yield per Ton of Cottonseed | Average Selling Price per Trade Unit |
|---|---|---|
| Oil.......................... | 300 lbs. | 40¢ per lb. |
| Meal........................ | 600 | $80 per ton |
| Hulls....................... | 800 | $50 per ton |
| Lint........................ | 100 | $ 5 per cwt. |
| Waste....................... | 200 | No value |

A marketing study has indicated that the company can expect to sell its maximum output during the coming year at the average selling prices listed above. The company's operating costs are as follows:

Processing costs:
   Variable—$25 per ton of cottonseed processed
   Fixed—$4,000,000 per year
Variable marketing costs—$60 per ton of output sold
Fixed administrative costs—$2,000,000 per year

From the foregoing information, you have prepared and submitted to management an analysis of the company's break-even point. In view of almost continually fluctuating prices in the cottonseed market, management has asked you to determine the maximum amount that the company can afford to pay for a ton of cottonseed and suffer an operating loss no greater than would be incurred if operations were shut down. You have determined that all fixed costs would still be incurred if operations were shut down.

*Required:*

a. Compute the maximum amount that the company can afford to pay for a ton of cottonseed during the coming year.

b. Compute the maximum amount that the company can afford to pay for a ton of cottonseed and still earn a net profit before taxes equal to 15% of sales revenue.

c. Assuming that the company does produce at full capacity during the coming year, what would the average price per ton of cotton-seed have to be in order for the company to break even?

(Adapted from CPA Examination)

14–16.  Shelley Hosiery Mills, Inc., manufactures and sells women's stockings. Productive capacity is 8 million pairs per year, and this limit cannot be exceeded during the next year. All pairs of stockings are carefully inspected. Twenty percent of the output is unavoidably flawed and must be sold as "seconds." The remaining 80% of the output is sold under the brand name "Shelley Sheers" for $2.50 per pair. The seconds are presently being sold under the brand name "Shelley Seconds" for $1.50 per pair.

Budgeted sales volume for the next year is planned as follows:

"Shelley Sheers".................... 5,600,000 pairs
"Shelley Seconds".................. 1,200,000 pairs

Budgeted costs for the coming year are as follows:

Variable production costs................. $.90 per pair produced
Fixed production costs................... $5,000,000
Variable selling expense.................. $.20 per pair sold
Fixed selling expense.................... $2,500,000

A marketing consultant has advised management that the sales of seconds under the Shelley brand name are hurting the sales of "Shelley Sheers." He has projected that the budgeted sales volume of "Shelley Sheers" could be increased by 25% if sales of seconds under the company's brand name were discontinued.

The sales manager has learned that the entire output of seconds could be sold to a chain of discount stores with no brand identification for $1.00 per pair. The usual variable selling expense would be avoided on these sales, but additional billing and shipping costs of $80,000 per year would be incurred.

There is no significant inventory of either "Shelley Sheers" or seconds as of the end of the current year.

*Required:*

Accepting the validity of the marketing consultant's estimates, prepare a report for management to show the most profitable method of selling seconds during the next year.

14–17.  In 1950, A. F. Slicko developed and patented a heat-resistant paint which has the additional properties of being long wearing and easy to clean. He found a ready market for this new paint among manufacturers of ovens and other equipment used under conditions of extreme heat. At the outset, Slicko and 36 employees produced this paint in a small rented plant and delivered it to customers in the Chicago area only. By 1955, however, it was apparent that a much broader market for this product existed and could be served only by a major expansion of production and distribution facilities. Accordingly, Slicko incorporated under the name Asbestone Paint Company and constructed a large plant in East Chicago. An expanded sales force began distribution of the paint under the trade name "Asbestone" throughout the East and Midwest.

In 1958, Slicko obtained a patent on a graphite-base industrial lubricant, subsequently marketed under the trade name "Glideze." The combined demand for this new product and for Asbestone soon exceeded the capacity of the East Chicago plant. In 1964, a new and larger plant was completed in Gary; and all paint production was shifted to that location. This left the East Chicago plant temporarily far below capacity. Growth in demand for Glideze and the introduction of another new product soon corrected this situation, however.

In 1972, the company introduced a lightweight heatproof liner for use in ovens, furnaces, and similar equipment. This liner, marketed under the trade name "Heatrap," quickly proved to be a good seller, particularly to customers who could also use Asbestone. Indeed, while the growth in sales of Asbestone had been very steady at an annual rate of 5% for the past several years, it accelerated significantly as the sales of Heatrap grew. Salesmen who found a customer for Heatrap soon found that they also had a good prospect for sales of Asbestone in place of competing products.

By the end of 1976, it had become apparent that the combined capacities of the two plants could no longer meet demand. In fact, the sales forecast for 1977 seemed to exceed present capacity. After careful study, the board of directors voted to construct a major new plant in Michigan City. This new plant will not be ready until the summer of 1978, however. Hence, it will not help to solve the short-term problem of inadequate capacity for 1977.

Sales in units of product for the ten years prior to 1977 were as follows:

| Year | Asbestone (gallons) | Glideze (pounds) | Heatrap (square yards) |
|---|---|---|---|
| 1967 | 2,000,000 | 800,000 | |
| 1968 | 2,100,000 | 860,000 | |
| 1969 | 2,205,000 | 910,000 | |
| 1970 | 2,315,000 | 960,000 | |
| 1971 | 2,431,000 | 1,050,000 | |
| 1972 | 2,633,000 | 1,100,000 | 400,000 |
| 1973 | 2,880,000 | 1,180,000 | 1,000,000 |
| 1974 | 3,214,000 | 1,250,000 | 2,000,000 |
| 1975 | 3,655,000 | 1,325,000 | 3,500,000 |
| 1976 | 4,303,000 | 1,400,000 | 6,000,000 |

Sales for 1977 have been budgeted as shown below.

Asbestone.................... 4,858,000 gals. @ $12.50
Glideze..................... 1,500,000 lbs. @ $10.50
Heatrap.................... 8,000,000 sq. yds. @ $1.00

Standard production cost data for the three products are as follows:

|  | Asbestone | Glideze | Heatrap |
|---|---|---|---|
| Standard production lot........ | 100 gals. | 50 lbs. | 1,000 sq. yds. |
| Standard labor hours per lot.... | 30 | 40 | 75 |
| Standard wage rate per hour..... | $4.50 | $4.50 | $4.50 |
| Standard materials cost per lot.. | $620 | $135 | $250 |

The flexible budgets for manufacturing overhead in the two plants are summarized below. The company uses absorption costing.

|  | East Chicago Plant | Gary Plant |
|---|---|---|
| Variable rate per direct labor hour....... | $    1.50 | $    1.50 |
| Fixed cost per year.................... | $4,000,000 | $8,000,000 |

The annual productive capacity of the East Chicago plant is 1,000,000 direct labor hours. Capacity in the Gary plant is 2,000,000 direct labor hours per year. Both of these quantities are also used as normal volumes. Both plants can produce any or all of the three products, although no paint has actually been manufactured in East Chicago since 1964.

Inventories of finished products and work in process at December 31, 1976, are the minimum stocks required for continuous sales and production operations.

*Required:*

Given the present capacity constraint, what would be the most profitable product mix for the company in 1977?

# chapter 15

# The Role of Costs in Pricing Decisions

ERHAPS THE most important single decision which the management of a business enterprise must make is setting the price for the firm's product or service. In a multiproduct firm, many pricing decisions must be made. The pricing decision is critical not only at the outset; it must be re-appraised and, possibly, revised regularly. The pricing decision affects the entire enterprise and must be made with this fact in mind. It is not simply a marketing or a financial decision. It is the genesis of the revenues which the firm realizes. If those revenues persistently fail to cover the costs of the firm, the enterprise as a whole will ultimately fail. The accountant, as a planner, compiler, and analyst of financial data, is importantly involved in the price-setting decision. Financial data and, more specifically, cost data are fundamental elements in the price-setting process; but they are only part of that process. Their relevance to the pricing decision must be neither exaggerated nor underestimated; either error could be financially fatal. This chapter is concerned with the proper role of cost data in price-setting decisions. It does not purport to offer a comprehensive analysis of pricing.

## ECONOMIC THEORY OF PRICE DETERMINATION

It is not the purpose of this section to expound or to summarize price theory as commonly developed in the discipline of economics. A few basic notions will be reviewed, however, to establish a general framework for the ensuing discussion of the pertinence of costs to pricing decisions.

## Supply and Demand

The basic factors determining price in economic theory are the supply of a product (or service) and the demand for it. If there is an actual market for a product, there must be some price at which the physical volume of product that suppliers are willing to sell is equal to that volume which customers (i.e., "demanders") are willing to buy. That is the price at which the product is traded. This relationship between supply and demand is commonly depicted graphically by a positively sloped

### FIGURE 15-1

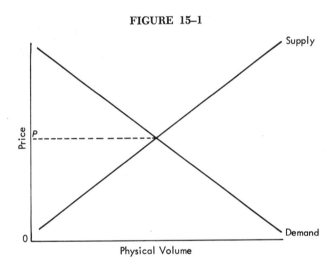

supply curve and a negatively sloped demand curve, as illustrated in Figure 15-1. (These curves need not be straight lines, of course.) The price of the product ($p$ in Figure 15-1) is determined at the point of intersection of the supply and demand curves. The conceptual validity of this analysis is readily apparent. Its practical applicability, however, is not always so apparent. Managers do not have access to neat supply and demand curves such as those in Figure 15-1. They may be able to estimate the general patterns of supply and demand for their products, but these estimates are subject to varying and indeterminate degrees of error.

*Elasticity of Demand.*  One of the most critical characteristics of the demand for a product is its price elasticity, that is, the relative degree to which changes in the price of the product cause changes in the volume of sales of that product. Obviously, knowledge of the elasticity of demand for a product is crucial to any price change decision. Yet, the elasticity of demand for most products is subject to a considerable degree of uncertainty. The demand for certain products, such as salt, is usually agreed to be highly inelastic. A substantial increase in the price of a pound of salt may have no appreciable impact upon consumers' purchases of it. Other products, however, have definitely elastic demand schedules. Substantially more units will be purchased at low prices than at high prices. Observing that the demand for a product is generally elastic or inelastic is one thing. Measuring its elasticity—determining the impact upon physical sales volume of a specific price change—is quite another. Yet, it is just this determination that is important to the business manager contemplating a change in the price of his product.

His problems are further complicated by the factor of cross-elasticity of demand. This is the relative degree to which the sales of one product are affected by changes in the price of a substitute product (e.g., the impact on the sales of steel of a reduction in the price of aluminum). The problem of measuring cross-elasticity is further clouded by the prior problem of identifying substitute products.

A review of the discussions in the preceding three paragraphs suggests that management cannot measure accurately the most basic factors underlying the price-setting decision. Nevertheless, these economic factors cannot be ignored. Subsequent discussions of the role of costs in pricing decisions will not deal extensively with the factors of supply and demand, but these factors will always be present as the basic constraints within which the pricing decision must be made.

## Competition

Pricing decisions must be weighed and evaluated with adequate consideration of the impact of competition upon the decision and the impact of the decision upon competition. In the perfect competition of economic theory, the individual seller is, in effect, the captive of competition. He has no price-setting discretion at all. One of the requisites of perfect competition is homogeneity of product; all sellers' products must be identical. If there exists an element of product differentiation among sellers, the market is described as imperfectly competitive. In an imperfect market, the individual seller has some range of discretion within which he may set his price. The extreme of price-setting discretion is the monopolist. He is the only one selling his particular product and, therefore, is limited in his pricing decisions only by the factors of supply and demand. However, as in the case of public utilities, the government may step in and impose additional constraints on the monopolist's pricing policies.

Subsequent discussions of pricing decisions in this chapter will assume some degree of imperfect competition in the market for the product whose price is in question. The seller will always be assumed to have some range of discretion in setting his price. This assumption is generally valid in respect to the operations of most American manufacturers and distributors.

## PRICING STANDARD PRODUCTS

Not all pricing decisions have the same dimensions. There may be great differences between a decision as to the price of one of a company's standard products and a decision regarding the pricing of a special order. The former type of decision will be considered here. Pricing special orders will be discussed in a later section. Standard products here include all items regularly produced and sold by the company, whether they are produced continuously for inventory or on individual customers' orders only.

### Cost-Plus Pricing

One of the simplest approaches to pricing decisions is to set the price at an amount equal to the standard or budgeted cost of production (or purchasing, in the case of a merchandising enterprise) plus a normal markup. This *normal markup* is usually a target gross profit, intended to cover nonmanufacturing costs and leave a remainder for net profit before taxes. The normal markup is customarily stated as a percentage, either of selling price or of cost. Normal markups are fairly widely employed in retailing, where they are regularly expressed as percentages of selling prices. Thus, in a retail store, a markup of 30% for an item with a cost of $3.50 means a selling price of $5. (If the markup is 30% of the selling price, then the cost of $3.50 is 70% of the selling price. Thus, the price is found by dividing $3.50 by 70%.) Whenever one encounters a normal markup percentage, he should be careful that he understands whether selling price or cost is the base of that percentage.

Although pricing at cost plus a normal markup is attractively simple, it lacks economic logic and is not generally valid for the pricing of standard products. Cost-plus pricing *may* result in a viable market price, but it cannot be relied upon to do so. There are two difficulties involved. First, the costs used as the base for pricing must be the appropriate costs. Since pricing is a decision, only relevant costs should be used. This problem is discussed in the following section. Even if relevant costs are used, it is possible that they will not reflect efficient production. If competitors' costs are lower, the firm is at a disadvantage. The second difficulty relates to the markup. While management may establish a target profit margin that it seeks to realize on all products, that margin may not be consistent with market conditions for some products. Adding the target profit margin to production costs to set a price implies either that there is no competition or that the resultant price is effectively competitive. A seller may find that the sum of his costs plus his normal markup is a price that is either too high or too low for the existing market. To the extent that his product is different from others, he may be able to justify some price differential. The range of his pricing discretion depends upon the ease with which buyers may substitute other sellers' products for his. If products are readily substitutable, the individual seller will have a narrow range of pricing discretion.

In a dynamic market, characterized by change and uncertainty, pricing at cost plus a normal markup is not a generally valid or sustainable policy. It may be a useful starting point for the pricing decision, but the seller must be prepared to deviate from such a target price and, perhaps, to deviate greatly from it. What is basically unsound in this approach is not its recognition of the need to cover costs but its insistence upon a normal margin.

## Relevant Costs for Pricing Decisions

*Direct Costs.* In a single product firm, all of the costs incurred may be regarded as traceable to the one product. Hence, all costs are direct costs with respect to the product. In setting a price for such a product, management would properly expect it to cover all of the company's costs and provide a profit margin. In a multiproduct firm, however, not all costs are directly traceable to individual products. Some are true common costs; any assignment of these to individual products is somewhat arbitrary. Which costs in the multiproduct firm, then, are relevant for pricing decisions? When a decision is to be made regarding the price of an individual product, only those costs directly traceable to that product and avoidable by discontinuing production and sale of the product should be considered directly. In other words, this type of pricing decision should be approached by means of the incremental profit analysis described in Chapter 14. In the incremental profit approach, the selling price must cover all direct costs—both manufacturing and nonmanufacturing, both variable and fixed—that are attributable to a product. The price should also contribute to the covering of common costs and the realization of a profit. The common costs are not ignored in this approach; they are provided for by the excess of the selling price over the direct costs. Common costs are not assigned to the individual products for the simple reason that they bear no direct relationship to those products. As noted in Chapter 5, allocations of common costs are not useful for decision making purposes. Thus, if cost plus a normal profit margin is to be the target price for a product, the cost involved should be the total of all costs directly traceable to that product. Once again, however, this target price may have to be regarded only as a starting point in the pricing decision.

For a short period of time is is tolerable for the price of a product to do no more than cover its direct costs or even, possibly, only the direct variable costs. This may be the case, for example, when a new product is introduced. The initial direct promotional costs may be unusually high relative to sales volume, and special price concessions may be granted in connection with introductory offers. In this case, the negligible contribution to common costs in the short run is accepted in anticipation of long-run profits. In other cases, a very low contribution from one or more products may be accepted for want of a more profitable alternative. A low contribution is better than none at all.

In the long run, of course, the aggregate revenues from all products must cover the common costs as well as the direct costs. Ideally, each product should make a significant contribution to common costs; but it is not possible to state any general rule for determining satisfactory and unsatisfactory contributions. If factors of demand and/or competition prevent a firm from setting a price for one of its products that will cover direct costs, there may be no alternative to discontinuation of that product. If a competitive price does cover direct costs and yields some contribution to common costs, however, how high must that contribution be to justify long-run continuance of the product in the company's line? This question can be answered only in light of the available alternatives. If the product is discontinued, are there others which may be substituted for it and which will yield a higher contribution to common costs? What effect will discontinuance of this product have upon the demand for other products in the line? The elimination of one product from the line may cause the loss of sales of other, complementary products. Product pricing decisions should be made with a view toward maximum company profit in the long run. This objective should be regarded as a total company accomplishment, not a piecemeal result of several independent pricing decisions.

**Full Cost Pricing.**  Obviously, pricing decisions should be made in recognition of the need for a firm to cover all costs, at least in the long run. An extension of this recognition is the concept of *full cost pricing*, in which all costs are assigned to individual products in order to ensure that they will all be covered by some price. This extension is not valid for standard products, however. It seeks to establish relationships between products and portions of common costs where no such relationships actually exist. Under the incremental profit approach to pricing, each product's price must cover its own direct, avoidable costs. Once these costs are covered, the sum of all products' incremental profits must cover common costs and provide at least a reasonable profit margin.

At this point, the reader may raise the question of how management can ensure that all common costs will be covered if individual products' prices are set on the basis of directly traceable costs only. To begin with, basing prices on direct costs is, at best, only a starting point in the pricing decision. Market conditions must be considered, and these may dictate prices that provide a very substantial contribution to common costs. In any event, to the extent that costs are relevant in the pricing decision, they must include only those costs that bear some definable functional relationship to the product in question. Allocations of common costs among products and prices based upon the resultant full costs must be regarded as nothing more than tentative targets. For certain products, such targets have proved realistic and attainable. For others, however, these targets must quickly be abandoned. A low contribution from a single product does not necessarily mean that the price is too low or that the product ought to be discontinued. If the economic determinants of price are such that the combined prices for all of a company's products are insufficient to cover common costs in the long run, the conclusion is not that the individual prices are wrong but, rather, that the firm is economically inefficient. Such a firm must either improve its operating efficiency or cease operations and liquidate.

## Pricing a New Product

The introduction of a new product in a company's line may entail some additional problems. If it is significantly different from any product already available, there is no established market for it. Until its introduction, there has been no supply of the product and, hence, no demonstrated demand for it. The company may believe firmly that the demand will be substantial, but this has yet to be proved in the market. In all likelihood, there are some near-substitute products currently on the market; but their actual degree of substitution is as yet unknown. Thus, the competitive influence on the price of the new product can only be estimated. Further, the firm may have no reliable estimate of the direct costs of manufacturing and marketing the new product. Its cost patterns are likely to change as the firm obtains experience with the product and as its sales volume increases. In summary, then, pricing decisions for new products involve essentially the same considerations as those discussed earlier for established products. These considerations are subject to considerably greater uncertainty, however.

*Test Marketing.* One fairly popular technique employed to obtain valuable experience with a new product is test marketing. The product is introduced in selected areas only, often at different prices in different areas. Such tests afford the firm's management some idea as to the amount and elasticity of the demand for the product, the competition it will encounter, and the contribution to common costs and profit it may be expected to yield at various prices and volumes. Test marketing, of course, is not a perfect simulation of full-scale production and distribution. It may, however, provide very useful information for better planning of the full-scale marketing effort. It also permits initial pricing mistakes to be made in miniature rather than on a large scale.

**Pricing for a Target Rate of Return on Investment.** In most cases, the introduction of a new product will involve the commitment of a significant amount of assets to the production and distribution of that product. Management will expect the price of the new product not only to cover the costs of producing and selling it but also to yield a reasonable rate of return on investment (ROI) in those assets. The rate of return depends upon the dollar amounts of revenues, costs, and investment in assets directly traceable to the product. Revenue, of course, is a function of unit selling price and physical sales volume. If sales volume were a fixed quantity, setting a price to yield a target rate of return would be quite simple. However, if there is any degree of elasticity of demand for the product, volume will vary inversely with price. In that case, attaining the target rate of return on investment may or may not be feasible.

To illustrate pricing for a target rate of return, assume that a company is planning to introduce a new product whose variable costs will be $.60 per unit, regardless of volume, and whose traceable fixed costs will be $4,000,000 per year. The investment in assets designed specifically to produce and market this new product will be $10,000,000. The company's target rate of return on investment is 20% before taxes. Now, if sales volume is given as 5,000,000 units per year and is independent of the selling price, the price ($p$) that will yield a 20% rate of return is computed directly as follows:

$$5,000,000p = 5,000,000(\$.60) + \$4,000,000 + .20(\$10,000,000)$$

Solving for $p$, we determine that the necessary selling price is $1.80 per unit of product. The problem with this analysis is that it presumes that the resultant price is compatible with the given sales volume or, in other words, that the point identified by the volume of 5,000,000 units and a price of $1.80 falls on the demand curve for this product. If market analysis or actual sales experience shows that the given volume cannot be attained at a price of $1.80 per unit, management will have to make some adjustment to their plans or forego the target rate of return.

One adjustment that management might make would be to lower the price of the product in the hope that a substantially higher sales volume would be realized and that the target rate of return would then be achieved. Alternatively, management might seek ways to reduce the costs and/or the investment directly traceable to the new product. Either or both of these options would tend to raise the rate of return at any given volume. However, these actions might also necessitate some reduction in the quality of the product or of the marketing effort devoted to it. Such consequences might be expected to reduce sales volume.

The simple analysis above yields a 20 percent rate of return on investment in a year in which sales volume is 5,000,000 units and the investment base is $10,000,000. Neither of these quantities is likely to be constant over time. In the case of the typical new product, sales volume will start at a fairly low level and then rise in future years as the product's market grows. The investment base may decline over time as the initial capital investment is recovered via depreciation. Thus, if sales volume increases and the investment base decreases over time, the successive annual rates of return would increase. In the illustration above, 5,000,000 units might be taken as the average sales volume and $10,000,000, as the average unrecovered investment over the market life of the new product. Then the average annual rate of return on investment over that market life would be 20 percent. A more appropriate approach to determining the average rate of return on investment in a new product would be to use the rate of return methodology explained in the next chapter. Management's projections, however, are still subject to the constraints of the market. For any particular product, no action by management may be able to produce the desired rate of return. If such is the case, management must either accept a lower rate of return or decide against the introduction of the new product.

## PRICING SPECIAL ORDERS

For purposes of the present discussion, special order pricing decisions include only nonrecurring, or "one time only," decisions. These will be classified according to two general types: orders for special products and orders for standard products at special prices. The important distinguishing characteristic of both of these types of special pricing decisions is that they pertain to individual sales only. They are not intended to influence the regular prices of the seller's standard products.

### Orders for Special Products

The first type of special order is for a custom-made product, designed and manufactured to a single customer's specifications by a firm that does not regularly handle such orders. If a firm routinely processes special items to customers' orders, it should set the price for each such order on the basis of an established general pricing policy, for it is then not a special situation. In firms regularly producing custom-made goods more than in any others, pricing at cost plus a normal profit margin has merit. There is no market and no competitive price for such goods. The producer quite reasonably seeks to recover his costs plus a profit. In this case, the producer's costs legitimately include a reasonable allocation of common costs; for only by such an allocation can those common costs be recovered as part of the price. The profit margin added on to the full cost of the order must be reasonable. If that profit is too great, other companies will win orders away from the producer. If the profit is too low, on the other hand, the producer will lose money on such orders. Thus, the profit margin will tend to be normalized by the threat of competition on one side and by the manufacturer's profit objectives on the other.

*Incremental Profit Analysis.*  The decision as to the price of an order for a custom-made item, when such orders are not the customary mode of sales in the firm, should be made in consideration of the alternatives. If such an order is received when a firm is producing at full capacity, acceptance of it would necessitate either a reduction in the output of standard products or overtime. If the order is taken at the cost of regular production, its price must be adequate to yield an incremental profit at least equal to that foregone on the standard products which cannot be produced because of the special order. In order to determine their respective incremental profits, management must know the direct costs of both the special order and the standard products. These will include variable costs and, possibly, direct fixed costs. Special setup and training costs incurred in connection with the special order must be assigned to it, even though they may derive from sources normally included in general manufacturing overhead. For example, indirect labor for machinery setup and maintenance is commonly a part of manufacturing overhead, charged to standard products at a normal or standard rate. If the special order requires setup and maintenance costs in excess of those that would routinely be incurred for production of standard items, that *excess* is a direct cost of the special order.

If an order for a custom-made product is received at a time when the firm is operating below capacity and its acceptance would involve simply the utilization of otherwise idle facilities, the price of such order need, at minimum, cover its own direct costs only. Here the alternative to the special order is no output at all. If the order yields any incremental profit at all, the firm's net income will be increased. The alternative of sales of regular products does not exist.

*Capital Investment Analysis.*  Acceptance of an order for a custom-made product was discussed above as a short-run decision. Implicit in this analysis is the assumption that the order could be produced without additional capital investment in production facilities. If new investments were necessary in order for the firm to accept the order, either the price of the order would have to cover the full amount of such investments or the firm would have to have reasonable expectations of further profitable employment of the new facilities. In the latter instance, those other profitable opportunities should be quantified; and the proposal should be evaluated as any capital investment decision.

*Other Considerations.*    Handling special orders occasionally may afford a company the opportunity of examining the possibilities of entering new markets without committing itself thereto. On the other hand, a firm's unfamiliarity with a special product may present peculiar difficulties. The costs of processing the order may be increased beyond the planned amount because of unexpected overruns on time and/or expenses. If the order is priced in advance on the basis of budgeted costs (as would often be the case), any significant cost overrun could convert a planned profit to a loss. With this possibility in mind, management may accept orders for new and unfamiliar items only if the buyer agrees to bear any reasonable and unforeseen additional costs.

*Cost-Plus-Fixed-Fee Pricing.*    Perhaps the extreme expedient in pricing special orders for special products is to charge the customer for the total actual costs of producing the goods plus a predetermined profit. That profit, agreed to by the parties in advance, would be the "fixed fee" added to cost in order to determine price. Obviously, such a contract benefits the seller, for he is guaranteed a profit. There is no risk of loss on the order. It is not necessarily beneficial to the buyer, however; for the seller has no incentive to control production costs on the order. At one time, cost-plus-fixed-fee contracts were quite common in government purchases of specialized goods—including very costly defense equipment. Recently, however, the government has sought to purchase such goods under cost-plus-incentive-fee contracts or other incentive arrangements. Under this type of contract, the seller will be reimbursed for actual costs plus a predetermined profit only if his actual costs equal the estimated costs that were used by both parties in negotiating the contract. If his actual costs are lower than estimated, his profit is increased by a predetermined percentage of the cost saving. Conversely, if actual costs exceed the estimate, his profit is reduced or even completely eliminated. These incentive contracts are intended to offer the seller part of the cost recovery advantages of cost-plus-fixed-fee contracts and, at the same time, to encourage him to cut costs and, thereby, benefit both himself and the government. Similar agreements would be equally appropriate in contracts between two private firms. The size of the predetermined profit margin will be established by negotiations. Presumably, the seller would seek a larger profit margin if there was a high degree of uncertainty associated with his cost estimate.

## Orders for Standard Products at Special Prices

*Incremental Profit Analysis.*    Not uncommonly, manufacturers are asked to supply large quantities of standard products to individual customers at prices below regular list prices. If such an order is received when a manufacturer is operating at full capacity, it will almost certainly be rejected. Why should a firm cut prices when it can sell the same quantity at regular list prices? If, however, the manufacturer is producing below capacity, the special order affords an opportunity to employ idle facilities in the production of the company's standard products. In this situation, any price that yields some incremental profit will increase net income and cash flow in the short run. From the viewpoint of incremental profit analysis, the only costs relevant to the decision are those direct costs that would be avoided if the order were not accepted. Ordinarily, these will be the variable production and delivery costs.

As an example, assume that a company operating at 70 percent of normal capacity is asked to produce 25,000 units of one of its regular products for a large drugstore chain at the special price of $1.65 per unit. The regular selling price is $2.25 per unit. The standard production cost of the item is as follows:

| | |
|---|---:|
| Raw materials | $ .48 |
| Direct labor | .65 |
| Variable manufacturing overhead | .29 |
| Fixed manufacturing overhead | .38 |
| | $1.80 |

Acceptance of the order would place no strain whatever on production facilities and would not affect output of items for sale at regular prices. The incremental administrative cost of handling this order is estimated to be $900. At first glance, the order might appear unprofitable, for the proposed selling price is less than the standard cost of the product. However, it must be remembered that the fixed manufacturing overhead will be incurred in any event. Whether it is charged to production or charged to the volume variance, it is incurred. The proposed price of $1.65 does exceed the variable production costs (raw materials, direct labor, and variable manufacturing overhead) by $.23 per unit. Thus, the total variable profit on the order would be $5,750 (25,000 units × $.23). After deducting the direct fixed administrative cost of $900, the incremental profit before tax would be $4,850.

*Capital Investment Analysis.* The illustration in the preceding paragraph involved a special order for a large quantity of a standard product at a lower price only once. However, a manufacturer might be offered a similar proposition on a continuing basis. A distributor might offer to purchase annually a minimum quantity of a particular product at a reduced price. Such an offer would involve a long-term commitment of resources to one sales contract. Hence, it would have to be evaluated as an investment opportunity.

*Other Considerations.* Before any decision is made to sell a regular product at a special low price, consideration should be given to the possible repercussion upon sales of that product at the regular price. If other customers learn that the item has been sold at a reduced price, they may demand a similar price or they may even threaten to cancel their orders. If it becomes common knowledge that a product is being sold at a "cut-rate" price, the image of the product's quality may be impaired. If the buyer at the low price is a private brand distributor, however, the manufacturer's name might never be associated with the item when resold below the usual selling price. Thus, if the special sale can be kept secret, the dangers suggested above might not arise. If the manufacturer enters into a long term contract to supply a private brand seller with a product, knowledge of the arrangement is likely to spread. To some extent, this depends upon the nature of the product. If the product is a radio, minor changes in the exterior of the cabinet might effectively mask the manufacturer's identity. If it is an automobile tire, however, the tread design might reveal the manufacturer despite the presence of the distributor's private brand name on the casing. As a manufacturer's sales volume is obtained increasingly from one or a few large buyers, his bargaining position with them deteriorates. Ultimately, his continued solvency may depend upon their will. Obviously, this possibility should be considered before entering into sales contracts of the type described here. As a final consideration, the offering of standard products to individual buyers at reduced prices might be in violation of the federal antitrust law.

## ROBINSON-PATMAN ACT

In 1936 the Congress passed and President Franklin D. Roosevelt approved the Robinson-Patman Act. This law amended the Clayton Act of 1914 and added to the federal government's arsenal of antitrust legislation. Specifically, the Robinson-Patman Act deals with price discrimination—situations in which a seller offers the same product to different buyers at different prices. Section 2(a) of this act provides that it is unlawful for a seller to discriminate in price between different purchasers of goods of like grade and quality if such discrimination would tend to lessen competition or to create a monopoly.[1] However, the seller who so discriminates may justify price differentials by showing that they are attributable to actual cost differences. This cost defense provision of the law reads as follows:

*Provided*, That nothing herein contained shall prevent differentials which make only due allowance for differences in the cost of manufacture, sale, or delivery resulting from the differing methods or quantities in which such commodities are to such purchasers sold or delivered.[2]

---

[1] 49 Stat. 1526 (1936).

[2] Ibid.

The Robinson-Patman Act is enforced and the cost defense interpreted by the Federal Trade Commission. The following paragraphs do not purport to contain an exhaustive discussion of the act or of the cost defense alone. They simply attempt to indicate the role of cost accounting in one important area of antitrust legislation.[3]

The cost defense has not played a major role in formal proceedings of the Federal Trade Commission in cases of alleged price discrimination. It has, however, been of considerable importance in many of the commission's investigations which have terminated without formal complaints.[4] Thus, managers responsible for pricing decisions should be cognizant of the relevance of the antitrust law to their work and of the particular pertinence of cost data to the legality of price differentials. As the Robinson-Patman Act deals with price discrimination between different buyers of the same product, it is relevant only to pricing decisions respecting standard products. The pricing of custom-made products does not come within the scope of the act.

Although the cost defense includes within its scope both manufacturing and nonmanufacturing costs, there is no question that distribution costs are the most important ones in establishing an effective cost defense. Some cost differentials are easy to show; lower freight charges on carlot shipments are examples. Other cost differentials may be more difficult to demonstrate. For example, it is generally agreed that the costs of order taking, invoicing, and billing are lower per sales dollar on large orders than on small orders. If the seller's cost accounting system is not set up so as to develop these costs as amounts per sales dollar, however, he may have difficulty in establishing an acceptable cost defense on such basis.

Earlier in this chapter, the prime importance of direct costs in pricing decisions was emphasized. For purposes of the cost defense in the Robinson-Patman Act, however, both direct and indirect costs are relevant. The Federal Trade Commission will not accept the assignment of only the direct costs of a product or of a particular method of distribution to that product or method in a cost defense. A reasonable allocation of common costs to all products or to all business activities of the firm is required.[5] In determining what is a reasonable cost allocation

---

[3] For more expansive treatments of this act and the cost defense in particular, see Corwin D. Edwards, *The Price Discrimination Law,* (Washington, D.C.: The Brookings Institution, 1959), chap. xviii on the cost defense; and Wright Patman, *Complete Guide to the Robinson-Patman Act* (Englewood Cliffs, N.J.: Prentice-Hall, Inc., 1963), pp. 70–83 on the cost defense. A detailed analysis of experience with the cost defense in actual cases may be found in Herbert F. Taggart, *Cost Justification* (Ann Arbor: Bureau of Business Research, School of Business Administration, The University of Michigan, 1959).

[4] Edwards, *The Price Discrimination Law,* pp. 587–89; and Patman, *Complete Guide,* pp. 75–76.

[5] Edwards, *The Price Discrimination Law,* p. 586.

scheme, the commission has shown a general inclination to accept widely employed cost accounting practices. If a seller wishes prior approval of his cost allocation practices, he may submit them to the commission's accounting staff for review. The commission may then indicate approval or suggest modifications. In order to avoid future difficulties, the seller probably will conform to the commission's suggestions. In this way, a cost defense is established before the fact. As costs and other operating conditions change, of course, cost differences justifying price differentials are likely to change also. In other words, a cost defense, once established, is not immutable; it must be kept current.

The cost defense provision in the Robinson-Patman Act offers a challenge to the cost accountant. It requires him to develop and defend detailed cost analyses that may go beyond the ordinary requirements of product costing or of managerial analysis. It demands more detailed analysis of distribution costs than many firms have yet developed. Finally, it imposes upon the accountant the professional responsibility for developing cost accounting systems that entail the most appropriate and reasonable cost classifications and allocations. To some extent, the reasonableness and equity with which the price discrimination law is administered depend upon accountants' acceptance of this responsibility.

## QUESTIONS FOR DISCUSSION

1. The suggestion that an individual seller's costs have some relevance to his pricing decisions implies that he can set his prices at his own discretion and based upon his own situation. Isn't this implication inconsistent with the generally accepted notion that prices are set by forces of demand and supply in markets?

2. The president of a medium-sized manufacturing corporation makes the following statement at a meeting of the company's policy committee: "When we get around to setting prices, every cost we incur had better be charged to one or another of our products if we expect to make any money. I don't care how or why a cost is incurred, if it's there it has to be covered by some price. Anybody who thinks differently just doesn't understand the realities of business." How would you respond to this statement?

3. Under what circumstances, if any, is pricing at cost plus a target profit margin a valid approach to the pricing decision?

4. What are the relevant costs in a decision regarding the price of one of a company's regular products?

5. How does the level of operating capacity affect a special order pricing decision?

6. What are the relevant costs in a decision regarding the price of a custom-made product?

7. What are the relevant costs in a decision regarding a special, low price for an order of one of a company's regular products?

8. "Although it may be conceptually valid, the practice of pricing new products so that they will yield a specified rate of return on their investments is extremely difficult, if not impossible, to implement effectively." Do you agree or disagree with this statement? Explain.

9. Your company is planning to introduce a new product in the home appliance market. Initial market research indicates that demand for this product will eventually be large enough to justify the expansion of the company's production facilities. Forecasted sales in the first year or two of the product's market life can probably be met by production in existing facilities, however. What factors should management consider in setting a price for this new product?

10. A manufacturer has been approached by a large chain of discount stores with an offer to purchase a large quantity of a particular electrical appliance at a price 20% below the regular price. This quantity would represent almost 25% of the manufacturer's current annual output of the appliance. Existing capacity is adequate if the offer is accepted, however. What costs and other factors should the manufacturer consider in its process of deciding whether to accept or reject this offer?

11. Assume that the manufacturer has accepted the offer described in Question 10. Another customer has learned of the 20% discount and has filed a complaint, alleging price discrimination, with the Federal Trade Commission. How should the manufacturer go about establishing a cost defense against the price discrimination charge? Would his cost analysis for this defense be the same as the cost analysis used earlier in deciding whether to accept the discount chain's offer? Explain.

## PROBLEMS

15–1. The Wellgunde Corporation plans to introduce a new product in 1977. Sales volumes, along with consistent selling prices and variable costs per unit, have been estimated as follows:

| Sales in Units | Selling Price | Variable Costs |
|---|---|---|
| 5,000 | $19 | $12.00 |
| 10,000 | 18 | 11.50 |
| 15,000 | 17 | 11.25 |
| 20,000 | 16 | 10.00 |
| 25,000 | 14 | 9.75 |
| 30,000 | 12 | 9.75 |
| 35,000 | 10 | 9.75 |
| 40,000 | 8 | 9.75 |

The volumes indicated are limits for their respective prices and variable costs. That is, any sales above each volume would have to be made at the next lower price and variable costs.

Fixed costs directly traceable to the new product are expected to be $40,000 for any volume up to and including 20,000 units. Above that volume, fixed costs would be $60,000.

*Required:*

At what price should the corporation introduce this new product if it wishes to maximize its short-run profit on the product.

15–2.  Woglinde Wineries, Inc., produces and sells a variety of wines. Among the company's products is a cocktail wine called Rhinegold. This wine has been on the market for three years. When it first appeared, it was the only wine of its kind in its general price range; and initial sales were very satisfying to management. In the most recent year, however, other producers have introduced their own lower-priced cocktail wines; and sales of Rhinegold have declined significantly.

Rhinegold was originally introduced at a retail price of $2.69 per bottle. Woglinde Wineries sold it to retailers for $21.50 per case of 12 bottles. The competing wines that have appeared in the past year sell at retail for $1.99 per bottle. Retailers pay $15.92 per case of 12 bottles for these other wines. Woglinde Wineries has received considerable feedback from retailers, who reported that many customers still came in for Rhinegold but finally chose another brand because of the substantial price differential. Some retailers have cut the price of Rhinegold to as low as $2.19 per bottle, but they contend that they cannot make a profit on it at that low a price. In recent months, Woglinde Wineries has begun cutting its price per case to retailers.

Summary sales data for Rhinegold during its three years on the market are as follows:

| Year | Cases Sold | Average Price per Case |
|---|---|---|
| 1974............ | 60,000 | $21.50 |
| 1975............ | 100,000 | 21.50 |
| 1976............ | 80,000 | 20.60 |

Variable production and distribution costs average $8.10 per case. Fixed manufacturing overhead is allocated to all wines at a normal rate of $3.90 per case. Fixed selling and administrative expenses are allocated among products at a rate of 20% of gross sales revenue. Production facilities are common to all of the company's wines. The only fixed distribution cost directly traceable to Rhinegold is special advertising budgeted at $200,000 per year. The company's management believes that this advertising is essential in order to maintain a substantial sales volume of Rhinegold.

A survey of retailers and consumers indicates that Rhinegold still has a superior product image in the cocktail wine market, but that it is not great enough to warrant the existing retail price differential. Retailers who sold Rhinegold for $2.19 per bottle reported that their sales of the product were not materially affected by the introduction of the competing wines. Woglinde Wineries has a generally acknowledged reputation for higher quality products than the producers of the competing cocktail wines. The president is concerned that reducing the price of Rhinegold in the face of low-price competition might adversely affect this reputation. He agrees, however, that even further sales declines may be expected if some positive action is not taken to reverse the recent trend.

*Required:*

a. What would be lowest price per case the company could accept if sales volume in 1977 were budgeted at 80,000 cases of Rhinegold? Why?

b. If $2.19 per bottle were considered an effectively competitive retail price for Rhinegold, what would be the highest competitive price per case that the company could charge to retailers? Why?

c. What price would you recommend that the company set per case of Rhinegold in 1977? Why?

15–3. Flosshilde Products, Inc., has recently developed a new automatic bottling machine. While operating on the same principle as machines currently on the market, it is faster and results in less spillage and breakage. The company's management is seeking the most advantageous price at which to introduce this new machine and has requested your assistance in making the pricing decision. You have been provided the following information:

1. There are four basically competitive bottling machines on the market at present. Their selling prices are shown below.

| | |
|---|---|
| Alberich Bottler...................... | $110,000 |
| Fafner Automatic Filler................ | 99,500 |
| Fasolt Bottling Machine................ | 107,500 |
| Mime Fast-Filler..................... | 114,000 |

Flosshilde management is convinced that the new machine will save users money in operations in comparison with these competing machines and, hence, believes that a higher price would be justifiable.

2. Cost estimates for producing and selling the new machine have been prepared by the product engineering staff. Variable production costs per unit have been budgeted as follows:

| | |
|---|---|
| Materials.............................. | $24,000 |
| Direct labor........................... | 20,000 |
| Manufacturing overhead................ | 15,000 |

Fixed manufacturing overhead is applied to all of the company's current products at a normal rate of 120% of direct labor cost. Variable distribution expenses are expected to average $1,000 per machine sold. Fixed nonmanufacturing expenses are allocated among products in proportion to total revenues. In recent years, this allocation has averaged 10% of sales revenues.

3. Additional fixed manufacturing costs of $600,000 annually will be required in order to produce the new machine. Otherwise, existing facilities are considered adequate to meet the expanding operations of the company.

4. The company's present products are yielding a net profit before tax of approximately 15% of revenues, after deductions for both direct costs and allocated indirect costs.

5. The total market for automatic bottling machines is about 1,500 units per year. This market is now shared by the four machines mentioned in paragraph 1 above.

*Required:*

a. Prepare a preliminary report summarizing your analysis of factors management should consider in this pricing decision.

b. What additional information, if any, would you want to have before making a specific price recommendation in this case?

15-4. The Ortlinde Company is planning to introduce a new product in 1977. Market research indicates that the total market for this product is about 50,000 units annually. However, management is planning a much more limited introduction designed to "skim the cream off the market." In other words, the company will arbitrarily restrict supply so that it can initially charge a relatively high price for the new product. Later, management expects to penetrate the mass market for the product with a reduced price. In its "cream skimming" strategy, management estimates that 10,000 units can be sold during each of the first two years of the product's market life at a price of $695 per unit. At this volume, variable production costs would average $275 per unit; fixed manufacturing and selling costs would amount to $1,200,000 annually; and the required investment in new facilities would cost $12,000,000.

The sales manager has cautioned that the policy of "skimming the cream" may prove self-defeating in the long run. Competitors may develop similar products and rush them into the mass market that the Ortlinde Company is presently planning to defer for at least two years. He has developed cost estimates for production and sale of the full 50,000 units of potential annual demand. Variable production costs could be reduced to $250 per unit. Fixed operating costs would be increased to $4,500,000 per year. The necessary investment in facilities for this larger volume would be $40,000,000. The sales manager is not sure what price would be appropriate for this mass market penetration, however.

*Required:*

a. What selling price would be necessary at a volume of 50,000 units annually in order to yield the same rate of return on investment before taxes that would be realized under the "cream skimming" strategy?

b. Irrespective of your answer to *a*, assume now that a selling price of $500 per unit has been determined to be consistent with a demand for 50,000 units annually. What factors should management consider before deciding between the "cream skimming" policy for two years and immediate mass-market penetration at the lower price?

15-5. For many years, the American automobile industry has generally followed a pricing policy that is tied to a concept known as standard volume. Auto manufacturers set a price that is designed to yield a target rate of return on investment if actual sales are at standard volume. If sales exceed standard volume, a higher rate of return will be earned; and lower sales will result in a rate of return below the target. Both fixed expenses and the target profit are allocated among units of a particular model at the standard volume. Adding variable costs per unit to the resultant figure produces the desired selling price.

To illustrate this pricing method, consider the following data for a hypothetical automobile model:

| | |
|---|---|
| Variable costs per unit...................... | $ 2,450 |
| Fixed costs per year........................ | $60,000,000 |
| Investment base: | |
|    Traceable working capital................. | $15,000,000 |
|    Traceable tools and dies.................. | 80,000,000 |
|    Allocated share of common facilities......... | 30,000,000 |
| Standard volume in units.................... | 50,000 |
| Target return on investment before tax........ | 20% |

*Required:*

a. Calculate the price of the hypothetical model in accordance with the formula based upon standard volume.

b. Evaluate this method of automobile pricing. Keep in mind that it has been used for many years and appears to work satisfactorily. What does it imply about the automobile market?

15-6. The Waltraute Manufacturing Company produces a variety of precision instruments and components. Most are sold to manufacturers of electronics equipment and to laboratories. The company's policy is to price all of its products at 150% of the total variable costs to produce and sell them. Because of the specialized nature of these products, this has proved to be a viable pricing policy.

Recently, the Coast Guard has requested bids on a compact, long-range radio direction finder for use on small craft. Specifications call for 400 units that are sufficiently durable to survive the pounding that they would receive in a small boat in heavy seas. The company's president has been interested in the possibility of the firm entering the government contract market as a prime contractor and has asked the controller to prepare a cost estimate for this radio direction finder. Based upon the Coast Guard specifications, the following cost estimate has been prepared:

| Direct materials | $160,000 |
|---|---|
| Direct labor | 110,000 |
| Variable manufacturing overhead | 40,000 |
| Fixed manufacturing overhead | 60,000 |
| Production setup costs | 25,000 |
| Special tools and dies | 60,000 |
| Clerical costs of processing government | |
| forms and reports | 5,000 |
| Total costs | $460,000 |

Unit cost ($460,000 ÷ 400 units) .............. $  1,150

Coast Guard specifications require delivery of all 400 radio direction finders within one year. In order to meet that schedule, Waltraute would have to forego regular sales orders totaling $450,000.

### Required:

What is the lowest price the company could bid on the contract for the radio direction finders without sacrificing short-run profit?

15–7.  In late 1976, the Gerhilde Corporation invited the Brunnhilde Company to submit a design for a fork-lift truck to meet the special requirements of Gerhilde's warehousing facilities and also to submit a bid for a contract to produce 60 of these trucks. Similar invitations were sent to four other equipment manufacturers.

The Brunnhilde Company has suffered from considerable excess capacity during the past two years and has seen little prospect of improving the situation in the near future. Consequently, it readily accepted the Gerhilde Corporation's invitation and has already spent $42,000 on design and cost studies in connection with it. As a result of this work, a bid of $7,667 per truck has been submitted. In support of this bid, the controller of the Brunnhilde Company has prepared the following budgeted profit statement for the contract:

| | | |
|---|---:|---:|
| Revenue (60 units @ $7,667) | | $460,000 |
| Costs: | | |
| Materials (60 @ $2,500) | $150,000 | |
| Direct labor (60 @ $1,750) | 105,000 | |
| Variable manufacturing overhead (60 @ $600) | 36,000 | |
| Fixed manufacturing overhead (60 @ $1,200) | 72,000 | |
| Shipping (60 @ $150) | 9,000 | |
| Design and cost studies | 42,000 | 414,000 |
| Profit margin before tax | | $ 46,000 |

The Gerhilde Corporation has replied that it prefers the Brunnhilde design to any of the others submitted but that the bid price of $7,667 is too high. It has made a counteroffer to award the contract to Brunnhilde at a price of $5,750 per truck.

### Required:

Would it be profitable for the Brunnhilde Company to accept the Gerhilde contract at the offered price of $5,750 per unit?

15-8. The Schwertleite Company produces a wide variety of plumbing and heating products. One of these is the Loge thermal control unit, the standard cost of which is as follows:

| | |
|---|---:|
| Materials................................... | $16 |
| Labor...................................... | 9 |
| Variable manufacturing overhead.............. | 3 |
| Fixed manufacturing overhead................. | 9 |
| | $37 |

The Loge thermal control unit is produced in a series of manufacturing departments, each of which also works on many of the company's other products. It is sold to distributors and industrial users at a unit price of $45. Variable selling expenses average $3.60 per unit. Fixed selling expenses are budgeted at 12% of sales revenue.

The Schwertleite Company has been approached by a large manufacturer of furnaces and boilers with an offer to buy 15,000 of the Loge units annually at a special price of $36 per unit. If accepted, this offer would increase Schwertleite's output considerably and would necessitate an increase in annual fixed manufacturing costs of $60,000. No new capital investment would be required, however.

*Required:*

a. On the basis of short-run profitability alone, would you recommend acceptance of this special-price offer?

b. What other factors should management consider before reaching a decision on this offer?

15-9. The Helmwige Corporation produces a single product. Its maximum annual productive capacity is 960,000 labor hours. Currently, it is producing at an annual rate of 750,000 labor hours. Normal volume is 900,000 hours.

Recently a private-brand distributor has offered to buy 120,000 units of the corporation's product at a special price of $29 per unit. The regular selling price is $40 per unit. The standard cost sheet for one unit of the product is as follows:

| | |
|---|---:|
| Direct materials (9 lbs. @ $.70)...................... | $ 6.30 |
| Direct labor (3 hrs. @ $4.40).......................... | 13.20 |
| Variable manufacturing overhead (3 hrs. @ $1.50)...... | 4.50 |
| Fixed manufacturing overhead (3 hrs. @ $2)........... | 6.00 |
| | $30.00 |

*Required:*

a. In the short run, would it be profitable to accept the private-brand distributor's offer?

b. Would your answer to a be different if the offer called for 90,000 units instead of 120,000? Why or why not?

15-10. The Siegrune Company manufactures an electric hair dryer, the standard unit cost of which is as follows:

| | |
|---|---|
| Materials................................... | $ 8.80 |
| Labor...................................... | 7.90 |
| Variable manufacturing overhead............. | 1.80 |
| Fixed manufacturing overhead............... | 1.50 |
| | $20.00 |

Variable selling costs of $1.25 per unit are incurred when the hair dryer is sold under the Siegrune brand name. The regular selling price is $29 per unit. Annual fixed selling and administrative expenses total $2,000,000.

The productive capacity of the company's plant is 720,000 units per year. Budgeted sales and production for 1977 are both 500,000 units. Normal volume has been set at 600,000 units per year.

The company has received three offers for special purchases of the hair dryer at reduced prices. These three offers, none of which has been included in the budgeted sales and output for 1977, are described below.

Offer A:   The prospective buyer would take 160,000 units during 1977 at a price of $21 apiece. He would sell the hair dryer under the Siegrune brand name.

Offer B:   The prospective buyer would take 200,000 units during 1977 at a price of $19.90 per unit. These units would then be sold under the buyer's private brand name and would have modified housings to conceal the manufacturer's identity. This modification would not change unit costs, however.

Offer C:   The prospective buyer would take 360,000 units during 1977 at a unit price of $21.75. These units would be sold in modified housings under the buyer's private brand name. Unit costs would not be affected by the housing modifications.

*Required:*

Evaluate each of the three offers from the point of view of short-run profit maximization in 1977. What other factors might be relevant to the decision to accept or reject any or all of the offers?

15–11.   The Rossweise Fruit Products Company produces and bottles four different fruit juices. Most of its output has been sold to grocery wholesalers. Sales of one of the products, lime juice, have never come up to management's expectations. Sales in cases during 1976 were as follows:

| Product | Cases | Price per Case |
|---|---|---|
| Prune juice.............. | 120,000 | $6.40 |
| Apple juice.............. | 180,000 | 5.25 |
| Lemon juice............. | 90,000 | 4.80 |
| Lime juice............... | 40,000 | 5.50 |

Actual operating costs for 1976 are summarized below. No price or cost changes have been budgeted for 1977.

|  | Variable Cost per Case | Fixed Cost per Year |
|---|---|---|
| Raw materials: |  |  |
| Prunes........................ | $2.00 |  |
| Apples........................ | 1.30 |  |
| Lemons........................ | 1.80 |  |
| Limes........................ | 2.20 |  |
| Bottles........................ | .60 |  |
| Direct labor...................... | 1.75 |  |
| Manufacturing overhead............ | .45 | $200,000 |
| Selling expenses.................. | .15 | 50,000 |
| Administrative expenses............ |  | 90,000 |

A chain of cut-rate liquor stores has offered to purchase 50,000 cases of lime juice in 1977 at a price of $4.95 per case. These sales would not involve any variable selling expenses. Further, because of the substantial increase in volume, the cost of limes would be reduced by $.25 per case.

*Required:*

a.  Would it be profitable for the company to accept the liquor chain's offer?

b.  Irrespective of your answer in *a*, assume that the company did accept the offer and that one of its wholesale grocery customers has now filed a complaint alleging price discrimination on the part of the Rossweise Company. Can an effective cost defense, as provided for in the Robinson-Patman Act, be established in this case? Support your answer with appropriate cost analysis.

15–12.  The Valkyries' Rock has long been one of the most famous and popular restaurants in Northern California. It is most celebrated for its aged steak served in a thick wine sauce prepared from a secret recipe. The national reputation of this particular dish has led to numerous requests from restauranteurs all over the country for the right to serve it in their establishments under The Valkyries' Rock name. Several years ago, the proprietor of The Valkyries' Rock sensed in these requests an opportunity for some very lucrative additional revenue at the cost of a fairly modest investment.

Thus, the proprietor set up a separate corporation, Wotan's Fare Well, Inc., to pack and ship aged steaks and jars of sauce. The sauce is prepared in the restaurant's kitchen and put into 2-quart jars. It is then transferred to a packing room built especially for the new corporation. In the packing room, two dozen 12-ounce steaks and three jars of sauce are packed in a specially designed case with dry ice. The cases are then taken by a company-owned truck to San Francisco for delivery to local restaurants or for air shipment to out-of-town customers.

Shipments of the aged steaks have increased steadily since this business was begun until, today, the packing room is operating at its practical capacity of 1,040 cases per month. Even so, orders frequently must be delayed because of a back-log of demand. Initially, orders were received only from "exclusive" restaurants with trade reputations similar to that of The Valkyries' Rock. Recently, however, some orders have come in from a greater variety of types of restaurants. In fact, two restaurant chains have asked the company to ship large orders at reduced prices. Thus far, the corporation has not been able to fill any such orders because of the heavy demand from regular customers. However, the owner has begun to wonder whether he may not have conceived the steak shipping business on too small a scale. He is currently considering the feasibility and financial advisability of packing and shipping large quantities at special prices and of selling to a wider variety of customers. Realistically, this course of action would lead to lower basic prices for all customers.

Each case of steaks is now sold for $144 plus air freight charges from San Francisco. This price was arrived at by assuming that restaurants serving the steak and sauce would price the meal at $9.50 per serving and that they would be willing to pay at least $6 per serving for the distinction of including the dish on their menus. Information from present customers suggests that they charge between $9 and $10.50 for this dish. The costs of producing, packing, and transporting the steaks have been estimated by the proprietor as follows:

| | |
|---|---:|
| Cost of empty packing case | $ 2.10 |
| Cost of empty 2-quart jar | .08 |
| Packing labor per case | .90 |
| Cost of preparing sauce: | |
| Ingredients per quart | 2.50 |
| Labor per quart | .40 |
| Truck operating costs per month | $1,500 |
| Packing room fixed manufacturing overhead per month | 750 |
| Cost of steaks (See below.) | |

The cost of aged steaks has varied widely since the business was established. Currently, the price is $3.60 per pound.

Several restaurants which regularly charge considerably lower prices than the corporation's present customers charge have indicated that they would be eager to buy if the price could be reduced to $4 per steak serving or even less. One restaurant chain has offered to purchase weekly quantities of at least 50 cases at a price of $90 per case plus air freight charges. The proprietor of The Valkyries' Rock believes that similar arrangements could be made with other chains.

*Required:*

a. Evaluate the corporation's present pricing policy with regard to shipments of steaks and sauce.

b. Identify the specific decisions facing the proprietor in connection with the growing demand for steaks and sauce. Suggest *approaches* to the resolution of each of these decisions.

c. If the proprietor does decide to reduce the selling price and to offer quantity discounts, would the prices of $4 per serving and $90 per case on large orders, as suggested by potential customers, be satisfactory? Discuss.

# chapter 16

# Capital Budgeting: Analysis of Investment Decisions

Long-term investment decisions, often called capital budgeting decisions, involve commitments of capital to specific assets or projects for long periods of time. Once made and implemented, such decisions ordinarily cannot be reversed easily without significant loss of the invested capital.[1] This does not mean that capital budgeting decisions are irreversible, of course; but it does mean that their implications are more extensive than those of the short-term decisions discussed in Chapter 14. Investment decisions typically require fairly long periods of time for their full financial justifications. A simple make-or-buy decision regarding components may be justified by cost savings almost at once. A decision to purchase a building, on the other hand, ordinarily can be justified financially only over a period of many years. The purchase is made in contemplation of continued economic benefits from occupancy of the building throughout a long useful life.

The critical element in an investment decision is time. It is the factor that necessitates analysis by techniques different from those explained in Chapter 14. The time factor requires financial planning into the fairly distant future, and it entails a long delay before the benefits of the investment are fully realized. The time factor injects the element of interest

---

[1] The types of investment decisions discussed here do not include decisions to invest in marketable securities. Since these securities may readily be resold, the investment decision is easily reversed. The possibility of a capital gain or loss still exists, of course.

on the invested capital into the decision. In Chapter 14, we saw that interest is theoretically irrelevant to the short-term decisions considered there. It is not possible to ignore interest in capital budgeting decisions, however. The commitment of capital to specific purposes for long periods entails an interest cost too large to be ignored. Indeed, interest is the crucial difference between the analyses of a long-term investment decision and a short-term decision. The time factor in capital budgeting may also inject a greater degree of uncertainty into the planning process than is usually encountered in annual budgetary planning.

## THE COST OF CAPITAL

In a broad context, capital budgeting may be thought of as comprising two principal types of decisions. One is the investment decision: How should the available capital be used? The other is the financing decision: How should the necessary capital be obtained? The former decision is concerned with uses of capital; the latter, with sources of capital. Obviously, there is an important interrelationship between the two decisions. Capital cannot be invested unless it is first obtained. Conversely, it would be pointless to obtain capital that could not advantageously be invested. Nevertheless, these are two separate and distinct decisions; they are not merely two facets of a single decision. Moreover, these two decisions must be analyzed separately by management. If the investment and financing decisions are combined, serious error may be the result.[2] This book focuses attention on the investment decision only. The financing decision is considered at length in business finance texts.

There is a very important link between financing and investment decisions that must be considered here, however. The sources of capital chosen in the financing decisions determine the cost of capital, and that cost of capital is the criterion for profitability of any investment of capital. An investment can be regarded as profitable only if it generates a return greater than the cost of the invested capital. Thus, financial analysis of an investment decision depends upon management's knowledge of the cost of capital.

All capital has a cost; any assumption that a particular source of capital is cost-free is erroneous. The cost of capital is not uniform, however. It may be different in different firms, at different times in a single firm, and for different sources of capital. Thus, one must be precise in discussing the cost of capital so that there is no confusion as to the particular cost in question. For purposes of discussion here, we shall identify two concepts of the cost of capital. The first is the *specific cost of capital*. This is the cost associated with one specific source of financing

---

[2] Cf. Chapter 17.

at one time. The second is the *average cost of capital,* a weighted average of all of the various specific costs of financing in a firm at one time. It is the average cost of capital that is the appropriate criterion for the profitability of investment decisions. Moreover, it is the *current* average cost of capital that is important. This is the cost that reflects current conditions in the capital markets. The cost that happened to be in effect the last time that the firm actually obtained capital in the markets is no longer relevant.

## Cost of Debt

The specific cost of debt capital is the effective after-tax interest rate on the market value of the outstanding debt securities of a firm. Since there may be several different classes of debt securities outstanding at a given time, there may be several different specific costs of debt. Interest on debt capital is unique among the various specific costs of capital in that it is deductible for income tax purposes. Thus, the actual cost to the firm is less than the effective market interest rate. It is the effective interest rate multiplied by the complement of the income tax rate (i.e., one minus the tax rate). For example, if the effective interest rate is 10% and the income tax rate is 40%, the net cost of that particular debt capital is 6% (10% × 60%).

The current effective interest rate is a function of three variables: the nominal interest, the remaining period of time prior to the maturity date of the debt, and the current market price of the security. For example, a $1,000 bond with a nominal interest rate of 8% pays nominal interest of $80 in cash per year. If this bond matures at the end of 15 years and is currently selling at a market price of $847.50, the effective interest rate currently is 10% before tax. If the bond issuer's income tax rate is 40%, the net interest cost of the bond is 6%, as explained above. This effective interest rate may be computed rather tediously by formula. It may also be computed from tables of present values in the same way that the effective rate of return on an investment is computed. This computation is presented later in this chapter. Finally, the effective interest rate may be read from very extensive published bond tables.

## Cost of Preferred Stock

Legally, preferred stock represents an ownership equity in a corporation. Economically, however, it has characteristics more like long-term debt than like common stock. There is a fixed annual dividend payable on preferred stock, and it must be paid before any dividends can be distributed to common stockholders. Further, the preferred dividend is not increased, regardless of the amount of profits earned and the dividends paid on common stock.[3] The cost of preferred stock is computed simply by dividing the amount of the fixed annual dividend by the current market price of the stock. For example, if the annual dividend is $7 per share and the market price is $78 per share, the specific cost of capital is 9 percent.

## Cost of Common Equity

The specific costs of debt and preferred stock derive from fixed periodic interest and dividend payments. There is no fixed periodic dividend on common stock. Common dividends are paid only when, in the judgment of the board of directors, they are warranted by earnings and by the size of the cash balance. Thus, the current dividend payout is not a valid indicator of the specific cost of common stock equity. When an investor purchases a share of common stock of a corporation, he is looking toward earnings and dividends over an indefinite future period. This is true whether he expects to realize his return by holding the stock indefinitely and receiving dividends or by reselling the stock to someone else at a gain. Thus, the relationship between expected future dividends and the current market price of the stock is the basis for determining the specific cost of capital. Inasmuch as future dividends may reasonably be expected to increase as time goes by, no single dollar amount readily represents those dividend expectations. Hence, the cost of common equity may be approximated by dividing the current dividend by the market price of the common stock and adding to that quotient a factor that represents the anticipated rate of growth of dividends in the future. The formula for the cost of common equity is as follows:[4]

$$k = \frac{D}{M} + g$$

where

$k$ = the specific cost of common equity capital,
$D$ = the current dividend per share of common stock,
$M$ = the current market price per share of common stock, and
$g$ = the expected average annual rate of growth in common dividends.

The great practical difficulty with this formula, of course, is the problem of estimating the value of $g$. The past growth rate may be a useful start-

---

[3] This statement is true of most preferred stock. There are some participating preferred stocks, however. That is, the preferred stockholders have the right to participate with common stockholders in distributions of relatively large dividends. In such a case, the specific cost of preferred stock tends to be equal to the specific cost of the common equity.

[4] Harold Bierman, Jr., and Seymour Smidt, *The Capital Budgeting Decision,* 3d ed. (New York: The Macmillan Co., 1971), p. 145.

ing point, but it cannot be assumed to continue indefinitely. Indeed, the past growth rate may depend upon which specific set of years one selects as the basis for computing that rate. Moreover, different persons may have different estimates of $g$. Presumably, the growth rate used would be the one estimated by management; but that estimate may be subject to some bias. Thus, this formula can be used only to compute an approximation of the cost of common equity. Such an approximation is essential, however.

The specific cost determined in accordance with the formula above is applicable to all of the capital provided by common stockholders. This includes both amounts invested directly by the stockholders (i.e., common stock at par value plus any additional paid-in capital) and amounts reinvested from profits (i.e., retained earnings).

## Average Cost of Capital

It is common practice to regard current liabilities as an offset to current assets rather than as a distinct portion of total invested capital. Thus, total invested capital (or capitalization, or capital structure) is usually considered to consist of long-term debt and stockholders' equity. The average cost of capital is then computed from the specific costs of these sources. It is an average of the specific costs, weighted by the respective market values of the total capital provided from each source. This weighted average computation is illustrated in Table 16–1. In lines

### TABLE 16–1
#### Computation of Average Cost of Capital

| | Source of Capital | | | | |
| | Bonds | | Stocks | | |
| | 1st Mortgage | Debenture | Preferred | Common | Total |
|---|---|---|---|---|---|
| Basic Data: | | | | | |
| 1. Maturity Value..... | $20,000 | $100,000 | | | |
| 2. Nominal Interest Rate......... | 6 | 7½% | | | |
| 3. Years to Maturity.. | 8 | 22 | | | |
| 4. Annual Interest or Dividend...... | $ 1,200 | $ 7,500 | $ 3,000 | $ 12,000 | |
| 5. Market Value of Capital........ | $17,700 | $ 85,800 | $40,000 | $200,000 | $343,500 |
| Specific Cost of Capital: | | | | | |
| 6. Preliminary........ | 8.0% | 9.0% | 7.5% | 6.0 | |
| 7. Growth Factor..... | — | — | — | 5.0% | |
| 8. After Tax at 40%... | 4.8% | 5.4% | 7.5% | 11.0% | |
| Percentage of Total Market Value...... | 5.2% | 25.0% | 11.6% | 58.2% | 100.0% |
| Average Cost of Capital... | .25% | 1.35% | .87% | 6.40% | 8.87% |

1 through 8 of the table, the specific cost of each source of capital is computed. Each specific cost listed in line 8 is then multiplied by the percentage that the market value of that particular source of capital is of the total market value of all capital. The sum of the resultant products is the average cost of capital for the firm. In this illustration, the average cost of capital is computed to be 8.87%. For practical purposes, this would probably be rounded to 9%. This illustration is not advanced as representative of what the actual cost of capital is likely to be in any particular company. It simply demonstrates the mechanics of computing the average cost of capital.

## THE INVESTMENT DECISION

Before considering the techniques of investment analysis, we must first identify clearly the objectives of investments, their natures, and the data that are pertinent to investment analysis.

### Optimum Allocation of Scarce Capital

The basic goal of long-term investment decision making is to maximize the wealth of the investor over the long run. In a business firm, this goal is usually stated as the maximization of long run profit. In a governmental agency, it would logically be stated as the maximization of public benefits from the available capital resources. Whatever the nature of the organization, it has a limited supply of capital available to it. Therefore, it must attempt to make the best possible use of that capital. Management must invest capital in projects most likely to achieve the basic goal of maximizing wealth. As capital is a scarce economic resource, it has a cost. The return from an investment must be at least equal to the cost of the capital invested. Otherwise, the firm would be financially better off if it didn't have the capital at all. The problem of capital investment may be more complicated than simply determining whether individual investment opportunities offer a sufficient return relative to the cost of capital. Frequently, the potentially profitable investment opportunities exceed the capital available for investment. Thus, management must select those investments that are *most* profitable.[5] In general, then, capital budgeting is the analytical process of allocating a firm's scarce capital to the most advantageous possible uses.

### Types of Investments

Before analyzing them, management must understand the natures of the various investment opportunities available and any relationships

---

[5] An excess of investment opportunities over available capital defines the condition known as "capital rationing." It is discussed more fully in Chapter 17.

among them. Some investments are complementary: making one investment either necessitates or, at least, suggests making another. The full benefits will not be obtained unless both are made. In this case, it is desirable (perhaps mandatory) that the two investments be combined into a single package for purposes of managerial analysis. For example, a decision to invest in mineral rights would be pointless (assuming that the rights were not to be held for speculative purposes) unless an investment in mining equipment were also made. Neither investment would produce any benefits unless the other were also made. Thus, there is really only a single investment decision to be made. As another example, a decision to invest in company-owned trucks may suggest a decision to invest also in a company-owned garage for repair and maintenance of the trucks. In this instance, the first investment could be made alone, although it might prove more advantageous if the second were made also. Similarly, the garage alone might offer some benefits; but its full justification depends upon the investment in the trucks.

Some investments are mutually exclusive: acceptance of one necessarily involves rejection of the other(s). For example, if either of two machines would perform a particular manufacturing operation satisfactorily but only one can be used, the decision to buy one automatically entails a decision not to buy the other. Where mutually exclusive investment opportunities exist, they should be identified and dealt with directly. A choice among the alternatives should be made first, and only then should the best alternative be considered along with other possible investments.

Finally, many investments are essentially independent. No significant interrelationship can be detected. For example, a decision to invest in a computer would appear to be independent of a decision to invest in a company airplane. Either or both investments might be made or rejected without regard to the other. The only relationship that might exist in such a case would arise if the otherwise independent investments were competitors for the firm's limited available capital. In this case, however, rejection of one investment would not be caused by acceptance of the other. Rather, it would be caused by the shortage of capital.

### Importance of Cash Flows

Investment decisions, like all decisions, should be analyzed in terms of the cash flows directly traceable to them. These cash flows include both receipts and outlays. They should be the *incremental cash flows* that will occur in the future if and only if the particular investment is made. Both the amounts and the timing of these cash flows must be estimated carefully if a sound investment decision is to be made. The natures of these future cash flows will vary. Almost every investment will require some substantial initial cash outlay; this is usually referred to as the amount invested. Subsequent receipts and outlays may differ considerably among investments. For example, a decision to purchase new production machinery may generate cash receipts in the form of reduced out-of-pocket operating costs. Such cash cost savings are, for practical purposes, equivalent to cash receipts. A decision to undertake a long-term promotional program is usually expected to generate cash flows in the form of increased variable profit—the net excess of increased sales receipts over the increased variable expenses of such sales. It is important to identify clearly those cash flows which are directly traceable to a specific investment decision. Some increase in sales and, hence, in variable profit may be anticipated as a normal consequence of a secular growth in demand. This additional variable profit should be separated from that directly attributable to a specific investment, such as a promotional program.

An investment in a new plant or in a plant expansion would entail an initial cash outlay for purchase or construction of the plant. (Actually, if the plant had to be constructed, the "initial" outlay would probably be spread over some period of time, possibly several years. Illustrations and problems in this book will assume that the initial outlay must be made in total immediately.) In addition to the initial outlay, periodic repairs and maintenance would necessitate fairly regular cash outlays throughout the plant's useful life. The principal expected cash receipts from the investment would be the cash profit realized from sale of products manufactured in the new plant. At the end of the plant's life, there might be some final cash receipt representing the terminal salvage or scrap value of the building. While the foregoing cash flows associated with an investment in plant are those that most readily come to mind, there is another that may be very significant. This is the investment in incremental working capital required for the operation of the plant. Plant operations will require, in most cases, an increased investment in inventories of raw material, work in process, and finished products. They will also necessitate a larger work force and other supporting activities. In order to finance these increased operations, the firm may have to increase its total investment in working capital. The incremental working capital should be included as part of the initial outlay for the new plant. Of course, at the end of the plant's life, that incremental investment in working capital would no longer be needed for the specific plant and it should be included as part of the cash receipt from terminal salvage value.

*Cash Flows and Income Taxes.* For a business enterprise, most cash receipts and outlays must be analyzed after consideration of their income tax implications. The relevant cash flows are after-tax cash flows. We shall continue to assume an income tax rate of 40% on all income. Thus, taxable cash receipts may be converted to their after-tax amounts by multiplying them by 60%. (This is equal to the amounts of the cash receipts before tax less the 40% income tax payable.) Similarly, tax deductible cash outlays must be multiplied by 60% to determine their after-tax amounts. Some cash flows have no direct tax effects because of the provisions of the Internal Revenue Code. These, obviously, have the same before-tax and after-tax values. It would be possible to treat all of the tax effects pertinent to an investment decision as a single cash flow. There are some analytical advantages in relating tax effects to individual cash flows, however; and this method will be employed consistently here.

Depreciation is a noncash expense and, as such, would not be relevant to capital budgeting analyses. However, depreciation is also a deductible expense in the computation of taxable income. Thus, although it has no before-tax cash implications, it does generate after-tax cash receipts for a business firm in the form of reduced income tax payments. That is, the cash outlay for taxes is lower because of the tax deductibility of depreciation. Different depreciation methods involve different time patterns of these after-tax cash flows. Accelerated depreciation methods cause higher depreciation deductions and lower tax payments in the early years of an asset's life than does the straight-line method. As we shall see, the timing of cash flows is an important determinant of their significance in the decision-making process. Consequently, the depreciation method to be used should be regarded by management as a part of the decision to invest in a depreciable asset. It is not merely a technical accounting matter.

The federal income tax law in the United States is extremely complex. It contains many special provisions that may be applicable to particular investment decisions. Certain gains, for example, are identified as long-term capital gains and currently are taxed at a rate lower than that applicable to ordinary income. The after-tax cash benefits from capital gains, thus, are greater than those from ordinary income of the same amount before tax. Operating losses of one period may be carried over to subsequent periods and offset against operating profits. Thus, tax effects are not always bounded by the limits of a single year. If, for example, a proposed investment in a subsidiary corporation is not expected to be profitable for the first year or two of its existence, the tax savings from the early years' operating losses need not be lost. They may be realized in a later profitable year. For purposes of the discussions, illustrations, and problems in this text, no technical knowledge of the income tax law is assumed. In the absence of any statement to the contrary, the reader may assume simply that all revenues and gains are taxable at 40% and that all expenses and losses are deductible at the same rate. Any special tax considerations pertinent to an illustration or a problem will be explained explicitly. To ignore tax implications altogether in these illustrations would be unrealistic. Tax planning is an integral part of good capital budgeting.

## TECHNIQUES OF INVESTMENT ANALYSIS

The mechanical process of analyzing the budgeted cash flows relevant to a particular investment proposal is only part of the total investment decision-making process, but it is an important part. It will be the subject matter of the remainder of this chapter. The assumptions underlying these analytical techniques, as well as their mechanics, should be clearly understood by managers responsible for decision making. Generally, all analytical techniques for capital budgeting may be classified in two broad categories: those that do recognize the time value of money and those that do not. Any technique that does not fall into the first category is thereby deficient. Money does have time value, and any analysis of money flows over extended periods of time that ignores this fundamental fact is consequently invalid. Our discussion will be devoted primarily to valid analytical techniques. We will, however, also consider two methods that ignore the time value of money, simply because these methods are fairly often used in practice. The techniques of analysis to be examined in the sections that follow include the following:

1.  Those that recognize the time value of money:
    *a.*   Net present value.
    *b.*   Present value index.
    *c.*   Discounted rate of return.
2.  Those that ignore the time value of money:
    *a.*   Payback period.
    *b.*   Simple rate of return.

Before turning to these analytical techniques, however, it is important that we clearly understand the concept of the time value of money. All of the valid methods of investment analysis depend upon this concept.

## TIME VALUE OF MONEY

Cash flows have both face values, or dollar values, and time values. Thus, $100 today is not equal to $200 today. This is obvious. Nor is $100 today equal to $100 one year from today. If this does not appear equally obvious, ask whether a rational person would be just as satisfied to wait a year for $100 as to receive the same amount immediately. Clearly, he would prefer to have the money now. If he receives it now, he can invest it to earn interest over the ensuing year. Thus, one year from now he can have the original $100 plus one year's interest on it. If he could earn interest at 10% compounded annually, $100 now could be invested to become $110 one year from now. Thus, $100 today is equal in time value to $110 one year from today at 10% interest. Likewise, $100 one year from today is equal to $90.91 today, because $90.91 plus 10% interest for one year amounts to $100. This is the essence of the time value of money. It is a consequence of the fact that money can be invested to yield a return. Therefore, one would prefer to have a given dollar amount of money sooner rather than later. Similarly, he would be unwilling to exchange a given dollar amount today for the same amount in the future. He would insist upon receiving a larger amount in the future. How much larger that amount would have to be would depend upon the interest rate applicable and the number of years he would have to wait for his money. The value to which $100, invested now at 10% interest compounded annually, will grow at the end of each of the next five years is computed thus:

| | |
|---|---|
| Year 0 (i.e., now) . . . . . . . . . . . . . . . . . . . . . . . . | $100.00 |
| Year 1 [$100 + .10($100)] . . . . . . . . . . . . . . . . . | 110.00 |
| Year 2 [$110 + .10($110)] . . . . . . . . . . . . . . . . . | 121.00 |
| Year 3 [$121 + .10($121)] . . . . . . . . . . . . . . . . . | 133.10 |
| Year 4 [$133.10 + .10($133.10)] . . . . . . . . . . . . | 146.41 |
| Year 5 [$146.41 + .10($146.41)] . . . . . . . . . . . . | 161.05 |

These same values could be computed from the following more compact formula:

$$F = \$100(1 + .10)^n$$

where $F$ is the value to which $100 will grow at the end of $n$ years at 10% interest. Obviously, any values for the initial dollar amount and the interest rate could be substituted for $100 and 10%.

In the tabulation above, all of the end-of-year values shown are equal insofar as time value is concerned. However, no two of them are directly comparable at any single moment in time, for each is expressed at a different time. One of the problems of capital budgeting is to express cash flows that will occur at various times in a common time dimension. This is done by converting all of these cash flows to their values at the same point in time. Mathematically, any point in time might be chosen. Thus, all six of the figures above are equal to $100 at year 0, to $110 at year 1, to $121 at year 2, and so forth. While any point in time might be used, logically one should use the point in time at which he must make a decision—that is, the present time. Thus, all of the cash flows would be stated in terms of their value at year 0, which is a common way of identifying the present time in capital budgeting analyses. Of course, all of the dollar amounts in the tabulation above have a present value equal to $100, so long as the appropriate interest rate is 10%. The process of converting a future cash flow to its present value by use of an interest rate is called *discounting,* and the resultant present value is frequently referred to as a *discounted present value.* The interest rate used may also be referred to as the *discount rate.*

Discounting future cash flows to their present values is essential in any analytical technique that properly recognizes the time value of money. It may be done by solving the appropriate present value formula, or it may be done by reference to published tables of present values, such as those in the Appendix to this book. The use of tables is a much easier alternative, for the present value formulas have already been solved for a large number of cases. The reader not already familiar with tables of present values is advised to read the introductory comments preceding the tables in the Appendix. These tables contain present values of $1. These may be converted to the present value of any given cash flow by multiplying the amount of that cash flow by the appropriate present value of $1. Hence, the tabulated present values are frequently referred to as *present value factors.*

There are two different tables for two different types of cash flows. The first type is a cash flow that occurs only once in a single future year. Present value factors for such a cash flow are found in Table A–1. The second type is a cash flow that occurs in the same amount each year for several successive years. Such a cash flow is called an annuity because it is an annual amount. Present value factors for annuities are found in Table A–2. Technically, the mathematics underlying both of these tables are based on the assumption that any cash flow in a future year occurs all at once in a lump sum at the end of that year. Obviously, this is an artificial assumption; cash flows actually would be more likely to occur at various times throughout the year. Nevertheless, the end-of-year cash flow assumption is implicit in most of the widely available published tables of present values. This simplifying assumption permits all cash flows occurring in a single year to be combined and discounted in one computation. Although not strictly accurate in most cases, the assumption does not seriously affect the present values computed. It is almost universally accepted in present value analyses for the purpose of investment decision making.

## TECHNIQUES THAT RECOGNIZE THE TIME VALUE OF MONEY

As was stated earlier, any valid method of analysis for purposes of investment decision making must recognize the time value of money. We shall discuss and illustrate three generally valid methods for investment analysis. Each of these methods deals with the present values of all of the cash flows relevant to an investment proposal. The only basic difference among them is in the interest rate used to discount cash flows to their present values. Both of the first two methods presented use the same predefined discount rate; hence, they are really two variations of a single basic method. The third method uses an unknown discount rate that must be determined in the analytical process.

## Net Present Value

The *net present value* of an investment is the difference between the present value of the budgeted cash receipts and the present value of the budgeted cash outlays directly traceable to the investment. If the net present value is positive (i.e., the present value of the receipts exceeds that of the outlays), the investment is profitable. If the net present value is negative (i.e., the present value of the receipts is less than that of the outlays), the investment is unprofitable. All future cash flows relevant to the investment are discounted to their present values by use of an interest rate equal to the enterprise's weighted average cost of capital. This cost of capital is the logical discount rate to use, for it is the break-even rate for long-term investments. That is, the interest rate earned on invested capital must equal the average interest cost of that capital if the firm is to break even on its investments. If the net present value of an investment is exactly equal to zero when the cost of capital is used as the discount rate, that is a break-even investment. The interest rate earned on it is exactly equal to the cost of capital. If the net present value is positive, the investment is profitable; and the interest rate earned on it is greater than the cost of capital.

The mechanics of computing the net present value of an investment proposal are quite simple when tables of present values are used. We shall illustrate this computation first for a very simple investment. An investor has the opportunity to purchase a truck now at a cost of $18,000. This truck would have a useful life of five years. It could be used to haul cargo and earn annual cash revenues of $12,000. The annual out-of-pocket costs of operating the truck would be $4,370. Thus, the principal cash receipt from operation of the truck would be a net $7,630 each year for five years. For income tax purposes, the investor would depreciate this truck by the straight-line method (i.e., $3,600 of depreciation would be deductible each year). His income tax rate is 40%. Therefore, the net receipts from operation would be reduced by 40% from $7,630 to $4,578 after tax. However, the investor would save income taxes each year in an amount equal to the annual depreciation deduction ($3,600) multiplied by the income tax rate (40%). This $1,440 annual tax saving is also an after-tax cash receipt. The tax saving derived from depreciation is commonly referred to as the *depreciation tax shield*. Finally, this investor's weighted average cost of capital is 10%.

The proposed investment in this truck is analyzed in Table 16–2. Each cash flow is discounted to its present value by using the appropriate

**TABLE 16–2**

**Analysis of Proposed Investment in Truck**

| | Cash Flow before Tax | Tax Effect | Cash Flow after Tax | Present Value Factor at 10%* | Present Value |
|---|---|---|---|---|---|
| Cash receipts: | | | | | |
| Annual net cash receipts from operations.......... | $ 7,630 | $(3,052) | $ 4,578 | 3.791 | $ 17,355 |
| Tax saving from depreciation............. | — | 1,440 | 1,440 | 3.791 | 5,459 |
| | | | | | $ 22,814 |
| Cash outlays: | | | | | |
| Purchase of truck.......... | (18,000) | | (18,000) | | (18,000) |
| Net present value............ | | | | | $ 4,814 |

* See Appendix, Table A–2.

factor from the 10% column of the tables in the Appendix. In this illustration, the only present value factor used is 3.791, the present value of a five-year annuity of $1 at 10%. Since the initial outlay to purchase the truck would be made at the present time, its present value is equal to its face value. No discounting is required. Alternatively, we might say that the present value factor applicable to a present cash flow is always 1.000, regardless of the discount rate used. In Table 16–2 and in subsequent illustrations, cash receipts are shown as positive cash flows and cash outlays or reductions in cash receipts are shown as negative cash flows. Negative flows are enclosed in parentheses. Note that the tax saving from depreciation is a cash flow only after tax; before tax, it is a noncash expense. Note also that the cash outlay for purchase of the truck has no direct tax effect. In fact, the tax effect of this purchase is the tax saving from depreciation of the truck. This tax effect cannot be combined directly with the purchase, however, because the timing of the two cash flows is not the same. Cash flows may legitimately be combined only if they have the same timing. In this illustration, thus, the two cash receipts might have been added together *after tax* and discounted by one multiplication instead of two. Note carefully, however, that these two items are totally dissimilar before consideration of their tax effects. Finally, it would be equally correct to include the operating revenues of $12,000 as receipts and the operating expenses of $4,370 separately as outlays instead of using only the net receipts of $7,630. This alternative would increase the present values of the receipts and of the outlays by the same amount. Hence, the net present value would remain exactly the same— $4,814 (cf. Table 16–4). It is unlikely that such additional detail would improve the analysis in any way, and it would involve slightly more work.

Confusion sometimes arises as to the correct use of the income tax rate in determining after-tax cash flows. As may be seen in Table 16–2, an item that is a before-tax cash flow and is directly taxable (a receipt) or tax deductible (an outlay) is reduced by the product of itself multiplied by the tax rate. The remainder is the amount of the after-tax cash flow, and it is equal to the before-tax cash flow multiplied by the complement of the tax rate. An item such as depreciation, that is not a cash flow at all before tax, is also multiplied by the tax rate to compute its tax effect. In this case, however, that tax effect *is* the after-tax cash flow. Thus, two general rules may be followed in determining after-tax cash flows. *If an item is a cash flow before tax, multiply it by one minus the tax rate to determine its after-tax amount. If an item is not a cash flow before tax, multiply it by the tax rate to determine its after-tax amount.*

A somewhat more complex illustration of the net present value method is presented in Table 16–3. The pertinent facts in this example are as follows: A corporation has an opportunity to purchase a labor-saving machine now at a cost of $110,000. The machine would have a useful life of eight years, at the end of which time it could be sold for a salvage value of $10,000. For tax purposes, the machine would be depreciated by the straight-line method. In order to keep the machine running properly, its motor and gears would have to be replaced at the end of the fourth year of its life. This replacement would cost $20,000 and would be deductible at that time for tax purposes. Use of the machine would save

**TABLE 16–3**

**Analysis of Proposed Investment in Labor-Saving Machine**

| | Cash Flow before Tax | Tax Effect | Cash Flow after Tax | Present Value Factor at 10% | Present Value |
|---|---|---|---|---|---|
| Cash receipts: | | | | | |
| Annual labor cost savings: | | | | | |
| Years 1–4............. | $  20,000 | $( 8,000) | $  12,000 | 3.170† | $  38,040 |
| Years 5–7............. | 25,000 | (10,000) | 15,000 | 1.698† | 25,470 |
| Year 8............... | 18,000 | ( 7,200) | 10,800 | .467* | 5,044 |
| Tax saving from depreciation | — | 5,000 | 5,000 | 5.335† | 26,675 |
| Terminal salvage value..... | 10,000 | | 10,000 | .467* | 4,670 |
| | | | | | $  99,899 |
| Cash outlays: | | | | | |
| Purchase of machine....... | (110,000) | | (110,000) | | $(110,000) |
| Replacement of motor and | | | | | |
| gears................. | ( 20,000) | 8,000 | ( 12,000) | .683* | (  8,196) |
| | | | | | $(118,196) |
| Net present value (negative).. | | | | | $(  18,297) |

\* See Appendix, Table A–1.
† See Appendix, Table A–2.

labor costs each year, but the amount of these cost savings would not be the same each year. The annual cost savings are estimated thus:

First four years (years 1–4)............. $20,000
Next three years (years 5–7)............ 25,000
Last year (year 8)...................... 18,000

While such a pattern may not be typical of most investment proposals, it will serve to illustrate the mechanical flexibility of the net present value method. The corporation's weighted average cost of capital is 10%. The applicable income tax rate is again assumed to be 40%.

A line-by-line examination of Table 16–3 will show how each of the various cash flows pertinent to this investment proposal is discounted to its present value. The principal cash receipt from the investment in this machine is the saving of annual labor cost. This cost saving is not received in a uniform annuity over the entire eight-year life of the machine, however. Hence, the cost savings must be discounted in three separate steps. The $20,000 that will be saved in each of the first four years constitutes a four-year annuity. After adjusting for the tax effect, the after-tax saving is discounted by the present value factor from the 10% column and the four-year row of Table A–2. The $25,000 cost saving in each of the next three years is also an annuity. However, it is a three-year annuity that will not commence for four years. It cannot be discounted by the three-year factor in Table A–2, because that factor is for a three-year annuity beginning at once. The proper discount factor must be computed by subtracting the four-year factor (3.170) from the seven-year factor (4.868). The remainder (1.698) is the factor for the intervening three years, that is, the years 5, 6, and 7. Since these are the years in which the $25,000 annual saving will be realized, this remainder is the appropriate discount factor.[6] Finally, the cost saving in the last year occurs in only one year. The present value factor for such a cash flow is found in Table A–1 in the 10% column on the eight-year row. This factor is then multiplied by the after-tax amount of the cash flow as in the previous instances.

Straight-line depreciation is handled in exactly the same way as in the preceding illustration. Annual depreciation expense is $12,500 (the

---

[6] This same factor may be computed by taking the three-year factor from Table A–2 and multiplying it by the four-year factor from Table A–1. In essence, this approach says that there is a three-year annuity that has a present value factor of 2.487 (from Table A–2). This present value will not exist until the end of the fourth year in the future, however. Hence, it is discounted by the present value factor for a lump sum at the end of four years—.683 (from Table A–1). This produces the same result as that obtained by subtraction in Table A–2: 2.487 × .683 = 1.699. The trivial difference is due to rounding. This approach is a bit more cumbersome, for it involves two tables instead of one and multiplication instead of subtraction.

difference between the $110,000 cost and the $10,000 salvage value divided by the eight-year life of the machine). As this amount is tax deductible at a rate of 40%, it produces an after-tax cash flow of $5,000 per year for eight years. This eight-year annuity is discounted to its present value by the eight-year factor in the 10% column of Table A–2. The terminal salvage value is a cash receipt at the end of the eighth year. Hence, it is discounted by the eight-year, 10% factor from Table A–1. This salvage value constitutes recovery of that portion of the cost of the machine not earlier charged to depreciation. Hence, so long as no more nor less than $10,000 is expected to be received, there will be no gain or loss on final disposition of the asset. Consequently, the terminal salvage value has no tax effect. Since the terminal salvage value occurs in the 8th year and there is a unique cost saving that occurs only in the 8th year, those two cash receipts might be added together and discounted in one computation. (Note that both use the same present value factor, .467.) The salvage value is shown separately in Table 16–3 to highlight it as a distinct type of cash flow. Further, in most cases it must be discounted separately.

The initial outlay for the purchase of the machine has a present value equal to its face value, for there is no time delay in its incurrence. Its tax effect has already been handled separately in the tax saving from depreciation. The outlay for replacement of the motor and gears at the end of the fourth year will be tax deductible in that year. Hence, the after-tax cash flow will be only $12,000. This is discounted by multiplying it by the present value factor for the fourth year in the 10% column of Table A–1. Since the present value of all outlays exceeds that of all receipts, the net present value is negative. At a cost of capital of 10%, the proposed investment in the machine would not be profitable.

## Present Value Index

The *present value index* is simply a variation of the net present value method. It is the ratio of the present value of cash receipts to the present value of cash outlays. The appropriate discount rate is still the weighted average cost of capital. If the present value index is less than 1.00, the investment is unprofitable; if it is greater than 1.00, the investment is profitable. This is consistent with the results of the net present value method, for the index could be less than 1.00 only if the net present value were negative. Similarly, an index of more than 1.00 follows from a positive net present value. An index of exactly 1.00 and a net present value of zero would be compatible and would indicate a break-even investment.

The present value index for the proposed investment in a truck (Table 16–2) is computed as follows:

$$\text{Present value index} = \frac{\text{Present value of cash receipts}}{\text{Present value of cash outlays}} = \frac{\$22,814}{\$18,000} = 1.27$$

The index for the investment in a labor-saving machine (Table 16–3) is calculated in the same way:

$$\text{Present value index} = \frac{\text{Present value of cash receipts}}{\text{Present value of cash outlays}} = \frac{\$ 99,899}{\$118,196} = .85$$

This index is sometimes referred to as a *discounted benefit/cost ratio*, since it is a ratio of the discounted cash receipts (benefits) to the discounted cash outlays (costs). Some writers call it the *profitability index* of an investment.

**TABLE 16–4**

| | Cash Flow after Tax | Present Value Factor at 10%* | Present Value |
|---|---|---|---|
| Cash receipts: | | | |
| Annual revenue.................. | $ 7,200 | 3.791 | $ 27,295 |
| Tax saving from depreciation....... | 1,440 | 3.791 | 5,459 |
| | | | $ 32,754 |
| Cash outlays: | | | |
| Annual operating expenses......... | ( 2,622) | 3.791 | $( 9,940) |
| Purchase of truck................ | (18,000) | | (18,000) |
| | | | $ 27,940 |
| Net present value................... | | | $  4,814 |

* See Appendix, Table A–2.

In connection with the example of the investment in a truck, we noted previously that cash flows having the same time dimension could be combined or handled separately with no change in the net present value. The operating revenue of $12,000 could have been treated as a cash receipt each year, and the out-of-pocket operating expenses of $4,370, as an annual cash outlay instead of combining them into a single net cash receipt of $7,630. This alternative would have increased the present values of both the cash receipts and the cash outlays by the same amount. Hence, the net present value would be unchanged. The present value index, however, would be different under this approach. This effect may be seen by recomputing the net present value in Table 16–2 as shown in Table 16–4, with cash flows shown initially at their after-tax amounts. This net present value is identical to the one determined in Table 16–2. However, the present value index computed from these data is lower than the one originally computed.

$$\text{Present value index} = \frac{\text{Present value of cash receipts}}{\text{Present value of cash outlays}} = \frac{\$32,754}{\$27,940} = 1.17$$

Obviously, an alternative method of processing exactly the same basic data cannot really reduce the profitability of an investment. It is simply a characteristic of a ratio that its value is affected by the absolute magnitude of the two variables (the present values of the cash receipts and outlays here), even though the absolute difference between them (the net present value here) remains the same. As a practical matter, the present value index is most accurate and useful when all of the cash flows that may legitimately be combined (that is, all that have the same timing) are combined. Thus, the proper index for the truck investment is 1.27, as originally calculated from the data in Table 16–2.[7]

## Discounted Rate of Return

The *discounted rate of return* on an investment is the true interest rate earned on that investment over the course of its economic life. It is a *discounted* rate of return because it specifically provides for the time value of money. This same measure is sometimes referred to as the *effective yield* of an investment. Economists usually refer to it as the *internal rate of return* on an investment. By whatever name, it is an interest rate determined from an analysis of all of the cash flows relevant to an investment proposal and their timings. *Operationally, the discounted rate of return is that interest rate which, when used to discount all cash flows pertinent to an investment, will equate the present value of the cash receipts to the present value of the cash outlays. In other words, it is that discount rate that will cause the net present value of an investment to be equal to zero.* While the calculation of the discounted rate of return does not involve the average cost of capital, any evaluation of its

---

[7] The superiority of the alternative that combines, or nets, all cash flows having the same timing may be seen from a comparison of two very simple investment proposals. Both have three-year lives and both require initial outlays of $40. Investment A will produce annual cash revenues of $250 and will require annual cash expenses of $225. Investment B will generate annual cash revenues of $100 and entail annual cash expenses of $80. (All of these dollars amounts are already stated after taxes.) It is already evident that investment A is more attractive, for it returns $5 more each year with no difference in the initial outlay. If both investments are discounted at 10%, the preference for investment A still appears. It has a net present value of $22, while investment B's net present value is only $10. This same ranking appears when the present value indexes are calculated from the net cash flows (i.e., $25 per year for A and $20 per year for B). The index for investment A is then 1.55, while that for investment B is 1.24. However, if the gross cash receipts and outlays are used in calculating the indexes, the ranking of the two investments is reversed. Investment A has an index of 1.037; and investment B, 1.042. Clearly, this second approach cannot be correct, for investment A is unquestionably superior. Of course, this particular pair of alternatives cannot be considered typical. One would not ordinarily expect two investments of the same initial outlay to produce such widely differing annual receipts and outlays. Nevertheless, the fact that a fallacious ranking *can* occur when the present value index is computed without first combining time-comparable cash flows is sufficient basis for using the other approach.

significance must. If the discounted rate of return is greater than the cost of capital, the investment is profitable. If the discounted rate of return is lower than the cost of capital, the investment is unprofitable. Thus, the cost of capital is just as important in this method as in the net present value and the present value index methods. The difference is that it enters the analysis after the mechanics of computation are completed rather than as a part of those mechanics.

The procedure for computing the discounted rate of return is essentially the same as that for the net present value. All of the cash flows pertinent to an investment proposal are discounted to their present value. The interest rate used as the discount rate is not specified in advance, however. Rather, it is an unknown rate that will cause the net present value to be zero. Thus, the procedure usually involves several trial-and-error discountings of the cash flows with successive guesses at the appropriate discount rate. When the net present value is equal to zero, the correct rate has been found. As a practical matter, it is sufficient to find a rate that will make the net present value of the investment almost equal to zero. This rate is then taken as a satisfactory approximation of the discounted rate of return.

We shall illustrate this trial-and-error procedure for the proposed investment in a labor-saving machine (Table 16–3). We have already seen that the investment has a negative net present value when its cash flows are discounted at the 10% cost of capital. Consequently, we know that the discounted rate of return must be less than 10%. It may be found by repeating the discounting procedure at interest rates lower than 10% until we find one that produces a net present value equal or close to zero. Suppose we guess that the approximate discount rate is 6%. After discounting all of the after-tax cash flows in Table 16–3 at 6%, we find that there is a negative net present value of −$2,077. This tells us that the correct rate of return is still lower than 6%. If we next discount all of the relevant cash flows at 4%, we find a positive net present value of $7,750. Thus, the correct rate must be higher than 4%. As a practical matter, knowing that the discounted rate of return is between 4% and 6% may be sufficiently precise for purposes of decision making. We have straddled the true rate and defined a range of only two percentage points within which it falls. Further, since the negative net present value at 6% is much smaller than the positive value at 4%, we may say that the discounted rate of return is closer to 6% than to 4%.[8]

Of course, there is no guarantee that the trial-and-error process will take us so quickly to the rate we seek. Particularly for a very complex investment proposal, many iterations of the process might be required

---

[8] By interpolation between 4% and 6% (cf., Appendix A), we can determine that the discounted rate of return is 5.58%. So precise a result from the discounting of estimated future cash flows is not really very meaningful, however.

before we found the discounted rate of return. While the tedium of repeated discounting may once legitimately have been considered a disadvantage of this method, it no longer is. The trial-and-error approach can be programmed for a fast and accurate solution by a computer. Also, there are now hand-held electronic calculators that are programmed to compute the discounted rate of return if the cash flows associated with the investment are fairly simple.

For certain investments, the discounted rate of return can. be determined very easily by reference to tables of present values. If the cash flows associated with an investment can be reduced to cash receipts in the form of an annuity of uniform value over the life of the project and cash outlays in a lump sum at the beginning of the project's life, the discounted rate of return can be found directly in Table A–2 after one simple computation. Fortunately, quite a number of investment proposals typically are of this type. The proposed investment in a truck (Table 16–2) is an example. Both of the two items of cash receipts are uniform annuities after taxes. Thus, they may be combined into a single after-tax annuity of $6,018 ($4,578 + $1,440) per year for five years. The only cash outlay, $18,000, occurs at the beginning of the life of the investment (i.e., at the present). Remember that, when the discounted rate of return is used to discount all cash flows to their present values, it will make the present value of the receipts equal to the present value of the outlays. Since the outlays all occur at the present time in our example, their present value is equal to their face value regardless of the discount rate used. Thus, our problem is to find an interest rate that will equate a five-year annuity of $6,018 to a present value of $18,000. If we had a table of present values of an annuity of $6,018, we would only have to find $18,000 in the five-year row to determine the rate of return. Of course, we have a table of present values of an annuity of $1 only. Thus, we must divide both the annuity and the original outlay, which is the present value of the annuity, by $6,018. The same discount rate that will equate $6,018 per year for five years to $18,000 will equate $1 per year for five years to $2.99 ($18,000 ÷ $6,018). In the five-year row of Table A–2, we find that a factor of 2.991 occurs in the 20% column. Hence, the discounted rate of return on this investment is 20%.

***Computing the Cost of Debt Capital.*** Earlier in this chapter, it was noted that the computation of the effective interest rate on debt is the same as the computation of the discounted rate of return. This may now be demonstrated. A bond with a face value of $1,000 is selling in the market for $847.50. The nominal interest is 8% and the bond matures at the end of 15 years. The effective interest rate on this bond is that rate which will equate the future cash receipts that the bondholder will realize to the amount that he must now invest to acquire the bond. His future receipts include $1,000 at the end of 15 years plus $80 of interest each year for the next 15 years. Thus, the problem is to find a discount rate that will equate a single payment of $1,000 after 15 years plus a 15-year annuity of $80 to a present value of $847.50. The discount rate that does this almost exactly is 10%. Hence, 10% is the effective interest cost of the bond before consideration of taxes. That this is the correct interest rate is proved as follows:

Present value of future cash receipts, discounted at 10%:
  Maturity value—$1,000 × .239 (from Table A–1) .............. $239.00
  Interest annuity—$80 × 7.606 (from Table A–2) ...............   608.48
  Total ....................................................... $847.48

Present value of initial investment in bond ..................... $847.50

## Critical Evaluation of Methods

All three of the analytical techniques discussed in the preceding sections are conceptually valid and complete methods of analyzing capital investment proposals. All explicitly recognize the time value of money; hence, they are sometimes described collectively as discounted cash flow methods. All three indicate whether the investment would be profitable, with the average cost of capital used as the criterion for profitability. That is, the investment must yield a return greater than the cost of capital in order to be considered profitable. The net present value and the present value index methods incorporate the cost of capital directly in their calculations, while the discounted rate of return is compared to the cost of capital. There are some differences among these techniques, however, and also some potential difficulties in the use of any one of them.

*Reinvestment Rate Assumptions.* The discount rate used in the net present value method and in the present value index method is the firm's cost of capital. The discount rate used in computing the discounted rate of return is that rate of return itself. This distinction is the source of a substantive difference. All three methods entail the implicit assumption that cash receipts from an investment are immediately reinvested in some project to yield a rate of return equal to the discount rate used in the basic analysis. Thus, the first two methods assume that cash receipts will be reinvested to yield a rate of return equal to the cost of capital. The discounted rate of return method, on the other hand, assumes that those cash receipts will be reinvested to earn the same rate of return as that calculated for the original investment. For example, the proposed investment in a truck (Table 16–2) has a net present value of $4,814 and a present value index of 1.27, when the cash flows are discounted at 10%, only so long as the cash receipts can be reinvested to earn 10%. Similarly, the discounted rate of return on this investment is 20% only if the cash receipts can be reinvested to earn 20%. If it appears that one or the other of these alternative reinvestment assumptions is more realistic, there is a logical argument for using an analytical technique that involves the better reinvestment assumption. Unfortunately, it is seldom practicable to make a reliable forecast of reinvestment opportunities several years in the future. Hence, reinvestment plans are not typically included in investment analyses in any explicit fashion. Thus, management might decide that the best implicit assumption is that the rate of return available on current investments will also be available in the future. Alternatively, management might prefer the more conservative assumption that cash receipts can be reinvested to earn no more than the cost of capital. Whichever method of analysis is chosen, its implicit reinvestment assumption should be recognized.

*Multiple Rates of Return.* The discounted rate of return method suffers a technical shortcoming that does not afflict the other two methods. The net cash flow associated with an investment in any single period is either positive (a net cash receipt) or negative (a net cash outlay). In a simple situation, the net cash flow is negative only at the present, the time of the initial outlay. Subsequently, the net cash flow is consistently positive, even though it may fluctuate somewhat in amount. In this simple case, the algebraic sign of the successive net cash flows over time changes only once; it is negative at the outset and then positive in all future periods. If the sign of the net cash flows in successive periods changes more than once, the discounted rate of return may be indeterminate. There *may be* (but not necessarily *will be*) as many rates of return as there are sign changes.[9] Each of these rates would equate the present value of total cash receipts with that of total cash outlays. Obviously, such a solution to the analysis of the investment proposal is not satisfactory. While multiple rates of return may be mathematically meaningful, only one rate is economically significant in determining whether an investment is profitable. As a matter of fact, if an adequate analysis of the multiple rates of return is made, one of them may be identified as the relevant one for purposes of investment decision making.[10] Fortunately, the majority of business investment proposals fit into the simpler case that produces a single, determinate discounted rate of return. Thus, the multiple-rate-of-return situation is not typical. It ought not be ignored, however; for when it occurs, its effect may be very important to the investment analysis. This problem has led some writers to reject the discounted rate of return as a generally useful technique of investment analysis.

---

[9] This phenomenon is an illustration of Descartes' rule of signs.

[10] An analysis to resolve the problem of multiple rates of return is described in G. David Quirin, *The Capital Expenditure Decision* (Homewood, Ill.: Richard D. Irwin, Inc., 1967), pp. 49–55.

*Practical Considerations.* On a very pragmatic plane, the net present value and present value index offer an advantage of simplicity. These methods require only one discounting of the cash flows relevant to an investment. As was demonstrated above, the determination of the discounted rate of return, except in very simple cases, is a trial-and-error procedure that might entail several discountings until the appropriate rate is found. While this is not a real problem for a manager with access to computing equipment, it may be a genuine consideration for the harried student. The problems at the end of this chapter and the next can be solved by any of the methods discussed here. The student who does not have access to a computer will find them solved more quickly in most cases by use of the net present value or the present value index.

The discounted rate of return does have one practical advantage of its own. It is stated as an interest rate, a very familiar concept to businessmen and to investors generally. The other two methods, while equally valid, present their results in less familiar forms. Of course, as these methods become more widely understood and used, this problem of unfamiliarity should disappear.

## TECHNIQUES THAT IGNORE THE TIME VALUE OF MONEY

As was stated earlier, any technique for analyzing investments is defective if it fails to consider the time value of money. The two methods discussed below are included here only because they are used with some degree of frequency in practice. Neither, however, may be relied upon to provide an indication of an investment's true profit potential.

### Payback Period

The *payback period* of a proposed investment is the length of time required for the net cash receipts from the investment to equal, in total, the amount of the initial outlay. It is often described as the time required for an investment to pay for itself. The basic premise of this technique is that, other things being equal, an investment that will pay for itself soon is better than one that will require a long time before the initial outlay is recovered. The payback is expressed in units of time, usually years. The customary formula for its computation is as follows:

$$\text{Payback period} = \frac{\text{Initial outlay}}{\text{Average annual net cash receipts}}$$

By this formula, the payback period for the proposed investment in a truck (Table 16–2) would be computed thus:

$$\text{Payback period} = \frac{\$18,000 \text{ initial outlay}}{\$6,018 \text{ annually}} = 3 \text{ years}$$

Since this period is less than the five-year life of the truck, one might be tempted to conclude that the investment would be profitable. As it happens, we know that this investment is profitable; but we cannot safely conclude that simply from the payback period.

The formula above is not appropriate in determining the payback period of the investment in a labor-saving machine (Table 16–3). In this case, the annual cash receipts vary considerably over time. Also, there is an additional cash outlay four years after the initial outlay. Hence, the payback period must be determined by accumulating positive and negative cash flows sequentially until the algebraic sum of all of them is exactly zero. This is done in the chronological analysis of the cash flows relevant to the labor-saving machine shown in Table 16–5. The positive

**TABLE  16–5**

|  | Cash Flow | Cumulative Sum |
|---|---|---|
| Present............................ | \$−110,000 | \$−110,000 |
| First year........................ | 17,000 | −93,000 |
| Second year...................... | 17,000 | −76,000 |
| Third year....................... | 17,000 | −59,000 |
| Fourth year...................... | 17,000 | −42,000 |
| End of fourth year................ | −12,000 | −54,000 |
| Fifth year....................... | 20,000 | −34,000 |
| Sixth year....................... | 20,000 | −14,000 |
| First 7/10 of seventh year......... | 14,000 | 0 |

cash flows for all years include the sum of the after-tax labor cost savings plus the tax saving from depreciation. If we assume that the $20,000 to be received during the seventh year is received in a steady stream throughout the year, $14,000 will have been received after seven tenths of the year is over. Thus, the payback period would be 6.7 years. This is shorter than the machine's life of eight years, but it does not indicate that the investment is profitable. We have already seen that, at a cost of capital of 10%, this is an unprofitable investment. The problem, of course, is that the payback computations ignore the very important fact that future cash receipts cannot validly be compared with an initial outlay until they have been discounted to their present values.

The payback period could be made a valid indicator of the time required for an investment to pay for itself, if all cash flows were discounted to their present values. This is seldom done, however. Even if it were done, the payback period would not be a complete measure of an investment's profitability. It could only indicate *whether* the investment was profitable, not *how profitable* it was. For example, an investment calling for an initial outlay of $1,000 and having annual cash receipts of

$300 for five years would have exactly the same payback period as an investment of $1,000 initially with annual cash receipts of $300 for 10 years. Yet, the latter investment, with its longer life, is obviously preferable. The payback period, however, even if computed from present values, would not show the advantage of the second investment. The net present value, present value index, and discounted rate of return methods all would show the greater profitability of the longer lived investment.

If the payback period has any value at all, it is as a supplementary indicator of investment risk. One of the techniques that recognize the time value of money should be used to determine the investment's profitability. The payback period might then be taken as one measure of the risk associated with that investment. The longer the payback period, the greater the risk of future cash flows not being realized as initially anticipated. This is only a rough notion of risk, however; for it is based on the premise that the risk of cash flows not being realized increases as the cash flows are planned further and further in the future. This premise need not always be valid.

## Simple Rate of Return

The *simple,* or *undiscounted, rate of return* is often called the financial statement method of computing a rate of return because it uses the type of data found in the conventional balance sheet and income statement. Unlike any of the methods discussed previously, it does not deal only with cash flows. Rather, it divides the estimated average annual net income (or contribution to net income) from an investment by the initial outlay for that investment. If the investment involves the purchase of a depreciable asset, depreciation is deducted from operating revenues along with cash operating expenses to determine net income. While this treatment of depreciation is entirely appropriate in the determination of periodic net income after it has been earned, it is incorrect in a forecast of future benefits from an investment. The simple rate of return on the proposed investment in a truck (Table 16–2) is computed below:

| | | |
|---|---:|---:|
| Annual revenue from operations...................... | | $12,000 |
| Annual out-of-pocket operating expenses................ | $4,370 | |
| Annual depreciation................................ | 3,600 | 7,970 |
| Income before tax..................................... | | $ 4,030 |
| Income tax at 40%.................................... | | 1,612 |
| Annual net income................................... | | $ 2,418 |
| Divided by initial outlay............................ | | 18,000 |
| Simple rate of return ($2,418 ÷ $18,000).............. | | 13.4% |

This result is significantly below the true (discounted) rate of return of 20%.

In an alternative method of computing the simple rate of return, the annual net income is divided by the average investment rather than the initial outlay. The average investment is defined as the unrecovered portion of the initial investment that remains at the midpoint of the life of the investment. It is computed by taking one half of the sum of the initial outlay plus the terminal salvage value. In cases such as the investment in a truck, where there is no terminal salvage value, the average investment is simply one half of the initial outlay. Thus, the simple rate of return on the average investment in the truck is 26.8% ($2,418 ÷ $9,000). This is still not the same as the discounted rate of return.

Possibly one attraction of the financial statement method of computing a rate of return is that it conforms to the methodology used in computing the rate of return on the investment in assets for a fiscal period.[11] There is no reason, however, why the computation of the rate of return in prospect on a proposed investment over its entire life should be the same as the computation of the rate of return in retrospect for a firm or a part of a firm during a single period. These two distinct rates of return are conceptually different. They are designed to serve different purposes, and it is entirely proper that they are computed in different ways. The discounted rate of return on an investment proposal is the annual interest rate earned on that investment *over its entire life*. There is nothing in the method that implies that the same rate is earned *in each individual year* of that life.

## QUESTIONS FOR DISCUSSION

1. What are the distinctive characteristics of an investment decision as contrasted with a short-term decision of the type discussed in Chapter 14?

2. This chapter is concerned almost entirely with the financial analysis of long-term investment decisions confronting business managers. While financial analysis is indispensable to an intelligent decision, it is not the sum and substance of the decision-making process. What other factors are relevant to the decision? Have these factors any financial implications? If so, why are they not incorporated in the formal financial analysis? If not, how should they be analyzed in the decision-making process?

3. Are the principles of capital budgeting discussed in this chapter relevant to governmental and other nonprofit organizations as well as to business firms? Discuss.

4. Discuss the relevance of each of the following expenses commonly appearing in corporate income statements to the financial analysis of an investment decision:
   a. Depreciation
   b. Interest
   c. Income taxes

---

[11] This after-the-fact rate of return was discussed in Chapter 12.

5. Why does money have time value? Is present value the same as time value? Explain.

6. Define the net present value of an investment in a way that should be clear to a reasonably informed layman (i.e., one who is not an accountant nor an expert in financial matters).

7. Why is the discounted rate of return preferable to the simple rate of return on an investment proposal?

8. What are some of the practical disadvantages in using the discounted rate of return as a method of evaluating capital investments?

9. Is it a safe generalization to say that any investment having a payback period shorter than its economic life is profitable? Why or why not? Is it a safe generalization to say that any investment with a payback period longer than its economic life is unprofitable? Why or why not?

10. Of what general utility is the payback period in capital investment analysis?

11. What are some of the advantages and disadvantages of the present value index as compared with the net present value?

12. What do the net present value, the present value index, and the discounted rate of return all have in common?

13. Your rich uncle has an opportunity to purchase for $100,000 a small retail store that will produce an annual net income after taxes of $10,000. He plans to make this investment, as it will yield a rate of return of 10% on his capital and, in his own words, "that beats government bonds." Criticize your uncle's analysis of this investment opportunity.

14. A friend of yours is planning to start his own business. He will have to purchase a store building, display counters, other furnishings, and an inventory. In talking with you about his plans, he mentions that he is fortunate in not having to worry about interest because all of the money he invests will be his own savings, which are now on deposit in his checking account. How would you react to this observation?

15. What is the difference between a specific cost of capital and a firm's average cost of capital? Why might the specific costs of various sources of capital differ from one another?

16. Does a charitable organization, whose only source of capital is donations, have a cost of capital? Explain.

17. "In the implementation of any long-term investment project, there is always some 'point of no return' beyond which it is impractical and unreasonable to abandon the project." Assuming for the moment that this assertion is valid, explain how one would identify this "point of no return." Now, is the assertion really valid? Explain.

## PROBLEMS

16–1. Following are the basic financial data pertinent to three independent investment opportunities:

Wholesale distributorship:

| | |
|---|---:|
| Initial cash outlay | $250,000 |
| Annual cash receipts | 40,000 |
| Economic life | 15 years |
| Cost of capital | 10% |

Diamond mine:

| | |
|---|---:|
| Initial cash outlay | $800,000 |
| Annual cash receipts | 200,000 |
| Economic life | 6 years |
| Cost of capital | 12% |

Farm:

| | |
|---|---:|
| Initial cash outlay | $500,000 |
| Annual cash receipts | 70,000 |
| Terminal salvage value | 500,000 |
| Economic life | 20 years |
| Cost of capital | 14% |

*Required:*

Compute the net present value and the present value index for each of these investment projects. Ignore income taxes.

16-2.  The basic financial facts pertinent to five independent investment proposals are outlined below.

Investment A:

| | |
|---|---:|
| Initial outlay | $ 300,000 |
| Annual cash receipts | 50,000 |
| Life | 8 years |
| Cost of capital | 10% |

Investment B:

| | |
|---|---:|
| Initial outlay | $ 75,000 |
| Annual cash receipts | 12,500 |
| Terminal salvage value | 9,000 |
| Life | 12 years |
| Cost of capital | 12% |

Investment C:

| | |
|---|---:|
| Cost of capital | 14% |
| Life | 15 years |
| Annual cash receipts: | |
| First five years | $ 50,000 |
| Next five years | 100,000 |
| Last five years | 80,000 |
| Terminal salvage value | 120,000 |
| Initial outlay | 400,000 |

Investment D:

| | |
|---|---:|
| Annual cash receipts: | |
| First year | $ 50,000 |
| Next 14 years | 90,000 |
| Last 15 years | 150,000 |
| Economic life | 30 years |
| Initial outlay | $1,000,000 |
| Outlay at end of 10 years | 350,000 |
| Outlay at end of 20 years | 450,000 |
| Cost of capital | 8% |

Investment E:

| | |
|---|---:|
| Initial cash receipt | $ 600,000 |
| Annual cash outlays | 150,000 |
| Cost of capital | 15% |
| Life | 8 years |

*Required:*

Compute the net present value and the present value index for each of these investment proposals. Ignore income taxes.

16–3. An investment proposal promises to yield $28,700 in cash annually for a period of 25 years and requires an initial expenditure of $175,000.

*Required:*

Determine the discounted rate of return on this investment proposal. Ignore income taxes.

16–4. An investment of $704,000 today promises to return net cash proceeds after all tax effects of $75,000 per year for the next 12 years.

*Required:*

What is the discounted rate of return on this investment?

16–5. An investor whose cost of capital is 10% has an opportunity to purchase a 30-year mortgage note that provides for annual payments of $5,000 over the term of the note.

*Required:*

What is the maximum amount that the investor could afford to pay for this mortgage note without suffering a loss on his investment? Ignore income taxes.

16–6. A mortgage note provides for a loan of $60,000 and a series of repayments of $6,610 at the end of each of the next 25 years.

*Required:*

What is the effective interest rate on this mortgage note, before consideration of income taxes?

16–7. A portable drilling rig has a useful life of 6 years and no terminal salvage value. It may be purchased for $125,000 cash, or it may be leased for 6 years. The lease contract would require annual payments of $27,145 at the beginning of each of the next 6 years.

*Required:*

What is the implicit interest rate before taxes in this lease contract?

16–8. A 20-year, $10,000,000 bond issue bearing interest at 8% was issued on January 1, 1969. On January 1, 1977, this bond issue is selling in the market at 86.4 (i.e., 86.4% of face value).

*Required:*

What is the effective market interest rate, before taxes, on this bond as of January 1, 1977?

16–9.  The Corcoran Corporation has the following capital structure as of December 31, 1976:

|  | Market Value of Outstanding Securities | Specific Cost of Capital before Taxes |
|---|---|---|
| Debenture bonds............ | $15,000,000 | 9% |
| Mortgage bonds............. | 6,000,000 | 7½% |
| Preferred stock............. | 9,000,000 | 8% |
| Common stock.............. | 30,000,000 | 15% |

The applicable income tax rate is 40%.

*Required:*

Compute the average cost of capital of the Corcoran Corporation.

16–10.  The Bobstay Chemical Corporation has the following long-term capital outstanding as of December 31, 1976:

Bonds with a face value of $20,000,000 were issued in 1964 and are due on December 31, 1993. The nominal interest rate on these bonds is 6%. They are currently selling in the market at a price of $817.32 for a $1,000 bond.

One hundred thousand shares of preferred stock with a par value of $100 are outstanding. The annual dividend is $8 per share. This stock is presently selling on the market at $88 per share.

One million shares of $5 par value common stock are issued and outstanding. The current market price per share is $20. Annual dividends per share for the past 10 years have been as shown below. The same rate of growth in dividends is expected to continue in the future.

| | | | |
|---|---|---|---|
| 1967.............. | $.50 | 1972.............. | $ .73½ |
| 1968.............. | .54 | 1973.............. | .79½ |
| 1969.............. | .58¼ | 1974.............. | .86 |
| 1970.............. | .63 | 1975.............. | .93 |
| 1971.............. | .68 | 1976.............. | 1.00 |

The income tax rate is 40%.

*Required:*

Compute the corporation's average cost of capital. Include all necessary preliminary computations.

16–11.  Following is a summary of the important financial data applicable to five independent investment proposals. All tax effects are already included in these data.

| Investment | Initial Outlay | Annual Cash Receipts | Life in Years |
|---|---|---|---|
| A............. | $ 55,000 | $ 8,000 | 25 |
| B............. | 64,900 | 19,000 | 7 |
| C............. | 83,700 | 12,000 | 16 |
| D............. | 137,000 | 5,000 | 40 |
| E............. | 69,500 | 33,000 | 3 |

The cost of capital is 10%.

*Required:*

Rank these five investments in the order of their:

a. Payback periods,
b. Discounted rates of return,
c. Present value indexes, and
d. Net present values.

16–12. The U.S. Coast and Geodetic Survey has been leasing the land for its Maui Test Station. The lease has five more years to run at the current annual rental of $250,000. A development company has recently purchased this land and has advised the government that it plans to construct a retirement community on it after ten years. Hence, the new owner would be willing to renew the government's lease for only five additional years when it expires. Further, it has notified the Coast and Geodetic Survey that the rent would then be increased to $400,000 per year. Under the terms of the lease, the government is committed to restoring the land to its natural condition at the termination of the lease at an estimated cost of $500,000. After further discussions, the development company has offered to sell the land to the government now for $2,600,000.

The Coast and Geodetic Survey does not plan to continue its testing activities on Maui for longer than ten more years in any event. If it did purchase the land, it would simply add it to Haleakala National Park after ten years; no restoration would then be required.

Federal regulations specify that major capital expenditures of this type must be evaluated by using a discount rate of 10%.

*Required:*

Present a financial analysis that will show whether it would be cheaper for the government to purchase the land on Maui or to continue renting it for ten more years.

16–13. Robin Oakapple has an opportunity to purchase a cabin cruiser that is used commercially for fishing parties off the Kona Coast. The boat has a remaining useful life of 15 years. It would cost $154,000 now and could be resold at a scrap value of $10,000 after 15 years. Annual receipts from passengers are expected to average $125,000, and annual out-of-pocket operating expenses are estimated at $80,000. Oakapple would pay incomes taxes at a rate of 40% and would deduct depreciation on the boat by the straight-line method. His cost of capital is 12%.

*Required:*

a. Compute the payback period for the investment in the boat.
b. Compute the simple rate of return (1) on the initial investment and (2) on the average investment.
c. Compute the net present value of the investment.
d. Compute the present value index of the investment.
e. Determine the discounted rate of return on the investment.

16–14. The Cholmondeley Building Products Corporation is considering the construction of a new plant to produce pre-cut framing for houses. The initial cost of the plant would be $12,000,000. It would have a useful life of 30 years and no terminal salvage value. Depreciation on this plant would be deducted by means of the straight-line method for tax purposes. Annual cash revenues from sales of the plant's output are budgeted at $10,000,000 and annual out-of-pocket operating costs, at $7,000,000. The corporate income tax rate is 40%. The company's cost of capital is 10%.

*Required:*

Would the investment in the new plant be profitable? Support your answer with appropriate financial analysis.

16–15. The Joseph Porter Realty Company is contemplating the purchase of an old apartment building on Nob Hill for $2,000,000, of which $500,000 would be the cost of the land. Extensive renovation of the building would be required at an estimated cost of $3,300,000. This work would take one year to complete and would be paid for upon completion. The renovated building would then have an economic life of 20 years. For tax purposes, it would be depreciated by the straight-line method.

The apartments would have a high prestige value. Hence, full occupancy may reasonably be anticipated over the entire 20-year period. Annual rental collections would total $2,966,000; operating and maintenance expenditures would average $684,000 per year. At the end of the building's economic life, the land could be sold for an estimated $800,000. The salvage value of the building materials would just cover the cost of demolition.

The company's cost of capital is 14%. The income tax rate is 40%.

*Required:*

Would the contemplated real estate investment be profitable? Support your answer with appropriate financial analysis.

16–16. Adam Goodheart, 50 years of age, has received an inheritance of $500,000 from his uncle. He currently is employed as the store manager of a large metropolitan haberdashery. His salary is $30,000 per year, and he does not anticipate that this will change if he remains in his present position until retirement at age 65. He is considering only two alternative uses of his inheritance. The first alternative would be to continue in his present job and to invest the $500,000 in safe 15-year term bonds yielding 10% interest. The second alternative would be to purchase and manage his own store.

Goodheart knows of a haberdashery that he could buy for $450,000, including $210,000 for inventory and the balance for the building and fixtures. The land is leased. He would have to invest an additional $50,000 for working capital purposes. Expected annual sales in this store would be $1,500,000. Annual out-of-pocket operating costs, including land rent, would total $1,380,000. Goodheart would quit his present job in order to devote full time to the management of the new store. At the end of 15 years, the land lease would terminate and the building and fixtures would become the property of the lessor. Goodheart would, however, recover his entire investment in working capital at that time.

The applicable personal income tax rate is 30%. Straight-line depreciation would be claimed for income tax purposes.

*Required:*

Prepare an analysis showing which of Goodheart's two alternatives would be more profitable for him. Accept his premise that there are no other alternatives.

16–17. The Buttercup Home Products Company has developed a new kitchen appliance that it plans to introduce in the coming year. It is estimated that this product will have a market life of 10 years. An initial expenditure of $1,500,000 for equipment to manufacture the product will be necessary. After two years, additional equipment costing $2,500,000 will have to be acquired. The original equipment will have no significant salvage value at the end of the product's market life. The equipment purchased two years later, however, will be sold for approximately $300,000 at the end of the market life. For tax purposes, straight-line depreciation will be used.

Projected annual sales volumes of this new appliance over the course of its market life are as follows:

| | |
|---|---:|
| 1st year.................................. | $  750,000 |
| 2d year................................... | 1,200,000 |
| 3d–7th years.............................. | 3,000,000 |
| 8th–10th years............................ | 2,000,000 |

Variable out-of-pocket costs to produce and distribute the product will average 60% of selling prices. Fixed out-of-pocket operating costs will average $400,000 annually. In addition, a special sales promotion campaign is planned. Its annual costs will be as follows:

| | |
|---|---:|
| 1st year.................................. | $750,000 |
| 2d year................................... | 400,000 |
| 3d–10th years............................. | 100,000 |

The applicable income tax rate is 40%. It may be assumed that the company, as a whole, will have net taxable income in every year, regardless of profit or loss on any single product line. The company's cost of capital is 10%.

*Required:*

Will it be profitable for the company to market this new appliance?

16-18. Montarrat Productions, Inc., is planning a new "disaster" motion picture to be titled *Claws*. It is the story of a killer bear that terrorizes the tourist communities around Lake Tahoe. Production is scheduled to begin at once and is expected to take one year to complete. Operating cash outlays, including actors' salaries (except as noted in the next paragraph), are budgeted at $8,000,000 during the year of production. In addition, the producers will have to make an immediate payment of $1,000,000 to the U.S. Forest Service for exclusive rights to the use of the Rubicon Canyon wilderness area during the filming of the picture.

The distinguished British actor, Earl Tolloller, has been signed to play the role of Flint, the misanthropic hunter hired to find and kill the bear. Tolloller has agreed to accept either a salary of $600,000, to be paid during the year of production, or 3% of the gross receipts from the film. The latter alternative would require annual payments to Tolloller during the period of the film's initial release. No salary or percentage for Tolloller has been included in the $8,000,000 production costs mentioned earlier.

Promotional costs of $2,000,000 will be incurred upon completion of production and release of the film. Thereafter, annual promotional outlays of $250,000 are planned throughout the period of initial release. The producers have estimated that the initial release will last for three years. Gross receipts from the film are expected to be $10,000,000 during the first year, $7,000,000 in the second year, and $3,000,000 in the third year. Also, at the end of the third year, television rights to the movie would be sold for about $2,000,000. Theater receipts thereafter would be negligible.

Montarrat Productions' cost of capital is 14%. The income tax rate is 40%. For tax purposes, the producers of a motion picture that is completed in less than two years have the option of charging production costs to expense as they are incurred or capitalizing them and amortizing them over the period of initial release.

*Required:*

a. Would it be more economical for the producers to pay Earl Tolloller the $600,000 salary or 3% of the gross receipts?
b. Would it be more advantageous to charge the production costs to current expense or to capitalize them for income tax purposes?
c. Would *Claws* be a profitable investment for the producers?

16-19. The Hildebrand Electronics Corporation has developed a revolutionary new remote control device for television sets. It can be installed easily on any set. The corporation plans to build a new factory for the production of the device. The initial cost of the factory will be $20,000,000. Its useful life is estimated at 30 years and its terminal salvage value, at $2,000,000.

The remote control device will be sold for $39 per unit. Variable costs of production and marketing will total $15 per unit. In addition, there will be annual fixed factory costs of $2,800,000, including salaries, maintenance, taxes, insurance, and straight-line depreciation on the factory.

An initial sales promotion campaign is planned. It calls for an immediate outlay of $500,000 and then subsequent outlays during each of the first three years of the product's market life in the following amounts:

| | |
|---|---|
| 1st year.................................. | $400,000 |
| 2d year................................... | 200,000 |
| 3d year................................... | 100,000 |

After the third year, promotion of this device will simply be a part of the company's regular annual advertising program at no additional cost. This advertising program currently costs about $1,250,000 per year.

Forecasted annual sales volumes for the device are as follows:

| | *Units* |
|---|---|
| 1st year.................................. | 100,000 |
| 2d year................................... | 200,000 |
| 3d year................................... | 300,000 |
| 4th–30th years............................ | 350,000 |

The income tax rate is 40%. The company's cost of capital is 10%.

*Required:*

Prepare a report showing the budgeted profitability of the proposed investment in the new factory.

16–20. The Maynard Company has developed a golfer's "cart bag," replete with handy devices. If the clubs are properly stored in the bag, the desired club is extended automatically at the touch of a button. There is a built-in ball washer, an 18-hole scorekeeper, and a retractable umbrella for sudden showers. The cart bag has its own handle and wheels and, because of its weight, is self-propelled by a small battery-powered motor.

Corporate management has decided to "skim the cream off the market" for several years before introducing the cart bag to the mass market at a price within the means of the average golfer. Consequently initial production facilities will be limited to produce an output below the expected total demand. Early promotional efforts will be directed at the high income golfer. Because of this very selective distribution plan, management believes it has very wide latitude in setting its price. There is no closely competitive product on the market.

The cost of the production facilities required to manufacture the

486     *Accounting for Managerial Analysis*

cart bag in the initial low volume will be $1,500,000. The annual output of these facilities will be 5,000 units, and management is confident that all of them can be sold. These facilities will have an economic life of only three years and no significant terminal salvage value. Promotional outlays are planned at $500,000 during each of these first three years. Variable costs of producing and distributing the cart bag will average $360 per unit. Additional fixed out-of-pocket costs incurred because of this new product are budgeted at $250,000 per year.

The company's profit goals call for a discounted rate of return of 20% after taxes on investments in new products. The cost of capital is 10%. The income tax rate is 40%. Straight-line depreciation will be used for tax purposes.

*Required:*

What initial selling price is necessary in order to obtain the target rate of return on investment?

16-21. Fairfax bought an apartment building 20 years ago for $800,000. It has a remaining economic life of 20 years and no terminal salvage value. His annual income statement for the current operations of this building appears as follows:

| Rent revenue | | $300,000 |
|---|---|---|
| Expenses: | | |
| Out-of-pocket | $160,000 | |
| Depreciation | 20,000 | 180,000 |
| Income before tax | | $120,000 |
| Income taxes at 40% | | 48,000 |
| Net income | | $ 72,000 |

Meryl has expressed an interest in buying this building "if the price is right." It may be assumed that rents and out-of-pocket expenses will continue as shown above for the remaining life of the building. Meryl is in the 30% income tax bracket.

Fairfax's cost of capital is 12%. Meryl's cost of capital is 10%.

*Required:*

a. What is the lowest price at which Fairfax can afford to sell the building?
b. What is the highest price Meryl can afford to pay for the building?

16-22. The Willis Land Development Company has an opportunity to purchase the mineral rights on a small plot of land known to be rich in limestone. It would have to pay $100,000 now for those rights, which it would then hold for 20 years. The company estimates that its net cash flow from extraction and sale of limestone would amount to $25,000 per year for the entire 20-year period. At the end of 20 years, the company would have to restore the land to its natural state; this would cost an estimated $600,000 at that time. The company's cost of capital is 12%.

All of the cash flows mentioned above are stated net of their income tax effects.

The controller of the company asked his new assistant to determine the return on investment that the company could expect to earn on the proposed investment. The assistant submitted a report showing a discounted rate of return of approximately 22%. The controller decided to double-check this new man's work. To his dismay, he came up with a discounted rate of return of about 6%. Annoyed, he returned his assistant's report with a sharply worded note attached to it. The next morning, the assistant walked into his office with a smile on his face. "Chief," he announced, "We are both right." With that, he placed the following report on the controller's desk:

Analysis of Limestone Mineral Rights
May 12, 1977

| Discount Rate | Net Present Value | Discount Rate | Net Present Value |
|---|---|---|---|
| 0% | $-200,000 | 16% | $+17,625 |
| 2% | - 95,025 | 18% | +11,625 |
| 4% | - 33,850 | 20% | + 6,150 |
| 6% | - 450 | 22% | + 100 |
| 8% | + 16,450 | 24% | - 5,650 |
| 10% | + 23,450 | 26% | -10,800 |
| 12% | + 24,325 | 28% | -15,550 |
| 14% | + 21,775 | 30% | -20,100 |

While the controller was pleased to have his faith restored in the new assistant, he now had a different concern. "How do we explain this?" he asked. "And what do I tell the board next week when they ask me whether that blasted piece of land would be a good investment?"

*Required:*

Answer the two questions posed by the controller in the last paragraph of the problem.

# chapter 17

# Capital Budgeting: Applications and Complications

IN THE PRECEDING chapter, techniques for analyzing the cash flows pertinent to an investment decision were explained and illustrated. The importance of recognizing the time value of those cash flows was emphasized. The subject of capital budgeting covers much more than techniques of financial analysis, however. It embraces the various types of investment decisions that may face managers and the problems of measurement and analysis that may be encountered. Some of these situations and problems will be discussed in this chapter. The potential implications and complications of capital budgeting decisions extend far beyond the scope of this discussion, however.

Most probably, the greatest practical problem of capital budgeting is the development of reliable estimates of the future cash flows relevant to an investment proposal. This is similar to the problems of forecasting for annual budgets, but it is more acute because of the long time horizon over which plans must be formulated. Unless reasonable cash flow estimates can be made, the most sophisticated analytical techniques will yield unreliable results. While the techniques provide correct analysis, they cannot compensate for inaccurate basic data. Also, the precision (to three decimal places) of the present value factors in the Appendix does not mean that the present values of future cash flows computed by use of those factors are very accurate. An approximation of a future cash flow may be discounted to a *precise* present value, but this does not increase the *accuracy* of the original estimate. Thus, care should be taken in the development of cash flow estimates. The validity of the subsequent capital budgeting analysis depends largely upon this critical first step.

## ASSET REPLACEMENT DECISIONS

A fairly common illustration of a capital budgeting decision is the asset replacement decision. Managers frequently must consider the possibility of replacing an asset presently in service with a new and presumably better one, even though the old asset's useful life has not expired. Obviously, if the old asset can no longer be used, the replacement decision takes on a different character. It is then a decision either to replace the asset or to discontinue the operation for which the asset has been used. Assuming that operations can be carried on with either the present asset or a new one, the replacement decision will depend upon which alternative is more profitable or otherwise more advantageous. Capital budgeting analysis, of course, can deal directly only with the matter of profitability. Such other legitimate considerations as safety and public responsibility can be incorporated in the financial analysis only if they have measurable effects on future cash flows.

The profitability of replacement may be indicated by a positive net present value, a present value index greater than 1.00, or a discounted rate of return greater than the cost of capital for the investment in the new asset *in place of* the old one. That is, the analysis will focus on the cash flows that will occur if the new asset is substituted for the old one. The relevant cash flows, then, are the incremental flows associated with use of the new asset instead of the old one.

For purposes of the replacement decision, whether the old asset is fully depreciated or has only recently been purchased is not normally a critical consideration. The original cost incurred for the old asset is now a sunk cost; it has no direct bearing on the decision. As a matter of fact, a loss on the disposition of an old asset has a favorable implication for the replacement decision if that loss is tax deductible. The basic factors entering into the analysis are the incremental cash flows from operating the new asset in place of the old one, the price that must be paid for the new asset, the incremental depreciation tax shield on the new asset, the current salvage value of the old asset, and the terminal salvage values of both. A typical replacement decision is illustrated in Table 17–1.

The data for this illustration are as follows: A corporation purchased a large production machine two years ago for $775,000. This machine was then estimated to have a useful life of 10 years and a terminal salvage value of $50,000. Now, a new automated machine is available to perform the same function as the two-year-old machine. It would cost $1,200,000, would have a useful life of eight years, and would have a

**TABLE 17-1**

**Analysis of Proposed Asset Replacement Decision**

| | Cash Flow before Tax | Tax Effect | Cash Flow after Tax | Present Value Factor at 10% | | Present Value |
|---|---|---|---|---|---|---|
| | | | | Table | Factor | |
| Cash receipts: | | | | | | |
| Incremental operating cost savings | $ 250,000 | $(100,000) | $ 150,000 | A-2 | 5.335 | $ 800,250 |
| Incremental tax saving from depreciation* | — | 28,000 | 28,000 | A-2 | 5.335 | 149,380 |
| Incremental terminal salvage value | 10,000 | | 10,000 | A-1 | .467 | 4,670 |
| Proceeds from sale of old machine | 250,000 | | 250,000 | | | 250,000 |
| Tax saving from loss on sale of old machine† | — | 152,000 | 152,000 | | | 152,000 |
| | | | | | | $ 1,356,300 |
| Cash outlay: | | | | | | |
| Purchase of new machine | (1,200,000) | | (1,200,000) | | | (1,200,000) |
| Net present value | | | | | | $ 156,300 |

\* Incremental tax savings from depreciation:

| | | |
|---|---|---|
| Depreciation on new machine | | |
| [($1,200,000 − $60,000) ÷ 8 yrs.] | $142,500 | |
| Depreciation on old machine | | |
| [($775,000 − $50,000) ÷ 10 yrs.] | 72,500 | |
| Incremental depreciation | $ 70,000 | |
| Income tax rate | 40% | |
| Incremental tax saving | $ 28,000 | |

† Tax saving from loss on sale of old machine:

| | |
|---|---|
| Original cost of machine | $775,000 |
| Accumulated depreciation (2 yrs. @ $72,500) | 145,000 |
| Book value at date of proposed sale | $630,000 |
| Proceeds from sale | 250,000 |
| Loss on sale | $380,000 |
| Income tax rate | 40% |
| Tax saving | $152,000 |

terminal salvage value of $60,000. It would reduce annual out-of-pocket operating costs by $250,000 as compared with continued operation of the old machine. The old machine could be sold now for $250,000. It is being depreciated by the straight-line method for tax purposes, and the same method would be used if the new machine is purchased. The corporation's cost of capital is 10%, and the income tax rate is 40%.

The largest cash receipt from the replacement investment is the present value of the operating cost savings. There is also a positive cash flow resulting from the greater tax deduction for depreciation. Note that only the excess of the tax saving from depreciation on the new machine over that on the old machine is included, for that is the amount by which the cash flow will change if the replacement decision is made. The proceeds from the sale of the old asset are also a positive cash flow. Although the old asset must be sold at a loss of $380,000, this loss involves no cash outlay. On the contrary, the tax saving from deduction of this loss is a positive cash flow, tending to make the replacement investment more attractive.[1] It would be a mistake to think of the loss on disposition of an old asset as a negative factor tending to inhibit replacement. A very minor cash receipt in this case is the present value of the incremental terminal salvage value of the new machine over that of the old one. It should be included in the analysis, of course. The only cash outlay in this illustration is the initial expenditure to purchase the new machine.

The analysis in Table 17–1 concludes with the determination of the net present value of the proposed replacement decision. The present value index might also be computed. If it is, the proceeds from the sale of the old machine and the tax saving from deduction of the loss on this sale should first be offset against the outlay for purchase of the new machine. The combination of cash flows with the same timing, it should be recalled, is appropriate in order to compute the present value index correctly. In this case, the effect of the combination is to reduce the present values of both the cash receipts and the cash outlay in Table 17–1 by $402,000. The present value index would then be calculated as follows:

$$\text{Present value index} = \frac{\text{Present value of cash receipts}}{\text{Present value of cash outlay}} = \frac{\$954,300}{\$798,000} = 1.20$$

If this same combination were used in computing the net present value, of course, there would be no change in that value. It would still be

---

[1] Losses on sale of assets used in business operations are generally deductible for tax purposes in the year of the sale. An exception is made, however, if the old asset is traded in for a new asset. In that case, a loss on the trade-in is not immediately deductible. Rather, it must be added to the cost of the new asset and then deducted in the form of depreciation over the life of the new asset. In total, the same dollar amount of tax deduction is allowed for the loss, but the timing is different. Since the present value of a cash flow diminishes the longer in the future that cash flow is deferred, there is a clear advantage in being able to deduct the loss all at once instead of having to include it as part of the depreciation allowed on the new asset.

$156,300. The discounted rate of return on the replacement decision might also be computed. In this case, the rate of return is slightly higher than 15%.

## SELECTION OF DEPRECIATION METHOD

In financial accounting, the primary criterion for selection of a depreciation method is the best possible matching of costs with revenue. In capital budgeting, this criterion is totally irrelevant. The only way in which depreciation is relevant to an investment decision is through its tax effect. Hence, the criterion for selection of a depreciation method to be used for income tax purposes in connection with a proposed new asset is maximization of the present value of the asset's depreciation tax shield. Whether the depreciation method chosen for tax purposes is the same as that used for financial reporting is irrelevant. One of the accelerated depreciation methods will produce a higher present value for the tax saving from depreciation than the straight-line method, so long as the income tax rate is not expected to rise substantially during the course of the asset's life. The advantage of the accelerated methods reflects the fact that they allow greater depreciation deductions in early years, and, of course, the present value of a cash flow is greater the earlier that cash flow will occur. The two popular accelerated depreciation methods are the double-declining balance method and the sum-of-years'-digits method. As a general rule, the double-declining balance method will result in a higher present value of the depreciation tax shield if the life of the asset is fairly short and/or the asset has a substantial terminal salvage value. The sum-of-years'-digits method tends to be more favorable in connection with an asset having a very long life and/or little if any salvage value. Both of these methods are illustrated below in comparison with the straight-line method that has been used in all of the investment analyses illustrated thus far.

Consider a depreciable asset with an original cost of $100,000, no terminal salvage value, and a life of five years. Assume that the company's cost of capital is 10% and its income tax rate is 40%. Regardless of the depreciation method chosen, the total depreciation deductible over the asset's life will be $100,000 and the total tax saving from this deduction will be $40,000—at face value! The present value of this tax saving will depend upon the timing of its realization, however. Under the straight-line method, $20,000 of depreciation will be deducted each year for five years. The tax saving, thus, will be in the form of a five-year annuity of $8,000. At 10%, the present value of this annuity is $30,328 ($8,000 × 3.791). If the double-declining balance depreciation method is used, depreciation each year is equal to 40% (i.e., double the straight-line rate) of the annually declining book value of the asset. Thus, the tax

**TABLE 17–2**

**Present Value of Double-Declining Balance Depreciation**

| Year | Beginning Book Value | De- preciation Rate | De- preciation | Tax Rate | Tax Saving | Present Value Factor | Present Value |
|---|---|---|---|---|---|---|---|
| 1...... | $100,000 | .40 | $40,000 | .40 | $16,000 | .909 | $14,544 |
| 2...... | 60,000 | .40 | 24,000 | .40 | 9,600 | .826 | 7,930 |
| 3...... | 36,000 | .40 | 14,400 | .40 | 5,760 | .751 | 4,326 |
| 4...... | 21,600 | .50 | 10,800 | .40 | 4,320 | .683 | 2,951 |
| 5...... | 10,800 | 1.00 | 10,800 | .40 | 4,320 | .621 | 2,683 |
| | | | | | | | $32,434 |

saving is not a level annuity. Each year's tax saving is unique in amount and, hence, each must be discounted separately by the appropriate factor from Table A–1. The calculation of the present value of the tax saving from double-declining balance depreciation is as shown in Table 17–2. Thus, the present value of the tax saving from depreciation by the double-declining balance method is $2,106 more than by the straight-line method. Notice that the company switches to the straight-line method in the fourth year of the asset's life. This switch is a standard part of the double-declining balance method. It should be made whenever the depreciation deduction would be greater by applying a new straight-line rate to the *remaining* life and book value than by continuing to apply the doubled rate used in prior years.

In the sum-of-years'-digits method, an annually declining depreciation rate is applied to the depreciable base of the asset (i.e., original cost less terminal salvage value, if any). The calculation of the present value of the tax saving from depreciation of the asset described above by the sum-of-years'-digits method is shown in Table 17–3. This result is $1,909 higher than the present value under the straight-line method, but it is $197 lower than that under the double-declining balance method. Hence,

**TABLE 17–3**

**Present Value of Sum-of-Years'-Digits Depreciation**

| Year | Depreciable Base | De- preciation Rate | De- preciation | Tax Rate | Tax Saving | Present Value Factor | Present Value |
|---|---|---|---|---|---|---|---|
| 1...... | $100,000 | 5/15 | $33,333 | .40 | $13,333 | .909 | $12,120 |
| 2...... | 100,000 | 4/15 | 26,667 | .40 | 10,667 | .826 | 8,811 |
| 3...... | 100,000 | 3/15 | 20,000 | .40 | 8,000 | .751 | 6,008 |
| 4...... | 100,000 | 2/15 | 13,333 | .40 | 5,333 | .683 | 3,642 |
| 5...... | 100,000 | 1/15 | 6,667 | .40 | 2,667 | .621 | 1,656 |
| | | | | | | | $32,237 |

management should select the double-declining balance method for tax purposes if this $100,000 asset is purchased. It is conceivable that the choice of a depreciation method might make the difference between an investment being profitable and it being unprofitable. For example, if the net present value of the proposed investment in the asset discussed above were positive but less than $2,100 when the double-declining balance method was used, that net present value would become negative if the straight-line method were used instead.

To illustrate the effect of a longer life, suppose that the $100,000 asset in the foregoing illustration had a life of 20 years instead of five and that all other facts remained the same. The present values at 10% of the tax saving from depreciation under each of the three methods illustrated would be as follows:[2]

| *Method* | *Present Value* |
|---|---|
| Straight-line............................ | $17,028 |
| Double-declining balance.................. | $20,615 |
| Sum-of-years'-digits...................... | $21,879 |

All three present values are lower than those in the previous illustration, because the same total tax saving is spread over 20 years rather than only five. As before, the straight-line method is the least advantageous of the three. This time, however, the sum-of-years'-digits method is the most favorable one to use. In every capital budgeting analysis involving a depreciable asset, the most favorable method of depreciation should be determined before the rest of the analysis is completed. Most of the problems at the end of this chapter and the preceding one specify the straight-line method in order to simplify the computations. This should not be interpreted to mean that this is the best method to use. Unless tax rates are expected to rise substantially in the future, the straight-line method is usually the *least* advantageous one to use.

## SEPARATION OF INVESTMENT AND FINANCING DECISIONS

The preceding chapter noted that there are two basically different types of decisions involved in the total capital budgeting process. One is the investment decision, relating to uses of capital. The other is the

---

[2] The computations underlying these present values are exactly the same procedurally as those illustrated above when the asset's life was five years. The computations for the double-declining balance and the sum-of-years'-digits methods are much longer, of course. This is unavoidable if one has access only to the tables in Appendix A. There are tables available elsewhere, however, that show the present value of the total (not the annual) tax saving from depreciation under the two accelerated depreciation methods directly by a single discounting calculation. See, for example, Tables C and D in Harold Bierman, Jr., and Seymour Smidt, *The Capital Budgeting Decision*, 4th ed. (New York: The Macmillan Co., 1975), pp. 444–51.

financing decision, concerned with sources of capital. It is important that these two decisions be analyzed separately in order to avoid possible errors. If the cash flows associated with financing are mingled with those pertinent to an investment, the result may be an erroneous conclusion that a basically unprofitable investment proposal is acceptable. This error is illustrated below in connection with a proposed investment in an asset that would generate after-tax cash receipts of $12,520 per year for five years and would require an initial cash outlay of $50,000. If the average cost of capital for the investor is 10%, this proposal's net present value would be determined as follows:

| | |
|---|---:|
| Annual cash receipts (5-year annuity) | $ 12,520 |
| Present value factor for 5 years and 10% (Table A-2) | 3.791 |
| Present value of cash receipts | $ 47,463 |
| Present value of cash outlay | (50,000) |
| Net present value | $( 2,537) |

The proposed investment would be unprofitable. This fact may also be seen by computing a present value index of .95 ($47,463 ÷ $50,000) or by determining that the discounted rate of return is only 8%.[3]

Logically, if an investment proposal is unprofitable at the average cost of capital, it should not be made profitable simply by changing the means of financing it. Yet, that is exactly the impression that may be created if the financing decision is confused with the investment proposal. Suppose that the investor is offered the alternative of purchasing this asset on an instalment plan. A down payment of $5,000 would be required. Thereafter, annual instalment payments of $10,684 after taxes would be required for five years. This instalment plan is merely one way of financing the proposed investment. As such, it should have no effect on the profitability of the investment itself. But see how the combining of the investment and the financing cash flows makes the investment *appear* to be profitable.

| | |
|---|---:|
| Annual cash receipts | $ 12,520 |
| Annual instalment payment | (10,684) |
| Net annual cash receipt | $ 1,836 |
| Present value factor for 5 years and 10% | 3.791 |
| Present value of net cash receipt | $ 6,960 |
| Present value of cash outlay (down payment) | ( 5,000) |
| Net present value | $ 1,960 |

---

[3] The discount rate that will equate $12,520 per year for five years to $50,000 is the same rate that will equate $1 per year for five years to $3.99. In Table A-2, a present value factor of 3.99 on the five-year row is found in the 8% column.

Similarly, the present value index would *appear* to be 1.39; and the discounted rate of return, between 24% and 25%. All of these apparent values are erroneous, however, and are inappropriate for purposes of investment decision making. The basic error is that the confused analysis implies that the only investment is the $5,000 down payment, and that is incorrect.

The investment was correctly analyzed to begin with, and it would be unprofitable as long as the average cost of capital is 10%. A separate analysis should be made of the proposed financing alternative. The five instalment payments of $10,684 are an alternative to expending an additional $45,000 immediately. This is equivalent to borrowing $45,000 now and repaying it with interest at a rate of 6%.[4] The fact that a single source of financing entails an interest cost of 6% does not mean that the *average* cost of capital is that low. In this case, the average cost of capital was 10%. There is no reason to expect that new borrowing at 6% will cause the average cost of capital to decline. As a matter of fact, it could increase. Additional borrowing increases creditors' claims relative to equity, or ownership, claims. Owners or potential investors in equity securities may interpret this change as increasing the risk of an equity investment in the firm. If so, the market price of the common stock will decline; and, as a consequence, the specific cost of the common equity capital will rise. Thus, when a new average cost of capital is computed, it might actually be greater than 10%. In any event, however, the average cost of capital is clearly not 6%.[5]

## MUTUALLY EXCLUSIVE INVESTMENTS OF DIFFERENT LIVES

Present value analysis of future cash flows is inherently involved with the time frame of those cash flows. For comparison purposes, it would be very convenient if all investment proposals had the same life, for this would provide a common time horizon for the capital budgeting process. Obviously, not all projects can be expected to have the same life. When two or more projects must be compared directly, however, a difference between their lives causes a complication. Mutually exclusive alternative investments typify projects that must be considered in direct comparison with each other. When such alternatives have different lives,

---

[4] The discount rate that will equate $10,684 per year for five years to $45,000 is the same rate that will equate $1 per year for five years to $4.21. In Table A-2, a present value factor of 4.21 is found in the five-year row and the 6% column.

[5] The relationship between the cost of any one source of financing and the average cost of capital is discussed more expansively in numerous books and articles. For example, see G. David Quirin, *The Capital Expenditure Decision* (Homewood, Ill.: Richard D. Irwin, Inc., 1967), chap. 6.

this comparison is made more difficult. A perfect comparison would require knowledge about future alternatives that will be available for the period of the difference in the lives of the projects currently under consideration. For example, assume that a company needs to replace its furnace. Two models are available. Model X would cost $25,000 now, would involve annual after-tax operating costs of $10,000, and would have a useful life of five years. Model Y would cost $40,000 now, would entail annual after-tax operating costs of $8,000, and would have a life of eight years. Comparison of these alternatives is complicated by the fact that they have different lives. Yet, complicated or not, the comparison must be made. The two models are genuine alternatives.

Since neither furnace will generate any cash receipts, it is not feasible to compute any of the customary measures of an investment's profitability. The financial objective of the investment in the furnace is to minimize total costs. One approach that might appear useful is to determine the present value of the total cost of each alternative. This is done in Table 17–4. The cost of capital is assumed to be 10%.

**TABLE 17–4**

|  | Model X | Model Y |
|---|---|---|
| Useful life............................. | 5 years | 8 years |
| Annual operating costs.................... | $10,000 | $ 8,000 |
| Present value factor for 10% and life of model (Table A–2)..................... | 3.791 | 5.335 |
| Present value of annual costs.............. | $37,910 | $42,680 |
| Initial purchase cost...................... | 25,000 | 40,000 |
| Present value of total costs................ | $62,910 | $82,680 |

Unfortunately, this comparison is not conclusive, for Model Y has a life three years longer than model X. Hence, its greater present value of total costs is not necessarily a disadvantage. Presumably, the company would need a furnace for the sixth, seventh, and eighth years in the future regardless of the model purchased now. Thus, if model X is chosen, a new furnace will be required after five years. The characteristics and costs of furnaces that will be available then cannot be predicted accurately now. A perfect solution to the present choice problem, however, requires complete knowledge about future replacement furnaces. In the absence of such knowledge, management must seek to convert the financial analysis of the present alternatives to a common time horizon. While such conversion is useful for decision making, it does not eliminate the problem of different lives. Rather, it simply removes that difference from the comparison.

## Replacement Chains

One method of achieving a common time horizon is to assume that each model, if purchased, would be replaced at the end of its useful life by an identical furnace. These sequential replacements, or replacement chains, would be continued as long as necessary to obtain a common time horizon. As a practical matter, this is usually done over a number of years equal to the lowest common multiple of the lives of the alternatives. In our illustration of the furnaces, this would be a period of 40 years. For model X, this analysis would involve a 40-year annuity of $10,000 plus an outlay of $25,000 at the beginning of the first year and every fifth year thereafter, through and including the 36th year. For model Y, there would be a 40-year annuity of $8,000 plus outlays of $40,000 now and every eighth year thereafter, through and including the 33rd year. When all of these cash flows were discounted to their present value at 10%, the present values of the total costs of the two alternatives over a 40-year time period would be as follows:

> Model X..................... $162,290
> Model Y.....................   151,592

In the absence of any compelling nonfinancial considerations, model Y, with its lower lifetime cost, would be selected. While this replacement chain analysis does neutralize the time differential, it also implies that technology and prices will stagnate for the next 40 years. This is hardly a reasonable implication.

## Salvage Values at End of Shortest Life

A second means of dealing with the time difference is to make a comparison of present values over the life of the shortest lived alternative. In the case of the two furnace models, that would be model X with a life of five years. The estimated salvage value of the longer lived alternative, model Y, would be included as a cash receipt in the present value analysis. The alternative with the lower net cost (i.e., operating cost over five years plus initial outlay minus salvage value after five years) would then be selected. This approach, of course, depends upon a reasonable estimate of the salvage value of the longer lived alternative(s). If that value is highly uncertain, the approach is not very satisfactory.

## Equivalent Annual Costs

A third technique for eliminating the time difference is to compute the annual cost that is equivalent to the present value of the total cost of each alternative. This entails adding to the annual operating cost an annuity whose present value over the life of the alternative is equal to the initial outlay for that alternative. This annuity is the *equivalent annual cost* of purchasing the asset. The equivalent annual costs of the two alternatives in our furnace illustration are computed as shown in Table 17–5.

**TABLE 17–5**

**Computation of Equivalent Annual Cost**

|  | Model X | Model Y |
|---|---|---|
| Initial purchase cost........................ | $25,000 | $40,000 |
| Divided by present value factor for 10% and life of model........................ | 3.791 | 5.335 |
| Equivalent annual purchase cost............ | $ 6,595 | $ 7,498 |
| Annual operating cost...................... | 10,000 | 8,000 |
| Equivalent annual cost..................... | $16,595 | $15,498 |

In other words, spending $6,595 each year for five years is equivalent to spending $25,000 now, if the cost of capital is 10%. Similarly, an annuity of $7,498 for eight years is equivalent to an immediate expenditure of $40,000 at a 10% cost of capital. The operating costs, of course, are already stated on an annual basis. We may now compare the alternatives directly and choose the one with the lower equivalent annual cost— model Y.

The foregoing analysis does not say that there would actually be an annual expenditure of $15,498 if model Y is selected. Rather, it says that such an annual expenditure is equivalent to the actual proposed expenditures of $40,000 at once and then $8,000 annually for eight years. Further, this procedure does not cancel the difference in the lives of the two models. It simply removes the difference from the analysis. It says nothing, however, about what might be done during the sixth, seventh, and eighth years if model X were purchased. Of the three techniques discussed here, the equivalent annual cost method is recommended as the simplest and as valid as either of the other two. It avoids the necessity for an estimate of salvage value, which is required in the second method above. Insofar as a choice among alternatives is concerned, it will give the same result as the replacement chain method. However, it usually requires fewer calculations; and it would probably be easier to explain to management.

***Equivalent Annual Net Value.*** The foregoing illustration of a choice between two furnace models was simplified in that it presents only costs as relevant data. Presumably, the cash receipts of the company would be unaffected by the selection of a furnace. Moreover, all cash flows were given directly at their after-tax amounts; thus, we did not have to deal with the depreciation tax shield as a separate amount. The method known generally as the equivalent annual cost method can be applied to any situation involving alternatives with different lives, however. Table 17–6 presents all of the relevant data and the appropriate analysis for two alternative computer investments that a data processing center is considering. In this case, the alternative machines not only have different lives and costs but also have different revenues and terminal salvage values. Both the cash receipts and the cash outlays must be converted to equivalent annual amounts. The difference between these might be called an *equivalent annual net value*. The more attractive investment alternative is then the one with the largest positive equivalent annual net value.

Annual revenues and out-of-pocket operating costs are already stated

### TABLE 17–6
### Illustration of Equivalent Annual Net Value

|  | Computer Model 200 | Computer Model 500 |
|---|---|---|
| *Basic data* | | |
| Useful life. . . . . . . . . . . . . . . . . . . . . . . . . . . . . . . . . | 7 years | 11 years |
| Annual revenue from services. . . . . . . . . . . . . . . . . . . | $ 250,000 | $ 375,000 |
| Annual out-of-pocket operating costs. . . . . . . . . . . . | 120,000 | 180,000 |
| Initial purchase cost. . . . . . . . . . . . . . . . . . . . . . . . . . | 400,000 | 970,000 |
| Terminal salvage value. . . . . . . . . . . . . . . . . . . . . . . . | 50,000 | 90,000 |
| Annual straight-line depreciation. . . . . . . . . . . . . . . . | 50,000 | 80,000 |
| Cost of capital—10% | | |
| Income tax rate—40% | | |
| *Financial analysis of alternatives* | | |
| Equivalent annual receipts: | | |
| Annual revenue after tax. . . . . . . . . . . . . . . . . . . . . | $ 150,000 | $ 225,000 |
| Annual depreciation tax shield. . . . . . . . . . . . . . . | 20,000 | 32,000 |
| Equivalent annual terminal salvage value*. . . . . . | 5,269 | 4,850 |
| | $ 175,269 | $ 261,850 |
| Equivalent annual outlays: | | |
| Annual out-of-pocket operating costs after tax. . . | $( 72,000) | $(108,000) |
| Equivalent annual purchase cost†. . . . . . . . . . . . . | ( 82,169) | (149,346) |
| | $(154,169) | $(257,346) |
| Equivalent annual net value. . . . . . . . . . . . . . . . . . . | $  21,100 | $  4,504 |

| * Computation of equivalent annual terminal salvage: | | |
|---|---|---|
| Terminal salvage value. . . . . . . . . . . . . . . . . . . . . . . . . . . . . . . . . | $ 50,000 | $ 90,000 |
| × Present value factor for end of economic life (Table A–1). . . | .513 | .350 |
| = Present value of terminal salvage value. . . . . . . . . . . . . . . . . | $ 25,650 | $ 31,500 |
| ÷ Present value factor for annuity over economic life | | |
| (Table A–2). . . . . . . . . . . . . . . . . . . . . . . . . . . . . . . . . . . . . . . . . | 4.868 | 6.495 |
| = Equivalent annual terminal salvage value. . . . . . . . . . . . . . . | $ 5,269 | $ 4,850 |

| † Computation of equivalent annual purchase cost: | | |
|---|---|---|
| Purchase cost. . . . . . . . . . . . . . . . . . . . . . . . . . . . . . . . . . . . . . . . . | $400,000 | $970,000 |
| ÷ Present value factor for annuity over economic life | | |
| (Table A–2). . . . . . . . . . . . . . . . . . . . . . . . . . . . . . . . . . . . . . . . . | 4.868 | 6.495 |
| = Equivalent annual purchase cost. . . . . . . . . . . . . . . . . . . . . . . | $ 82,169 | $149,346 |

in annual amounts and need only be reduced to their after-tax amounts by multiplying them by the complement of the tax rate. The depreciation tax shield is found by multiplying annual depreciation by the income tax rate. It, too, is already an annual figure. The original purchase cost of each computer is annualized by dividing it by the present value factor for an annuity of the life of that machine (as already illustrated in Table 17–5). In the case of terminal salvage value, it must first be discounted to its present value, as we have seen before. This present value is then divided by the present value factor for an annuity over the life of the computer in order to annualize the terminal salvage value.

The analysis in Table 17–6 shows that computer model 200 would be the more profitable of the two alternatives. The equivalent annual net value of that machine would be significantly greater than the equivalent annual net value of model 500.

## MUTUALLY EXCLUSIVE ALTERNATIVES WITH DIFFERENT INITIAL OUTLAYS

When two or more mutually exclusive alternative investments have different initial outlays, even though they have equal lives, a question

**TABLE 17–7**

|  | Machine L | Machine M |
|---|---|---|
| Net present value................. | $11,450 | $12,175 |
| Present value index................ | 1.23 | 1.15 |
| Discounted rate of return........... | 15% | 13½% |

arises as to the appropriate method of comparing them. The net present value method tends to favor the larger alternatives, although these are not necessarily the better ones. The net present value is affected directly by the absolute size of the cash flow associated with a proposal. This is not true of the present value index and the discounted rate of return. Both of these are relative measures of profitability. That is, they express the profitability of an investment in relation to the amount invested. Which technique is best for choosing among mutually exclusive alternatives depends upon the circumstances surrounding the investment and the investor. An example will help explain the problem of choice of a technique. A company with an average cost of capital of 10% is considering buying one or the other of two labor-saving machines; it could not use both. Both machines have lives of 10 years. Machine L costs $50,000 and saves costs of $10,000 per year after tax. Machine M costs $80,000 and saves costs of $15,000 per year after tax. Table 17–7 shows a comparison of the results of determining the profitabilities of these alternative machines by the three techniques. By the net present value method, machine M appears more profitable. By either of the other two methods, machine L seems preferable. Which actually is the better alternative?

The answer to that question depends upon the answer to another. Will the choice between these two alternatives affect the company's ability to make any other investment? If it will not, machine M should be chosen. While it is not as profitable per dollar invested as machine L, it would increase the total wealth of the investor by a larger amount. In other words, in this case, the greater net present value indicates the investment to be selected. However, if investing in machine M would limit the firm's ability to make other investments because of a limitation on the total amount of capital available for investing, the net present value is not a suitable basis for the choice between these mutually exclusive alternatives. In this situation, the fact that machine L would consume $30,000 less of the firm's investible capital becomes significant. The choice now depends upon what return might be obtained by some other investment of that $30,000 if machine L were chosen in preference to machine M. Thus, the two machines cannot now be compared all by themselves. Machine M must be compared with machine L plus some other profitable investment of the differential $30,000.

The best way to make the choice between mutually exclusive investment proposals, when that choice has an effect on other investment possibilities, is to compute the profitability of the additional investment required to make the larger of the alternative investments under consideration. In the example of machines L and M, this would entail determining the return from investing an additional $30,000 in machine M. This is often referred to as the *incremental investment*. The incremental investment of $30,000 in this case will produce an incremental annual cash receipt of $5,000 ($15,000 − $10,000) for 10 years. The three measures of profitability for this incremental investment are as follows:

| | |
|---|---|
| Net present value...................... | $725 |
| Present value index.................... | 1.02 |
| Discounted rate of return.............. | 10½% |

These measures should now be compared with those for other possible investments of the same $30,000. If this incremental investment proves to be more profitable than any alternative use of capital, machine M should be purchased. On the other hand, if the incremental investment is found to be less attractive than other projects that would use the $30,000, machine L should be chosen.

## CAPITAL RATIONING

In all of our discussions and illustrations of investment decisions thus far, with the exception of that in the immediately preceding section, we have been concerned simply with determining whether an investment would be profitable. By implication, then, if the investment was profitable, it would be undertaken. This rule is valid so long as the firm is able to obtain all the capital necessary to make all profitable investments available to it. In such a situation, the capital budgeting process is relatively simple—once estimates of future cash flows have been made. First, choices among mutually exclusive alternatives would be resolved by selecting the one with the largest net present value in every case. Then, all investments with positive net present values would be made. This statement assumes that unprofitable investments would not be made. This may not be realistic. It may sometimes be necessary to make certain investments (e.g., installation of warning signals at railroad crossings) because they are required by law. Actually, such an investment might be truly profitable if it would avoid recurring fines or other financial penalties. Also, a firm may make investments (e.g., a cafeteria or plant landscaping) to improve its relations with employees or with the community at large. Such investments may be thought to yield certain intangible benefits that are hoped to enhance profits in the long run, although not in any measurable amount.

It may happen, however, that a firm is not able to obtain all of the capital necessary to make all potentially profitable investments. In this case, the firm is faced with the necessity of rejecting some investments that meet established criteria of profitability. Such a situation is described as *capital rationing*. That is, the capital available to the firm is rationed to it in an amount less than the firm might profitably invest. Consequently, management must allocate the limited available capital in a way that produces the greatest possible benefit. It is no longer sufficient to determine *whether* an investment is profitable. Management must also *rank* the alternative investment opportunities according to their relative profitabilities. Only the most profitable investments will be made. (Again, exceptions may be made for "necessary" or desirable investments not offering identifiable financial returns.) Thus, under conditions of capital rationing, the analytical technique used for evaluating investment opportunities must be capable of ranking the alternatives or of determining the optimal combination of investments that fits the constraint of limited capital.

## Causes of Capital Rationing

Capital rationing may be caused by factors external to the firm or by internal restrictions imposed by management. The primary external cause of capital rationing is an imperfect capital market. In a perfect capital market, every firm will be able to obtain all of the capital it needs as long as it has profitable uses for that capital. The total amount of capital available to all investors at a given time is fixed, of course.

Consequently, the average cost of capital to any single firm is partially determined by the aggregate supply of capital in the market. Given its cost of capital, however, the firm will then be able to obtain capital so long as it has investment opportunities offering rates of return greater than the cost of capital. In an imperfect capital market, each firm may not be able to obtain all of the capital it could profitably invest. Imperfection may be caused by deficiencies in market information, by rigidities that hamper the free flow of capital between firms, and by a difference between the interest rate at which the firm can obtain capital in the market (i.e., the borrowing rate) and the interest rate it could earn by loaning its own capital to others in the market (i.e., the lending rate). One reason why the borrowing rate is typically greater than the lending rate is the costs that must be incurred when a firm seeks additional capital by selling securities in the market. Fees must be paid to register the securities with the appropriate federal and/or state authorities, and a fee must be paid to the investment banking syndicate that will handle the marketing of the securities. In a government agency, the funds authorized by the legislature constitute an external limitation on the amount that the agency may invest.

Internal causes of capital rationing are sometimes more difficult to justify, as they reflect self-imposed restrictions on potentially profitable investments. Nevertheless, where they exist, the capital budgeting analysis must recognize them. A firm's management may decide that it will not incur debt to obtain additional capital, perhaps as a matter of conservative financing policy. A closely held corporation may reject the opportunity of selling additional shares of common stock, for this would threaten the present stockholders' control of the firm. In a large, decentralized corporation, top management may arbitrarily limit the funds it is willing to make available for investment by the division managers. Finally, management may insist that any investment undertaken yield a rate of return greater than the average cost of capital. The reason for requiring a rate of return greater than the cost of capital may be to provide for overly optimistic estimates of cash receipts or simply to enforce a conservative investment policy. Whatever the reasons for or the logic of internal capital rationing, it constrains the capital budgeting process in the same way as external rationing.

### Effects of Capital Rationing

Regardless of its cause, capital rationing affects the investment decision-making process in several important ways. First, as has already been observed, it requires that independent investment opportunities be ranked according to profitability. This is largely a technical problem and is discussed in the next section. Second, under conditions of capital rationing, a firm really should extend the decision process to include investment opportunities both at the present time and in the future. Unless capital rationing is considered to be a temporary constraint, the investments chosen now may constrain the choices of future periods. Thus, management might decide to make a minimally profitable investment today because it has a very short payback period. Thus, additional funds will be available in some future period to permit the firm to take advantage of a particularly profitable investment then. Unfortunately, few firms are likely to have enough information about future investment opportunities to make this multiperiod analysis practical.

Finally, capital rationing changes the effective cost of capital relevant to investment decisions. It raises that cost from the average cost of capital to the rate of return that must be foregone on the most profitable investment proposal that is rejected because of the limitation on available capital. This is an opportunity cost. For example, if a firm's weighted average cost of capital, determined in the usual manner, is 10% and if that firm must reject investment opportunities offering rates of return of 12%, 13%, and 14%, its effective cost of capital has increased to 14%, the highest yield that had to be foregone because of the capital rationing constraint. This is the effective cost of capital, for it measures the sacrifice the firm had to make in order to use its limited capital for the investments that it was able to undertake.

## Methods of Ranking Independent Investment Proposals

The ranking of investment opportunities according to their relative profitabilities may vary with the technique of measuring profitability that is used. The net present value method, for example, tends to make investments of large amounts appear relatively attractive because it expresses profitability in absolute dollar amounts. Thus, unless all investments are of equivalent size—an unlikely situation—the net present value cannot be relied upon for ranking purposes. Both the present value index and the discounted rate of return are relative measures and are not affected by the size of the investment. Thus, they tend to produce accurate rankings. It is possible that these latter two methods will not produce the same ranking, however, because of their different implicit reinvestment rate assumptions.[6] Difficulties of ranking independent investments will be seen in the illustration below.

Suppose that a company operating under the constraint of capital rationing has six independent investments from which to choose. For simplicity, we shall assume that each alternative requires an initial cash outlay and will generate cash receipts in the form of a level annuity over

---

[6] Chapter 16.

**TABLE 17–8**

| Investment | Annual Cash Receipts | Present Value of Cash Receipts | Initial Cash Outlay | Net Present Value | Present Value Index | Discounted Rate of Return |
|---|---|---|---|---|---|---|
| A....... | $20,691 | $127,146 | $100,000 | $27,146 | 1.27 | 16% |
| B....... | 9,962 | 61,216 | 50,000 | 11,216 | 1.22 | 15% |
| C....... | 9,542 | 58,636 | 40,000 | 18,636 | 1.47 | 20% |
| D....... | 8,401 | 51,624 | 30,000 | 21,624 | 1.72 | 25% |
| E....... | 3,834 | 23,560 | 20,000 | 3,560 | 1.18 | 14% |
| F....... | 1,770 | 10,877 | 10,000 | 877 | 1.09 | 12% |

the next 10 years. All cash flows are stated after consideration of tax effects. The company's average cost of capital is 10%. The six alternatives and their profitabilities according to the three analytical techniques are summarized in Table 17–8. If these six alternatives are now ranked by the three measures of profitability, we find the same ranking by the present value index and the discounted rate of return methods. The ranking by the net present value method is different, however, as shown in Table 17–9.

Which investments will actually be made depends not only upon the ranking but also on the amount of capital available for investment. Suppose that exactly $100,000 is available. Neither of the rankings above directly indicates the investments that should be made. The net present value ranking suggests investment A, but that is actually the least profitable possible use of the $100,000. The other two methods suggest investments D and C, but their selection precludes the making of either of the next two investments in that ranking because of the limit on available funds. Thus, the best way to determine the optimal investment program is to determine the net present values of the various combinations of investments that would sum to $100,000 and to choose the largest. The four feasible investment packages that total $100,000 and their net present values are given in Table 17–10. Any other combination would either exceed $100,000 or would use less than all of the available capital.

**TABLE 17–9**

| Ranking by Net Present Value | Ranking by Present Value Index and Discounted Rate of Return |
|---|---|
| A | D |
| D | C |
| C | A |
| B | B |
| E | E |
| F | F |

The first alternative is considered impossible here; the second would be inefficient. Given another set of alternatives, however, it is possible that the optimal investment package would include projects totaling less than $100,000, with the balance simply loaned to other firms to earn a rate of return equal to the cost of capital. In this particular illustration, however, no other combination of projects totaling $100,000 or less would be more profitable than the package of C, D, E, and F.[7] Exactly the same conclusion would be reached if the four feasible investment *packages* were compared by their aggregate present value indexes or discounted rates of return.

Of course, capital rationing does not necessarily imply that a fixed amount of money is available for investment. It simply means that not enough is available to fund all potentially profitable projects. Presum-

**TABLE 17–10**

| *Investments* | *Net Present Value* |
|---|---|
| C, D, E, and F. . . . . . . . . . . . . . . | $44,697 |
| B, D, and E. . . . . . . . . . . . . . . . | 36,400 |
| B, C, and F. . . . . . . . . . . . . . . . | 30,729 |
| A. . . . . . . . . . . . . . . . . . . . . . . . | 27,146 |

ably, the amount available is somewhat flexible. Thus, management might be able to obtain sufficient funds to make the top group of investments on a list ranked by the present value index or the discounted rate of return. With this kind of flexibility, a ranking by one (or both) of these methods could be a valid basis for direct selection of projects to be undertaken.

## RISK AND UNCERTAINTY

In our discussions and illustrations, we have tacitly assumed that the future cash flows pertinent to an investment can be budgeted accurately. Any such budget, or course, is actually subject to some degree of risk or uncertainty. The financial analysis of a proposed capital investment is typically based upon one particular outcome of that investment. There may be alternative outcomes, and the actual one may prove to be different from the outcome upon which the analysis was based. This is the essence of *risk*. There are two or more alternative outcomes of some

---

[7] This particular illustration is quite simple. In even a modest sized organization, there may be so many investment proposals that the search for the optimal investment program by listing all possible packages would be too tedious to be practicable. In such cases, the optimal investment package may be found by the use of linear programming or, perhaps, integer programming. For a discussion of this approach to the capital rationing problem, see H. Martin Weingartner, *Mathematical Programming and the Analysis of Capital Budgeting Problems* (Englewood Cliffs, N.J.: Prentice-Hall, Inc., 1963).

event (e.g., an investment), and the probability of each alternative occurring is known or can be estimated. The approach to decision making under the condition of risk is to weight each possible outcome by its probability and compute an expected value of the outcome. This expected value is then used as the basis for the financial analysis.[8] A more difficult situation to deal with is one in which the decision maker does not have information permitting him to assess the probabilities of the alternative outcomes. Indeed, he may not even be able to define all of the possible outcomes. This is the situation of *uncertainty*. One approach to decision making under uncertainty is to seek to protect the firm against the worst conceivable outcome. Such an approach is defensive and basically conservative in nature. An alternative approach is to make subjective estimates of the probabilities of several alternative outcomes—usually a pessimistic, an optimistic, and a median outcome—and then to treat the problem as one of decision making under risk. An illustration of this approach is presented below.

A decision maker faces risk when the outcome of his decision will depend partly upon conditions over which he is unable to exercise any control. For example, suppose that a trucking company is considering the construction of a truck depot at the terminus of a small railroad's freight spur. This railroad is presently the principal source of transportation of goods into and out of the region beyond the terminus. Like most railroads, its financial condition is not very secure. However, it is currently negotiating a possible merger with a larger and more stable railroad. If this merger is consummated, shipment of goods on the freight spur would be increased considerably. On the other hand, if the merger fails, it is possible that the small railroad will discontinue operations on this marginally profitable freight spur. The trucking company can do nothing about the railroad's situation, but that situation will significantly affect the profitability of the investment in a trucking depot. Construction of the depot would cost $500,000 now, and the facilities would have an economic life of 20 years. The annual variable profit (a cash receipt) from the depot would depend upon the railroad's situation. If the railroad continues to operate as it presently is doing, the trucking depot's annual variable profit would be $200,000. Should the merger with a larger railroad be consummated, the trucking depot would produce an annual variable profit of $300,000. However, if the railroad were forced to discontinue operations on the freight spur, the variable profit from the truck depot would be only $100,000 per year. The trucking company's management has estimated that the probability of the railroad's continuing to operate as at present is .5 (i.e., 5 chances out of 10); the probability of the merger is .3; and the probability of closing down operations on the

_____

[8] The concept of expected value was explained and illustrated in Chapter 7.

freight spur is .2. Regardless of the outcome of the railroad's situation or the volume of operations, there would be fixed out-of-pocket costs of operating the trucking depot in the amount of $90,000 per year. The company's cost of capital is 10%. The income tax rate is 40%, and the trucking depot would be depreciated by the straight-line method for tax purposes.

The analysis of the proposed investment in a trucking depot is shown in Table 17–11. The first part of the table shows the computation of the expected value of the annual net receipts from operation of the depot. The second part of the table shows the determination of the projected profitability of the investment in the same way as in previous illustrations. The various cash flows are adjusted to their after-tax amounts and then discounted to present values in the usual way. The results of the analysis show that the proposed investment is profitable. This projection of profit depends not only upon the estimates of future cash flows but also upon the subjective estimates of the probabilities of the alternative operating volumes. If management expected the worst to happen (i.e.,

**TABLE 17–11**

**Analysis of Proposed Investment in Trucking Depot**

A.  *Computation of expected value of net operating receipts*

| Situation | Variable Profit | Probability | Expected Value |
|---|---|---|---|
| Continuation of *status quo* | $200,000 | .5 | $100,000 |
| Railroad merger | 300,000 | .3 | 90,000 |
| Closing of freight spur | 100,000 | .2 | 20,000 |
| Expected value of variable profit | | | $210,000 |
| Fixed operating costs | | | 90,000 |
| Expected value of net operating receipts | | | $120,000 |

B.  *Analysis of profitability of investment*

| | Cash Flow before Tax | Tax Effect | Cash Flow after Tax | Present Value Factor at 10%* | Present Value |
|---|---|---|---|---|---|
| Cash receipts: | | | | | |
| Expected value of net operating receipts | $ 120,000 | $(48,000) | $ 72,000 | 8.514 | $ 613,008 |
| Depreciation tax shield | — | 10,000 | 10,000 | 8.514 | 85,140 |
| | | | | | $ 698,148 |
| Cash outlay: | | | | | |
| Construction of depot | (500,000) | | (500,000) | | (500,000) |
| Net present value | | | | | $ 198,148 |
| Present value index | | | | | 1.40 |
| Discounted rate of return | | | | | 15–16% |

\* See Appendix, Table A–2.

the railroad to close down the freight spur), the investment would be very unprofitable.

In addition to the probabilistic analysis illustrated above, there are other more sophisticated approaches to decision making under conditions of risk or uncertainty. These are beyond the scope of this text, however.[9] There are also some simpler approaches to the problem that are sometimes employed. One of these is to use a discount rate higher than the cost of capital in evaluating risky investments. For example, a company whose cost of capital is 10% might use that as the discount rate only for investments whose outcomes are fairly well assured. Higher discount rates might be used for risky investments—perhaps 15% for investments considered somewhat risky and 20% for high risk investments. The amount by which the discount rate exceeds the cost of capital in such a case is referred to as a *risk premium*. The effect of using a higher discount rate in the analysis is to reduce the present value of future cash flows. As a consequence, an investment will appear profitable only if future cash receipts are greater than would be necessary if a lower discount rate were being used. In effect, this approach requires greater prospective benefits from relatively risky investments. There is, of course, something logical about that notion. However, this approach implicitly treats all future cash flows from the investment as equally risky. Such is not likely to be the case. For example, in the illustration of the trucking depot investment above, the revenues and variable costs that depend upon the volume of operations were considered risky. The fixed costs of operations and the depreciation tax shield, however, were regarded as virtually certain. The use of probability factors for specific cash flows permits different degrees of risk to be associated with different cash flows. The inclusion of a risk premium in the discount rate does not.

## CHANGES IN PRICES AND INTEREST RATES

Even after discounting, dollars received or paid in the future may not be directly comparable to cash flows at the present. Inflation and deflation alter the real values of cash flows. If the rate of general price inflation or deflation can be predicted, future cash flows can be adjusted for it before they are discounted to their present values. The impact of price changes on investment decisions can be significant, particularly if the annual rate of price change is expected to be substantial. Some investments generate future cash flows that may be expected to change approximately in direct proportion to the general price level. Investments

---

[9] For a more expansive discussion of decision making under conditions of risk and uncertainty, see David W. Miller and Martin K. Starr, *Executive Decisions and Operations Research,* 2d ed. (Englewood Cliffs, N.J.: Prentice-Hall, Inc., 1969), pp. 104–20.

in common stocks, production facilities, and retail stores typically fall into this category. If the cash flows from the investment would follow the pattern of the general price level exactly, then price changes could be ignored in the capital budgeting process. Future cash flows would be adjusted "automatically" for price inflation or deflation. Other investments, such as in bonds, generate cash flows that are fixed in dollar amount. Consequently, the real value of these cash flows declines in periods of price inflation and rises during periods of deflation. For example, investment in a bond that yields a rate of return of 6% is unprofitable, regardless of the cost of capital, if the annual rate of inflation is higher than 6%. Obviously, expected price changes are factors to be considered in the investment decision-making process.

Interest rates, the price of money, may change over time just as any other price. Such changes have important implications for capital budgeting. To begin with, they mean that the cost of capital for a firm cannot be expected to remain constant over time. Similarly, future investment opportunities may be expected to have different rates of return than current investments. This fact complicates the precision of investment analysis, for we know that all of the analytical techniques that recognize the time value of money entail an implicit assumption about the interest rate that will be earned on the reinvestment of the cash receipts from a current investment. Changes in interest rates tend to undercut the validity of such assumptions. Also, prospective interest rate changes should be considered when investment alternatives have different lives. An expectation that interest rates in the future will be lower than currently would tend to make the longer lived investment more attractive. Conversely, anticipated increases in interest rates tend to favor shorter lived investments now. Of course, these expectations must be weighed carefully with other pertinent factors, including any differences between expected rates of return on the current investment opportunities.

## INTANGIBLE BENEFITS FROM CAPITAL INVESTMENTS

Not every investment may be expected to generate specific cash receipts. If an investment produces neither revenues nor cost savings, it cannot be justified on financial grounds. Yet, such investments cannot be rejected out of hand. Corporations frequently invest in such nonremunerative projects as plant beautification, art objects in executives' offices, and employees' recreational facilities. Apparently, these firms believe that such investments will yield intangible benefits that more than justify the outlays. They are unable to assign a specific financial value to those benefits, however.

Intangible benefits are particularly important in investments made by governmental and nonprofit organizations. For example, the primary benefits of government funded public housing developments are usually alleged to be the physical and psychic satisfactions that the residents derive from living in decent conditions. In effect, the majority, through their tax payments, invest in facilities intended to benefit personally a minority. Even such public investments may produce some recognizable financial benefits, however. Elimination of substandard slum dwellings may reduce the public cost of fire protection. Particularly if coupled with expanded job opportunities, public housing projects may lead to reduced crime rates and, hence, lower costs of police protection and lower property insurance rates. The incremental earnings of construction workers and contractors are also relevant financial benefits to the public as a consequence of the public housing project. Similar evaluations might be made of other public investment projects, notably dams, harbors, recreational facilities, and waste-treatment plants. Of course, the more explicitly financial techniques of capital budgeting are also applicable to investments intended chiefly to produce intangible benefits. Present value analysis can indicate which of various alternatives is the least costly means of achieving a specified goal. Such analysis is extremely important in the public sector, for it may lead to savings of capital on certain projects so that more is available for other beneficial investments.

## MANAGEMENT OF CAPITAL INVESTMENTS

The discussions in this chapter and in the preceding one have focused almost entirely on financial analysis of proposed investment decisions. This focus is consistent with the objectives and scope of the book. It would be a mistake, however, to think that financial analysis is all there is to the capital investment process. Hence, we shall present a brief overview of the total process so as to place financial analysis in its proper context. The total process of capital investment may be described as comprising six significant phases.

*1. Definition of an Investment Project.* Obviously, investment decision making cannot begin until a specific project has been proposed as a potential capital investment. Since capital investments are essential to the sustained operations and the growth of an enterprise, this is a phase that deserves explicit attention by management. Employees at all levels should be encouraged to submit proposals for capital investments that would improve operations in their areas of work. Obviously, not all such proposals will result in investments; but there can be no investments without good ideas for projects.

*2. Estimation of Cash Flows.* We have already noted that this is a crucial stage in the total process. If reasonable cash flow forecasts cannot be made, the remainder of the process is reduced to pure guesswork. Management should provide competent technical assistance in this respect to employees who propose capital investments. A production department foreman, for example, might have a good idea for an investment; but he might not be capable of preparing a realistic cash flow forecast. It would be most unfortunate if employees refrained from offering good suggestions because they were intimidated by the technical work that would have to be done in order to complete the proposal.

**3. *Financial Analysis of Cash Flows.*** This is the phase of the process to which these last two chapters are devoted. It is the phase that is particularly within the province of the management accountant. No further elaboration is necessary here.

**4. *Decision.*** The decision to make an investment or not to make it should be based largely upon the financial analysis. However, many such decisions are also based partly or even wholly on nonfinancial considerations. If the decision is against the proposed investment, then the process is terminated for that particular proposal. If the decision is to go ahead with the investment, however, two very important phases remain.

**5. *Project Implementation.*** Once a favorable decision has been made regarding an investment proposal, some very substantial management problems must be faced. Implementation of the project involves the expenditure of funds to obtain an asset or to inaugurate a program. Serious difficulties may be encountered at this stage. Earlier cash flow projections for the initial expenditure may prove to be substantially in error. As an example, the original plans for the motion picture "Cleopatra" called for an investment of less than $10 million. The picture ultimately cost more than $40 million before it was ready for distribution. In some cases, careful control of expenditures may keep a project within the original budget. In other cases, circumstances beyond management's control may cause cost increases. In such cases, management may be faced with the choice of committing additional funds to complete the project or accepting the complete loss of funds expended to date. Of course, that choice should be made in consideration of only the additional costs and the prospective benefits from the investment. The funds already invested are now sunk costs and are irrelevant to any further decision.

**6. *Post-Completion Audit.*** Once a project has been implemented and is in operation, management should review it to determine whether it is actually producing the benefits that had been planned. If it is not, specific action may be possible to correct the situation. The post-completion audit may be easy in some cases and very difficult in others. If the investment stands by itself as an operating entity, the accounting system will usually provide revenue and cost data directly traceable to it. For example, an investment by an oil company in a new service station is an independent operating entity. Comparison of actual cash flows with the budgeted cash flows used to make the investment decision should be quite easy. However, if an investment, once implemented, becomes an integral part of a larger operation, it may be impossible to trace actual cash flows directly to it. For example, a new production machine may be installed and operated as one link in a long production chain. Specific cost savings may have been projected for its use. However, other factors in the total production operation may be changing at the same time that the new machine is being put into service. Thus, there will be no practical way of tracing changes in costs to any single change in operations. The new machine is inextricably combined with all other facets of the production process. At best, the post-completion audit may be able to determine that there is no evidence that the anticipated benefits are *not* being realized. This is something of a negative assurance, but it is better than no post-completion review at all.

## QUESTIONS FOR DISCUSSION

1. A small manufacturing corporation has two machines of the same basic type. One was purchased 10 years ago and is now fully depreciated, although still in service. The other was purchased just one year ago and is being depreciated over a useful life of 10 years. A revolutionary new machine has recently appeared on the market. It really makes the old type of machine obsolete, even though still physically usable. Both of the old type machines the corporation is now using could be sold for the same low scrap value. Management is planning to scrap the machine used for 10 years and replace it with one of the new type. The machine purchased one year ago will be retained, however; for management does not believe the company can afford to bear the loss that would be incurred by scrapping it now. Evaluate the two decisions management has made regarding the two machines now in service.

2. "Because of the time value of money, it is always advantageous for a taxpayer to elect one of the accelerated depreciation methods rather than the straight-line method." Do you agree with this assertion? Why or why not?

3. Why is it so important for management to distinguish clearly between investment and financing decisions?

4. What are the alternative methods for analyzing mutually exclusive investment proposals that have differing economic lives? What limitation is inherent in all of them?

5. "The discounted rate of return and the present value index are common denominators of investment profitability. They are not affected by the size of the initial investment. The net present value, on the other hand, tends to vary directly with the size of the investment. Hence, it is a biased measure of investment profitability." Discuss this statement.

6. How should mutually exclusive alternative investments of different initial amounts be compared?

7. What are the implications of capital rationing in the capital budgeting process?

8. What are some of the principal problems encountered in an attempt to rank several independent investment proposals in the order of their profitability?

9. Weighting alternative estimates of the cash flow associated with an investment proposal by their respective probabilities of occurrence is one way of coping with the problem of uncertainty in capital budgeting. The results, of course, are no better than the data used in the analysis. How might management go about determining the probabilities of two or more alternative patterns of cash flows from a single investment proposal?

10. Some firms have attempted to incorporate uncertainty in their capital budgeting analyses by using higher discount rates on investments considered to be relatively more risky than others. Evaluate this method of coping with the problem of uncertainty.

11. Assume that the general price level in the economy will rise at an annual rate of 5% for the foreseeable future. How should this inflation factor be included in the analysis of an investment of $100,000 in—
   a. A public utility's bonds?
   b. A department store?
   c. Commercial real estate?

12. When a state legislature appropriates public funds for the construction of new academic facilities on the campus of a state college, it is making a capital investment decision. How might such an investment be justified financially?

13. This chapter described six stages in the total capital investment process and suggested that all of them require explicit attention by management. Which of these six stages do you feel would be easiest to implement as part of a formal management system? Which would be most difficult to formalize? Explain.

14. How would the post-completion audit of each of the following capital investments be performed:
   a. A new store in a retail grocery chain?
   b. An automated material-handling system in a warehouse?
   c. A new computer in an accounting department?

## PROBLEMS

17-1. The Palmieri Brothers Winery is now using a bottling machine purchased three years ago for $300,000. This machine has a remaining useful life of five years and no terminal salvage value. Accumulated depreciation on the machine totals $112,500. Annual out-of-pocket operating costs associated with the use of this machine are $750,000. The machine could be resold today for $67,500.

A new bottling machine has recently appeared on the market. It sells for $500,000, has an economic life of five years, and would have a terminal salvage value of $50,000. The company has estimated that annual out-of-pocket operating costs with this new machine would be $600,000.

The company's cost of capital is 10%. The income tax rate is 40%. The company's policy is to use straight-line depreciation for tax purposes.

*Required:*

Prepare a financial analysis to show whether it would be profitable for the winery to replace its bottling machine now with one of the new model.

17-2.   The Gama Tool & Die Corporation now uses a die stamping machine that was purchased two years ago at a cost of $250,000. It is being depreciated by the straight-line method over a life of ten years and is assumed to have a terminal salvage value of $30,000. Recently, an equipment manufacturer has developed a new machine that performs the same operations much more efficiently. This new machine could be purchased for $400,000. It would reduce annual out-of-pocket operating costs by $100,000 throughout its useful life of eight years. The new machine would have a terminal salvage value of $64,000. The old machine could be sold now to a scrap dealer for $16,000.

The corporation's cost of capital is 10%. The applicable income tax rate is 40%. Straight-line depreciation would be used for the new machine if it were purchased.

*Required:*

Would it be profitable for the corporation to replace its old die stamping machine at this time?

17-3.   The Pointdextre Corporation manufactures small electronic components largely by hand labor. Recently, a machine has been developed to automate part of this work. The machine would cost $750,000, delivered and installed, and would have a useful life of ten years and a terminal salvage value of $50,000. Acquisition of this machine would render useless a number of work benches now in use. These benches originally cost $20,000 ten years ago and are being depreciated over a useful life of 20 years with no assumed salvage value. The benches now have no market value. If the machine were acquired, the benches would be donated to a local correctional facility.

A comparison of annual operating costs under the present hand labor method and with the machine in service is as follows:

|  | *Hand Labor* | *Machine* |
|---|---|---|
| Raw materials.............. | $360,000 | $375,000 |
| Direct labor................ | 500,000 | 125,000 |
| Indirect labor.............. | 80,000 | 100,000 |
| Heat, light, and power........ | 40,000 | 90,000 |
| Depreciation............... | 1,000 | 70,000 |
|  | $981,000 | $760,000 |

The corporation will use straight-line depreciation for both financial accounting and income tax reporting. The applicable income tax rate is 40%. The corporation's cost of capital is 12%.

*Required:*

Would it be profitable for the corporation to purchase the machine?

17-4. The Bunthorne Dredge and Dock Company is currently using a harbor dredge purchased five years ago at a cost of $9,000,000. This dredge was then estimated to have a useful life of 25 years and a terminal salvage value of $500,000. A substantially improved dredge is now available at a cost of $15,000,000. It operates faster than the one presently in service and would increase the corporation's annual revenues by $5,000,000. It would also increase annual operating costs, exclusive of depreciation, by approximately $3,000,000.

The new dredge would have a useful life of 20 years and an expected terminal salvage value of $1,000,000. If the new dredge is purchased, the company would have no further use for the old one, which can be sold currently for about $2,300,000.

The firm's cost of capital is 14%. The income tax rate is 40%. Straight-line depreciation is used on all assets for income tax purposes.

*Required:*

Prepare an analysis showing whether it would be profitable to replace the old dredge at this time.

17-5. The Sangazure Printing Company is considering replacing its present press with a new one that would double capacity and improve the overall quality of the printing work done. The new press would cost $90,000 and would have a useful life of 10 years, with an expected terminal salvage value of about $10,000. The old press has a book value of $36,000. It could be sold now for $6,000. If held for the remaining 10 years of its useful life, the old press would have a terminal salvage value of $3,000.

Annual operating costs under each press at the present volume of work are compared below.

|  | Old Press | New Press |
|---|---|---|
| Variable costs: | | |
| Materials and supplies........... | $60,000 | $60,000 |
| Labor........................ | 40,000 | 50,000 |
| Fixed costs: | | |
| Maintenance................... | 22,000 | 20,000 |
| Taxes and insurance............. | 3,000 | 10,000 |

While the new press would double capacity, management estimates that actual volume would increase by only 80%. The company now bills all jobs at variable cost plus 50% thereof. Even though product quality would be improved by the new press, increased competition would make it impossible for the company to raise its prices.

Straight-line depreciation has been used on the old press and would be used also for the new one. The income tax rate is 40%. The company's average cost of capital is 12%.

*Required:*

Prepare an analysis to assist management in deciding whether or not to replace the printing press.

17–6.   The Pitti-Sing Nursery has just ordered a new sprinkler system. This system will cost $150,000 and will last for five years. The terminal salvage value of the materials will then just cover the cost of removing the system. The nursery has a cost of capital of 10% and is subject to an income tax rate of 40%.

*Required:*

What would be the most advantageous depreciation method for the nursery to use in its income tax returns?

17–7.   Pish-Tush Products, Inc., has plans to purchase a new machine for $900,000. This machine would have a useful life of four years and a terminal salvage value of $100,000. The company's cost of capital is 12%, and the income tax rate is 40%.

*Required:*

What would be the most advantageous method of depreciation for the corporation to elect for income tax purposes?

17–8.   The Katisha Company is contemplating the acquisition of several new machines at a total cost of $990,000. These machines would have useful lives of ten years and no significant terminal salvage values. If they are purchased and put into service, the company would save out-of-pocket operating costs of $240,000 each year.

The income tax rate is 40%. The company's cost of capital is 15%.

*Required:*

a.   Which method of depreciation of these machine would be most advantageous for income tax purposes?

b.   Would the investment in the machines be profitable?

17–9.   The Hilarion Company is considering the purchase of a 25-year lease on mineral rights for $500,000. It would finance this purchase by signing a 25-year note payable in the amount of $450,000 and paying the balance in cash immediately. Annual cash income from operations, including all income tax effects, would be $82,000. The net after-tax annual payment on the note would total $42,155.

*Required:*

Determine the discounted rate of return on the investment in mineral rights.

17–10. Calverley Products, Inc., was considering the purchase of a labor saving machine that would increase its after-tax cash flow by $25,000 per year for nine years and would cost $133,200, installed. Inasmuch as the proposed investment appeared to yield less than the company's cost of capital of 14%, management decided against buying the machine. When the machine salesman learned of this decision, he proposed that the company buy the machine on an instalment contract. Under the terms of this contract, Calverley would pay only $5,000 down and would then make annual instalment payments of $22,260 for nine years. The salesman pointed out that this arrangement offered the company an increase in its annual cash flow of $2,740 for the next nine years in return for an investment of only $5,000—a rate of return of more than 50%. Management decided to reconsider its earlier decision.

*Required:*

Advise Calverley's management as to the profitability of the proposed investment and the desirability of the instalment contract.

17–11. J. W. Wells has an opportunity to purchase a lease on a service station for $90,000. The purchase would be financed by a cash payment of $30,000 and a 12-year note for the balance. Monthly payments of $663.50 would be required for the term of the note. The lease has a remaining term of 12 years and is not renewable. All property rights revert to the lessor at the termination of the lease. Annual cash receipts from operation of the station are budgeted at $50,000, and annual out-of-pocket operating costs, at $33,000.

The income tax rate is 40%. Wells' cost of capital is 12%.

*Required:*

a. Compute the net present value of this investment.
b. Determine the discounted rate of return on the investment.
c. What is the specific interest cost on the 12-year note?

17–12. The Grosvenor Corporation sells computer services to its clients. The company recently completed a feasibility study and decided to obtain an additional computer on January 1, 1977. Information regarding this new computer is as follows:

1. The purchase price of the computer is $2,000,000. Maintenance, property taxes, and insurance would cost the purchaser $150,000 annually. Alternatively, the computer may be rented at an annual rental charge of $750,000 plus 5% of gross billings to clients. The rental contract includes maintenance, taxes, and insurance.

2. Because of competitive conditions, the company feels that it would have to replace the new computer at the end of three years with

one that is larger and faster. It is estimated that the computer will have a resale value of $500,000 at the end of three years. If purchased, the computer would be depreciated on a straight-line basis for both financial reporting and income tax purposes.

3. Estimated annual billings for the services performed on the new computer will be $1,600,000 during the first year and $2,000,000 during each of the next two years. The estimated annual expenses of operating the computer are $600,000, in addition to the expenses already mentioned above. Also, start-up costs of $75,000 would be incurred as soon as the computer is installed.

4. The corporate income tax rate is 40%. The company estimates that its average cost of capital is 15%.

*Required:*

a. What is the nature of the decision facing the Grosvenor Corporation?

b. Should the new computer be purchased or rented? Support your answer with appropriate financial analysis.

(Adapted from CPA Examination)

17-13. The Murgatroyd Corporation must construct acid bath facilities for cleaning the tools and dies that it uses in molding aluminum parts. It has a choice of either a dip process or a spray process. Dip process facilities would cost $420,000 and would have a useful life of 14 years. Annual operating costs for this process would average $40,000. Spray process facilities would cost $175,000 and would have a useful life of seven years. Their annual operating costs would average $70,000. Neither facilities would have any terminal salvage value. The straight-line depreciation method would be used in either case.

The corporation's cost of capital is 10%. The applicable income tax rate is 40%.

*Required:*

Which type of acid bath facilities would be more economical for the corporation to acquire and operate?

17-14. The Maybud Diaper Laundry can buy either a Saf-T-Steam boiler for $22,500 or a More-Heat boiler for $15,000. The Saf-T-Steam model has a service life of 9 years and would cost about $900 per year to operate and maintain. The More-Heat model would last for 5 years and would cost about $1,500 per year to operate and maintain. Either would be depreciated by the straight-line method, and neither would have a significant terminal salvage value.

The laundry has a cost of capital of 12%. Its income tax rate is 40%.

*Required:*

Which boiler would be more economical for the laundry to install?

17-15. The Dunstable Memorial Hospital, a nonprofit institution, is planning a modern radiology laboratory. It is considering three alternative X-ray machines for this laboratory. Each machine would serve the hospital's purposes adequately, but there are some significant differences in their costs and useful lives. Pertinent data for these three X-ray machines are as follows:

|  | Interprobe | Medi-Vue | Radiscope |
|---|---|---|---|
| Original cost.............. | $240,000 | $360,000 | $500,000 |
| Annual operating and |  |  |  |
| maintenance cost.......... | 50,000 | 44,000 | 38,000 |
| Terminal salvage value...... | 20,000 | 40,000 | 25,000 |
| Useful life................. | 4 years | 8 years | 12 years |

The hospital estimates its cost of capital at 10%.

*Required:*

Which would be the most economical X-ray machine for the hospital to acquire?

17–16.  The Yum-Yum Pizza Parlor is expanding its facilities and is currently deliberating the purchase of a new oven. The larger model would cost $64,000 and would have an economic life of 6 years and a terminal scrap value of $4,000. This model would have a capacity of 60 pizzas per hour, and the cost of electricity to operate it would be $.75 per hour. The alternative smaller model would cost $48,000 and would have a useful life of 9 years and a terminal scrap value of $3,000. The smaller model would have a capacity of 40 pizzas per hour, and electricity would cost $.60 per hour.

The Yum-Yum Pizza Parlor is open for business 50 hours each week. Pizzas are sold for $3.95 each. Variable ingredients costs are $.75 per pizza. Fixed operating costs total $12,500 per month. Weekly sales demand is estimated at 2,500 pizzas.

The cost of capital is 14%. The income tax rate is 40%.

*Required:*

Which oven would be the more profitable investment?

17–17.  Jack Point, a truck driver, would like to be his own boss. He wants to buy his own moving van and become a Venetian Van Lines contractor. There are two trucks available to him. He could afford either one, but he would have no interest in buying both, as he does not want to be anyone's boss either.

A Putterbuilt truck would cost $36,000, has a cargo capacity of 3,000 cubic feet, and would have a useful life of six years and a terminal salvage value of $3,000. An Internal Harder truck would cost $17,000, has a cargo capacity of 2,400 cubic feet, and would have a useful life of four years and a terminal salvage value of $1,000.

From the experience of others, Point estimates that his annual operating receipts would be about $30 per cubic feet of cargo space. His annual out-of-pocket operating costs would be about $15,000, regardless of which truck he bought.

Point has estimated his cost of capital to be 15%. He is in the 30% income tax bracket.

*Required:*

Assuming that Jack Point wishes to maximize the present value of his net annual cash flow, which truck should he buy?

17-18. The Partlett Corporation has exactly $15,000,000 available for investment in its 1977 capital budget. The six independent investment proposals listed below are the only ones being considered by management. Each of these six proposals would have an economic life of ten years and no terminal salvage value. The corporation's cost of capital is 10%. If the entire $15,000,000 are not invested, the remainder will be loaned to other firms on short-term notes yielding an after-tax rate of return of 10%.

The six investment proposals and their budgeted cash flows are as follows:

| Investment | Initial Outlay | Net Annual Cash Receipts after Tax |
|---|---|---|
| A............ | $2,500,000 | $ 596,400 |
| B............ | 5,000,000 | 1,112,600 |
| C............ | 2,000,000 | 611,800 |
| D............ | 4,500,000 | 931,100 |
| E............ | 6,000,000 | 1,431,300 |
| F............ | 3,600,000 | 977,700 |

*Required:*

a. Rank the six investment proposals in the order of profitability. Which investments should the corporation undertake?
b. What is the corporation's effective cost of capital for 1977?

17-19. The Poo-Bah Products Company has a total of $8,000,000 available for investment. The cost of capital is estimated to be 12%. The company is considering the following five independent investment opportunities, each having the budgeted financial characteristics indicated below:

| Investment | Initial Outlay | Net Annual Cash Receipts after Tax | Life in Years |
|---|---|---|---|
| A............ | $5,000,000 | $1,812,250 | 6 |
| B............ | 3,000,000 | 779,000 | 12 |
| C............ | 2,000,000 | 662,470 | 9 |
| D............ | 4,000,000 | 1,019,630 | 10 |
| E............ | 4,500,000 | 1,351,750 | 8 |

No salvage values are anticipated.

*Required:*

a. Rank these five investments in the order of their profitability.
b. What would be the most profitable investment program for the company to undertake?
c. What factors complicate investment decision making in this case?

17-20. The Dauntless Company plans to introduce a new product in 1977. Initial market tests indicate that the product might be sold at any of four alternative prices and volumes. Pertinent data for each price-volume combination are as follows:

| | | | | |
|---|---|---|---|---|
| Price..................... | $4.20 | $4.40 | $4.75 | $5.99 |
| Variable cost per unit... | 2.52 | 2.62 | 2.80 | 3.00 |
| Annual sales in units.... | 2,000,000 | 1,600,000 | 1,200,000 | 800,000 |
| Annual fixed costs...... | $2,000,000 | $2,000,000 | $1,500,000 | $1,500,000 |
| Initial capital investment........... | 2,800,000 | 2,400,000 | 2,000,000 | 1,600,000 |

Whatever the amount of the capital investment, it will be amortized by the straight-line method over a useful life of eight years. The applicable income tax rate is 40%. The company's cost of capital is 12%.

A total of $500,000 has already been invested in research and development of this new product over the past year.

*Required:*

Prepare an analysis of the alternative prices and volumes for this new product. Which price would be the most profitable for the company?

17-21. The Deadeye Distillery Corporation is considering three alternative promotional plans for its new products. They involve various combinations of prices and promotional expenditures. High, medium, and low forecasts of revenues under each plan have been formulated; and their respective probabilities of occurrence have been estimated. These budgeted revenues and probabilities, along with other pertinent data, are summarized below.

| | Plan X | Plan Y | Plan Z |
|---|---|---|---|
| Budgeted annual revenue (with probability): | | | |
| High.............. | $6,000,000 (.2) | $5,000,000 (.1) | $4,000,000 (.3) |
| Medium.......... | 4,000,000 (.5) | 3,000,000 (.7) | 2,500,000 (.6) |
| Low.............. | 2,000,000 (.3) | 1,000,000 (.2) | 0 (.1) |
| Variable cost as percentage of revenue.... | 55% | 57½% | 60% |
| Initial investment...... | $5,000,000 | $3,500,000 | $2,000,000 |
| Life in years.......... | 5 | 5 | 5 |

The corporation's cost of capital is 15%. The income tax rate is 40%. Investments in promotional programs will be capitalized and amortized by the straight-line method for income tax purposes. The corporation will have net taxable income in every year, regardless of the success or failure of its new products.

*Required:*

a. Which promotional plan would be expected to be the most profitable? Present appropriate financial analysis in support of your answer.

b. In the event the worst happened, which plan would result in the lowest total loss?

17–22. The Carruthers Cartage Company is considering expanding its fleet of river barges by purchasing 20 new shallow-draft barges, each with a freight capacity of 900 tons. Maximum operating capacity for one barge is 1,800,000 ton-miles per month. Each barge would cost $1,200,000 and would have an estimated useful life of 25 years. Depreciation would be computed by the straight-line method for income tax purposes.

The company's standard freight rate is $.12 per ton-mile. Variable out-of-pocket operating costs average $.05 per ton-mile. Fixed monthly out-of-pocket costs are $50,000 per barge. The income tax rate is 40%, and the company's cost of capital is 14%.

Management has estimated that the chances are 5 out of 10 that the new barges will be utilized at a normal volume of 75% of maximum capacity. (Routes and schedules would make it impossible for the company to operate 15 barges at 100% of capacity instead of 20 barges at 75% of capacity.) The actual operating rate, however, may be affected by the outcome of a situation over which the company has no control. One of the company's principal competitors is the financially-troubled Penzance Railroad, which is currently discussing a merger with the larger and stronger G&S Railroad. If this merger is approved, the Penzance Railroad's competitive position will be substantially improved; and it will be able to attract customers away from river barges. In that event, Carruthers' new barges would be operated at only 50% of their maximum capacity. Management estimates that the chances are 3 out of 10 that this will occur. On the other hand, if the merger does not take place, the Penzance Railroad may be forced to discontinue operations. In that event, the new barges would be utilized at 90% of their full capacity. Management figures the odds are 2 in 10 that this will be the result.

*Required:*

Would the proposed investment in the new barges be profitable? Present a supporting analysis to assist management in reaching a decision.

17–23. Alhambra Aluminum Products, Inc., is a medium-sized manufacturer of aluminum and aluminum products. Corporate sales volume in 1976 totaled $96 million, on which the company earned $6.7 million after taxes. Most of Alhambra's customers were relatively small users of aluminum extrusions and/or custom-designed aluminum products. Thus, Alhambra had found a segment of the aluminum market in which it was able to compete quite effectively with the three giants of the industry.

Alhambra fared less well in competition for bauxite, the basic raw material of aluminum production, however. Getting the bauxite required to meet the company's annual production requirements was one of its biggest problems. The demand for aluminum products was fairly stable. Unfortunately, the supply of bauxite was neither stable nor predictable. The causes of this supply problem were both natural (weather conditions and discoveries of new bauxite deposits) and economic (widely varying outputs from marginal mines in various parts of the world). There seemed to be no way that anything could be done about this supply situation; it was just a fact of life that had to be faced.

It was a problem that hit Alhambra harder than it did the big three aluminum producers, however. These companies had their own bauxite mines and, in addition, long-term supply contracts with large independent mines. Alhambra, on the other hand, relied entirely upon bauxite produced by smaller independent mines. But it was precisely these mines that were the most unstable sources of supply. In some years, they could meet all of Alhambra's needs at very favorable prices. In other years, they were able to mine little if any bauxite. Then Alhambra had to "beat the bushes" to find the supplies that it needed, and it had to pay premium prices for them. What was worse, the bauxite that the company could get in the bad years was usually a low grade of ore that yielded less aluminum and caused higher conversion costs as a result. Following is a summary of Alhambra's bauxite purchases over the preceding 10 years and the net costs per ton:

| Year | Tons Purchased | Net Cost per Ton |
|------|----------------|------------------|
| 1976 | 518,000 | $35.40 |
| 1975 | 402,000 | 32.00 |
| 1974 | 390,000 | 31.60 |
| 1973 | 493,000 | 33.25 |
| 1972 | 385,000 | 30.50 |
| 1971 | 484,000 | 32.90 |
| 1970 | 473,000 | 32.50 |
| 1969 | 457,000 | 32.70 |
| 1968 | 350,000 | 29.30 |
| 1967 | 342,000 | 29.25 |

Thus, the market for bauxite was an aggravated "feast or famine" situation. In a good year, such as 1975, Alhambra could fill its requirements by purchasing relatively smaller quantities of high-grade ore at favorable prices. In a bad year, such as 1976, the company had to buy larger quantities of low-grade ore and pay higher prices. Competitive conditions in the aluminum products market did not allow the company to pass those higher prices on to its customers. It simply had to accept lower profits in the bad years.

For several years, one of Alhambra's important bauxite suppliers had been del Bolero Mines, Ltd., a Brazilian corporation. Recently, del Bolero's American representative advised Alhambra that his firm was investing heavily in newly discovered deposits in Indonesia and felt that it had to cut back on some of its operations in the Western Hemisphere. Accordingly, del Bolero planned to sell its Plaza-Toro mine in Honduras. The American representative knew of Alhambra's supply problems and suggested that del Bolero would be willing to sell the Plaza-Toro mine directly to Alhambra for $30 million, without soliciting competing bids. This mine was a known producer of high-grade ore, and reliable geological surveys indicated that it had the capacity to continue producing an annual output of about 750,000 tons for the next 20 years.

The market research staff at Alhambra estimated the company's bauxite requirements for the next 20 years at an annual average of 520,000 tons of high-grade ore. If it had to buy low-grade ore, annual requirements would be about 650,000 tons. An average market price of $40 per ton was forecast for the same 20-year period. This price was an average of the lower and higher prices that could be expected in good and bad years. Inasmuch as the productive capacity of the Plaza-Toro mine exceeded Alhambra's own requirements, the excess output could

### EXHIBIT 1
#### Capital Budgeting Analysis of Investment in Plaza-Toro Mine

*Cash receipts:*

| | | | |
|---|---:|---:|---:|
| Cost savings from use of high-grade ore: | | | |
| Annual tonnage saved (650,000 − 520,000).. | | | 130,000 |
| Estimated market price per ton............ | $ | 40.00 | |
| Estimated conversion costs per ton......... | | 3.20 | $    43.20 |
| Annual saving.......................... | | | $ 5,616,000 |
| Profit on sale of excess output: | | | |
| Excess tonnage mined (750,000 − 520,000).. | | | 230,000 |
| Market price per ton..................... | $ | 40.00 | |
| Variable mining costs per ton.............. | | 28.00 | $    12.00 |
| | | | $ 2,760,000 |
| Gross annual cash receipts.................. | | | $ 8,376,000 |
| Less income taxes, net of percentage depletion*. | | | 2,838,000 |
| Net annual cash receipts.................... | | | $ 5,538,000 |
| Discount factor for 20 years at 10%.......... | | | 8.514 |
| Present value of cash receipts............... | | | $47,150,000 |

*Cash outlays:*

| | | |
|---|---:|---:|
| Investment in mine....................... | $30,000,000 | |
| Additional working capital needed to operate mine............................... | 6,000,000 | 36,000,000 |
| Net present value of investment............ | | $11,150,000 |
| Present value index of investment............. | | 1.31 |
| Discounted rate of return on investment........ | | 14.3% |

* Income taxes are charged at a rate of 50%. The net tax due is substantially reduced by a percentage depletion allowance of $1,350,000 per year, however.

readily be sold at prevailing market prices. With data provided by the market research staff, his own cost accounting department, and the management of the del Bolero mining division, the corporate controller prepared a financial analysis of the proposed investment. This appears in Exhibit 1. There was general agreement within the corporation that the basic estimates underlying this analysis were as good as could be obtained in the circumstances. There was some controversy about the question of risk, however.

For some time, Alhambra had used 10% as its cost of capital. This was used as the discount rate for proposed capital investments only when they were relatively riskless, however. In other cases, a higher discount rate was used to compensate for the element of risk. In the case of the Plaza-Toro mine, the president of the company wondered whether a discount rate of at least 15% would not be more appropriate. If that were used, of course, the investment would appear to be un-profitable. The controller defended his use of 10% on the grounds that purchase of the mine would actually reduce risk by eliminating the year-to-year fluctuations in materials purchase quantities and prices. In fact, he contended that 10% was a conservative discount rate in view of the fact that the company would use capital borrowed at an after-tax interest rate of only 5% to finance the acquisition of the mine.

*Required:*

a. Evaluate the capital budgeting analysis prepared by the controller. Indicate any revisions you believe should be made in it.
b. What do you believe the appropriate discount rate for the investment in the mine should be? Explain.

# APPENDIX

# Tables of
# Present Values

$T$HIS APPENDIX contains two tables of discounted present values of amounts to be paid or received in the future. These tables are included here for use in the solution of problems in Chapters 16 and 17 of this text. They do not purport to be a complete set of present value tables useful for all financial and managerial purposes. They are based upon principles of compound interest and of discrete periodic discounting of cash flows. That is, interest is assumed to compound only once each period at the end of that period. The effect of discrete discounting is to treat all cash flows occurring during a period as though they had occurred all at once at the end of the period. While this treatment is admittedly an artificial simplification of reality, it is the conventional method of discounting and does not introduce a significant error into the resultant analysis.

Each of the tables contains three basic data: interest rates, time periods, and present values of $1. Given any two of these data, one can find the third in the tables, unless either the interest rate or the time period is beyond the limits of the tables. For most of the problems in this book, the interest rate and the time period will be known; and the unknown quantity will be the present value of some future cash receipt or payment. For some problems, the present value and the time period will be known; and the interest rate will be the unknown quantity. As a practical matter, the time period would rarely be unknown; but it could be found easily enough if the interest rate and the present value were given.

Although these are tables of present values of $1, they can be used very easily to determine the present value of any amount. The tabulated present values of $1 are often referred to as *present value factors*. These factors can be used to determine the present value of any dollar amount by simple multiplication. For example, the present value of $100 is 100 times that of $1; the present value of $.50 is half that of $1. The nature and the usage of each table are explained briefly in the sections that follow. Additional illustrations of their use are found in Chapters 16 and 17.

## TABLE A–1: PRESENT VALUE OF $1

Table A–1 contains present value factors for a single cash flow at one moment in time in the future. Examples of such a cash flow for a typical capital investment are the net cash receipts of a single period in the life of the investment, a major expenditure to replace part of an asset in the future, and the terminal salvage value realized when an asset is sold at the end of its useful life. Each present value factor is computed by means of the following formula:

$$p = \frac{1}{(1 + i)^n}$$

where

$p =$ the present value of a $1 cash flow,
$i =$ the interest (or discount) rate, and
$n =$ the future period in which the cash flow will occur.
This formula may be used to compute present values for interest rates and time periods not tabulated. An inspection of the table shows that the present value factors decrease as the interest rate rises and as the time period increases (i.e., as the cash flow is deferred further into the future). Beyond certain points (e.g., beyond 25 years at 35%) no factor is tabulated. This omission indicates that the present value is so small that it may be regarded effectively as zero.

The use of this table is quite simple. For example, suppose that the sale of an asset for $20,000 is expected at the end of the 10th year in the future and that the appropriate interest rate is 15%. Management wishes to know the present value of that future cash receipt. The relevant factor is found at the intersection of the 10-year row and the 15% column— .247. This factor is then multiplied by the amount of the future cash flow, thus:

Present value = $20,000 × .247 = $4,940.

In other words, $20,000 at the end of 10 years and discounted at 15% is presently worth $4,940.

Sometimes, the future cash flow and the present value are known; and management wishes to determine what the interest rate is. For example, suppose that an investor is offered the opportunity to invest $50,000 now (the present value) in return for $114,500 at the end of five years. He wants to know what interest rate he would earn on the investment. It would be whatever interest rate would equate a future cash flow of $114,500 after five years to a present value of $50,000. The relevant present value factor ($f$) would be computed as follows:

$$\$50,000 = \$114,500 \times f$$
$$f = \$50,000 \div \$114,500$$
$$f = .437$$

A present value factor of .437 is found on the 5-year row of Table A–1 in the 18% column. Thus, the proposed investment would earn an interest rate of 18%.

An investment may offer annual cash flows of differing amounts each year. In such a case, the present value of the future cash flows must be computed individually for each year and then summed to determine the total present value of the future cash flows. For example, suppose that an investment in a new machine is expected to result in operating cost savings over the 5-year life of the machine; but the savings are expected to decrease in amount each year as the machine ages. The projected savings are as follows:

| Year | Cost Saving |
|---|---|
| 1 | $20,000 |
| 2 | 16,000 |
| 3 | 12,000 |
| 4 | 10,000 |
| 5 | 8,000 |

Each annual cost saving is equivalent to a cash receipt. If the relevant discount rate is 10%, the total present value of the savings would be computed as follows:

| Year | Cost Saving | × | Present Value Factor at 10% | = | Present Value |
|---|---|---|---|---|---|
| 1 | $20,000 | | .909 | | $18,180 |
| 2 | 16,000 | | .826 | | 13,216 |
| 3 | 12,000 | | .751 | | 9,012 |
| 4 | 10,000 | | .683 | | 6,830 |
| 5 | 8,000 | | .621 | | 4,968 |
| | | | | | $52,206 |

The investment in this machine would be profitable if the machine costs less than $52,206. The initial investment in the machine would have a present value equal to its face amount, for it would occur at once; there would be no time period in which interest could operate. In effect, the present value factor for any cash flow that occurs at the present time is 1.000, regardless of the interest rate.

## TABLE A–2: PRESENT VALUE OF AN ANNUITY OF $1

Table A–2 is a table of present values of annuities of $1 to be received or paid in the same amount each period for a given number of consecutive periods. The word "annuity" implies that the time periods involved are years. Indeed, in most capital investment analyses, the cash flows are budgeted on an annual basis. However, the periods could be either longer or shorter than a year, if interest is compounded at the end of each such period. Each present value factor in Table A–2 is the present value of an annuity of $1 for the interest rate and the number of periods tabulated. For example, the present value of a 20-year annuity discounted at 12% is 7.469. That is, the present value of an annual cash flow of $1 at the end of each of the next 20 years is $7.47. Note that the factors decrease as the interest rate increases, just as in Table A–1. The factors continue to increase as the number of periods increases, but they increase at a decreasing rate. For every interest rate, the annual increment to the present value factor is less each year as the number of years increases.

The present value factors in Table A–2 are computed by means of the following formula:

$$P = \frac{1 - \dfrac{1}{(1 + i)^N}}{i}$$

where

$P =$ the present value of a $1 annuity,

$i =$ the interest (or discount) rate, and

$N =$ the number of periods in which the annual cash flow will occur (i.e., the term of the annuity).

This formula may be used to compute present values for interest rates or periods not included in the table.

Mechanically, the use of this table is very similar to that of Table A–1. Of course, the cash flow to which the present value factor is applied here is always an annuity. For example, suppose that an investment in a machine is expected to produce annual cost savings of $25,000 throughout the 8-year life of the machine. The appropriate discount rate is 10%. Management wants to know the present value of these cost savings in order to compare it with the $120,000 initial cost of the machine. The present value of the annual cost savings is computed thus:

$$Present\ value = \$25,000 \times 5.335 = \$133,375.$$

Since this present value is greater than the cost of the machine, the investment would be profitable.

The interest rate earned on an investment that generates future cash receipts in the form of a uniform annuity for a given number of periods may be found directly in Table A–2. For example, an insurance company may purchase a jet airliner and immediately lease it to an airline for the economic life of the plane, at the end of which period title to the aircraft passes to the airline. Obviously, what the insurance company is really investing in is an annuity in the amount of the annual lease payments; it is the airline that is investing in the aircraft. The cost of the plane is $22,000,000; the term of the lease is 10 years; and the annual lease payment is $4,217,791. The interest rate that the insurance company would earn on this investment may be found by determining the present value factor that will equate the present value of the 10-year annuity to the initial cost of the plane. This factor $(f)$ is computed as follows:

$$\$22,000,000 = \$4,217,791 \times f$$
$$f = \$22,000,000 \div \$4,217,791$$
$$f = 5.216$$

A present value factor of 5.216 is found on the 10-year row of Table A–2 in the 14% column. Thus, the insurance company would earn a rate of return of 14% on its investment.

The factors in Table A–2 are for annuities that begin at the end of the first year in the future and terminate at the end of the $N$th year. Occasionally, an investment may involve an annuity that begins later than the first year. For example, suppose that an initial investment of $100,000 would generate a 20-year annuity of $40,000 per year but that the annuity would not begin until the end of the 11th year in the future (i.e., it would run from the 11th through the 30th year). The discount rate is 12%. The factor found at the intersection of the 20-year row and the 12% column is not appropriate, for it assumes that the annuity would commence in the first year. The pertinent factor must be computed by subtracting the factor for 10 years from the factor for 30 years. The remainder is the factor applicable to the intervening 20 years, that is, the years 11 through 30. This factor is 2.405 (8.055 − 5.650). The present value of the annuity, then, is $96,200 ($40,000 × 2.405). Since this is less than the initial outlay of $100,000, the investment would not be profitable.

## INTERPOLATION BETWEEN TABULATED FACTORS

In the example of the investment in an airliner, the appropriate interest rate was determined exactly, because the present value factor derived from the initial investment and the 10-year annuity was exactly equal to a factor in the table. More often in practical situations, the factor determined will fall between two tabulated factors. For example, suppose that an initial investment of $100,000 will produce a 15-year annuity of $22,000. The present value factor for this annuity is 4.545 ($100,000 ÷ $22,000). This factor cannot be found on the 15-year row of Table A–2. It falls somewhere between 4.675 and 4.315, the factors for 20% and 22%, respectively. Thus, we may conclude that the correct interest rate is between 20% and 22%. For many purposes, this may be a sufficiently precise answer. If a more exact figure is desired, it could be found by solving the basic formula for Table A–2 for an unknown $i$, with $P$ set equal to 4.545 and $N$ equal to 15. A simpler, though not quite as accurate, method of finding the exact interest rate is to interpolate between the two tabulated factors. In our example, the interval between the two tabulated present value factors is .360 (4.675 − 4.315); and the corresponding interval between the tabulated interest rates is 2% (22% − 20%), or .02. The interval between the factor of 4.675 for 20% and the computed factor of 4.545 is .130, and this corresponds to the interval between 20% and the unknown interest rate on the annuity in question. Let this interval be represented by $x$. It is then computed as follows:

$$\frac{x}{.02} = \frac{.130}{.360}$$

$$\frac{x}{.02} = .361$$

$$x = .361 \times .02 = .00722$$

The exact interest rate $(i)$ for this annuity is then equal to 20% plus $x$, or

$$i = .20 + .00722 = .20722$$

Thus, by interpolation, the discount rate has been found to be 20.7%.

The foregoing interpolation is quite accurate, as it is done between two factors only two percentage points apart. Interpolation between two more widely separated interest rates (e.g., between 10% and 30%) would be much less accurate. The mathematics of the interpolation are linear, whereas the actual change between tabulated interest rates is nonlinear. If the interval is small, the error introduced by the linear assumption implicit in interpolation is minimal. Over a larger interval, however, the error might be considered significant. For example, if the present value factor for a 15-year annuity were computed to be 4.675 and one interpolated between 10% and 30%, the interest rate would be computed to be 23.5%. Actually, the interest rate is only 20%, as may be seen directly in Table A–2.

## TABLE A-1
### Present Value of $1 at End of n Periods

| n | 1% | 2% | 4% | 6% | 8% | 10% | 12% | 14% | 15% | 16% | 18% | 20% | 22% | 24% | 25% | 26% | 28% | 30% | 35% | 40% | 45% | 50% |
|---|----|----|----|----|----|-----|-----|-----|-----|-----|-----|-----|-----|-----|-----|-----|-----|-----|-----|-----|-----|-----|
| 1 | 0.990 | 0.980 | 0.962 | 0.943 | 0.926 | 0.909 | 0.893 | 0.877 | 0.870 | 0.862 | 0.847 | 0.833 | 0.820 | 0.806 | 0.800 | 0.794 | 0.781 | 0.769 | 0.741 | 0.714 | 0.690 | 0.667 |
| 2 | 0.980 | 0.961 | 0.925 | 0.890 | 0.857 | 0.826 | 0.797 | 0.769 | 0.756 | 0.743 | 0.718 | 0.694 | 0.672 | 0.650 | 0.640 | 0.630 | 0.610 | 0.592 | 0.549 | 0.510 | 0.476 | 0.444 |
| 3 | 0.971 | 0.942 | 0.889 | 0.840 | 0.794 | 0.751 | 0.712 | 0.675 | 0.658 | 0.641 | 0.609 | 0.579 | 0.551 | 0.524 | 0.512 | 0.500 | 0.477 | 0.455 | 0.406 | 0.364 | 0.328 | 0.296 |
| 4 | 0.961 | 0.924 | 0.855 | 0.792 | 0.735 | 0.683 | 0.636 | 0.592 | 0.572 | 0.552 | 0.516 | 0.482 | 0.451 | 0.423 | 0.410 | 0.397 | 0.373 | 0.350 | 0.301 | 0.260 | 0.226 | 0.198 |
| 5 | 0.951 | 0.906 | 0.822 | 0.747 | 0.681 | 0.621 | 0.567 | 0.519 | 0.497 | 0.476 | 0.437 | 0.402 | 0.370 | 0.341 | 0.328 | 0.315 | 0.291 | 0.269 | 0.223 | 0.186 | 0.156 | 0.132 |
| 6 | 0.942 | 0.888 | 0.790 | 0.705 | 0.630 | 0.564 | 0.507 | 0.456 | 0.432 | 0.410 | 0.370 | 0.335 | 0.303 | 0.275 | 0.262 | 0.250 | 0.227 | 0.207 | 0.165 | 0.133 | 0.108 | 0.088 |
| 7 | 0.933 | 0.871 | 0.760 | 0.665 | 0.583 | 0.513 | 0.452 | 0.400 | 0.376 | 0.354 | 0.314 | 0.279 | 0.249 | 0.222 | 0.210 | 0.198 | 0.178 | 0.159 | 0.122 | 0.095 | 0.074 | 0.059 |
| 8 | 0.923 | 0.853 | 0.731 | 0.627 | 0.540 | 0.467 | 0.404 | 0.351 | 0.327 | 0.305 | 0.266 | 0.233 | 0.204 | 0.179 | 0.168 | 0.157 | 0.139 | 0.123 | 0.091 | 0.068 | 0.051 | 0.039 |
| 9 | 0.914 | 0.837 | 0.703 | 0.592 | 0.500 | 0.424 | 0.361 | 0.308 | 0.284 | 0.263 | 0.225 | 0.194 | 0.167 | 0.144 | 0.134 | 0.125 | 0.108 | 0.094 | 0.067 | 0.048 | 0.035 | 0.026 |
| 10 | 0.905 | 0.820 | 0.676 | 0.558 | 0.463 | 0.386 | 0.322 | 0.270 | 0.247 | 0.227 | 0.191 | 0.162 | 0.137 | 0.116 | 0.107 | 0.099 | 0.085 | 0.073 | 0.050 | 0.035 | 0.024 | 0.017 |
| 11 | 0.896 | 0.804 | 0.650 | 0.527 | 0.429 | 0.350 | 0.287 | 0.237 | 0.215 | 0.195 | 0.162 | 0.135 | 0.112 | 0.094 | 0.086 | 0.079 | 0.066 | 0.056 | 0.037 | 0.025 | 0.017 | 0.012 |
| 12 | 0.887 | 0.788 | 0.625 | 0.497 | 0.397 | 0.319 | 0.257 | 0.208 | 0.187 | 0.168 | 0.137 | 0.112 | 0.092 | 0.076 | 0.069 | 0.062 | 0.052 | 0.043 | 0.027 | 0.018 | 0.012 | 0.008 |
| 13 | 0.879 | 0.773 | 0.601 | 0.469 | 0.368 | 0.290 | 0.229 | 0.182 | 0.163 | 0.145 | 0.116 | 0.093 | 0.075 | 0.061 | 0.055 | 0.050 | 0.040 | 0.033 | 0.020 | 0.013 | 0.008 | 0.005 |
| 14 | 0.870 | 0.758 | 0.577 | 0.442 | 0.340 | 0.263 | 0.205 | 0.160 | 0.141 | 0.125 | 0.099 | 0.078 | 0.062 | 0.049 | 0.044 | 0.039 | 0.032 | 0.025 | 0.015 | 0.009 | 0.006 | 0.003 |
| 15 | 0.861 | 0.743 | 0.555 | 0.417 | 0.315 | 0.239 | 0.183 | 0.140 | 0.123 | 0.108 | 0.084 | 0.065 | 0.051 | 0.040 | 0.035 | 0.031 | 0.025 | 0.020 | 0.011 | 0.006 | 0.004 | 0.002 |
| 16 | 0.853 | 0.728 | 0.534 | 0.394 | 0.292 | 0.218 | 0.163 | 0.123 | 0.107 | 0.093 | 0.071 | 0.054 | 0.042 | 0.032 | 0.028 | 0.025 | 0.019 | 0.015 | 0.008 | 0.005 | 0.003 | 0.002 |
| 17 | 0.844 | 0.714 | 0.513 | 0.371 | 0.270 | 0.198 | 0.146 | 0.108 | 0.093 | 0.080 | 0.060 | 0.045 | 0.034 | 0.026 | 0.023 | 0.020 | 0.015 | 0.012 | 0.006 | 0.003 | 0.002 | 0.001 |
| 18 | 0.836 | 0.700 | 0.494 | 0.350 | 0.250 | 0.180 | 0.130 | 0.095 | 0.081 | 0.069 | 0.051 | 0.038 | 0.028 | 0.021 | 0.018 | 0.016 | 0.012 | 0.009 | 0.005 | 0.002 | 0.001 | 0.001 |
| 19 | 0.828 | 0.686 | 0.475 | 0.331 | 0.232 | 0.164 | 0.116 | 0.083 | 0.070 | 0.060 | 0.043 | 0.031 | 0.023 | 0.017 | 0.014 | 0.012 | 0.009 | 0.007 | 0.003 | 0.002 | 0.001 | |
| 20 | 0.820 | 0.673 | 0.456 | 0.312 | 0.215 | 0.149 | 0.104 | 0.073 | 0.061 | 0.051 | 0.037 | 0.026 | 0.019 | 0.014 | 0.012 | 0.010 | 0.007 | 0.005 | 0.002 | 0.001 | 0.001 | |
| 21 | 0.811 | 0.660 | 0.439 | 0.294 | 0.199 | 0.135 | 0.093 | 0.064 | 0.053 | 0.044 | 0.031 | 0.022 | 0.015 | 0.011 | 0.009 | 0.008 | 0.006 | 0.004 | 0.002 | 0.001 | | |
| 22 | 0.803 | 0.647 | 0.422 | 0.278 | 0.184 | 0.123 | 0.083 | 0.056 | 0.046 | 0.038 | 0.026 | 0.018 | 0.013 | 0.009 | 0.007 | 0.006 | 0.004 | 0.003 | 0.001 | 0.001 | | |
| 23 | 0.795 | 0.634 | 0.406 | 0.262 | 0.170 | 0.112 | 0.074 | 0.049 | 0.040 | 0.033 | 0.022 | 0.015 | 0.010 | 0.007 | 0.006 | 0.005 | 0.003 | 0.002 | 0.001 | | | |
| 24 | 0.788 | 0.622 | 0.390 | 0.247 | 0.158 | 0.102 | 0.066 | 0.043 | 0.035 | 0.028 | 0.019 | 0.013 | 0.008 | 0.006 | 0.005 | 0.004 | 0.003 | 0.002 | 0.001 | | | |
| 25 | 0.780 | 0.610 | 0.375 | 0.233 | 0.146 | 0.092 | 0.059 | 0.038 | 0.030 | 0.024 | 0.016 | 0.010 | 0.007 | 0.005 | 0.004 | 0.003 | 0.002 | 0.001 | | | | |
| 26 | 0.772 | 0.598 | 0.361 | 0.220 | 0.135 | 0.084 | 0.053 | 0.033 | 0.026 | 0.021 | 0.014 | 0.009 | 0.006 | 0.004 | 0.003 | 0.002 | 0.002 | 0.001 | | | | |
| 27 | 0.764 | 0.586 | 0.347 | 0.207 | 0.125 | 0.076 | 0.047 | 0.029 | 0.023 | 0.018 | 0.011 | 0.007 | 0.005 | 0.003 | 0.002 | 0.002 | 0.001 | 0.001 | | | | |
| 28 | 0.757 | 0.574 | 0.333 | 0.196 | 0.116 | 0.069 | 0.042 | 0.026 | 0.020 | 0.016 | 0.010 | 0.006 | 0.004 | 0.002 | 0.002 | 0.002 | 0.001 | 0.001 | | | | |
| 29 | 0.749 | 0.563 | 0.321 | 0.185 | 0.107 | 0.063 | 0.037 | 0.022 | 0.017 | 0.014 | 0.008 | 0.005 | 0.003 | 0.002 | 0.002 | 0.001 | 0.001 | | | | | |
| 30 | 0.742 | 0.552 | 0.308 | 0.174 | 0.099 | 0.057 | 0.033 | 0.020 | 0.015 | 0.012 | 0.007 | 0.004 | 0.003 | 0.002 | 0.001 | 0.001 | 0.001 | | | | | |
| 40 | 0.672 | 0.453 | 0.208 | 0.097 | 0.046 | 0.022 | 0.011 | 0.005 | 0.004 | 0.003 | 0.001 | 0.001 | | | | | | | | | | |
| 50 | 0.608 | 0.372 | 0.141 | 0.054 | 0.021 | 0.009 | 0.003 | 0.001 | 0.001 | 0.001 | | | | | | | | | | | | |

## TABLE A–2

## Present Value of an Annuity of $1 for N Periods

| N | 1% | 2% | 4% | 6% | 8% | 10% | 12% | 14% | 15% | 16% | 18% | 20% | 22% | 24% | 25% | 26% | 28% | 30% | 35% | 40% | 45% | 50% |
|---|---|---|---|---|---|---|---|---|---|---|---|---|---|---|---|---|---|---|---|---|---|---|
| 1 | 0.990 | 0.980 | 0.962 | 0.943 | 0.926 | 0.909 | 0.893 | 0.877 | 0.870 | 0.862 | 0.847 | 0.833 | 0.820 | 0.806 | 0.800 | 0.794 | 0.781 | 0.769 | 0.741 | 0.714 | 0.690 | 0.667 |
| 2 | 1.970 | 1.942 | 1.886 | 1.833 | 1.783 | 1.736 | 1.690 | 1.647 | 1.626 | 1.605 | 1.566 | 1.528 | 1.492 | 1.457 | 1.440 | 1.424 | 1.392 | 1.361 | 1.289 | 1.224 | 1.165 | 1.111 |
| 3 | 2.941 | 2.884 | 2.775 | 2.673 | 2.577 | 2.487 | 2.402 | 2.322 | 2.283 | 2.246 | 2.174 | 2.106 | 2.042 | 1.981 | 1.952 | 1.923 | 1.868 | 1.816 | 1.696 | 1.589 | 1.493 | 1.407 |
| 4 | 3.902 | 3.808 | 3.630 | 3.465 | 3.312 | 3.170 | 3.037 | 2.914 | 2.855 | 2.798 | 2.690 | 2.589 | 2.494 | 2.404 | 2.362 | 2.320 | 2.241 | 2.166 | 1.997 | 1.849 | 1.720 | 1.605 |
| 5 | 4.853 | 4.713 | 4.452 | 4.212 | 3.993 | 3.791 | 3.605 | 3.433 | 3.352 | 3.274 | 3.127 | 2.991 | 2.864 | 2.745 | 2.689 | 2.635 | 2.532 | 2.436 | 2.220 | 2.035 | 1.876 | 1.737 |
| 6 | 5.795 | 5.601 | 5.242 | 4.917 | 4.623 | 4.355 | 4.111 | 3.889 | 3.784 | 3.685 | 3.498 | 3.326 | 3.167 | 3.020 | 2.951 | 2.885 | 2.759 | 2.643 | 2.385 | 2.168 | 1.983 | 1.824 |
| 7 | 6.728 | 6.472 | 6.002 | 5.582 | 5.206 | 4.868 | 4.564 | 4.288 | 4.160 | 4.039 | 3.812 | 3.605 | 3.416 | 3.242 | 3.161 | 3.083 | 2.937 | 2.802 | 2.508 | 2.263 | 2.057 | 1.883 |
| 8 | 7.652 | 7.325 | 6.733 | 6.210 | 5.747 | 5.335 | 4.968 | 4.639 | 4.487 | 4.344 | 4.078 | 3.837 | 3.619 | 3.421 | 3.329 | 3.241 | 3.076 | 2.925 | 2.598 | 2.331 | 2.108 | 1.922 |
| 9 | 8.566 | 8.162 | 7.435 | 6.802 | 6.247 | 5.759 | 5.328 | 4.946 | 4.772 | 4.607 | 4.303 | 4.031 | 3.786 | 3.566 | 3.463 | 3.366 | 3.184 | 3.019 | 2.665 | 2.379 | 2.144 | 1.948 |
| 10 | 9.471 | 8.983 | 8.111 | 7.360 | 6.710 | 6.145 | 5.650 | 5.216 | 5.019 | 4.833 | 4.494 | 4.192 | 3.923 | 3.682 | 3.571 | 3.465 | 3.269 | 3.092 | 2.715 | 2.414 | 2.168 | 1.965 |
| 11 | 10.368 | 9.787 | 8.760 | 7.887 | 7.139 | 6.495 | 5.937 | 5.453 | 5.234 | 5.029 | 4.656 | 4.327 | 4.035 | 3.776 | 3.656 | 3.544 | 3.335 | 3.147 | 2.752 | 2.438 | 2.185 | 1.977 |
| 12 | 11.255 | 10.575 | 9.385 | 8.384 | 7.536 | 6.814 | 6.194 | 5.660 | 5.421 | 5.197 | 4.793 | 4.439 | 4.127 | 3.851 | 3.725 | 3.606 | 3.387 | 3.190 | 2.779 | 2.456 | 2.196 | 1.985 |
| 13 | 12.134 | 11.343 | 9.986 | 8.853 | 7.904 | 7.103 | 6.424 | 5.842 | 5.583 | 5.342 | 4.910 | 4.533 | 4.203 | 3.912 | 3.780 | 3.656 | 3.427 | 3.223 | 2.799 | 2.468 | 2.204 | 1.990 |
| 14 | 13.004 | 12.106 | 10.563 | 9.295 | 8.244 | 7.367 | 6.628 | 6.002 | 5.724 | 5.468 | 5.008 | 4.611 | 4.265 | 3.962 | 3.824 | 3.695 | 3.459 | 3.249 | 2.814 | 2.477 | 2.210 | 1.993 |
| 15 | 13.865 | 12.849 | 11.118 | 9.712 | 8.559 | 7.606 | 6.811 | 6.142 | 5.847 | 5.575 | 5.092 | 4.675 | 4.315 | 4.001 | 3.859 | 3.726 | 3.483 | 3.268 | 2.825 | 2.484 | 2.214 | 1.995 |
| 16 | 14.718 | 13.578 | 11.652 | 10.106 | 8.851 | 7.824 | 6.974 | 6.265 | 5.954 | 5.669 | 5.162 | 4.730 | 4.357 | 4.033 | 3.887 | 3.751 | 3.503 | 3.283 | 2.834 | 2.489 | 2.216 | 1.997 |
| 17 | 15.562 | 14.292 | 12.166 | 10.477 | 9.122 | 8.022 | 7.120 | 6.373 | 6.047 | 5.749 | 5.222 | 4.775 | 4.391 | 4.059 | 3.910 | 3.771 | 3.518 | 3.295 | 2.840 | 2.492 | 2.218 | 1.998 |
| 18 | 16.398 | 14.992 | 12.659 | 10.828 | 9.372 | 8.201 | 7.250 | 6.467 | 6.128 | 5.818 | 5.273 | 4.812 | 4.419 | 4.080 | 3.928 | 3.786 | 3.529 | 3.304 | 2.844 | 2.494 | 2.219 | 1.999 |
| 19 | 17.226 | 15.678 | 13.134 | 11.158 | 9.604 | 8.365 | 7.366 | 6.550 | 6.198 | 5.877 | 5.316 | 4.844 | 4.442 | 4.097 | 3.942 | 3.799 | 3.539 | 3.311 | 2.848 | 2.496 | 2.220 | 1.999 |
| 20 | 18.046 | 16.351 | 13.590 | 11.470 | 9.818 | 8.514 | 7.469 | 6.623 | 6.259 | 5.929 | 5.353 | 4.870 | 4.460 | 4.110 | 3.954 | 3.808 | 3.546 | 3.316 | 2.850 | 2.497 | 2.221 | 1.999 |
| 21 | 18.857 | 17.011 | 14.029 | 11.764 | 10.017 | 8.649 | 7.562 | 6.687 | 6.312 | 5.973 | 5.384 | 4.891 | 4.476 | 4.121 | 3.963 | 3.816 | 3.551 | 3.320 | 2.852 | 2.498 | 2.221 | 2.000 |
| 22 | 19.660 | 17.658 | 14.451 | 12.042 | 10.201 | 8.772 | 7.645 | 6.743 | 6.359 | 6.011 | 5.410 | 4.909 | 4.488 | 4.130 | 3.970 | 3.822 | 3.556 | 3.323 | 2.853 | 2.498 | 2.222 | 2.000 |
| 23 | 20.456 | 18.292 | 14.857 | 12.303 | 10.371 | 8.883 | 7.718 | 6.792 | 6.399 | 6.044 | 5.432 | 4.925 | 4.499 | 4.137 | 3.976 | 3.827 | 3.559 | 3.325 | 2.854 | 2.499 | 2.222 | 2.000 |
| 24 | 21.243 | 18.914 | 15.247 | 12.550 | 10.529 | 8.985 | 7.784 | 6.835 | 6.434 | 6.073 | 5.451 | 4.937 | 4.507 | 4.143 | 3.981 | 3.831 | 3.562 | 3.327 | 2.855 | 2.499 | 2.222 | 2.000 |
| 25 | 22.023 | 19.523 | 15.622 | 12.783 | 10.675 | 9.077 | 7.843 | 6.873 | 6.464 | 6.097 | 5.467 | 4.948 | 4.514 | 4.147 | 3.985 | 3.834 | 3.564 | 3.329 | 2.856 | 2.499 | 2.222 | 2.000 |
| 26 | 22.795 | 20.121 | 15.983 | 13.003 | 10.810 | 9.161 | 7.896 | 6.906 | 6.491 | 6.118 | 5.480 | 4.956 | 4.520 | 4.151 | 3.988 | 3.837 | 3.566 | 3.330 | 2.856 | 2.500 | 2.222 | 2.000 |
| 27 | 23.560 | 20.707 | 16.330 | 13.211 | 10.935 | 9.237 | 7.943 | 6.935 | 6.514 | 6.136 | 5.492 | 4.964 | 4.524 | 4.154 | 3.990 | 3.839 | 3.567 | 3.331 | 2.856 | 2.500 | 2.222 | 2.000 |
| 28 | 24.316 | 21.281 | 16.663 | 13.406 | 11.051 | 9.307 | 7.984 | 6.961 | 6.534 | 6.152 | 5.502 | 4.970 | 4.528 | 4.157 | 3.992 | 3.840 | 3.568 | 3.331 | 2.857 | 2.500 | 2.222 | 2.000 |
| 29 | 25.066 | 21.844 | 16.984 | 13.591 | 11.158 | 9.370 | 8.022 | 6.983 | 6.551 | 6.166 | 5.510 | 4.975 | 4.531 | 4.159 | 3.994 | 3.841 | 3.569 | 3.332 | 2.857 | 2.500 | 2.222 | 2.000 |
| 30 | 25.808 | 22.396 | 17.292 | 13.765 | 11.258 | 9.427 | 8.055 | 7.003 | 6.566 | 6.177 | 5.517 | 4.979 | 4.534 | 4.160 | 3.995 | 3.842 | 3.569 | 3.332 | 2.857 | 2.500 | 2.222 | 2.000 |
| 40 | 32.835 | 27.355 | 19.793 | 15.046 | 11.925 | 9.779 | 8.244 | 7.105 | 6.642 | 6.234 | 5.548 | 4.997 | 4.544 | 4.166 | 3.999 | 3.846 | 3.571 | 3.333 | 2.857 | 2.500 | 2.222 | 2.000 |
| 50 | 39.196 | 31.424 | 21.482 | 15.762 | 12.234 | 9.915 | 8.304 | 7.133 | 6.661 | 6.246 | 5.554 | 4.999 | 4.545 | 4.167 | 4.000 | 3.846 | 3.571 | 3.333 | 2.857 | 2.500 | 2.222 | 2.000 |

# index

# Index

*This book has been set in 10 and 9 point Modern #21, leaded 2 points. Part numbers are 24 point (large) Helvetica Medium and chapter numbers are 16 and 30 point Helvetica. Part and chapter titles are 24 point (small) Helvetica. The size of the type page is 27 × 45½ picas.*